D1609912

DISPOSED OF
BY LIBRARY
HOUSE OF LORDS

Drink in Great Britain 1900 to 1979

BY

GWYLMOR PRYS WILLIAMS

MBE, BCom, FIS, FSS

and

GEORGE THOMPSON BRAKE

ARHistS

Indexed by
ELIZABETH WALLIS

EDSALL LONDON

ISBN 0 902623 26 5.

Published by B. EDSALL & CO. LTD, LONDON

Printed by The Pitman Press, Bath, Avon, England.
Typeset by Wayside Graphics, Clevedon, Avon, England.

DRINK IN GREAT BRITAIN 1900–1979

CONTENTS

Part I

Part II

FOREWORD

by

The Very Reverend, The Dean of Westminster, Edward F. Carpenter, DD.

In all social studies, in particular when they relate to matters of grave public concern, it is important as we say "to get at the facts". Of course, in the process of doing so, complete objectivity, if it were possible would be undesirable. All facts so teazed out represent a response to some prior question already regarded as important. It is seldom that facts speak for themselves except to those who have an existing built-in set of values which make the facts come alive and be significant.

However, in no area, I suspect, is it more important to try as best we may to find out what the facts are than in the area of concern which is dealt with in the study *Drink in Great Britain 1900 to 1979*, the joint work of Gwylmor Prys Williams and the Reverend George Thompson Brake. Much research, conscientious and sustained, has gone into the writing of this book, research which is as honest and objective as integrity can make it within the area of a deeply felt concern. Nowhere, it must be allowed, is this approach more urgent and necessary than in relation to what is popularly known as the "drink problem". That there is such a problem, and that this nation, *inter alia*, has lived with it for centuries, is as certain as regrettable. That the nature of this problem has changed with changing social circumstances, differing economic and environmental pressures and with new moral and cultural mores, is equally self-evident. Also, it is important to recognize that this problem spills over into politics, religion, economics, psychology, and ethical attitudes, amongst others. "Am I my brother's keeper?" remains a significant question within this context, nowhere more so than to the responsible citizen who feels that he cannot be indifferent to the social scene, rather that he must involve himself in it.

Drink in Great Britain 1900 to 1979 is an authoritative work compiled by two men who have spent long years in this particular area in the life of society, and have researched extensively into its origins, character and effects. The intention of the present volume is to update G. B. Wilson's authoritative study *Alcohol and the Nation* (London 1940), and to do this by a historical survey which in its narration is fully documented by means of a massive statistical analysis. The result is a comprehensive examination of a highly complex situational problem which has thrown up new and disturbing facets in the course of the twentieth century. *Drink in Great Britain 1900 to 1979* shows clearly how many are the areas and the motivations which lead to addiction and resort to excessive drinking; therefore how diverse the remedies and the therapies to deal with them once identified.

As I read these pages I must confess that many thoughts and reflections crowded in upon me. I couldn't but recognize how severe this problem is in its total cost in terms of human happiness and personal fulfilment, to say nothing of its wastage of human resources, all of which could be harnessed to the common good. Hence the prime need to lay bare its causes, both primary and secondary and undertaking the probing and research necessary to this end. Such a grievous evil, I became more convinced than ever as

I read, cannot be swept under the carpet in the naively optimistic hope that somehow or other it will disappear if left to itself. Nor does the evidence suggest that individual conversion, highly desirable though this must be, is in itself an adequate approach to deal with this problem in the highly complex, pressurised, unstable world of today. Contemporary living brings with it excessive strain. Nor can we ignore the fact, in a democratic society such as we have in Britain, that the protection of the few cannot be purchased by the denial of responsible freedom for the many. To keep options open means risking the abuse of them. How to preserve the former and limit the latter demands a nice and discriminating judgment. Alleviation, and where possible, the cure of this evil in the body politic – and *Drink in Great Britain 1900 to 1979* illustrates this – must be dealt with in the spheres of parliament, mass communication, advertising, teaching in schools, medicine and psychiatry: the list is endless. In other words, alcoholism must be tackled on many fronts. Here the appendices will be found of great interest as a commentary on the text. Whatever our views and diagnoses so concluded, the last thing that a community should do, be the problem ever so severe, is to adopt an attitude of defeatism or to regard this problem as so intractable as to be incapable of resolution or indeed alleviation. If, in its contemporary setting, alcoholism may be regarded as a disease of affluence it must not be regarded as a necessary concomitance of affluence.

The Reverend George Thompson Brake is secretary and Gwylmor Prys Williams is statistical adviser of the Christian Economic and Social Research Foundation which was founded by the Reverend Harold S. Goodwin, FJI. It became an educational charity in 1966. The Foundation has never sought to over-simplify complex situations or to suppose that there is any one known practical cure universally appplicable in every area of this long-standing problem. Facts must not be forced to fit *a priori* theories. We must do our best to follow whither the argument leads.

Drink in Great Britain 1900 to 1979 is directed towards those who entertain a general social concern as well as to those who in their professional capacity are charged with particular responsibilities in this field and are brought into daily contact with it. To such I commend this book with complete confidence as a serious, informed and illuminating contribution to a subject of grave concern.

Edward F. Carpenter

London
Autumn 1980

INTRODUCTION

Two books have been essential reading for students of what has often been called "the alcohol problem". One is *Alcohol and the Nation* (1940) by G. B. Wilson and the other is *Drink and the Victorians* (1971) by Brian Harrison. Wilson's book will remain a source book especially for statistical information for the period 1800 to 1935. Harrison's book is massively comprehensive as a history of "The Temperance Question in England, 1815–1872" to quote the book's subtitle. There is one other book which is widely consulted, this is *Paterson's Licensing Acts*, which is revised annually. In the work which follows there are references to licensing laws, but no attempt has been made to supplant or supplement *Paterson's* and for specific information readers are directed to this standard work.

This present book has been written with the intention of up-dating Wilson and of providing a historical account of drink and society's response to it from 1900 to the time of publication. The statistical tables had to be ruled off at 1974 because in that year there was a major change in the constitution of the police districts and so the basis of comparison was no longer valid. A note has been added to indicate certain trends since then. It will be seen that the two parts of the book have been written by different authors. Part I is the work of the Revd G. Thompson Brake, honorary secretary of the Christian Economic and Social Research Foundation. Part II is the work of Gwylmor Prys Williams, the honorary statistical adviser to the foundation.

There can be few aspects of British social history about which more has been written than "Drink". This means that an author, attempting to do justice to any aspect of the history of this vast subject, has to be selective in his treatment and, indeed, in the sources he consults. In this particular field, being selective need not result in the omission of vital matters. Some of the events of the twentieth century have been documented by authors with a historical interest in the subject, but mostly interest was expressed dynamically in protest and propaganda. And so, much of the source material is in newspapers, temperance and trade journals and propaganda material. The issue was frequently raised in parliament so that the records of debates are another important source of information. In Part I the author has set out to provide a comprehensive but not exhaustive account of the major features of the subject from the beginning of the century. The then Professor John Ferguson read the manuscript of Part I and his valuable recommendations have been incorporated.

The principal indebtedness of the authors is to their respective wives who have done so much typing and checking. Special mention must be made of the enormous amount of work in sifting material and checking facts done by Celia Hudson, the research assistant of the Christian Economic and Social Research Foundation, and to the back-up provided by Lois Brown the foundation's librarian. Gratitude must be expressed to the United Kingdom Temperance Alliance Limited for initial financial encouragement. The authors were fortunate in securing Brian Edsall as their publisher and his early comments were invaluable in making it possible to revise essential parts of the book before publication. The chairman of the foundation, the Dean of Westminster (The Very Reverend Edward F. Carpenter DD), has shown his eager interest in this project and has generously contributed a foreword. To him and the councillors of the foundation the authors record their deep appreciation.

London 1980

PART I

CHAPTER 1

THE EMERGENCE OF AN ALCOHOL PROBLEM IN BRITAIN

The reign of Henry VII, the first of the Tudors, is important because it saw the beginning of licensing administration as we have known it in Britain for nearly five hundred years. In 1495 an act was passed which empowered two justices of the peace to suppress ale houses. This was the beginning of the legislative control of liquor. It was appropriate that this beginning was made during Henry VII's reign because his household was largely free from the extravagance and revelry of the courts of Edward III and Richard II. There is some evidence that this lack of excess was reflected in the hospitality of the nobility. The visitation of the monasteries which had been entrusted to Thomas Cromwell, revealed a different situation. The discovery of gluttony and drunkenness led to the dissolution of the smaller monasteries. Outside the monasteries the clergy, from the archbishop downward, were notorious for the time they spent in taverns. In the succeeding reign of Henry VIII, Irish settlers in Pembrokeshire introduced the distilling of spirits. This, too, was appropriate, for Henry VIII was to be remembered for his excessive drinking. "The court was rotten, and its influence filtered then, as always, to the masses."[1]

Although drunkenness was widespread there is no record of it as a civil offence until 1552. From that time a number of statutes were passed for the prevention or punishment of drunkenness. The role of the justices was strengthened, so that they could ensure the supervision of ale houses as well as their suppression. Later an act was passed to control the price and accessibility of wine and to discourage the opening of too many retail outlets. No wine could be retailed without a licence and the price was fixed. Only two taverns could be opened in a borough, except in larger centres where the number, although increased, was specified.

Accounts of the drinking habits during the Elizabethan period which began in 1558 are varied. Some observers of the time portrayed Elizabethans as disciplined in respect of drink. However, the legislation of the period supports a different conclusion. There is much evidence of an extension of the British taste for imported wines, while distilling also increased. Elizabeth herself did not indulge extensively and properly retained a reputation for disciplined living. Her principles were shared by not a few prominent persons close to the throne. The most notable, Sir Walter Raleigh, who wrote:

> *Take special care that thou delight not in wine, for there was not any man that came to honour or preferment that loved it; for it transformeth a man into a beast, decayeth health, poisoneth the breath, destroyeth natural heat, deformeth the face, rotteneth the teeth, and to conclude, maketh a man contemptible, soon old, and despised of all wise and worthy men, hated in thy servants, in thyself, and companions; for it is a bewitching and infectious vice.*[2]

The example of the court and certain nobility did not receive support from the Church. Drink flowed freely at church festivals and drunkenness was a common feature of such events. There were, however, powerful advocates of temperance among the outstanding literary men of the Elizabethan period, in the writings of Bacon, Gascoigne and particularly in Spenser's *Faerie Queen*, in the second book of which there is a legend of Sir Guyon, or temperance, although Spenser was ambivalant in his attitude and wrote lines in praise of drink. The references in Shakespeare's writings to the value of temperance and the foolishness of heavy drinking are too numerous to mention in this short review. There are detailed studies of this aspect of his writings.

The contemporary literature of the early years of the Stuarts reflected the increasing indulgence of the British people in the consumption of liquor. There were also powerful pleas for sobriety, notably in the writings of George Herbert. By this time too, the effectiveness of legislative measures had been tested and further action in this field was taken. Drunkenness became an offence punishable by fines and a period of confinement in the stocks. Although attempts to deal with the problem of drunkenness by legislation were made, they were not, it seems very effective. A statute in 1609 admitted that despite previous legislation excessive drinking and drunkenness increased. The trend continued throughout the reign of Charles I and gave rise to literature which described the social consequences of the widespread habit. Various reasons were advanced for this trend. The drinks themselves were attractive and, because of the numerous taverns, were readily available. Social customs, such as toasting and the Wakes, were positive encouragements to drinking. As in previous periods, there were powerful voices raised against the habit. Possibly none was more notable than that of Jeremy Taylor, and the example of John Milton, who lived an extremely disciplined life, must have had some influence.

Of the measures taken to control the consumption of liquor, none was more important than the introduction of the excise in 1643. It was first imposed on the makers and retailers of ale, beer, cider and perry. Introduced by parliament after its breach with the Crown, it was adopted also by the Royalists. Intemperance continued during the Commonwealth and Protectorate, even though, in the popular mind, the sobriety of the Roundheads is contrasted with the excess among the Cavaliers. Certainly under the Protectorate stern action was taken against drunkards. In 1650, or thereabout, coffee was introduced as a social drink, and in 1657 chocolate was first advertised. A reference in Pepys's diary, 28th September 1660, to tea, suggests that it was about this time that it was introduced to England. It was Catherine of Braganza, after her marriage to Charles II, who made tea drinking fashionable, but none of these alternatives to liquor made a significant impact on the drinking habits of the people who, by this time, had developed a thirst for alcoholic beverages.

The Restoration and after

The Restoration was marked by pageants and festivals at which liquor was consumed in large quantities. Naturally the custom of toasting the monarch received a new impetus; and so far as liquor consumption was concerned the gesture was more than reciprocated. Charles II set an example of drunkenness which was followed in every section of the community. Although many drinking customs were preserved under James II, the king himself hated hard drinking. Historians of the period, such as Macaulay and Lecky, confirmed that the principal drink was beer. In 1688 the production of beer amounted to 12,400,000 barrels for a population of a little over 5,000,000. The production and consumption of spirits was small. In 1689, however, the government of the Revolution stopped the importation of spirits from other countries and threw open the distillery trade. On payment of comparatively small duties and the giving of ten days' notice to the excise, any person could open a distillery. As a result there was a large increase in the distillation of spirits, a massive increase in consumption and a deterioration in behaviour and public health. There was no improvement in the situation during the remainder of the Stuart period, nor, indeed for some time during the following dynasty. Indeed, the permission to open distilleries, which was continued by William III, was positively encouraged by George I. Spirits were sold so cheap that excessive indulgence was widespread and after 1724 gin drinking spread like an epidemic. Some indication of the extent of the growth of spirit drinking is that in 1684 about 527,000 gallons were distilled, but by 1727 the figure had risen to 3,601,000 gallons. The imposition of heavy duties on imported spirits gave rise to smuggling on a large scale. Thus by one means or another, liquor was readily available. At this time, also, public houses were numerous. Most historians of drink in Britain quote figures produced by a committee of Middlesex magistrates who stated that in 1725 there were 6,187 houses in London, not including the City of London and Southwark, where "geneva, or other strong waters" were sold retail. The population then was about 700,000. The consequences of the availability of relatively cheap liquor were poverty, murder, robbery and other offences. To check the excessive consumption, in 1728 such a high duty was placed on spirits as to impose almost a prohibition on its consumption, and the act which introduced this high duty made other provisions which are of special interest to students of licensing legislation. For the first time, licences which, by this act, applied to dealers in spirits as well as to publicans, were required to be renewed annually. Further applications were to be made at a general meeting of justices of the division to avoid decisions being made by justices at a distance. After only four years, the act was repealed because it was being evaded.

Intemperance became so widespread and intense that in 1736 a petition was presented to parliament from the quarter sessions of magistrates of Middlesex. This petition stated that for some years the drinking of geneva and other distilled liquors had greatly increased, that constant and excessive consumption had destroyed thousands of people and made others unfit for work and degraded in behaviour. The retailing of such liquors had corrupted not only distillers, but others who were drawn into its distribution. It had become a threat to public welfare and safety. The petition was referred to a committee of the whole house, which resolved:

> *That the low price of spirituous liquors is the principal inducement to the excessive and pernicious use thereof.*

That in order to prevent this excessive and pernicious use, a discouragement be given thereto by a duty to be laid on spirits sold by retail.
That the selling of such liquors be restrained to persons keeping public brandy-shops, victualling houses, coffee houses, ale-houses, innholders and to such surgeons and apothecaries as shall make use of it by way of medicine only.

The "alcohol problem" emerges

In the face of such an unequivocal indictment of the retailing of spirits the government was forced to take action. Not even a cursory account of the drinking habits of the British people and the legislation relating to it, could omit a reference to the Gin Act of 1736 which prohibited the sale of spirits in quantities of less than two gallons without a licence on the payment of £50, which had to be applied for annually. The duty per gallon was raised to £20.

This was prohibition in all but name. Initially there was a decline in consumption, but the people were too addicted to the drinking habit for even such a severe measure to be effective. Despite 12,000 convictions in two years for breaking the law, an illicit trade flourished. Spirits were sold disguised as wine or medicine. "In short, the repressive Act gave a great stimulus to the traffic."[3] Consumption in England and Wales rose from 11,000,000 gallons in 1733 to nearly 20,000,000 in 1742. One effect of making spirits almost inaccessible was to divert people to beer. Drinking problems increased. In 1743 amending legislation was passed which repealed certain duties. Legislation in other directions was introduced which prohibited distillation from grain, malt or flour. It was resolved to test these measures by keeping them in force until 1759. The success of this action was seen in the reduction of consumption of spirits in England and Wales from almost 20,000,000 gallons in 1742 to an average of about 4,000,000 between 1760 and 1782.

At a time when the consumption of liquor was widespread and heavy, it is not surprising to discover that men prominent in public life and literature became victims of the drinking habit. Among those who practised and advocated restraint was Dr Samuel Johnson. In his early life he drank wine, but on medical as well as on moral grounds he gave it up. But he described himself as "a hardened and shameless tea-drinker." Another author who exposed the vice of drinking was Oliver Goldsmith. However, it was an artist who will be remembered most for capturing the scenes of drunkenness, debauchery and poverty of the period. This was William Hogarth (1697–1764), famed for *A Rake's Progress*, a series of eight satirical pictures of gin drinking.

During the second half of the eighteenth century various modifications to the duty on liquor were effected, but the general level of consumption remained high and so did that of the adverse consequences of excessive indulgence. It was, perhaps, a sign of the times that George IV, who was born in 1770 and came to the throne in 1820, was an example of dissolute behaviour, especially in regard to drink. His reign was short (just ten years), yet during that time, in 1828, a consolidating Licensing Act was passed.

This made several provisions which, with minor variations, are in force today. These were that licences could be granted only from year to year at a special session of magistrates, with a right of appeal to quarter sessions. Public notices of intended applications had to be fixed to the door of the premises and of the parish church. No persons of bad character were to be admitted to public houses, and publicans were required not to allow drunkenness and disorder on their premises. Besides these provisions, which basically are in force today, two justices could direct the publican to close his house in cases of disorder.

Reference is made elsewhere in this book[4] to an act passed at this time which proved to be one of the most notable in the history of licensing. This was the Beerhouse Act of 1830, which permitted virtually any householder to sell beer in his house on the payment of *£2. 2s* to the Excise Office without a licence issued by the magistrates. The proliferation of beer houses as a consequence led to a further act in 1834 requiring the issue of a magistrates' licence. The intention of the 1830 Act, which vastly increased the accessibility of beer, was to wean drinkers from spirits, but in fact the demand for them was even greater. Between 1821 and 1830 the consumption of British spirits was 57,970,963 gallons. During the next ten years it increased by 32 per cent to 76,797,365 gallons. When, three years later, a select committee of the House of Commons was appointed and subsequently reported, its first recommendation was "That it is the opinion of the committee from the evidence that has been adduced that considerable evils had arisen from the present management and conduct of beer-houses." The committee made recommendations, none of which were incorporated in legislation, and in 1834 a further select committee was appointed to inquire into the prevailing state of drunkenness "among the labouring classes".

Their report provides a student of the drinking habits of the British people with a graphic description of drinking patterns and their social consequences, and the recommendations for dealing with the problem are exceedingly interesting, especially one urging the formation of temperance societies throughout the country. What the report did establish, beyond serious dispute, was the right of legislative interference, in the the public interest, for the correction of any evil in society.

More legislation

Queen Victoria's accession saw the beginning of a period of great activity in the promotion of licensing legislation. During the early part of her reign the first steps were taken to regulate hours during which liquor could be retailed. In 1853 yet another select committee of the House of Commons was appointed to examine how public houses were regulated and whether any alterations to the law could be made to improve their conduct and administration. The committee reported in 1854. It concluded that the distinction between beer shops and public houses gave rise to unhealthy competition; that drinks were both adulterated and diluted and in many places beer was sold without a licence; that beer houses set up to enable people to drink away from the disorderly conditions of public houses, had failed; that drunkenness was the main cause of crime, disorder and distress in England and that magistrates rarely enforced the law.

The most immediate legislative action was the passing of the Sunday Beer House Act by which public houses and beer shops were closed on Sunday from 2.30 p.m. to 6 p.m. and from 10 p.m. on Sunday to 4 a.m. on Monday. This act, whose early beneficial results were not maintained, was the first of numerous attempts to regulate the sale and consumption of liquor in the second half of the nineteenth century, and it was in this same period (1853) that the United Kingdom Alliance, which became a formidable force for the pursuit of legislative measures to prohibit the sale of liquor in the United Kingdom, was formed. Among those who wrote of the bane of drunkenness of this period were Charles Kingsley and John Ruskin, but once more it was an artist, George Cruikshank, who may have done most to arouse the nation's conscience to the evils of drink. His series of eight prints called *The Bottle* were dramatized in eight theatres in London at the same time. The prints were published in one volume in 1848.[5]

In the second half of the nineteenth century innumerable local and national temperance societies were formed, and of this period French observes:

> *Every species of counter-attraction is being furthered. Education is made possible, nay, compulsory, almost to all. Better dwellings are being provided for the poor, and solid security for their savings . . . Recreations are being provided for the masses; and a vastly improved system of sanitation. The medical world is giving the subject its close attention, and as the result of its labours of close observations and analysis, the fallacies of a past and less scientific age are being dethroned; and as a tangible outcome, temperance hospitals and homes are being erected.*[6]

As the turn of the century approached there was evidence that the tide of drunkenness was slowing down, if not halted. The revenue from taxation on liquor was diminishing. Moreover, the Temperance Movement itself was in flood-tide. Was it possible that the twentieth century would see the inauguration of a period of national sobriety?

The Royal Commission, 1896–1899

In 1896 a Royal Commission on Liquor Licensing Law was set up, its membership being drawn from three groups, the trade, the temperance forces and persons without specific interests. It would have been remarkable if such a commission had produced a unanimous report, and in the event the Majority Report went further in the direction of temperance reform than might have been expected, and recorded this judgment: "It is undeniable that a gigantic evil remains to be remedied, and hardly any sacrifice would be too great which would result in a marked diminution of this national degradation."[7] This unequivocal statement increases in significance when it is recalled that of the seventeen signatories of the Majority Report, eight were directly connected with the liquor trade.

The main recommendations included a further large reduction in the number of licensed premises; extensions of magisterial control; the reconstitution of the Licensing Authority; further reduction of hours of Sunday trading in liquor with power to the Licensing Authority to close licensed premises on Sunday; the prohibition of the sale of liquor to children under sixteen; the strengthening of the law relating to drunkenness and to offences committed by licensees and the registration of clubs supplying liquor.

The recommendation which aroused most controversy and ultimately deterred members of the commission with temperance convictions from signing the Majority Report was "Compensation." It was proposed that, in order to effect a reduction in the number of licensed premises, those which had to surrender their licences should receive compensation. The report said, ". . . . we desire to express – in the case of the suppression of licensed houses under the proposed scheme – our general adhesion to the principle of compensation equivalent to the fair intrinsic selling value of the licence and goodwill, apart from the extreme inflation of prices caused, in some cases, by excessive competition."[8] The report also recommended that the funds for the provision of compensation should be raised from the trade itself by some form of taxation. The opposition in principle to compensation was that it created a vested interest and was in breach of the principle of liquor licensing in Britain that licences were granted annually. There had never been in liquor licensing a recognition of the perpetuity of licences, and compensation implied that there had, and that licences had intrinsic value.

Lord Peel, Chairman of the Commission, was one of nine members who did not sign the Majority Report, but a Minority Report whose recommendations included all those of the Majority Report mentioned above but in some instances with more emphasis. In addition they urged later opening and earlier closing of licensed premises on weekdays; the creation of a specific hotel, as distinct from a publican's licence; the prohibition of the sale of liquor on premises where groceries and other articles were offered for sale; the granting of "on" licences on a ratio of one to every 750 persons in towns and one to every 400 in the country; and the extinction of all surplus "on" licences beyond the statutory ratio within a term of seven years. Five members of the commission added two further recommendations, one on local option and the other on the closing of premises entirely on Sundays.

Because, as Chairman, Lord Peel had signed the Minority Report, it came to be identified with his name. With the backing of such notable temperance-minded commissioners, it was to be expected that the temperance organizations would unite behind it, but on the contrary, Lord Peel's proposals proved divisive. The contentious issue was compensation, which was not a novel recommendation because in 1888 the government had introduced a local government bill one of the provisions of which was to provide compensation for a licensee whose application for the renewal of his licence was turned down. But even with government support the bill failed.

Two years later the government brought forward another scheme, the Chancellor of the Exchequer proposing to devote £350,000 to provide compensation for extinguished licences. This bill was withdrawn. The same year (1890) Lord Randolph Churchill drafted a licensing amendment bill, of which compensation was a feature. This bill, too, made no progress. This debate was now resurrected by the publication of the 1896–1899 Report of the Royal Commission, continuing to be an issue and reaching a climax, as we shall see, when A. J. Balfour's government introduced a licensing amendment bill in 1904 which included a provision for compensation.

So far as the Royal Commission's Report was concerned, what began as a controversy about compensation, developed into a public debate about temperance reform, which was reflected in the national press, and in trade and temperance journals. It prompted lobbying of members of parliament by all who had taken sides on the issues involved. Temperance reform became a political issue; some would say a party political issue, with the Liberals on the side of temperance reform and the Tories opposing any measures which might embarrass the trade.

Temperance reaction

With so much evidence in favour of reforming legislation, even in the Majority Report of the Royal Commission, one would have expected to find unity among the temperance advocates and organizations. In fact within the temperance movement there was division. *Alliance News*, the major temperance journal, which at that time was published weekly, provided a medium for the controversy. The more uncompromising advocates were so committed to the pursuit of prohibition by means of the exercise of local veto that they were unwilling to contemplate any measures of licensing reform. Others, while not yielding in their zeal for temperance reform, saw value in the achievement of limited objectives. This view was well expressed by the Connexional Temperance Secretary of the Wesleyan Church, the Revd G. Armstrong Bennetts, in a letter to *Alliance News:*

> *We must be practical men. Even if we could calculate that the Teetotallers will at the next election subordinate all other questions to Temperance, and vote only for such candidates as will support vigorous Temperance legislation, the teetotal vote is not sufficient to carry the election. As practical politicians, our plan should be to go for such measures as will carry with us a large number of persons who are eager that something should be done, but are not yet ready to accept the programme which commends itself to teetotallers.*[9]

There were, he said, a great many such people who would not accept any scheme of licensing reform which did not include some concessions to the principle of compensation. He urged his "Temperance friends" to "unite upon Lord Peel's report as a basis of union for immediate legislation". While many declined such an invitation, a very considerable body of opinion supported Lord Peel. Well-attended conferences and public meetings were held in many places providing opportunities for Lord Peel's proposals to be explained and supported. The assemblies of the major Christian churches all passed resolutions in support of the proposals.

These proposals were the main subject for discussion at the annual meetings of the United Kingdom Alliance, at Manchester in November

1900. The President, Sir Wilfrid Lawson, had just been defeated at the general election. He gave a characteristic presidential address, characteristic for him, that is. He was well known for his humour and flashes of satire, which ensured that he held the attention of audiences whether he was on a temperance or a political platform. His speeches to temperance audiences were contrived not only to capture attention, but to arouse fervour. By the time of the annual meeting of 1900 it was widely known in the Temperance Movement that he was a reluctant supporter of those who were pressing for the adoption of Lord Peel's proposals as a basis of temperance policy. At heart he was a prohibitionist. It was this conviction which prompted his unswerving resolve to secure legislation which would introduce the local veto. It was not surprising that he made scarcely any reference to Lord Peel and his Minority Report, but chose to give prominence to the addendum to the Majority Report, signed by what Sir Wilfrid described as "five of the best men in the country I know". The addendum favoured two measures which were not recommended in the Majority Report. These were local veto and the closure of licensed premises on Sundays. The signatories were, the Archbishop of Canterbury*, Charles Cameron, W. C. Caine, J. Herbert Roberts and Thomas P. Whittaker, but not, be it noted, Lord Peel. In a satirical passage, Sir Wilfrid said, "I admire greatly the licensing reformers. They have been at it for three hundred and fifty years and are not tired yet. Well, let them go on, I wish them God speed. If they can find a way of carrying on the trade without doing harm, the Alliance will be dissolved tomorrow. But until then, we are not going to be shifted by licensing reformers or anyone else."[10]

It was rousing stuff. And the address ended, as might be expected, with an uncompromising appeal to the troops. "There stands the liquor traffic" he declared, "here stands the army, the Prohibition army, marshalled for the noblest work ever allotted to humanity. Turn aside, if you please, by the by-paths of compromise and you are lost. Go straight and your ultimate triumph is as certain as the rising of tomorrow's sun."[11]

Sir Wilfrid had not been explicit, but his lukewarmness towards Lord Peel's proposals was implicit in his references to "reformers" and "the by-paths of compromise". His views were reflected in the resolution which was brought to the annual meeting from the UKA executive:

> *That this Council heartily welcomes the Report of the Minority of the Royal Commission on Licensing, and pledges itself to give the recommendations of that Report a cordial yet discriminating support, whilst reiterating its declaration that no legislation can be adequate which does not confer upon the people of the United Kingdom power to veto the grant or renewal of licences for the sale of intoxicating liquor in their respective localities.*[12]

This resolution was moved by T. P. Whittaker MP, who had been a member of the Royal Commission and was one of the signatories of the Minority Report. His speech was perceptive and diplomatic. He did not speak to the Minority Report, but to the resolution. This enabled him to say at the beginning that ". . . we do not intend to drop the Veto. We are going to advocate it still. We are going to press for it . . . . We are not going to adopt or take up Lord Peel's report as the basis of our policy".[13] The aim of

* *Frederick Temple.*

the UKA had always been to secure prohibition, and the means of getting it was "not a question of principle so much as of tactics and expedience". In view of the situation created by the publication of the Minority Report, the following passage from Whittaker's speech seems important:

> *The Alliance recognised more than forty years ago that Prohibition cannot be got at a step, at a bound, and we all admit that. There is the intervening ground between the position we are in today and the position we are aiming at, and that intervening ground has to be covered. The question is how can we traverse that space most quickly and most easily? We want the readiest road to it. Is taking at any time less than we wish lowering our flag?*[14]

He thought not, and the audience agreed with him. The Alliance had always been ready to adapt its resolution and its policies and readjust its demands in the light of what was deemed expedient and possible. He gave some illustrations of actions taken by the Alliance in which Sir Wilfrid Lawson had played an active role. Whittaker had prepared the way for the annual meeting to pass the resolution and to support Lord Peel's proposals.

"I have frequently stated from this platform that it is not the business of the UKA, as an organisation, to propose licensing reform" declared Whittaker. "But we are deeply interested in it. On this point, perhaps Sir Wilfrid and I do not altogether agree, though I think we might if we talked in private, but we are deeply interested in licensing reform."[15] He said that he knew Sir Wilfrid was interested in the Children's Bill and that everyone was interested in such matters as the question of appeal being removed from Quarter Session, and in reducing the number of public houses. It was not the business of the UKA to respond to every irresponsible licensing scheme, but the Report of the Royal Commission was different. The country, and certainly everyone in the Temperance Movement, would expect the UKA to give some guidance and advice on these matters. The annual meeting was clearly with him when he said:

> *We should not allow the impression to be created throughout the country that we are against any of the proposals, against the Report, because now our opinion is challenged. If we decline to say anything it will be urged all over that it is simply because we are opponents, and do not care to say so. That would be a very damaging result. That would alienate from us a large number of people, who are not what we may call Temperance stalwarts, but are amongst the great mass of the community which we must carry with us, if we are to carry our measures – and if we alienate that element we weaken our power. Yes, rather we must carry them with us.*[16]

Influential members of the UKA, such as Lief Jones (later Lord Rhayader), Guy Hayler, W. S. Caine and Joseph Malins spoke in the debate and expressed the view that it would have been better not to have made a pronouncement on either the majority or minority reports, but since the resolution they were being asked to support contained a reference to "discriminating support" and reiterated the plea for local veto, they would vote for it. When it was put to the vote the resolution was carried with only two or three dissentients.

This was an important policy decision, not only for the United Kingdom Alliance, but for the future course of temperance reform in Britain. The plea for full-blooded prohibition remained the message of the

Alliance, but it did not again inhibit it from engaging in initiating and drafting bills for specific and limited reforms. The debate about Lord Peel's proposals had enabled the Temperance Movement to see that much could be achieved by realizing limited objectives. For instance, it was shown that if Lord Peel's proposals for the reduction in the number of licences with compensation were adopted the number of licensed premises would fall dramatically over the seven-year statutory period.[17] As we have seen, this was an exceedingly controversial matter and was not one of the limited objectives which would have united the Temperance Movement. However, one which did was that to prohibit the sale of intoxicating liquor to children under sixteen.

Concern for children

As the law stood in 1900 the following provisions were made as far as children were concerned: (a) children of any age might buy beer and spirits for consumption off the premises, (b) children of thirteen and upwards might buy and drink beer on the premises, (c) children of sixteen and upwards might buy and drink either beer or spirits on the premises. At the beginning of the new session of parliament on 13th January 1900 no less than thirteen bills on various aspects of licensing were presented. Two bills to prevent the sale of intoxicating liquor to young children, either for their own consumption, or as messengers for others, were tabled by Sir Joseph Leese and Robinson Souttar. Neither obtained a good position in the ballot for private member's bills, but unexpectedly an opportunity came for Souttar to present his bill on 6th March 1900. After a brief discussion it was read a second time on 9th March without division, but it was still on the order paper when parliament was prorogued and so it made no further progress. In the next session a bill with similar provisions was introduced by J. W. Crombie (Kincardinshire) and on 20th March 1901 came up for second reading when the vote was 372 in favour and 54 against. Although the bill was read a second time, the operation of the time rule prevented it from going to committee. Only government intervention could ensure further progress, and the government view was that progress could only be facilitated if the bill was made uncontentious. They insisted on various amendments, but eventually on 14th August 1901 a third reading was given to the bill, the main provision of which was to forbid the sale of intoxicating liquor to children under fourteen, save in quantities of not less than one reputed pint, corked and sealed. This protected children from the temptation to "swig" a drop from an open jug or similar container. The title of the legislation was The Intoxicating Liquors (Sale to Children) Act 1901, but it was often called the "Child Messenger Act".

References

1. *Nineteen Centuries of Drink in England*, R. Valpy French p. 138.
2. *French* op cit p. 151.
3. *Drink, Temperance and Legislation*, Arthur Shadwell p. 26.
4. See pp. 207, 221.

5. The complete series, including eight further prints of a sequel to *The Bottle* are displayed at the Temperance Research and Information Centre, 12 Caxton Street, London S.W.1. See also *The Man Who Drew the Drunkard's Daughter. The Life and Art of George Cruikshank (1792–1828)* Hilary and Mary Evans (1978).
6. French op cit p. 382.
7. Report of Royal Commission on Liquor Licensing Laws 1899 p.2.
8. Op cit Part V chapter 1 (vi) p. 51.
9. *Alliance News* 4th January 1900 p. 3.
10. *Alliance News* 7th December 1900 p. 778.
11. *Alliance News* 7th December 1900 p. 779.
12. *Alliance News* 7th December 1900 p. 779.
13. *Alliance News* 7th December 1900 p. 780.
14. *Alliance News* 7th December 1900 p. 780.
15. *Alliance News* 7th December 1900 p. 780.
16. *Alliance News* 7th December 1900 p. 780.
17.

	1900	**After 7 years**
Liverpool	2,109	839
Manchester	2,361	720
Sheffield	1,187	475
Birmingham	1,703	680
Newcastle	568	300
Leeds	783	547

CHAPTER 2

NEW OBJECTIVES FOR A NEW CENTURY

The popular estimate of the mood of the nation at the turn of the century is that people believed then that "every day and in every way the world was getting better and better". In so far as this mood applied to the drink problem there was certainly need for optimism. In the latter half of the nineteenth century its dimensions had vastly increased, and drunkenness was a major feature of the social scene. There were threats to the welfare of children, not only from drunken parents, but from the accessibility of liquor to the children themselves, so that the magnitude of the problems had prepared the public for legislation to mitigate the destructive consequences of excessive drinking.

In the chapter devoted to "Children and Drink"[1] we have referred to the passing of the Intoxicating Liquor (Sale to Children) Act 1901. This was the first piece of liquor legislation to be passed in the new century. It was also brought in by a new parliament elected in October 1900. The general election was notable for temperance reformers because their leader, Sir Wilfrid Lawson, lost his seat, his failure to be elected depriving the house of one of its most entertaining parliamentarians. However, in the annual report of the United Kingdom Alliance, of which Sir Wilfrid was the President, it was declared: "There is nothing whatever in the result of the election which needs to cause the Temperance party any discouragement." If the house had lost Sir Wilfrid Lawson, it had gained "a number of young men, more thoroughly educated on the "Temperance" question than were even the friends of temperance of a former generation the in the House".[2]

The candidates at the general election had been canvassed for their views about the introduction of local option, which Sir Wilfrid Lawson had campaigned for throughout his parliamentary career. Local option would have given people in any locality the opportunity to decide whether they wished to have licensed premises in their neighbourhood or not. Temperance reformers believed that given the option the day would come when the people would choose to prohibit the sale of liquor. In 1900, of the 960 parliamentary candidates who expressed an opinion, 365 were in favour of local option, 480 against and 115 were doubtful. Of the 567 who were returned, 181 were in favour, 341 were against and 45 were doubtful. These figures give some indication of the number of MPs who could have been counted on to support not only local option, but other legislation to implement temperance reform. However, it was the concept of local option for which the United Kingdom Alliance and its supporters in parliament campaigned throughout the latter part of the previous century, and which was their principal objective in the new century and the new parliament, but with the composition of the House of Commons as it was, the prospect for such legislation was not favourable.

One measure which did gain support was the Intoxicating Liquor (Sale to Children) Act, 1901. Although it was criticized for not going far enough, it did prohibit the sale of liquor in unsealed vessels to children under fourteen years of age.[3]

Licensing Act 1902

In 1902, the government introduced a major licensing bill. This was presented to parliament on 30th January by C. T. Ritchie (Home Secretary). At that time there was considerable agitation among those concerned with liquor licensing, as retailers, magistrates and temperance reformers, about the reduction of licences and compensation for licences declared redundant, which the Home Secretary said the new bill did not purport to deal with. The bill was in three parts. The first dealt with the individual drunkard, making the way for this transgressor harder, though it also increased the responsibility of the publican as regards serving an already drunken person, or a declared inebriate. The second part sought to deal more gently with the licensee as to endorsements, and substituted a justices' record of convictions to be produced at each annual meeting of the licensing justices. Five convictions in five years would place the renewal of a licence in jeopardy. The third part was concerned exclusively with clubs and a proposal that they should be registered under certain conditions. Although this bill did not represent radical licensing reform, the United Kingdom Alliance concluded that it was "from a Temperance point of view unobjectionable".[4] The UKA executive passed a resolution recording its "hearty approval of the several provisions of that measure, and recommends the friends of the Alliance throughout the country to give the bill their cordial support."[5]

The second reading of the bill took place in April and it was referred to committee. Although it had a protracted passage it was finally passed on 8th August and came into force on 1st January 1903.

The new act amended the law on drunkenness, making it an offence to be drunk and incapable in a public place. It was also made unlawful for a person to be drunk while in charge of a child under seven. Such a person, on summary conviction, would be liable to a fine not exceeding two pounds or to imprisonment for any period not exceeding one month. Under the act persons declared to be habitual drunkards were prohibited from purchasing liquor. These were persons who had been convicted under the Inebriates Act 1898, and who in the twelve months prior to the offence in question had been convicted three times. In such instances the record of their offences could be taken into account. This procedure was often referred to as "black-listing". Black-listed persons were liable, on summary conviction, to a fine not exceeding, for the first offence, twenty shillings and for a subsequent offence, forty shillings. Anyone selling liquor to a black-listed person was liable to a fine not exceeding ten pounds for a first offence, and for subsequent offences fines not exceeding twenty pounds. "A black-listed convicted person is thus liable to a penalty if he purchases or obtains, or attempts to purchase or obtain, intoxicating liquor at any retail 'on' or 'off' licensed premises or at a registered club. He cannot even lawfully obtain at such premises a bottle of wine for consumption at home."[6]

The act brought in new regulations regarding so-called "Grocers' Licences". As the law stood, such a licence was obtained as a right of being a shopkeeper, and the justices had no power to refuse it. This referred to the sale of wine, spirits and beer to be consumed off the premises, until 1882 when a bill was introduced which gave justices the power to refuse licences for the sale of beer. The justices still had no power to refuse a licence for the sale of wine and spirits. Should the grocer die before the expiration in any year of a licence, the commission of Inland Revenue was required to direct the executors, or administrators, or widow or child of the deceased grocer, to continue the business without additional duty. At the next licensing session, and subsequent sessions, the justices would have no power to withhold the licence from the person carrying on the business. This represented holding a licence in perpetuity. Under the new act, no new licence could be obtained without the will of the justices, and then held for one year, with a liability of being refused renewal at any future licensing session. The justices would, of course, grant a new licence to the person carrying on the grocery business, but all the privileges of the old licence died with the holder.

There were various new licensing procedures incorporated in the new act. Plans for proposed licensed premises had to be deposited with the clerk to the justices before an application was made. No justices clerk could act for an applicant outside his own petty sessional district. Annual licensing sessions were to be held in the first fourteen days of February throughout the country. In future special licences, which could be obtained from one magistrate, had to be obtained from a petty sessional court, or from two magistrates sitting together. No licensing session could be held on licensed premises, and coroners' juries could not meet in public houses.

An attempt was made to deal with the vexed question of clubs. The act provided that clubs should be registered and powers given to strike off the list any unsatisfactory club. Unregistered clubs could be prosecuted for selling liquor without a licence. No liquor could be sold for consumption off the premises except to a member on the premises.

A person supplying or obtaining liquor in contravention of this part of the act was liable to be fined ten pounds. It was in the area of the clubs that the effects of the act were first seen. There were a great many "bogus" clubs, especially in London, and many of these succumbed to the operation of the new measure. The provisions relating to club registration required all applications to be made by 2nd February, the month of January being allowed for club proprietors to comply with the new requirements. *Alliance News* reported, "Of the numerous sham clubs which have made Soho notorious, nearly all failed to apply for registration on Monday (February 2), and some of them had even put up their shutters in January."[7]

Enforcement of the act

Magistrates lost no time in enforcing the new act. On New Year's Day the senior magistrate at West London took his seat with a copy of the act in front of him. As charges of drunkenness were brought before him he referred to the act and applied the clause relating to black-listed habitual drunkards. In two cases the gaoler proved that the offenders had been convicted three times within the last twelve months. The magistrates, in imposing a fine, announced that in each case the conviction would be notified to the police and the defendant would be debarred, under pain of heavy penalty, from purchasing liquor for a period of three years.[8] Such cases were not without humour. At Southwark, 36-year-old Mary Murphy (Snuffy Annie) pleaded guilty to being drunk and disorderly. The gaoler gave evidence of six convictions in the last twelve months and forty others. When sentenced to one month's imprisonment the defendant responded joyfully – "Thank you". Matilda Murray, a 35-year-old flower seller, charged with being drunk and disorderly was extremely voluble at Marlborough Street Magistrate's Court, until she was given the option of a fine of forty shillings or a month in prison. Then she was removed from the court without uttering a word, sobered, no doubt, by the magistrate's warning – "If you get liquor for the next three years it will be at your peril." The husband of a 50-year-old woman who said his wife had been convicted 20 times before told the magistrate at Clerkenwell – "Take her away from me for God's sake". When asked if he wanted to take a summons against her, the husband replied – "Do as you like with her. Burn her!"[9] Similar cases were reported from provincial courts, indicating the determination of magistrates to apply the act vigorously and immediately. In the West London court on New Year's Day, a young woman was convicted of being drunk in charge of a child under the age of seven. The magistrate warned that in all such cases the law would be rigidly enforced. For several weeks *Alliance News* carried news from all parts of the country, proving that the new act was welcomed by the courts and was being rigorously enforced.

The act itself was a "best seller". It was on sale at twopence a copy from the parliamentary printers Eyre and Spottiswoode. On Tuesday, 6th January it was reported that over 60,000 copies had been sold. The previous day there had been an unceasing stream of purchasers. Publicans, temperance workers, secretaries of clubs, grocers and husbands and wives, "flowed through all the crooked lanes and alleys and squares and passages" to the printing works. Here half-a-dozen clerks were kept hard at work all day selling copies of the act. It was so popular that a parody of it, carrying the Royal Arms, appeared on the streets of London and was purchased by many people as the real thing. Six people were later fined for this sale of indecent literature.[10]

The impact of the act can probably be seen in statistics for convictions for drunkenness in England and Wales. For the years 1895 to 1899 the average per 10,000 for all persons, that is male and female, was 54.30. From 1900 to 1904 the average was 59.35, which probably reflects the application of the new law. From 1905 this ratio began to decline. In the period 1905 to 1909 the average was 54.92 and in the following five-year period 50.97. This seems to indicate that the new act had had an effect. During the period 1900 to 1905, when the act was first applied, the number of publicans' licences declined only slightly in England and Wales, from 7,202 to 7,025. The decline in convictions was more dramatic from 1915 onwards, but this can be attributed to the severe restrictions, particularly on opening hours, which were introduced as wartime measures and subsequently retained after the First World War. This may be seen from the following table:[11]

1915–19 average per 10,000 persons 21.34
1920–24 average per 10,000 persons 21.86
1925–29 average per 10,000 persons 16.01
1930–35 average per 10,000 persons 11.04

Death of Archbishop Temple

We shall return to a consideration of the introduction and impact of wartime restrictions, but any account of the early years of the twentieth century ought to include a reference to the influence of Frederick Temple, the Archbishop of Canterbury, who died on 23rd December 1902, at the age of eighty-two. An obituary described him as "the only Archbishop for half a century at least who was a total abstainer". The *Westminster Gazette* reported that he was not a teetotaller in his early days.[12] He became one, as he explained on more than one occasion, because he believed his example would be a help to the cause. "For years and years past Dr Temple was, in virtue of his position, the most powerful and conspicuous of all temperance advocates, and no one can deny that he himself was a splendid illustration of its virtue."[13] And yet he had "a breadth of Temperance view not exercised by all Temperance men".[14] A guest at Lambeth Palace was told by the Archbishop, "You know my principles. You will find nothing but water on my dinner table, but my servants have orders to see that wine is placed in your bedroom." A curate, an intolerant teetotaller, who was invited to lunch at Lambeth Palace observed, "I am astonished to see wine on your table, my Lord." To which the Archbishop sharply replied, "You are not asked to drink it." On his travels, if he gave a luncheon, he ensured that sherry and claret were liberally supplied for those who wanted it.[15] His own tolerance of other people's views strengthened his advocacy of a principle which in his own life was never in jeopardy. Canon Edward Lee Hicks, in an appreciation in *Alliance News,* said that Archbishop Temple felt himself to be the leader of churchmen on the temperance question. "He was anxious not to break with any church friends who would join him, nor to alienate or alarm any who were willing to follow him even with halting steps".[16] The national press too, acknowledged that it was his genuine tolerance linked with his personal integrity which drew to the causes he espoused the support of people prominent in various areas of the nation's life. This was particularly true in respect of temperance reform. Whereas some earlier temperance advocates had antagonized public opinion by their vehemence, Archbishop Temple and others who shared his approach won widespread respect for this cause. This was seen in the quite remarkable growth of the temperance sentiment in the years after William Temple's death and on into the second and third decades of the twentieth century.

Resistance from the trade

The progress of the temperance sentiment was made in the face of powerful resistance from the trade. This opposition was directed particularly against the increasing inclination of justices to reduce the number of licensed premises. Considerable impetus was given to this movement by the action of the Licensing Justices of Farnham in 1902 when they introduced a ratio of one licensed house for every 155 adult persons in the community, and proceeded to declare licences redundant without compensation.[17] There was a swift reaction from the trade. In February 1903 the Licensed Victuallers' Central Protection Society called a mass meeting of London licensees at the Queen's Hall to discuss the question of the reduction of licences and compensation. The chairman of the Central Board, Edward Johnson, surprised the audience at the beginning of his speech, when he said, "I appeal to the gentlemen present to abstain . . . ." After a momentary pause, he added ". . . . from smoking". On the main theme of his speech, the reduction of licences, he said that the assumption was too often made that the reduction of licences led to a reduction of drunkenness. The Majority Report of the Royal Commission had in fact given statistics which showed that far from reducing drunkenness the reduction of licences appeared to lead to an increase in intemperance. Johnson thought it was an inopportune time to clamour for a reduction of licences to decrease drunkenness. Would it not have been better to wait and see what was the effect of the new act? He admitted that while the act added to the burden and responsibilities of licensees it was a fair and reasonable effort to punish the drunkard, and he was sure that they were willing to give it a fair trial. To these views the audience responded with applause.

Why was a licence granted, he asked. Surely because the justices thought it was necessary for the comfort and social requirement of a particular place. The publican was enlisted in a form of public service at his own expense, he was risking his capital in the enterprise. When the justices reached the conclusion that the licence was no longer needed in the public interest, they were surely under an obligation to restore the publican to his former state. He rejected the concept of a "redundant licence". No licence carried on at a profit, even a small one was redundant. He agreed that in certain older parts of London there were more licences than were necessary. If, however, some of them were to be removed the holders were entitled to compensation. This might take one of two forms, direct cash or the option of the transfer of the licence to premises in an area to which people had moved and where there was greater necessity for one. If there was to be monetary compensation, this should come from public funds and not from the licensees. Reginald Mortimer, barrister-at-law, said he was tired of hearing magistrates say that licences were renewable year by year. Every licensee had almost a sacred right to have his licence renewed, unless he was guilty of misconduct. A resolution expressing the views of the meeting was passed and sent to the government. Sir Thomas Dewar thought there was a prospect of parliamentary action in their favour because, he said, "I think we have now far more friends in the House of Commons than we ever had, and this is entirely owing to the drastic measures adopted by magistrates in various parts of the country."[18]

On 18th March 1903 the Prime Minister, A. J. Balfour, received a deputation composed of representatives of all sections of the trade in England and Wales regarding the recent action of magistrates in the suppression of licences. The deputation included a large number of members of parliament. Introducing the deputation, John Gretton MP said the trade had become very agitated about the recent action of magistrates in this matter. It was the view of the trade that legislation was needed to remedy the grievances. Another MP, J. G. Groves, made two points which were later taken up by the Prime Minister. The first was that magistrates seemed to be acting upon a constraint, apparently laid upon them by quarter sessions, that it was desirable to reduce the number of licences. The second was that many magistrates regretted that because the matter of compensation for redundant licences had not been dealt with in the 1902 Act, they were precluded from taking this into account. On the first point the Prime Minister said, "I cannot conceive it to be the business of quarter sessions to give instructions of that character to the brewster sessions; they are a court of appeal from the work of the brewster sessions, and they ought not, I conceive, to lay down any judgments until the matter comes before them in their judicial capacity as a Court of Appeal."[19] On the second point, he did not know how the inference arose that because the matter of compensation had not been included in the 1902 Act the government had no particular interest in it.

However, Balfour regarded these issues as subsidiary to the main issue, that of the policy recently adopted by magistrates in reducing the number of licences. He regretted their action, not least because it was not giving the 1902 Act a chance to work: an act which had the support of the Temperance Movement and of the trade. Since the matter of the reduction of licences had now become a controversial issue he was afraid it was going to be difficult to follow a smooth path. "If for that reason alone (and I have strong reasons besides), I confess I regret the course the magistrates have pursued."[20] The deputation could not have been other than delighted by the statement which followed. The Prime Minister clearly accepted the argument that publicans and owners of public houses laboured under severe injustice. Because of the insistence that a licence was for one year only, the property could not be regarded as an investment nor was it insurable. Moreover, the taxation system worked unjustly against them. He was also concerned that a bench of magistrates were the successors of those who had granted the licences in the first place, and created the situation which the present benches felt constrained to change. Although they were not bound to the letter by the action of their predecessors "they must consider themselves as in-part trustees of the past, and that any change which is made should be made gradually, and with a full regard to those interests which their predecessors themselves have called into existence". He feared that a consequence of a too-rigorous pursuit of the reduction of licences would mean that the insecurity created would drive out of the trade men of position and substance. If that happened the trade could fall into the hands of men who had nothing to lose; and so the best interests of temperance would not be served. The Prime Minister said he could not disclose the intentions of the government to deal with so recent a development, but it seemed to them that what was happening was "little short in its practical effect of injustice and confiscation of property" and to this neither the government nor parliament could remain indifferent.

The Prime Minister's speech was widely reported in the press, and newpapers carried substantial editorial comments on his views. If Balfour's intention was to arouse a public debate on the issue of compensation and prepare the way for implementing legislation, he certainly succeeded. *The Times*, while accepting that "the conditions of capricious insecurity which is threatened should be averted", wondered where the proposed compensation would come from.[21] It was not surprising to find the *Daily Telegraph* supporting the Prime Minister, and commenting that his remarks would serve as a useful reminder to magistrates to curb their excess of reforming zeal, and would "stay the panic which was spreading through a most important industry".[22] The *Manchester Guardian* and the *Daily News* were exceedingly critical of the Prime Minister's speech. Said the *Manchester Guardian,* "His speech reads like an echo of the speeches usually made at licensed victuallers' trade dinners and meetings."[23] In a long editorial the speech was "taken apart" and the fallacies thoroughly exposed. "At the bottom of all these fallacies" it declared, "is the fallacious notion that in consenting to accept a licence to sell drink a man places his countrymen under an obligation to ensure his future. But the acceptance of a licence to sell drink is not a perilous or arduous public service. The grant of a licence is simply an enormously valuable gift, and the gratuitous bestowal of such a gift imposes an obligation not on him who gives but on him who receives it." The *Daily News* was outraged by the attack on the magistrates, which for a man in Balfour's position was "without parallel in the annals of modern politics". "We regard the speech as nothing less than the prostitution of the greatest office in the British Empire" declared the editorial.[24]

Compensation

The first attempt to introduce legislation to provide compensation to publicans for redundant licences was made by J. G. Butcher (York) in a Private Member's Bill. The object of the bill was to provide compensation in all cases where licences were suppressed for reasons other than the misconduct of the licence holder, in order to reduce the number of licensed houses in the country. The provisions were intended to include the licences of the ante-1869 beerhouses. The amount of compensation would be the fair value of the licence and the goodwill, and the compensation would be provided out of contributions from the trade. In each county or borough a compensation authority would collect and distribute the compensation. At the second reading debate on 24th April 1903 the familiar arguments for and against the principle of compensation were clearly expressed and at the end of the bill was read a second time. The controversy over this issue which had been aroused by the Prime Minister's speech to the trade deputation was given fresh impetus by the successful second reading of Butcher's Bill. Churches and temperance organizations held protest meetings and passed resolutions condemning the bill. At Leeds, for instance, nearly four thousand people crowded the coliseum for a "no compensation" public meeting.[25] Similar public meetings were held in many cities and towns throughout the country. In London a conference to protest against interference with the powers of magistrates over licences was held at Caxton Hall, London.[26] The list of those present indicated the strength of opposition from persons in various areas of public life, and the list of those who did not attend, but expressed their support for the resolution passed at the conference, read like an extract of *Who's Who.*[27] The campaign organized by the churches and temperance organizations which had mobilized thousands of people at meetings in most of the principal provincial cities reached its climax on 17th July 1903 at the Albert Hall in London. This was attended by representatives from nearly 5,000 temperance, religious and social organizations. The purpose of this large convention was to register an emphatic protest not only against Butcher's Bill to introduce compensation, but also against another Private Member's Bill, introduced by Sir W. Hart Dyke, which aimed at suspending the power of magistrates to refuse renewal of licences. There was an afternoon session at which certain resolutions were passed and an evening demonstration at which the Bishop of London* presided. In reporting the convention the *Daily News* said, "Yesterday ten thousand men and women entered their protest against the scheme for establishing a vested interest in the drink traffic . . . . the great meeting in the Albert Hall last night is one of many signs that the brewers, though they have captured the government, have not yet captured the country." It is worth mentioning that on the very day of the convention, Sir William Hart Dyke's Bill was abandoned in the House of Commons. It was later restored to the Order Paper. However, in August, in answer to a question, the Prime Minister announced that "it would be quite impossible for the Government to give facilities for either of the Bills interfering with the discretion of justices in granting licences."

A report in the *Yorkshire Post* on 12th January 1904 foreshadowed that although the government would not facilitate the progress of these bills, it had its own intentions to introduce legislation. In what was described as a "rough general summary" it indicated the anticipated provisions of a new licensing bill to be introduced during the approaching session of parliament. On the major issue of compensation it was reported that no statutory scheme would be introduced. Instead, the licensed victuallers would be left free to frame their own scheme, the funds for compensation being found from the trade, none being provided by the exchequer. The bill would provide for a period of five years, during which magistrates would be deprived of all power to take away a licence on the sole ground that it was not needed in the neighbourhood. During this period it was hoped the trade would effect sensible reductions in the number of licences. The basis for granting new licences would be one for the price of two. That is, for the surrender of two old licences, one new one would be granted. However, the area in which such a scheme would operate would be that covered by quarter sessions instead of petty sessions. Ante-1869 beer houses would be placed on the same footing as others, that is, placing their renewal at the absolute discretion of the justices. The report that the government had such legislative intentions brought an immediate reaction from the temperance forces. A meeting of representatives of temperance organizations was held in London to initiate a strategy.[28]

In an objective account of the "alcohol problem" in the early part of the twentieth century the response of the Temperance Movement must be given prominence. We have noted already that the campaign launched against a Private Member's Bill was on a massive scale by any standards. Few causes at that time could have guaranteed filling the largest halls in

* *A. F. Winnington-Ingram.*

provincial towns and cities as well as the Albert Hall in London. With this in mind, it is not surprising to find that a month before the publication of the government's bill, the temperance forces were into a campaign to oppose any erosion of the discretion of justices and the introduction of a scheme of compensation. A national conference and demonstration was convened at Exeter Hall, London by some of the principal temperance organizations. *Alliance News,* which reported it fully, described it as "the most representative of its kind ever held in the metropolis".[29] The judgement is borne out by the list of organizations represented and by the range of speakers from the churches and parliament. Fifteen bishops of the Church of England who were unable to be present sent messages of support for the intention of the meetings.

Balfour's Compensation Act

The bill which had been promised in the King's Speech was published on 23rd April 1904. It was entitled "A Bill to amend the Licensing Acts 1828 to 1902 in respect to the extinction of licences and the grant of new licences". The main provisions were that the power to refuse the renewal of a licence on grounds other than that the licensed premises had been ill-conducted, or that they were structurally deficient or unsuitable, or on grounds connected with the character or fitness of the proposed licence-holder should be vested in quarter sessions and not the local licensing justices. The grounds for the refusal of an on-licence by the justices would be specified in writing to the applicant. The local justices would be required to refer to quarter sessions any application for renewal on grounds other than those with which they were competent to deal. Refusals in either courts would be accompanied by compensation as determined in the act. The scale of compensation would be laid down in the act and in default of agreement the amount to be paid would be determined by the Commissioners of Inland Revenue in the same manner and subject to the same appeal as on the valuation of an estate for the purpose of estate duty. The compensation would be divided among the interested parties by agreement, or if not by the quarter sessions. The compensation fund would be raised by charges on the licensed premises in the area. In presenting the bill on its first reading, the Home Secretary (A. Akers-Douglas) said there might be different views as to the methods to be employed for reducing licences, but he did not think that anybody thought a reduction was not necessary. He expounded the reasons why the government thought such a measure was necessary, and described the provisions of the bill. Sir Henry Campbell-Bannerman, leader of the Liberal opposition, promised the most strenuous resistance to the bill. There were three provisions on which the opposition would insist. These were, first, no tampering with, or modification of, the discretion of local magistrates. Second, nothing should be done to assign anything in the nature of a vested interest or right to the licensee, and third, that no compensation should come from public funds. In the debate, the arguments for and against the intentions of the bill were cogently expressed and the voting at the end was 314 in favour and 147 against.

The bill, which was generally welcomed by the trade, had a mixed reception in the national press. The temperance organizations, as we have seen, were already mobilized for opposition. Their campaign against this bill is the clearest possible illustration of the strength of the temperance movement at the turn of the century, and its ability to mount nationwide action "at the drop of a hat". By the time of the second reading, which commenced on 9th May 1904 and was concluded on 11th May 1904, the campaign against the bill was in full flood. Once more massive meetings and demonstrations were held in the major cities. In Liverpool the St. George's Hall was crowded, as was the Coliseum at Leeds and the Free Trade Hall in Manchester. In Birmingham, ten processions, headed by two bands each, and carrying hundreds of banners, converged on the area outside the town hall. It was estimated that 10,000 people took part in the processions and that 20,000 more lined the route. The climax of this nationwide campaign was a demonstration in Hyde Park, London. On Saturday, 25th June 1904 processions of demonstrators from seventy different meeting places throughout London converged on the Embankment where they were marshalled four-abreast. "For over an hour-and-three-quarters they marched steadily on, while the side-streets, and even Park Lane itself, were choked with raging motorists and aristocratic broughams, landaus and victorias."[30] As the great procession reached Hyde Park it was met by the contingent from Battersea. With them were three van-loads of drunkards' children in native costume and carrying a banner with the striking slogan, "Say, Guv'nor, who is going to compensate us?" At the park the crowd, estimated by one newspaper correspondence at 40,000 at least, dispersed round fourteen or more platforms. In all there were 200 speakers. By any standards, for any cause at all, this demonstration was almost unparalleled.

According to experienced parliamentary observers the scenes in the House of Commons during the committee stage, when the Prime Minister sought to carry a closure motion by compartments on the bill, were also unparalleled. The Prime Minister was constantly interrupted and there were lively exchanges between various members on either side of the house, in one of which Winston Churchill was engaged in opposing the government "I do not remember witnessing such earnest, nervous emotion manifested by the whole dense mass on the opposition side as was shown during this notable sitting" commented the lobby correspondent of *Alliance News*.[31] News of the debate on the closure motion spread outside the house and after the adjournment for dinner, and on the resumption of the debate, the outside lobby became crowded with London constituents. They had come immediately to urge their MPs to vote against the closure. Hundreds of people could not get in and messengers and officials found it difficult to get through the crowd. Eventually the closure order was passed and limits set to the committee stage, during which most of the amendments proposed were not adopted. The bill went to the Lords where it had an easy passage, and having passed through the final stages it received the Royal Assent on 15th August 1904. It came into force on 1st January 1905.

The chief effects of the new act were to curtail the absolute discretion of the local justices in respect of the renewal of existing licences, though this was retained as far as new licences were concerned; to introduce the concept of the perpetuity of licences because of the virtual surrender of annual licensing; and the provision of compensation which helped to establish a vested interest in licensed premises. The extent to which the justices' discretion had been set aside by the act was seen in a case at Birkenhead. The Birkenhead justices had asked the applicants for the renewal of their licences to give six undertakings before the issuing of the licences. These were, that intoxicating liquor should not be supplied on credit; that no drink should be supplied to any child under fourteen; that no games, draws or raffles should be allowed on the premises, except billiards; that back doors should be kept locked except for domestic purposes; that licensees should give the whole of their time to the business, and that clubs for the distribution of drink at Christmas or other periods should not be allowed. The justices announced their willingness to renew the licences but to deposit them with the clerk until the applicants had given assurances that these undertakings would be carried out. Before the new act the justices followed this practice because the discretion of the licensing authority was absolute and unlimited. The unanimous opinion of the Court of King's Bench Division was that the old practice was still lawful. However, when the trade took the matter to the Court of Appeal, the court decided by two judges against one that the action of the Birkenhead justices could not stand. Thus justices could no longer withhold licences until undertakings had been given by applicants. This judgment applied to renewals only and did not affect the justices' discretion in respect of new applications.

As to compensation, the act provided for the setting up of compensation authorities. These might consist of the entire body of licensing justices or a smaller group set up by the justices. The compensation authority had two duties to perform each year: first, to collect a compensation fund, and then to distribute it. The fund was to be obtained by a levy on each licensed house, and paid by the tenant or licensee in accordance with a gradual scale, as follows:

Under £15 annual value, levy £1 a year
Under £50 annual value, levy £10 a year
Under £100 annual value, levy £15 a year
Under £500 annual value, levy £50 a year
Over £900 annual value, levy £100 a year

Brewery companies with interests in large numbers of public houses paid this out of income. In some cases this payment was reckoned to be equal to about 2 per cent interest on the share capital. The distribution of the compensation was a more complicated process. In the first instance, a number of licensed houses were selected for non-renewal of their licences. Two sets of valuations were required, one prepared by valuers for the claimants and one prepared by the compensation authority. When the valuation was finally fixed by the compensation authority that amount was paid, provided such sum was in the compensation fund. In the event of the compensation authority being unable to agree the amount to be paid the case was referred to the Inland Revenue.

The declared object of the act was to reduce the number of licences. In May 1906 the government published some licensing statistics which brought the official figures up to the end of 1905.

These showed that in the two years immediately preceding the coming into force of the Licensing Act 1904 the reduction in the number of on-licences, from all causes such as refusals by justices, surrender schemes, street improvements and those not applied for, was 1,850. Against this, 361 new on-licences were granted in the same period. So the total reduction in England and Wales during that two-year period was 1,489 or 744 on-licences per annum, and it is interesting to compare these figures with those for the two-year period after the coming into force of the act. For the latter two-year period the total reductions was 1,924. Thus the government promise that the new act would effect a reduction "incomparably larger" than anything which had previously occurred had not been fulfilled.

Landslide victory for Liberals

In view of the strength of the Temperance Movement at this time the death of its parliamentary leader, Sir Wilfrid Lawson, calls for special mention. He had been president of the United Kingdom Alliance since April 1879 until his death on 1st July 1906. He was seventy-six and although his close associates had noticed his physical powers were declining, he was in his place at the House of Commons for a late sitting on Thursday, 28th June. He went home feeling unwell and died peacefully early on the Sunday morning. We have noted elsewhere his persistent advocacy of local option, and although he never succeeded in securing legislation to give effect to it, his series of Private Member's Bills kept the matter before parliament and the country. The memorial service at St. Margaret's, Westminster, attended by the Prime Minister, the Speaker of the House of Commons, many members of the government and almost one hundred MPs, was itself a tribute to the position Sir Wilfrid had won in public life. This is not the place to record a biographical note, but no reference could be made to any event in temperance reform in the year 1906 without reference to the death of the most outstanding temperance leader of his time.

It was fitting that he should have won back his original seat at Cockermouth in the general election held early in 1906, when the Liberals under Sir Henry Campbell-Bannerman won a notable victory. The Unionist Government under Balfour resigned in November 1905 and Campbell-Bannerman agreed to form a ministry. "The ensuing election of 1906 resulted in an utter rout of the Unionist Party, due not so much to the conversion of the electorate to Radicalism, as to a widespread feeling that the South African War, if it could not have been avoided, was grossly mismanaged in its earlier stages; to the determination of the industrial parts of the country not to abandon Free Trade, which at least gave them cheap food, for the alleged benefits of Protection; to the dissatisfaction of the Nonconformists with the Education Act of 1902; and to the unpopularity among the organised workers of Chinese labour and of the Taff Vale judgment, which deprived Trades Unions of the position which they supposed themselves to have."[32] This was the view of a historian. Those interested in licensing legislation and temperance reform interpreted the Liberal victory differently. The trade was hoping for a return of the

Unionists. "At this general election it behoves you to understand what your duty is, and to do it," declared a manifesto of the National Trade Defence Association to those engaged in the liquor trade. "The Unionist Government during the ten years of its tenure of power has not done all that you wanted, it has given you the half loaf which is better than no bread." The manifesto also stated that the interests of the licence-holders were threatened by the Liberal Government, "members of which have within the past twelve months declared themselves antagonistic to the trade". The Board of the Licensed Victuallers' Central Protection Society of London published a circular to its members which stated that if the Liberal party was returned to power the trade would be called upon to pay additional taxation and be threatened with confiscation. Their fear was the extinction of licences without compensation, the introduction of Sunday closing and local option. The circular concluded, "Therefore vote yourself, and tell your customers that if the Liberals get in, and the trade is subjected to further taxation, their beer will cost them more." The various trade journals carried the same message.

The election strategy of the Temperance Movement was formulated at the first hint of a general election. Candidates were questioned about their attitude to various reforms of the licensing laws. A series of ten special election leaflets was prepared of which 2,000,000 copies were distributed. As early as 12th December 1905 the United Kingdom Alliance Executive called a conference of representatives of national and other temperance organizations to formulate a declaration of temperance policy for the general election. This re-iterated the primary objective of prohibition for the direct vote of the people, and the securing of this end by legislation introducing local option. The declaration welcomed the pledge of Sir Henry Campbell-Bannerman, if returned, to repair the damage done by the 1904 Licensing Act. It also declared the opposition of temperance organizations to any municipalization of the liquor trade. The temperance campaign followed the established pattern of public meetings, distribution of literature and the questioning of candidates. It would be tedious to describe these activities in any detail, because earlier references in this chapter to the capability of the Temperance Movement to mount a national campaign provide sufficient evidence of the scale and scope of their actions.

The result of the general election was not only a landslide victory for the Liberals but a quite notable victory for the forces of temperance. Of some 1,200 candidates, only 262 declared support for the interests of the liquor trade. Of these only 81 were elected and this meant that only one-eighth of the House of Commons was committed to liquor interests. The comparative figures of trade and temperance support were particularly striking in London. "The trade endorsed the candidature of 60 out of 123 candidates in London, of whom, however, only 19 were elected. On the other hand, the Alliance recommended and supported 47 candidates, of whom 33 are now members of the House."[33] Inquiries by the parliamentary agents of the United Kingdom Alliance showed that of the 430 liberal and labour MPs, only one declared himself in favour of the Licensing Act 1904 and 18 declined to express their views. Over three hundred pledged their support for local option legislation and only 23 could be found to oppose it.

Some other interesting figures had been published in the *Daily News* on 20th April 1904 when it was reported that 129 members of the previous House of Commons were financially interested in the liquor trade, either directly or indirectly as trustees, directors or shareholders. Of that number 75 were either defeated in the 1906 general election or for some other reason were not members of the new house. In the previous parliament there were 88 declared total abstainers, but in the new parliament there were 156. Reviewing the losses on 17th January 1906 the *Morning Advertiser* said, "It is a sickening tale altogether." On 19th January it confessed, "No intelligible reason is brought forward to account for any of these changes, and we are left to suppose that a certain proportion of the electors have gone absolutely off their heads". The defeat of J. G. Groves at Salford South, a brewer who had been one of the chief spokesmen of the trade in the previous parliament, was described by the *Morning Advertiser* as "an almost unintelligible result", one of the "manifold disasters which have befallen trade candidates at this election". The defeat of Balfour, the former Prime Minister was seen by the temperance organizations as the inevitable consequence of his misguided and undisguised support for the trade. And so there could be no doubt that the 1906 general election resulted in a great shift of parliamentary power from the trade to the temperance cause.

Prospect for licensing legislation

It was curious, therefore, that no reference was made to licensing reform in the King's Speech. The omission was referred to by two speakers in the debate on the Address, J. Chamberlain and J. Keir Hardie. This omission drew an editorial comment in *The Times,*

> *The importance of Temperance legislation figured very largely in pre-election controversy. Everyone remembers the tremendous outcry about the Compensation Bill, and the frequent declarations that one of the first tasks of the Liberals would be to sweep out of existence that iniquitous endowment of "the trade" out of its own subscriptions. These declarations were doubtless very useful, though based upon an entirely inaccurate view of the scope of the measure. Now we hear nothing at all about the burning question.*[34]

The Parliamentary Temperance Committee, consisting of members of parliament supporting temperance legislation was formed as soon as the new parliament had assembled. At its second meeting (15th March 1906) twenty-nine MPs were present. Bearing in mind the commitments of MPs this attendance was high by normal standards. At this meeting it was decided to seek an interview with the Prime Minister to urge on him that temperance reform should be given priority in the next session. All members of the committee, free to do so, were requested to ballot for a motion in favour of English Sunday Closing. It was also resolved to press for legislation to secure greater control of clubs. The Prime Minister responded to the invitation to meet a deputation. This meeting was planned for 5th April 1906 at the Foreign Office where there was adequate accommodation for the numbers expected. In a leading article, *Alliance News,* on the day of the meeting, said, "The object of the deputation is not to ask the Prime Minister to declare the policy of the Government Bill, still less to dictate to him what that policy shall be; but to indicate the urgency of the question and ask for the Bill to have the first place in the programme of 1907."[35] This editorial also contained a note of caution. Just because the Liberal Party had such a big majority it was exposed to the dangers of "security and of vagueness". The result was that they might "expect at times to find a less definite lead given to the house than the earnest reformer might desire". In view of what happened later, this warning was not misplaced. However, at this time the temperance forces pinned their faith in Sir Henry Campbell-Bannerman. "One thing, however, is abundantly clear" declared *Alliance News* "viz, that the Prime Minister himself is a consistent, convinced and fearless reformer, and may be trusted – if left to himself – to lead his party and the House with courage and clearness of vision."[36]

Around eighty members of parliament formed the deputation led by Sir Wilfrid Lawson whose death occurred later in the year. He said they had not come to find fault with the fact that it was not proposed to introduce licensing reform during the first session of the new parliament, but to urge that it should be given first place in the new session. T. P. Whittaker, who spoke for members from the English constituencies reminded the Prime Minister that it was more than thirty years since a liberal government had carried even as a second reading any measure of temperance reform in England. This was an unintentional confession that temperance opinion, strong as it was in the country, had failed to achieve significant legislative reform. Now, however, the situation seemed more propitious. Whittaker did not doubt the will of the government to initiate reforming legislation which would restore old powers and bring in new ones to facilitate sobriety and temperance. The members of the deputation wanted to demonstrate their support on which the government would have to rely if the measures needed were to be passed in parliament. The newly-elected members of the labour party were also represented in the deputation, and speaking for them, D. J. Shackleton said his party contained a greater proportion of total abstainers than any other section of the house. His party, too, would support reforming legislation. Speakers from Wales, Ireland and Scotland also pledged support. The response of the Prime Minister and of the Home Secretary (Herbert Gladstone) was unequivocal. They believed that what was needed was a comprehensive licensing act which would deal with all anomolies and omissions in the present legislation. They could not promise that it would be the first business of the new session, but what they would promise was that it would be of first importance. The intention, they said, was to was to base new legislation on "inviolable principles".

Later in the year, in November, a deputation from the Licensed Victuallers' National Defence League met the Prime Minister. The main points they put to him were, (a) that it seemed unjust that magistrates with any interest in the liquor trade were not permitted to serve as licensing justices, whereas persons with strong temperance views were so permitted; (b) there was the need for stricter control of clubs; and, (c) the time limit on licences which had to be applied for annually was unfair in that it jeopardized the true value of a publican's business. Sir Henry Campbell-Bannerman welcomed the deputation but said they would realize he did not see eye to eye with them on many things. However, he promised that legislation would be introduced to deal with anomalies of clubs. He did not accept their arguments about justices with trade connections, nor their views about annual licences. He stressed that the first consideration of the government in framing a new licensing bill would be the interests of the general community. However, the government would not wish to deal harshly or unfairly with the trade, which had been justified by law.

References

1. See pp. 177–192.
2. United Kingdom Alliance Annual Report 1900 p. 7.
3. See p. 12.
4. United Kingdom Alliance Annual Report 1902 p. 6.
5. Op cit p. 6.
6. *Paterson's Licensing Acts.* Eighty-fifth edition 1977 J. N. Martin pp. 281, 282.
7. *Alliance News* 5th February 1903.
8. *Alliance News* 8th January 1903 p. 20.
9. *Alliance News* 8th January 1903 p. 20.
10. *Alliance News* 8th January 1903 p. 24.
11. The statistics in the paragraph are taken from *Alcohol and the Nation* G. B. Wilson 1940 pp. 430–433.
12. Quoted in *Alliance News* 1st January 1903 p. 11.
13. *Alliance News* 1st January 1903 p. 11.
14. Op cit p. 8.
15. Op cit p. 11.
16. Op cit p. 9.
17. See p. 226.
18. *Manchester Guardian* 24th February 1903 p. 5.
19. *Alliance News* 26th March 1903 p. 203.
20. Op cit p. 203.
21. *The Times* 19th March 1903.
22. *Daily Telegraph* quoted in *Alliance News* 26th March 1903 p. 206.
23. *Manchester Guardian* 19th March 1903.
24. *Daily News* 19th March 1903.
25. *Alliance News* 14th May 1903 p. 321.
26. *Alliance News* 21st May 1903 p. 236.
27. *Alliance News* 28th May 1903 pp. 354, 355.
28. Report in *Alliance News* 21st January 1904 pp. 48, 49.
29. *Alliance News* 17th March 1904 p. 187 ff. and 24th March 1904 p. 202 ff.
30. *Alliance News* 30th June 1904 p. 439.
31. *Alliance News* 7th July 1904 p. 459.
32. *A Short History of the English People* J. R. Green, Dent 1934 pp. 836, 837.
33. United Kingdom Alliance Fifty-fourth Annual Report 1906 p. 13.
34. 20th February 1906 p. 10.
35. *Alliance News* 5th April 1906 p. 216.
36. Op cit p. 216.

CHAPTER 3

TEMPERANCE TAKES OVER

The first test of strength for temperance reform came on 10th April 1906 when Leif Jones (Westmorland, Appleby) moved a resolution in the House of Commons which noted the successful working of local option laws in the colonies and which invited approval of the principle "that the people ought to possess the power through a vote of the local electors to protect themselves against the admitted evils of the liquor traffic".[1] Leif Jones gave an account of how the system of local option in Canada, Australia and New Zealand had resulted in a reduction of licences and the provision of some areas where there were now no licences at all. At the end of a brief debate the Prime Minister intervened to say that as he had supported similar motions in the past, so he would vote for this one. When the vote was taken the result was 271 in favour and 44 against, a majority for the resolution of 227. The ability of the house to carry temperance reform legislation was demonstrated on 25th May 1906 when the Sale of Intoxicating Liquors (Ireland) Bill came up for second reading and was passed by 246 votes to 52. The bill provided for early Saturday closing and complete Sunday closing in Ireland. There had been Sunday closing in Ireland since 1878 except in five exempted cities where there was evidence of a desire to be brought within the general provision. The bill reached the Statute Book in November 1906. Its main provisions were (a) the Sunday Closing Act was made permanent; (b) the hours of sale in the five exempted cities were reduced from five to three; (c) there were new regulations for bona fide travellers; (d) on Saturdays in all towns under five thousand, licensed premises were to close at 9 p.m. and in towns over five thousand at 10 p.m.

Evidence of the firm intention of the government to bring forward a comprehensive licensing bill, and of a majority in parliament to carry it through encouraged the temperance forces to launch a campaign for the kind of reforming measures they believed were needed. *Alliance News* carried regular extensive lists of public meetings in various places throughout the country,[2] some of them being fully reported in the journal. In Leeds, for example, a conference was held which was attended by nearly one thousand representatives from two hundred societies. Every parliamentary division in the West Riding was also represented. Commenting on the conference, the *Yorkshire Daily Observer* said, "the Prime Minister's definite promise that the government would deal comprehensively with the licensing question next session has aroused temperance workers all over the country to a high pitch of hope and expectation. The result of the new prospect is an energetic propaganda with the object of enlisting on the side of reform the vast mass of public opinion which has not hitherto been identified actively therewith . . . ."[3]

The "high pitch of hope and expectation" referred to by the *Yorkshire Daily Observer* was extended by the announcement in the King's Speech for the new session of parliament. – "A measure of licensing reform will be introduced with the object of effectively diminishing the evils which result from the sale and use of intoxicating liquors under the present conditions".

The temperance forces responded immediately and so did the trade. At the annual meeting of the Central Sunday Closing Association at Bristol the two forces met. Several local licensed victuallers and other trade associations distributed leaflets urging their customers and sympathizers to attend the meeting and to be there early. The response from both parties was immense so that more than thirty policemen were required to maintain order. Over three thousand people crowded the Colston Hall. As the meeting proceeded there were interruptions which increased until the uproar was so great that speakers could not be heard. Representatives of the licensed victuallers appealed for order but their efforts were in vain.[4] At Hyde, near Manchester, there was similar disruption of a meeting in support of local option by people who had been goaded by local publicans.[5]

Medical Manifesto

In April 1907 the attention of those interested in the alcohol problem was diverted, temporarily at least, from legislation to the medical aspect. Sixteen distinguished medical men published a pro-alcohol "Manifesto" in *The Lancet.*[6] The principal paragraphs in this manifesto read as follows,

> *Recognising that, in prescribing alcohol, the requirements of the individual must be the governing rule, we are convinced of the correctness of the opinion so long and generally held, that in disease alcohol is a rapid and trustworthy restorative. In many cases it may be truly described as life-preserving, owing to its power to sustain cardiac and nervous energy, while protecting the wasting nitrogenous tissues.*
> *As an article of diet we hold the universal belief of civilised mankind that the moderate use of alcoholic beverages is, for adults, usually beneficial, is amply justified.*
> *We deplore the evils arising from the abuse of alcoholic beverages. But it is obvious that there is nothing, however beneficial, which does not, by excess, become injurious.*

The manifesto led to considerable public reaction, not least from other medical men who dissented from it. Sir James Barr, Chairman of the Medical Faculty of Liverpool University wrote a scathing reply in *The Lancet.*[7] He said he knew most of the signatories of the manifesto, was acquainted with their work and their writings, but he did not know one of them who had ever done any experimental work of any value either on the use or abuse of alcohol. He confessed he took a little alcohol himself, and had had two glasses of champagne while he had been writing his letter to *The Lancet.* He thought the manifesto was impertinent in presuming to dictate to the medical profession on the value of alcohol. He concluded, "Today some shrewd business men asked 'How many cases of Scotch whisky did this manifesto represent?' I resented the suggestion, but the signatories have only themselves to thank if the public put a commercial value on this document." Some of the leading newspapers were contemptuous of the manifesto. The *Daily Mirror* said "In future no one will be taking to drink. He will be sustaining 'cardiac and nervous energy.' He will not be indulging in a destructive instinct, but will be 'protecting the nitrogenous tissues'. The solemn verdict will simply result in a run on the public-houses. The only people it will serve will be the publicans."[8] As if to prove it, the Licensed Victuallers' Central Protection Society of London had the manifesto printed as a pamphlet for distribution.

Temperance faith in government promises

When the controversy about this medical manifesto had subsided public attention was drawn to legislation, but not immediately to the government's promised licensing bill. Local option in Scotland temporarily occupied parliament. This was a private member's bill to give ratepayers in Scotland a direct control of the liquor trade in their respective areas. The bill received a second reading on 26th April 1907 with a majority of 156. The Scottish vote in the house was 51 for and only seven against. The bill was then referred to the Scotch Grand Committee, consisting of all the Scottish members and fifteen others. The Secretary for Scotland supported the second reading, but found fault with some details and hinted that it might not make progress beyond the committee stage. In fact it made no further progress and was an example early in the new century of what had consistently happened in the previous one to the attempts by Sir Wilfrid Lawson to secure support for local option legislation.

Even with this setback, the United Kingdom Alliance retained its implicit faith in the intentions of Sir Henry Campbell-Bannerman. Had he not given his pledge to introduce a licensing bill of temperance reform? And was not that pledge fulfilled in the King's Speech? The faith of the leaders of temperance opinion was somewhat shaken when, at the beginning of June 1907, the Prime Minister made a statement in the house about the inability of the government to bring forward promptly some of the legislation foreshadowed in the King's Speech. In this, thirteen bills were mentioned, a large programme, but not an impossible one. The passage in his statement which attracted the attention of the liquor trade and the temperance forces related to the inevitable postponement of licensing legislation. The Prime Minister said, "The first measure named in the speech was a Bill for the reform of licensing, and the fact that it occupies the first place is a proof of our earnestness, and of our desire to proceed with it with as little delay as possible. We have departed in no degree whatever from the opinion we have held on that subject. We believe this is perhaps the most important and immediate matter to which the House can address itself . . . The introduction of this Bill has been so long delayed that, although very great progress has been made in sketching a number of provisions which might be constituted into a Bill, it has been practically crowded out this session. But the obligation laid upon us remains." The temperance organizations felt somewhat reassured by this statement and by the personal pledge with which the Prime Minister concluded it. "I myself made last year a most positive pledge on this subject" he declared, "one from which I do not recede for a moment. We feel ourselves bound by these pledges, as well as by our own instincts and desires, to promise that this great measure shall be the very first measure of the next session."

Although retaining faith in the integrity of the government and in particular of the Prime Minister, the executive of the United Kingdom Alliance passed a resolution which, while making allowance for the pressure of public business, nevertheless could not perceive any justification for the continued delay in dealing with "a question of unparalleled importance, involving highest interests of the national sobriety, health, economy and domestic welfare". An editorial in *Alliance News*[9] said that the temperance reformers were not men to desert a leader or think of revolt, but they could not always be fed on promises, they needed substantial measures of reform. If these measures were to be achieved, pressure would have to be stepped up as the new parliamentary session drew near. In the last issue of *Alliance News* in 1907, it was announced that the headquarters of the United Kingdom Alliance would move from Manchester to London for the period January to October 1908. The office in Manchester would be retained and additional office accommodation had been found in Tothill Street, Westminster where the London Office of the UKA was situated. In the struggle over the 1904 Licensing Bill it had been a disadvantage not having the key personnel of the UKA in London continuously. Since the centre of interest during 1908 would be parliament at Westminster, it was necessary for the principal campaigners to be close to the scene of action.

A bill is published

The promises of the government and the expectations of temperance reformers were realized when in January 1908 the King's Speech for the new session of parliament included a reference to the introduction of a new licensing bill. The bill was published and introduced to parliament by the Chancellor of the Exchequer, H. H. Asquith on 27th February 1908. The provision which most pleased the temperance forces was that of local option. The principal object of the bill was to reduce the number of on-licences and it would be obligatory on justices to reduce, by the end of the next fourteen years, the number of such licences by about 30,000, at the rate of some 2,200 a year, compensation being given in such cases. The reduction would conform to a ratio of one licence to every 400 of the population in country districts, and one licence to between 500 and 1,000 of the population in urban areas. The selection of licences under the reduction schemes was put back into the hands of the justices from quarter sessions. A licensing commission would be set up in which the compensation fund would be vested, and schemes of reductions would be submitted by the justices to the commission for financial consideration. Compensation levies would be on a national basis and would cease to be managed by the Committee of Quarter Sessions. After a period of fourteen years all on-licences, whether new or old, would be treated as new ones, subject to any conditions justices might impose, and after the expiry of fourteen years no compensation would be paid. Local option would be introduced immediately for both on- and off-licences. A poll could be demanded by one-tenth of the parochial electors. If a prohibitory vote was obtained, a new poll could be taken after three years. Other provisions of the bill were the extension of Welsh Sunday Closing to Monmouthshire, outside London, and in England, public houses would be opened on Sundays for only one hour in the middle of the day and for not more than two hours in the evening and justices would be empowered to attach conditions to renewal of licences to exclude children, employ women and close on polling days. As for clubs, they would have to be registered in January each year, police in plain clothes would have access to inspect them, and the sale of drink in clubs for consumption off the premises would be prohibited.

Campaigning for and against the bill was stepped up as soon as the text had been published. An appeal for a fighting fund of £100,000 was launched by the trade, a modest sum when seen in relation to the massive vested interests which might have been threatened by such legislation. The temperance organizations spearheaded by the United Kingdom Alliance, mobilized support throughout the country. Their campaign was launched at a national convention at the Queen's Hall, London, More than fifty members of parliament, as well as leaders in public life and the churches were on the platform, among them Lloyd-George and Ramsey MacDonald, two future Prime Ministers. Winston Churchill was active in the campaign.[10] Scarcely had the process begun to secure the passage of the bill through parliament than, at the beginning of April 1908, Sir Henry Campbell-Bannerman resigned through ill-health as Prime Minister and died two or three weeks later. He was succeeded by H. H. Asquith who, on 28th April, moved the second reading of the bill, referring to what he had said when as Chancellor of the Exchequer he had introduced it. The government had two objectives. The first was to improve, primarily by a reduction in the number of licences and by other changes, the conditions under which the liquor trade was carried on. The second was to recover to the state its dominion and control over the monopoly enjoyed by the liquor trade.

The second-reading debate occupied four days of parliamentary time in the House of Commons, at the end of which the house divided. The voting was 394 for and 148 against, a majority of 246 and the bill was accordingly sent to a committee of the whole house. The outcome of the second reading gave impetus to a renewal of the campaigns run by the trade and by the temperance movement. In May, the Bishop of London* presided at a demonstration at the Albert Hall in favour of the bill. Again, the support was impressive. As we have observed, filling the Albert Hall presented no difficulty to the temperance forces, but what was also striking was the great support for public meetings in villages and small towns as well as in the major cities. Some demonstrations were held in the open air, as for example one at Heaton Park, Manchester in June 1908, when there were twenty-five platforms and where one estimate was that at least 50,000 people and twenty-five bands took part in the procession.

The trade also staged an open-air demonstration in Hyde Park, London, on 27th September 1908. The *Alliance News* correspondent who covered the event estimated that the number exceeded that of the temperance demonstration in favour of the bill which had been held at Heaton Park, Manchester, and that there were evidently more present than at the recent one at Hyde Park over which Winston Churchill had presided. Brewers and licensed victuallers' organizations booked special trains to bring supporters to London. In many instances ridiculously low prices were paid for tickets on the understanding that passengers would attend the demonstration and vote for a resolution condemning the bill. In many cases sums of money were given for expenses, and it was even hinted that unemployed men had been paid 2*s.* to join the demonstration.

* *A. F. Winnington-Ingram.*

Progress through parliament

In the House of Commons the committee stage of the bill began on 20th July 1908 and was not completed until October. The report stage began on 10th November and the bill received a third reading on 18th November when there was a majority in favour of 237 and the bill went to the Lords. Before it came to the floor of the House of Lords, a meeting of peers was held at Landsdowne House, the home of Lord Landsdowne. Ostensibly this was to test the opinion of the Lords, but effectively this meeting sealed the fate of the bill. At the second reading in the House of Lords, Lord Lansdowne, the leader of the Unionist Party in the House of Lords, moved that the bill should not be permitted to proceed further. In the debate which followed, a number of peers, the Archbishop of Canterbury and several bishops opposed the motion, but when the house divided the bill was rejected by 272 votes to 96, a majority of 176.

The progress of the bill and its ultimate defeat had several lessons for reformers. It showed that however excellent the reasons for reform, however strong the support for change, if vested interests were involved, there was often sufficient influence in the corridors of power to thwart progress. The temperance forces had never been stronger, more ably led or supported with so much parliamentary influence as in 1908. There was no inclination to accept defeat and, as we shall see, up to the outbreak of the First World War the Temperance Movement remained a real threat to the liquor trade and a force to be reckoned with in parliament.

The strength of this movement was demonstrated when, on 10th March 1909, Asquith received a deputation in the Grand Committee Room of the House of Commons. There were between 300 and 350 people in the deputation, thirty of them being members of parliament. More than eighty temperance societies sent representatives. The meeting had been called by the United Kingdom Alliance, following the Prime Minister's response to a request to receive such a deputation. In addition to this deputation, the Prime Minister received at the same time one consisting of over one hundred representatives of constitutent bodies of the National Temperance Federation. When he spoke, the Prime Minister said he believed the licensing bill, which was contemptuously rejected without any attempt even to consider its provisions, let alone amend them, by the House of Lords, was considered by most people in the house and in the country as the least measure of reform that ought to be contemplated. He gave his pledge that its defeat in the House of Lords was not the end of the matter. He believed that once it had been established that the elected representatives of the people were masters in their own house, the passage of legislation of temperance reform would be one of the first fruits of that victory.

The issue of the powers of the House of Lords came to a head when the upper house declined to pass the Finance Bill in 1909 until its provisions had been put to the electorate. Asquith responded by calling a general election in January 1910 and made the question of the Lord's veto and the budget the main issue. The Liberals were returned to power with a reduced majority.

As the Finance Bill had provided for greatly increased taxation of liquor, the trade and the temperance forces were involved in conflict in the 1910 general election, the National Trade Defence Association issuing a manifesto which dealt with the position of the trade under the budget proposals. The licensed trade, it was claimed, collected nearly 30 per cent of the tax revenue of the country, that had the 1908 Licensing Bill been passed, the property of the licensed trade would have been confiscated and 30,000 licences would have been lost for "fractional compensation", and that because this bill had been rejected by the House of Lords, the government had become vindictive. "A policy of taxation, nominally for revenue, but substantially for revenge, was thus foreshadowed. It was realized in the budget. The Finance Bill would place crushing burdens on licensed houses, while leaving other means of supplying excisable liquor comparatively free, thus revealing its real intention."[11] Electors were warned that the government, if returned, would implement the budget proposals. This would mean increases in the price of liquor and the cutting back of public-house facilities. In addition to this, the Licensed Victuallers' National Defence League published a questionnaire to parliamentary candidates. They were asked whether they would resist any further taxation of the trade; oppose any interference with the present hours of trading; press for the modification of the Children's Act so that it did not apply to children in the personal care of the parent, support efforts to enable licensed premises to provide not only refreshments but amusements; and secure adequate protection for the trade.[12]

The trade had no doubt about the party which would be most sympathetic to their views, and its literature and its spokesmen urged people to vote tory, but members of the Barman's Union held a different view. "What has the Tory party every done for you?" asked a statement issued to members. The answer was "Nothing. Why? Because the Tory party is the bond slave of the brewer and tied house owner. Surely the time has arrived when you ought to shake off your political yoke and strike for liberty." In support of this view the statement offered some facts. "It is well known that in the liquor trade a smaller proportion of gross profits goes to the wage earners than is the case with trade in general. A well-known brewery company held their annual meeting a short time ago, when the following revelations were made. The gross profit for one year amounted to £83,187. Out of that the shareholders dividends amounted to £72,300. The managing director's salary and commission amounted to £3,171. The other directors' fees amounted to £2,052, whilst other salaries and wages amounted to £5,664. Or in other words the capitalists and big-salaried officials pocketed £77,523, and the wage-earners were paid the handsome sum of £5,664."[13]

Barmen were advised to vote liberal because they and the newly-elected labour MPs had secured compensation for licensees of tied-houses and much better treatment for tenants than the Tories had attempted to secure. In fact the compensation received by licensees had been grotesquely small compared with that secured by the brewers. In 1907, for instance, out of £578,911 paid in compensation, the licensees received only £70,828. For the years 1906, 1907 and 1908 the licensees only received 12.5 per cent of the amout paid out for licences which had been withdrawn.

The result of the general election was a victory for the government, which implied a defeat for those who wished to retain the power of the House of Lords, as well as for those who were the chief supporters of the liquor trade. The final figures were 396 seats for the Liberal Government and its Labour and Nationalist supporters, and 271 for the Tories. The total votes cast indicated a more closely-run contest than was reflected in the distribution of seats. The figures for the United Kingdom were:

Liberal	2,858,687
Labour	498,289
Socialist	18,316
Nationalist	118,435
Total	3,493,727
Conservative	3,094,354
Government majority	399,373

A study of the results showed that the support for the retention of the powers of the House of Lords came largely from "landed" agricultural areas, whereas what may be described as the "democratic" vote came from the industrial areas, which was hardly unexpected. But the constitutional issue was not resolved by the return of a liberal government and later, in December 1910, Asquith went to the country again on the single issue of the Lords' veto when his party was returned with a similar majority and with a clear mandate to reform the powers of the House of Lords, which was effected in the Parliament Act of 1911, and the temperance forces were confirmed in their conviction that a comprehensive licensing act would now be passed.

Facts and figures

The year 1910 marked a notable change in an annual provision of statistics on the consumption of liquor in Britain. For many years Dr Dawson Burns of the United Kingdom Alliance had written annually to *The Times* newspaper giving facts about the nation's drink bill. After his death in 1909 G. B. Wilson, the secretary of the UKA, took over this role. His first letter appeared in *The Times* on 31st March 1910. In estimating the national expenditure on alcoholic liquor for 1909, he pointed out the difficulty which had arisen because of the alteration in prices of beer and spirits during the year. However, he estimated that the increase in the price paid for spirits consumed was £4,500,000 and for beer £750,000, making a total overall of £5,250,000. "In other words, if the total amount of beer and spirits consumed in 1909 had been equal to the total amount consumed in 1908, the actual expenditure on the same amount would have been £5,250,000 more in 1909 than it was in 1908." In fact consumption had fallen. Wilson concluded, "I estimate the total expenditure of the United Kingdom on alcoholic liquors during 1909 at £155,162,485, as compared with £161,060,482 in 1908. There has therefore been a decrease in expenditure of £5,897,997. On spirits the decrease was £4,800,000, with a decrease in consumption of 7,022,775 gallons. On beer the decrease was £1,186,000 with a decrease in consumption of 645,396 barrels. On wines, on the other hand, there had been an increase of £93,000 with an increase in consumption of 103,744 gallons. If there had been no increase in prices, the reduction on total expenditure would have been £11,147,977."[14] Some commentators in national newspapers concluded that these were remarkable figures, but could not accept the inference that the decrease in consumption was accounted for entirely by increased taxation. There had been a decline in consumption over a period of ten years. Wilson admitted that there were other causes and quoted a parliamentary paper issued in anticipation of the 1909 Budget which said, "The diminishing consumption of alcoholic liquors, though to some extent attributable to the recent depression in trade, is principally the result of a continuous change in the habits of the people which has been in progress for some time, and seems likely to be permanent."

The impact on consumption of taxation on liquor was likely to be increased once the Finance Bill which had been rejected by the Lords was finally passed, which it was, through all its stages on 28th April 1910. Since this was one of the objects to be achieved as a result of the return of the Liberal Government at the 1910 general election, some consideration must be given to its provisions for a revised scale of duties on liquor licences payable by retailers, wholesale dealers, manufacturers and also by registered clubs. It was estimated that the new duties would yield an additional revenue of £2,100,000 of which some £400,000 would come from manufacturers' duties on brewers and distillers, and £1,700,000 from duties on publicans, dealers, off-licence holders and clubs. The duties were to be levied in the first instance on the licence-holders, but in the case of "tied" licence holders they would be able to recover the whole or part of the duty paid from the brewer or whoever held the "tie". The tax would fall on the monopoly values of licences which were in the hands of those to whom the licence was tied. Public houses, beerhouses, hotels and restaurants would be subject to new minimum rates of duty. The rate in rural areas was raised slightly from £4. 10*s*. to £5 in the case of public houses. In urban areas the duty was related to the population at the last census. The minimum scale varied as between publicans' licences and beer-house licences, the former paying somewhat more than the latter. There were certain variations in respect of hotels because of income derived from letting rooms and serving food. Restaurants, too, were subject to variations. So far as registered clubs were concerned, the duty would be charged not on annual value, but at the rate of sixpence in the pound on the club's purchases of liquor for supplying to its members during the preceding year. Maximum duties were fixed for railway refreshment rooms, picture galleries, exhibitions and other places where the licence was auxiliary. Before the act, duties paid by off-licences were regarded as anomalous and a new system was introduced based on the annual value of the licensed premises and varying only in relation to the type of liquor sold, that is, spirits, beer or wine. For the first time a distinction was drawn between a wholesaler's licence and a retailer's licence, the wholesaler being allowed to sell not less than two gallons or not less than one-dozen reputed quart bottles in the case of wine and spirits, and not less than four-and-a-half gallons or two-dozen reputed quart bottles in the case of beer and cider.

Retailers might sell in amounts at or below these quantities. Manufacturers of beer who had been paying a duty of £1 irrespective of output would in future pay on the number of barrels brewed. Similarly, distillers who had been paying £10. 10*s.* for a distiller's licence would pay on the number of gallons distilled. The basis for new assessments would be what was referred to as "Annual Licence Value". The change meant, in effect, that licence duties were to be charged not on the value of the site or structure, but on the amount of alcoholic trade done, which brought in an important element of consistency. The same factors, that is annual rent paid and annual trade profit, would be ascertained both for purposes of compensation and to fix the licence duty. Thus compensation and taxation would be on the same basis.

One matter of note was the passing of the Licensing Consolidation Bill in August 1910. It was originally a government bill which two years earlier had made no progress. It was introduced again as a Private Member's Bill, contained 113 clauses and seven schedules and consolidated the law found in nine acts of parliament going back to 1828, the opportunity being taken at the same time to introduce points of minor administrative convenience.

Significant comments

Although there was the expectation that, in view of Asquith's pledges, a comprehensive temperance reform bill would be introduced, this did not happen in the remaining years before the First World War. Two Royal Commissions reported in 1912 and both contained significant statements relating to matters with which our present study is concerned.

The Report of the Royal Commission on the Selection of Justices of the Peace contained the following judgment,

> *It was strongly urged on behalf of those engaged in the liquor trade that but few are appointed justices. There is no disqualification for appointment of brewers and licensed victuallers by statute. The number of these is entirely within the discretion of the Lord Chancellor, and within the exercise of that discretion we cannot recommend any interference. Objection was taken to the appointment of total abstainers and particularly of advocates of total abstinence, who, it was alleged, fail in the discharge of their duties when dealing with licensing or cases affecting the liquor trade. We cannot recommend that an advocate of total abstinence should be disqualified for appointment as a justice. His interest is only one of opinion which does not disqualify any judge. By our law, the interest that disqualifies must be pecuniary or material. If such a person refused to exercise his discretion as a justice, as he would do if he refused to sanction all licences, such negation of his duty would be dealt with by the Lord Chancellor.*[15]

The Report of the Royal Commission on Divorce and Matrimonial Causes reporting in the same year made several references to the involvement of drinking on marital relationships.

> *302. It is the view of all witnesses examined on this point that the use of alcohol to excess is a source of misery of the most serious character.*
> *303. It seems probable from the evidence given before us that habitual drunkenness produces much, if not more, misery for the sober partner and the children of a marriage as any other cause in the list of grave causes.*

Temperance resolve and power

The determination of the temperance reformers not to allow the government to forget its pledge to introduce a major licensing bill was seen when a national convention was called to meet in the recently-opened Central Hall, Westminster on 13th November 1912. Within a fortnight of the decision to hold it, 2,565 delegates had been appointed from almost every religious denomination and from large numbers of social and temperance organizations throughout the country. Over 400 towns and districts, and practically every county in England and Wales sent representatives. The Scottish and Irish National Temperance organizations sent observers. Leif Jones MP, the president of the United Kingdom Alliance, presided. *Alliance News,* in its issue of 21st November, not only carried a full report of the speeches, but a list of those who attended and who they represented, and the names of local temperance organizations which sent delegates. The convention passed a resolution which pleaded with the government to introduce and pass a measure of temperance reform in the 1913 parliamentary session. It expressed gratitude to the Prime Minister for his strenuous efforts in this matter, and sympathy with him that pressure of business had compelled him to postpone the introduction of such a measure. Nevertheless, the time had come for the government to carry out its pledge. Following the convention, a deputation was appointed[16] to meet the Prime Minister, which it did on 11th December 1912.

In responding to the plea of the deputation the Prime Minister referred to the failure of the bill introduced in 1908 to reach the Statute Book because of its rejection by the House of Lords. Since the passing of the Parliament Act 1911 the power of the House of Lords to impede reforming legislation had been removed. However, Asquith said, there was a serious backlog of legislation which, having been frustrated by the House of Lords, must now be processed. The session which was drawing to an end had put enormous strain on members of parliament. It was idle to suppose that the next session could be given anything in the nature of a large extension of the legislative programme. "The machine will break down; the men will break down; the thing cannot be done," he told the deputation, "and all reformers must be content – I issue the caution not only to you, but to others – they must be content to see such progress made as can be made within the limits of human power and Parliamentary possibility, and I should be doing a very ill-service to you, and not acting honestly to my colleagues, if I made any promise of any sort or kind as to legislation for next session." He was even more specific. "It would be a most dishonest thing, under these conditions, if I were to say to you now that there is any reasonable prospect, I will not say of introducing, but of attempting to carry through the House of Commons into law any large measure of temperance legislation."[17] He said that this must not be taken as discouragement, but simply a recognition of parliamentary conditions. The Executive of the United Kingdom Alliance was not content with the Prime Minister's reply. His assurance that licensing legislation was still part of the government's programme was welcomed. However, his reply in general had been received with "profound dissatisfaction". The Executive requested the Prime Minister to introduce the promised bill in 1913, or at the very latest in 1914. The Executive's reply to the Prime Minister concluded, "But in the face of grave and admitted evils, it is our plain duty frankly to warn the government that the patience of the temperance electors must not be misunderstood or overstrained."[18] In the event the pleas and pressure of the temperance forces were to no avail. The government did not introduce legislation for England and Wales.

The Scotland Act

If a comprehensive licensing act for England and Wales did not reach the Statute Book, one for Scotland was at last achieved. This was the Temperance (Scotland) Act 1913. It had been a long time coming. The first attempt to secure the support of parliament for local veto in Scotland was made in 1883. Since then a bill had been introduced every year. In 1907 Robert Balfour (later Sir) sponsored a bill in which the term "option" was substituted for "veto" and at a second reading it secured a majority of 156 votes. It made no further progress and nor did any subsequent Private Member's Bills. On the eve of the general election of 1910 the Permissive Bill Association appealed to the Prime Minister to renew his promise of a government measure of temperance reform for Scotland. Asquith responded favourably. In October 1911, Lord Pentland, Secretary of State for Scotland and Alex Ure, Lord Advocate, received a deputation of national and denominational temperance bodies which asked the government to redeem the promise made by the Prime Minister. The deputation was told that Asquith intended that a Scotland bill would be introduced in the next session. A government bill was introduced by the Secretary of State for Scotland on 12th March 1912. After passing through all stages in the House of Commons it went to the Lords where it was read a second time on 6th November 1912. In committee, the Lords added some amendments which were unacceptable to the government and the House of Commons and the bill was in consequence dropped and introduced again in the new session. Under the Parliament Act the bill went formally through its various stages in the House of Commons. In the House of Lords a compromise was reached and on 15th August 1913 it received the Royal Assent. It was provided that the act came into force "eight years from the first day of June nineteen hundred and twelve".

The act gave the people of Scotland the right of local veto after the expiry of the eight-year period. A poll could be requisitioned by not less than one-tenth of the electors in a local authority area. Three questions were to be submitted to the electors:

1. *No-change resolution* which would mean that the powers and discretion of the existing licensing Court would remain unchanged.
2. *Limiting resolution* which meant a reduction of at least one-quarter of the number of licences for the sale of liquor.
3. *No-licence resolution* which meant that no licence would be granted except for inns, hotels or restaurants in special cases.

The act specified the percentage vote required in each case for the principle to be adopted. If a "No-Licence" was not carried the votes cast for it would be added to those for the Limiting Resolution. Once carried, a resolution would remain in force until superseded by a resolution carried at a further poll. No further poll could be held unless requisitioned by ten per cent of the electors who desired a change. Other provisions were that all licensed premises in the area must be kept closed for the sale of liquor during polling hours, and after May 1914 the sale of intoxicants must not take place before 10 a.m. and as closing time was at 10 p.m. throughout Scotland, the sale of liquor would in future be restricted to 72 hours per week (in England it was 123½ hours). Other minor reforms included a strengthening of control over clubs, power for the sheriff to close drink shops in case of threatened riot or where it was taking place, and the exclusion of drunken persons from public houses.

The Scotland Act was welcomed by the temperance forces and in November a thanksgiving demonstration was held in St. Andrew's Halls, Glasgow, at which the principal speaker was T. McKinnon Wood the Secretary of State for Scotland, who had introduced the bill to parliament. The placing of the act on the Statute Book was the first conspicuous achievement of those who had pressed the case of local option for many years. Perhaps it was this achievement which was one reason for a comment in *The Brewers' Gazette,* "For teetotalism is a greater power in the land, exerting over Governments no small sway. He who thinks otherwise allows his belief to be mastered by his desire."[19] This was a comment which was substantiated by any objective survey of the pre-war period of the twentieth century.

References

1. See *Alliance News* 19th April 1906 p. 244.
2. *Alliance News* 10th January 1907 p. 21, 17th January 1907 p. 42, 24th January 1907 p. 51, 31st January 1907 p. 75.
3. Quoted in *Alliance News* 31st January 1907 p. 72.
4. *Alliance News* 14th February 1907 p. 108.
5. *Alliance News* 21st February 1907 p. 118.
6. *The Lancet* 30th March 1907 p. 894.
7. *The Lancet* 6th April 1907 p. 972.
8. *Daily Mirror* 30th March 1907 p. 7.
9. *Alliance News* 6th June 1907 p. 360.
10. See his speech at Darwin reported in *Alliance News* 9th April 1908, Pontypool *Alliance News* 16th July 1908, Hyde Park *Alliance News* 30th July 1908.
11. *The General Election and the Licensed Trade* National Trade Defence Association.
12. *The Appeal of the Licensed Victuallers Defence League* featured in *The Trade Paper* 23rd December 1909 p. 25.
13. Quoted in *Alliance News* 20th January 1910 p. 34.
14. *The Times* 31st March 1910 p. 3.
15. *Report of Royal Commission on the Selection of the Justices of the Peace* 1912 pp. 13–14.
16. List of deputation in *Alliance News* 21st November 1912 p. 777.
17. United Kingdom Alliance Annual Report 1913 pp. 9–11.
18. Op cit pp. 11, 12.
19. *The Brewers' Gazette* 18th December 1913.

CHAPTER 4

THE FIRST WORLD WAR: A LESSON IN CONTROL

No event of the twentieth century had more far-reaching and permanent effects on the control of the retailing and consumption of liquor than the 1914-1918 war which, as we shall see, also marked the beginning of the decline of the numerical strength of the temperance organizations in Britain. In the early months of 1914, before the war broke out, the temperance forces pressed the government to redeem their pledge to introduce major legislation for the stricter control of the liquor trade. In February 1914 the National Temperance Federation sent a memorial to the government, which pointed out that five years had elapsed since the House of Commons passed the Licensing Bill of 1908 and since it had been summarily rejected by the House of Lords. Four years had passed since the government had promised that "one of the first fruits of a recovered Constitution" would be the re-introduction of the bill. And it was two years since the passing of the Parliament Act, which had opened the door for the placing of the promised licensing legislation on the statute book. The memorial said that the National Temperance Federation was not unmindful of the passing of the Scottish Temperance Act, nor of the hindrances in bringing in legislation for England and Wales. Nevertheless, the government was reminded of repeated pledges to introduce legislation which would include the principle of local option. The memorial was backed up with public meetings at the Queen's Hall and elsewhere to press for a bill to be introduced in 1914. In the House of Commons on 13th February 1914, Leif Jones, the President of the United Kingdom Alliance made a speech urging government action. In reply, Asquith, the Prime Minister, said he had kept strictly within every pledge he had given on the subject. "I repeat what I said to a deputation two years ago," he declared, "that it is our intention, within the lifetime of the present Parliament – I do not say anything more – to prosecute legislation of this kind".[1] The defeat at the second reading of a bill to prohibit the sale of liquor on Sundays was, perhaps, an indicator of the hesitation of members of parliament to pass further licensing legislation. The voting was close, 179 for the bill and 198 against.

When war was declared on Germany on 4th August 1914, there appeared to be no prospect of the intentions of the government over licensing legislation being fulfilled until after the war. In fact, the war resulted in the introduction of new controls of the liquor trade, some of which have not been rescinded. In December 1914 the brewers issued their own manifesto, as though in anticipation of sterner controls. "The extent of drunkenness in this country at the present time is grossly exaggerated" declared the manifesto, "and investigation of such drunkenness as there is would show that only a negligible part of it was due to the drinking of beer".[2] The Brewers' Society manifesto rebuked the teetotal forces for pursuing their campaign "with more virulence than ever before", at a time when, in the face of a common peril, a truce had been called in domestic controversy. Theirs, it said, was the old "indiscriminate campaign" against any beverage which contained an appreciable amount of alcohol, regardless of its dilution or other characteristics. In fact, whatever might be said of other liquors, beer was a temperance drink. And so its consumption should be encouraged. This manifesto had first appeared in the *Daily Telegraph* on 9th December 1914, but surprisingly not in the *Morning Advertiser.* Publicans were asked to display the manifesto on their premises, together with posters in support of the brewers' campaign.

Threat to security

Because drinking, especially at ports and in the vicinity of war establishments, created a threat to national security, there was pressure for a restriction of hours for the opening of public houses. In September 1914 the Intoxicating Liquor (Temporary Restrictions) Bill was passed to come into immediate effect. It gave power to the licensing justices for any district "temporarily to restrict the sale, consumption and supply of intoxicating liquor" through licensed premises and clubs. The justices could only issue such an order on the recommendation of the Chief of Police that it was desirable for the maintenance of order or the suppression of drunkenness in an area. If such an order was to take effect before nine-o-clock at night it needed the approval of the Secretary of State. It was naval and military authorities who had pressed for such a measure to check the way in which publicans had been serving recruits and soldiers to excess. Lord Kitchener, himself, having more than once appealed to the public to observe the principle of temperance issued a further appeal in November 1914. This said,

> *The men who have recently joined the Colours are doing their utmost to prepare themselves for active service with the least possible delay.*
> *This result can only be achieved if by hard work and strict sobriety they keep themselves thoroughly fit and healthy.*
> *Lord Kitchener appeals to the public, both men and women, to help the soldiers in their task. He begs everyone to avoid treating the men to drink, and to give them every assistance in resisting the temptations which are often placed before them. Lord Kitchener suggests that in the neighbourhoods where soldiers are stationed committees should be formed to educate public opinion on this subject, and bring home its importance to those who prevent our soldiers from being able to do their duty to their country in a thoroughly efficient manner.*[3]

Powerful support for government action came from the Shipbuilding Employers Federation. On 29th March 1915 the Chancellor of the Exchequer, Lloyd George, and the Secretary of State for Scotland, M'Kinnon Wood, met a deputation from the federation. The ministers were accompanied by high-ranking officers from the Navy and the Army. The deputation consisted of some twenty representatives of the major shipbuilding companies and the members were unanimous that what was required, if the needs of the nation were to be met, was a total prohibition during the period of the war of the sale of excisable liquors. The mere restriction of hours or even total prohibition within certain areas was not sufficient, as this would leave certain classes unaffected. The total prohibition should apply not only to public houses, but to private clubs and other licensed premises. The members of the deputation assured the ministers that they believed the workers themselves would favour total prohibition.

What impressed the Chancellor of the Exchequer was the statement by the leader of the deputation that not one of the members was a teetotaller. They approached the matter not from the point of view of a principle, but because they were facing the realities of the situation. It was the view of the deputation that the grave loss of production being experienced in the industry was principally due to drink. It was stated that in many cases the number of hours being worked was actually less than before the war. In spite of Sunday working and overtime, almost all shipyards reported that fewer hours were being worked than in a normal week. Although the shipyards were working night and day there was less overall production. Many were working conscientiously, but they could not make up for the production lost by those who were drinking instead of working. Speaking with experience in the industry ranging from twenty to forty years, the members of the deputation believed that 80 per cent of the avoidable loss of time could be ascribed to no other cause but drink. The figures for weekly takings in public houses near the shipyards provided further evidence of the truth of their conclusions even when allowance had been made for the increased cost of liquor, the larger number of men employed in shipbuilding and the reduction of opening hours. As long as public houses were open, there would be found men to break the rules of the yard and come to work late in order to secure a drink beforehand. And the indisposition to work after the excessive consumption of alcohol was too obvious to need elaboration.

The Chancellor of the Exchequer said that statements made by the deputation were of the gravest possible character in the national interest. Their statements had been supported by irrefutable evidence. He wished it might have been possible to cast some doubt upon them, but information from other sources corroborated what had been said. The action recommended was more severe than had been contemplated, and before such action was taken it was essential to have every class of the community behind it. He was glad to find that the country was beginning to realize the gravity of the situation. "Having gone into this matter a great deal more closely during the last few weeks" he said, "I must say that I have a growing conviction based on accumulating evidence, that nothing but root and branch methods will be of the slightest avail in dealing with this evil. I believe that to be the general feeling. The feeling is that, if we are to settle German militarism, we must first of all settle with the drink". And then came the most quoted of all the statements of Lloyd George on this subject, "We are fighting Germany, Austria and the drink, and as far as I can see, the greatest of these deadly foes is drink".

The views of so important a body as the shipbuilders would be taken very seriously into account as the government decided how to respond to the problem. Lloyd George told the deputation before they left that he had that morning had an audience with the King. "I am permitted to say by him that he is very deeply concerned on this very question – very deeply concerned – and the concern which is felt by him is, I am certain, shared by all his subjects in this country" concluded the Chancellor.[4]

The Transport Workers' Federation, with a membership of nearly a quarter of a million, backed the Shipbuilding Employers Federation. A letter from them to the Chancellor said, "We are prepared to support the Government in any drastic restrictions they may deem desirable, provided that they affect all districts alike and all classes alike, thereby removing any suggestion of favourite treatment. We are convinced that, although excessive drinking is indulged in by only a small minority, so interdependent is modern labour that the diminished efficiency of this minority has a marked influence upon the output of the total number of men engaged in any set of operations."[5] The Secretary of the Licensed Victuallers' National Defence League, H. G. Robinson, swiftly reacted to the call for prohibition. He accused the United Kingdom Alliance of being responsible for the current agitation. In fact, when the first restrictions on the sale of liquor were introduced the government spokesman was at pains to make it clear that the temperance organizations had not been consulted. When referring to the Temporary Restrictions Bill in the House of Commons on 28th August 1914, McKenna said, "I have not consulted any single honorary member representing what might be termed the total abstinence party with regard to this bill. I have not consulted one of them, and I do not think that one of them has spoken to me about it".

The King's response

Quite the most significant response to the plea by the Shipbuilding Employers Federation came from King George V. A letter from Buckingham Palace to the Chancellor of the Exchequer thanked him for so promptly giving the King a full report of the meeting with the employers. Written the day following the Chancellor's meeting, the letter said, "His Majesty has read it with interest, but also with the deepest concern. He feels that nothing but the most vigorous measures will successfully cope with the grave situation now existing in our Armament Factories. We have before us the statements, not merely of the employers, but of the Admiralty and War Office officials responsible for the supply of munitions of war, for the transport of troops, their food and ammunition. From this evidence it is without doubt largely due to drink that we are unable to secure the output of war material indispensable to meet the requirements of our Army in the field, and that there has been such serious delay in the conveyance of the necessary reinforcements and supplies to aid our gallant troops at the front. The continuance of such a state of things must inevitably result in the prolongation of the horrors and burdens of this terrible war".[6] The action of the Shipbuilding Employers Federation and the King's response to it, with corroborative evidence from the Admiralty and the War Office, could not be explained, as some sections of the liquor trade attempted to do, as the result of the action of teetotal fanatics. The letter from King George V disposed of this fallacy. However, it was the final paragraph in the King's letter which established the drink question as a national issue to which every citizen was called to make a response. It concluded, "I am to add that if deemed advisable, the King will be prepared to set an example by giving up all alcoholic drink himself and issuing orders against its consumption in the Royal Household, so that no difference shall be made so far as His Majesty is concerned between the treatment of rich and poor in this question".[7] This unequivocal statement came to be known as the King's

Pledge. A few days after the letter was written the King ordered the wine cellars in the Royal Household to be closed. Lord Kitchener took similar personal action. The Royal initiative was taken up widely throughout the country. For example, there was a movement among South Wales mine officials and miners, led by the general manager of the Cambrian Combine Colleries, which resulted in the immediate enlistment of 1,000 for the King's Pledge.[8]

Britain was not alone in having a drink problem in wartime which required government action. In Russia, for example, where the state had a monopoly in the sale of vodka, prohibition was introduced, first for limited periods and finally as a permanent measure. France, also, took severe measures, first, in common with Italy, by prohibiting the production and sale of absinthe and second, the sale of spirits to women and young people under-eighteen was prohibited, and severely restricted to men. Germany reduced the quantity of beer to be brewed, first by 48 per cent of pre-war production and then by 25 per cent. The main reason was to conserve barley for bread. For a similar reason Austria decreed that corn should not be used for brewing during the war. The United States of America, once it came into the war in 1917, prohibited the sale and supply of liquor to their forces. The manufacture and sale of spirits was prohibited and the alcoholic strength of beer was reduced to 2¾ per cent. In 1918 a coal shortage in the U.S.A. led to the closing of breweries, and from 1st July 1919 there was complete prohibition for the period of demobilization. In Canada, Australia and New Zealand drinking was forbidden among troops in training, and in Canada one province after another opted for no liquor above 2½ per cent proof spirit being available. Even neutral countries like Denmark and Switzerland imposed various controls.

Drink and defence

A month after the meeting with the Shipbuilding Employers Federation[9] the Chancellor of the Exchequer presented to the House of Commons the Defence of the Realm (Amendment No. 3) Bill which was concerned with the control of the sale of intoxicating liquors. Lloyd George defended the government against the charge that they had singled out the drink question for unnecessary precipitate action. This was not the case. The government's principal concern was to mobilize the total resources of the nation for the war effort. This was the object of the Defence of the Realm Act. It was a strong measure. First, it gave the government power to commandeer all the works of the country and to take away plant and machinery from any workshop in order to increase the output of munitions of war. That was the first step. The second was to summon all leaders of the unions involved in the output of munitions and war materials to discuss the best method of suspending restrictions and regulations which, although they had been operating for years, would have the effect perhaps of diminishing production. The Chancellor explained, "The third step we are taking is the removal of another obstacle in the way of the increase of the output of munitions and armaments, and that is the excessive drinking amongst a section of those who are engaged in these works." He stressed the vital importance of building up the supplies of armaments and ammunition, especially in view of the great offensive which would have to take place to drive the enemy out of Flanders. In his speech Lloyd George expounded in some detail, and with statistics from various official sources, the reasons the government felt compelled to take action. In a finance bill provision would be made for increasing taxation on spirits and on beer over a certain strength. In a new drink restriction bill other provisions would be proposed for discouraging the consumption of liquor, but the proposal for prohibition was not one which the government felt could be implemented at that time.

The text of the new bill was duly published. It was to "extend the Defence of the Realm Consolidation Act 1914". The most far-reaching outcome of the eventual act was the taking into public ownership of breweries and licensed premises in specific areas, notably in Carlisle. This emerged out of the extensive powers which the act conferred on the Central Control Board[10] which was set up as the prescribed authority. The Carlisle scheme is dealt with in the chapter on "public ownership".[11] Here we will deal with the main provisions of the act which preceded the setting up of the board. Where it appeared expedient to His Majesty that for the successful prosecution of the war the sale and supply of intoxicating liquor in any area should be controlled by the state, because war material was being made, loaded, unloaded or transported, or where naval or military personnel were stationed, His Majesty by order in council could define the area and impose any regulations provided for in the Defence of the Realm Consolidation Act 1914. These regulations could be declared to be in force for the duration of the war and for twelve months afterwards. When the prescribed authority had been set up it could be given powers to take over completely the sale and supply of intoxicating liquor in any defined area. Further, it could compulsorily acquire all licensed premises in the area, either temporarily or permanently. Refreshment rooms for the use of the general public and for any section of the public such as employees in factories, could also be opened. The prescribed authority would have power to modify provisions for the regulation of persons with an interest in licensed premises. Finally, the act would give effect to the transfer of the control of the liquor trade in any area to the prescribed authority.

The serious misgivings of some temperance organizations about the powers conferred on the Central Control Board were expressed by Leif Jones during the second reading debate on 10th May 1915. He said they were prepared to accept the measures proposed, with some serious reservations, and only with the chancellor's assurance that they were of a temporary nature. They were designed to deal with the particular situation of excessive drinking among people upon whose efficiency the supply of war materials depended. The overall problem of drink in our society required more drastic measures. Leif Jones said he saw grave dangers in the state taking responsibility for running the drink trade, and for providing alcoholic refreshment through canteens which might be opened. At the third reading, Leif Jones said he could not let the bill leave the House of Commons without expressing regret that the government was not prepared to introduce countrywide regulations, such as the reduction of hours for the sale of liquor.

The Central Control Board

Shortly after 19th May 1915 when the Defence of the Realm (Amendment) Act became law, the prescribed authority was set up in the form of the Central Control Board (Liquor Traffic) with Lord D'Abernon as Chairman. On 10th June 1915 the government issued the statutory rules and orders, defining the functions, constitution and powers of the board. Although the Minister of Munitions appointed the Chairman and the members, and the Treasury controlled the size of the staff, the board was virtually autonomous. It could, for instance, acquire property to be vested in trustees appointed from its membership. It could not, however, designate any area for control. This required an order in council. Apart from this, its powers were very extensive. The board could close any licensed premises or club, regulate hours of sale, prohibit the sale of any particular liquor, impose conditions of sale, regulate the supply and transport of liquor, establish supervision of licensed premises, create its own monopoly, prohibit treating, establish refreshments rooms, acquire permanent or temporary possession of premises, carry on businesses, provide entertainment or recreation facilities, grant excise licences, and inspect licensed premises or clubs. These were the main provisions of the statutory rules and orders; there were others. These powers were exercised with such discretion that no serious opposition was encountered.

Although arbitrary action could have been taken by the board to schedule areas for control, this was not done. The initiative came from authorities such as the Admiralty, the Army or the Ministry of Munitions. When such requests were received, the board held a local inquiry at which representations could be made by interested parties and when expert witnesses could provide information. These inquiries had three objects: (a) to determine whether control was necessary; (b) to decide what restrictions were appropriate; and (c) to fix the geographical limits of the control. In the first instance, the areas designated for control were quite small, and were confined to the immediate vicinities of naval and military bases and installations or munition factories. After the board's recommendations had been endorsed by order in council, ten days elapsed before the order took effect. This was to enable the authorities, the trade and the public to prepare for change. The first areas related to seaports and, later, inland industrial areas were scheduled. By the end of 1915 about half the population of Great Britain was affected and by the end of 1916 control had been extended to affect something like 38 millions of the total population of 41 millions. Eventually control applied to virtually the whole country.

The regulations which were applied to controlled areas affected hours of sale, treating and credit. The most far-reaching effect was on hours of sale. These had varied according to districts from 16 – 19½ hours per day. The Control Board reduced these to five and a half in all districts, two and a half at midday and three in the evening. These hours applied to all licensed premises including clubs. Hours for off-sales which had been the same for on-sales, were reduced even further, to four and a half hours. This was to prevent people drinking on licensed premises until closing time and then taking liquor home. There were stringent regulations introduced in respect of sales of spirits. Canvassing for custom, the widespread habit of treating and the practice of credit were all prohibited under the regulations.

Drink and victuals

These various regulations of effective public control established a precendent for state interference in the running of the liquor trade. If this interference appeared negative, the same conclusion would not be reached about other action by the Control Board. While the regulations enumerated applied to the supply and consumption of liquor, the restriction of hours, for example, did not apply to the provision of food. In its second report, published in May 1916, the Control Board explained its policy on facilities for meals in public houses which might remain open all day. from as early as 5 a.m. or 5.30 a.m. for the sale of food and non-intoxicants. The board reminded licensed victuallers of the original meaning of the title, that is, to provide victuals. Many public houses, declared the board, were not fulfilling their traditional role as victualling houses, the object of the owners seeming to be to push the sale of liquor. It was pointed out that the English licensing system laid upon licensees the obligation to provide food for travellers, and that justices had power to close or withdraw licences from houses which failed to make such provisions. The attempt by the board to encourage an extension of eating facilities in public houses was only partially successful. By long tradition the public house was regarded as a place where people went to drink.

The determination of the board to encourage the provision of meals, especially for munition workers, directed attention to the establishment of canteens. In its second report (1916) the board referred to three possible methods by which such provisions could be made. Such canteens could be established by the employers, by voluntary agencies or by the board itself if the other two methods failed. The first response came from voluntary agencies financed by public subscriptions. In its third report in 1917 the board stated, "At first sight it appeared that the voluntary system was susceptible of practically unlimited development provided that the necessary funds were forthcoming, and in order to ease the situation in this respect the board obtained Treasury authority to pay grants-in-aid to approved voluntary societies and up to one-half of their capital expenditure on canteens for munition and transport workers".[12]

Even with this substantial assistance the voluntary agencies were not able to maintain the initial momentum because of a fall-off in public subscriptions. The Control Board concluded that another method would have to be found, though the voluntary agencies would still be employed to manage the canteens provided by employers. It was recognized that some incentive would have to be given if employers were to be persuaded to erect canteens for their workers, especially as they were to receive only their standard pre-war profits plus one-fifth. The Control Board secured for controlled employers the concession to charge to revenue the expenditure they might incur with the board's approval to establish canteens in their works. This meant that the cost of establishing canteens in works would be borne by funds which would otherwise have gone to the Exchequer. At government establishments it became the duty of the Control Board to make similar provisions at state expense. A year after these arrangements were agreed, 780 establishments had canteen facilities. In February 1918 the canteen system was transferred from the Control Board to the Ministry of Munitions, where a special department was set up. Official opinion was that the provision of canteens resulted in marked improvement in the health of employees, less absenteeism, less tendency to alcoholism and increased efficiency and output. Although no liquor was supplied at canteens, they became to only a limited extent an alternative to public houses.

Effects of control

An indication of the immediate effects of the measures taken by the Control Board was given in a report in *The Times:*

The liquor regulations which have lately been applied to some of the most important transport and munition areas have had striking results. Figures which have come to hand from several of these areas show that there has been a very considerable reduction in the number of prosecutions and convictions for drunkenness.
The following comparitive table gives the number of convictions before and after the application of the regulations to four important boroughs on the North East Coast:

	Coverage 4 weeks before order	First week of order	Second week
Newcastle	76	36	43
Gateshead	28	9	5
South Shields	19	12	8
Middlesbrough	45	14	17

The first week's returns for Liverpool are very similar. There were 217 prosecutions for drunkenness in the week before the order came into force. In the next week the number fell to 118. Birkenhead showed the same tendency, but not to so great a degree. The average number of convictions for the four weeks before the order came into force was 20. During the first week the order was in force it was 17.[13]

Three days later *The Times* drew attention to the contrast between the effects of the board's actions in provincial cities and in London. "The prevalence of excessive drinking among the wives of soldiers and sailors is forcing itself with increasing insistence upon social workers in the poorer districts of London".[14] *The Times* quoted clergy and police in areas of the East End who said the problem of open drunkenness among women was serious and was increasing. "The general question of the evil is now receiving the careful consideration of the Home Office and the police. The condition of things in the neighbourhood of the Victoria Docks might very well engage the attention of the Central Control Board, whose liquor regulations have already achieved the striking results in the Newcastle and Liverpool areas as recorded in the *Times* of 28th August."[15] There were reports, too, of disgraceful scenes at London railway termini, and near public houses in the vicinities of Waterloo, Victoria and Euston.

The first report of the Central Control Board was published in October 1915. It listed fourteen areas in respect of which orders had been issued for the regulation of the liquor traffic. These were almost without exception port areas and included three in Scotland. In the report, Lord D'Abernon said that although the orders were not identical the main provisions were substantially the same. Broadly they were under six heads. (1) Hours were restricted to two-and-a-half in the middle of the day and three in the evening, which meant that the sale of alcohol was prohibited before 12 noon and throughout the afternoon from 2.30 p.m. to 6 p.m. or 6.30 p.m. (2) The sale of spirits was prohibited in the evenings and on Saturday. (3) "Treating" and credit sales, with certain minor exceptions, were prohibited. (4) Clubs were included in the restrictions. (5) Licensed premises could open to supply non-alcoholic drinks and solid refreshment during the hours when they would otherwise be closed for the sale of intoxicating liquor. (6) Spirits could be diluted to 35 degrees under proof instead of 25 degrees under proof as allowed by general law. Lord D'Abernon reported that consideration was being given to special regulations for London.

The board had received reports from chief constables, medical officers of health, employers, workers' representatives and from officers appointed to make inquiries on behalf of the board. One conclusion reached from the brief experience of the regulations was that prosecutions and convictions for drunkenness had diminished. Another was that drinking in many areas had declined. It had also been shown that in the scheduled areas trade in articles commonly required by the working classes had increased, no doubt because of the diversion of purchasing power. It was too early to assess the effect on efficiency in factories, but from harbour areas there were reports of improved working conditions. Drunkenness among sailors and shipyard workers had decreased and ships were leaving with much less delay. Chief constables had been particularly appreciative of the no-treating order, and even the *Brewers' Gazette* had reported little difficulty in enforcing the ban.[16] Barmaids had complained that this regulation meant more running about for them to give change to customers. Otherwise the board seemed justified in their conclusion that "the orders have taken effect with but little friction and without any breach of public order".[17] After three years working on the no-treating order, Lord D'Abernon was able to say, "The evidence received from responsible authorities is convincing that the No-treating Order, even imperfectly carried out, has in large measure achieved its objectives, and has played an important part in the great advance of the last three years. I hope that the good sense of the community will not permit the return of this foolish and pernicious fashion after the war. Good fellowship is not reduced to such straits that its only mode of expression is the reciprocal administration of a narcotic!"[18]

It would be wrong to conclude that the only function of the Central Control Board was to impose stricter controls on the licensed trade. As we have seen, there was a positive role. This was to encourage the provision of non-alcoholic drinks and food and the establishment of works' canteens. There seems no doubt that the effect of the work of the Control Board and other measures directed towards increased sobriety were effective. While statistics for drunkenness are not conclusive they are an important element

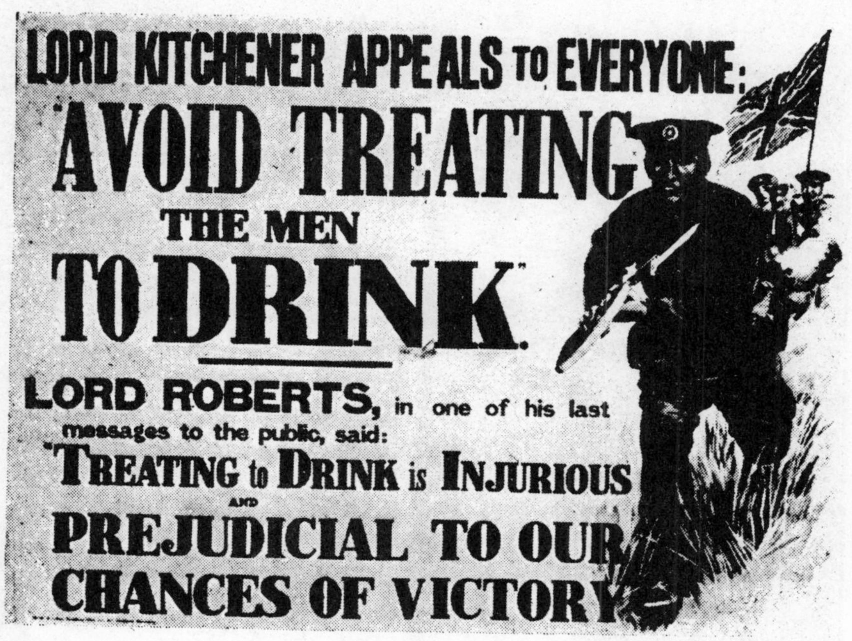

Poster, First World War, 1914–1918. In some areas treating was prohibited.

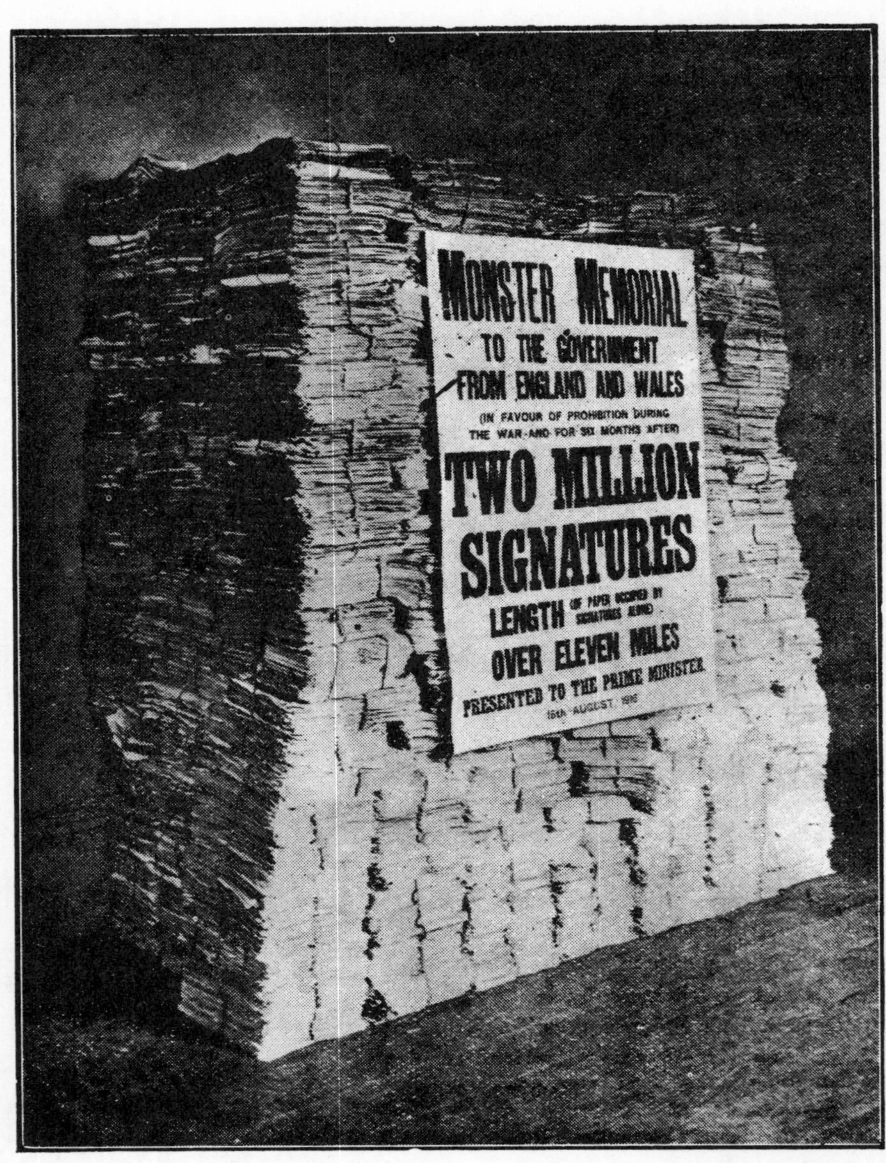

This photograph illustrates the enormous, purely physical, dimensions of the petition to the Prime Minister in 1916, urging the introduction of prohibition during the First World War, 1914–1918.

in the data upon which judgement has to be based. In this instance the statistics for 1915, 1916 and 1917 for drunkenness are striking. Henry Carter quoted figures from the official *Licensing Statistics 1916*, "Taking 1913 – the year before the War – as a standard, the convictions for drunkenness in England and Wales fell in 1915 by 28 per cent, in 1916 by 56 per cent and in the first quarter in 1917 by 66 per cent".[19] There were factors other than restrictions imposed by the Control Board which affected the statistics. One was the change in the strength of the police force, many members enlisting in the forces. Another was the removal from civil life of many men because of enlistment, and a third was the leniency with which members of the forces were dealt with by magistrates. In this latter instance, servicemen found drunk by civilian police were often handed over to the service authorities. There were two other types of statistics which cast some light upon the increase in sobriety. These were medical statistics which gave the incidence of deaths caused by an alcohol induced condition, and those relating to duty on alcoholic drinks for home consumption.

The main object of the restrictions imposed by the Central Control Board, that is to safeguard the nation's security and ability to prosecute the war, was achieved. There were other beneficial effects. "Family life, and public health and order gained substantially under the policy of Liquor Control".[20] These benefits were substantial, but among the temperance forces there were those who did not think the restrictions went far enough. In 1916 a national campaign for prohibition during the war was launched. The following petition was devised,

> *We the undersigned, being impressed with the necessity of avoiding all waste, and of utilising fully the moral and material resources of the Nation, and being convinced that the present enormous consumption of intoxicating drink is the most dangerous enemy of National efficiency, health and economy, hereby urge His Majesty's Government to prohibit the manufacture, import, export and common sale of intoxicating liquors during the War, and for six months afterwards.*[21]

This petition was widely circulated by temperance societies and appeared in several religious newspapers. *Alliance News* reported that "a good number of signatures" had been obtained from persons who had never signed a temperance pledge. "On one form 20 signatures came from non-abstainers, and there have been not a few such cases".[22] The campaign forms were published in the *Christian Herald* and other journals. In many places house-to-house canvassing was undertaken by members of local temperance organizations. In six weeks over two million signatures had been secured and on 16th August 1916 a deputation presented this massive memorial to the Prime Minister at the House of Commons.[23] Asquith admitted to being impressed by the size of the petition and promised to give it his most careful consideration. The intention of the petition was not, in fact, carried out by the government, though the setting up of the Central Control Board and its subsequent imposition of restrictions was evidence that the alcohol problem was being taken seriously.

Almost simultaneously with the collection of signatures to the prohibition petition, a more broadly-based appeal was made to the nation. This was the launching of the Strength of Britain Movement. The memorial to the government which was the basis of the movement was a comprehensive assessment of the alcohol problem as a threat to national security and the prosecution of the war. Its first signatories were prominent high-ranking officers of H.M. Services, politicians, Fellows of the Royal Society, leading scholars and other well-known public figures. The memorial was not simply a recital of the evil effects of drinking intoxicating liquor, it was a call to moral integrity. It said:

> *We are convinced that the dangers confronting us arise from the sudden possession of abundant wages rather than from a lack of patriotic feeling; untrained in spending or in thrift, large numbers of our workers waste their resources on drink. The greatest good a Government can render to its people is to strengthen their right purposes and weaken the power of their temptations, and there lies upon us now the double duty of protecting our people from the temptation to drink away their earnings and of protecting the State from the intolerable folly of high wages turned to the advantage of our enemies.*[24]

Britain, it was urged, should follow the example of Russia and France in suspending the liquor trade for the duration of the war. "We are no temperance reformers as such, "declared the signatories to the Memorial. "We stand for the great desire of all good people to strike the mightiest blow for freedom of which Britain is capable"?[25] A deputation of the Strength of Britain Movement met Lloyd George soon after his appointment as Prime Minister at the head of a new coalition government early in 1917, and there was a dispute afterwards about his interpretation of their case. He seemed to believe that the Strength of Britain Movement was prepared to accept state purchase of the liquor trade provided this was followed by the granting of local option. In a letter to the Prime Minister (11th April 1917), Dr C. W. Saleeby, chairman of the Executive of the Strength of Britain Movement corrected the impression. The movement stood for wartime prohibition, he said, and for nothing less.

Strength seemed to be an early characteristic of the movement. On 21st March 1917 the Queen's Hall, London could not accommodate all who wished to attend a public meeting in support of it. The smaller hall, where an overflow meeting was held, also proved inadequate and many people failed to gain admission. The supporters at the meeting included representatives of 20 British universities, 243 headmasters of schools, 100 admirals and generals, 250 directors of munition factories, 100 members of parliament and privy councillors, 200 baronets and knights, 90 members of the Royal Society and the Royal Academy, 200 leaders of finance and industry, 100 persons distinguished in the arts and in literature, 450 doctors, 500 magistrates and 100 municipal leaders. There were nine holders of the Victoria Cross in the audience which totalled over four thousand.[26] These statistics are significant as supporting the claim: "We are no temperance reformers as such". Various speakers at the demonstration advanced as a major argument in favour of prohibition, the fact that valuable foodstuff was being wasted in the production of beer. Both at home and at the front there was urgent need for maintaining supplies of food. It was this need which prompted an editorial in the influential journal *The Spectator.* It said:

> *We have stated over and over again our strong conviction that it is almost hopeless for the Government to appeal to the country with an appearance of sincerity when they*

themselves not only tolerate but encourage a widespread waste of food. For this is what the brewing of beer means. It consumes barley, and it also consumes sugar. It does this at a time when sugar is short in every household in the land, and housewives are being urged to shut down their consumption of bread to the last possible crumb. We do not write as teetotallers. We have no idea of condemning beer as a drink. All we say is that brewing of beer automatically carries its own condemnation in such times as these on terms which the Government themselves have stated. There is no food to waste, yet food is being wasted in the form of beer.[27]

One official response was a letter from the Ministry of Food, in November 1917 to all hoteliers. It said, "I am instructed by the Food Controller to request you to post in a prominent place in your hotel a strong appeal to all those of your customers who require alcoholic drinks, to drink light *Wine*, and to refrain from drinking beer in order that there may be more beer for the working classes."[28] This seemed a strange piece of advice, if besides a curb on the misuse of foodstuff it was also important to restrict the excessive consumption of liquor in general.

Trends and statistics

A review of the 1914–18 war period might end appropriately with a reference to the trends in consumption during that time. G. B. Wilson provided the required statistics in a review of "The National Drink Bill for 1918".[29] He summed up the situation in one paragraph, "The consumption of alcoholic liquors in the United Kingdom during 1918, measured in terms of absolute alcohol, shows a decline of approximately 60 per cent as compared with a pre-war consumption in 1913". However, the expenditure on intoxicants in 1918 "calculated on a very conservative basis" was practically the same as in 1917, and at least 54 per cent higher than in 1913. This was the highest on record in the history of the United Kingdom. Two comments are necessary to complement these figures. First, although there was a falling off in employment in some industries after the war ended, wages continued to rise. There was an aggregate increase of nearly £2,800,000 in the weekly wages of over 5,650,000 workpeople, giving a total weekly advance of over £5,000,000 during 1917–18 compared with £1,300,000 in 1915–16 and less than £400,000 in 1910–14. The second comment is that the maintenance of the restrictions on the output of beer and the release of spirits from bond effectively controlled consumption during 1917–18. Prices tended to increase but, as we saw, so did average wages. The trends in the quantities of alcoholic liquor retained for consumption during the period 1913–18 inclusive are shown in the following table. The figures for beer are given in both "standard" and "bulk" barrels; spirits are given in imperial proof gallons; and wine, cider and perry in imperial gallons, all to the nearest thousand.

Liquor	**1913** '000s	**1914** '000s	**1915** '000s	**1916** '000s	**1917** '000s	**1918** '000s
Beer (standard)	35,324	34,193	29,148	26,676	16,134	12,791
Beer (bulk)	36,843	35,661	30,960	29,855	21,054	21,960
Spirits	31,845	31,694	35,020	28,163	18,549	15,123
Wine	11,368	10,630	10,175	9,910	7,099	11,346
Cider & perry (dutiable)					8,098	8,714

The number of licensed premises for the same period 1913–18 were:

	On-licences	Off-licences	Clubs
1913	88,739	23,632	8,457
1914	87,660	23,408	8,738
1915	86,626	23,202	8,902
1916	85,889	22,977	8,520
1917	85,273	22,719	8,167
1918	84,644	22,473	7,972[30]

The other figures for the same period which are relevant at this point are those for convictions for drunkenness:

	Total	Males	Females
1913	188,877	153,112	35,765
1914	183,828	146,517	37,311
1915	135,811	102,600	33,211
1916	84,191	62,946	21,245
1917	46,410	34,103	12,307
1918	29,075	21,853	7,222

It will be seen that there was a marked decrease in convictions once the restrictions of the Control Board came into effect. It was not surprising, therefore, that after the war it was regarded prudent to retain many of them as peacetime measures.

Lord D'Abernon, speaking in Paris in April 1919 on the "Effects of War-time control on liquor traffic in England" gave some other interesting statistics. Taking the year 1913 as the standard he produced the following table on convictions and other related consequences of drinking.

	Standard 1913	1917 Male	1917 Female
Convictions for drunkenness	100	22	34
Deaths from alcoholism	100	32	31
Deaths from cirrhosis	100	66½	49
Attempted suicide	100	33	47
Cases of delirium tremens in certain districts	100	4½	3
Suffocation of infants	100		57
Absolute alcohol consumed	100		(1918) 40

One lesson to be learned from the drinking habits and their consequences in Britain as a result of the imposition of wartime restrictions is that society can take effective measures to control the "alcohol problem".

References

1. *Alliance News* 19th February 1914 p. 117.
2. See *Alliance News* January 1915 p. 3 for the text of the Brewers' Manifesto.
3. *Alliance News* November 1914 p. 592.
4. *Alliance News* April 1915 p. 68.
5. *Alliance News* April 1915 p. 62.
6. Quoted verbatim in *Alliance News* May 1915 p. 83.

7. Op cit p. 83.
8. *Alliance News* May 1915 p. 95.
9. 29th April 1915.
10. The full text of the powers of the Central Control Board is published in *Alliance News* July 1915 pp. 142, 143.
11. See pp. 99–113.
12. *Drink in 1914–1923 A Lesson in Control.* Arthur Shadwell (1933) p. 6 ff.
13. *The Times* 28th August 1915 p. 8.
14. *The Times* 31st August 1915 p. 3.
15. Op cit p. 3.
16. *Brewers' Gazette* 19th August 1915 p. 465.
17. The report of the Central Control Board was published in *Alliance News* December 1915 pp. 246, 247.
18. "Principles of Drink Reform" speech by Lord D'Abernon to the Church of England Temperance Society (Women's Section) on 25th October 1918. Quoted by Henry Carter in *The Control of the Drink Trade. (second edition)* p. 159.
19. Carter Op cit p. 238.
20. Carter Op cit p. 273.
21. *Alliance News* August 1916 p. 123.
22. Op cit p. 123.
23. *Alliance News* September 1916 p. 140.
24. *Alliance News* August 1916 p. 132.
25. Op cit p. 132.
26. *Alliance News* April–May 1917 p. 56.
27. *The Spectator* 13th October 1917 p. 375.
28. *Alliance News* January 1918 p. 7.
29. *Alliance News* April 1919 p. 30.
30. *Alliance News* October 1919 p. 84.

CHAPTER 5

"LEASE-LEND" REFORM

During the Second World War Britain and America entered into an imaginative scheme which came to be known as "lease-lend". It was a reciprocal relationship by which the United States provided warships for Britain in exchange for bases in the West Indies. It was the beginning of a system of mutual help, though the outcome was that Britain materially benefited from the arrangement to an extent that enabled her to prosecute the war more effectively and to make a more hopeful recovery afterwards. "Lease-lend" is a term which might apply to other ways by which Britain has been influenced by the U.S.A., not least in ideas which find their way across the Atlantic. The Americans may have inherited our democratic procedures, but the British have received the impact of the results of the application of those procedures in the United States.

Prohibition

A concept which created a social revolution in America at the time of the First World War was "Prohibition". After fifty years of campaigning for the prohibition of the liquor traffic in the U.S.A. the Eighteenth Amendment embodying this principle was adopted in 1919. Several states had already introduced prohibition, but by 1919 the requisite number of states had opted for prohibition for it to be put to all the states. Thereafter, it was this issue which dominated thinking in Britain and elsewhere so far as the "alcohol problem" was concerned. It will be helpful, therefore, to give a brief account of the progress of prohibition in America.[1]

Legislation designed to discourage the excessive use of alcohol in America was enacted in many areas during the colonial period. In particular, laws were passed prohibiting the sale of ardent spirits to Indians. After the War of Independence in 1783 and before the Constitutional Convention in 1787, an essay was published by Benjamin Rush of Philadelphia which is recognized as the foundation document of the Temperance Movement in the United States. It appeared in 1785 under the title "Effects of ardent spirits upon the human mind and body." The first temperance society was formed in Morean, Saratoga County, New York in 1808. It was initiated by a local physician, Dr Billy J. Clark. "We shall all become a community of drunkards in this town unless something is done to arrest the progress of intemperance", he told his minister, the Revd Lebbeus Armstrong. His action led to the formation of a temperance society on 13th April 1808 with twenty-three men members enrolling. However, the year in which temperance in America became a crusade was 1826, when the American Temperance Society was formed in Boston. There followed a phenomenal growth in temperance societies throughout America, so that the Eighth Annual Report of the American Temperance Society recorded that more than 8,000 societies had been formed with a total membership of over one and a half million.[3]

By the late 1830s the effects of the Temperance Movement were being seen in a decline in granting licences, in the abandonment of the sale of ardent spirits and in the reduction of the number of distilleries. Convictions for various crimes also declined.[4] However, there were other more sinister trends to be noted. Up to about 1835, very little beer or wine was consumed, the predominant intoxicants being distilled liquors. It was against the use of spirits that the temperance societies were formed. Producers of beer and wine was quick to seize the opportunity to provide alternatives which, so far, were not condemned by temperance societies. It soon became clear that the increased consumption of beer, cider and wine created an extension of the alcohol problem and the Temperance Movement reacted by bringing in the principle and pledge of total abstinence.

The next development was to attack the producers of liquor. Lyman Beecher, whose *Six Sermons on Intemperance,* published in 1826 and which proved to be one of the influential factors in the creation of the Temperance Movement in America, said that "the traffic in these liquors is wrong and should be abandoned as a great national evil is evident".[5] He saw "legislative interference" as one of the remedies. So did many of the early leaders of the Temperance Movement, and increasingly references were made to the need for prohibition.

First steps towards prohibition

The first notable action towards this end was taken when General James Appleton was elected to the legislature of Maine in 1836. He had advocated prohibition earlier when he lived in Massachusetts. In 1837, by which time he had become chairman of a joint special committee to consider the licensing system of the state, he urged that the traffic in ardent spirits should be prohibited. The report of this committee is of immense interest to the historian.[6] It argued that the effect of prohibition legislation would be to make the traffic in ardent spirits disreputable, as well as to impose an effective control. Some limited prohibition legislation was enacted in some states, but progress towards out-and-out prohibition was halted in 1840 by a movement of such "spectacular interest that it swamped efforts for legislation for several years and in fact submerged most of the earlier temperance organizations".[7]

This was the Washington Movement which started on Washington's birthday in 1840 among a group of reformed drunkards in Baltimore. It was a pledge-signing movement directed to drinking men. So many signed the pledge that in many cities saloons were closed and distilleries either went out of business or were forced to work half-time. The initial success of this movement encouraged temperance leaders to pin their faith in what came to be known as "moral suasion". The method employed was not to use an appeal for total abstinence on grounds of health, but by the personal testimony of reclaimed drunkards. The movement did not seem able to sustain reformed drunkards in their abstinence, and many lapsed. Saloon bars began to reopen because the liquor traffic was protected by law. The plea for some kind of legislative reform began to be heard again, first in advocacy of legislative control and then for full-blooded prohibition. In 1851 the Fourth National Temperance Convention came out in favour of legal prohibition based on the Maine Law.

Moral suasion and prohibition

For some years there was controversy between temperance reformers who favoured moral suasion and those who advocated prohibition. The experience of Neil Dow, whose advocacy eventually resulted in the passing of prohibition legislation in Maine, illustrates the progress from moral suasion to legislative action. He emerged as a temperance advocate in 1829 at the age of twenty-five. Thereafter his reputation increased and he is generally recognized as the Father of Prohibition. His first attempt to secure legislation in the State of Maine was not successful, but in 1846 the first of a series of bills was passed by the legislature. It was Neil Dow's persistence which in 1851 secured the passage of the major legislation which became known as the Maine Law. This prohibited the manufacture, sale and keeping for sale of intoxicating liquors. The law was backed up with severe penalties which included imprisonment for a third offence. Seeing the benefits to public health and order in the State of Maine, other states adopted similar measures. Between 1851 and 1855, thirteen states had passed such measures. In 1853 President Lincoln endorsed the principle of prohibition. At this time campaigning for prohibition was confined to individual states. There was no national movement. Suddenly, in 1856, the progress of the previous years was halted. Several states reverted to licensing. Even Maine returned to licensing from 1856 to 1888. "So by the middle of the Civil War only five of the thirteen prohibition states were left and within the next dozen years two of these, Massachusetts and Connecticut, backslid."[8]

For the student of the course of temperance reform in Britain, the reasons for this recession in the United States are important. Some may be seen to apply to the recession of the fortunes of the temperance cause in Britain at a much later period. The principal reasons were (a) the diversion of reforming zeal from liquor to the anti-slavery issue; (b) court decisions which declared some features of prohibition as unconstitutional; (c) failure to enforce the law vigorously; and (d) the issue became divisive politically.[9] In Britain, after the First World War reforming zeal was largely devoted to the peace issue. " . . . . overwhelmingly the most significant 'cause' to which people pledged themselves in their thousands was 'Peace'. So much like a temperance organization was Dick Sheppard's Peace Pledge Union that it could have been charged with plagiarism. What happened, in fact, was that peace ousted temperance as the cause above all causes to advocate."[10] At least one of the other causes of the recession in the temperance cause in the U.S.A. applied in Britain: "the issue became divisive politically". This emerged in our consideration of the period from 1900 to the outbreak of the First World War.

Having noted this similarity, the remainder of our account of the Prohibition Movement in America will have increased significance. The chief lesson of the attempt to secure State-by-State prohibition was that the ultimate purpose would not be achieved without powerful national political action. This was necessary not only to secure the passage of suitable legislation, but to guarantee support in the legislature for other measures which would ensure fiscal policies which did not depend upon revenue from liquor, and the provision of adequate enforcement services. The passage of the Internal Revenue Act of 1862, with its provisions for drawing revenue from the sale of liquor, acted as a spur to the United States Brewers' Association to become more active politically; and this, in turn, was an additional reason for the Temperance Movement to enter the political arena. The success of the anti-slavery campaign also had lessons for the prohibitionists. In 1869 the first steps were taken to form a national political party with a principal aim of securing prohibition legislation. Progress was impeded by lack of funds and by the division among temperance supporters on the objectives of political action. Some were content to pursue the limited objective of local option for their own state, some believed it was sufficient to secure a temperance vote in the existing political parties, while others believed in the formation of a prohibitionist party, which was formed, but its early successes in election for state legislatures were few. In 1872 a prohibitionist candidate was put up in the presidential election, but he secured very few votes. In subsequent presidential elections the experiment was repreated, with little success. The fortunes of the temperance cause and of the liquor interests in the 1870s were summed up by Leigh Colvin, "While in the seventies prohibitory legislation went backward and the whole temperance movement was characterised by vacillation and defeat, the liquor interests, confident because of their victories, went forward like a conquering army, each year attaining additional political power."[11] The intention of the liquor interests to secure effective control of state and national legislatures by securing the election of representatives sympathetic to their cause was vigorously expounded at their conventions. The success of this policy was revealed in a sinister form between 1873 and 1875, when it was shown by investigation that highly-placed persons in administration were involved in whisky frauds which deprived the government of $4,000,000 in revenue.[12]

Constitutional prohibition

After various setbacks the prohibitionists rallied their forces again with the formation of the Prohibition Home Protection Party. This adopted the policy of securing constitutional prohibition in the states as distinct from statutory prohibition which could be changed by the legislature. The first state to adopt constitutional prohibition was Kansas in 1881 and a similar result was obtained in Iowa in 1882. In Maine, in 1884, where prohibition had been tried for almost a quarter of a century, constitutional prohibition was carried by a vote of nearly three to one. At that time it seemed to many observers that prohibition would prevail. Leigh Colvin wrote lyrically about the mood of the times. "It was the beginning of a period which in many respects is the most inspiring in the history of the reform. For a whole-hearted devotion to the cause, for deep conviction, for moral earnestness, for able championship, for advocacy of high principle and for spontaneous enthusiasm no period has excelled it. From the standpoint of great and commanding personalities and masterly promulgation of the prohibitionist philosophy and argument the half-dozen years following 1884 were in many respects the golden age of reform".[13] It was at the National Convention of the Prohibition Party at Pittsburg in 1884 that a campaign emerged which gave the party significance in national politics. In the next four years more prohibition legislation was passed than in the previous twenty-five years. Opposition to the party came from both republicans and democrats. Supporters of prohibition were ostracized socially and in business. However, in the election of 1886 support for the Prohibition Party enabled it to hold the balance of power in fourteen states and in forty-eight congressional districts. Between 1884 and 1888 the vote for the party rose rapidly, but this was not the extent of its influence. The two major parties saw the importance of appealing to the prohibition voters and both engaged in various methods of securing their support. The lengths to which opponents were prepared to go was seen in the theft by two clerks in the subscription department of the party's journal *Voice* of the lists of subscribers. These lists were then sold to the Republican Party and used to send literature to prohibition voters.[14] Despite what seemed to be an increase in support for prohibition between 1887 and 1890 votes were taken and prohibition lost in twelve states. The reasons for the halt in the advance of prohibition included the reorganization of the liquor traffic's campaigning methods, unfair tactics such as subsidizing the press and fabricating news, the purchase of politicians and corruption in elections.[15]

So thorough is Leigh Colvin's treatment of the subject that his judgement as to the effects of prohibition where it was tried are important.

> *A careful and comprehensive study of the history of state prohibition in every State where it has been tried reveals the fact that no matter how hostile or indifferent the officers, it has almost uniformly been followed by an immediate and decided decrease in drunkenness and arrests for drunkenness, has diminished crime and pauperism, and lessened child dependency. Prohibition has stimulated business, increased sales of legitimate commodities and improved collections; it has bettered homes and made social life more wholesome; it has increased school attendance and in general has brought about decidedly improved social, economic and moral conditions.*[16]

Then why, if the benefits were so conspicuous and evident, did not prohibition prevail universally through the U.S.A.? The answer seems to be that the vested interests learned how to nullify the gains. They persisted in stressing that prohibition had been a failure. They magnified every small incident of drunkenness and evasion of the law in support of their main contention that it had failed.

As the new century approached, two extensions of the liquor problem gave fresh impetus to the prohibition movement. One was drunkenness and evasion of regulations in army canteens, and the other was the introduction of liquor to the new American colonies. It was at this time that a new approach to the liquor problem emerged as an alternative to prohibition. This was the Anti-Saloon League which differed both in objective and method from the Prohibition Party. The Anti-Saloon League campaigned for the elimination of the local saloon and pinned its faith in local option as the means of achieving it. Instead of advancing nationwide with a party political platform, it urged temperance-minded electors to vote for the individual candidates in the two main parties who supported the suppression of saloons in their areas. The Anti-Saloon League was formed at Oberlin, Ohio in 1893 by a group who had earlier shown interest in local option. Most important of all they were republicans in a town which had been one of the centres of anti-slavery. They were reluctant to abandon their party affiliation to join the prohibitionists. The Anti-Saloon League achieved sporadic success, but never emerged as a threat to the liquor traffic as a whole. However, its existence tended to draw off support from the prohibitionists, especially from those with otherwise strong party affiliation.

The movement moves into the twentieth century

The Prohibition Party survived this embarrassment and gathered strength in the first decade of the twentieth century. At a national conference at Indianapolis in 1913 it adopted "one of the most ambitious programs undertaken . . . for a number of years."[17] The aim was to raise one million dollars before the close of the campaign in 1916; to organize prohibition clubs; to increase circulation of prohibitionist periodicals; to concentrate in not more than ten congressional districts to secure the election of prohibitionists to congress in 1914; and to enrol five million voters to support the Prohibition Party. By concentrating on selected congressional districts the party achieved its most notable and influential successes. In 1914 it polled nearly half-a-million votes in various states for governors and congressmen. Most important, their candidate in the ninth congressional district of California was elected to congress. Switching the campaign to Massachusetts, the prohibitionists very nearly succeeded in securing the election of their candidate as governor. The tide of support for nationwide prohibition was rising again and in 1913 the Anti-Saloon League came out in favour of it. This was a great turning point in the strategy for temperance reform. A national conference was called at which more than ninety organizations were represented. The outcome was the formation of the National Temperance Council and the adoption of a common objective, the national prohibition of the liquor traffic.

The Eighteenth Amendment

This account of the cause of prohibition in America shows how fluctuating were its fortunes. For over five years before 1914 there had been no net gain in the number of prohibition states, which remained at nine.[18] And then in 1914 five states adopted prohibition by popular vote, five more followed in 1915 and four more in 1916. On 6th April 1917 the United States entered the First World War and there was an immediate and widespread demand for wartime prohibition. This re-enforced the strength of the demand for the permanent adoption of this principle. On 22nd December 1917 the issue was submitted to the states in the form of the Eighteenth Amendment. This read:

> **Section 1.** *After one year from the ratification of this article the manufacture, sale or transportation of intoxicating liquors within, the importation thereof into, or the exportation thereof from the United States and all territory subject to the jurisdiction thereof for beverage purposes is hereby prohibited.*
> **Section 2.** *The Congress and the several States shall have concurrent power to enforce this article by appropriate legislation.*
> **Section 3.** *This article shall be inoperative unless it shall have been ratified as an amendment to the Constitution by the Legislatures of the several States, as provided in the Constitution, within seven years from the date of the submission hereof to the States by the Congress.*[19]

It was ratified on 16th January 1919 and came into force a year later. Leigh Colvin commented, "The Eighteenth Amendment was ratified by the largest number of States, and by the largest percentage of States that ever ratified any amendment to the Constitution in the entire history of our country, and, with the exception of the Twelfth, Thirteenth and Fifteenth Amendments, it was ratified in the shortest length of time."[20] Forty-six states, that is all but two, voted in favour of ratification. The total vote of both houses in the forty-six states was 5,084 to 1,265 or more than 80 per cent majority. The National Prohibition Act, which came to be known as the Volstead Act, to enforce the amendment, passed congress in October 1919 and against the veto of President Wilson. It was fitting that this should happen in 1919 when the Prohibition Party was celebrating its 50th anniversary.

The immediate results of prohibition were very impressive. Statistics for the first year compared with 1917 showed dramatic reduction in arrests for drunkenness, committals to prison, criminal offences, arrests of women and young persons for drinking offences, incidences of alcoholism and deaths generally. Positively it led to increased productivity in industry and demands for labour. There was also a rise in the standard of living. Unfortunately these signs of hope were not maintained in the years immediately following 1920. The reasons for the failure to sustain the benefits of prohibition were analysed by many observers, and they fell into three categories. There were some deficiencies in the law itself, but the chief reason for failure to fulfil the highest hopes was unsatisfactory enforcement procedures which were often lax and open to corruption. Finally, although constitutional prohibition had been achieved the political system upon which its implementation depended remained almost unchanged. For many politicians their support for the Eighteenth Amendment had been prompted by expediency and not conviction.

Bearing in mind the division between the Prohibition Party's commitment to a national policy and the Anti-Saloon League's stress on local option, it is interesting to note that when the Campaign for Prohibition was launched in Britain, it was based on the conviction that a nationwide policy could best be ensured by the application of local option. This was not surprising, since the temperance forces in Britain, and notably the United Kingdom Alliance, had been pressing for local option legislation since the middle of the nineteenth century. And so in the wake of the introduction of prohibition in America, the "Campaign for Prohibition by Local Option" was launched in London in November 1919 and culminated in a meeting at the Central Hall Westminster. A group of temperance leaders from

America were there and two of them, Dr A. W. Hamilton and Dr George A. Henry, spoke of the success of the prohibition movement in their country. It was, however, another American who made the deepest impression in Britain. This was W. E. (Pussyfoot) Johnson who, though not able to be at the Central Hall meeting, sent a message. It was a poignant message. He said that before prohibition American insurance companies had calculated that over 60,000 deaths each year occurred as a result of the consumption of intoxicating liquors.

> *In other words each year, in America, the liquor traffic put out sixty-thousand pairs of eyes. These eyes were destroyed and these lives snuffed out, in order that the liquor traffic might further profit thereby. By discontinuing the liquor traffic the greater proportion of these unnecessary deaths are avoided. In America we simply terminated the business of destroying human lives for profit. When it comes home to me to lose one single eye, I am overwhelmed with thankfulness that I have been permitted by God's good will to contribute in some measure to the ending of a traffic in my country whose business it was to put out each year sixty-thousand pairs of eyes.*[21]

"Pussyfoot" Johnson in Britain

This reference to "Pussyfoot" Johnson provides a natural introduction to one of the most remarkable temperance advocates to contribute to the cause in Britain as well as in America. William Eugene Johnson was born in the village of Coventry, New York on 25th May 1862.[22] He began his active working life in journalism and earned a reputation for his tenacious investigation into corruption and injustice. This was a suitable preparation for his eventual work as a special officer of the government Indian Bureau for the Suppression of the Liquor Traffic in Indian Territory. To say that the methods he employed were unusual is an understatement. He did not flinch from physical force to root out, intimidate and apprehend those who were engaged in the illegal pushing of liquor in Indian territory. When he and his colleagues believed the battle for prohibition had been won in the U.S.A. they turned to the prospect of securing worldwide prohibition. He came first to Britain in September 1918. After helping in the Local Option Campaign in Scotland, he established an office in Fleet Street, London, with financial backing from America he launched a Campaign for Prohibition in Britain. The *Daily Mail* assigned a reporter to "trail" Johnson and carried extensive features about him and reports of his meeting and activities. The *Brewing Trade Review*, one of the prominent monthlies of the trade, referred to "Pussyfoot" Johnson in almost every issue in the most scathing terms.

To British observers it must have seemed a forlorn hope that prohibition would follow swiftly in the wake of its success in America. An article in the *Daily Mail* gave Johnson's campaign a new aspect, and explained that the American Anti-Saloon League had sent "its best man" to Britain, with *carte blanche* in strategy, tactics and finance and others would follow him. Controversy was aroused by a reported statement, based on a misunderstanding of what Johnson said, that the Anti-Saloon League was going to engage actively in British elections. When this story broke Johnson was in Finland, but on his return he was beseiged with newspapermen asking for an explanation. "Neither myself nor the Anti-Saloon League has had the slightest intention of interfering in any way with British affairs. We will not take any part whatever in any British Election", he told the *Manchester Guardian.* His purpose, he said, was to explain American action against drink, why and how it was taken, and with what result. His explanation did not remove suspicion and representatives of the liquor trade combined to form an anti-prohibition organization. The country was flooded with literature and temperance meetings were broken up.

The campaign against "Pussyfoot" Johnson reached its climax in tragedy. On 13th November 1919 he was invited to take part in a debate on American prohibition at the Overseas Club in Kingsway. So numerous were the applications for tickets that the meeting was transferred to Essex Hall.[23] The meeting coincided with a period when the students of University College and St. Bartholomew's Hospital were engaged in demonstrations. Students from the hospital schools and from King's College and University College decided to "rag" Pussyfoot Johnson at the meeting at Essex Hall. They had no intention of injuring him. Everybody was instructed not to cause damage and if objects were thrown they were to be confined to little bags of flour. The organizers of the meeting knew nothing of other plans, but information had been leaked to the press. Students occupied as many seats in the hall as possible and kept up a chant which the chairman's appeals failed to quell. Neither was Johnson, with his customary good humour, able to disarm the students. Flour bags were thrown at him, and then chairs were smashed and tables overthrown. Eventually he and the chairman were carried from the hall and taken to King's College. Realizing it was no more than a rag, Johnson entered into the spirit of the event and allowed himself to be carried in procession through the West End. At Great Portland Street the good-humoured event turned sour. Someone from the edge of the crowd threw a stone and hit Pussyfoot Johnson in the eye. The following day he was taken to a nursing home. He told reporters, "Don't let the boys think that I am a martyr. I am not. I am fifty-seven, but last night the boys made me feel twenty years younger. I am feeling today a bit stiff, and the eye gave me a bad night, but the only thing that really bothers me is that the doctors won't let me read the story of the rag in the papers". A fortnight later his eye had to be removed. The students assured him of their deep sorrow at the outcome of what they intended to be a rag. Even the Chairman of the Wine and Spirit Defence Fund sent a letter of sympathy. The London *Evening News* opened a fund as an expression of sympathy, but although Johnson appreciated the sentiment, he asked for the money to be sent to St. Dunstan's Hostel for the work of Sir Arthur Pearson for blinded solders, and this was done. On 17th January 1920 he was present at a meeting called by the Strength of Britain Movement at the Central Hall Westminster. In a reference to the meeting *Alliance News* commented, "We are sorry, however, to find that Mr Johnson is far from well". He had "by no means recovered from the serious injuries he suffered at the hands of the students".[24] However, in May *Alliance News* reported "We are glad to see Mr Johnson back again, looking wonderfully fit".[25]

He was by no means the only American to come to Britain to join the campaign for prohibition. At almost every campaign rally in the major cities and especially at those held in London, leaders of the Prohibition Movement in the United States were among the speakers.

The trade in Britain responds

The trade, through its established organizations and new ones formed to counteract the prohibition campaign, responded to the challenge. The main trade organizations were formed at about the same time or later than the United Kingdom Alliance which spearheaded the campaign for prohibition. The very earliest of the trade bodies was in fact the Licensed Victuallers' Protection Society of London formed in 1833. Its main purpose was to watch all proceedings in parliament which affected the retail liquor trade and take action to promote measures for its benefit or to defeat measures which threatened it. It was also devoted to securing representation at all levels of government to protect the trade's interests. In London it acted as a federal organization to represent all local branches of licensed victuallers. The body which represented licensed victuallers outside the Metropolitan area was the Licensed Victuallers' National Defence League which was established in 1872. The other main body to represent the retailers of liquor was the National Federation of Off-Licence Holders' Associations, founded in 1886 to safeguard the interests of the off-licence trade. Another body which represented the beer and wine trade and consisted of twenty-four local societies was the Beer, Spirit and Wine Trade National Defence League, founded in 1873. Its objects were "to promote, support or oppose Bills in Parliament, and to assist in the return to Parliament of candidates favourable to the interests of the trade". Possibly the main organization was the National Trade Defence Association, which was established in 1888. It represented all sections of the trade in alcoholic liquor in the United Kingdom.

Its objects were,

> *to watch at all times the general interests of the Trade as a whole in and out of Parliament; to secure by all legal means, regardless of party politics, the return to the House of Commons and other elected bodies of candidates favourable to the Trade interests; to federate existing societies; to decide upon the general policy of defence; and generally to do all things that the committee shall deem to be for the interests of the Trade.*[26]

These were not the only organizations with close ties with the trade. There were some whose names gave no indication of this connection, no more, indeed, than there was any indication from the name of the "Strength of Britain Movement" that it had close ties with temperance organizations. Best known of the organizations which had strong backing from the trade was The Fellowship of Freedom and Reform which was founded in November 1920. Its main principles were to stand for personal freedom as opposed to restriction or prohibition, to promote "True Temperance" and to work for the reform of public houses and thus eliminate drunkenness. The Fellowship had a close association with the Order of Buffaloes, which claimed a membership of nearly three millions. Most Buffalo lodges held their meetings at public houses. The Fellowship declared its belief in the repeal of the Children's Act which excluded children from public houses. There was no doubt that this organization received considerable financial support form the trade. Reference to "True Temperance" is not confined to a principle. As we have seen, there was an organization created which was called The True Temperance Association. Among its aims were:

1. *To create a healthy and reasonable public opinion on the subject of Temperance in drinking.*
2. *To encourage the development of the public-house in the direction of making it in the best sense a place for the present-day needs of the people, and to help in the removal of all legislative and administrative hindrances to such developments.*
3. *To promote fairness, justice and common sense in dealing with the problem of intemperance.*

Several brewers were actively associated with the organization.

The direct confrontation in the prohibition controversy was between the Campaign for Prohibition by Local Option, sponsored by the United Kingdom Alliance, and the Anti-Prohibition League which was formed in June 1919. This described itself as "a public and non-trade organisation which has been formed to combat the activities, public and secret, of those so-called 'temperance' bodies which aim at introducing prohibition of alcoholic beverages in this country". On its own admission it came into being as a direct challenge to the temperance movement for prohibition. A circular declared, "A strong and influential combination of various temperance bodies, including those which claim the credit of having obtained prohibition in the United States, is actively at work in this country. The funds at its disposal already amount to several million pounds, whilst guarantees of unlimited support have been given for trade or other motives by various wealthy individuals and firms."[27] The league stated it had a dual policy, (a) combative and (b) constructive.

The combative policy was,

1. *To meet misleading propoganda with scientific evidence, and with the fullest forces of properly organised publicity.*
2. *To give active support to Parliamentary candidates who pledge themselves to support the interests of the moderate consumers, and to keep constituents informed as to the attitude on this question of those members who represent, or who seek to represent, them in Parliament.*
3. *To resist the passage through Parliament of any Acts intended to restrict or affect the rights of the moderate consumer.*
4. *To bring into the light of publicity the methods adopted by the prohibitionists.*

The constructive policy was,

1. *The Improved Public House Policy.*
2. *To demand that an adequate supply of beer and spirits of an approved strength shall be made available for public consumption.*
3. *To demand that one of the most common causes of intoxication and physical injury, viz, immaturity of spirits and adulteration of beer shall be prevented by securing through suitable legislation, a high standard of purity.*[28]

The league claimed to have more than 500,000 members. This was probably accounted for by the fact that there was an alliance with the Working Men's Club and Institute Union whose total membership was corporately affiliated to the league. It arranged its own public meetings, but encouraged its members to attend prohibition meetings to challenge and disrupt the speakers. Courses were held to train people in the art of speaking and interruption. These were arranged by the National Trade Defence Association and the curriculum was based on *The handbook of the so-called Temperance question* which was regularly revised. The courses ended with examinations. The Fellowship of Freedom and Reform had similar courses. After a period of testing, during which a fee of £2. 2*s.* plus expenses were paid, speakers were placed on the salaried list and received £6. 6*s.* a week and often more.

Policy after the First World War

Inevitably, as Britain returned to normality after the war, the question was raised as to what form of licensing administration should succeed the Liquor Control Board. The trade and the temperance bodies were equally interested in this matter. On 22nd April 1921 a Private Member's Bill sponsored by Colonel John Gretton was down for second reading. The objectives of the bill were,

(a) *To destroy the administrative power of the justices in licensing matters and to change Quarter Sessions into a licensing court with a paid president.*
(b) *To limit effectively local opposition to the grant, removal or renewal of licences.*
(c) *To extend the hours of sale and relax the stringency of the present regulations as to conduct of licensed premises.*

Specific proposals in the bill would have introduced far-reaching changes in licensing administration. It was proposed that, instead of annual licences, they should be granted for a term not exceeding twenty-one years. Changes in the basis of compensation would have considerably increased what could be claimed for redundant licences. Variations of hours were proposed. In regard to children in bars of public houses, it was proposed that Section 120 of the Children's Act 1908 should be modified to enable an adult to take a child into any part of licensed premises, not being an open drinking bar, provided provision was made for "suitable refreshment". It was proposed that the onus of proof of permitting drunkenness or disorder should be shifted from the defendant to the prosecution by the addition of the word "knowingly"; that is, "knowlingly sell any intoxicating liquor to a drunken person".

Although Colonel Gretton who sponsored the bill was associated with Bass and Co., and although two of his fellow sponsors were Sir W. Reginald Hall (Barclay, Perkins and Co.) and Henry B. Betterton (Brunt, Bucknall and Co.) were also in the trade, the Colonel insisted it was "*not* a Trade Bill". Far-reaching as it was, it "did not meet entirely and fully the views of the trade on some questions". The second reading debate was courteous, bearing in mind the strong views held on either side of the issue. After the Attorney-General had reviewed its provisions commending some points and criticizing others, Colonel Gretton was granted leave to withdraw the motion and the bill. It was useful to have heard the views of those interested in licensing administration as they saw it following the end of the war.

It was understandable that the government wished to deal with post-war licensing legislation on a more satisfactory basis than by supporting a Private Member's Bill. On 26th May 1921 the Under Secretary of State for the Home Department, Sir John Baird, made a statement in the house announcing the publication of recent orders issued by the Central Control Board. These were modifications to the existing regulations. The statement read,

> *The Central Control Board (Liquor Traffic) have made Orders dated April 25th and operating on Monday May 2nd applicable to all scheduled areas in England and Wales consolidating the existing Orders and amending them in the following particulars:*
>
> *(1) The prohibition of the sale and supply of spirits for consumption off the premises on Saturday is removed, and such sale and supply during the midday period (12 to 2.30 pm) on that day is allowed.*
>
> *(2) The provision which fixes a reputed quart as the minimum quantity of spirits which may be sold for off consumption together with the requirements as to the labelling of bottles is revoked.*
>
> *(3) The hours after 10 pm for which magistrates (or in London, the Commissioner of Police) may grant an Order or licence in pursuance of Section 57 or Section 64 of the Licensing (Consolidation) Act 1910, are extended beyond the present limit of 11 pm.*
>
> *(4) The extent to which spirits may be diluted without notice to the purchaser is limited to a strength falling between thirty degrees and thirty-five degrees under proof.*
>
> *(5) The sale of intoxicating liquor to authorised messes of officers or non-commissioned officers is exempted from the operation of the Order.*
>
> *(6) The requirement that copies of the Board's Orders must be exhibited in every club and in every public room, in licensed premises is revoked, and a requirement that copies must be kept on the premises and produced on demand is substituted therefor.*[29]

The next important, and novel, event was the Licensing Reform Conference which was set up by the government in July 1921. It was the first time such a round-table conference had been held to advise the government on licensing legislation. Its terms of reference were: "To consider, with reference to the Law of Licensing, how best to adapt to time of peace the experience obtained during the period of the war". The Attorney-General was chairman and the discussions and recommendations were confidential. The Parliamentary Correspondent of *The Times*, in the issue of 30th June 1921, speculated on some of its recommendations. "The round-table conference concluded its sittings yesterday" it was reported, "It has reached agreement as to the lines on which a non-contentious licensing Bill can be framed with a prospect of its reaching the Statute Book in the current session". *The Times* understood that there was to be a general eight-hour day for the opening of public houses, the closing hour to be not later than 10 p.m., except when licensing justices, having regard to local circumstances, might determine otherwise. In London the closing hour could be 11 p.m. and elsewhere 10.30 p.m. The earliest opening hour would be 11 a.m. and there would be a two-hour compulsory closing in the afternoon. The Carlisle properties were to be placed under the control of parliament through the Home Office. When the round-table conference agreement was given statutory effect the Central Control Board would disappear. *The Times* reported that the atmosphere of the conference, which represented a wide-ranging interest in licensing matters, was so amicable that there was the basis for agreement on a comprehensive licensing measure in the next session of parliament.

In due time the Licensing Act 1921 was passed. Its principal provisions were concerned with permitted hours. For on- and off-licensed premises these were to be eight hours commencing not earlier than 11 a.m. and ending not later than 10 p.m. with a break of not less than two hours after noon on weekdays outside London. In the metropolis the permitted hours were to be nine and the closing time 11 p.m. On Sundays, Christmas Day and Good Friday the hours would be confined to five, of which not more than two were to be between twelve (noon) and 3 p.m. and not more than three between 6 p.m. and 10 p.m. In Wales and Monmouthshire such premises would be closed on Sunday. Permitted hours could be extended for one hour at the end of normal permitted hours for consumption of liquor with a meal in those parts of the licensed premises reserved for the serving of meals. The act provided for certain exemptions, as for example the serving of liquor by the licensee to private friends. The distribution of liquor was forbidden unless it was previously ordered and the details of the sale documented. Sale of liquor on credit was prohibited, the "long pull" was abolished, and dilution of liquor was restricted to not more than thirty-five degrees under proof. Liquor of original gravity not exceeding 10.16 degrees or 2 per cent proof spirit was not to be regarded as intoxicating liquor if an excise licence was not required for its sale. There were certain other supplementary provisions in the act.

The political climate changes

The result of a general election towards the end of 1922 reflected the changing disposition of trade and temperance forces in parliament. The Conservatives were now in the ascendency and secured 344 of the 615 seats, and traditionally they were sympathetic to the trade. By this time the Labour Party had overtaken the Liberal Party as the main opposition, securing 138 seats to the Liberals' 60, and for the future it was among the Labour members of parliament that the temperance cause found its chief support in parliament. The basis for temperance reform among the Labour MPs was different from that of the traditional Liberal approach. The trade was seen as part of the capitalist system which had to be destroyed. This was made clear in a policy statement issued in 1923:

> *It must be recognised, even by those holding diverse views as to the plan or method of temperance reform, that the enormous vested interest in the manufacture and sale of alcoholic beverages constitutes, in itself, a serious obstacle to every kind of reform. It can be forcibly argued that no effective temperance reform is possible so long as so great an interest as the liquor interest is in private hands. If, therefore, we do nothing on this point, we must look forward to a long period during which the efforts of private persons who desire any kind of temperance reform will be opposed by the money and organisation of one of the most formidable vested interests in the country. In fact, the political power of the "trade" is now a standing menace to promoters of reform of any kind in Parliament or at Parliamentary elections.*

The statement advised against any attempt at dealing with the problem by the adoption of one method of reform. Diverse measures were needed. However, the Labour Party came out in favour of local option which, if adopted, would enable the necessary reforms to be effected. Localities should have conferred on them the freedom, (a) to prohibit the sale of alcoholic drink within their own boundaries; (b) to reduce the number of places of sale and regulate the conditions of sale; and (c) to determine, within the fundamental conditions prescribed by statute, the manner in which the public places of refreshment and social intercourse in their own districts shall be organized and controlled.[30]

It was with strong Labour Party support in the House of Commons that the Intoxicating Liquors (sale to persons under eighteen) Bill became law on 31st July 1923. Although the bill was sponsored by Lady Astor, it was the initiative of a group of schoolmasters which was mainly responsible for its introduction. Chief credit went to J. L. Paton, the High-Master of Manchester Grammar School, whose concern about the effects of drinking on schoolchildren was shared by others in his profession. At the second reading, the labour supporters were joined by many independents and national liberals and, most remarkably, by 120 unionist members. As Lady Astor explained in her speech, the bill had a very simple objective. "As the law now stands" she explained, "a publican can sell beer to children over fourteen for consumption inside his public-house as well as to be taken away. Spirits can only be sold for consumption on licensed premises to young people over sixteen. This Bill proposes to make it illegal to sell to anyone apparently under eighteen any kind of intoxicant for consumption in a public-house. That is all the Bill proposes". At the end of the second reading debate the motion to approve the bill was carried by 338 votes to 56. Some amendments were made in committee, and at the third reading an attempt was made to secure from Lady Astor a pledge that this bill represented the legislative demand of the temperance opinion, but she declined to give such a pledge.

The four provisions of the act were:

1. *No intoxicating liquor may be sold to or consumed by any young person under eighteen in a "bar" as defined by the Children Act 1908, Section 120, that is, 'any open drinking bar or any part of licensed premises exclusively or mainly used for the sale and consumption of intoxicating liquors' no matter who pays for it.*
2. *No intoxicating liquor may be sold to or purchased by any young person under sixteen anywhere on licensed premises for on-consumption.*
3. *No intoxicating liquor may be sold to or purchased by any young person over sixteen and under eighteen anywhere on licensed premises for on-consumption,* except *beer, porter, cider or perry when consumed at a meal on a part of the licensed premises set apart for the service of meals and not being a bar as defined above.*
4. *Breaches of the Act are offences not merely for the licence-holder but for the young person, but the licence-holder's liability is limited to offences knowingly committed by him or his servants.*

This was a significant piece of legislation. In the decade following the end of the First World War attempts were made to introduce other measures. In 1926 a Hotel and Restaurants Bill, designed to give to hotels certain more favourable conditions than those of ordinary licensed premises, was introduced but did not reach the statute book. This was the fate of a series of bills introduced in 1927, one to confer local option on Wales, one to remove anomalies in respect of clubs, as well as a further attempt by Colonel J. Gretton to restrict the power of justices to control licensed premises. During this period the United Kingdom Alliance continued its campaign for local option, but without success. The period as a whole was relatively quiet, in that it was free from the kind of heated controversy which characterized some of the decades before the war. *Alliance News* and trade journals such as the *Morning Advertiser* and the *Brewing Trade Review* continued their editorial skirmishes. But the public debate was carried on in a low key. There were reasons for this. First, as the statistics show, the problem of public drunkenness had receded and there were those who thought the problem had been licked in Britain. Second other issues, particularly economic ones, were dominant. Sir Keith Feiling summed up the post-war situation, "meantime" he wrote, "the post-war boom had broken, unemployment on a scale hitherto unknown hit our basic industries, and a series of strikes pointed the contrast between Labour ideals and post-war facts".[31] The nation was too pre-occupied with economic and political issues to be over-concerned about the liquor problem which, compared with unemployment for instance, was peripheral. Third, there was the decline of the Liberal Party, where support for temperance reform had been strongest. In 1924 the first Labour government was formed under Ramsey Macdonald and licensing reform was not high on its list of priorities.

The achievement of prohibition in America kept the issue alive, but few entertained the possibility of similar legislation in Britain. One who did was Edwin Scrymgeour, Member of Parliament for Dundee. In 1931 he introduced the Liquor Traffic Prohibition Bill. The second reading debate took place on 13th February 1931. The bill provided for the prohibition of the manufacture, importation and sale of alcoholic liquors for beverage purposes. The intention was that when an act came into force all existing licences should cease and no new licences should be granted. It would be illegal for any person to manufacture import or sell alcoholic liquors except for scientific or industrial purposes. When required for medicinal purposes it should be dispensed in bottles labelled "Poison". The debate rehearsed the usual arguments for and against such a measure. The response of the government was to say that the whole matter was one which should be dealt with by the Royal Commission which had been appointed in 1929. When the house divided 18 voted in favour of Scrymgeour's bill and 137 against it. And so the whole question was referred to the Royal Commission which, as we shall see, occupied the debating ground on the "alcohol problem" until the menacing political situation in Europe began to dominate public thought and discussion.

References

1. Numerous books have been published on prohibition in America, and many give facts about the concept and its progress. Most references in this chapter relate to *Prohibition in the United States* by D. Leigh Colvin. George H. Doran and Co., New York (1927).
2. *Prohibition in the United States* D. Leigh Colvin pp. 14, 15.
3. Op cit p.15.
4. Op cit p. 16.
5. Op cit p. 18.
6. Op cit pp. 19 ff.
7. Op cit p. 23.
8. Op cit p. 39.
9. Op cit pp. 39, 40.
10. *Drink — Ups and Downs in Methodist Attitudes to Temperance.* G. Thompson Brake. Oliphant (1974) p. 125.

11. Leigh Colvin op cit p. 103.
12. Op cit p. 105
13. Op cit p. 145.
14. Op cit p. 197.
15. The evidence produced by Leigh Colvin is compelling and disquieting.
16. Op cit p. 217.
17. Op cit p. 406.
18. Op cit p. 430.
19. Op cit p. 449.
20. Op cit p. 449.
21. *Alliance News* January 1920 p. 4.
22. His story is told in *"Pussyfoot" Johnson.* F. A. McKenzie, Hodder and Stoughton.
23. For a full account of the meeting see *Alliance News* December 1919 p. 107.
24. *Alliance News* February 1920 p. 25.
25. *Alliance News* May 1920 p. 69.
26. *Alliance News* March 1921 p. 39.
27. *Alliance News* March 1921 p. 40.
28. *Alliance News* March 1921 p. 40.
29. *Alliance News* July 1921 p. 99.
30. *Alliance News* July 1923 p. 102.
31. *A History of England.* Sir Keith Feiling. Book Club Associates (1975). First published 1950. p. 1080.

CHAPTER 6

THE ROYAL COMMISSION, 1929–31

In September 1929 a Royal Commission under the chairmanship of Lord Amulree was appointed to "inquire into the working of the laws relating to the sale and supply of intoxicating liquors, and into the social and economic aspects of the question, and to examine and report upon proposals that may be made for amending the law in England and Wales in the public interest". The commission, which reported in January 1932, held 97 meetings, of which 70 were devoted to the hearing of evidence. Oral evidence was given by 189 witnesses representing many and varied interests, of which the principal were government departments, police, magistrates, the trade, temperance organizations and the medical profession. Very considerable evidence was given in the form of memoranda and correspondence. As it was the first major inquiry of the twentieth century into the licensing system, and the social and economic consequences of the supply and consumption of intoxicating liquors, account had to be taken of the many changes in all aspects of these matters since the report of the previous Royal Commission in 1896–1899. The major change in the intervening period had been the introduction of wartime restrictions, many of which had been retained. Chief among them was the provision of "Permitted Hours".

Restriction of hours

Many witnesses spoke in favour of the restrictions of Permitted Hours. There was some difference of opinion about confining "closing time" to 10 p.m. and many advocated extending this to 10.30 p.m. Some witnesses agreed with the view expressed by Cecil Whitely, Chairman of the Licensing Committee for Surrey, who recommended that evening closing hours should be fixed by statute and made universal, though in London there might be some variation. One of the chief arguments for having a nationwide closing time was to prevent people crossing boundaries of adjacent licensing districts where there might be a variation of half an hour. Some licensed victuallers urged the commission to recognize the special needs of certain areas where, for example, men came off a late shift after the public houses had closed. Magistrates' representatives seemed to favour retaining the "afternoon break"[1] which had been introduced as a wartime measure and retained. However, Lt. Col. Sir Hugh Turnbull, Commissioner of Police for the City of London said, "I should be just as glad if they (the public houses) were kept open all of the time for the sale of drink. I do not think there would be any abuse and I think it would tend to make supervision easier".[2] The Chief Constable of Bradford, Joseph Farndale, agreed, and for the same reason that it would make administration easier. His experience was that the afternoon break was difficult to enforce. He would favour continuous opening from 12 noon to 10 p.m.[3] The Clerk to the Licensing Justices for the Tower and Paddington Divisions of the County of London, Richard E. Bruce Beal, while agreeing with dispensing with the afternoon break, believed that 10 p.m. closing had been of great benefit. His main plea was that justices should have complete discretion over "permitted hours", and should be able to make different orders for different licensed premises and areas. He also reminded the commission of the pressures under which many licensees worked. He said, "It must not be overlooked that brewers can, and generally do, compel a publican to keep his house open for all the hours he is permitted to sell beer . . . The allegations that 'the trade' as a whole desires later and longer hours has not been proved. In my opinion it is not true. The wishes of the brewers and of a well-organized but small minority must not be confused with the desires of the licensees as a whole".[4]

Powerful support for retaining the restrictions of hours came from Sir Alfred Thomas Davies of the Council of Magistrates' Association of England and Wales:

> *The danger now and in the immediate future in my opinion, lies, and will lie in any ignoring, firstly, of past experience and, secondly, of the overwhelming body of public opinion which favours the maintenance, in the public interest, of proved safeguards such as the restricted hours of opening now in operation. Unless deterred by the findings of this Commission, Parliament in a weak moment and in deference to clamour and the demand of a small, interested and noisy minority, reinforced, in some cases by political pressure – may be tempted to repeat some of its past notorious errors in its dealing with the liquor problem and to check the good done by reduction and restriction. To do so would, in my opinion, be a colossal blunder amounting almost to a crime. I have a fairly large experience of my fellow magistrates (I am one in two counties) and I do not know, and cannot recall, one who would be in favour, for example, of extending the present hours. They have been an untold and inestimable source of good.*[5]

The Royal Commission concurred with this judgment. There was much merit in the restriction of hours and evidence of strong public support for it. "We think that to a vast section of the public, including public-house clients, the present scheme is acceptable, and is becoming more, and not less, so".[6] Taking account of the disorder which occurred, particularly in some areas of London, after 10 p.m. and up to 11 p.m. the commission recommended no exceptions to the latest closing hour of 10 p.m. In rural areas there should be some discretion given to justices to fix closing time at 9.00 p.m. No recommendation was made to vary the "afternoon break". Some slight variations were proposed for the convenience of customers who had ordered drinks in association with meals. Pleas had been made that trade done by off-licences should be treated as "shop business" and therefore should be dealt with separately. These pleas were rejected as were those for exempting clubs from observing the permitted hours fixed by local justices. Especially among witnesses from Wales, the question of Sunday opening seemed important, and the commission, while rejecting arguments in favour of Sunday closing, drew attention to the provision for new licences to be six-day licences and for old licences to be converted to six-day licences, thus ensuring one free day each week for publicans.

So far as clubs were concerned the same general provisions applied, but each club, instead of having to conform to the hours laid down by the licensing justices, could fix their own hours. According to a return obtained by the commission, of all registered clubs 8,686 had hours differing from those of other local licensed premises, and 4,827 adopted the same hours.

Clubs had the same privileges on Sunday as on weekdays. Other licensed premises had more restricted hours on Sundays, five instead of eight or nine, and these had to be taken as two between 12 noon and 3 p.m. and three between 6 p.m. and 10 p.m.

Drinking habits

We shall return to other matters relating to public houses and clubs, but clearly at an early stage in any discussion of licensing and related matters some consideration must be given to prevailing drinking habits and their social consequences. The commission noted the substantial increase in the United Kingdom in the per capita consumption of beer and spirits during the last twenty years of the nineteenth century, from 27.72 gallons of beer and 1.06 proof gallons of spirits in 1881, to 32.53 gallons of beer and 1.09 proof gallons of spirits in 1899. In contrast the similar period at the beginning of the twentieth century showed a remarkable decrease. The consumption of beer in 1899 in the United Kingdom was 36,840,000 standard barrels, representing 32.53 gallons per head. In 1929 it had fallen to 20,300,000 or 16.42 gallons per head. The consumption of spirits in England and Wales in 1899 was 31,195,000 proof gallons or 0.97 gallons per head. In 1929 the comparable figures were 10,053,000 proof gallons or 0.25 gallons per head. The decrease in the consumption of wine was less spectacular, 0.41 gallons per head in 1899 and 0.31 per gallons per head in 1929. Following the 1914–18 war consumption of wine tended to increase, but this may be in part explained by the increase in duty on spirits. The Commission commented, "The general decrease in the consumption of intoxicants has been accompanied by a marked decrease in insobriety".[7]

The commission's report included a judgment which, alas, could not be sustained in the second half of the twentieth century. "It was a matter of general agreement amongst the witnesses who appeared before us" it declared, "that the present century has seen a distinct advance in sobriety. The change has been particularly noticeable amongst the younger people."[8] The main evidence for this judgment was in the figures for convictions for drunkenness. In 1899 there were 189,633 convictions in England and Wales, and in 1903 209,385. A more comprehensive statistical system was adopted in 1905 when convictions were 207,171. Thereafter they declined and in 1910 were 161,992. For a year or two after that they increased and then began to decline, so that by 1929 the figure was 51,966. This decline was reflected in statistics for both men and women, which confirmed the oral evidence given to the commission. Chairmen of licensing justices from many parts of the country testified to an appreciable decline in the cases of drunkenness in their districts. Stipendiary magistrates gave similar evidence. The views of them all could be summarized in the statement by Bertram C. Brough, stipendiary magistrate for North Staffordshire who said "There has been quite clearly a great decline (in drunkenness). In earlier days I used to expect some cases of drunkenness, or of drunk and disorderly conduct, every day. Nowadays it is a comparatively rare thing. I do not suppose I get more than two or three cases a month now."[9] He believed the change was due to the increased cost of drink, its diminished strength, unemployment, increased cost of living, restrictions of permitted hours, establishment of institutes and clubs, the spread of education and the influence of social workers and probation officers. Most cases of drunkenness, he said, concerned people over forty years of age. The offence was comparatively rare among young people. The habit of young people was not to stay in public houses, though they might call in for a drink on the way home from a cinema.[10]

Commenting on possible reasons for the decline in insobriety the commission recalled those advanced by the Royal Commission of 1896–99 for a similar decline. These were the labours of temperance workers, the spread of education and the passion for games and athletics. To these the 1929–31 Royal Commission added such diversions as the cinema, wireless, gardening, playing fields and travel. Better housing, public health, and education might have been contributory factors. Whatever the reasons, the result was an alteration in public attitudes towards drunkenness. The commission concluded "Drunkenness has gone out of fashion and a drunken person is not tolerated as he used to be."[11] Besides social reasons for the improvement, the commission noted legislative and taxation factors. One result of the 1904 Licensing Act, which provided for the reduction of the number of licences, with compensation, was to discourage excessive drinking. The reduction of hours, which we have seen was introduced as a wartime measure and retained in the Licensing Act 1921, also had an effect. The commission's judgment was that the effects of reduced hours had been beneficial.[12] Increases in taxation had also played a part. During the period reviewed the price of beer had more than doubled, and the cost of spirits had been multiplied between three and four times.

In the light of a very different situation at the beginning of the last thirty years of the twentieth century the comments of the commission on the effect of drinking on industrial efficiency are striking indeed. The commission said, "The magnitude of the change in former habits has been apparent in industry . . . there appears to be wide support for the view that alcohol is not at the present time and under the present abnormal industrial conditions a serious cause of industrial inefficiency. Absenteeism in particular, which formerly was a feature in many industries and which was attributed in large degree to excessive drinking, particularly at weekends, has in large measure disappeared."[13] The commission believed the improvement had been substantially helped by new techniques and methods of organization in industry. Mechanization, for instance, called for powers of concentration and judgement with which the drinking of alcohol was not compatible. Improvements of conditions of work had reduced strain which often induced people to drink. It was also recognized that the high level of unemployment meant that people could not afford to drink. It was hoped that the changed drinking habits, for whatever reason, might be a permanent feature of British life.

One person the commission saw as a possible major contributor to this prospect was Major Isidore Salmon CBE, MP, chairman and Managing Director of Messrs J. Lyons and Co. Ltd. The chairman told him that his firm had been described to the commission as "one of the great temperance reformers of the present time". Major Salmon said he believed the improved conduct of people in respect of drink had been contemporaneous with the improvements in the facilities and amenities provided for the service of food and drink. He said "I am therefore of the opinion that the abuse of drink will disappear as the habit of consuming it under these better conditions is fostered. . . . We have proved that serving liquor as an adjunct to food has had the effect of considerably reducing the consumption of drink per capita. We have tried to anticipate the wants of the public and to educate the public. We believe that it is possible to provide refreshments in proper surroundings, and at the same time to give facilities for the serving of drink, if people so desire it, without any abuse."[14] He said the secret of keeping down the consumption of alcohol was to make liquor as easily available as coffee or tea. People ought to be able to sit at the same table with different drinks without embarrassment.

Having noted the evident decline in drunkenness and the possible reasons for it, the commission reached the following conclusion:

"What appears to be beyond question, and is shown even by the figures of convictions, with all their limitations, is that a substantial amount of excessive drinking, over the country as a whole, still exists. So long as that continues to be the case, it cannot, in our view, be maintained that there is no problem of drunkenness."[15] While acknowledging the probability that so long as the sale of alcoholic liquors was permitted, insobriety would continue, the commission believed that there were still options open to the government to reduce excessive drinking "to the lowest dimension possible."[16]

Earlier the report had made a judgment of great significance to everybody concerned with liquor licensing reform. The commission said that readers of their report would find historical evidence, if such was needed, "for certain basic truths, the neglect of which must prejudice any attempt at licensing reform: for example, that undue relaxation of control produces intolerable social evils; that legislative regulation which goes too far beyond current public opinion is simply not administered; and that cheapness of intoxicants is always a powerful stimulant to consumption."[17]

The Commission's conclusions

At the conclusion of its preliminary survey of the extent of the alcohol problem the commission set out seven main recommendations which it believed would "contribute materially towards the elimination of the problem."[18] These were (i) the provision of machinery for the reduction of the number of licences; (ii) the improvement of the public house especially as a place of general refreshment; (iii) the creation of special hotel and restaurant licences; (iv) experiments in public ownership of the liquor trade; (v) the creation of a National Licensing Commission; (vi) more effective control of the supply of liquor in clubs; and (vii) the encouragement of specific education in alcohol.

Before surveying the evidence presented on these various matters, and the response of the Royal Commission, it may be helpful to note the dimensions of liquor trade and how it conceived its role. The dimensions of the trade were outlined to the commission by Frank Nicholson of the Brewers' Society.[19] He estimated that the total number of people employed directly or indirectly was 617,000. Of these 112,000 were engaged in brewing, distilling, malting and bottling, 350,000 were employed in retailing on the premises with a further 54,000 in off-licences, 12,000 were employed in registered clubs and he estimated that 35,000 were concerned with barley growing and a further 35,000 in other allied trades. He gave other statistics. In 1929 the quantity of malt used was 10,525,902 hundredweights, acreage under barley was 1,048,926 while 23,805 acres of hops produced 330,662 hundredweights. For the year 1928–29 the number of standard barrels of beer on which duty was paid was 19,436,399. The average alcoholic content of beer was between 3 per cent and 4 per cent of absolute alcohol by weight. He claimed that, although there was a demand for strong beers, the average beer sold, which was of a gravity of about 10.39 degrees to 10.42 degrees was not to any extent alcoholic, although he would not say it was not intoxicating. However, the restriction of gravity had made brewers concentrate on the necessity for producing a fine-flavoured beer of low gravity. In a reference to demand, he said that he did not believe advertising led to an increase in consumption, but only to preference for one product against another. He would have been glad to see advertising done away with. Cecil Lubbock, another spokesman for the Brewers' Society,[20] concentrated on demonstrating the great improvement that had taken place in the retailing of liquor, and the need to maintain liberal licensing laws. The physical state of public houses had vastly improved and attempts had been made to provide increased facilities, such as meals. At one time the hours were too long, which was no longer the case. Consumption, too, had decreased with the consequence that convictions for drunkenness had also fallen. He believed that, although certain amendments to the law were desirable, no drastic changes were needed in order that the trade might be further improved.

Compensation and reduction of licences

The commission based their consideration and recommendations concerning the question of the reduction of licences on the categorical statement that they found no grounds, nor any great demand, for a fundamental change in the constitution of the local licensing authority. They accepted the role of licensing justices. However, they were required to administer licensing laws, not change them. It was one of the functions of the Royal Commission to recommend any changes that seemed desirable in the public interest. To enable it to make recommendations, the laws as they stood had to be studied. The commission paid particular attention to the Licensing Act 1904 which provided for compensation to be paid when licences were not renewed. Until 1904 any on-licence, except a beer-house licence granted before 1869, could be refused renewal by the renewal authority, subject to appeal to quarter sessions. Under the 1904 Act, refusals of renewal of all existing on-licences were divided into two categories (a) misconduct; and (b) all other grounds.

In respect of (a) the law remained unchanged, that is refusal by the renewal authority subject to appeal. For refusals under (b) a special compensation scheme was introduced. Under this scheme all old on-licences were required to contribute to a fund from which compensation could be paid if the renewal was refused. Contributions to the fund were on a fixed scale varying with the annual value of the premises. The aim of the act was to reduce the number of licensed premises. The Report of the Royal Commission summarized the results. They said they were "bound to record that in the period between 1904 and 1930 the number of licences was diminished by some 22,143 only; viz, from 99,478 to 77,335, and that this reduction was not wholly due to the operation of the scheme instituted in 1904. The number actually dealt with under the scheme was 16,907. In addition, 573 were refused renewal without compensation, and 6,774 lapsed from various causes. The gross decrease was 24,254 but 2,111 new licences were granted, making a net decrease of 22,143."[21] Figures for the years immediately following 1904 showed that the number of licences refused, with compensation, was substantially less each year. The average amount of compensation granted in each case increased during the same period. In 1905 the average was £614 and by 1929 it was £1,975. There was wide disparity in the amounts awarded. For example, in 1930 they ranged from £114 for a beer house in a country district, to over £6,500 for a publican's licence in a county borough.

The Royal Commission considered that the compensation scheme failed to achieve the results anticipated. For example, the suppression of licences depended not on the merits of the case of an excessive number of licences, but on the limits of the compensation funds in particular districts. There was also the disparity between the basis on which compensation was calculated. Another defect was that the machinery devised for operating the scheme was complicated. Moreover, the administration was piecemeal rather than comprehensive. Despite the difficulties, the commission concluded that some such compensation scheme would have to be retained. It was recommended that it should be a duty of licensing justices, within say two years, to review their areas and determine the extent of the reduction of licences required. Their plans should be considered by interested parties and a plan subsequently submitted to the proposed National Licensing Commission whose approval would be necessary. It should be the duty of the National Licensing Commission to moderate excessive proposals, or strengthen those which seemed inadequate.

At the time of the commission's work, there were two forms of licence, "annual" and "term" licences, the latter being granted for periods of, say, seven years. The commission concluded that the existence of these two types of licence created unnecessary complication, and they recommended that "term" licences should be discontinued, and that monopoly value which was the difference between the value of the premises when licensed and their value if not licensed, should no longer apply in respect of new licences. In practice this value was difficult to calculate in advance and it favoured the companies with large capital resources, and appeared to confer uninterrupted renewal of the premises.

In considering the reduction of licences, the commission had to take into account the expansion of development areas. It was concerned to ensure that the wishes of the inhabitants of the area should be considered before the transfer of licences or the granting of new ones were effected. While not endorsing the principle of "local option" generally, it was thought that the new housing areas were a special case. The main recommendations of the commission were[22] (i) that the National Licensing Commission should have power to designate any development area as a special area; (ii) no licence should be granted until a substantial number of residents had arrived; (iii) the justices should cause a popular vote to be taken for their information; and (iv) the justices should declare a close period after licences had been granted. Closely associated with these matters was the question of "removals". This referred to the practice of transferring a licence from premises where one was no longer required to premises in a different and, sometimes, distant area within the same licensing district. In all instances, it seemed to the commission, there was no justification for such a system. There was no sense in which a licence for one area was by "removal" the same licence in another area. It was recommended that such cases should be treated as new applications.

Character of public houses

A subject to which many witnesses referred was the character of public houses. There was considerable divergence of view as to the extent to which public houses had been improved, and what effects the improvements had had on the drinking habits of customers. The view of Richard E. B. Beal, the Clerk to the Licensing Justices of the Tower and Paddington Division of London, was that the character of the public house had only marginal significance for the customers. He said, "The beer sold is the real test and a house with modern, comfortable, light airy bars will stand empty while customers will crowd into an ill-ventilated, badly arranged, dirty, dilapidated old place if the beer is to their taste and they like the licensee."[23]

There were those who thought that the provision of larger floor space and recreational amenities led to more people visiting public houses and purchasing more liquor, while others took the opposite view that these improvements resulted in less drinking. Fred J. Crawley, Chief Constable of Newcastle upon Tyne, argued for the continental cafe type public house to which the whole family could be taken. He believed the adoption of such a policy would lead to greater sobriety.[24] James A. Wilson, Chief Constable of Cardiff, was not the only witness to say that proprietors would embark on improvements if it were not for the fact that many justices did not encourage or facilitate such policies because they believed it would lead to more drinking.[25]

It was not surprising to find Barry Holderness, General Manager of the People's Refreshment House Association Limited, supporting the provision of more congenial licensed premises. His company was formed with the express intention of providing alternatives to public houses which were used simply for the consumption of alcohol. He wanted to see the government encouraging the sale of non-intoxicants which was one of the purposes of the kind of establishments run by his company, whose managers were paid a salary without bonuses related to liquor turnover.[26]

Having heard such conflicting evidence and many different opinions, the commission expressed dissatisfaction with the general condition of public houses. It commended the initiative of the Public House Trust Companies and similar enterprises in giving a lead to a new concept for public houses. Instead of their almost exclusive use as places for the sale of intoxicants, the commission favoured them becoming places "where the public can obtain general refreshment, of whatever variety they choose, in decent, pleasant and comfortable surroundings."[27] It was the judgment of the commission that the absence of facilities for eating, the cramped conditions and the encouragement of perpendicular drinking at the bar contributed greatly to excessive drinking and drunkenness. Living accommodation for the licensee and his family was another feature often neglected and there was concern about the lack of training and experience of many licensees. The commission believed there were two levels at which the main deficiencies could be remedied. One was at state level by a possible extension of public ownership and the appointment of a national licensing commission which would lay down guidelines, the other was at the level of licensing justices who could ensure that improved standards were maintained.

If any group had entertained a hope that the commission would recommend a relaxation of gaming regulations in respect of licensed premises, they were disappointed. Gaming of any kind on licensed premises had been forbidden for a very long time, at least since the Alehouse Act 1828, and probably before. The reasons for this prohibition were obvious since "winnings" could be spent on drink and disputes over results could lead to assaults. To obviate this danger police, and sometimes justices, had taken action to suppress even lawful games on licensed premises. The commission, while condemning this practice, nevetheless, upheld the view that all gaming even for trivial stakes, should be forbidden.[28]

In view of the strong representations made by some witnesses to improve the amenities of public houses the commission was bound to give consideration to the provisions of entertainment. The term "entertainment" was capable of wide interpretation. Did it refer to informal singing to the accompaniment of a piano, or to a song by a patron for a consideration? And did the regulations apply to "mechanical" entertainment such as gramophones and wireless sets? So far as recommendations were concerned, the commission felt it was limited, and the best that could be hoped for was a greater uniformity of interpretation of the existing law by the authorities in the different districts concerned. So far as dancing was concerned, no relaxation of existing requirements were proposed. There was, however, one danger, which was the service of intoxicants in rooms where dancing was actually going on, and in particular on the occasion of an occasional licence.[29]

The judgment of the Royal Commission on the state of the hotel industry is of great interest when read after a period of vast expansion of the tourist trade and hotel building and improvements. It said, "The majority of hotels in this country are out of date, the accommodation is unattractive and the catering is primitive; and there is obviously an absence of trained hotel management. These conditions apply all over England and Wales and they are especially noticeable in our large industrial and commercial centres. We are not convinced that the various restrictions on the sale of intoxicants have in fact, as has been suggested, acted in any substantial degree as a deterrent, to tourist traffic from abroad. On the other hand, we appreciate the argument that the hotel industry may have been cramped to some extent by being treated in nearly all respects on the same basis under the licensing laws as a public house."[30]

The commission recommended the creation of two new forms of licence, a hotel licence and a restaurant licence. In each case it was recommended that a limiting factor should be the receipts for the sale of liquor in relation to the rest of the takings. In the case of hotels, the receipts for liquor should not exceed 50 per cent and in the case of restaurants, not more than 60 per cent. Modifications of "hours" were also recommended. In both hotels and restaurants the sale of liquor should be permitted on weekdays with meals until midnight in London and 11 p.m. in the provinces, with an additional half an hour drinking up time. It was also recommended that where the first period of permitted hours terminated before 3 p.m., hotels and restaurants should be allowed to serve intoxicants with meals up to 3 p.m. Various other recommendations were made, two of which appeared to be concessions to representations by temperance organizations. These were, (a) no commission should be received by any member of the staff on the sale of intoxicants; and, (b) that fresh drinking water should be available on all tables when meals or refreshments were served. Strong recommendations were added concerning the provision of training schemes to make up for the lamentable standard of service referred to earlier in the report.

Public ownership

In view of the experiment, as a wartime measure, of state ownership of the liquor trade, it was inevitable that this was a matter on which the Royal Commission was required to report. The first excursion of the state into this field was at Carlisle and a small adjacent area where, because of the exposure of munitions workers to a free-for-all in the retailing of liquor, it was deemed right in the interests of the nation for the state to take over the local breweries and public houses. This enterprise did not end with the Armistice in 1918 but continued until 1971. Before surveying the evidence submitted to the Royal Commission, and summarizing its findings and recommendations, it is necessary to refer to the system which largely prevailed. This was the "tied house" system in which the tenant of licensed premises undertakes to purchase from the landlord, who is invariably a brewer-owner, either all his beers, or all his beers and other commodities such as wine, spirits and tobacco, at agreed prices. The system was established because brewers wanted to ensure outlets for their products. By 1816 it had become very extensive. In 1898 it was estimated that the proportion of tied houses was 75 per cent of licensed premises; and in 1931 it was reckoned to be 95 per cent. In 1817 it had become the subject of an inquiry by a select committee of the House of Commons. Although this committee reported adversely on the system and recommended legislation to curb it, no effective action was taken. It expanded considerably, and as the figures quoted indicate, it remained a prominent feature of the liquor trade. Its expansion was remarkable, especially in view of its condemnation by the Royal Commission of 1896–99. The Royal Commission 1929–31 shared the view that the "tie" had led to abuse, but it also recognized that the operation of a simple tie by which a tenant agreed to purchase beers from his landlord was fundamental in the retail trade. The commission's recommendations were centred on the various abuses and extensions of the "tie system".

The commission had no serious criticism of "the simple tie". In recent times various extensions to such ties had been brought in by some brewer-owners. They might lend money to licensees to begin their business, and then insist on the purchase from them of not only beers but a considerable range of other commodities in which they had no interest as producers. They often imposed such narrow profit margins that licensees were driven to methods of selling which took them to the limits of the law. In the event of offences being committed the tenant might lose his licence, and with it his investment and livelihood. There were other threats which the tenant had to face. For instance a club in the vicinity of his house might also do a deal with the same brewer and undercut the licensee. The "tie" frequently adversely affected the ability of a tenant to trade competitively if well-known proprietary brands were not available at his house.

Having considered the possibility of the system being reformed by direct negotiation between the brewer-owners and the tenants, or between their respective associations, the Royal Commission concluded that this was not possible. The remedy lay in legislation. The commission said, "the right course is to be found, we think, in the limitation of the scope of the tie and in conferring on licensing justices of wider powers to take note, in the interests either of the tenant or of the public, of the terms of agreement."[31] They recommended that licensing justices should be able to require brewers operating a tie to ensure supplies of malt liquors for which there was a public demand at reasonable prices. With regard to other intoxicants, these should be sold at normal market prices, with the usual profit margins. The commission could see no good reason why articles other than intoxicants should be subject to the tie. "We therefore, recommend that in all future contracts, a tie for articles other than intoxicating liquors should be null and void and incapable of enforcement."[32] Another main recommendation was that the licensing justices should be kept informed of all changes in tenancy agreements.

The alternatives to private ownership were, at the time, (a) the trust company system; and (b) state ownership, as the Carlisle scheme. There were two common features of these systems, viz; disinterested management and disinterested ownership. However, there were also significant differences. The public house trust companies worked within the limits of the licensing system, and they were in open competition with other houses both in respect of the purchase of property and supplies. The so-called Carlisle system brewed its own beer and supplied its own public houses. Except in outlying areas it enjoyed a virtual monopoly.

Space must be given elsewhere to the commission's consideration of this matter, because it was its recommendations on public ownership which chiefly characterized their report, and which gave rise to controversy which caused a serious division in the Temperance Movement.[33]

One of the main recommendations of the Royal Commission was the establishment of a National Licensing Commission. Its duties would be to consider, approve and, where necessary, amend proposals from local justices for the reduction of the number of licences and the delimitation of special development areas. It would oversee preliminary proposals for public ownership and the regrouping of licensing districts. The commission would also be concerned with standards of medication in medicated wines and spirits. It would collect data on the administration of licensing law, and make an annual report to parliament.

Clubs

Quite the most contentious issue, apart from that of public ownership was licensing in relation to clubs. When the Royal Commission was taking evidence, the clerk to the justices in each petty sessional division kept the register of clubs. He could exercise no discretion in registering a club, provided that all the rules relating to clubs had been observed and duly furnished. The registration had to be renewed annually. In the case of any irregularity it was doubtful whether the clerk had any power to withhold renewal of registration. Once a club had been registered it could not be removed from the register except as a result of court proceedings. There were three grounds on which action could be taken to remove a club from the register:

(a) serious breaches of good order which could be the subject of prosecution;
(b) serious breaches of good order which could not be the subject of prosecution;
(c) technical breaches of good order.

A serious hindrance to taking proceedings was that the police had no right of entry into clubs to obtain evidence. Search warrants could be issued, but only if reasonable grounds could be established for suspecting irregularities. Even when a club was struck off the register there was nothing to prevent a similar club of a different name being registered for the same premises. Summarizing the position, the commission concluded that the registration of a club, with resulting legal facilities for the supply of intoxicants, could be effected with such ease as to be a mere formality, that although there were various grounds on which a club might be removed from the register, in practice it was difficult to establish them by evidence, and that the consequences of being struck off had little deterrent value. These conclusions were borne out by statistics. In 1905 the number of registered clubs in England and Wales was 6,554, by 1930 13,526. Many were well conducted, but many more were not.

Naturally, representatives of the club movements sought to persuade the commission of the superiority of clubs over other retail outlets for liquor. Robert Chapman, secretary of the Working Men's Clubs and Institute Union gave an account of the origin and ideas of working men's clubs, of which there were 2,626 in his union.[34] The number of registered clubs of all kinds was about 12,700. He did not deny that the major portion of the clubs' income came from the supply of intoxicants. However, with the average expenditure per member of 2*s* 8*d* a week, he thought this was very moderate consumption and showed that their clubs were not "drinking dens". Indeed, he claimed that the clubs had been a most potent factor in temperance advance. He said the attention of the commission had been drawn to the remarkable fact that concurrently with an increase in clubs there had been a diminution of drunkenness beyond the average in particular areas. As to the conduct of the clubs in his union, there was a rule which prohibited gambling, drunkenness, bad language or other misconduct. Offenders under this rule were expelled. He contrasted the working men's clubs and proprietory clubs which existed not as communal bodies but to promote gain for private individuals. His union thought that in such clubs there was a danger of irregularities. Mr Frank Solbé,[35] who represented the Association of Conservative Clubs, said that most of the criticisms of the clubs to which the commission had listened were based on hearsay. He took the Chief Constable of Glamorgan to task for saying that clubs in his area were "a continuous source of trouble to him". Solbé said he had made enquiries about these allegations and had found there were only twenty-five registered clubs in Glamorgan, and during the last completed year of official police statistics only one club had been proceeded against. He had a similar rebuttal for Sir Henry Jackson, chairman of the Monmouthshire Quarter Sessions, who had told the commission that from statements made by members of the Licensing Committee of which he was the Chairman, he was satisfied that "the great majority of clubs were merely drinking houses" and that excessive drinking was by no means uncommon. Solbé replied that in 1928 in Monmouthshire there were 174 registered clubs and during the year there had been two proceedings against clubs. In the 36 conservative clubs in the county the weekly expenditure on all forms of refreshment was 4*s.* 11*d* per member. Other witnesses from club associations stressed the recreational and cultural facilities provided by clubs, which enabled them to encourage temperate habits away from squalid homes and public houses.

Charles Barker, Clerk to the Justices of Birmingham,[36] told the commission that the present law relating to clubs was futile from the point of view of the control of liquor. He believed the registration and licensing of clubs should be in the hands of the licensing justices and they should have the power to grant licences for the supply of intoxicating liquor in clubs. The same point was made by Frederick Burlington Dingle, Clerk to the Licensing Justices of Sheffield.[37] He quoted a resolution of the Council of the Incorporated Justices Society in 1922: "That in the opinion of this Council the time has arrived when registered clubs should be placed under the jurisdiction of the licensing justices." The importance of this proposal was illustrated by a number of witnesses who were magistrates and said that since the introduction of compensation for closure orders on public houses, it was becoming increasingly common for the premises to be opened again as a registered club. Police representatives thought it was "permitted hours" which accounted for some growth in clubs, because they were an attempt to overcome the restrictions on drinking in the afternoon and late at night. James H. Hudson, Member of Parliament for Huddersfield, said the issue of clubs was an urgent one because of the extraordinary increase in their number in the post-war years. It was highly undesirable in the public interest that, side-by-side with a regulated system of retail distribution of alcoholic drinks under licence, there should be growing up a system of drink distribution through clubs, at the will of any small group of persons entirely independent of magistrates or any public supervision.[38]

The unsatisfactory nature of the law in respect of clubs was set out with great candour by the commission in its report:

> *. . . . the ease with which registration can be effected under present law offers a strong temptation, and we are satisfied that there are many clubs in all parts of the country which have been brought into existence solely for the purpose of supplying intoxicants. . . . We recognise, moreover, that the possibilities of the position have not yet been fully exploited, and we think that the process of exploitation is growing. We have received conclusive evidence that some sections of the brewing industry have not failed to appreciate these possibilities and have, by means more or less direct, lent financial and other assistance towards the formation, with a view to registration, of clubs in which their wares may find an outlet. In short, it seems to us that, if the law remains unaltered, it is, theoretically at any rate, possible that by the multiplication of clubs the effective administration of licensing laws may be seriously prejudiced. This is the light in which licensing justices in many districts view the matter.*[39]

It was the view of the commission that the special privileges enjoyed by clubs tended to promote and prolong irregularities. While most bona fide clubs were of a satisfactory character, many were not. A system of discretionary registration, to be renewed annually was necessary. However, this ought not to be entrusted to the licensing justices, but to a committee of not less than three and not more than five justices in each petty sessional division. Such discretion should be exercised within certain limits.

Registration should depend on evidence of satisfactory premises, the good character of the management, the legitimacy of the objects of the club, and submission of the names and addresses of not less than fifty members. There should be no "tie" and the supply of the intoxicants should be controlled by the members. Provided these conditions were observed the renewal of the registration should be virtually automatic. Objections to renewal could be made on grounds of frequent instances of drunkenness, habitual admission of members after an insufficient period of waiting, disorderly conduct and illegal sales of intoxicants. It was further recommended that in a case in which a prosecution against those responsible for the club resulted in conviction it should be within the discretion of the court to direct that the club be struck off the register. Various other recommendations were made, including the important one that police should have a right of entry on the written authority of the Chief Constable or his authorised deputy, no "off" sales should be permitted, and premises which had lost their licence ought not be used for club purposes until after a lapse of five years.

Education

The section on education in the commission's report was brief but pertinent, quoting evidence given by the Senior Medical Officer of the Board of Education which referred to the syllabi available and the importance of incorporating appropriate teaching into general health education. There should be specific *ad-hoc* courses, especially for older children, but also such instruction should be incorporated into science, history and geography lessons. Children should also have set before them the advantages of temperance for health and physical fitness. While tributes paid to visiting temperance instructors had been endorsed by the commission, it was felt to be wiser to leave it to qualified members of the regular staff of the schools. To this end the commission urged the authorities to ensure that the introduction of this subject into the curricula of teacher-training colleges should be maintained and extended.

Local option

Besides the seven matters on which the commission made specific recommendations it took up other issues which, in any comprehensive survey of the report, must be mentioned. Temperance representatives had urged the commission to come out in favour of local option by which the people in a locality could decide whether the sale of liquor should be conducted in their locality, but the commission rejected this, one of the chief reasons for doing so being that such a referendum could apply only to public facilities for obtaining intoxicants, while private cellars and private stores would remain untouched. "It may be a doubtful advantage to drive drinking from the public house into the private home" the commission concluded.[40] The question of boundaries was also taken into account, and the likelihood of anomalies between adjacent areas. The real debate about local option took place much earlier and it is therefore not appropriate to make more than a passing reference to it. In one sense the commission made a concession to the views of particular localities in its comment about Wales and Monmouthshire.[41] It was accepted that the claim for a distinct licensing system for Wales might be part of a general national movement in Wales. The real issue was "whether, in opinion and sentiment in regard to licensing policy", Wales differed materially from England. "We think there can be no doubt that it does" declared the report. This was especially so in regard to Sunday closing, and there was no recommendation made to change this practice. Although it had been put to the commission that Monmouthshire should be included within the English licensing system, the commission concluded that "the outlook of that county in regard to licensing questions is Welsh rather than English". It was, therefore, recommended that Monmouthshire should be subject to the same licensing law as Wales.

Off-licences and occasional licences

Two specific licensing matters were also referred to in the report: off-licences and occasional licences. There was one exception to the general requirement that all sales by retail must be authorized by a justices' licence, which was the "bottle shop",[42] which differed from a normal "off-licence" in that it was a retail extension of a wholesale dealer's business. An exemption in the 1910 Act permitted such a dealer to sell, for off-consumption, wines or spirits provided that only intoxicating, or in addition, non-intoxicating drinks were sold in self-contained premises. This could be done by taking out a retail excise licence without first obtaining a justices' licence. Such premises were called bottle shops. The commission recommended that this exemption be abolished and that persons trading in this manner should obtain a justice's licence. Bona fide off-licence proprietors had a further trading disadvantage because they were required to sell wine in quantities of not less than a half bottle, and of spirits in not less than the normal bottle. The commission recommended that the law should be amended to permit the sale by off-licence holders of spirits in quantities of one reputed pint. There were various ways by which the law in respect of minima quantities was being evaded. These were dealt with by recommendations of the commission. An anomaly recognized by the commission was that whereas the justices could attach conditions when granting an on-licence, they had no similar discretion with reference to off-licences. The other licensing matter was the occasional licence.[43] "An occasional licence is an authority granted to the holder of an on-licence to carry on sales of intoxicants at some place other than his ordinary place of business."[44] The authority was granted by the Board of Customs and Excise with the previous consent of the petty sessional court (or in certain circumstances by two justices). The board asked to be relieved of their discretion to refuse a licence, which was agreed with a recommendation that the discretion rest with the justices. The board also called the attention of the commission to the fact that selling liquor outside the hours specified in the occasional licence was a revenue offence, and the commission accepted their view that the police, and not the board's officers, should initiate proceedings.

Other matters

Two other matters which were dealt with in a few paragraphs of the report have since become major issues in any consideration of the sale and consumption of intoxicating liquor. One was "Motorists".[45] The fact that this was dealt with as a sub-paragraph in a section on drunkenness consisting of fifteen lines, is evidence that at the time the relation between drinking and road accidents had not been fully appreciated. It seemed sufficient to know that "a large majority of motor transport undertakings" had a total abstinence rule for drivers while on duty. "We think this practice wise, and would welcome its universal adoption", commented the commission. The other matter was "Advertising".[46] This was dealt with in less than a page and a half of the report! It stated "According to evidence, it seems it would be a conservative estimate to put the figure of annual expenditure on such advertisements at £2,000,000".[47] The commission accepted that advertising tended to increase consumption. Other comments were that considerable numbers of such advertisements were directed to young people, that liquor advertising in the press might affect editorial policy and that many advertisements contained scientific untruths. Another astonishing omission, or nearly so, was any reference to alcoholism. In the index to the report there is not a single reference to it. The section on "habitual drunkards" was so brief that it can only be concluded that at the time the problem of "alcoholism" had not been identified.

Henry Carter's reservations

The Revd Henry Carter, the head of the department of the Wesleyan Church dealing with temperance issues was a member of the Royal Commission and entered certain reservations which were published as an addendum to the main report. While expressing agreement with the commission's recommendations he had reservations particularly on the question of referenda on the drink question and he did not share the commission's conclusions about Sunday opening.

The Royal Commission recommended that referenda should be held to ascertain the views of the electorate in two respects, (i) in new housing areas, on applications for new licences; and (ii) in Wales and Monmouthshire ten years after the appointment of a Welsh National Licensing Commission to discover the view of the electorate on such issues as local veto or public management. Carter approved both recommendations, but wished the principle to be extended to England. "The results of the referendum, to be reported by counties and county boroughs, would be for the guidance of Parliament which by this means would know, without uncertainty, the trend of English public opinion on the drink question"[48] As distinct from an informative vote, the Royal Commission also considered the merits of a determinative vote and rejected it. Henry Carter disagreed. He conceived that it was possible, in the future, that the nation might conclude that it did not wish to have a liquor trade operating at all. A determinative vote would allow the people to decide whether or not the trade in intoxicants was desirable in the public interest. "For this reason", Carter said, "I do not accept the adverse conclusion expressed in the chapter on 'Local option'. The door to future freedom of public decision must not be closed – indeed it cannot be closed".[49]

His other main reservations were (i) he did not share the commission's conclusions about "Sunday opening" and argued for accepting as the norm for England, as it was in Scotland, Wales and Northern Ireland, the "six-day licence", with a similar six-day certificate for clubs; and (ii) he wished to see it made illegal to display liquor advertisements on public hoardings, vehicles or other public places.

In another minority report, F. P. Whitbread dissociated himself from the commission's recommendations concerning the proposed National Licensing Commission and the extension of public ownership.

References

1. The Licensing Act 1921 perpetuated the system of permitted hours, the main features of which were (a) an earliest morning hour and a latest evening hour; (b) a maximum number of hours; and (c) a compulsory break of at least two hours commencing at or after midday.
2. 5488.
3. 7628.
4. 9541 (4).
5. 10,907 (11).
6. *Royal Commission on Licensing (England and Wales)* 1929–31 p. 95.
7. Report p. 8.
8. Report p. 8.
9. 6542.
10. 6549–50.
11. Report p. 9.
12. Report p.10.
13. Report p. 11 (cf also p. 20).
14. 18,719 and 18,730.
15. Report p. 18.
16. Report p. 19.
17. Report p. 3.
18. Report p. 23.
19. 14,448.
20. 15,318 ff.
21. Report p. 25.
22. Report p. 39.
23. 9541 (11).
24. 8238.
25. 9180 (7).
26. 18,139.
27. Report p. 45.
28. Report p. 54.
29. Report p. 57.
30. Report p. 58.
31. Report p. 72,
32. Report p. 73.
33. See pp. 99–113.
34. 23,509 ff.
35. 24,188 ff.
36. 3324.
37. 3823.
38. 28,731 ff.
39. Report p. 106.
40. Report p. 92.
41. Report p. 113.
42. Report p. 127.
43. Report p. 131.
44. Report p. 131 quoted from Licensing (Consolidation) Act 1910, Section 64.
45. Report p. 149.
46. Report p. 156.
47. Report p. 156.
48. Report p. 186.
49. Report p. 186.

CHAPTER 7

PUBLIC OWNERSHIP

It has already been said that one of the principal recommendations of the Royal Commission 1929–31 was to extend public ownership of the liquor trade on the basis of the so-called Carlisle Scheme. This was not the first attempt to take the trade out of private hands. What came to be known as the Gothenburg scheme had been introduced in Norway and Sweden in the previous century. At Gothenburg in Sweden a company was set up to run licensed premises for the benefit of the community. A major portion of the profits, equal to about one-third of the total municipal revenue, was off-set against the city rates. When the principle was applied in Norway in 1871, the dangers of the rate-payers having an interest in making the liquor trade prosper were seen, and the profits were devoted to "objects of public utility" instead of the relief of the rates. Temperance reformers in both countries were apprehensive about a scheme which made rate relief or town improvements dependent on profits from the local liquor trade, but the Gothenburg scheme naturally attracted attention in Britain at the end of the nineteenth and the beginning of the twentieth centuries, because of a widespread desire to reduce the number of licensed premises.

Disinterested management

The first major attempt to apply the Gothenburg scheme in Britain was made in 1896 when the Bishop of Chester* became chairman of a new company called the People's Refreshment House Association Limited. By 1901 it had eighteen houses under its management. It sought to acquire leases of existing public houses and to secure new licences where growth in population demanded such facilities. The main features of the scheme were that the managers should be paid a fixed salary and not benefit from profits on the sale of liquor but, to encourage the sale of non-intoxicants, were allowed a profit on food and other drinks. Capital was raised by one-pound shares from the public and the annual dividend was limited to not exceeding five per cent. Surplus profit was devoted to objects of public utility. The houses, mainly in rural areas, provided the usual facilities of public houses.

The scheme in Britain which attracted most interest was one associated with Earl Grey. On 6th September 1900 he wrote to the licensing magistrates in various petty sessional divisions of Northumberland following his successful application, as the principal landowner in the district, for the licence for a new public house at Broomhill. It was only then that he discovered, he told the magistrates, that such a monopoly licence was a big commercial asset. He continued, "I was informed that if I would consent to sell my licence I could, without spending a single sixpence, obtain nearly £10,000. Now it appears to me that large monopoly values arising out of the possession of a public licence conferred upon a private individual by the State, ought to belong, not to any private individual, but to the community. I am, accordingly, making arrangements by which the surplus profits, after

* *Francis Jayne.*

a dividend of 10 per cent has been paid per annum (5 per cent for interest and 5 per cent for redemption of capital) shall be expended by the Trustees, to be appointed, in such a manner as they may direct, for the inhabitants of Broomhill."[1] Lord Grey asked the magistrates to give the first refusal of new licences to applicants prepared to run them on the Scandinavian principle. At first he thought such licences should be acquired by the People's Refreshment House Association, but he announced in a letter to *The Times*[2] that a new body had been formed, the Public-House Trust Companies for London and the provinces.

The objects of the Public-House Trust Association were similar to those of the People's Refreshment-House Association, already described. In a further letter to *The Times*[3] Lord Grey explained that his proposals were not an attack on the licensees of public houses, and he was not asking licensing authorities to alter their practice in respect of the renewal of licences. He added, "We do not ask the Legislature to come to our assistance. We are content to make the best use of the opportunities which the law allows us."[4] In discussing the merits of this scheme, Rowntree and Sherwell asked, "In what way can the Trust Company secure licences? The number of "on" licenced houses in Great Britain is a diminishing quantity, and in settled districts the full number of licences likely to be granted has already been allotted."[5] It was their view that even if, by various means, a considerable number of licences were acquired, "the relation they would bear to the existing licences of the country must be insignificant".[6] It was part of Lord Grey's scheme that where necessary the Trust Company should purchase existing licences, but Rowntree and Sherwell believed that a sum far in excess of the 5 per cent per annum suggested by Lord Grey would have to be set aside as a redemption fund.

These were the attempts made at the turn of the century which came to be known as "dis-interested management". The debate on this issue had begun earlier. It was initiated by Joseph Chamberlain who was elected for Birmingham in 1876. He visited Sweden and returned as an enthusiastic advocate of the Gothenburg scheme. On 13th March 1877 he moved a resolution in the House of Commons in favour of empowering town councils of boroughs to acquire compulsorily, on payment of fair compensation, the existing retail outlets for liquor, and thereafter to carry on the business for the convenience of the inhabitants and without profit to any individual.

United Kingdom Alliance policy

It is interesting and important to note the change of attitude of the United Kingdom Alliance on this issue. In 1869 the *Report* of the UKA executive contained this reference to the Gothenburg scheme.

> *The excellent results of this wise policy may be imagined, and it is perhaps the most satisfactory attempt at regulation that has ever been made. Pending the adoption of total prohibition, your committee would gladly see the friends of licensing reform intent on carrying out the Gothenburg scheme. The transition from such a scheme to one of prohibition would not be a very difficult task, seeing that there are but few liquor-sellers who would care to be in the trade when nothing can be gained by it, either by themselves or the community."*[7]

By 1893 the executive had changed its mind and report that year criticized the Gothenburg scheme,[8] and in their 1901 report there was an extensive critical appraisal of the schemes for disinterested management which had been set up in the country. The People's Refreshment House Association had been in existence for about five years. The report said:

> *In 1900 it had a capital of £5,000 and controlled eighteen public-houses. The yearly cash takings of these must, we should suppose, have been more than the capital; yet somehow the total amount which the Association was able to devote to "purposes of public utility" was only £100, or about £5. 5s. for each house. So much for the gain in money to the people of the 18 villages.*[9]

Was there, however, a great increase in sobriety? It would seem not. This was the conclusion reached by the UKA about Lord Grey's Public House Trust Association, and it was particularly contemptuous of the financial arrangements he proposed.

> *His Lordship's scheme proposed that at least three times as large a return on the money invested should be derived from it as can be obtained from investments in the public funds; more, certainly, than can be obtained from investments, at the prices ruling in the market today in the shares of the liquor syndicates, and quite 2 ½ times as much as the average yearly return from investments in ordinary railway shares. Does not this demonstrate that it is possible to serve both God and Mammon?*[10]

The fundamental temperance objections to these schemes were that they involved the community in what was acknowledged by many to be a "dangerous trade", that any scheme to reimburse the rates or to provide public amenities from the profits of the retailing of liquor was an incentive to increase the sale, that instead of reducing the number of licensed premises it would increase them, and especially in areas where previously there had been none and that the evidence from Scandinavia was that drunkenness and other offences induced by the consumption of alcohol had not diminished since the introduction of the scheme.

Other views

What was purported to be a more detached view than that of the temperance reformers was given in *The Commonwealth as Publicans* by John Walker.[11] He examined in considerable detail the various experiments in Britain to apply the Gothenburg system, and he appraised the advocacy for the scheme of Rowntree and Sherwell. Like them he had visited a number of the establishments and it is interesting to compare his impression of specific premises with those of Rowntree and Sherwell. His general conclusion was that the system failed on almost all counts, and on none so manifestly as the trend in sobriety. Because it had been claimed that the chief reason for applying the Gothenburg system was to stem the tide of drunkenness, this was the crucial test. Walker stated that the general tenor of the data available showed that since 1855 there had been an improvement in the sobriety of the country, but after the system had been established the improvement had slowed down, and in the last decade there had been a "return towards the former state of degradation". He believed the present-day advocates were blind to the current retrograde movement, and arrests for drunkenness, the figures for the consumption of spirits, and other data seemed to bear this out. Walker's visit to, and enquiries about, British "Gothenburgs" produced evidence which showed that standards of management were no better than in the usual public houses and the abuses were equally common, and, although the sale of non-alcoholic drinks and other refreshment were reckoned to be a special feature of the Gothenburg establishments, these facilities were sparsely patronized. The distribution of profits for the public good, another feature of the scheme, was patchy; and instead of being used to provide counter attractions to the public house, went to street-lighting, water wells or to the maintenance of a district nurse. Walker concluded that the scheme failed to achieve its principal objects.

Rowntree and Sherwell published a reply to their critics and to John Walker in particular. They examined the statistics he used and showed they were basically inaccurate or erroneously calculated. It is not necessary to make extensive reference to the controversy between Walker and Rowntree and Sherwell who in their book did stress the importance of distinguishing between, for example, the trust companies set up in Britain and the system in Scandinavia. In their earlier book[12] they had said that the authorities in Norway had learned from the experiments in Sweden and had been able to improve on the original scheme. Instead of a number of isolated "take-overs" which remained in competition with free houses, the Norwegians instituted a system of true control. The company system could be efficient only in so far as it was a controlling system. And so the companies were not left to their own devices, but were required to work under the joint supervision of the Crown and of the local authorities. Rowntree and Sherwell commented, "It is in the wise combination of central control and local initiative that the singular excellence of the Norwegian System consists."[13]

They then described what happened in Norway when a town wished to establish the company system.[14] The right of retailing ardent spirits was only granted to societies whose articles of incorporation had been confirmed by a resolution of the magistracy and municipal council, and had been sanctioned under the royal seal. This guarded against the introduction of ill-considered schemes not in harmony with what had been determined by the Norwegian people. The appropriation of profits was also defined by statutory law. Sixty-five per cent was to go to the central government and twenty-five per cent of the remainder to the administration of the company. None was to be applied to objects for which the municipality itself was responsible. It could only be applied to objects of "public utility" not chargeable to the rates. The balance of fifteen per cent was for the municipality as an allowance in lieu of the much larger sums previously derived from the licence tax which had been abolished. The accounts of the Samlags, as the companies were called, had to be audited by official auditors, and representatives of the Crown, the magistracy and the Municipal Council were entitled to inspect the books and accounts at all times. So strict was the supervision that the choice of local managers was also subject to the approval of the magistracy and the Municipal Council. The municipality was the ultimate licensing authority, determining the number of licences issued, as well as being strongly represented on committees of management. Along with this strict control was a measure of freedom not enjoyed under some other systems, because localities were left to work out their own deliverance from the threat of the drink interests by whatever method seemed best.

Rowntree and Sherwell's criticism of the Public House Trust Companies of the United Kingdom was that such safeguards did not apply, and there was no statutory law defining and limiting the sphere and character of a trust company's operations. "The control exercised by the State over their articles of association is similar in character to that exercised over the articles of association of a cycle company."[15] The special danger of the drink trade was not taken into account. Such companies had no need to be sensitive to public opinion, neither the state nor the local authority had any control over the appropriation of the profits, and no public audit was required.

They quoted reports by foreign observers of the Scandanavian scheme, one of the most important of which was that of Dr E. R. L. Gould of the Department of Labour at Washington published in 1893. Gould said he was a convert to the scheme. "The testimony of the facts and the object lessons afforded on every hand were so conclusive that I could not help feeling that the Scandinavian method is the only really practical means of dealing with the liquor evil in this generation. This opinion is fortified by knowledge and observation of other systems, gained from nearly five years' experience as an investigator of social problems in Great Britain and on the continent of Europe. It is far in advance, too, of any method which has been tried in the United States. I do not regard the Scandinavian plan as perfect, but I do believe it contains the 'promise and potency' of higher things. It is a measure of progressive reform, sound in principle, operating harmoniously with well-defined laws of social advance, and is easily adaptable to English and American conditions. Its trial will do more than anything else yet suggested to mitigate an intolerable social curse."[16]

As we have seen, not everybody concerned with licensing reform was so enthusiastic, and the issues of "disinterested management" and "public ownership" caused deep divisions and, at times, acrimonious controversy. The opposition of the United Kingdom Alliance became even more determined, the grounds of its opposition being set out in the 1905 report of the UKA executive.[17] It said the term "management" meant the regulation of the liquor trade, "the toleration of it, the making of it something respectable, the exalting of it into a public institution". It rejected the argument that disinterested management, by eliminating the element of private profit, would remove the greatest evil of the liquor trade. All "management", however disinterested, involved private profit for the brewers and distillers.

The debate on these issues continued up to the outbreak of the First World War, and as a consequence of the Carlisle Scheme of public ownership, introduced as a wartime measure, it received new impetus. The Carlisle Scheme was one outcome of the passing of the Defence of the Realm (Amendment) Act which became law on 19th May 1915. As we have seen,[18] among its provisions was one which enabled the control of the liquor trade in any area to be transferred to "the prescribed authority". It was this provision which provoked most controversy. Henry Carter records, "The temperance party was divided on the question of state purchase".[19] He explained that some who represented moderate opinion were in favour of it. The strongest opposition came from the United Kingdom Alliance. Their president, Leif Jones, during a parliamentary debate, said that in the bill there was a phrase which implied that there might be a permanent purchase of the trade in certain areas. "I think that is to be deprecated" he said. "Any purchasing that may be done should be for the period of the war, and no longer. . . . There is a large section of the community which would object strongly to anything like public ownership of the liquor trade after the war is over."[20]

The main objection to public ownership was that the state ought not to be involved as a participant in the liquor trade. Leif Jones introduced a number of amendments to prevent the inclusion in the bill of a provision for public ownership. The Chancellor's reply was twofold. First, to introduce temporary purchase was impracticable, and second, the state was already deeply involved because it was drawing large sums from the trade in taxation. The state, by purchase, would exchange partnership without effective control, for ownership with complete control. Lloyd George, Chancellor of the Exchequer, replied to the critics: "I am fully alive to all the conscientious suggestions which my hon. friends urge, but the idea that you are not to touch the unclean thing when, through the Chancellor of the Exchequer, we are touching £60,000,000 and to that extent relieving the duties on tea, sugar and everything else, I have never been able to appreciate. You will not touch it direct, but as long as it goes through the refining fires of the Exchequer you can take it. That is an argument I do not care to describe."[21] The government's proposals included provision for compensation for all interests taken over or adversely affected. This and the fact that they had some sense of patriotic duty, enabled the trade to accept the proposals.

First experiments in public ownership

The intervention of the state, through the Control Board, prepared the way for the introduction of the first experiments in true public ownership. Wartime conditions prompted the experiment, but although it succeeded it did not lead to a general extension of the principle. Such limited action might not have taken place had there not been a ready-made and convenient instrument to hand. This was the Central Control Board which, as we have seen, possessed powers to purchase and manage licensed premises. The first excursion into state purchase was at Enfield Lock, Middlesex. After the outbreak of war, the Royal Small Arms factory there was vastly extended and the workforce was multiplied several times. Although a canteen was erected within the works to accommodate one thousand people, it was quite inadequate. The result was that at meal times the four public houses were crowded, and many work-people were driven to eat sandwiches on the roadsides. These conditions led to weariness and irritation. The Control Board received a deputation of workers from the factory, and as a result it was decided to provide extended facilities and take over the local public houses. Thus on 4th January 1916 the state, for the first time, entered into the business of retailing liquor. In addition to the four public houses, the state also took over an off-licence and so controlled all retail outlets adjacent to the factory.

Two principal objects were fulfilled, (a) to limit the sale of liquor to mealtimes and (b) to extend accommodation for meals in comfortable surroundings. The hours were limited to 4½ per day and arranged to coincide with various working shifts. Two of the public houses, the Greyhound and the Royal Small Arms were practically rebuilt and the two others acquired, the Ordnance Arms and the Swan and Pike were closed early in 1919. The reconstruction of the Greyhound enabled a thousand meals a day to be served. Henry Carter observed that "although the increased accommodation made it possible to deal with four or five times the former number of customers, the liquor receipts in the first half-year only doubled, while the food sales increased almost sevenfold".[22] The reconstruction of the Royal Small Arms was completed in June 1917 when the new facilities enabled between two thousand and three thousand men per day to be accommodated. A committee of workers was elected to assist in the management of these canteens which in 1918 were serving on average 12,000 meals per week. The social benefits were evident in increased sobriety, greater contentment and higher efficiency.

A second area to which state purchase was applied was Cromarty Firth which had had summer visits by the fleet, but whose two peaceful villages of Invergordon (population 1,100) and Cromarty (1,200) were transformed when Cromarty Firth became a naval base and dockyard. Invergordon became an industrial town, and although Cromarty was not developed to the same extent it became a resort for sailors and soldiers. With the arrival of so many workmen to build the installations, and then the influx of members of the forces the control of the drink trade was important, and in April 1916 the state took over the licensed premises in the two places. At that time there were two hotels with public bars, two public houses and three licensed grocers in Invergordon, while at Cromarty there were two hotels with bars, three public houses and one licensed grocer. After state control was introduced "on" and "off" sales were separated. "Off" sales were confined to one licensed premises in each town. Of the four licensed grocers, two lost their licences and two were closed for groceries and used as the depots for the "off" licensed premises. Five of the thirteen licensed premises were declared redundant and closed. Special hours were arranged of 4½ hours per day, 2½ at midday and 2 in the evening. Until these measures were taken drunkenness was a problem, but gradually sobriety was achieved. At the request of the Admiralty, public control was extended to Alness, which was three miles from Invergordon, and to Novar, both on the north of the Firth, and to three villages on the south. Five of the nine licences taken over were withdrawn as redundant, and "on" and "off" sales were separated. In 1918 the control was extended to Dingwell and the remainder of the Firth. In this additional area ten of the seventeen licences were extinguished. Again the level of drunkenness and disorder was greatly reduced.

The Carlisle scheme

"The Carlisle Scheme", as it came to be known, was a much bigger enterprise. The scheduled area in the Solway Firth included Carlisle, with a population at the time of 52,000 and a surrounding district encompassing Gretna which raised the total population affected by the scheme to 140,000. It was the erection of a large explosives factory in the area which prompted the Ministry of Munitions to ask the Control Board to step in. This was in November 1915, when it was estimated there would be a work force of 10,000, leading to an overall increase in population of 20,000 to 30,000. In fact, as the construction of the factory progressed the influx of people increased to more than double the original estimate. The high wages paid to workers, and the absence of alternative recreational facilities, meant that the public houses were crowded. Drunkenness became a major problem, and some indication of its escalation may be seen in the number of convictions in Annan and Carlisle before the Gretna workers arrived and after. In the six months January to June 1915, convictions in Annan were six and in Carlisle seventy-two. The comparable figures for the same period in 1916 were 146 and 564, which indicated the need for drastic action.

The first action of the Central Control Board was to introduce its customary scheme of restrictions. The hours of sale were reduced, "off" sales restricted, limits set on amounts to be retailed, the sale of spirits at railway refreshments rooms prohibited, and various other controls introduced. Henry Carter commented, "It should be emphasised that all these regulations were imposed by the Board within a few weeks of the first influx of labour. Critics of the State Purchase Scheme have implied that the life of the district was allowed to drift into wild disorder. The fact is that if a policy of restriction would of itself have met the need, no disorder would have arisen."[23]

It was because these regulations proved inadequate that the Board felt compelled to introduce another method. In January 1916, following a conference of interested parties with the board, the first licensed premises to come into the possession of the state were acquired. They numbered four breweries and 119 public houses in Carlisle itself. The process continued until October 1916, by which time the last purchases were made, and the area of control further extended to include Maryport. In the whole area 368 licensed premises of various kinds, as well as breweries, maltings, bottling stores, wine and spirit merchants' premises, and other properties, were taken over. A total of £883,265 compensation was paid to the owners of the properties, including the two schemes at Enfield and Cromarty. The Carlisle scheme was administered by a general manager with an advisory committee of twenty-four persons representing the civic authorities of Carlisle and the surrounding area. Because the area extended both sides of the England-Scotland border a separate general manager was appointed to administer the Scottish section.[24]

According to policy statements,[25] the aims of the administration were to reduce the number of licensed premises, effect their re-arrangement where necessary, improve the premises especially to provide meals, introduce salaried managers and effect other minor changes. The general manager's reports record the progress made towards the fulfilment of these aims. In July 1916 there were 340 licences in the whole area and by 1920 all but 47 had been acquired by the board who had suppressed 123 of them. The three other factors taken into account in suppressing licences, were redundancy, unsuitability of premises either in structure or location, and unprofitability. What was called re-arrangement would in more recent times be called rationalization. It was the process by which specific operations such as malting, blending or bottling were concentrated for efficiency in distinct departments, and on the retail side it meant the separation, as far as possible, of the retailing of liquor from that of other commodities. The improvement of facilities was mostly concerned with the provision of meals, even to the extent of restaurants. The encouragement of public houses to remain open outside permitted hours to provide meals without drink met with little success. An experiment of some importance which state purchase made possible, was the appointment of disinterested managers, instead of licensees, to Carlisle public houses, which had been urged for some time because it was said that salaried managers would have no incentive to encourage excessive drinking, and under the Carlisle scheme this system was introduced. The general manager's reports commented favourably upon the working of the system. Other minor, but important, actions taken by the board were to improve the outward appearance and interior furnishings of public houses, to prohibit the sale of spirits in Carlisle on Saturdays and to prohibit temporarily the sale of spirits at Langton and the area adjoining the Gretna Green factory.

The first public examination of various schemes of disinterested management was undertaken by the Southborough Committee appointed in June 1925. Its terms of reference were to "consider the various systems of disinterested management of public houses which have been put into practice, whether in connection with private enterprise or otherwise, and to report whether the experience already gained affords ground for the development of any such system by an amendment of the licensing laws". It concluded, "We are not satisfied that a case has been established for the extension of the scheme to any other particular area or place". It advocated the continuance of the present schemes "until such time as it is possible to make a more final estimate of the results achieved." The whole matter was dealt with extensively by the Royal Commission 1929 to 1931.

Before considering the findings of the Royal Commission on the Carlisle scheme, it will be useful to refer to the conclusions of Henry Carter who was a member of the Control Board. It was his view that the Carlisle State purchase scheme demonstrated the following advantages: (a) freedom to suppress swiftly and permanently all redundant and undesirable licences; (b) the elimination of private interest in the sale of liquor; (c) a closer regard to the law; (d) economy in business management; (e) a free hand to effect reform suited to local requirements; (f) the association of local progressive opinion with the control of the drink trade.[26]

Carlisle and the Royal Commission

The 1929 Royal Commission received considerable evidence on how the Carlisle scheme had progressed and what its effect had been on the drinking habits of the area. Sir John G. Sykes, of the Home Office gave the commission a detailed account of the reasons for establishing the Carlisle scheme, how it had been set up and what some of the effects had been. The Local Advisory Committee, which met regularly, had proved of great value.[27] Further information about the administration of the scheme was given by A. E. Mitchell, general manager of the Carlisle and District State Management Scheme, who also gave evidence for the Home Office. He referred to the system of inspection by whole-time inspectors, who made daily checks of the premises for cleanliness, the condition of equipment and repairs. There were fortnightly meetings with managers. Inspections were also made at night during the midweek and also at weekends. Reports were prepared every week on all aspects of the undertaking, including behaviour on licensed premises. Mitchell described how the Carlisle public houses were responding to the intention of the scheme to create more than mere drinking houses. Dining rooms were separate from the bars and smoke-rooms had separate entrances. Some houses had separate compartments for the sale of cooked hot food to be consumed off the premises. Many children called at midday with plates or basins for soup or some other dish which cost twopence or threepence. The mothers of such children were employed in local factories, so they were unable to cook a midday meal for their family. In the country areas, public houses reserved rooms for teas, and these were well advertised. Recreation facilities were provided in all houses as part of the policy of the scheme. In a personal survey, he had discovered that in an "improved" house, that is one with more space and with recreational facilities, expenditure per head on liquor was lower than in the normal public house.[28]

Sir Edgar Sanders, formerly general manager of the Carlisle and District State Management Area, said spirit drinking was reponsible for a great deal of the drunkenness in the north of England, and he thought the working classes had a real grievance about the excessive price of beer. Referring specifically to the Carlisle scheme, he said that in the winter of 1917 the sale of spirits on Saturdays was banned in the area. Before the ban, Saturday was the worst day of the week for arrests for drunkenness, but after the ban it headed the list for sobriety. He thought the Carlisle area was too small and more experience would have to be gained from much larger areas before a conclusion could be drawn for the whole country. The success of the Carlisle scheme had been due to the fact that the "personal touch" could be maintained. "We started with everybody against us" he said, "and the two most bitter enemies were, I think, the trade on the one side and the prohibitionists on the other". In between, the great body of public opinion was not, at first, sure about the merits of the scheme. Now, he thought, the vast majority were in favour of its retention. Asked by the commission what were the real qualities of beer and why people enjoyed drinking it, he said the chief quality was alcohol, which was the staple constituent of beer. People did not drink it because it was intoxicating, but because it was a good beverage and its goodness depended on a certain percentage of alcohol. They had tried all "near" beers, or two per cent beers, in Carlisle, but the ordinary beer drinkers would not have them at any price. It made them ill, or so they said.[29]

Andrew A. Johnston, Chief Constable of Carlisle, described some of the social amenities provided by the state-owned public houses. Bowling greens and billiard tables not only provided recreation for those who were playing, but also for spectators. These were useful diversions. The food rooms, separate from the licensed areas were an important amenity, and he especially commended the provision of hot meals for consumption off the premises, which were patronized by children whose mothers were at work. He said there had been a marked decrease in convictions for drunkenness since the introduction of the scheme. He confirmed the view of Sir Edgar Sanders that for a time the Carlisle scheme was very unpopular with the mass of citizens, especially consumers, the working class and middle class men who frequented public houses. They complained of the extra restrictions, the quality of drink and sometimes of the service. As time went on these views were modified. The initial restrictions such as Sunday closing and spiritless Saturdays, had been lifted. On the whole the service had been good and the improvement in the premises had been welcomed.[30] Another police witness was Superintendent Ernest Stewart, who had been with the Carlisle Division of the Cumberland and Westmoreland Constabulary since 1922. He said people who became drunk in the district were generally of the tramping kind. It was an area through which many travellers passed. Asked how public houses were equipped to provide tea and other refreshments for motoring parties the superintendent said every facility was provided and encouraged.[31]

Two former chief constables of Carlisle were able to provide evidence for the period between the inception of the scheme and the time when the Royal Commission was at work. Eric Spence was Chief Constable of Carlisle from 1913 to 1928. He said that for ten years preceding the war, convictions for drunkenness averaged 250 per annum. This was a reasonable figure for an industrial town of a little over 50,000. In 1916, when the Greta munitions factory was opened, convictions rose to 953 and could easily have trebled if police action had not been seriously depleted by officers joining the forces.[32] In his evidence Andrew A. Johnston had shown how convictions decreased with the introduction of state control. In 1917 there were 320 convictions, in 1918 there were 80 and in 1919 there were 78. Spence told the commission that he thought the current number of licensed premises in Carlisle was sufficient and that their improved standards were conducive to good order. He said,

> *I am also satisfied that the brewers would welcome the opportunity for carrying out far reaching improvements to their premises if they were not consistently obstructed by individuals, and organisations, who oppose any structural alterations, and send protests, or appear before the licensing justices with this object in view, and try to explain, often successfully – that increased floor space makes for increased drinking. In my opinion, after studying the question for many years, this is a complete myth, better premises make for sobriety and self-respect, and I should welcome the opportunity of being able officially to explain to licensing justices, the advantages I have observed as the result of improved premises.*[33]

He also made this observation about Carlisle public houses,

> *You also have to remember that the Carlisle Public-houses are very much like clubs, because a man can go into a Carlisle public-house, take a paper and have a soft drink, or no drink at all, and can sit and watch other people playing billiards for as long as he likes and no question is asked about what he is going to have to drink. That is a very strong factor. There is no suggestion that a man must have a drink or that he must have another drink.*[34]

He made the same point as Johnston that people can watch games being played without participating themselves and without pressure to drink. The other former Chief Constable of Carlisle was Archibald Kennedy Wilson who was at Carlisle in 1929 before being appointed Chief Constable of Plymouth. Before going to Carlisle he had been in the Cardiff City Police Force for nineteen years. He was asked by the commission whether, as compared with Carlisle, there was any redundancy of public houses at that time or when he left it. He said there was not. Did Cardiff compare well with Carlisle in its system of control? Yes, he replied, but he was speaking of one particular brewery company in Cardiff which had made a practice of no participation in the profits by people who managed the trade. They only participated in profits from food. He thought the standard of management in the two areas was comparable.[35]

The commission heard the views of various local representatives of the community about the scheme, including the Mayor of Carlisle, Robert C. Chance. He was Deputy Chairman and Managing Director of Ferguson Bros. Ltd. who were cotton manufacturers. He summarized the effect of the scheme as follows: (a) If public houses are necessary it is better to try to make them decent, respectable places of refreshment rather than drinking houses. It must be a public gain to have all possible done to discourage drinking in excess. He thought those who frequented public houses in Carlisle were generally satisfied with the way in which public houses were at present conducted. (b) It appeared to be a great gain to be able to dispense with private interests, whose main concern must be to bring about the maximum consumption of alcohol. (c) Reforms would be very much easier to bring about under public ownership. (d) There was great gain in the elimination of competition, which must have the effect of encouraging a public house to press the sale of drink and to go to the limits of the law in the retailing of it. (e) The principle of public ownership should be extended to one or two larger areas to secure more information upon which a decision could be reached about public ownership. (f) He believed public opinion in Carlisle was in favour of the scheme.[36]

Councillor John R. Potts, a locomotive engine driver and member of the Carlisle City Council for ten years, and a member of the Local Advisory Committee of the Carlisle State Management Scheme, shared the view of the Mayor that public opinion in Carlisle, and especially of working men who used the public houses, was favourable towards the scheme.[37]

The views of churchmen illustrated the division of opinion in the churches on the question of public ownership. The Revd G. Bramwell Evans, a Wesleyan minister who lived in Carlisle from 1914 to 1926, told the commission he was not a temperance worker and he spoke as a resident.

He described how the drink problem in Carlisle became very much worse after the influx of 12,000 work people, many of whom were hard-drinking navvies. Taking this and other factors into account, he said of the Carlisle scheme that he had never come across any system which had more hope in it, and at the same time functioned better, in the public interest. He thought that any system which could be a success in a crisis could be relied on more fully when conditions were normal. He felt that if the scheme was in vogue all over the country there would be a far greater chance of a sober England than under the old regime.[38]

An opposite view was taken by the Revd A. Jeans Courtney, another Wesleyan Minister, formerly of Loxton, Cumberland, and Temperance and Social Welfare Secretary of the Carlisle District of the Wesleyan Church from 1923 to 1926. He also represented the United Kingdom Alliance. He described how between January 1925 and August 1926, he paid 200 visits to various public houses in the area and subsequently gave evidence to the Southborough Committee.[39] When he first went to Cumberland, he said, he was in favour of the scheme, but this judgement had been based on literature he had received and reports from the police. He had been challenged to visit Carlisle personally, which he did, visiting public houses dressed as a normal frequenter of such establishments. He discovered a considerable body of opinion that the results of the Carlisle scheme did not justify its extension to other areas. The available figures did not prove that consumption was less in Carlisle and district than in the rest of the country. He quoted from Section 45 of the Southborough report, "As regards the consumption of intoxicating liquor in Carlisle, it does not appear to be established that the reduction of public houses by approximately 50 per cent and the improvement of those retained has led to a reduction in the quantity of intoxicating liquor consumed beyond that common to the rest of England, Scotland and Wales in the post-war period." He also referred to the surprise expressed by the Select Committee on Public Accounts in their examination of Sir John Sykes in 1928 that the percentage of food sold in Carlisle public houses was so very low, especially in view of the declared aim of the Control Board "to provide cheap and good food so as to discourage the drinking of alcohol apart from meals". The turnover on food in 1928 was only four per cent of the ordinary public-house trade. He also referred to the loss of magisterial control of the licensed trade in Carlisle. He quoted the *Cumberland News,* "No citizen of Carlisle outside the Committee (i.e. The Advisory Committee) knows what the Board proposes to do until a bare paragraph appears in the newspapers stating that such and such a house is to be closed, another re-built or a new one opened. There is no appeal against these decisions. To the people of Carlisle alone is the right denied of being heard as to whether measures which are being ostensibly taken for their convenience and betterment have their approval. In all other towns, not a partition may be moved in a licensed house, or a fresh door broken, without the sanction of the licensing justices. In Carlisle, houses may be opened in virgin districts and others re-built at an expenditure of £25,000 – the cost of the new 'Apple Tree' in Lowther Street – as the management thinks fit."[40] The Local Advisory Committee was not completely independent, he said. Its constitution made it very difficult for public officials to criticize or take action against irregularities or definite law infringements where their own colleagues were indirectly concerned. For example, the presence of the Mayor gave immediate civic and official sanction. Moreover, the Advisory Committee had no real power, all decisions having to be ratified by the Home Office.[41]

An Anglican point of view was put by the Very Reverend Henry V. Stuart, Dean of Carlisle. He said the opinions generally of the citizens of Carlisle were that they preferred the scheme to the only other one which obtained in the country. He had visited the public houses and had found them much cleaner and better cared for than the average houses in working-class districts in other areas he had known. He believed the system was conducive to greater sobriety and more temperate habits. In 1925 the Bishop had conducted a survey among clergy in the parishes affected by the scheme. The majority were in favour: 25 out of 40. Of six who were against the scheme, three were against the principle of state-trading in liquor.[42]

Conclusions of the Commission

Having considered all the evidence, the Royal Commission concluded that the Carlisle scheme had provided well-appointed and well-conducted public houses which offered a satisfactory service, and efficient business management had contributed to its success from a financial point of view. The commission also accepted evidence of social advantages accruing to the community, not least a decrease in drunkenness. Two conclusions were reached, (a) that it was likely to reduce excess, while meeting the requirements of the moderate consumer; and (b) that monopoly under public ownership was likely to effect a much more rapid development of the policy of public-house improvement than was probable, or indeed possible, under the existing system.[43] The commission came out strongly in favour of public ownership. "It is our view that a prima-facie case of considerable strength has been made out in its favour. We think it theoretically sound: and that experience in Carlisle has gone far to show it to be sound in practice also."[44] Besides recommending the continuance of the Carlisle scheme it was thought desirable that public ownership should be applied elsewhere in circumstances which would submit the system to a further test both in the social and the financial sense. This did not imply a repetition of the Carlisle scheme, but a modification of it. Instead of it being under the control of the state and treasury, an independent board of management should be established which would report to parliament through the Home Secretary. A feature of the Carlisle scheme which could be incorporated in an extension of the principle was the Local Advisory Committee, composed of representatives of local authorities and other bodies. One of the difficulties revealed was the continuance within the prescribed area of licences which were not held by the state enterprise. It would be necessary for all licences to be taken over, and this might raise the question of severence compensation. The commission discussed the most appropriate procedure for initiating schemes of public ownership. It rejected the idea of a general enabling Act of Parliament delegating to a subordinate authority the right to take decisions. Instead, the commission favoured a National Licensing Commission having power to initiate inquiry and formulate schemes and that these schemes should not have force until parliament had had the opportunity of considering them.[45]

References

1. *British Gottenburg Experiments and Public House Trusts,* Rowntree and Sherwell (1903) pp. 93, 94.
2. 12th December 1900.
3. 16th January 1901.
4. Rowntree and Sherwell op cit p. 96.
5. Rowntree and Sherwell op cit p. 97.
6. Rowntree and Sherwell op cit p. 98.
7. UKA Report 1869 p. 29.
8. UKA Report 1893 pp. 53, 54.
9. UKA Report 1901 p. 18.
10. UKA Report 1901 p. 20.
11. *The Commonwealth as Publican* John Walker (1902).
12. *Public Control of the Liquor Traffic* Rowntree and Sherwell (1903).
13. Rowntree and Sherwell op cit. p. 184.
14. Rowntree and Sherwell op cit. pp. 185–88.
15. Rowntree and Sherwell op cit. p. 189.
16. Rowntree and Sherwell op cit. p. 173.
17. UKA Report 1905 p. 17 ff.
18. See p. 51.
19. *The Control of the Drink Trade* Henry Carter (2nd edition) 1919 p. 73.
20. 10th May 1915.
21. 11th May 1915.
22. Carter op cit. p. 174.
23. Op cit p. 199.
24. In view of the later role he played it is interesting to note that he was E. C. Sanders (later Sir Edgar Sanders, Director of the Brewers' Society).
25. General Manager's report 1920.
26. Carter op cit p. 222 ff.
27. 19,197 ff.
28. 19,644 ff.
29. 20,033 ff.
30. 20,879 ff.
31. 20,999.
32. 20,486 (3) ff.
33. 20,486 (7).
34. 20,580.
35. 20,750.
36. 21,190.
37. 22,869.
38. 23,155.
39. The Southborough Committee was set up in 1925 to consider various schemes of disinterested management. See *Alcohol and the Nation* George B. Wilson. Nicholson and Watson (1940) p. 177.
40. February 1927.
41. 21,586 ff.
42. 21,052.
43. Royal Commission on Licensing (England and Wales) 1929–31 Report p. 77.
44. Op cit p. 86.
45. Op cit pp. 86–88.

CHAPTER 8

THE TEMPERANCE SOCIETIES AND THE ROYAL COMMISSION

Twenty or more temperance spokesmen gave evidence to the Royal Commission, either in an individual capacity or as representatives of temperance and kindred organizations. It should, perhaps, be made plain at the outset that the temperance organizations did not ask for the appointment of the Royal Commission, but once it had been appointed there was no reluctance on their part to ensure that the temperance view on the main issues was presented to it. The principal organizations which had a tradition for legislative action were the United Kingdom Alliance, the Temperance Council of the Christian Churches, and the National British Women's Total Abstinence Union. Their representatives were among the prominent persons who appeared before the commission. There were others, whose evidence was possibly more compelling because it was better researched and, in one or two instances, more competently presented.

UKA evidence

The United Kingdom Alliance was represented by its Political and Literary Secretary, George Bailey Wilson, a graduate of London University who had practised as a solicitor in the Licensing Courts at Birmingham for ten years before joining the UKA. He later secured a doctorate for a thesis which was subsequently published[1] and which stood for a very long time as the definitive work on the many aspects of the supply and consumption of alcohol and the fiscal and legislative controls which had been introduced. Besides the UKA he spoke for the Temperance Committee of the Houses of Parliament, which consisted of members of both houses, who had expressed an interest in temperance reform legislation. Wilson told the commission that the problem they were concerned with differed from all other forms of social reform because it had to do solely with the operation and effects of a material agent, beverage alcohol. He assumed it was now proven, beyond all reasonable doubt, to be a disturbing factor in every sphere of human activity. Nevertheless, he wished to make it clear to the commission that he did not assume that alcohol was the only disturbing factor. The issue was not as clear cut. For example, was poverty due to drink, or drink to poverty? They did, in fact, react upon each other, and yet it was a well-established fact that most drinking and most drunkenness occurred when trade was good and the country was prosperous. Neither was it possible to isolate the drinking problem of individuals from society as a whole. He quoted the *Brewers' Gazette* which indicated that the trade itself was aware of the far-reaching social consequences of drinking, "We deal in a ware, the misuse of which brings sorrow in its train; and modern conditions have made the exigencies and affairs of society so interdependent that it is no longer possible for the individual to work out his own damnation, in whatsoever fashion he chooses to do it, without society as a whole being subtly affected."[2] He dealt, too, with the economic wastage of materials in the manufacture of all forms of liquor, particularly in the distilling of spirits. He quoted Sir Daniel Hall of the Ministry of Agriculture who in 1926 said, "Another item of waste which would have to be eliminated in case of stern necessity is the conversion of potential food into alcoholic drink. Without going so far as to say that beer possesses no food value, it has certainly not half that of the materials which could have been grown from the land thus used for the production of drink".[3]

Although later in his evidence Wilson referred at some length to the impact that temperance societies had had in persuading large numbers of people to be total abstainers and thus reducing consumption, he dealt fairly with a number of legislative measures. A controversial issue, particularly in the early part of the twentieth century, had been the granting of compensation for redundant licences. The United Kingdom Alliance had been foremost among the temperance bodies in opposing it. He acknowledged that the intention of those who had initiated the legislation which had made it possible to pay compensation, was to get rid of an immense number of redundant licences quickly. It was also the intention of parliament that the licensee should receive decent compensation. In fact the licensee received only 13.2 per cent of the compensation; 86.8 per cent going to other people, chiefly the brewers. The average sum received by licensees was £126 and by others £986. He told the commission that in the administration of the act the wishes of parliament had not been met. Members of parliament, he said, never intended the publican to receive such a small share of the allocation of compensation.

The brewers seemed to be doing well not only in respect of compensation, but in their normal trading, and he cited statistics which referred to breweries in the Lancashire area. In 1913 the dividends for these companies was very low, but by 1927 they were much higher, indicating what he called the "enormous prosperity" of the Lancashire breweries. Even so, he thought the present time was not one in which reliable deductions could be made about trends in consumption of liquor. Statistical studies had shown that this depended upon the condition of trade generally, which was almost a more powerful governing factor than price. Consumption at that time appeared to be low, but they were not entitled to say that the situation was satisfactory until it had been tested by a period of expanding trade. Another aspect of the economy of drinking was the proportion of personal income, on average spent on intoxicants. If a man drank a quart of beer a day, he spent a shilling a day on drink. This worked out at £18 a year. If a man earned £3 per week, six weeks of his earnings would be spent on beer. This meant that a man and his family would have to exist on 46 weeks' pay per year. On such an income there would be no money for holidays, for saving or for provisions for the future. It had been shown that in many cases the proportion of income spent on alcohol was greater as the social status of the person became lower. Thus manual labourers spent proportionately more than did non-manual workers, and efficiency suffered. Besides this, there were other economic factors. Revenue from tax on intoxicating liquors was not net revenue because the cost of collecting it was heavy. Moreover there had to be taken into account the costs of ill health, deaths attributable to drink, domestic unhappiness, crime, lunacy and poverty.

Wilson told the commission that economic factors were not the only ones which affected the level of consumption. He quoted the opinion of Sydney and Beatrice Webb in their *History of Liquor Licensing in England*, that the most important part of this history since 1830 was to be found in "the wonderful story of the growth of temperance organizations, and their effect in changing public opinion." This change, they said, had been reflected to only a small extent in legislation and in total consumption. In fact, since the Webbs made this judgement in 1903, the changed attitude had been reflected in a fall in consumption. A Labour Party Committee report published in 1923 said it was not clear to what extent the aggregate decline in total consumption had been due to an increase in the proportion of total abstainers, and to a diminution in the daily consumption of moderate drinkers. That the growth of the temperance sentiment was an important factor in the decline in consumption seemed beyond dispute. The wonderful thing was, he declared, the small cost in money of the actions of the temperance societies. While the liquor trade was spending £2 million to £4 million in a year on drink advertising, the total expenditure of all temperance societies in England and Wales since 1860 had not reached £4,500,000. The strength of the temperance movement was in the voluntary activity of the tens of thousands of people who worked unstintingly for it. There had also been a big change in the attitude of the churches. He said that in the early days of the United Kingdom Alliance it had been difficult to secure even a free church schoolroom for a meeting. The Primitive Methodists had been the only ones to allow it. One final indication of the role played by the temperance movement was the presence in the House of Commons of a substantial number of abstainers which showed that constituencies did not consider total abstinence to be a bar to political success.[4]

Temperance medical evidence

One of the main spokesmen for the temperance organizations was Dr Courtenay C. Weeks, who said that while he recognized there had been a great improvement in the last century so far as the results of drinking were concerned, there remained a grave national problem. Contributing to this improvement had been the spread of education, the increased amenities of life, the extension of social services, and wider opportunities for culture and travel. Of themselves, there had been and there must continue to be, progressive education as to the true nature of alcoholic liquor and its effect on individual and social life. He admitted that alcoholic indulgence was not the only cause of social deterioration, but it was certainly one of them.

He spoke of his wartime experience among the forces. "I was at Fort Pitt military hospital at Chatham" he said, "and in those days it was really terrible to see the effect of alcoholic indulgence had upon some of our wounded who were well enough to go out." He quoted the 1920 report of the civil medical authority which took over examining recruits which said, "there was not a sufficient number of men perfectly fit in the country to supply all needs as laid down by the Government". It was reckoned that there were over one million men so mentally or physically defective that they could render no direct help to this country, and the three most serious factors to account for this were alcoholism, venereal disease and mental deficiency. It was his view that the consumption of alcohol was a major cause of the low state of public health. He gave examples from private practice and from hospital service of how, in recent years, the use of alcohol in the treatment of all manner of conditions had been abandoned, often with outstanding beneficial results. He quoted the judgement of the book *Alcohol: its action on the human organism;* published by the government for the Medical Research Council, "The popular belief in alcohol as a remedy is largely based on the illusion that it has an important stimulant action on the heart, on the respiration and on the vital activities in general. Rational medicine has long abandoned this belief, but it still lingers in popular practice". In the light of such a judgement, Dr Weeks saw something wholly misleading in advertisements which had appeared at that time, e.g. "Whisky is the best protection against and remedy for influenza: a direct heart stimulant of great value" and "A glass of good beer is as nourishing as a glass of good milk." (Those were the days before the Advertising Standards Authority!)

He devoted considerable time to the effect of drinking on home life and the welfare of children, and insisted that alcohol was a menace to child life at all stages of its existence. He referred to the work of Dr Bertholet on the effects of alcohol on the sex glands, which was to produce changes in the gland cell. The germ cell if and where it came to birth was affected by the alcoholic habits of the parents. When there was gross excess of drinking, sterility might result. He also quoted the work of Stockard and Pearl. Sir Benjamin Stockard became a teetotaller as a result of his experiments with guinea pigs. He found that although there appeared to be no deleterious effect on their bodies, the germ cells were definitely affected. He proved statistically that alcohol could affect the male germ plasm to the detriment of the child. Alcohol was a selective poison, it picked out the weak and destroyed them, and left the strong. At the foetal stage the child was utterly dependent upon the blood of the mother for the supply of oxygen through the plasma. Three poisons are able to pass through the placenta into the unborn child, lead, syphilis and alcohol. Alcohol is so diffusible that within ten minutes it passes into the blood and thence into the placenta and the blood of the unborn child and later the mother can give it through the milk. "The law of the land prohibits giving alcohol to an infant under five years" observed Dr Weeks. "But a pregnant and nursing mother gives it to her baby every time she takes alcohol." In the post-natal period the effect of drink in the home can also have serious consequences for the psychological stability of the child.

He dealt at length with some of the social consequences of the excessive consumption of alcohol and from a historical point of view it is important to refer to some of the evidence and the inferences drawn, chiefly because it is doubtful whether some of it would be as confidently advanced today. In support of the statement that "alcohol inhibits and interferes with normal growth in all forms of life", Dr Weeks quoted various opinions, particularly from Herefordshire, of the effect of cider drinking among schoolchildren. Letters from headmasters expressed the view that the prevalence of cider drinking at home seemed to result in children being stunted in growth and mentally dull. The County Medical Officer of Health for Herefordshire was quoted as saying that dandelion and cowslip wine were common drinks for children at home and these also had a deleterious effect on the growth of the child, as well as on health generally. Samples of home-made ciders and wines taken from various parts of Herefordshire and Radnorshire had been analysed and showed a high-alcoholic content. Dr Weeks said that one of the results of cider drinking in Herefordshire had been to produce in the past, and to a certain extent in the present, a good deal of insanity. No doubt the inter-marriage of Herefordshire people, and the hereditary effect of more extreme alcoholism in by-gone generations, were powerful factors. He said there were still signs of the effect of these factors in Herefordshire where figures for insanity were higher than in Wiltshire or Lincolnshire which, apart from cider drinking, were comparable agricultural counties. They were also higher than for the whole of England. He said he wanted to press the point of insanity because successive medical officers for the Herefordshire county mental hospital had, in the past, referred to alcohol in cider as a very powerful co-operating factor in the production of insanity. It had to be remembered that at that time farmers paid part of their workers' wages in the form of free cider.

The effect of drinking on industrial and commercial efficiency was another aspect to which Dr Weeks called attention. He said that even small quantities of alcohol interfered with the actual co-ordination of hand and eye, while at the same time it gave the individual a false sense of his performance. He quoted the results of various surveys which indicated that efficiency increased and accidents decreased in factories where consumption of alcohol had been reduced. At the time the commission was taking evidence, the relation between drinking and driving had not the significance it had later. Even so, Dr Weeks referred to rules which applied to some public and private transport companies. Of 405 replies received from local authorities and public and private companies, 88 per cent of municipalities had an absolute binding rule or understanding that there was to be no drinking of liquor or entering public houses while on duty. Of public and private companies who replied, 72 per cent had a definite rule or understanding that there was to be no drinking while on duty. It had also been found that these employers had a much lower accident rate and death rate both from accidents and from cirrhosis. Many managers stressed that any breach of these regulations led to instant dismissal.

Having dealt with various other aspects of the matter, such as the prevalence and control of drinking in H.M. Forces, the evidence from insurance companies of the greater expectation of life of abstainers, and the relation between alcoholic indulgence and prostitution, Dr Weeks addressed himself to "Alcoholism". This he defined as, "The morbid effects of the excessive use of alcoholic beverages, as manifested in abnormal states of body and/or of mind".[5] There were four main manifestations of alcoholism:

1. Acute, which was either simple drunkenness, or sudden maniacal outburst, with homicidal or suicidal tendencies.
2. Chronic, which was a general condition of deranged bodily function with some impairment of mental powers. Such a condition rendered the

person less resistent to infection, and accentuated the incidence and severity of such diseases as gout, arterial degeneration, diabetes, rheumatoid arthritis, and skin infection. This can also be a more specific condition in which alcoholic influence fastens on one organ of the body, for example in cirrhosis of the liver.

3. Delirium tremens which is the end result of continuous alcoholic indulgence brought on by shock.
4. Dipsomania, which is a periodical yielding to a desire for alcohol by someone who may be abstinent between attacks.

He quoted a recent statement of Sir William Willcox, a leading toxicologist, that alcohol was the first poison in England. At one time alcoholism was thought to be a problem confined to the lower classes, in fact, education of the upper classes was now an urgent need. He referred the commission to the *Lancet* of June 1929 where it was stated, "Alcoholism has for several generations been regarded as a disease of the poorer classes. It is, however, becoming increasingly obvious that the balance is shifting, and some authorities consider that before long the incidence will preponderate among persons of wealth and leisure." He thought this was already the case and that the upper classes of society needed specific education as to the properties and effects of alcohol.[6]

Evidence from women

The representative of the National British Women's Total Abstinence Union, with 160,000 members, was Mrs Randolf Clarkson. She said that the policy of her organization had always been local option. She argued that owners of land might, if they chose, insert clauses in their deeds forbidding the sale or lease of land for buildings which were to be licensed for the sale of intoxicating liquor. The privilege of the few should be extended to all. The wishes of the inhabitants of an area should be ascertained by ballot before any licence was granted. This should particularly apply to new housing estates, where the inhabitants had often moved from slum areas devastated by the influence of public houses, and hoped to get away from them. Social amenities which were free from alcohol ought to be provided on new housing estates.

It was appropriate that a women's temperance organization should refer especially to the influence of alcohol on home life. Mrs Clarkson described how people living on small incomes were often ill-fed and ill-clad because money went on drink. Parents who went drinking at night deprived children of companionship, security and sleep. She quoted the Principal of the National Children's Home, who had said, "In this work we have constant and abundant evidence of the close connection between drinking and child destitution. Very many children who are in the Home at the present time would not be in our care but for intemperance on the part of one, and sometimes both parents."[7] Mrs Clarkson supported her case with evidence provided by the National Children's Home at Highbury Park, London, by social workers, by a medical officer of health, by a Liverpool sanitary inspector and by a probation visitor. The sanitary inspector had said, "My experience was that the houses of teetotallers were more comfortable, the children healthier, happier, better fed and clothed than where parents indulge in alcoholic drink . . . I have found such contrasts in conditions where men are earning the same money – comfort in one house, and next door, confusion, broken furniture, children unhealthy, crippled, and ill-fed".[8] The deleterious effects of drink were seen not only in home life, but in the incidence of moral downfall among young women. The evidence of a social worker was that young prostitutes said they could not live the life they were living without drink.

Among the recommendations of the National British Women's Total Abstinence Union was the provision of non-alcoholic refreshment facilities at shipyards, docks and markets. Where such canteen facilities had been provided they had been extensively used, with evident beneficial results in efficiency. A farmer had testified that since a canteen had been provided at Hereford, there had been a "marked diminution of drunken drovers, and dumb animals have gained thereby". Since the supply of coffee, "the lads no longer acquired a taste for beer". Mrs Clarkson did not think that improved public houses would have the same beneficial effect.[9]

Salvation Army evidence

Because no group of people came in closer proximity to drunkenness than the Salvation Army, the evidence of Commissioner David Lamb was particularly important. He said that the Salvation Army had come to the conclusion that hard drinking and drunkenness were not now the greatest social evil. There had been a marked improvement in recent years in the appearance and conduct of both men and women, and in the general condition of the districts usually described as slums. Salvation Army officers believed that the earlier closing of public houses and the higher prices charged for liquor had contributed greatly to the improved conditions. Gambling and betting were great curses in slum areas. Commissioner Lamb thought the moral effect of the *black list* had been considerable on a large number of people. What was needed so far as licensing administration was concerned was a more thorough scrutiny of the "black spots" where a reduction in the number of public houses was very desirable, and attention given to clubs so that police had the power of inspection of such premises. With regard to children and public houses, the opinion of Salvation Army officers was that it was better for children to be left outside the premises than to make special provision for them inside. Where such provisions had been made, Commissioner Lamb saw little difference between the accommodation for children and the public bars. What he had seen was simply an evasion of the act.[10]

Temperance Council of the Christian Churches

The views of the temperance societies were predictable, and when the Revd E. Benson Perkins, Superintendent Minister of the Birmingham Central Mission of the Wesleyan Church presented the case for the

Temperance Council of the Christian Churches, he reiterated much of what other temperance spokesmen had said. The main policy of the council he represented was local option based on the principle that the decision on the provision of licensed premises in an area should be in the hands of the people who lived there.

A parliamentary temperance view

Quite the most well-documented evidence was presented by Ernest Winterton, Member of Parliament for Loughborough who, though he was not representing a particular temperance organization, spoke as a well-known "temperance man".[11]

He told the commission that he had made a special study of the relation between the liquor problem and housing conditions. He had carried out a survey himself of different housing situations. At the outset of his evidence he said that the conclusion he had drawn was that things were "very much better than they were", but that the propinquity of a public house had an exceedingly bad influence on any district. It affected the morale of the people, inducing them to dirtiness and lack of care of property. In a poor area of Leicester which had many public houses, he saw the contrast between two adjoining streets. In one, with a chapel at a corner of the street, the property was tidy and well cared for, and when he visited, it was quiet and clear. Enquiries showed that a number of the residents and still more of the children attended the chapel. In the next street, where there was an off-licence, the property was dilapidated and dirty, and at the time of his visit groups of women were gossiping, and dirty children were playing in the gutter.

In Nottingham he visited very bad housing conditions in an area with numerous public houses. Statistics relating to various areas in the city showed that both the general death rate and infant mortality rate bore some relation to the number of public houses, as well as to the air space available. He told the commission that while the drink factor could not be isolated and separated from other factors, it was clear that the drink trade must be under serious suspicion as an accomplice and an accessory to every other enemy of health and well-being. His surveys included a study of Ancoats in Manchester. This was a district of small and very overcrowded houses, many of which were old, dark, dilapidated and lacking either larders or bathrooms. Some were infested with rats and beetles. Although grossly overcrowded, a team of investigators from Manchester University Settlement found that two-thirds of householders and lodgers expressed themselves as having no desire to move to newer districts. The usual reason for this attitude was that they could not afford the rent and there were undoubtedly cases where actual low wages prevented such a removal. However, even if the people of Ancoats spent no more on intoxicating liquor than any other district in England and Wales, its average expenditure per family of five at 13*s.* 3*d.* a week would have been sufficient to pay the extra rent on a new housing estate. In the area covered by the survey there were 138 retail establishments, of which 18 were public houses, one was a licensed shop and there were four pawnbrokers. In the area were eleven grocers and nine bakers. The Medical Officer of Health had said that of several hundred families which had been transferred from Hulme, another over-licensed area of Manchester, to the "unlicensed" Wilbraham Road estate, a large proportion of people from the slum area had made satisfactory tenants.

Surveys in Liverpool, Birkenhead, Birmingham and the East End of London had confirmed him in the belief that the necessary preliminary to all schemes of housing improvements was to clear out the public houses from the district. When he visited the Custom House area near the Victoria Dock he found ten public houses in the Victoria Dock Road (thirty years earlier there had been 19). In spite of drizzling rain he found many children in the streets. They were sitting on the pavement outside public houses. On Saturdays he discovered they were there from 2 p.m. to 10 p.m. In Bethnal Green he found the public houses thronged with people. The effect on children was baneful. It was the practice of young mothers to go out shopping at about 10.30 a.m. when they would meet their friends and make their way to the "pub" for "just one drink" when it opened at 11 a.m. Often they became oblivious to the passage of time and remained drinking and talking until it was almost time for the children to go back to school. When the children appeared at the public house asking for their dinners they were given a penny for some chips. This was the midday meal for hundreds of children.

Winterton told the commission that he concluded there was an intimate and inseparable relation between drink, bad housing, dirt and neglect of home and children. He said, "I believe it to be impossible for any human being who conscientiously and with an unbiased mind investigates these conditions to arrive at any other conclusion than that there is no hope of improving the social conditions of these districts so long as the public house remains as a constant menace to the health and well-being of the people who live there."[12] People were attracted to the public house for its warmth, its light, music or entertainment, because their own homes were so denuded of these advantages, and conversely sometimes their homes were so denuded of these advantages because they were habitués of the public house.

Turning to the current legislation, Winterton said that under the 1904 Licensing Act there had not been the rapid reduction of licences as compared with the pre-1904 period which the country had been led to expect. The act had operated to consolidate the trade rather than weaken its position. At the commencement of the act the consumption of beer was 34,220,000 standard barrels, ten years later it was 34,130,000 barrels. The consumption of spirits had continued to decline, as it had for the past 35 years. The chief reason beer consumption had been maintained was because when justices chose licences for extinction they adopted the "spread-over" method; that is, the closure of, say, one of 50 public houses simply meant that custom was spread over the remaining 49; thus there was no appreciable reduction in consumption. Winterton quoted Joseph Chamberlain, "a very acute licensing reformer" who held it was necessary to give a shock to the drinking habits of a neighbourhood if one was to see an improvement. The trade had simply got rid of worthless licences without great sacrifice. It was an excellent bargain for the brewers, for every licence extinguished carried with it not only its own inherent value and compensation, but also the accumulated value of the consumption. The "Compensation Act" (i.e. the 1904 Licensing Act) even after nine years' operation did not reduce beer output at all. In 1904 production was 34,220,000 barrels, and in 1913 it was 35,250,000 barrels, an increase of 103,000. Yet over £4 million in compensation had been paid on the presumption that the barrelage of some 12,000 on-licences had been extinguished. The consumption of the extinguished licences had been spread to the public houses which remained, and so, compensation had been paid for nothing. In the same decade the population rose from 33,378,000 in 1903 to 39,919,000 in 1913, an increase of about ten per cent. Beer consumption did not go up at the same rate.[13]

Temperance reaction

Having studied the evidence presented to the Royal Commission, by representatives of the Temperance Movement it is difficult not to reach the conclusion that it suffered from lack of co-ordination. Too many representatives demanded a hearing and so the temperance point of view became diffused and repetitive. If one legislative objective emerged more clearly than others it was to secure local option. This was really a legacy of Sir Wilfrid Lawson's relentless campaign as a member of parliament to secure prohibition of the liquor trade by the will of the people. In every session of parliament while he was in the house he introduced a bill to effect this reform. Usually it made little progress, and there never was a chance that such a measure would reach the statute book. It was surprising, therefore, to find such an astute temperance leader as the Revd Henry Carter inserting Reservations to the Report of the Royal Commission pleading for a determinative referendum on proposals affecting liquor licensing. He was hopeful that at some time the people would vote for the elimination of the trade. It was a vain hope. Had the necessary legislation to effect local option been passed, there was little prospect that the British people would have voted in favour of outright prohibition. Indeed, some of the restrictive legislation passed by parliament might have had a different fate had it been submitted to the will of a fickle electorate. In the event, the Royal Commission did not recommend local option in any form. It did, however, recommend more effective control of the supply of liquor in clubs, and this pleased the temperance reformers. However, since the temperance representatives appeared to have no major common objectives, it was not surprising that the Royal Commission's recommendations offered them very little for mutual congratulations.

The uncompromising attitude of the United Kingdom Alliance was reflected in an editorial comment on the Royal Commission's Report in *Alliance News.*

> *The fundamental assumption made in the Report is that the liquor traffic in one form or other is, and will forever continue to be, a necessary and permanent English*

Institution. The Report does not seem to consider that the consumption of intoxicating liquors is essentially bad for the nation, though it may be dangerous for the individual, and its attention is therefore directed entirely to its regulation and not to its elimination, which is quite clearly ruled out even in the subsidiary form of local veto. The Report is therefore fundamentally disappointing to all who believe that drink is a bad thing and ought to be got rid of. It will, however, be especially interesting to those who indulge the vain hope that it is possible so to regulate the traffic that it shall be practically harmless to the nation.[14]

Having said that, the editorial admits that from the standpoint of legislative control, many of the commission's recommendations for the amendment of the licensing system were undoubtedly useful. It gave qualified support to the recommendation to appoint a National Licensing Commission. The real danger was that such a commission could cripple the work of local justices. As might have been expected *Alliance News* rejected totally any extension of the Carlisle scheme. While admitting the need to improve the accommodation for the licensee and his family, the editorial was suspicious of indications that recommendations to improve the general facilities at public houses were intended to encourage "a much larger concept".

We believe it to be true to say that the number of persons using public-houses is steadily diminishing, and that today a majority of the adult population – particularly under twenty-five years – never enter a public-house; and it is because we desire that the public house population shall continue to diminish that we feel compelled to protest against any schemes for rehabilitating these places which will make them general places of resort for the future youth and parenthood of our land, as indicated in the ominous statement (para. 681) that "as the standard of conditions in licensed premises advances there will be a justification for a progressive, though carefully guarded, extension of the facilities at present allowed by law in respect of the admission of children. From the year 1830 the legislature has steadily advanced in its restrictive policy as to the relation of children to the liquor trade, and temperance reformers throughout the country and many others will oppose strongly a retrograde policy which contemplates even the possibility of the progressive extension foreshadowed.[15]

The editorial expressed the disappointment generally felt in the Temperance Movement at the rejection by the commission of the policy of local option. There was equal disappointment that the commission had come out in favour of public ownership of the liquor trade. However, the recognition by the commission that there was public approval for the present "permitted hours" was welcomed, as was the decision not to interfere with the powers of licensing justices. Naturally the commission was congratulated on having almost stepped outside their terms of reference to recommend that "every child ought to receive specific and systematic instruction as to the properties of alcohol", and to urge the adoption of *Alcohol: its action on the human organism,* an official publication of the Education Department, as the basis of the instruction. The editorial concluded on a generous note, "Our strong objections to certain important recommendations do not blind us to the good points in the Report".[16]

The conciliatory sentiment expressed did not prevail in the discussion which arose in the Temperance Movement following the publication of the report. In 1932 Wilson Black succeeded Lord Rhayader as President of the United Kingdom Alliance. This coincided with the publication of the Royal

Commission's Report, and with a nine-point programme of temperance reform associated with the name of Henry Carter which appeared in the *Christian World*, 11th February 1932 (p. 7).

1. Reduction of Licences by closing all redundant licensed premises following a survey by Justices.
2. Informative polls on applications for new licences in new housing areas.
3. Abolition of removals of licences as e.g. from centre of city to its suburbs.
4. Control of supply of intoxicants in clubs setting up a clubs Registration Authority.
5. Appointment of 10 p.m. throughout the country as the normal closing hour of liquor bars.
6. Increase of powers of Local Licensing Authorities over the liquor trade.
7. Provisions to deal with menace of 'medicated' wines and prohibition of unsigned medical testimonials published to advertise any kind of intoxicant.
8. New endorsement of Sunday closing of licensed premises in Wales and inclusion of registered clubs within scope of Welsh Sunday closing law.
9. Setting up of National Licensing Commissions for England and Wales.

In his biography of *Robert Wilson Black,* Henry Townsend commented "Mr Carter's policy was in sharp opposition to the Declaration of Principles by the United Kingdom Alliance. The Nine-Point Programme in the *Christian World* deeply disturbed Black, and after consulting several friends he went into action".[17] His reply to the Nine-Point Programme was also published in the *Christian World*[18] and copies of it were sent to twenty-eight leading Free Church ministers and laymen inviting their signatures. Only five declined. The chief issue of controversy was the Royal Commission's recommendation for public ownership of the liquor trade, which Henry Carter, as a member of the commission, had supported.

The issue aroused what seemed at times to be a traditional antipathy between the United Kingdom Alliance and the Wesleyans on what turned out to be the fruitless argument about whether the alcohol problem would be solved by "moral suasion" or legislation. When the United Kingdom Alliance was founded in 1853 to campaign for the suppression of the liquor trade by legislation, the Wesleyan Conference was reluctant to support it. However, in the September issue of the *Methodist Temperance Magazine* in 1870 it was reported that "for the first time" a respectful and pleasant response had been sent from the conference to the United Kingdom Alliance. The Wesleyan Conference reiterated its conviction that "moral suasion" rather than legislation was the best method to adopt, but also admitted that the legalized facilities were a hindrance to the work of the churches and the well-being of society. In 1872, in reply to another memorial from the United Kingdom Alliance, the conference reaffirmed the principles embodied in its Resolution of 1870.[19] The relationship between the Wesleyan Conference and the United Kingdom Alliance was never one of complete cordiality. The Revd Henry Carter, the acknowledged temperance leader in the Wesleyan Church, was not forgiven by the United Kingdom Alliance for accepting an invitation to serve on the Liquor Control Board set up by the government during the First World War, on which a brewer also served. And so it was not difficult for the United Kingdom Alliance to fall out with him when, as a member of the Royal Commission, he signed the majority report which included the recommendation for public ownership of the liquor trade. This was the issue which locked the Temperance Movement in controversy in the 1930s and which led to a serious breach between the Wesleyan Conference and the United Kingdom Alliance.

On 18th October 1932 the alliance called a National Convention in association with its annual meetings in Manchester. Every temperance organization was invited to appoint delegates, and these included the churches. About two hundred bodies were represented.[20] Of the main Protestant denominations the Wesleyan Church was the only absentee. Presumably because Henry Carter was so closely identified with it, the Temperance Council of the Christian Churches was not represented either, though the corresponding council in Wales did send a delegate. Wilson Black presided. Although the convention was in one respect a centenary celebration of the founding of the Temperance Movement in Britain by the Seven Men of Preston, its main purpose was to respond to the report of the Royal Commission. The first resolution passed by the convention was a salute to the Seven Men of Preston who, in 1832, had signed what was thought to be the first total-abstinence pledge.[21] The second resolution adopted by the convention may be regarded as the official response of the Temperance Movement to the Royal Commission's report. It read:

THAT

i. *This convention notes that the evidence and findings of the Royal Commission on Licensing constitute a grave indictment of the drink traffice, and justify the call for its suppression.*

ii. *The Convention regrets therefore that the Commission base all their Recommendations on the assumption that the Traffic must and will continue, and make no proposals whereby the electorate, if so minded, could rid themselves of the drink evil.*

iii. *Among the Recommendations the Convention finds useful proposals for the reform of the Licensing System and for the stricter supervision of clubs.*

iv. *It warmly endorses the Recommendation that all children shall receive systematic instruction in the nature and effect of alcohol.*

v. *While welcoming the Commission's approval of Sunday Closing in Wales, and its Recommendation that it should be extended to clubs there, it regrets the refusal of the Commission to recommend the same reform for England.*

vi. *It finds no grounds for reversing its considered objections to all forms of State Management and Public Ownership of the Traffic.*

vii. *The Convention notes that the Commission devoted much attention to the 'Improved Public-House' but is convinced that the mischievous results of the Traffic are due almost wholly to the nature of drink rather than to the conditions under which it is sold, and that the added attractions of the "Improved Public House" are designed to increase the number of drinkers.*

viii. *The Convention protests against the suggestion of the Commissioners that it would be desirable to provide increased facilities for children on licensed premises, and urges every Temperance Society to resist this retrograde suggestion.*

ix. *While therefore, the Convention recognises as valuable certain of the Recommendations, it cannot find in them an adequate basis for Temperance agitation. It refuses to accept the view underlying the Recommendations of the Commission that the drink traffic is a permanent part of the National life, and it calls upon the Temperance workers of the country for renewed vigour in pressing home the overwhelming case against drink, which has been established by a hundred years of Temperance agitation and education.*[22]

Although it seems that neither the Wesleyan Church nor the Temperance Council of the Christian Churches were represented at the convention to endorse the policy relating to the Report of the Royal Commission, a serious split in the temperance forces was avoided. In 1932 the three main branches of Methodism, the Wesleyans, the Primitive Methodists and the United Methodists came together to form the Methodist Church. Henry Carter became General Secretary of the Temperance and Social Welfare Department of the new church, and no doubt, found his views being modified in the new situation. Discussions were opened between his department and the United Kingdom Alliance with the object of finding common objectives. On 9th November 1933 "An agreed Temperance Programme" was signed by the Revd Luke Wiseman (President of the Conference), the Revd Henry Carter and Lord Rochester (General Secretary and Treasurer of the Temperance and Social Welfare Department), representing the Methodist Church and R. Wilson Black, Lord Rhayader and H. Cecil Heath, representing the United Kingdom Alliance.

The text was as follows:

We, the undersigned, have considered carefully the means by which unity of action within the English Temperance Movement may be achieved, and recognizing that there have existed, for many years past, honest divergences of judgement as to certain legislative proposals, are none the less convinced that there is substantial unity within the movement regarding a wide range of important reforms urgently needed in the public interest.

We present, therefore, the following plain statement for the consideration, and we hope, the endorsement of our colleagues in the Temperance movement throughout the country. The statement defines a common aim, and indicates that, with mutual respect for differing convictions on certain named subjects, we believe that a union of forces can straightway be effected in support of an agreed programme of educational and legislative Temperance work. We affirm as follows:

1. *Our common aim is the abandonment of the use of intoxicating liquors throughout the country.*
2. *We recognise that differences exist among social reformers regarding the policies of National Prohibition, Public Ownership and Control of the drink trade, and public house improvement. A common policy on these wide issues is not in sight, but a frank recognition of this diversity of judgement makes more necessary active co-operation in promoting the reforms specified in the final paragraph.*
3. *We are in agreement that people should be given the right to protect themselves, through a vote of local electors, against the liquor traffic in their own areas.*
4. *We are prepared actively to co-operate also in the public advocacy on the following immediate programme of educational and legislative Temperance reform:*
    1. *Advocacy of personal total abstinence from all intoxicating liquor.*
    2. *Efficient Temperance instruction in all schools on the basis of the new manual of the Board of Education –* Handbook of Suggestions on Health Education.
    3. *More rapid reduction of liquor licences.*

4. *Abolition of 'Removals' of licences, in accord with the Recommendations of the Royal Commission on Licensing.*
5. *Polls in new housing areas on application of new licences.*
6. *Effective control of the supply of liquor in registered clubs.*
7. *10 p.m. to be the latest normal closing hour for liquor bars.*
8. *Legislation to counter the mischief created by the sale of so-called 'medicated wines'.*
9. *Extension of Welsh Sunday Closing Act to registered clubs.*
10. *The advocacy for Sunday closing for England.*
11. *More effective and more uniform administration of the licensing laws.*
12. *Prohibition of the public advertisement of intoxicating liquors.*

To the foregoing Programme we invite the adhesion of the Temperance movement.

Wilson Black was frequently quoted as saying that the right policy for the Temperance Movement to adopt in respect of legislation was "to ask for what we want, and take what we can get". This might have applied to the "Agreed Temperance Programme". For the sake of agreement with the Methodist Church the United Kingdom Alliance was prepared to accept differences of opinion on such major issues as prohibition, public ownership of the liquor trade and public-house improvement. And the Methodist Church found no difficulty in agreeing with the remainder of the manifesto. The signing of this agreement registered the comprehensive response of the Temperance Movement to the findings and recommendations of the Royal Commission, and the end of controversy and division. Nearly half a century later, it seems that this agreement also marked the end of effective action for temperance reform, for none of the twelve points of the " 'programme' of educational and legislative temperance reform" has been achieved.

References

1. *Alcohol and the Nation* George B. Wilson, Nicholson and Watson (1940).
2. 1916.
3. Quoted in 25,541.
4. 25,632.
5. 24,946.
6. 24,673 ff.
7. 25,331.
8. 25.340.
9. 25,309 ff.
10. 34,423 ff.
11. 27,881 ff.
12. 33,790.
13. 33,736 ff.
14. *Alliance News* February 1932 p. 15.
15. *Alliance News* February 1932 p. 15.
16. *Alliance News* February 1932 p. 16.
17. *Robert Wilson Black* Henry Townsend (1954) p. 178.
18. Henry Townsend op cit. p. 178.
19. *Drink: Ups and Downs of Methodist Attitudes to Temperance* Thompson Brake (1974) p. 17, 18 see also p. 19 ff.
20. *Alliance News* November 1932 p. 122.
21. Thompson Brake op cit p. 18 (Note 1).
22. *Alliance News* November 1932 pp. 122, 123.

CHAPTER 9

THE SIXTIES AND LICENCE FOR LIBERATION

A leap in sequence from the 1930s to the 1960s which we have now taken requires an explanation. In the first place, the impact of the Second World War on the alcohol scene in Britain was in no way as far reaching as was that of the First World War. In the second place, it has seemed most appropriate to incorporate the main features of the period between the thirties and the sixties in subsequent chapters which deal with such specific matters as the purpose of licensing legislation, drink advertising, drink and the young and some of the contemporary responses to the alcohol problem in the second half of the twentieth century. The sixties were so distinctive sociologically, and especially in regard to the development of drinking habits, that a separate chapter is now devoted to that decade.

In the perspective of history the 1960s will almost certainly be seen as the decade in which the alcohol problem in Britain began massively to increase, and when some of the official inquiries initiated at the time and soon after into its causes and possible remedies were, almost without exception, wrong in their conclusions and recommendations. As we shall see, it was left to independent researchers to produce the evidence on which more well-considered judgements began to emerge in the 1970s.

The ethos of the period

The Licensing Act 1961, the first major revision of licensing law for forty years, needs to be seen in relation to the ethos of the period. There were clear signs of the emergence of a new culture, brought in by the generation of "the bulge". The dimension of this phenomenon was described in *The Youth Service in England and Wales,*[1] the report of a committee appointed by the Minister of Education in November 1958. This stated that the release of young men from the obligation of national service, plus the arrival of "the bulge" would make the Youth Service responsible for about a million *more* young people in 1964 than it had to cater for in 1958. The absolute increase on the 1958 figures would have dropped to about 770,000 in 1973, but thereafter the number was likely to increase. "In 1960 the number of young people aged 15–20 inclusive will be over three and a half million."[2] There had never been so many teenagers as there were in the late 1950s and early 1960s. They were everywhere. They did not so much take over the society in which they had been brought up, as create one of their own. The young were caught up in what is sometimes called "Beatlemania", a cult of hysterical adulation for their folk heroes, the Beatles from Liverpool. This was the most dramatic expression of the new culture, but "mania" could have been applied to obsessions of dress, of coffee bars, of scooters and other short-lived characteristics of behaviour.

The committee which produced *The Youth Service in England and Wales* was not the only group which addressed itself to "the problem of youth". They all appeared to reach similar conclusions: young people were taller and heavier than those of previous generations, they matured earlier, and faced emotional developments and strains at an earlier age. At the same time they were facing the prospect of manhood and womanhood when the older generations were less sure of their behavioural norms. "There does not seem to be at the heart of society a courageous and exciting struggle for a particular moral and spiritual life – only a passive neutral commitment to things as they are. One cannot, in fact, indict the young for the growth of delinquency without also indicting the older generations for apathy and indifference to the deeper things of the heart."[3] Frightened of losing the respect and affection of the young, the parents in particular posed as admirers of the new generation. Reluctantly they were driven to admit that there was no way of recalling their children to the kind of fixed standards which had largely determined their own early life style. And so was born the permissive society. This is meant to be a statement of fact and not a value judgement on the life style of the sixties. In that decade, and since, there has been a revolution in the realms of personal and social ethics. New "norms" have been adopted which prior to the sixties would have been unacceptable. In many instances these have found sanction in legislation.

Although in the 1950s there were the first signs of an increase in drunkenness among young people, there was no evidence that in their quest for liberating experiences the young would turn to drink as they have done. At that time there was no really serious drinking problem among young people. Had there been, it is likely that the Licensing Act 1961 would have been a less cautious measure. Either it would have expressed the liberating spirit of the times, or it would have been a severely restrictive emergency measure. In fact, it was neither. Its main provision was to restrict the discretion of licensing justices to refuse to grant on-licences to restaurants and residential hotels. In this respect it may have given rise to a sense of freedom from control. More retail outlets emerged, despite a decrease in the number of public houses, but in the early sixties the social consequences of the consumption of intoxicants seemed under control. Between 1963 and 1966 there was a steady decrease in the number of convictions of drunkenness per 10,000 of the population aged fifteen years and over. This is seen in the following table,[4]

1962	23.26 per 10,000
1963	22.83 per 10,000
1964	20.97 per 10,000
1965	19.80 per 10,000
1966	19.04 per 10,000

The trend indicated a return to the comparitively low rates of the 1950s.

Earlier surges in drunkenness

Before turning to note and consider a dramatic change in trends, it is important to refer to two previous periods when similar dramatic changes occurred. These took place in the decade 1954 to 1964. Prys Williams observed that they were "without parallel in the last hundred years of records of conviction for drunkenness in England and Wales."[5] The first was between 1955 and 1957 when the number of convictions for drunkenness suddenly rose by 23 per cent and then fell slightly. The second was between 1960 and 1962 when they rose again by 23 per cent, held steady in 1963 and then fell by 7 per cent in 1964. Earlier there had been two similar fluctuations. Between 1872 and 1873 convictions rose by 25 per cent, but this was associated with the coming into force of the Licensing Act 1872. The other instance was between 1930 and 1935, when between 1930 and 1933 convictions fell by 40 per cent and then rose by 40 per cent by 1935. This is generally accounted for by the great economic depression which had such deep and far-reaching effects on employment and earnings. Similar reasons could not have accounted for what happened between 1954 and 1964. The total number of convictions in England and Wales for pedestrian and motorized drunkenness increased from 56,900 in 1954 to 90,300 in 1963, a rise of nearly two-thirds. However, it must be noted that (a) the population of England and Wales rose during that period; (b) convictions for motorized drunkenness rose proportionately, much more than those for pedestrian offences. Having studied the statistics, Prys Williams concluded that the real increase among pedestrians was "rather under 50 per cent than over it"; and that most, if not all, of the increase in motorized drunkenness was "probably attributable to the increase in the number of motor vehicles in the same period".[6]

In this decade there were, as we have noted, two distinct surges of drunkenness offences. In neither did the consumption of beer play a role. "Indeed, the consumption (of beer) tends to be depressed at the commencement of both surges and, in 1964, an increase of beer consumption occurs as convictions fall."[7] What is evident, however, is that the start of both surges was associated with a substantial rise in the consumption of spirits. The first coincided with the end of an effective rationing of whisky in 1955 and 1956, by which time sufficient stocks of matured spirits to support a big export trade had been accumulated following the dearth of the war years. This also coincided with the appearance of a new generation of consumers who had not tasted whisky before and had no experience of handling it. The second surge, even when it reached its peak in 1962, was geographically localized. "The areas affected coincided broadly with those where vodka enjoyed a sudden popularity. All spirits tend to trap the unwary and the inexperienced into excess and inebriety; vodka is notorious in this respect."[8]

The 1967 surge in drunkenness

In 1967, another dramatic change occurred. There was an increase in convictions for drunkenness of 7 per cent. Almost half the police districts of England and Wales showed a continuation of the decline which nearly all had experienced in the previous five years, but in other specific police districts an increase occurred. This trend did not emerge clearly until March–April 1967 to the end of the year, by which time there was a sustained increase of some 600 convictions per month, over the broad 1965/66 levels. This phenomenon is described by Prys Williams in *Social effects of the ending of Resale Price Maintenance of alcoholic beverages 1966 and 1967.*[9] In August 1966, the distillers considered appealing to the Restrictive Practices Court for the retention of resale price maintenance on liquor. However, in October 1966 they decided not to do so, and the Restrictive Practices Court had no option but to declare that the maintenance of the resale price of wines, spirits and other alcoholic drinks was thenceforth illegal. Immediately the shop windows of supermarkets and discount stores with off-licences were stacked with cut-price liquor. Backed up with newspaper publicity, sales increased enormously and so did the incidence of drunkenness. The boom was short-lived, but once stocks were replenished and Christmas approached, the sales increased again. Because supermarkets have to make profits, price margins can be cut only in relation to demand, and after Christmas, in February and March, figures for convictions for drunkenness declined even lower than those for 1965.

What then accounted for the subsequent rise in convictions later in 1967, and which has continued ever since? Prys Williams pointed out the importance of recognizing that while resale price maintenance was in operation very few supermarkets had off-licences.[10] The annual register prepared by the trade periodical *Self-service and Supermarket* listed only 102 stores of 2,000 square-feet areas and over as possessing off-licences in 1966. "It was these 102, and a few discount stores, that made the headlines in the autumn of 1966."[11] At the end of 1967 the number had increased to 264 and it further increased in 1968. The cut prices offered by the supermarkets drove the traditional off-licences to make price concessions.

Having established a relationship in time between the escalation of sales and drunkenness statistics, Prys Williams discovered that there was a relation of place. He re-grouped the police districts on the basis of the Home Office statistical reports of pedestrian and motorized drunkenness offences into four categories:

Group A: Metropolitan police district

Group B: Forty-four police districts with a combination of new off-licences at supermarkets in 1967, and a 1967 total of two or more licensed supermarkets; that is where price-cutting and supporting publicity was greatest.

Group C: Twenty-two other police districts which had only one licensed supermarket or had no addition in 1967, and where extensive publicity of cut-prices was doubtful.

Group D: The remaining twenty-four police districts where there were no supermarket off-licences listed.

The picture which emerged can be seen in the following table based on Home Office figures,[12]

	Licensed supermarkets			**Total convictions**		
Police Districts	**1966**	**1967**	**% inc.**	**1966**	**1967**	**% inc.**
Group A	11	20	81	28,170	31,694	+ 12.5
Group B	78	217	178	30,568	32,649	+ 6.8
Group C	13	27	101	7,421	7,061	− 4.8
Group D	Nil	Nil	Nil	4,337	4,130	− 4.8

Other tables show that the largest increases in pedestrian offences were among males under 18 and males between 18 and 21 in Groups A and B. Pedestrian drunkenness among women also showed big increases in Group A (8 per cent) and Group B (13.5 per cent).

This suggests that the behaviour of the public as a consequence of the consumption of alcohol is induced by publicity and competition. It is significant that the increases in drunkenness occurred in the police districts where there had been the largest increases in the number of supermarket off-licences. This indicates that the apparent sudden increase in drunkenness offences in the latter part of 1967, and which has been sustained ever since, is not unrelated to the increase in supermarket off-licences and price-cutting backed up by publicity. Prys Williams concluded, "Social statistics are subject to so many varying influences that the effects of particular factors never emerge with the precision of scientific laboratory tests. But there can be few examples of change in social behaviour being so directly and consistently related to cause and effect. Time, place and most subsidiary elements combine clearly to demonstrate that to advertise price reductions of alcoholic beverages is to cause deterioration in the social behaviour of the most gullible and most inexperienced and irresponsible."[13]

Supermarkets and drunkenness

At this point it is appropriate to refer to a major survey into the relation between supermarket sales of liquor and the growth of drunkenness among young women and young persons since 1966.[14] This was carried out by the Christian Economic and Social Research Foundation who had been invited to give evidence to the New Zealand Royal Commission on Liquor which was appointed in 1973. In its evidence the foundation drew upon an earlier survey which was up-dated. In the six years preceding 1967 in England and Wales the trend of convictions for drunkenness of people of all ages and sexes was steady or downward. Even after 1967 this trend persisted for men aged over 21 and for women over 30; but a remarkable change occurred among younger women and males under 18. Convictions of women aged between 21 and 30, fell in number up to 1967 and then more than doubled by 1973; those of women between 18 and 20, also fell up to 1967 but by 1973 they had increased almost three times; at the same time girls under 18 were being convicted over three times as frequently. Convictions of youths under 18 more than doubled in the same period. We have seen already that in selected areas there was a close correlation between the proliferation of supermarket off-licences selling cut-price liquor and the increase in drunkenness offences. What was the special influence which gave rise to an overall increase in drunkenness offences?

It is important to dispose of a number of possible causes. First it could not be accounted for by price-cutting in liquor. Price-cutting did occur, but by the time the main effects became visible the once-for-all reductions in retail margins had been made, and the unit prices were rising steadily. Second, increasing numbers in the affected age groups could not have produced the effect because, over the period, the number did not increase. Third, the ordinary public houses were not an influence because their number was declining before 1967 and continued to decline: from 70,875 in 1956 to 66,373 in 1966 and to 63,732 in 1972. Fourth, although the number of registered clubs increased after the passage of the 1961 Licensing Act, the increase of 8 per cent between 1962 and 1967 was a little higher than the 7 per cent increase between 1967 and 1973. Fifth, the 1961 Act introduced a new retail outlet in the restaurant licence. These increased initially, but so many proved unprofitable that the rate of increase fell away sharply. Sixth, it could not be attributed to an overall increase in consumption, which was slow and gradual. The report of the Christian Economic and Social Research Foundation analyses the relevant statistics and concludes that the greater accessibility afforded to young persons and women by the supermarket off-licence was the principal factor to account for the increase in pedestrian drunkenness among young women and young persons after 1966.

By the end of the 1960s public concern about the escalation of the "alcohol problem" prompted the government to appoint a departmental committee "to review the liquor licensing laws of England and Wales, taking account of the changes recommended by the Monopolies Commission and of any other changes that may be proposed, and to make recommendations."[15] Lord Erroll of Hale was appointed chairman and the subsequent report is best known as the "Erroll Report". We shall give space to a consideration of this report in the next chapter, but now reference must be made to the Monopolies Commission's report mentioned in the terms of reference for the Erroll Committee.

The Monopolies Commission and the tied house

The Monopolies Commission was asked to consider whether the tied-house system of retailing beer constituted a monopoly. After two years deliberations the commission published its report in April 1969.[16] Its chief finding was that a monopoly did exist, but that within the framework of licensing legislation there was no way of breaking it. The commission therefore proposed that licensing administration should be so relaxed as to make it possible for any retailer whose character and premises satisfied certain minimum standards, to sell liquor on or off the premises.

The commission's report gave a very clear picture of the liquor trade, and especially of the brewing and retailing of beer in the United Kingdom. In 1967 the U.K. was the third largest market in the world for beer. The U.S.A. market accounted for 2,758,932,000 gallons, Federal Germany 1,682,824,000 gallons, and the U.K. 1,132,000,000 gallons. In consumption per head of the population the U.K. was seventh in the world. Of the beer consumed in the U.K. 95 per cent was produced in the U.K. One of the most striking statistics given in the report was concerned with excise licences for producing beer. These dropped from 16,798 in 1881 to 244 in 1967. There were, said the commission, two reasons for this. First, the reduction in the number of licensed premises which brewed their own beer, and, second, the amalgamation of breweries. At the end of 1967 there were 111 separate brewing companies operating 240 breweries. Seven brewers together accounted for 73 per cent of the total production of beer in 1967. They were, Bass Charrington, Allied Breweries, Whitbread, Watney Mann, Scottish and Newcastle Breweries, Courage, Barclay and Simonds, and Arthur Guinness Son and Co. The balance of 27 per cent in 1967 was accounted for by 104 brewery companies or groups of companies.

Despite the claims of some brewers for their products, there was no overall favourite brand or type among beer drinkers. There were reckoned to be 3,000 different brands. In the course of time, types and methods of beer retailing had changed. In addition to "draught" beer, "keg" beer had become popular, and because of more drinking at home, bottled and canned beers had increased in sales.

The wholesale trade was operated mainly under brewer-for-trade licences. These were obtained by brewers under Section 125 of the Customs and Excise Act 1952. The commission observed, "While there exists non-brewery-owned wholesales and bottlers in the U.K. industry, the brewery companies themselves have assumed a dominant role in the wholesaling trade for several reasons."[17] Chief of these was the development of brewers producing beer of better quality than that which the individual publican could produce for sale over his own counter. The bigger brewer was able to expand his trade, whereas the local publican could not do so. This trend continued until the greater part of the beer sold in the U.K. was sold through retail outlets owned by the brewers, that is, the tied-houses. Of the total amount of beer retained in the U.K. in 1967, that is approximately 32.5 million bulk barrels, approximately 66 per cent was sold through licensed premises owned by brewers. From the point of view of the terms of reference of the commission, the following finding was important, "Although arrangements for the sale and purchase of beers between brewers are widespread, in 1967, approximately 90 per cent of the beer sold by brewers was the seller's own brew. . . . In some cases, brewers make some of the beers they have purchased from other brewers available only to their free-trade customers and not to their own licensed premises; in other cases they are made available to some but not all of the licensed premises of the brewers concerned."[18] The commission noted that brewers had extended their activities into the wine and spirits trades. Two other types of drinks were also distributed through the licensed trade, these were cider and "soft" drinks. Soft drinks were made by nearly seven hundred manufacturers in the country, and it was estimated that about a quarter of the sales were through the licensed trade. The two biggest producers of the so-called "soft" drinks were the Beecham Group and Schweppes. Over one-third of the brewers also manufactured these types of drinks, mostly through subsidiaries.

A chapter in the report on "Brewer-ownership of licensed premises" contains some interesting historical material.[19] It begins, "In their *History of Liquor Licensing in England Principally from 1700 to 1830,* Beatrice and Sidney Webb noted that 'the purchase of tied houses by the brewers was admitted and defended in 1802'. A select committee of the House of Commons in 1817 found that half the licences in London and a greater number in the provinces were tied. But the great bulk of brewery acquisitions of licensed premises in England and Wales took place between 1850 and 1900." As we have seen already,[20] in 1830 the Beerhouse Act established "free licensing", that is, any ratepayer wishing to sell beer on his own premises could do so without a justices' licence on the payment of a fee of two guineas to the local excise officer. Free-licensing continued until the Beerhouse Act of 1869, and during that period, and thereafter until the early 1900s, the brewers continued to acquire licensed premises. Many of the new businesses founded as a consequence of the 1830 Act failed. Their owners took out mortgages from their supplying brewers on condition that most, if not all, beer was obtained from lender. In time, many were forced to sell out to the brewers. By 1900 there were over 102,000 on-licences in England and Wales, the majority of which were for premises owned by brewers. Today, virtually all brewery companies or groups own licensed premises. More than 97 per cent of the beer supplied within the U.K. for retail sale on licensed premises is supplied by brewers who also own premises in the U.K. Out of the total of 139,966 licensed and registered outlets in the U.K. on 31st December 1967 brewers owned 67,649. Approximately 81 per cent of the total of 72,550 full on-licences and 30 per cent of off-licences in Great Britain were owned by brewers mostly in the hands of six groups.

With only minor exceptions all the brewer-owners of licensed premises operated "tied-supply" arrangements. An undertaking by the tenant to buy beer only from his brewer-landlord was an essential feature of almost every tenancy agreement. Although the tie on beer was of long standing, the extension to wines and spirits and other goods was a post-war development. Tenancy agreements almost invariably included clauses binding tenants to observe retail prices fixed by the brewer-landlord. These conditions usually apply also to non-alcoholic drinks and tobacco.

The commission found that while they received many complaints and criticisms about the different aspects of the tie for beer, there were few, if any, expressions of feeling that the tie should be abolished. Chief criticisms were of the system of price fixing, the low margin of profit allowed and in particular of the tie on wines and spirits which it was thought ought to be broken. Various other means of maintaining the brewers' control were mentioned in the report. These included the deposit by the tenant of a sum of about two to four times the value of the weekly order from the brewer-landlords.

Outlets not involved in the tied system are called "free trade". The chief of these outlets was the registered club in which the brewers also had a big interest. A number of clubs were "tied" because money had been borrowed from the brewers. The other major outlet was the off-licence, and in recent times the supermarket. In 1967 there were 30,365 off-licences in the U.K. of which 21,000 were owned by the free trade.

The brewers, naturally, supported the retention of the tied-house system. In their summary of the case presented by the Brewers' Society, the commission reported, "The Society maintains that the tied house system is in the public interest. The arguments advanced to support this contention may be briefly summarised as follows. In the Society's view, the public interest lies in a system which provides the consumer with the best balance, in relation to his requirements of quality, choice, amenity and convenience, at a price which he is prepared to pay. The Society claims that the tied house system is the best adapted to give the consumer what he wants, where he wants it, at the lowest price consonant with the quality of the goods and the standard of surroundings desired today. Ownership of licensed premises brings the brewer into direct contact with the public, to whom he has responsibilities."[21] The Brewers' Society argued that the tied-house system did not preclude competition in the industry. There were over one hundred independent brewers in the country; and the free trade, with which they had to compete, accounted for 35 per cent of all sales of beer in the country.

The Monopolies Commission exceeds its brief

The commission found it impossible to form a judgment on the restrictions on competition in the supply of beer to public houses without taking into account the tied-house system as a whole. This involved consideration of the functions of brewers as producers, wholesalers, retailers and landlords of retailers, not only of beer, but also of wines, spirits, cider, mineral waters and various other goods which licensed houses retailed to the public. The commission commented on all aspects, summarized the disadvantages of the tied-house system, and concluded, "We have found that the tied house system, as operated in the conditions of restricted competition which in any case result from the licensing laws, has certain disadvantageous effects. These effects derive from the ownership by brewers of large number of licensed outlets." The principal disadvantages were that the elimination of inefficiency and redundancy was retarded, that it prevented the growth of competition particularly the entrance of new competitors, that what competition there was existed between brewers competing for portions of the retail market as captive outlets, and in the on-licensed retail trade price competition was practically absent.[22]

The commission concluded that "the conditions we have found to prevail operate and may be expected to operate against the public interest since the restrictions on competition involved in the tied house system operated by the brewer suppliers concerned are detrimental to efficiency in brewing, wholesaling and retailing, to the interests of independent suppliers (including potential new entrants) and to the interests of the consumers."[23] What, therefore, did the commission recommend to break the prevailing system? It confessed that in making any recommendations for the relaxation of the licensing system, ". . . . we are treading here upon ground that may be regarded as outside the scope of our judgment. It is certainly not our function to criticise the social objectives or effects of the licensing laws."[24] Many observers wondered, therefore, why the commission proceeded to recommend what amounted to the dismantling of the licensing system.

> *The principal change we have in mind, declared the Commission, is that the present licensing system should be substantially relaxed, the general objective being to permit the sale of alcoholic drinks, for on or off consumption, by any retailer whose character and premises satisfy certain minimum standards. Various regulations would still be necessary in relation to the premises concerned in the interests of health and safety, but it should be possible to lay down and enforce standards in these respects and for such other purposes as may be deemed socially desirable – e.g. as to opening hours, the suitability of the premises and even the character of the retailer concerned – without a system of licensing controlled by justices. Insofar as restrictions on opening hours were necessary, these could be operated more flexibly than at present; and restrictions on access by children might become unnecessary if retailers were free to provide environments for drinking which were different from those of the public house. If the purpose of the laws was to maintain the minimum standards referred to above, without any intention, explicit or implicit, to limit numbers of outlets, the administration of the laws would appear to be a function which might be undertaken by local authorities and the Government Departments concerned.*[25]

These recommendations, if implemented, would mean that shoe-shops, boutiques, hairdressers, launderettes, hardware stores, any shop in the High Street, in fact, would be free to retail liquor provided the premises were suitable and the proprietor was a person of good character. Even supposing premises could be suitably adapted, how could most retailers comply with the insistence maintained for so long by licensing justices, that drinks should be dispensed by suitably-experienced and qualified persons? And is the experience of centuries of licensing administration by justices to be set aside on the recommendation of a commission whose competence in this field is, to say the least, suspect? This is one of the inquiries referred to in the first paragraph of this chapter.

Our judgement is supported by a leading article in *The Times*,

> *It is just as well to remember that the licensing laws grew up to curb a grave social evil and that – illogical though they may often seem – they are the envy of governments trying to cope with that evil today. They ought not to be relaxed out of an impulse to promote freer competition. The Monopolies Commission, who in this field is utterly unqualified, has produced a recipe for fewer pubs, more drinking and many more alcoholics.*[26]

Although the Erroll Committee was asked to take account of the changes recommended by the Monopolies Commission, it found itself in some difficulty in interpreting what aspects of the commission's report were proper matters to be considered in a review of licensing law. The Monopolies Commission was concerned solely with the issue as to whether the tied-house system and virtual monopoly of licensed retail outlets by a small number of brewers was in the public interest. The conclusion of the Erroll Committee was that this was a matter of marketing method and generally fell outside the scope of licensing law, and so it did not feel justified in embarking on a fresh investigation into the merits of the system. Commenting on their decision not to investigate this matter, it said, "The suggestion has been made that we are entitled to undertake such an investigation because the issue is somehow of wider significance. This represents, in our view, merely a pretext which on closer examination has little, if any, validity."[27]

Alcohol and road safety

We shall postpone a full consideration of the Erroll Report until the next chapter, and include here reference to a major piece of legislation, the Road Safety Act 1967, the object of which, declared Barbara Castle, the then Minister of Transport, was to change the drinking habits of the public. In a period of general relaxation of the control of the consumption of liquor, this act, while not a piece of licensing legislation, might well have had a greater impact on the excessive consumption of alcohol than more restrictive controls of the retailing of liquor.

The antecedents of this act may be traced back to 1932 when Professor Widmark, of the University of Lund, Sweden, discovered how to determine by a scientific test the level of alcohol in the blood. By this time, some tests had shown how the consumption of alcohol affected such matters as reaction time, accuracy of performance and the co-ordination of mental and bodily functions. Because police statistics indicated that some persons involved in road accidents had been driving "under the influence", the Minister of Transport, Hore Belisha, announced in the House of Commons on 30th January 1935 that he intended asking the British Medical Association to say whether it could usefully make any observations on the place of alcohol in the causes of road accidents. The B.M.A. appointed a special committee to consider the matter, and in July 1935, published its report on the *Relation of Alcohol to Road Accidents.*[28] This referred to alcohol as "from first to last a narcotic drug."[29] Having taken account of various tests that had been carried out, the B.M.A. concluded that the consumption of alcohol even in small amounts of, say, two or three ounces of whisky, diminished attention and control, reduced capacity to learn and adversely affected reasoning powers and the power to make movements which were dependent on rapid and accurate co-ordination. It concluded that the kind of skills required for driving a motor car were precisely those which had been shown to be adversely affected by the presence of alcohol in the body. The committee believed it to be "Highly desirable in the public interest to draw attention to the effect of amounts of alcohol, commonly regarded as without deleterious effect on the driving capacity of persons in charge of motor vehicles."[30] Even taking account of the intervention of the Second World War, it seems incredible that it took thirty years for it to become an offence to be in charge of a motor vehicle with a prescribed excess of alcohol in the blood.

It did not take long for the United Kingdom Alliance to launch a campaign to secure such legislation. At its annual meeting at Manchester on 20th October 1936 it passed a resolution expressing "the imperative need of determining responsibility of alcohol for road casualties by requiring a scientific test for the presence of alcohol in the blood to be made in all cases where drivers are concerned in accidents involving injury to any person."[31] The initiator of the resolution and subsequently the relentless campaigner for this legislation was Wilfrid Winterton, a prominent member in later years of the executive of the United Kingdom Alliance. It was gratifying to him in his old age to see the Road Safety Act 1967 on the statute book, with its prescribed limit of 80 mg. of alcohol in 100 ml. of blood, road-side breath testing and blood or urine tests to determine the blood/alcohol level in drinking motorists.

Road safety legislation

The first attempt at legislation on these lines was an act of 1962 for which the then Minister of Transport, Ernest Marples, was responsible. This gave legal recognition for the scientific blood/alcohol test to be used in the courts. However, it failed to make its use compulsory or to provide a figure for the guidance of the courts by which they might determine the prescribed limit of alcohol in the blood beyond which any offender would have no defence against conviction.

It was surprising that this act did not incorporate a prescribed limit because one had been firmly recommended by the British Medical Association in another report which had been published in 1960. This report, *Relation of Alcohol to Road Accidents* studied the results of research and experience since the previous report of 1935. The conclusion reached was "On the basis of the evidence examined in the preparation of this report, the Committee is satisfied that a concentration of 50 mg./100 ml. of alcohol in the blood of a driver of a motor vehicle is the highest that can be accepted as consistent with the safety of other road users."[32] A further report from the British Medical Association was published in 1965. In 1951 the Council of the B.M.A. appointed a special committee to revise and bring up to date the association's reports on *Tests for drunkenness (1927)* and *Relation of Alcohol to Road Accidents (1935).* In 1964 the terms of reference of the committee were amended as follows, "To advise the Council on the medical aspects of the prevention of traffic accidents with reference to the part played by alcohol or other drugs, and to keep up to date the reports which have so far been published by the Association on the subjects."[33] The report considered all medico-legal aspects of the matter and on the question of the prescribed limit concluded, "We believe that analysis of the concentration of alcohol in the body affords the best available scientific evidence of impairment of the ability to drive properly due to alcohol, and we recommend that it should be an offence for a person with a blood/alcohol concentration in excess of 80 mg./100 ml. to drive a motor vehicle on the public highway."[34] The suggested limit was higher than that recommended in 1960. The reason for the higher limit was that at this level it was believed that no person was in a fit state to drive a motor vehicle, and that prosecutions could with confidence be pursued on this basis.

It was this recommendation which was embodied in a bill presented to parliament on 10th February 1966 by Barbara Castle. She reminded the house of the gravity of the situation to which the proposed legislation was addressed. She said, "In 1964, the latest complete year for which figures are available, 7,820 people in Britain were killed in road accidents and over 95,000 were seriously injured. In all, more than 380,000 people were road casualties. This was the highest number in our whole history. And of these, 60,000 were children under 15 years of age." The following passage in her speech is particularly important in view of the form of the eventual Road Safety Act,

> *We have come to the conclusion that it would be far less invidious and less offensive to the individual to be stopped completely at random, without any stigma being attached to it. Passers-by seeing that test being conducted will know that this is a decent citizen collaborating in carrying out a social duty in the interests of road safety. If we want a deterrent, then there could be no more effective way than for people to realise that there will always be a possibility of their being asked to undergo a random test. I know that there are strong feelings about this and we shall debate it fully in committee. But to those who maintain that there is a great principle involved, I say that there is no difference in principle between random breath tests and random tests on goods vehicles.*

Random tests on goods vehicles were also provided in the same bill and at no stage in either the Commons or the Lords was this provision questioned.

The opposition spokesman on transport matters was Sir Martin Redmayne. Somewhat belatedly, he confessed, his party had come round to accepting compulsory scientific testing. However, he declared, "If we ourselves, when we come to power, go on with this bill, it will be with the one important amendment that we shall knock out the random check." In the spring of 1966 parliament was dissolved, but Harold Wilson's government was returned with an increased majority. The Road Safety Act had reached the committee stage, and so a new bill had to be introduced. In the meantime opposition to random tests was organized. The trade and the motoring organizations made much of what the Director-General of the Automobile Association called "the serious encroachment of personal liberty involved in random tests". To most people's surprise, when the new bill was introduced after the general election it did not include random tests. At the third reading on 20th February 1967 an amendment which sought to re-introduce random tests was defeated. However, Castle resolutely stood by the provision for automatic disqualification for a year for motorists found guilty of excess alcohol in the blood. There was a hint of "pressures" which had made her change her mind about random tests. The Road Safety Act received the Royal Assent on 11th May 1967 and come into force on 9th October 1967.

In the first three months of the breathalyser, casualties dropped by 16 per cent and road deaths by 23 per cent. For an anlaysis of the figures for the first full year of the breathalyser readers are directed to a study of the Official Home Office statistics by Prys Williams.[35] Although the initial impact of the new act was dramatic, this impact was not maintained and lawyers found ways of exploiting loopholes in the law. Police began to feel inhibited from prosecuting in many instances because of anomalies in the law. Eventually, in 1974 the Blennerhassett Committee was set up to study the administration of the law and to recommend amendments to close the loopholes so that the intentions of the act could be fulfilled. Although the government fully accepted the Blennerhassett recommendations, parliamentary time has not been available to secure their implementation. Until appropriate amending legislation is passed the full force of the Road Safety Act 1967 will not be exerted on the serious problem of drinking-driving offences.

Road safety and personal liberty

It may be thought that the consideration of the Road Safety Act does not properly belong to a chapter concerned with "Licence for Liberation". It does fall within the sixties, and has relevance to the theme of this chapter from a number of points of view. First, for many people the Road Safety Act raised the important issue of the encroachment of the law upon personal liberty. The motoring organizations, in particular, attempt to show that every new restriction imposed on the motorist is an infringement of personal liberty. The breathalyser was not the first piece of equipment to be seen as a threat to the motorist's freedom. Parking meters are, perhaps, the most recent example, but one-way streets, speed limits and pedestrian crossings have all been maligned for the same reason. What opponents to the breathalyser failed to see was that the drunken motorist interfered permanently with the liberty of a person fatally injured in a car crash. A second factor raised by the new act was the issue whether the slight infringement of the motorists' personal liberty was a sufficient ground for failing to safeguard the liberty of other road-users from the menace of the drinking driver. Certainly the question of personal liberty was raised by the Road Safety Act, but not just for the driver.

The fact that it was passed at all in the form in which it reached the statute book was surprising in view of the mood of the times. Legal sanctions in several realms of personal and social ethics had been relaxed, and one might have expected the Road Safety Act to have reflected the trend. In one respect it may be said that it did adopt a less rigorous stance than was at first anticipated, and related to random tests which were omitted, no doubt under pressure from the lobby for more liberal licensing laws. However, the great achievement was that the public and parliament placed a high premium on the value of human life, and the need for its protection on our highways. What is the value of human life, or personal liberty, if people are not alive to enjoy either? In the context of the times, the Road Safety Act was a triumph of discipline over permissiveness.

References

1. H.M.S.O. February 1960.
2. Op cit p. 14.
3. Op cit p. 18.
4. *Social effects of the ending of Resale Price Maintenance of alcoholic beverages 1966 to 1967.* Prys Williams. Christian Economic and Social Research Foundation (1968).
5. *High spirited years.* Christian Economic and Social Research Foundation (1966) p. 5.
6. *Decade of Drunkenness: England and Wales 1954 to 1963.* Prys Williams. Christian Economic and Social Research Foundation (1965) pp. 6, 7.
7. *High spirited years.* Prys Williams p. 18.
8. *Social effects of the ending of Resale Price Maintenance of alcoholic beverages 1966 to 1967.* Prys William. Christian Economic and Social Research Foundation (1968) p. 3.
9. Op cit p. 4.
10. Op cit p. 5.
11. Op cit p. 5.
12. Op cit p. 6.
13. Op cit p. 7.

14. *Supermarket off-licences and the growth of drunkenness among young women and young persons since 1966.* Christian Economic and Social Research Foundation and *Alliance News* 1975.
15. *Report of the Departmental Committee on Liquor Licensing* H.M.S.O. (1972) p. iii.
16. *Beer: a report on the supply of beer.* H.M.S.O. (1969).
17. Op cit p. 12.
18. Op cit p. 14.
19. Op cit p. 46 ff.
20. See p. 5.
21. Op cit p. 77.
22. Op cit p. 113.
23. Op cit p. 119.
24. Op cit p. 116.
25. Op cit p. 117.
26. *The Times* 29th April 1969 p. 11.
27. Erroll op cit pp. 260, 261.
28. *Relation of Alcohol to Road Accidents.* B.M.A. (1935).
29. Op cit p. 5.
30. Op cit p. 4.
31. *Breath-taking history.* Wilfrid Winterton (1968) p. 9.
32. *Relation of Alcohol to Road Accidents.* B.M.A. (1960) pp. 31, 32.
33. *The Drinking Driver.* B.M.A. (1965) p. 4.
34. Op cit p. 39.
35. *1968 – The First Full Year of the Breathalyser.* G. Prys Williams. Christian and Economical Social Research Foundation.

CHAPTER 10

THE ERROLL COMMITTEE: A REVIEW OF SUBMISSIONS

When the Departmental Committee on Liquor Licensing was appointed by the Home Secretary, Reginald Maudling, in 1971 to review the liquor licensing laws of England and Wales and to make recommendations, it was the first major inquiry into the administration of the licensing laws since the Royal Commission 1929 to 1931. This committee will hereafter be referred to as the Erroll Committee after the name of its chairman Lord Erroll of Hale. A Home Office statement announcing the setting up of the committee said, "In their present form the Licensing laws are designed to prevent the misuse of intoxicants by providing public supervision over those who sell them and by limiting the opportunities for over-indulgence." The statement went on to say that the committee would be expected to "examine the social and economic implications of the present law and of any proposals for change, and determine what will be in the best interests of the public."

The composition of the committee

After the publication of the Erroll Report in December 1972 it became plain how crucial had been the composition of the committee which was different from the Royal Commission 1929–31, which had members with considerable experience in the trade, in the judiciary and in temperance reform and who were competent to consider licensing law and all aspects of the manufacture and retailing of liquor and the personal and social consequences of the consumption of alcohol in the context of history and experience. It is true that the Royal Commission's report was not a unanimous one, but this did not detract from the importance of its findings and recommendations on which there was unanimity. On the release of the Erroll Report it was said by members of the committee that they had set out with the intention of being unanimous, and the significance of this intention will be seen as we give an account of the membership of the committee.

The chairman, Lord Erroll, was a former member of conservative governments and his deputy, Lord Shepherd, had been a minister of the previous labour government. Best known of the members of the committee was Graham Hill, the racing driver. Not so widely well known, but nevertheless prominent, was the headmaster of Harrow school, Dr Robert James. Two members were from the legal profession, Richard John, formerly clerk to the Glamorgan County Council, and Sir Robert Bayne, who had been president of the law society 1969–70. In Professor Alan R. Prest, the committee had a professional economist with a special interest in the economics of the public sector. Two members had strong links with consumer marketing, Sheila Black, a journalist specializing in consumer affairs on the *Financial Times,* and David Wolfson, managing director of Kaye and Co., a mail order firm and a director of Great Universal Stores. Derek Gladwin, a regional secretary of the General and Municipal Workers

Union, was also a member of the British Tourist Board. There were three other members of the committee, Robert Clough, director of Thomson Newspapers who began a lifetime in journalism as a reporter on the *Northern Mail*, Dr M. M. Sabir, formerly of Kenya, but a general practitioner in London, and Bishop Simon Phipps. Three assessors were also appointed, a magistrate, a chief constable and a magistrates' clerk. The obvious criticisms of the membership of the committee were that there was only one woman, that consumer interests appeared to outweigh historical and sociological considerations, that there was no one with experience in the medical diagnosis and treatment of alcoholism, and that in addition to the three assessors appointed, there should have been a social historian. In attempting to appoint a thoroughly independent committee, the Home Secretary lost sight of the need for expertise in the essential areas for consideration. *Alliance News* commented,

> *Inevitably the committee will learn a great deal they did not know initially about the drinking patterns in this country, the reasons for legislation and the views of the various interested parties. Some sections of the trade press have criticised the Home Secretary's choice on the grounds of their lack of experience of the economic and other factors of the licensed trade. They may well be only partially informed about the temperance point of view. However, we shall suspend judgment until they have completed their work and produced their report. Only then can their competence be judged.*[1]

The hesitancy in reposing complete confidence in this committee was justified when the Erroll Report was subjected to expert criticism. However, since it was a serious attempt to assess the contemporary state of the retailing of liquor and the social consequence of its consumption we must devote this chapter to it.

Erroll and the Monopolies Commission

In their consideration of the nature and powers of the licensing authority and the operation of the licensing system, the Erroll Committee was able to take account of the report of the findings of the Royal Commission on Assizes and Quarter Sessions which was published in September 1969. This proposed a new procedure for appeals against decisions of licensing justices. For some time the Licensed Victuallers and representatives of temperance organizations who opposed applications for licences in magistrates' courts found themselves united in their dissatisfaction with the system of appeals to Quarter Sessions. Too often the decision of local licensing justices not to grant an application was overturned on appeal to quarter sessions. In many instances the quarter sessions were held at a place remote from the locality to which the application applied, and the appeal was heard by magistrates with no local knowledge, and who might not themselves be licensing justices. In 1969 an unprecedented deputation went to the Home Office to discuss the issue with Lord Stonham, an under secretary of state. It was unprecedented because it was a joint deputation of representatives of the National Federation of Licensed Victuallers and of the National Temperance Federation. The deputation urged the Minister to incorporate in new legislation special appeals tribunals, composed of licensing justices and including licensing justices from the area affected by the application. In its report the Royal Commission not only accepted the recommendation of the joint deputation, but incorporated other improvements in appeals procedures. "We recommend that Licensing Tribunals, convened by the Circuit Administration, shall sit whenever they are needed, and that solicitors shall have the right of audience before them. We recommend that each tribunal should consist of a Circuit Judge as Chairman and four justices, two of whom shall be drawn from the petty sessional division concerned in order to provide local knowledge, and two should be drawn from elsewhere."[2] The Courts Act 1971 reflected this recommendation with one important variation. Appeals against licensing decisions by licensing justices now go to crown courts, where in these matters a judge presides, but sitting with him are two justices from the area affected by the appeal, but who did not sit on the original case, and two other justices. The crown court decision is made by the five members' votes. There is general satisfaction with these procedures, which indicates the value of having persons with experience involved in early discussions of possible changes in licensing administration.

Archaic licensing laws

The Erroll Committee met for the first time on 5th April 1971. This information was given to William Price, Member of Parliament for Rugby, who on 24th June 1971 asked the Home Secretary when the Erroll Committee held its first meeting and when he expected to receive its recommendations. Price was the licensed victuallers' spokesman in the House. In a supplementary question he asked whether the Home Secretary was aware of the "considerable concern about the independence and scope of the committee in view of the fact that he has already made up his mind and announces that our licensing laws are archaic." "If the committee denies they are archaic does not that leave the right honourable gentleman in a curious position half-way up a gum tree looking stupid?" Maudling replied, "I am prepared to take that risk. I think the laws are archaic. If the committee comes up with the view that they are perfect, I and many others will be surprised." They would, indeed, have been surprised after such a statement by the Home Secretary which virtually pre-empted any other view being taken. Even before the committee met, Miss Sheila Black told *Alliance News,* "I might say that all licensing laws ought to be relaxed."[3] In particular she said she was in favour of children being permitted to accompany their parents as freely as possible where drinks were served.

The view that licensing laws were archaic had been most strenuously advanced by the English Tourist Board. In its submission to the Erroll Committee it conceded that while it had no real evidence that prohibition on the sale of alcoholic drinks at motorway restaurants was in any way detrimental to tourist activities, it was aware of the argument that the sale of drink might increase the hazards of driving. "We realise that there are strong feelings on this matter," said the ETB, "and we do not think in any event that the tourist interests should prevail in this instance." The main recommendations of the ETB were, (a) restrictions on the hours for the sale and service of alcoholic drinks should be abolished; (b) if the liquor licensing regulations were retained, they should be standardized throughout the country; (c) there should be greater flexibility in the permitted opening hours to meet the requirements of tourists, particularly at resorts, railway stations, coach stations, airports and passenger terminals at ports; (d) it should be possible to obtain and consume drinks with meals at any time; (e) at the management's discretion, children should be allowed in those parts of licensed premises ancillary to catering services, the licensing procedures should be reviewed and simplified and consideration should be given to the transfer of responsibility to the local authority.[4] The Erroll Committee firmly rejected this last recommendation, which had also been made by the Monopolies Commission, but which found little favour among those directly involved in the trade.

The brewers' views

The submission of the Brewers' Society and the National Federation of Licensed Victuallers were, of course, important. The Brewers' Society submission began by recognizing that the personal and social consequences of drinking excessive amounts of alcohol inevitably created issues as to the control of establishments selling liquor, which did not exist in the case of ordinary shops or places where only non-intoxicating refreshments were supplied. The laws in Britain had long recognized this fact, and had sought to "counter the social problems of the excessive consumption of liquor by sanctions aimed at the drinker himself and, more importantly, by careful control of the establishments which supply it". The law had to strike a balance between restraints which were necessary to prevent abuse and mischief, and the legitimate demand for individual freedom of choice. Whatever was done as a result of the review by the Erroll Committee, the Brewers' Society believed it could not fail to have important sociological effects, depending on the balance struck. The submission declared, "This does not mean that the Brewers' Society advocates that changes should not be made in the licensing system, if such are desired by the public. The Brewing Industry regards its function as to follow, not lead, public opinion and to provide the facilities the public requires in accordance with whatever laws best give effect to this public opinion and with due sense of the social responsibilities involved."

The Brewers' Society made submissions on the main items with which the Erroll Committee were bound to be concerned. First, concerning the considerable growth of registered clubs in the twentieth century, it observed that this provided a significant alternative choice to the public which was in direct competition with public houses. There were then 23,000 registered clubs in England and Wales, compared with 9,000 at the end of the First World War, whereas in the same period the number of public houses had declined from 83,000 to 65,000. In some areas there were arrangements by which members of one club were entitled to use virtually all the other clubs in the same area. This made club drinking facilities as readily available to the public as public houses, and yet there was a great difference between the legislative treatment of clubs and public houses. For instance, (a) clubs were immune from the detailed time controls imposed on public houses; (b) they were not subject to the law concerning the supply of liquor to children and young persons; (c) they were not subject to police supervision; and (d) they were allowed more attractive gaming machines than those in public houses. Two of these anomalies would have been removed had the Brewers' Society recommendations about permitted hours and children in public houses been implemented. The plea was for the same regulations in these matters to be applied to clubs and to public houses.

As to opening hours, the Brewers' Society had given much thought to the matter. It had considered the proposition that all that was required was to give licensees an option to stay open in the afternoon, and to close at a later hour at night. This variation of practice had been rejected by the brewers in favour of a consideration of the simplification of the law to remove anomalies. What was recommended was that the hours during which a public house would normally be open should be specified by the licensee, although he should not be allowed to sell liquor before a statutory commencement hour or after a statutory terminal hour. It would not be compulsory to provide for an afternoon break in these hours. The normal opening hour should be 10 a.m. on weekdays and 12 noon on Sundays, and the normal terminal time should be midnight. The specified hours of any public house should include at least six hours daily between the commencement hour and the terminal hour. The law should not require public houses to be open either at all or for a minimum period on Christmas Day or Good Friday. Licensees should be required to exhibit a notice outside their premises stating the opening hours. In general such provisions should apply to all on-licensed premises, except that there should be no time controls on the sale of drinks to hotel residents or their guests.

One of the matters on which the Erroll Committee was expected to make recommendations was the presence of children in licensed premises, and the minimum legal age at which young persons might purchase intoxicating liquor. Although there had been some demand for reducing the age from eighteen to sixteen, the Brewers' Society did not believe there was any real public demand for such a change, and the society recommended the retention of eighteen as the legal age. Its remaining recommendations were that, (a) the licensee of a public house should be allowed to propose to licensing justices that either his whole premises or specific parts of them should be available for the accommodation of children (i.e. persons under 14) accompanied by adults; (b) areas available in this way for the accommodation of children should be identified by a notice; (c) the minimum age at which persons could be employed in bars should be reduced from eighteen to sixteen; and (d) it should be possible for liquor to be supplied to persons under eighteen on behalf of others for consumption off the licensed premises.

On the general licensing system, the society understandably made complimentary comments about the place of the public house. It said that the present-day English public house was much admired, it had an unprecedented standing in the community and provided a valuable social amenity, which derived from the high degree of social amenity and the way in which restrictions on disorderly behaviour were enforced. These advantageous features owed much to the fact that licensing justices had complete discretion as to the issue of new on-licences and a wide discretion as to their renewal. If this discretion were curtailed the high standards of amenity and conduct would be substantially reduced. It followed that it would be most undesirable to transfer liquor licensing administration from the justices to the local authorities.

On various other related matters the Brewers' Society expressed its judgement. It did not believe there was wide public support for a new kind of licensed catering establishment in which the supply of drink would be subsidiary to the supply of other forms of refreshment, and which would have no restrictions on the admission of children. It was its view that the statutory system of licensing planning had served its purpose and should be replaced by a system of consultation. The special rules relating to "old licences" had also served their purpose and should be discontinued, and the compensation funds should be wound up.

Licensed victuallers' submission

The National Federation of Licensed Victuallers told the Erroll Committee that the soundness of the present licensing legislation was more pronounced than was generally understood. They based this claim on the fact that since the process of drastically reducing the number of licensed houses had begun nearly seventy years previously, drunkenness convictions had declined even though, at the same time, the average intake of alcohol had increased. "Could there be any better recommendation of the licensing system than this: that the national sobriety and the pub trade, in volume and quality should have improved together?" the N.F.L.V. asked in its submission. The common impression of the licensing law as harsh, unreasonable and oppressive was one which needed to be corrected. The law was not that severe. It had no control over how much or how often people drank in private. The law controlled only social drinking. It was, in fact, decidedly more permissive than the law in countries from which many tourists came to Britain. Some of the changes in the law recommended by tourist bodies, such as the abolition of permitted hours, changing the character of the public house to conform to continental ideas and the admission of children to public bars, were totally unacceptable to the Licensed Victuallers. The grounds for their opposition were, of course, economic. Widespread relaxation of hours and the provision of other facilities would require larger staffs and increased overheads. Many public houses would be unable to meet these extra costs.

In a reference to the report of the Monopolies Commission, the Licensed Victuallers made two principal criticisms. First, that the recommendations of the commission were not based on evidence it had accumulated, but upon some personal impressions or prejudices. Second, that the evidence was incomplete. In spite of its terms of reference, the commission had neglected to investigate the extent of the "tie" in the so-called free trade. "With these errors, and in reaching a conclusion in regard to licensees incomes which was later flatly contradicted, in effect, by the National Prices and Incomes Board, the Monopolies Commission, we submit, must lose claim to a serious consideration of its recommendations".

The submission recognized some of the serious social consequences of the excessive consumption of alcohol, such as alcoholism and the relation of drinking and the incidence of road-accident casualties. Serious though the problem of alcoholism was in Britain, the Licensed Victuallers believed its incidence to be lower than in countries where the consumption of alcohol was much higher. The problem was of special concern to the French government. The campaign of the Mendes France government to persuade people to drink more milk and less alcohol presumably owed a great deal to the shocking disclosures of alcoholism among children. A statement in the British press that a report on the drink problem in France was being treated as confidential, if true, was no doubt because of the powerful alcohol lobby in France. This was a somewhat striking statement coming from a vested interest such as the Licensed Victuallers.

The submission was less objective in its consideration of the relation between drinking and road accidents. The Licensed Victuallers discounted the connection made. They believed the initial improvement in road-accident figures following the introduction of the breathalyser may have been due to the shock of the legislation which made all drivers, including teetotallers, drive more carefully. Nevertheless, the submission stated that the matter of road safety ought to be borne in mind "when developments calculated to place a drink at everyone's elbow at all times of the day and night are apparently being serious contemplated". It was recognized that road-safety experts would want to retain the "afternoon break" and the ban on the sale of liquor on motorways. The conclusion reached was that any impairment of the present licensing system would be at variance with the need for improved road safety.

The Licensed Victuallers agreed with the general principle of licensing legislation as stated by R. A. Butler, the Home Secretary, when he introduced the Licensing Bill 1961, "To strike a balance between the restraints which are still necessary to prevent abuse or social mischief and the legitimate demand for individual freedom of choice and behaviour in an adult and responsible society." If, as the N.F.L.V. had suggested, the aim of the present licensing law was correct and was being achieved, it followed that some powerful reasons must be given for major changes in the present controls.

> *"We can think of none" it was declared emphatically, "We suggest rather that the controls of the public-house should be extended to registered clubs as so many of them function as unlicensed pubs. What needs particularly to be said about the controls, in our opinion, is that taking into account our freedom from serious national insobriety and drunkenness and from any interference with our private drinking lives, they constitute as responsible, effective and progressive a system as any in the world. The demand of changes too often has its source in minor irritation at some control and a complete ignorance of the purpose of that control. We submit that the Departmental Committee has an exceptional opportunity of educating the public on the subject. We see no reason for attempting by changes in the law to alter our drinking habits merely because they are distinctive to other people particularly as those habits seem to interest and even appeal to tourists from abroad. If as a result of some changes in the national character, there should arise a demand for a different scheme of things, substantial alterations would be possible even under the present law."*

The only specific recommendations made by the Licensed Victuallers were concerned with variation in the administration of "permitted hours". These were (a) permitted hours should be 9½ per weekday between the hours of 10.00 and 24.00 and to be selected by the licence holder; (b) the licensing authority should be required to grant the hours selected by the licence holder unless there was good reason to refuse; (c) the licensing authority should be required to grant special orders for exemption of not more than two hours in any day to meet any special need (e.g. catering for tourists or other holiday makers); (d) the present system of special hours certificates should continue but without the requirement that premises be licensed for music and dancing; (e) the selected permitted hours should apply for a minimum period of sixteen weeks, and any variation be subject to the licensee giving one month's notice to the licensing authority; (f) a notice should be clearly displayed outside the premises setting out the permitted hours.

Temperance representation

Having outlined the main features of the submission from the principal trade bodies, it is appropriate to turn to representatives of the temperance organizations, and here it is interesting to note the change of method of receiving submissions from temperance organizations compared with that followed by the Royal Commission 1929 to 1931. Then the representatives of numerous organizations appeared before the commission to give separate evidence. The Erroll Committee made it known that if this method were followed, there could be no undertaking given that the representatives of numerous organizations would meet the full committee and that in addition their time would be limited. The suggestion was made that a joint deputation representing the major temperance bodies should meet the full committee, and this was readily agreed.[5] The Temperance Council of the Christian Churches, the United Kingdom Alliance and the National Temperance Federation had sent in written submissions and they were, of course, represented on the joint deputation which was convened by the National Temperance Federation.

The deputation expressed anxiety regarding the serious personal and social manifestations of the excessive consumption of alcohol such as alcoholism, drunkenness, drink and driving and the emerging problem among young people. Effective controls were absolutely necessary. So far as the temperance organizations were concerned the main planks of their platform were, (a) alcohol is recognized by the medical profession as a dangerous drug; (b) the incidence of alcohol-caused problems is related to the availability and the per capita consumption of the drug; (c) the necessary controls are best exercised in a legal framework; (d) the existing framework might well be simplified so that all liquor outlets are controlled within the ambit of a single law regulating hours of sale, age below which sale is illegal, etc. with no exceptions.

Their reply to those who pleaded for longer hours and easier access by young people was expressed in a six-point statement.

It was necessary to recognise:

1. The practical interpretation of later hours as longer hours.
2. The increasing under-age drinking and juvenile crimes deplored by chief constables – and the still larger potential if the legal age was lowered.
3. The growing percentage of younger men and women among alcoholics.
4. The inconsistency of the 'double-standard' wherein drug trafficking is officially deprecated as 'a violence against the human spirit.'
5. The dubious policy of creating new opportunities for drinking while urging motorists not to drink.
6. The vast burden of expenditure already committed to the National Health Service on behalf of the chronic sick and disabled, the NHS being in no position to be saddled with the added cost of preventable illness due to increased alcohol consumption.

No doubt members of the deputation were able to bring substantial evidence in support of this outline when they met the Erroll Committee, otherwise on the basis of the written submission of the joint deputation, one is bound to conclude that the temperance case was not a compelling one. Something more than an expression of general principles is required; but both with regard to the temperance organizations' submission to the Royal Commission 1929 to 1931, and their representations concerning the eventual Licensing Act 1961, there was inadequate marshalling of facts and an inability to be specific in comments about proposals for changes in licensing law. Bearing this in mind it is not surprising that the temperance organizations' achievements in licensing legislation have been limited.

Christian Economic and Social Research Foundation evidence

It was the genius of an observer of the well-intentioned efforts of temperance organizations to initiate reforms of the licensing laws to ensure more effective control that led Harold S. Goodwin to create, with one or two others, the Christian Economic and Social Research Foundation in 1953. It was important that such a body should be independent and capable of assembling facts without bias. Although largely financed by the United Kingdom Temperance Alliance Limited, with additional specific grants from the Rowntree Social Service Trust, it remained wholly independent, its objectivity being secured by the integrity of Gwylmor Prys Williams, co-author of this book, who had been honorary statistical adviser to the foundation since its inception.

The foundation made a submission to the Erroll Committee which is a model of the marshalling of relevant statistics and other material, and the exposition of their implications for a committee charged with studying licensing laws and making recommendations for changes.[6] The submission was in two parts. The first included some background observations and a summary of the main conclusions. The second, and much longer, gave the statistical and other evidence from which inferences and deductions could be drawn.

The submission said that for over 150 years it had been generally acknowledged that the manufacture, sale and consumption of alcoholic beverages must be legally controlled. However, what had emerged in the way of legislation and regulation did not form a systematic code. It included acts of parliament and *ad-hoc* regulations devised to deal with specific situations and to get rid of anomalies. In several instances these changes had been conceived in response to what were thought to be the spirit and changing conditions of the times. Recent representations made by the Consumer Council and the British Tourist Authority fell into this last category, because they held that the spirit of the times called for a further "liberalising" of licensing laws. The foundation submitted "The arguments presented are frankly improvisations; and we applaud the Home Secretary's decision that the total licensing situation in all its complexity needs to be surveyed before wise decisions can be made as to whether in fact licensing reform has again become expedient and, if so, what forms it shoud take."[7] Whatever criticisms might be offered about the manner in which the present miscellany of controls had accumulated, it may still be true it serves the purpose well enough, or nearly so.

Believing that the intention of the Home Secretary was to secure a comprehensive report, the foundation assembled information on a wide-ranging scale. This included international trade and tourism, the social function of the "local", and the adequacy of the present permitted hours and of licensed premises. It dealt also with the various economic factors involved in production, marketing and ancillary services. A considerable section of the submission dealt with the various controls of fire risk, sanitation, hygiene and public order, and the means of control were also dealt with. There were two other sections of the submission, one indicating the lines on which licensing amendments might proceed, the other being concerned with proposals for the minimum safeguarding of overall public interest in the context of provisions of safeguards out of private profits. The principal conclusions of the foundation were summarized as follows:[8]

The tourist aspect
Total of foreign visitors, business and tourist, to the United Kingdom have been growing faster and for longer than in any other country. This remained true in 1970. Visitors from countries with little or no liquor licensing are increasing as fast as any. Not only is there no basis for saying that our liquor licensing puts tourists off: the 'English pub', which has emerged from our system is unique and a matter of positive interest to many tourists.

The public house as a social institution
Whatever the social detriment involved in the use of alcoholic drinks, they are most effectively controlled through the moderation imposed upon patrons of the public-house by the licensee's need to safeguard his licence. Also it may be claimed for the public-house that it functions as a local club for adults, and has therefore a social value. But to survive and meet its obligations it must remain profitable, and the economics of the public-house therefore become highly relevant.

Adequacy of present licensing hours
The present licensing hours are more than adequate in total as measured by actually observed patronage. Many of the 'opening hours' are in fact not needed and constitute a costly extravagance which customers at popular times effectively subsidise.

Adequacy of present licensed premises
On the experience of the last eleven years, the present number of licensed premises, in total and in category, seem to be as much economically, as the population will bear.

Restaurants and public-houses
These serve different needs, and their internal economics differ. Establishments attempting both services are seldom viable commercially. Both institutions, however, being places of public assembly and consumption, need to meet standards of hygiene and safety. They require to be profitable to be able to do so, and inspection and judicial assessment are needed to ensure conformity.

Need for 'closed periods'
Hygiene and maintenance of public amenity necessitate regular periods during which the public is denied access to the premises. Another public concern, the relative safety of people on the roads, requires that one such closed period should be 15.00 to 17.30 hours on working weekdays. On the established evidence since the introduction of the breathalyser, it would be a crime against society to bring about the injection of drunken motorists into the evening weekday rush-hour traffic.

An indicated solution consistent with the facts
From the economic viewpoint, patronage of licensed premises over the whole range of permitted hours is inadequate. The cost of keeping on-licensed premises open when there is little or no patronage must be reflected in (a) higher prices to the consumer; (b) reduced service; (c) lessened amenity; (d) low return personnel or combination thereof. It is good economic sense to help the licensee to operate most efficiently. It would be more profitable for him to close for some substantial part of present permitted hours. It would also make economic sense for licensees to open for longer at certain periods of the year, and at different times in different places, so long as public patronage is sufficient to cover costs. These costs include the provision of the services and labour necessary to preserve public order and safety in places of public assembly.

The foundation then made specific suggestions, rather than proposals, in regard to more flexible hours[9] and urged the retention of the general principle of control of on-licences by licensing justices and supervision by police and local authorities as appropriate. In the final section of its submission the foundation recommended that whatever decisions were made concerning licensing-law revision, there should be provision made for the central collection and publication of already available statistics, so that future decisions can be based on fact rather than conjecture.

The Magistrates' Assocation's submission

Since the administration of licensing legislation has been the responsibility of the licensing justices for centuries, the views of the Magistrates' Association were important among the various submissions made to the Erroll Committee.[10] Justices of the Peace, said the submission, were primarily concerned with the maintenance of the Queen's Peace, and committed to upholding law and order. It was from that standpoint that magistrates approached liquor licensing. While the main structure of the existing system was reasonably satisfactory there were anomalies and sources of irritation. There was need for simplification where the law was unnecessarily complex. The association pointed out that factors other than the law acted as controls of liquor consumption and abuse. Price was an important factor, especially the element of taxation. Before the introduction of heavy taxation the law may have been the principal constraint. Now taxation was such an effective control that it raised the question how far the ramifications of liquor licensing were really needed. There were other controls such as various requirements as to suitability of the licence-holders and premises, as well as restrictions of "permitted hours".

The Magistrates' Association said plainly that they did not think it was their function to discuss the economic issues of the matters being considered by the Erroll Committee. However, they did discuss what the Erroll Committee clearly regarded as a related issue, that is who should be the effective licensing authority, the licensing justices or some other body such as the local authority. (This was in fact related to economic factors, as we shall see when we discuss the report of the committee in the next chapter.) The case in favour of the justices retaining control of licensing rather than the local authority, was that the latter was more likely to be subject to outside pressures, to changes of policies with changing party control and to "interest" in the sense that local authorities were often applicants for licences. Against the justices retaining control was the argument that their role was judicial, whereas licensing was largely administrative, moreover, magistrates were overworked in any case and ought to be relieved of their licensing responsibilities. "There is certainly force in both views", said the magistrates whose conclusion was expressed in one sentence, "Inasmuch as licensing justices are concerned with demand for outlets for the sale of drink we believe that we are in a fair position to assess the wishes and requirements of the public."[11] This discussion anticipated one which occupied much of the time of the Erroll Committee.

On specific issues the Magistrates' Association made comments which, no doubt, were of special interest to the Erroll Committee. For instance, it was their view that the recent increase in outlets had not had any great effect on consumption or on drunkenness. This reinforced their view that controls might be eased, perhaps to a single form of licence. Certainly more flexible hours might be introduced, "If a maximum number of hours were fixed . . . ., but without the present requirements of an afternoon break of at least two hours, this would allow licensees to arrange their hours as they thought best in order to meet local demand."[12] New procedures for the issue of "occasional" licences to save bringing every application to the licensing justices were recommended.

Numerous associations and organizations submitted written evidence and some were invited to give oral evidence, but the summaries of selected bodies which have been included in this chapter bring out most of the major opinions expressed. In the next chapter we shall see how the committee dealt with the evidence, the conclusions it reached and the recommendations it made.

References

1. *Alliance News* May 1971 p. 8.
2. *Report of Royal Commission on Assizes and Quarter Sessions 1966–69.* H.M.S.O. para 230 p. 80.
3. *Alliance News* May 1971 p. 9.
4. *Alliance News* October 1971 p. 15.
5. For membership of the deputation see *Alliance News* March 1972.

6. *Evidence submitted by the Christian Economic and Social Research Foundation to the Home Office Departmental Committee on Liquor Licensing.* Priory Press for the Christian Economic and Social Research Foundation (1971).
7. Op cit p. 2.
8. Op cit pp. 3, 4.
9. Op cit p. 4.
10. Memorandum of evidence to the Departmental Committee on Liquor Licensing. Annual Report 1971–72 of the Magistrates' Association pp. 33–40.
11. Op cit p. 36.
12. Op cit p. 36.

CHAPTER 11

THE ERROLL COMMITTEE AND ITS RECEPTION

The Erroll Committee published its report in December 1972. It was unanimous, and in that respect was probably unique so far as public inquiries into liquor licensing law are concerned, and began with a review of current licensing legislation,[1] which included the identification of features of licensing law which had strongly influenced the committee's analysis of it.

The first was the discretion of the licensing justices in granting various types of licences. This was absolute in the case of full on- and off-licences, but limited in the case of licences to restaurants and hotels or in the issue of registration certificates for clubs by magistrates' courts. In the view of the committee both types of discretion carried with them certain legislative consequences.[2] The second characteristic was the way in which particular provisions of the law owed their existence to specific and often remote historical events. Though still relevant, they bore marks of their historical origins even when incorporated into a Consolidation Act. The onus on the committee was to examine not only whether the various provisions were justified in principle, but also whether they were in a form appropriate to modern legislation.[3]

A third characteristic was the "clear emphasis in current legislation on public order and safety,"[4] and fourth, the licensing system was operated by a judicial body and the extent to which this was appropriate was one of the more important issues the committee would have to consider.[5] A sixth characteristic was the absence of any central authority to issue advice and directions.[6] Finally, there were parts of the law, such as those relating to children and permitted hours, which raised important social issues.[7]

The social context

It was the social context to which the committee addressed itself first, and it began with references to the commercial background.[8] Consumption of all types of intoxicating liquor had increased considerably in recent years, and since 1960 the increase had been much more rapid than the upward movement of population in the same period. In 1960 consumption of spirits per head of the population was 0.39 proof gallons and ten years later it was 0.47 proof gallons. It was, however, the consumption of wine which showed the most dramatic increase from 0.68 gallons per head of the population in 1960 to 1.14 in 1970, but the increase accelerated more rapidly from 1966 (0.89) onwards. What caused fluctuations in consumption was a complex issue to which the committee gave more detailed consideration later in their report. In view of the detailed account of the structure of the liquor industry in the Monopolies Commission's report, the Erroll Committee did not think it necessary to go over the same ground, though it did think there were some details it might incorporate. Most usefully it included the following table:[9]

Premises in England and Wales licensed for the sale of intoxicating liquor by retail, and registered clubs at 30th June 1971

	Types of premises	Scope of licence		No. in existence
A (i)	On-licences (other than licensed clubs and part IV licences)	A (i) only		
		All intoxicating liquors (full on-licences)	63,640	
		Beer, cider and wine or beer and cider	395	
		Wine only/and or cider	52	64,087
(ii)	Restaurants			7,100
(iii)	Residential			1,804
(iv)	Combined residential and restaurants			2,324
(v)	Licensed clubs			2,563
		Total on-licensed premises		**77,878**
B	Registered clubs			23,985
C	Off-licences			28,166
		Total retail licensed and registered outlets in England and Wales		**130,029**

(Source: Home Office Liquor Licensing Statistics)

The committee thought that at the time of the publication of their report the number of public houses in England and Wales should be revised to 61,000. There was a process of rationalization in the provision of public houses. Although new ones were being built and new licences granted, these were more than off-set by reductions due to closures. This process had been influenced in the early years of the century by the administration of the law and the provision of compensation for redundancy. More recently standards required for building, fire precautions, health and various facilities for patrons had tended to discourage the proliferation of sub-standard premises. Moreover, the licensing justices had exercised discretion in respect of "need" and their powers to impose conditions. "The result has been to produce a type of premises which, in structure, operation and clientele, has evolved directly in step with various changes in the licensing law."[10]

Taking 1960 as the break point, there had been a steady increase in the number of off-licences since then. In 1960 there were 23,670 in England and Wales and in the decade to 1970 this had increased to 27,910. Before 1960 the number of off-licences had remained generally constant at around 23,500, though the number in the years between the wars had hovered at about 22,000.[11] It was the Licensing Act 1961 which led to the increase in the number of off-licences, particularly in supermarkets. Before 1961 off-licences had to observe the "permitted hours" of the district. The 1961 Act changed this and enabled off-licences to open during normal shop hours. Supermarkets felt inhibited from securing off-licences for a section of the store which had to observe the licensing hours when the rest of the store was open for business.

The other major outlet was the clubs. These were of two types: proprietary clubs which differed from public houses only in that they purported to restrict admission, and in many cases (as with bingo clubs) use the premises for other purposes than the sale and consumption of alcohol; members' clubs, in many of which the supply of liquor was ancillary to the main purpose of the club, though the supply of liquor was an important factor in the financial viability of the club. In 1971 there were reckoned to be 2,563 proprietary clubs and 23,985 members' clubs.[12] In addition to clubs there were what the Erroll Committee called "Ancillary outlets". These included hotels, restaurants, theatres, cinemas, ballrooms and railway catering facilities. The restaurant and hotel licences accounted for the largest number of ancillary outlets. The following figures indicated the trends:[13]

	Combined Restaurant and Residential Licences	**Residential Licences**	**Restaurant Licences**
1967	1,769	1,191	4,590
1971	2,324	1,804	7,100

In concluding their preliminary consideration of the commercial background the Erroll Committee referred to the difficult task of relating the changing pattern of consumer demand and the marketing response to it, and the need for legislation to safeguard the public from the adverse social consequences of the consumption of alcohol. It was these actual and potential consequences which had to be considered before any recommendations for changes in legislation could be made. And the most serious consequence of what the report called "abnormal drinking" was "alcoholism" or "alcohol dependence". The seriousness of this problem had only fairly recently been recognized. Its prevalence was higher than most people would expect, and its causes included the availability of liquor. "Given this" said the report, "we make no apology for considering the possible link between changes in the law and the actual prevalence of alcoholism."[14] It was not easy to express statistically the incidence of alcoholism, but the report quoted the World Health Organization's estimate that in 1951 there were 86,000 alcoholics in England and Wales. The Office of Health Economics would update this figure for 1971 as 350,000. Other authorities quoted different figures, but it might be assumed that there were between 200,000 and 400,000 alcoholics in the country. The major possible causes or contributory factors were availability, constitutional or biological factors, and environmental and cultural influences. While hesitating to endorse the equation availability = consumption = the incidence of alcoholism, the Erroll Committee said it was simply necessary "to establish that the availability of liquor is a factor in the genesis of alcohol dependence which has to be taken into account."[15] Further, "any overall increase in consumption tends to produce more heavy drinkers".[16] The committee concluded, "The picture we get, particularly over the last twenty years, is of rising overall consumption, accompanied by increases in alcoholism death rates and in offences of drunkenness, all of which, however, are still below the peak levels reached towards the end of the last and the beginning of this century."[17]

Inconsistency and conflict

Others have taken the Erroll Committee to task for the inconsistency, and at times the conflict, of its various statements,[18] and it would be tedious to repeat this process in detail, but some of the more obvious examples can be given. For example, the committee said it was not easy to express the incidence of alcoholism statistically, but, later concluded that the increase in alcoholism death rates was still below the peak levels reached toward the end of the last century and the beginning of this one. Again, while it complained of a lack of research into "the historical pattern of our own licensing legislation,"[19] yet it made its own selection of historical material to support a conclusion;[20] even though there was no member of the committee, or an assessor, qualified in the relevant field of history.

Despite these deficiencies, the conclusion was nevertheless reached, at the end of the section called "The relevance of licensing law" that "We have to conclude, therefore, that decisive evidence is lacking as to the likely impact of changes in the law on levels of alcohol consumption and abnormal drinking."[21] If, in fact, the evidence was indeed lacking on such a crucial issue, it may be thought that the committee should have required the Home Office researchers to prepare, from all available sources, the kind of documentation upon which solid judgements could be made.

Again, at the end of their consideration of the social context of the matter, the committee reached far-reaching conclusions and propounded general principles to be brought to the rest of the report justified by the astonishing statement that "In the absence of any substantial research guidance on the results of recent liquor control policy in this country, we have had to make our own judgments on the degree of change which is acceptable."[22]

The statement was astonishing because in the absence of any substantial research guidance on the fundamental issue with which the committee was concerned, and bearing in mind the lack of expertise on the committee, it did not occur to them to question their qualifications as right to make judgements on the degree of acceptable change.

Controls

Part III of the report was the core of the committee's case. This was concerned with "Controls". It began, as might be expected, with a discussion of the need for and the purposes of control. It was admitted that the issue of control or no control might seem hardly worth discussing.

However, it was important to a committee which was later going to recommend greater sensitivity to market forces. The way was cleared for this approach to "control" by the statement, "It is not entirely frivolous to ask whether the sale of intoxicating liquor really needs to be regulated by act of parliament. None of the memorandas submitted to us seriously argued that all control was unnecessary, but underlying many was an impatience with what was frequently cited as an unduly restrictive regime – an impatience which some people would argue can be met only by a system of complete and unrestricted *laissez faire.*"[23] The credibility of the Erroll Committee would have been utterly destroyed had it come out in favour of removing all controls. It did, however, recommend that licensing justices should no longer have the power to assess "need" in considering applications for licences, and we shall return to this part of the committee's recommendations. The report stated quite firmly that "the sale of intoxicating liquor is *not* like that of any other commodity."[24] It required of the person operating an establishment as a retail outlet, particularly for on-consumption, that he should maintain adequate standards of conduct. Since drinking often implied a convivial social activity, wherever it took place standards of hygiene and safety, as well as public order had to be recognized and enforced. "We are unable to accept, therefore, that so far as on-consumption is concerned, the sale of intoxicating liquor is so like other forms of retail activity as to justify complete freedom from controls designed to prevent potential abuse" concluded the report.[25] In the next few sentences it seemed that the committee was not going to be firm. They said, "The proposition is easier to argue in the case of off-licences. Here the nature of the trade is akin to ordinary shop business, and an analogy frequently drawn from sales of ordinary groceries or, for that matter, any retail commodity."[26] The apprehension aroused by such argument was, however, dispelled when the report concluded that "some form of control is still necessary for off-sales, even though the case for special treatment is not nearly as strong as for on-sales."[27]

The question of "Need"

The crunch issue was the question of "need". The Licensing Act 1904 gave licensing justices absolute discretion in respect of all types of licensed premises. In general this was still the position, though the 1964 Act limited this discretion in respect of restaurant licences and residential licences. Such applications could be refused only on grounds of the character of the applicant and the suitability and convenience of the premises. The committee conceded that the main trade organizations were opposed to any relaxation of the justices' discretion, the organizations advocating its abolition being predictably the Consumer Council, the British Tourist Authority and the English Tourist Board. Similar proposals for restricting the justices' discretion were made by Berni Inns Limited, Grand Metropolitan Hotels Limited and the British Hotels and Restaurants Association. The committee inquired of various petty sessional divisions what criteria were observed by justices in determining "need" and they found considerable variation. Some conceived it their duty to restrict to a minimum the number of licensed premises in their area, others saw it to be their duty to ensure that there were enough licences of all descriptions to cater for the needs of the public, while others regarded themselves primarily as justices of the peace, even as licensing justices. The committee said they found that the attitude of licensing justices was a disincentive to potential entrants into the licensed trade. Further, they found sufficiently numerous cases to confirm their impression of the restrictive effect of the justices' wide powers. "Far from encountering areas in which there could be said to be too many licensed premises, we found some where there were quite obviously too few."[28]

It is in the "Conclusions" at the end of the chapter "The question of need" where the Erroll philosophy is expounded. Having raised doubts already about the validity of the justices' discretion, the ground was prepared for declaring that "need" was "a meangingless expression" which had "little or no commercial or economic significance".[29] It then became plain how crucial was the composition of the committee and how persuasive had been the members with commercial marketing predilictions. This is plain from the following important quotation from the report – "In our view, the only relevant commercial consideration is that of market demand. A licensing authority is hardly qualified to assess whether such a demand exists, and we see no reason why any licensing process should interfere with the ordinary operation of market forces."[30]It was the view of the committee that the power of justices should be confined to such matters as the fitness or competence of an applicant, the external and internal suitability of the premises and its implications for public order and the environment of the immediate locality. And so it was recommended that it was no part of the justices' responsibility to consider "need". "The point we seek to establish at this stage" declared the report, "is simply that the interests of the consumer are more likely to be met than they are at present in the sort of a more open and flexible situation which we see emerging from the proposed re-definition of the licensing authority's discretion. These interests are distinct from, but no less important than, the more esoteric considerations of certainty and simplicity in the administration of the law. The abolition of the need criteria, in our view, is an essential pre-condition of ensuring that the brewing industry and the licensed trade, as well as potential new entrants, are more responsive to public demand."[31] Again in discussing off-licences the committee said, "In the final analysis, it must be left to the public to demonstrate what type of outlets they prefer, and the licensing law cannot, in our view, be used to control these market forces."[32] The recommendation in respect of both on- and off-licences was that, in principle, the justices' present absolute discretion be replaced by "specific grounds for the refusal of applications for and renewals of licences".[33]

Who should administer the law?

In considering who should be the licensing authority the committee said that in their view there were only three possible candidates: (a) the local justices of the peace (whether sitting as a whole bench or as a committee of the justices); (b) a local authority (leaving aside, for the moment, the question of the category of the authority); (c) a statutory body set up specially for the purpose.[34] The committee set out the various points in favour of each of the three contenders. Then it concluded that the case for change had not been made out, and that "given some modification of the present arrangements to allow for a more positive role by local authorities in licensing applications, the case for retaining the justices as the licensing authority is overwhelming."[35]

It did, however, recommend a new licensing system. There should be two types of licence, (a) a personal licence, to the operator of the premises; and (b) a premises licence, held by the owner of the premises. Any differences between types of outlets should be specified by way of conditions attached to the licences. In the case of a premises licence the local authority should be required to issue a notice to the applicant and to the Clerk to the Justices certifying the suitability or otherwise of the premises.

On the question of appeals against decisions of local licensing justices the Erroll Committee had doubts about the complete impartiality of the procedure adopted in the Courts Act 1971.[36] This provided for appeals to be made to the Crown Court with two justices from the district from which the appeal came sitting with a judge and two independent justices. On this procedure the Erroll Committee commented, "We think it debatable, however, whether it is right in principle for an appeals body to be composed, if only in part, of representatives of bodies who are respondents to an appeal. Even given the safeguard that the licensing justices concerned should not have sat during the case which is the subject of the appeal, their presence could cast some doubt on the impartiality of the appeal court."[37] Accordingly the committee recommended that this procedure should be reconsidered.

Permitted hours

Possibly no other aspect of licensing law has given rise to more discussion and controversy than the question of "hours". The existing "permitted hours" are described in the chapter on "The purpose of licensing legislation".[38] The Erroll Committee found that there were two main complaints about existing permitted hours, one concerning the "afternoon break" and the other the terminal hour at night. The plea for more flexibility of hours was usually for the abolition of the afternoon break and the fixing of a later closing time.[39] Before recommending more flexibility the committee recognized that a number of factors had to be taken into consideration. For instance, the freedom to open implied a freedom to close, which would rule out uniformity and thus create confusion for the consumer and problems of enforcement by the police. Such freedom would not only lead to differences of hours between neighbouring districts, but also between premises in the same district. It had been put to the committee that any proposed combination of longer hours and flexibility would result in excessive drinking. The committee recognized this possible danger, but thought safeguards could be introduced by legislation without harming the principle of flexibility. The pressure on licensees to remain open longer was also a factor to be considered. Again it was believed that safeguards could be introduced.

There was also the question of road safety. Would the abolition of the afternoon break lead to the release onto the roads at peak home-going times a large number of motorists who had been drinking in the afternoon? And would a later closing time create further road hazards late at night? The recommendation of the committee was that the justices should have discretion to order individual public houses to close for a specified period, or to impose such an order on all licensed premises in the district. Similar orders could be issued in respect of closing times. The committee made specific recommendations in respect of the various types of licensed premises, but it was hoped that their recommendations would be taken as a whole. "It would be unfortunate, in our view, if one particular proposal was taken out of its context and presented by itself, as an indication of what this committee has sought to achieve."[40]

Children and young people

In turning to the matter of access of children to licensed premises, which in some respects is the most complex area of licensing legislation, the committee recognized that this was a subject which aroused strong feelings. There is no need at this juncture to reiterate the existing law which temperance organizations and trade associations were united in urging should not be changed, while tourist associations and various entertainment interests wanted considerable relaxation. In the end the Erroll Committee, recommended that it should still be an offence to allow a person under fourteen years of age in a bar during permitted hours, with specific exceptions. In particular it was proposed that the licensing justices should be empowered to issue a certificate to a personal licensee for the parts of the premises from which children need not be excluded. Related to the question of access by children was the age at which a young person might purchase liquor on licensed premises or consume at a bar. The committee received numerous opinions on this matter and the well-known arguments were advanced both for retaining the age at eighteen and reducing it. Erroll came out in favour of reducing it to seventeen, while under certain circumstances someone of sixteen years of age should be able to purchase beer, porter, cider, perry or wine for his own consumption. It was further recommended that there should be no change in the law in regard to the degree of responsibility placed on licensees for under-age drinking.[41]

Perennial problem of clubs

There were several other matters on which the committee received submissions, and made comments and recommendations. The chief of these was the perennial problem of the registered clubs. These were not subject to the same legislative controls as fully on-licensed premises, and yet the facilities so far as the supply of liquor was concerned were so similar as to be indistinguishable. It had been a grievance shared by licensees, public-house managers, the police and temperance reformers that separate registration of clubs was an anomaly which ought to be removed. Both the Association of Police Officers and the Metropolitan Police Commissioner told the Erroll Committee that the registered clubs should be assimilated into the licensing law which was opposed by the various club association representatives.

The recommendations of the Erroll Committee were that the proposed "premises licence" should apply to registered clubs, and should be capable of being issued to the committee for the time being responsible for the management of the club, a "personal licence" should be held by the officer of the club nominated for that purpose or by some nominated employee who was acceptable to the justices. The committee also recommended that the police should have a general right of entry into all licensed premises. Gaming clubs should be treated as a special case. Where a club registered under the Gaming Act 1968 applied for a liquor licence, the justices should attach a condition imposing a 48-hour gap between nomination and application for membership and admission.[42]

Research

Throughout their report the Erroll Committee referred to the paucity of research material on various matters with which they were concerned. Their complaint was that either the research material was non-existent or inadequate. And yet, as we have observed, they proceeded to make recommendations for massive changes in licensing law and administration. Their final plea for more adequate monitoring and research services seemed insincere and perhaps if they had been more familiar with the subject, they would have known that some data they required was readily available or could have been provided. That having been said, their recommendations on this matter were admirable,

(a) that the social effects of any future liquor licensing legislation should be monitored;

(b) that the necessary research should be carried out under the direction and supervision of an interdepartmental working party;

(c) that, if necessary, a contribution to the costs of research should be met from the proposed trust to administer the balance of funds at present held by compensation authorities.[43]

The intentions of the Erroll Committee were succincty expressed by Sheila Black, a member of the committee. Writing in the *Financial Times*[44] she said, "We all knew that what we wanted basically, was total freedom for all, to drink when and where they liked." The committee's hypothesis was that while the dangers of the extremes of prohibition on the one hand and total permissiveness on the other were known, there was an intermediate area which was neutral. This ignored the report's own reference to "the picture we get, particularly over the last twenty years, of rising overall consumption, accompanied by increases in alcoholism and in offences of drunkenness."[45]

Press opinion

The report was received in many quarters with extreme caution. On the day the report was published *The Times* in a leading article said, "In general it would be wise not to go as far as the Committee would in satisfying the consumer. It is better to have a few thirsty throats than to provide further unnecessary encouragement to heavy drinking."[46] The relation of the Erroll proposals to road safety was referred to in an article in the *Financial Times.* It said "the biggest question raised by the report is whether its concept of social realities is unduly narrow in that it gives far too little weight to the highly relevant connection between drinking and our greatest modern bugbear – slaughter on the roads."[47] A particularly interesting comment appeared in the *Investors Chronicle:* "There are basically three directions in which the proposed alterations to the law could affect trading conditions. First, by abolishing the requirement to prove 'need' when applying for a licence, the business would be opened to many new potential licence-holders. Second, licensing hours would be lengthened greatly. Third, children would be allowed to enter many bars, while young people of at least 17 would be allowed to consume alcoholic drinks. All these are factors which it might be felt would increase consumption."[48] The *Daily Telegraph* published the results of a Gallup Poll on some of the recommendations of the committee. From a sample of 1,023, 62 per cent disapproved of public houses being open up to 14 hours a day, 68 per cent were against lowering the legal age from 18 to 17, and 77 per cent did not want children to be allowed in bars. Just over half, 58 per cent, were in favour of all restaurants and cafes being allowed to serve alcohol. In the same issue, a leading article in the *Daily Telegraph* advised the government to ignore the findings of the poll.[49] The *Police Review* accepted that the Erroll Committee's confession that there was often a lack of information and research on which to make considered judgments invalidated their recommendations for changes in the law. "In spite of the lack of information the committee has gone ahead to make the most sweeping proposals," commented the *Police Review,* "but belatedly as though trying to make amends its final recommendation is to set up a monitoring service to measure changes in consumption, drinking habits and abuse, after new legislation has been introduced." In a reference to "permitted hours", the *Police Review* said, "The extension of hours is principally intended to encourage the continental cafe-type of establishment but it will also encourage 'vertical' drinking without eating and this could be a serious menace and could disrupt a great deal of work in industry during the day. The French have plenty of experience of this, as they have of alcoholism, and these social evils may be aggravated here if facilities are increased. At a time when the Government is becoming increasingly concerned about the effects of drink and driving it is doubtful if it will introduce legislation which will extend drinking facilities for drivers."[50]

Conservative lawyers' views

While acknowledging that the Erroll Report included many of the proposals contained in their original submission, the Society of Conservative Lawyers reacted against some of its principal recommendations. On the lowering of the age limit the society commented, "The Erroll proposal to permit 17 year olds to buy and drink intoxicating liquor in bars is put forward in order to 'adjust the law so that it corresponds with social facts.' But statutes also can create social facts. The age of 18 has become a significant moment of transition into adulthood in other spheres of law. Enforcement of the present limit may be difficult; but this will be true of any limit. We express the view that a change in limit will have a creeping effect on drinking habits; the 17 year olds' life style becomes the model for the boy who is a year younger. We would leave the limit as it is."[51] The Conservative Lawyers believed a maximum of freedom should be maintained both in the sale and the consumption of liquor, but there were three reasons why a degree of control was necessary. "These are that alcohol is potentially dangerous to health; complete freedom could lead to widespread drunkenness and public disorder; and as it can lead to addiction, children should not have unrestricted access to it."[52]

Medical opinion

It was from the medical profession that the most serious criticisms came. An editorial in *The Lancet* described some aspects of the Erroll Report from the health angle as "disquieting". Having acknowledged the serious dimensions of the problem of alcoholism, and the trend towards more consumption and the resulting increase in drunkenness and drink offences, the Erroll Committee proceeded to make what *The Lancet* believed were astonishing recommendations. It said, "For the Committee then to suggest that pubs should have the right to open continuously from 10 a.m. to 12 midnight, and off-licences from 8.30 a.m. to midnight closing: to propose that bingo halls, dance places, and cinemas should have licensing hours co-extensive with hours of opening, which licences are rather easily obtainable: to suggest that the pub should now be supplemented by the "cafe-pub" so that parents can take the children along: all this, in terms of commonsense, can hardly be seen as a well-derived public strategy to meet a currently serious situation. If the committee has its way we seem headed to catch up with our Victorian ancestors. It is not only a number of the individual proposals which are ill-conceived but it is also the general tone, the ethics, which seems inappropriate to the problem. There are certainly bows in the medical direction, and the report has included a chapter on alcoholism: but in the light of much else in its pages, the bowing has the look of pretty empty posturing."[53]

The Lancet editorial referred, for instance, to the Erroll Committee's acknowledgement that breathalyser offences had increased from 27,972 in 1970 to 39,840 in 1971; and then the committee, without any awareness of inconsistence, proceeded to recommend "cafe-pubs" because it would make it easier for parents out on a family drive with their children to go in and have a drink. "Such a suggestion" commented *The Lancet,* "seems in the context of all we know about drinking and driving to convey an ethic of almost rollicking irresponsibility." And the same editorial referred to the recommendation of Erroll that in future it should be put " 'beyond doubt' that the use of credit cards on on-licensed premises is lawful." This, too, seemed further evidence of "rollicking irresponsibility". It also pointed out the bizarre situation which would arise if at the time when the Secretary of State at the Department of Health was spending a further £2 million on alcoholism treatment services, the Home Secretary recommended the acceptance of the Erroll proposals.

Equally critical comments were made in the *British Medical Journal.* The first consideration of parliament when it came to consider the proposals should be the consequences to public health, declared the journal. Taking up the statistics incorporated in the Erroll Report from which the committee reached certain conclusions, the *British Medical Journal* expressed surprise at the proposals for the relaxation of licensing based on the information accepted by Erroll. "The impression is given that the committee is set on policies of relaxation for reasons other than those concerning the public health," the BMA journal concluded. "From the public health point of view the report's main proposals must be condemned as untimely. Their adoption in practice would be to risk a further increase in alcoholism, with its attendant dangers to harmony in the home and life on the roads."[54]

The most detailed and devastating appraisal of the Erroll Report came from a group of ten psychiatrists and researchers of the Addiction Research Unit of the Institute of Psychiatry at the University of London.[55] In the introduction to their commentary the authors said their particular interests were in the areas of medicine and public health. It was with the implications for these aspects that their comments were, in part, concerned. In addition they accepted the invitation of the Home Office to express their view on the Erroll Committee's recommendations in general. They did so for two reasons. First, because they worked in a research unit, and, therefore, were interested in the evidence which the committee had available to it, in the way in which that evidence was commented upon and handled, and in the committee's recommendations as to the nature and organization of future research which might be carried out in this area. Second, because particular medical and public-health issues could not, with profit, be considered in isolation from the social, economic and legal context in which they were set.

The authors were particularly critical of the way in which the public-health aspect was dealt with by the committee. Although health was raised as a contender for consideration, the way in which it was discussed was quite different from the way in which other factors were considered. "The committee's certainty as to the importance of public disorder, public safety, public hygiene, problems of policing, upset beer and crisp litter, is unfortunately not extended to the matter of health."[56] "It appears that 'Health' having been the last to join the list of the committee's concerns seems also to have been the first to leave it."[57]

It was noted that in considering the important question of "need" (referred to earlier) the Erroll Report deferred to the penultimate paragraph of this section, the aspect of health. Here it referred to evidence presented by the Christian Economic and Social Research Foundation which it said had "attempted to demonstrate some relationship between the end of Resale Price Maintenance and the increase in the number of supermarket/off-licences and in statistics of drunkenness." The report went on, "We have also heard it suggested from the Temperance organisations that off-licences provide an unnecessary temptation to shoppers. We find ourselves unable to accept either of these arguments."[58] The staff of the Addiction Research Unit commented, "There is no presentation of an argument against the CESRF or Temperance positions, or even the hint of what criteria were used to reject these arguments."[59] Again, the committee said, "This is an area in which research is notably lacking, and we do not feel it can be said with any certainty that increases in consumption among particular groups are due to increases in outlets rather than to more fundamental factors."[60] "If evidence is lacking" replied the psychiatrists, "upon what grounds are the CESRF and Temperance organisations' arguments rejected? In such circumstances surely the only possible position is one of agnosticism rather than selective rejection of arguments."[61] Concluding their comments on the chapter of the Erroll Report dealing with "need" they said, "The committee's decision to abolish the justices' absolute discretion is felt by us to be symptomatic of a vital change of emphasis in relation to liquor licensing which the recommendations taken as a whole represent. The likely resultant expansion in the number of outlets once the "need" criterion is abandoned is, we feel, treated too lightly by the committee, while the committee's rejection of contra-arguments without comment or evidence is a matter of concern."[62]

The two proposals of the Erroll Committee which gave the authors of the commentary most cause for concern were the conditions associated with the extension of sale to young people and those associated with the extension of sale facilities to premises primarily used for other purposes. "Both betray the committee's apparent lack of concern for the possible adverse social consequences of liberalising and simplifying liquor licensing legislation", they said. As to the arguments advanced by the Erroll Committee for greater flexibility in the hours of opening, "they neither demonstrated that there was substantial public support for greater flexibility, nor guaranteed that applications for extensions or exceptions would be diminished."[63] It was also pointed out that while the committee acknowledged that there was little hard evidence to suggest that increasing the hours of opening would increase consumption and adverse consequences, no evidence was provided to show that the recommendations would *not* result in such consequences. The commentators added, "The opinions which are most pursuasive derive in the main from the Brewers' Society and those commercial interests likely to benefit from increased sales, together with the Commissioner of Metropolitan Police, whose main preoccupation was with the difficulty of administering the present legislation, none of which can be construed as reflecting in any way public-health considerations."[64]

When the team from the Addiction Research Unit considered the Erroll Committee's arguments for recommending greater access for children to licensed premises, it made this devastating comment, "It is interesting that in a situation where the Committee consider that 'the arguments we have had to evaluate have been largely value judgments' (Para 1209) that it should be the value judgments of those with a financial investment in the relaxation of licensing laws which should eventually be incorporated in the committee's recommendations."[65] It was also pointed out that the Erroll Committee was unclear whether children should be accompanied by an adult on licensed premises. If so, what did the term "accompanied" mean? As to the committee's dealing with the question of the age at which a young person could be served and drink in a bar, the Addiction Research Unit team exposed the inconsistency of Erroll's arguments and conclusions. The Erroll Committee admitted that most of the views expressed were in favour of retaining the age at eighteen, and this was supported by two-thirds of those questioned in a survey by the Office of Population Censuses and

Surveys. And yet, the Erroll Committee decided to recommend lowering the age to seventeen. Two considerations prompted this decision. First, when were young people sufficiently mature to purchase liquor? Second, the question of the enforceability of the law. Neither of these considerations was adequately explored in the report. In one place the committee criticized the way in which liquor advertisements appealed to young people to drink, and in another recommended lowering the age to seventeen and allowing children on licensed premises.[66]

The team of psychiatrists and researchers was particularly critical of the way in which research evidence was either ignored, dealt with inconsistently or misrepresented. They said, "The Committee's faith in its own observations is, in our view, exaggerated. Altogether the Committee's handling of the research material tends to have been frequently guided by the principle that such material is acceptable only if it accords with the Committee's own observations. This is a rather disturbing aspect of the report and is, surely, a matter which should be considered by all government departments who are 'good enough, to make available' to departmental committees of inquiry 'the results of a survey by the Office of Population Censuses and Surveys'."[67] The whole section of "Research" in the ARU team's critique of the Erroll Report, should be read by all who are especially interested in this aspect of it. They felt there should be a monitoring unit able to design and conduct co-ordinated research which would be of the quality demanded by the committee. Any changes in legislation which such a unit would monitor should be either temporary, and conditional upon a satisfactory research report, or at least accompanied by a commitment that the law would be reconsidered in the light of the results of such research.[68] The conclusion of this team was that the Erroll Committee received insufficient evidence from medical and related bodies, that it paid insufficient attention to the public-health aspect of the revision of licensing law, and that its handling of research material relating to the health aspect was deficient.

The report was criticized by almost every body which had an informed interest in the matter. The temperance organisations, notably the Temperance Council of the Christian Churches and the United Kingdom Alliance produced reasoned statements, commending where they could some of the judgments made but coming down firmly against the principal recommendations. Government statements in both Houses of Parliament gave a cautious welcome to the report but in debates following the statements there was almost unanimous hostility. As time passed, and the government gave no indication of introducing legislation to implement some of its major recommendations, the conclusion was reached that Erroll had been put on ice. This was confirmed by the failure of Private Member's Bills to make progress which, had they been successful, would have begun a process of bringing in Erroll reforms one by one.

References

1. *Report of the Departmental Committee on Liquor Licensing.* H.M.S.O. (1972) pp 819.
2. Op cit p. 17.
3. Op cit p. 18.
4. Op cit p. 18.
5. Op cit p. 19.

6. Op cit p. 19.
7. Op cit p. 19.
8. Op cit pp. 20–33.
9. Op cit p. 24.
10. Op cit p. 28.
11. Op cit p. 28.
12. Op cit pp. 29–31.
13. Op cit pp. 31–32.
14. Op cit p. 34.
15. Op cit p. 38.
16. Op cit p. 39.
17. Op cit p. 42.
18. *Where Erroll went wrong on Liquor Licensing.* Camberwell Council on Alcoholism (1973).
19. Erroll op cit p. 42.
20. Op cit p. 43.
21. Op cit p. 46.
22. Op cit p. 70.
23. Op cit p. 71.
24. Op cit p. 72.
25. Op cit p. 72.
26. Op cit p. 72.
27. Op cit pp. 72, 73.
28. Op cit p. 89.
29. Op cit p. 90.
30. Op cit pp. 90, 91.
31. Op cit p. 91.
32. Op cit p. 94.
33. Op cit pp. 92–94.
34. Op cit p. 97.
35. Op cit p. 107.
36. See p. 229.
37. Op cit p. 130.
38. See pp. 221–231.
39. Op cit p. 143.
40. Op cit p. 161.
41. Op cit pp. 163–180.
42. Op cit pp. 201–220.
43. Op cit p. 282.
44. 6th December 1972.
45. Op cit p. 42.
46. *The Times* 6th December 1972 p. 17.
47. *Financial Times* 11th December 1972 p. 46.
48. *Investors Chronicle* 8th December 1972 p. 998.
49. *Daily Telegraph* 27th December 1972 p. 10 (Gallup p. 11).
50. *Police Review* 5th January 1973 p. 4.
51. *Liberty and Licensing* Conservative Political Centre p. 4.
52. Op cit p. 5.
53. *The Lancet* 16th December 1972 p. 1297.
54. *The British Medical Journal* 16th December 1972 pp. 625, 626.
55. *Where Erroll went wrong on Liquor Licensing* (1973).
56. Op cit p. 13.
57. Op cit p. 13.
58. Erroll op cit p. 95.
59. Op cit p. 18.
60. Erroll op cit p. 95.
61. Op cit p. 18.
62. Op cit p. 19.
63. Op cit pp. 34, 35.
64. Op cit p. 35.
65. Op cit p. 36.
66. Op cit pp. 37, 38.
67. Op cit p. 44.
68. Op cit p. 55.

CHAPTER 12

CHILDREN AND DRINK

Towards the end of the nineteenth century there was increasing concern about the effects on children of excessive drinking by their parents and the lack of control over the sale of liquor to children. There was, no doubt, a connection between the prevalence of drunkenness and cruelty to children, but even the general problem of the maltreatment of children had remained hidden from the public. It was through the pressure of the National Society for the Prevention of Cruelty to Children that Acts of Parliament were passed in 1889 and 1894 which made such cruelty an offence. Until these acts were enforced the extent of the problem was not generally known. After the passing of these acts "and the building up of a systematic organization to enforce them through the greater part of the country, the cruelty and neglect which lurked unknown have been dragged into light."[1]

The facts

And what were the facts? The N.S.P.C.C. reported that during the eleven years from 1st April 1889 to 31st March 1900, the total number of complaints was 190,811 of which 176,230 were found to be true, affecting the welfare of 487,819 children, and involving 245,795 offenders. The following table[2] gives a breakdown of these figures:

	Complaints	**Children Involved**
Neglect and starvation	134,414	374,428
Manslaughter	63	
Abandonment	2,817	
Exposure	5,179	
Illtreatment and assault	32,734	66,395
Causing to beg	6,665	27,114
Moral wrongs	5,606	11,697
Other wrongs	3,333	8,185

This was not a complete picture. By 1900 the network of committees and inspectors of the N.S.P.C.C. covered only two-thirds of the country. To illustrate the extent of the problem the N.S.P.C.C. imagined a city of some 500,000 people of various social classes and occupations, with approximately one-third adults and two-thirds children. "One-half of the streets of the vast place are inhabited by notorious drunkards,"[3] they concluded. The society estimated that 50 per cent of the cases of cruelty were directly attributable to drink, and among the remainder there were bound to be cases indirectly the result of drink. It would be wrong to blame drink for all cases of cruelty to children, because there was a plurality of causes, of which drink was a dominant one.

Cruelty was not the only experience of children exposed to drink. In 1901 a committee under the chairmanship of the Bishop of Hereford published a report *The children and the drink*, from which we have already quoted.[4] This committee stated, "The drink-traffic is responsible directly for a great annual slaughter of infants and children; indirectly it works out into a stunted and undergrown physique, and a lowered standard of health; it is largely responsible for neglect of educational chances; it helps to produce the wretchedness of the tramp-children and the workhouse "ins and outs" and the juvenile street-traders; it hampers and complicates and overtaxes the efforts of those engaged in the work of child rescue; and it fills unnumbered places in voluntary homes and reformatories and industrial schools. Scratch the surface of degradation anywhere, and you will at once light upon the drink traffic."[5] This committee's report identified some of the other injuries inflicted upon children as a result of drink and gave some horrifying statistics.

Research by a Revd J. W. Horsely into infanticide revealed that of 136 cases investigated, 114 children had pre-deceased their parents, many being stillborn and many dying early in infancy. His conclusion was that the mortality among infants of intemperate parents probably accounted for more deaths than all other cases of preventable mortality put together. The report of the Medical Officer of Health for Liverpool (1899) contained the results of a survey carried out on a number of female drunkards in Liverpool prison to discover the effects of the mother's inebriety on infant mortality. The effects of incidental cruelty and neglect were ignored. It was found that out of 600 children of inebriate mothers, 335, including stillborn, died below two years of age, only 265 surviving beyond that age. Further inquiries showed that in a series of cases of children born of drunken mothers 55.2 per cent of the children died under two years of age against 23.9 per cent of children born to sober mothers in similar circumstances of life. Other studies in Liverpool had shown that the infantile death rate in specific districts bore some relation to the accumulation of licensed houses and the consumption of liquor in those districts.

There were other hazards for children in intemperate homes, some, such as accidents, being hard to state statistically. Hospitals in dealing with cases of minor injuries, scalds and burns, might detect a smell of liquor on the parents when the child was brought for treatment, "but" as the Bishop of Hereford's committee observed, "a burn is a burn to a hospital doctor who has neither time nor machinery to inquire further."[6] The hazard of babies dying as a result of overlying by drunken mothers was a serious one at the time. It was reckoned that in England and Wales some 1,550 infants were annually suffocated in bed. Not all were due to unintentional killing through intoxication. In a Manchester court on 26th December 1898, the Coroner, who had six cases of suffocation in bed to investigate, "strongly commented upon the unusually large number of cases of this kind at this period of the year." "Of course," he remarked, "there was no direct evidence to incriminate the parents, but there could be no doubt that the majority of the deaths was due to the excesses of parents and want of proper care."[7] It was not only at Christmas and other festive times that the number increased, but figures which began to be issued by the Registrar General in 1890 showed that there was a higher incidence at weekends.[8]

Henry Carter reported in his book "The Control of the Drink Trade" p. 274, that infant deaths from overlying declined by 43 per cent between 1914 and 1917 during which period the Central Control Board imposed severe restrictions on the sale of liquor.

Expenditure by parents on drink meant that many children were underfed, and this resulted in deterioration of health affecting a large section of a whole generation. Children were not only deprived of health, but of education. Attendance officers found that often children with irregular school attendances came from homes where there was evidence of excessive drinking. Money spent on drink might have been spent on clothes to enable children to go to school. Many children were deliberately kept from school to become street-traders to provide income for the family. Not all instances of child street-trading were for reprehensible reasons, but, of course, many were. The Bishop of Hereford's committee found that out of a list of thirty-seven cases of child street-hawkers submitted by the Chief Constable of Manchester to the city Watch Committee, thirty-three showed one parent or both was intemperate or a drunkard. Finally, there was evidence of juvenile alcoholism. The cases were not numerous, but that they existed at all was an indication of the availability of liquor for children.

Accessibility and legislation

It was the accessibility of intoxicants for children to which reformers and parliament addressed themselves at the turn of the century. As we have seen,[9] under existing law in 1900, children of any age could be served with beer or spirits or liquor of any kind for consumption off licensed premises; children of thirteen and upwards could buy and drink beer on the premises; and children of sixteen and upwards could buy and drink any kind of liquor on the premises. It was a common practice for children to be sent as messengers to buy liquor in open jugs or other containers for their parents and others, which led many to take a swig on the way home. Surveys of public houses showed that a high proportion of unaccompanied children engaged in this practice, and it was to be expected that the trade would oppose any measure to interfere with anything which so materially increased the sale of liquor. When the bill to prohibit the sale of liquor to children was going through parliament, it was customary for such measures to be opposed as an unwarrantable interference with parental right or parental convenience, but this argument no longer carried weight, having been disposed of by earlier legislation to protect child workers in factories, mines, chimneys, brickfields and the circus. Moreover, the Cruelty to Children Acts of 1889 and 1894 had established the right of the nation to confer upon children rights which even their parents had denied them. Even so, there were members who advanced these outmoded arguments during the second reading of the bill on 20th March 1901, but they were supported by only 56 members of the House of Commons and with 374 voting for the bill, there was a second reading majority of 318.

With such overwhelming support it seemed certain that the bill, or something very much like it, would reach the statute book, but leaders of temperance opinion who had experience of parliamentary procedures warned their colleagues not to suppose the battle had been won. They urged the Temperance Movement throughout the country to maintain the momentum of the campaign which had carried them thus far. The trade was equally active, so it was imperative that public meetings should be held to advocate the acceptance of the bill, petitions should be organized, and personal letters written in their thousands to members of parliament, three methods of campaigning which were followed zealously. *Alliance News*, for the period leading from the successful second reading through the committee stage, carried accounts of crowded meetings in some of the main cities of the United Kingdom. Some indication of how the plea for petitions was taken up was given by the secretary of the United Kingdom Band of Hope Union at its 46th annual meeting in May 1901. He reported that 1,397 petitions from school-boards, county and borough councils and benches of magistrates and others had been sent. In addition, 2,451 general petitions with 257,761 signatures had been sent,[10] those in favour of the bill contrasting with only four petitions against.

But these figures might have been misleading. Figures given in a report from the Select Committee on Petitions up to 28th June 1901 showed that 5,119 petitions had been sent on the bill to the House of Commons, and of these, 143 with 354,634 signatures were against and 4,975 petitions with 533,759 signatures were in favour. Thus although there was a big disparity between the number of petitions, the totals of signatures showed that there was no room for complacency among supporters of the bill, which was further stressed as the bill proceeded through committee, when delaying tactics of the opponents to the bill were condemned by many leading newspapers.

Various amendments were proposed, some of which eroded the original intention of the bill, which was to prohibit the sale of liquor to children under sixteen, the most damaging so far as the original intention of the bill was concerned, being one which provided that the sale of intoxicants to children was illegal, except in corked and sealed containers. With this, and other amendments, the bill was presented for third reading in the House of Commons on 14th August 1901 and was passed by the Lords on 16th August 1901, and came into operation on 1st January 1902 as The Intoxicating Liquors (Sale to Children) Act 1901.

This new act repealed the Intoxicating Liquors (Sale to Children) Act 1886 which had prevented the sale of intoxicating liquors to children under thirteen for their own consumption on the premises, and substituted a prohibition of the sale of any kind of intoxicating liquors to children under fourteen for consumption on or off the premises, except in corked and sealed containers of not less than a reputed pint. The new act did not prevent the employment by a licensed person or a member of his family or his servant or apprentice as a messenger to deliver intoxicating liquors, but it made it an offence for any person to send a child under fourteen to purchase liquor. The act did not fulfil the intentions of its originators who wanted to protect children from the purchase of liquor altogether, and so prevent them from becoming familiar with licensed premises, but it was generally recognized, except by the more militant representatives of the trade, as a valuable and necessary reform. A month after the act came into force J. W. Crombie, who piloted the bill through parliament, was reported as saying that the act was working splendidly, and that publicans had been much more sensible than those who purported to represent their views in parliament. They had found they could not carry out the elaborate arrangements of corking and sealing bottles, and so they were carrying out the original intentions of the bill and refusing to serve children at all.[11]

On 1st April 1909 another act, introduced by the government, further to protect children came into force. The intention of this act was not to exclude children altogether from licensed premises, but only from such parts of them where consumption of liquor was the chief feature. The jug and bottle department was exempt, as was the dining room where bona fide meals were served. It seemed also that a separate room for children was also exempt. As soon as the act came into force notices began to appear in the bars of public houses forbidding the presence of children and stating the penalties for a violation of the law. Newspapers reported that the act had had a dramatic effect in almost all public houses and children were no longer to be seen with parents in the bars.

The response of moral reformers and others

The threat of strong drink to children had been realized by moral reformers before the 1901 Act had been initiated in parliament. By that time the Band of Hope, which was founded in 1847, had grown phenomenally. Its purpose was to instruct boys and girls as to the properties of alcohol and the consequences of its consumption. By 1855 there were so many local Bands of Hope that a London Union was formed, and in 1864 this was expanded to become the United Kingdom Band of Hope Union. At its 46th annual meeting in 1901 it was reported that in the United Kingdom there were 28,894 local societies, with a total membership of 3,536,000 boys and girls. The local Bands of Hope provided a midweek meeting with a programme of music, magic-lantern slides, competitions and addresses on the importance of total abstinence. To the children it must have been the one bright spot of the week bearing in mind the drab conditions of the times, when the public house was the only place of "good cheer" in so many communities. By any standards with which the success or failure of a movement may be judged, the Band of Hope has to be reckoned as a success, almost in a class of its own. What other youth movement in the United Kingdom has ever had a membership of over three and a half million? For five years before 1901 a "school scheme" had been sustained by a special fund of £10,000. During that time 3,987 addresses had been given in schools in 741 towns and villages and these had been attended by 399,184 scholars and 13,492 teachers. In response to the school lectures, children had written 232,776 essays.[12] It is appropriate to make this reference to the strength of the Band of Hope at the beginning of the twentieth century, in order to correct an impression which might be drawn from the early part of this chapter, that nothing was being done positively to instruct boys and girls to encourage them to live sober lives.

But it was not only moral reformers who were concerned about the menace of drink to the children of the nation. In July 1904 a deputation representing the medical profession in Britain met the President of the Board of Education, Lord Londonderry, and presented him with a petition signed by 14,718 registered medical practitioners, in favour of the teaching of hygiene in schools. It stated that the signatories had constantly before them the serious physical and moral conditions of degeneracy and disease resulting from the neglect of the elementary laws of hygiene. It urged the educational authorities to consider including in school curricula such teaching as would encourage children to appreciate the value to health of cleanliness, pure air and proper nourishment from food and drink. Sir William Broadbent, a member of the deputation, told the minister that the petition represented almost the entire medical profession and that the signatures were spontaneous and had been secured without prolonged effort. Ignorance, he said, was almost as big a cause of suffering and ill-health as vice, indeed ignorance led to vice. This was particularly the case as regards alcohol, with respect to which not merely ignorance but a large number of perverted ideas prevailed. It was desirable that this subject should be a compulsory one, though not necessarily a new subject for examination. Lord Londonderry replied that although he was unable to give the deputation definite answers to their proposals, this must not be construed as rejecting them or regarding them as unimportant. One difficulty was that properly-trained teachers of hygiene did not exist and his department was endeavouring to secure the training of such teachers. His department was also about to issue a volume containing practical instruction on the subject. Before knowing exactly what remedies were required he would have to wait for the report of the commission appointed to study the physical conditions of the people.[13]

A syllabus for schools

It was in 1909 that the Board of Education issued the first syllabus for "temperance" education in public elementary schools.[14] In the introduction to this syllabus the Minister said it was hoped that instruction based on the syllabus would be given by the staff as part of the curriculum for personal health in every school. Hygiene, which included instruction relating to alcoholic drinks, was one of the regular subjects for two-year students at teacher training colleges. Some schools had no teachers on the staff qualified to give this kind of teaching, but various societies and organizations provided peripatetic teachers who were recognized by the education authorities. However, such visiting teachers were usually not qualified, and the material they used did not conform to the standards expected in public education. The intention of the Board of Education was that all such instruction, whether given by members of schools staffs or by others, should conform to the standards of accuracy and method embodied in the syllabus. The recommendation of the board was that at least three lessons based on the syllabus should be given each year. Thus there were three sections to the syllabus – 1. Eating and drinking: food and its use; 2. Alcohol: effects of alcoholic beverages on the body; 3. Evil consequences of intemperance to the individual, to the home, and to the state. The introduction indicated how the syllabus could be used for different age groups. There was a considerable appendix which provided teaching material for the help of teachers. What seems to be a striking feature of the syllabus, after a period of seventy years, was the use made of the word "temperance". At that time it was manifestly an acceptable term, whereas later it seemed to lose its credibility. Certainly the Board of Education understood the classic meaning of the word and intended its meaning to be conveyed to children. The concluding sentence of the introduction still has relevance for those who wish to inculcate the "temperance" sentiment – "Instruction on the subject of Temperance should itself be temperate and should make a sober appeal to such reasoning capacity as a child possesses and to the ideas of decent, self-respecting and dutiful living which every good teacher endeavours to present to and cultivate in the children under his charge."[15] The syllabus was reprinted without substantial alterations in 1916.

By 1922 the Board of Education concluded that there had been such an advance of knowledge since the issue of the syllabus that the time was opportune for a complete revision. This resulted in the publication of a new syllabus which set temperance education within the context of the hygiene of food and drink.[16] "The question of the misuse of food and its abuse is not less important than the question of the abuse of alcohol, and there is little doubt that the two subjects should be dealt with in a proper and well-balanced relationship" declared the new syllabus.[17]

Here it is interesting to interject the observation that, whereas in 1922 it was thought that the abuse of alcohol was related to the abuse of food, it is related today to the abuse of drugs. Alcohol is not now regarded as a food but as a narcotic. This, as we shall see, affects the educational approach to the consumption of intoxicating liquor in the second half of the twentieth century. The new concept of alcohol as a drug was taken up by the Advisory Committee on Alcohol of the Central Control Board when, in 1918, it produced *Alcohol: its action on the human organism,*[18] to which we shall give some consideration later. It is mentioned here because the syllabus on the hygiene of food and drink recommended it as essential reading for all engaged in temperance education.

The new syllabus set "temperance" instruction in a broader context. While the syllabus itself was formal, it encouraged less-formal instruction. Opportunities would arise incidentally in connection with other subjects. "In the science course; in the History lesson in connection with the social life of the people. in the Geography lesson when the influence of climate is being explained; or, perhaps, during the periods of rest in the course of Physical Exercises, or in connection with organized games or 'training' for sports."[19] Because the presentation could be affected by the "personal predilictions and prejudices" of the teachers they needed to be constantly on their guard and to follow the lines of the syllabus. There were four sections: 1. The uses of food and drink; 2. Alcohol: 3. The misuse and abuse of food and its results: 4. The misuse and abuse of alcohol. In this syllabus there was a more extensive section of teaching notes than in the previous one. Although the syllabus did not present "temperance" overtly as its predecessor did, the classic concept was retained. "It is perhaps hardly necessary to state that the one idea that should dominate any school teaching in hygiene is the paramount importance of self-discipline" it declared and continued, "The wise teacher will lose no opportunity of impressing upon his scholars the vital importance of habits of self-control and it will be his constant aim to afford plain, simple and satisfying reasons which the child will understand and appreciate."[20] The contemporary educational concepts of motivation and decision-making had not then been developed, but those who drew up the syllabus were clearly moving towards them.

The first textbook

Alcohol: its action on the human organism, to which reference was made in the syllabus became the acknowledged textbook for a generation. In 1916 the Central Control Board appointed an advisory committee "to consider the conditions affecting the physiological action of alcohol, and more particularly the effects on health and industrial efficiency produced by the consumption of beverages of various alcoholic strengths, with special reference to the recent Orders of the Central Control Board, and further to plan out and direct such investigations as may appear desirable with a view to obtaining more exact data on this and cognate questions".[21] The response of this committee was to produce *Alcohol: its action on the human organism.*

Bearing in mind the amount of money spent on the purchase of alcoholic beverages, it seemed remarkable to the committee, composed of eminent scholars, "that, throughout the world, lack of knowledge still prevails about the action of alcohol on the human system".[22] The committee observed, "No authoritative scientific work gives or seeks to give the required information: on many important points, which it is requisite to elucidate in order to regulate the proper guidance to the individual consumer, little of substantial value has been published in a form accessible to the general reader."[23] One reason there was no authoritative work was that science itself had not established the essential data. Many questions remained unanswered, some of which were mentioned in the preface to the book. The committee of scientists who prepared it, began by summarizing the current state of knowledge of alcohol, and concluded that its main action was confined to the nervous system, that in its action it was a narcotic rather than a stimulant, that its nutritional value was limited, that its habitual use as an aid to work was physiologically unsound, and that its ordinary use should not only be moderate, but limited by dilution and adequate intervals of time.

The book dealt with the scientific data on which these conclusions were reached, and in particular discussed what evidence there was for regarding alcohol primarily as a food, which had been the prevailing view. It then considered the evidence for treating it as a drug. Setting the evidence side by side, the conclusion was that its food value was negligible and its drug action primary, its direct effect upon the nervous system, in all its stages and upon all parts of the human system, being to depress and suspend its functions. In short, alcohol was "from first to last a narcotic drug"[24] and, taken persistently in a concentrated form acted as a poison in the system. Its harmful effects could be minimized by allowing a sufficient interval of time between consumption to prevent its persistent presence in the body, and by taking it in a dilute form and with food. The committee concluded, "The temperate consumption of alcoholic liquors in accordance with these rules of practice may be considered physiologically harmless in the case of the large majority of normal adults."[25] However, so far as children were concerned the committee was quite emphatic that alcoholic drinks were definitely injurious.

This new book became widely used in schools and colleges and so fulfilled one of its principal intentions. In 1921 the Central Control Board was dissolved. The Secretary of State for Home Affairs then invited the Medical Research Council to reappoint the Advisory Committee which produced *Alcohol: its action on the human organism,* as one of its own investigation committees and so enable its work to continue. Since the Medical Research Council had assisted in the original work this was a satisfactory arrangement. Using unpublished revision material, the newly-appointed Alcohol Committee of the M.R.C. brought out a second edition of the original book in 1924 and a third in 1938.[26] These followed the same schema and included most of the original material. The conclusions reached were the same.

Throughout, the work was confined to a consideration of the physiological aspects of the consumption of alcohol. It was recognized that there were other aspects, but these did not fall within the brief of the committee appointed. This was fully recognized by bodies such as the United Kingdom Alliance whose concern was with the social effects of the consumption of alcohol and how these could be mitigated by legislation. In its annual report in 1918 the UKA executive devoted a section of comment to the book[27] and earlier, in March 1918 *Alliance News* had carried an extensive review. Generally, both the review and the annual report welcomed it, while recognizing the self-imposed limitations placed on its scope.

The first survey

Between the second (1924) and the third (1938) editions of this book the Report of the Royal Commission on Licensing 1929 - 1931 made some firm recommendations on alcohol education in schools and colleges which we refer to in the chapter on the commission.[28]

Practical steps to implement the commission's recommendations were halted by the outbreak of the Second World War. It was not until after the war that the threat of alcohol to children was once more a matter of public concern. A report by Mass-Observation in 1943 drew attention to the problem.[29] In two areas of London it was found that three-quarters of the children between seven and fourteen included in the survey said they had tasted beer at some time. The results were similar in other parts of the country. It was further found that the great majority of children were introduced to alcoholic drinks by their parents. Later surveys[30] showed that the proportion of children who had tasted liquor was greater than in the Mass-Observation survey, but the other results were similar. In particular it was confirmed that most children were introduced to alcoholic drinks by their parents. Although some researchers were concerned to discover the drinking patterns of the young, it is wrong to isolate this phenomenon from the general drinking patterns of society as a whole. An important feature of the Mass-Observation report was the change in the drinking habits of young people and women reflected in replies from a London borough to the question, "Do you go to pubs more, or less, or about the same as before the War?"[31]

	Age 30 and over		Age under 30	
Frequency of Pub-going	**Men**	**Women**	**Men**	**Women**
More often	10%	28%	23%	45%
Less often	45%	28%	32%	7%
Same amount	35%	44%	35%	37%
Don't know	10%	0%	10%	11%

This showed there was a trend for pub-going to have increased among the younger more than the older generation; and the young women were going to public houses more often than before the war. In the same London borough the prejudice against young women frequenting public houses was rapidly diminishing. The social acceptance of the public house, especially by the young was almost bound to be reflected in the drinking patterns of the next generation. It needs to be remember that at the time Mass-Observation conducted its survey the public house was the main retail outlet for liquor. There were off-licences, but these tended to be patronized by a selective clientele among whom were few young people. In 1943 the youngsters were picking up cues about drinking from their parents and from the young adults who would be the parents of the next generation. It was the children of 1943 who became the drinkers ten years later, and who gave rise to an escalation of drunkenness between 1953 and 1955[32] and a similar increase in other offences.

Handbooks on health education

It is not surprising that with evidence of an increasing threat to children, the matter of education was constantly before the authorities. *Alcohol: its action on the human organism* had been widely used as a textbook for alcohol education, but since the beginning of the century there had developed a more comprehensive concept of health education, which resulted in the publication of a *Handbook of suggestions on Health Education,* the first edition of which was soon revised with a series of revised editions appearing in 1933, 1939, 1956 and 1968. It is interesting to note the way in which the use of alcohol was incorporated into the various editions. In the first three it was included in the section "Hygiene of food and drink". This meant that even after the publication of *Alcohol: its action on the human organism,* which so clearly placed alcohol outside the category of food and identified it as a drug, those reponsible for education suggested that it should be dealt with in the context of food and drink. One-half of the chapter on this aspect of health education was devoted to alcohol.

This section underwent only minor revision in the first three editions. It began with the facts about the nature of alcohol and a consideration of its food value. Although it was classed as a food, in fact its nutritional value was very limited. It might have a temporary effect, but it was not capable of being stored in the body and so could not be viewed as a source of nourishment. Its depressant effect on the brain and central nervous system was accurately described, as were its effects on work capacity and resistance to disease. The handbook said plainly that continued alcoholic indulgence resulted in some permanent affects on the human system so that the character of the individual was modified. "Thus mental activity is generally reduced and the work that is done becomes increasingly inaccurate, careless and untrustworthy."[33] There was evidence that people who drank excessively did not have the same life expectancy as normal healthy persons. Finally, it was recognized that there were social consequences to heavy drinking, notably poverty. It needs to be noted that although the amount of space devoted to alcohol was adequate, it was dealt with in a comprehensive context. Health education was concerned with the nature and condition of bodily and mental health, the practice of health habits, biology and health, mothercraft and infant care, preventive medicine, the importance of environment and the prevention of infectious diseases. Moreover, there was the important matter of methods and schemes of health education.

If the space devoted to a specific topic in a comprehensive handbook is the criterion by which its importance is to be judged, then the two most recent editions of the *Handbook on Health Education* must be reckoned as deficient in their treatment of alcohol, their method of dealing with it marking an evident departure from that of their predecessors. Alcohol was no longer regarded as falling within the sphere of food and drink. It was considered in a chapter on "Drugs, alcohol and tobacco". In the 1956 edition this chapter occupied five pages in which two paragraphs dealt specifically with alcohol.[34] The criticisms of the inadequacy of this chapter were met in 1968 when the most recent edition appeared, the chapter headings remaining the same, but twice as much space being devoted to it.[35] However, the space given to alcohol was just over one page compared with six and a half devoted to drugs and two and a half to tobacco, proportions of space which may be seen as a sociological comment on the period in which the handbook was produced. There were fears in the 1960s that the "drug problem" would escalate in Britain in the same fashion as it had in America. Hasty and in some respects ill-conceived, legislation was rushed through parliament in anticipation of an epidemic of drug misuse, and in the circumstances, it was understandable that health educationists reacted in the way reflected in the 1968 edition of a *Handbook of Health Education*. Ten years later the threat of the widespread consumption of alcohol was greater than that of drug misuse, while there was a considerable change in public attitudes to the use of tobacco, which made smoking a much less acceptable habit.

A new approach

A clue to a new approach to alcohol education was found in the 1968 *Handbook*. "Health Education should attempt to inform young people about the risks of misuse of both tobacco and alcohol and, even more important, should try to impart attitudes which allow young people to make independent decisions and free them from the necessity of always following their social group."[36] The concept of "decision making" lies at the heart of a new approach to alcohol education. Formerly it was thought that if young people were given the facts about the nature of alcohol and its effects they would, on the basis of these facts, reach conclusions about its use and it was only later that educationists recognized that this did not happen. "Young people cannot be inoculated against the pressures and problems of real life by merely being given a basis of factual material. Education about alcohol is far more complicated than this simplistic approach, which has been tried and tried again with little evidence that it has been effective. If we are going to educate young people about alcohol, then we have to accept that this is also part of education about life. Young people must be given a chance to discuss the situations they have met or are likely to meet and to learn to cope with them."[37] This is the philosophy of TACADE (Teachers' Advisory Council on Alcohol and Drug Education). TACADE is not concerned exclusively with specific instruction on alcohol and drugs, but with the development of decision-making skills which will equip young people to act responsibly in personal and social situations in which choices are vital. The materials produced by TACADE are in increasing demand. Their courses for teachers begin with the premise that, if they can be equipped to do so, members of staff are in the best position to give this kind of education. Other bodies, such as the Alcohol Education Centre, have become engaged in alcohol education, but TACADE has the merit of being highly professional, and for this reason is wholly accepted by education administrators and headteachers.

Statistics relating to drinking and drinking offences by young people, the increasing number of complaints by headteachers of drinking by pupils during lunch breaks, are alarming, but they are indicators of a widespread problem which cannot be isolated according to age. As we have seen, young people are greatly influenced in their drinking patterns by parents and peer groups. Enough research has gone on to establish the fact of this influence. What is now required is the insight to introduce concepts and attitudes which will save another generation from making the wrong decisions about the place of alcohol in personal and social life.

The threat to the child

We have surveyed some of the steps taken by education and legislation in the twentieth century to shield the child from alcohol. Recent studies have shown that the protection of the child from acquiring habits of excessive drinking is more difficult when consumption generally is high. Susan Dight in her survey of Scottish drinking habits[38] found that regular drinking among informants increased directly with both mothers' and fathers' frequency of drinking. There was some evidence that sex stereotyping in drinking behaviour took place, sons following their fathers' habits and daughters their mothers'. The greatest quantities of alcohol were consumed by those male drinkers whose fathers drank at least four times a week and whose mothers did not drink. An earlier survey of drinking habits in a London suburb also showed that among men the proportion of heavy drinkers increased in step with the heavy drinking of the father although the mother's drinking exerted no significant influence. Derek Rutherford, director of the National Council on Alcoholism, in a paper delivered at a seminar in London in December 1979 commented, "Concern is often expressed about the drinking of children and young people, but little attention has been paid to the effects of adult problem drinking upon children. Yet these effects are traumatic and can have long-lasting disabilities on a child's development, physically, mentally and socially. It is an area which can no longer be neglected. It is estimated that there are some 740,000 people in the United Kingdom with a serious drinking problem. Since alcohol affects three to four members of the family, then almost 3,000,000 people know the true cost of alcohol, that is one in fifteen of the population. Taking the number of individuals with children seen by local councils on alcoholism, there could be a minimum of 500,000 children under fourteen experiencing one or more parents with a drinking problem."[39]

Various studies have shown that children with alcoholic parents are prone to suffer emotional problems at school, difficulties in making friends, involvement with the police and drinking problems of their own. Margaret Cork's study[40] of 115 children of alcoholic parents showed that almost all had experienced serious problems with relationships inside and outside the family (98 per cent and 96 per cent respectively). Among 49 per cent, school work had been adversely affected, while nine per cent had suffered physically. Cork observed the following emotional anxieties,

1. Lack of self-confidence (98 per cent).
2. Felt unwanted by one or both parents (97 per cent).
3. Often ashamed, upset and crying (77 per cent).
4. Angry and hostile to parents (65 per cent).
5. Worried about being different (65 per cent).
6. Generally anxious and afraid of the future (61 per cent).
7. Uncomfortable or fearful with the opposite sex (48 per cent).
8. Defiant and angry and ambivalent towards authority (47 per cent).
9. Wished to escape from the family (42 per cent).
10. Worried at not being liked by peers (41 per cent).
11. Unable to trust or depend on anyone (27 per cent).

Of the 115 children, Cork thought that 48.6 per cent were fairly seriously damaged and 43.4 per cent very seriously damaged. Other studies in Britain confirm these findings. It is noteworthy that the Council of Europe estimates that 60 per cent of child cruelty has a background of alcoholism. In view of the often ill-informed comparisons which are made between drinking behaviour in Britain and France it is interesting to note that since 1958 the French government has encouraged French parents not to give alcohol to their children under fourteen, and, when it is done, to water the wine.

The lesson from all recent surveys leads to the conclusion that the role of parents is vital in the protection of the young from the effects of excessive consumption of alcohol in the community and the development of safe norms for their own consumption in later life. This is the more important because whereas at one time most drinking was done in public houses where the publicans are required by law to exercise control, it is now done in the home. A survey "Alcoholic drinks in the home", published by I.P.C. Magazines, showed that in 1977 total licensed turnover growth through supermarkets increased by more than 30 per cent. The survey was carried out in June 1978 by Communications Research Limited and covered a sample of 1,464 households in Great Britain where the housewife was under 65. Households where there were only men were excluded. The survey showed that almost 50 per cent of all drinks were sold in supermarkets. In a breakdown of home consumption of specific drinks it was shown that 62 per cent of main vodka drinkers and 56 per cent of main gin drinkers were women. Comparitive figures for other drinks were: main brandy drinkers 53 per cent women and 47 per cent men; sherry 67 per cent women and 36 per cent men. However, men dominated whisky consumption (67 per cent). The drinks trade executive of I.P.C. Magazines told a conference in London in September 1979 that a survey carried out for his company showed there were 8½ million regular women drinkers. With women earning wages their influence on buying drink was increasing. In the five years ending 1977 this had led to a 330 per cent increase in turnover for licensed supermarkets. It was found that more women than men were likely to buy from supermarkets: 50 per cent as against 33 per cent for men. These figures for supermarkets were confirmed by other surveys. In 1977 there was a 12.2 per cent increase in the take-home drinks trade in England and Wales compared with 1976. The total sales, including beer and cider, amounted to £1,047 million. Grocery multiples, that is supermarkets, showed an increase in their share of the turnover increased from 24.3 per cent to 25.7 per cent. These various surveys indicate a big increase in liquor consumption at home and, therefore, in situations in which children are involved. The responsibility of parents in these circumstances is to decide whether drink should be kept in the home and, if so, how much and under what circumstances. They ought to lay down firm ground rules for themselves, their guests and their children. "We all tend to show enthusiasm for educational programmes which have no immediate restrictive effects on ourselves, then hamper those programmes which would cut down our own freedom to drink or cause us to reflect more seriously about our own drinking habits".[41]

The exposure of young people to drink in the home is one factor in the increasing consumption of alcohol by the young persons themselves and their involvement in the personal and social consequences. This is dramatically illustrated in the fact that between 1959 and 1977 proved offences of drunkenness among young males in England and Wales under eighteen increased from 949 to 4,920 an increase of 518 per cent. Among young females the comparable figures were 59 and 442 or an increase of 749 per cent. Another consequence has been the rise in the number of young persons involved in serious road accidents. The trend for young people to become mobile has been one of the features of the past two decades, at least. The scooter craze of the 1960s has been followed by a massive increase in the purchase of motor cycles and "bangers" by young people. A survey conducted by Dr J. Havard of the British Medical Association for the World Health Organization, and published in 1979, showed that in fifteen years the number of young people killed in car accidents had more than doubled and many deaths were caused by drink. Mortality rates from car accidents for two age groups, the 15–24 and all ages were compared over two five-year periods, 1955–59 and 1970–74. In all but two of the thirty countries studied, there were increases of more than 50 per cent in deaths among young people. In Portugal the increase was 300 per cent. In the U.S.A., 8,770 young drivers died in the first period and 17,440 in the second, an increase of 54.9 per cent. Between 1970 and 1974 road deaths of people of all ages in the United Kingdom totalled 8,492. Only six other countries had worse figures, U.S.A. (70,581), Japan (23,636), West Germany (21,539) France (16,000) and Italy (15,581). Abuse of alcohol was reckoned to be the main cause of the rising death rate. An indication of the proportion of those who were young people who had been drinking can be gauged from the fact that during 1976 in England and Wales, 40 per cent of all drivers under 30 killed had a blood-alcohol level above the legal limit. The experience of Alcoholics Anonymous and various alcoholic assessment agencies is that in recent years there has been an increase in the number of young persons presenting themselves for help. It is these factors which have restrained the government from implementing the recommendations of the Erroll Committee that the legal age for the purchase of liquor should be reduced from eighteen and that in some circumstances children should be allowed in bars of licensed premises.

References

1. *The children and drink* – a report of a committee under the chairmanship of the Bishop of Hereford, R. Brimley Jones, London (1901) pp 30, 31.
2. Op cit p. 30.
3. Quoted op cit p. 31.
4. See para. 1 above.
5. Op cit p. 43.
6. Op cit p. 53.
7. *Manchester Guardian* 27th December 1898
8. *The children and drink* p. 55 ff.
9. See p. 12.
10. *Alliance News* 16th May 1901 p. 307.
11. *Alliance News* 30th January 1902 p. 65.
12. *Alliance News* 16th May 1901 p. 307.
13. *Alliance News* 14th July 1904 p. 477.
14. *Syllabus of lessons on 'Temperance' for scholars attending public elementary schools* H.M.S.O. (1909).
15. Op cit p. 4.
16. *The hygiene of food and drink* H.M.S.O. (1922).
17. Op cit p. 2.
18. H.M.S.O. 1918.
19. Op cit pp. 2, 3.
20. Op cit p. 3.
21. *Alcohol: its action on the human organism* H.M.S.O. (1918) p. i.
22. Op cit preface p. iii.
23. Op cit preface pp. iii, iv.
24. Op cit p. 38.
25. Op cit p. 133.

26. *Alcohol: its action on the human organism* by a committee originally appointed by the Central Control Board (Liquor Traffic) and later reconstituted by the Medical Research Council. H.M.S.O. (1924).
27. *Alliance News* November 1918 p. 88.
28. See p. 95.
29. *Mass-Observation on Juvenile drinking:* published by Livesy-Clegg Youth Club, Sheffield (1943).
30. *A survey of teenage drinking patterns and attitudes to drink:* Institute for Social Research (1964).
    Profile of alcohol usage by young persons in Coventry: Coventry and Warwickshire Council on Alcoholism (1976).
    Indications of alcohol usage and attitudes to alcohol by young persons of school and college age in Somerset (1977).
    Teenagers and Alcohol. John Davies and Barrie Stacey. H.M.S.O. (1972).
    Adolescents and Alcohol. Ann Hawker. B. Edsall and Co. Ltd (1978).
    The Young Drinkers Joyce O'Connor. Tavistock Publications. (1978).
31. Op cit p. 24.
32. See *Drunkenness among young persons aged under 21 by Police Districts in England and Wales 1953–1955:* Economic Research Council (1956), and *Social problems of post-war youth:* Economic Research Council (1956). 1st edition. H.M.S.O. (1928).
33. *Handbook of suggestions on Health Education.* H.M.S.O. (1933) p. 51.
34. *Health Education:* H.M.S.O. (1956) p. 112.
35. *A handbook of Health Education:* H.M.S.O. (1968) p. 132 ff.
36. *A handbook of Health Education:* H.M.S.O. (1968) p. 138.
37. *Teaching about alcohol and drinking:* S. Caruana, James C. P. Cowley and D. Rutherford. TACADE (1978) p. 1.
38. *Scottish drinking habits: A survey carried out for the Scottish Home and Health Departments* S. E. Dight. H.M.S.O. (1976).
39. Reproduced verbatim in *Alliance News* March/April 1980.
40. *Forgotten Children:* Margaret Cork. Addiction Research Foundation. Canada (1969).
41. Rutherford op cit.

CHAPTER 13

LIQUOR ADVERTISING

Modern liquor advertising can be traced to a specific origin. In 1933 the director of the Brewers' Society, Sir Edgar Sanders, addressed a meeting of the Midland Counties Wholesale Brewers Association in Birmingham. His career was a particularly interesting one. He was clerk to the Liverpool Justices before being chosen as the person best qualified to take charge of the Carlisle scheme of state ownership of the liquor trade. Later he became director of the Brewers' Society.

In view of what turned out to be a famous speech in Birmingham on the subject of liquor advertising, it is interesting to note what he said to the Royal Commission on Liquor Licensing 1929–31. He was asked, "What is your view about the amount of advertising that is done now recommending the purchase of alcoholic beverages?" He replied, "I think it is a bad thing."[1] His speech at Birmingham was at a private meeting and, according to Lord Askuith in a House of Lords debate,[2] only 400 copies of the speech were distributed. Lord Askuith said, "A copy was purloined and typewritten copies were made from it, and the speech was made use of in pamphlets circulated in the country, a proceeding which was denounced by a famous temperance advocate, Arthur Sherwell, as not a fair thing to do." Fair or not, Sir Edgar Sanders admitted that the speech published was the speech he delivered,[3] and one of the pamphlets which contained extensive quotations from it was *The "Trade", the Press and the Nation.*[4]

Before discussing in detail the speech which launched modern liquor advertising it is important to refer to the judgment of the 1929–1931 Royal Commission on Liquor Licensing. The significance of liquor advertising at that time, perhaps being judged by the space accorded to it in their report,[5] which was less than a page and a half. The commission concluded that a conservative estimate would put the figure of annual expenditure on such advertising at £2 million, and that the effect was to increase, or at least to prevent a decrease, in the total consumption of liquor. They did not accept the argument that the effect was merely "to transfer demand from unadvertised to advertised beverages". They thought advertising of specific brands tended to increase overall demand, and they noted that many advertisements were directed towards young people, some advertisements containing statements "which amount to palpable scientific untruths."

The brewers' campaign is launched

The starting point of Sir Edgar Sanders' speech was that since 1920 the consumption of beer in Britain had been falling. This was understandable, he said, because of the new interests which had catered for the surplus earnings of the working classes. These included dog-racing, the cinema, betting and such spectator sports as football, and it seemed that people preferred to spend their money on such attractions, rather than on beer. "This is confirmed very largely by the fact that the chief customers of public houses today are elderly and middled-aged men". He said, "Unless you can attract the younger generation to take the place of the older men, there is no doubt we shall have to face a steadily falling consumption of beer," and told his audience plainly that if the trend continued, three-quarters of the value of the investments in licensed houses would disappear. "That is what might happen unless we do something to attract and secure the younger customer, who, in turn, will become the mainstay of the public-house," he said. "Unless steps are taken to say to him that England's beer is the best and healthiest beverage he can consume and to bring before him all the goodwill and contentment that the public house imparts in England, and to carry on this goodwill, we shall certainly see the trade on a declining basis." Then came the oft-quoted declaration of intent for the brewers, "We want to get the beer-drinking habit instilled into thousands, almost millions of young men who do not at present know the taste of beer."

The remedy for a declining trade was the launching of a great advertising campaign, and he instanced the success of campaigns to promote the sale of fish, of fruit, of gas, and in prospect, electricity, which were all examples of what was known as "collective advertising", credit for the concept of which was claimed by *The Brewers' Journal* which said that "In 1919 *The Brewers' Journal* suggested the collective publicity of beer – indeed that phrase was coined in these columns,"[6] since when it had devoted much time and energy to its study. There was no reason why the collective publicity of beer should not succeed, as had those for "Eat more Fish", "Eat more Fruit" and "Use more Gas". It seems from this reference that Sir Edgar Sanders relied heavily on *The Brewers' Journal* editorial – unless he also wrote it! The pull of advertising was extraordinary he told his audience, and laid before them the plans for launching a campaign. The main lines proposed were press advertising, bill-posting, illuminated signs, distribution of literature, lectures and articles by prominent persons, and supporting news and comment in newspapers.

The campaign was launched on 1st December 1933. The advertisements, all of which carried the slogan "Beer is Best", appeared simultaneously in the national and provincial newspapers, and on posters on hoardings throughout the country. There were four main themes: Beer for Health; Beer for Refreshment; Beer for Good Fellowship; Beer as a staple product of vital importance to British Industry, Agriculture and Revenue. *The Brewing Trade Review* reproduced the first designs of advertisements[7] and thereafter reproduced the designs of each phase of the campaign. Later brewers were advised to put up posters on their premises and vans. Other advertising items, such as rubber mats for use in bars, all bearing the slogan "Beer is Best" were produced and could be obtained from the Brewers' Society.[8] When the King George's Jubilee Trust was launched in 1935 the Brewers' Society donated all their poster sites to the Trust for a fortnight. The Advertising Committee of the Brewers' Society also had three-colour stickers to affix to their own sixteen-sheet posters, and invited other advertisers to use them to promote donations to the King George's Jubilee Trust. The brewers' own posters and newspaper advertisements not only expressed the four main themes of the campaign, but were related to the seasons of the year during which the advertisements appeared. Thus in the summer, outdoor and sporting themes were taken up and towards

Christmas convivial scenes were portrayed. *The Brewers' Journal* also published a synopsis each month of the extent of the campaign. In the issue of 1st September 1934, for instance, it was reported that during the month approximately 8,500 posters would be displayed throughout the country and more than 92,000,000 impressions of "Beer is Best" would be published in the national and provincial press. In its comments on the campaign *The Brewers' Journal* stressed that the aim was not to persuade people to drink *more* beer, but, rather, to persuade *more* people to drink beer.[9]

A passage in Sir Edgar's speech which did not pass the notice of either the press or the temperance organizations, referred to the editorial support newspapers would be expected to give in consideration of the purchase of advertising space. He said that in anticipation of a reduction in beer duty, the advertising representatives of newspapers had approached him about the possibility of an advertising campaign to boost the sale of beer, and commented, "I said that we first had to get a reduction in beer duty, and I think there is no doubt whatever that this had some effect, because the commercial side are always pestering the editorial side. In the same way, if we begin advertising in the press, we shall see that the continuation of our advertising is contingent upon the fact that we get editorial support as well in the same papers. In that way it is wonderful how you can educate public opinion, generally without making it too obvious that there is a publicity campaign behind it at all."

This statement revealed a naiveté which was not apparent in some other statements and actions of the director of the Brewers' Society, and any newspaper man could have disabused his mind of the belief that editorial policy could be deeply affected by sources of advertising revenue. Certainly no editor of professional integrity would have capitulated in the face of the demand implied in Sir Edgar's statement, which is not to say that no editorial support would be forthcoming, but that is very different from the demand of Sir Edgar Sanders.

The temperance advocates, often it seems equally naive, quickly pounced upon the implication that the national press was fettered by the brewers, a possibility which had been in the minds of the 1929–1931 Royal Commission on Licensing who said "As regards press advertisements, it has been contended that certain sections of the press are likely to shape their policy so as, at least, to give no offence to an industry which supplies them with much advertisement revenue." They did not say if they accepted the truth of this contention, but Sir Edgar's statement gave credence to it, especially in the minds of temperance advocates, one result of which has been an ingrained suspicion of the press in temperance circles which has often lost their cause a powerful ally.

The trade press did not disguise its attitude to teetotalism, which it regarded as a threat to be taken seriously. For example, in urging the need for a beer advertising campaign, *The Brewers' Journal* made the point that such a campaign would differ from those to promote the sale of fruit, fish, milk and other commodities because, unlike beer, they had no "fanatical enemies". People had not been going up and down the country for a century telling other people not to have anything to do with these products.

"But they have been doing so in relation to beer. And there has been no effective and organized retaliation. The resilient, absorbent minds of countless thousands of British children have been unscrupulously exploited by the enemies of beer for at least a century."[10] In this they had the support of the government in an offical syllabus for schools, of which a revised edition was in course of preparation. At last, with almost the entire press open to counteract this propaganda, there was the chance for "the seed of truth and fact . . . for the first time to be sown".[11] This was a recurring theme, "Than beer there is no more maligned and misunderstood beverage;"[12] there was the need for the public to be informed of the pure, health-giving virtues of beer. To the teetotal element "the advertising of beer would be the greatest blow that could be dealt at the fallacious foundations of their fortresses".[13] This sentiment was repeated as *The Brewer's Journal* celebrated what it called a "red letter day for the trade", which was 1st December 1933 when the "Collective Advertising" campaign was launched. The *Journal* said, "There can be no doubt that the decision to advertise beer aims the greatest blow at the teetotal element that it has encountered in the present generation."[14] The sensitivity of the trade to the teetotal element seemed to have had interesting psychological implications. Describing the appearance of the Brewers' float in the Lord Mayor's Show in 1935 the *Brewing Trade Review* reported, "Whatever our teetotal friends may tell us, our National beverage is very popular with the man in the street, for even the gravest face relaxed as the brewing car passed with its friendly and convivial crew aboard."[15]

Sir Edgar Sander's speech, the publicity it received, and the launching of the collective advertising campaign made the advertising of liquor a matter of considerable importance, not only to the trade and to the temperance organizations, but to the legislators. Early in 1935 the United Kingdom Alliance took initiatives to bring before parliament a bill designed to restrict liquor advertising. On 21st February 1935, Lord Arnold, who was closely associated with the United Kingdom Alliance, presented the Intoxicating Liquor (Advertisement Regulation) Bill to the House of Lords. It came up for second reading on 28th March 1935. The main provisions were:

1. No advertising material to be sent through the post except at the written request of the person receiving it. Such a provision should apply to material relating to liquor and to places with a view to consumption.
2. Advertisements in newspapers, on hoardings or leaflets and other promotion material should be confined to giving the name and address of the manufacturer whether wholesale or retailer, and the name of the product.
3. No canvassers should be employed, though this should not apply to persons engaged in the distribution of liquor.
4. Penalties would be one month's imprisonment or £20 fine or both on summary conviction, and three months' imprisonment or £100 fine or both on indictment.

The *Brewing Trade Review* noticed the similarity between this bill and the draft of one which appeared in *Alliance News* in January 1935[16] and commented, "This was honestly entitled "Intoxicating Liquor (Advertisement Restrictions) Bill," which at all events gave a sufficient indication of its scope and object. The title substituted by Lord Arnold's Bill gives no such indication and is, in effect, so entirely misleading that it may even be doubted whether the greater part of the bill is in order. For it does not amend the law with respect to manufacturers and distributors of liquor. It prohibits liquor advertisements and scatters penalties broadcast over everybody, whether personally connected with any branch of the liquor trade or not, who has anything to do with their publication."[17] *Brewing Trade Review* took delight in unmasking the apparent disguise of Lord Arnold's Bill, and in taking a mild swipe at the lord himself. "It must, of course, perish by its own savage and grotesque absurdity" an editorial commented acidly, and wondered if the bill was a joke, concluding that, because Lord Arnold had resigned in 1931 as paymaster general in the Labour Government in order to devote himself to the causes of temperance and free trade, he must have been acting with serious intentions. His speech at the second reading of the bill was not persuasive, and the speeches both in favour of the bill and against it were not marked by great insight into the issues involved. After a brief discussion it failed to be read a second time.

Changes in presentation

The Brewers' Collective Publicity Campaign continued, but in 1937 with a change in presentation, when a series of advertisements prepared the way for the introduction of "Mr XXX". "Who is Mr XXX?" was the question which appeared in the new advertisements. The slogan "Beer is Best" was retained, but a cheerful face superimposed on a glass beer mug began to appear, *Brewing Trade Review* describing the new figure as "the industry's new spokesman." He was introduced to the public in January 1937. "His many and various activities in praise of beer will appear regularly in the press," announced *Brewing Trade Review.*[18] Also launched was a new type of advertisement for *The Times.* Each month, the season of the year would be illustrated, so that in March 1937 the theme was a sowing scene on a farm. This was reproduced in *Brewing Trade Review,*[19] and was, in fact, the last of the reproductions of advertisements used in the Collective Campaign to appear in that journal. Throughout 1938 no reference was made to advertising in general nor to the Collective Campaign in particular, neither was there any reference in *The Brewers' Journal.* This did not mean the end of the collective advertising of beer. It continued into the 1960s.

In 1938 the *Advertisers Weekly*[20] published the results of a survey of forty public houses in various parts of London to discover the views of the trade on collective advertising and possible alternatives. Licensees were asked the following three questions:

1. You have now had four years' experience of group advertising for beer and this, it is claimed, has increased sales. Do you think group advertising for whisky and wines, such as port and sherry, would be more likely to increase consumption than the present competitive advertising of individual brands?

2. If you had a fund for advertising in local papers and cinemas, by local posters etc., do you think such local advertising of the amenities of your house would increase custom?
3. Do you think local direct mail advertising of your off-licence department would increase off-licence sales?

There was a division of opinion about the likely value of group advertising for whisky and wines. More than half the licensees interviewed (52.5 per cent) thought that such a scheme would not help them in any way, 32.5 per cent were in favour, and 15 per cent did not express an opinion. Among the views put forward against the scheme was the argument that while group advertising was suitable for beer, it was not so for wines and spirits because they were generally asked for by their brand names. However, in the case of Guinness advertisements they were highly praised, and as a result of this constant publicity by such brand names the sales increased daily. Others, without mentioning specific brands, found that sales of beer had increased. Half the licensees who did not express an opinion thought the present advertising methods were satisfactory.

Responding to the second question, only 20 per cent thought that local advertising would increase their custom, and five per cent of these stated that unless full co-operation from mother houses and brewers was forthcoming the cost would be prohibitive. 80 per cent were against local advertising to increase custom. One licensee said he would be prepared to subscribe to a scheme for press, cinema and poster advertising locally to compete with milk bars and cafés which already did this. Five per cent thought the results would not be commensurate with the cost, and that custom was built up by personal service. Two-and-a-half per cent stated that such a scheme had been tried without success. The reaction to the idea of local direct mail advertising of off-licences was distinctly unfavourable.

The collective campaign did not replace brand advertising which had been considerably used by some breweries, notably Bass and Guinness. The early advertisements sought to link drinking with good health, fitness and strength. In 1925 Bass had an advertisement in the national newspapers which claimed: "Bass gives an edge to your appetite and promotes good digestion – therefore cultivate the Bass habit and be well."[21] Ten years later, the slogan was "Get more out of life – have Bass daily."

Before 1928 Guinness appeared to advertise "very little except for the distribution of samples to doctors and others to see whether it was worthy of recommendation as a pick-me-up."[22] Later it made use of slogans which became as well known as "Beer is Best". These were usually associated with striking illustrations and fixed in people's minds such claims as "Guinness is good for you" and "Guinness for strength" as well as "My goodness – my Guinness". In 1925 Worthington introduced limericks into their advertisements.

In the years immediately before the Second World War, Guinness and Bass, Ratcliff and Gretton became the big spenders in press display advertising. "Both companies were distinctive in that they owned no tied houses, and for that reason their sales depended on the widest degree of customer acceptance for their products. Advertising on a large scale throughout the country was the basis of ensuring that consumers asked for their products."[23] Some indication of the extent of brand advertising before the collective campaign was launched was given in quarterly statements published in *Advertisers Weekly*. In the months of October, November and December of 1932 the amount spent on press advertising by Bass, Guinness, Worthington and Younger was £60,000.

Post-war growth in advertising

After the 1939–45 war there was a vast increase in the amount spent on all forms of liquor advertising, an indication of the growth being given in the following table by the compilers of the report *Advertising Alcohol*.[24]

	Press display advertising as percentage of: Total consumer spending	Total consumer spending excluding tax
1948	0.04	0.09
1950	0.10	0.22
1952	0.14	0.28
1954	0.21	0.42
1956	0.25	0.48
1958	0.21	0.39
1959	0.24	0.41

A further table[25] indicates how expenditure on press display advertising was distributed among four main breweries and the Brewers' Society.

	£'000					
Product	**1955**	**1956**	**1957**	**1958**	**1959**	**Average 5 years 1955–9**
Bass	58.7	104.3	91.4	61.8	40.1	71.3
Guinness	287.6	290.2	321.0	329.7	333.3	312.4
Ind Coope	94.5	120.3	102.0	105.6	108.4	106.2
Mackeson's Stout	96.7	85.7	144.8	73.1	177.2	115.5
Brewers' Society	94.2	151.7	83.0	89.0	113.4	106.3
Total	**631.7**	**752.2**	**742.2**	**659.2**	**772.4**	**711.5**

Compared with the pre-war period the Brewers' Society's share of advertising expenditure fell from 12 per cent to 8 per cent.

Besides beer there was a great variety of other alcoholic drinks on the market, the consumption of which also increased. *Advertising Alcohol* reported, "In 1929, total spending on drinks other than beer came to just over £100 millions, of which nearly four-fifths went on spirits. By 1938, expenditure was somewhat lower at £90 millions, but by 1959, it had risen to £388 millions."[26] This trend continued, so that although beer consumption increased the increase in consumption of other liquors outstripped it. The compilers of *Advertising Alcohol* "tentatively estimated" that total spending on advertisements for drinks other than beer amounted to between £10 million and £11 million in 1959, or at least £4 million more than was spent on advertising beer in the same year. "Compared with 1935, advertising of other alcoholic drinks had increased 5½ times, whereas the comparable increase for beer advertising was around 5 times."[27] It was also concluded that advertising and consumer spending had been more closely related for other alcoholic drinks than for beer.[28]

Possibly encouraged by the success of the collective advertising campaign for beer, the wine merchants decided to launch a similar campaign in 1950, details of which were revealed in the *Morning Advertiser*.[29] A survey had shown that of the people who drank at all the day previous to the count, 86 per cent had taken beer and only one per cent had tasted wine. Alarmed by this discovery, the Wine and Spirit Association launched a Wine Education and Publicity Fund. It was being admitted among members of the association that, if the trend continued there would soon be no demand for wine, and an appeal was made to them for funds to launch the campaign, the scope of which could not be determined until it was known how much money was available. It was hoped to raise at least £20,000 in the first year. The association told its members that the education of the public to drink more wine would not be achieved overnight, but only by a determined effort over a considerable period and by substantial contributions. It was hoped that when they realized their livelihood was at stake wine merchants and shippers would contribute generously. They were told that donations would be treated as legitimate trading expenses by the Inland Revenue, and so firms could afford to be generous.

At this time the potential of television as a trend-setter was being appreciated. *Harper's Wine and Spirit Gazette* commented, "The man with a television set is likely to order more from his merchant as friends drop in to see the big television features and accept the usual hospitality. It seems, however, that some set-owners are economising in their hospitality bills by serving tea or coffee. Probably it won't be long before the radio industry is advertising television sets guaranteed to make each purchaser a leader of the social set in her street; and we trust that the amazingly fine types they will photograph grouped round the television will all be holding a sociable glass. This is one of the post-war social trends on which a Wine Education and Publicity Fund could exercise a beneficial influence."[30]

When £9,000 had been contributed to the Wine Education and Publicity Fund, the Wine and Spirit Association announced how this sum would be spent.[31] A black and white film for general distribution and public showing would cost between £2,500 and £3,000. The draft script, which had been prepared, envisaged a story centred round wine production and shipment to Britain. It would stress the fact that wine was a natural drink in most parts of the world. Some £5,000 was earmarked for wine samples and publicity for local tastings when the film was shown. Lectures to trade audiences would cost another £500. Any balance would be retained towards the cost of another film.

In 1964 the Advertising Inquiry Council produced a second study called *Report on Drink Advertising*.[32] This stated that each year between

1959 and 1962 expenditure on liquor increased by an average of over £50 millions. In the same period the total advertising bill increased by about £5 millions, "but in relation to total consumer spending on alcoholic drink, the relative importance of the advertising expenditure has increased only slightly."[33] The liquor advertising scene at that time was described in the following paragraph,

> *The division of the total advertising bill between beer and other alcoholic drinks on the one hand, and between the various types of media on the other shows a number of changes between 1959 and 1962. In the first place, beer claimed a larger proportion of total expenditure in 1962 than in 1959, increasing its share from 41 per cent to 44 per cent. Secondly, the relative importance of press advertising has fallen during the period from 45 per cent to less than 43 per cent, and this trend was common to beer and other alcoholic drinks. Thirdly, television has increased its share of total expenditure from just over 13 per cent in 1959 to around 19 per cent in 1962, making its gain from poster and outdoor advertising rather than from the other heads of expenditure. Fourthly, expenditure on television has increased somewhat faster in the case of beer than of other alcoholic drinks.*[34]

It is interesting to note that the cover of a third study of liquor advertising published in 1969 and called *Ten Years of Advertising Alcohol*[35] depicted two lads watching a television screen, which epitomised the new factor in the advertising of alcohol, namely television. During the decade under review the expenditure on television advertising was 43 per cent of the total but by 1967 it had risen to 80 per cent. What was striking about this period was the considerable difference in the proportion of the combined spending claimed by television for other drinks as compared with beer. In 1959 television's share of beer advertising was under 50 per cent, but was over 80 per cent in 1967. For other alcoholic drinks it was less than 30 per cent in 1959 and little more than 35 per cent in 1967. The difference was due, of course, to the voluntary agreement among manufacturers of spirits not to advertise on television.

Advertising and controversy

In the decade since 1967, despite the voluntary ban in respect of spirits, liquor advertising became an emotive and controversial issue. The inevitability of this was anticipated by Lord Moyne, vice chairman of the Guinness Company. In a House of Lords debate on television policy on 25th and 26th November 1953, he spoke and voted against commercial television. In his speech he said,

> *There is no such thing as free television. Somebody has to pay for it. In some cases it will be the consumer, in some cases the shareholders, in some cases the smaller concerns who would fall by the wayside. Insofar as it was borne by shareholders, approximately half the cost would fall directly on the Exchequer in reduced income and profit tax. If commercial television simply increases the sales of one manufacturer as against another it will cost the nation and the state a pretty penny: if it succeeds in increasing consumption it brings us nearer to that inflationary disaster which the party to which I am so proud to belong has worked so hard to prevent. We, as one of the six largest advertisers in the country, have never been asked whether we wish to see television advertising introduced. It would appear that industry is to stand beside the state as a milch cow, whether it likes it or not. It is no use saying that no advertiser need go on to the television screen if he does not want to, competition is likely to drive him there.*

Competition did drive him there. *Ten years of Advertising Alcohol* published a table showing leading beer advertisers' spending on press and television advertising between 1962 and 1967. By this time television had become the major medium for eight leading advertisers, including the Brewers' Society. In 1962 the total was £3,296,000 (press display £1,403,000, TV £1,893,000). By 1967 the total had risen to £4,227,000, but press display advertising had dropped to £712,000 and TV advertising had increased to £3,514,400. In 1962 Guinness headed this league table, but by 1967 had been replaced by the new group Bass-Charrington. As we have already stated, there was virtually no advertising on television of "hard liquor" such as whisky and gin, because in 1954 the distillers decided not to use this family medium for promoting sales of these products. Besides this voluntary ban the Independent Television Authority had its own rules to avoid the direct encouragement of young people to drink alcohol. Actors and actresses appearing in alcohol commercials had to be seen to be in their twenties, at least. There must be no encouragement of over-indulgence and nothing in any advertisement that could possibly associate drink and driving.

A later form of liquor advertising was sponsorship. This was by no means confined to activities by members of the liquor trade, some of the best known examples of sponsorship being those undertaken by cigarette manufacturers, for example the John Player League and the Benson and Hedges Cup in cricket. Trophies and prizes in horse-racing have become associated with donors from the liquor trade. No doubt some of the most inventive ideas for sponsorship have come from Cutty Sark Whisky, whose best known promotion is *The Times* Crossword Competition. This came at the end of a long line of lesser sponsorships, like the 1969 Waitress Race at Sandown Regatta in the Isle of Wight, the Cutty Sark Shield played for by the South Hants Licensed Victuallers Golfing Society and the Cutty Sark Whisky One Lap Cycle Race at Paddington. When the M.C.C. touring team left for their tour of Pakistan and Ceylon in 1969 the members of the team were photographed on the steps of their plane with carrier bags of bottles of Cutty Sark Whisky. In the *Daily Mirror* of 16th July 1969 an unusual Cutty Sark venture was reported. This was the promotion of a new kind of literature in France. Because of the powerful wine lobby in France the advertising of whisky was difficult, and Cutty Sark found a way of overcoming the difficulty. Said the *Daily Mirror* report, "At least two publishing houses in Paris (La Fleuve Noire and Arabesque) have been putting out thrillers whose common factor is plugging Cutty Sark. In three months, La Fleuve Noire has published thirty-three thrillers which have mentioned Cutty Sark at more or less appropriate moments. Arabesque, in the same period, published twelve novels, each of which mentioned the product. The books run to about 20,000 copies each."

Whereas at one time drinking was principally an activity for men, during the war, while in the services or the factories women acquired the habit. In the first of the three studies of liquor advertising[36] already mentioned, it was acknowledged that it had become accepted by the brewers that beer drinking among women should be encouraged by advertising,[37] and increasingly, beer advertisements involved the association of women with drinking. In 1973 the I.P.C. Womens' Magazine Group reported that advertisement investment by the liquor trade in its magazines increased by 55.17 per cent over the previous total of £271,402. In 1976 I.P.C's *Womens Market* magazine reported that grocery outlets accounted for almost half the current £860 million take-home drink trade. "It is clear women have become the big spenders in the alcoholic drinks market" commented the magazine. A Target Group Index survey showed that the big rise in the number of licensed supermarkets was the main reason women bought alcoholic drink. Women drank more sherry, port, table-wine, champagne, aperitifs, vermouths and liqueurs, than men. With such a potential market is was inevitable that liquor advertising would be directed towards women. In 1976 it was reported that Bols, the world's largest producer of liqueurs, had changed their advertising from TV to women's magazines. Benedictine's advertising aimed at women went up by 75 per cent, and the firm's advertising agency were quoted as saying that the reason was simply that women were more important than men to the sale of liqueurs. Target's survey showed that over half Britain's liqueur drinkers were women. Between 1971 and 1976 liqueur drinking by men went up by 10 per cent, but among women the increase was 17 per cent. In the same period the consumption of vermouths and aperitifs went up among women by 66 per cent, but among men by 40 per cent. Even Guinness reckoned that at least 30 per cent of their customers were women. In 1976 Guinness spent £150,000 advertising in women's magazines.

Youth target for advertising

From the late 1950s onwards young people became the target for liquor advertisers. This was not surprising since "the bulge" was one of the principal features of population trends. There were simply more young people everywhere, and they had a large surplus income to spend. Dr Mark Abrams estimated that the nation's 4,200,000 working teenagers disposed of about £17 millions a week of "uncommitted spending power."[38]The brewers were quick to respond to the potential demand of the young. William Younger's used a pun on their name in their message – "Join the Younger set. a younger taste is a taste for life." However, it was the Ind Coope advertisements for Skol lager which were most evidently directed to young people and women. A front page advertisement in the *Morning Advertiser* featured two young people drinking Skol with the explicit caption: "The boy and girl shown below will be appearing throughout June in the biggest advertising campaign Britain has ever seen for any lager. A £325,000 campaign that is changing the taste of Britain. Newspapers, magazines, posters and television – all the power of modern publicity and advertising is making this a boom year for Skol."[39]

During the 1960s and on into the '70s the young people fulfilled Sir Edgar Sanders' hope that they would become "the mainstay of the public-house." Realizing the massive market potential of young people, the public houses which had adjoining facilities introduced discotheques and attracted incredible numbers of young people. Although taking place on licensed premises the discotheques were patronized by hundreds of young people under the age of eighteen. Drink was easily conveyed from the bars to the discotheques, and according to *Which?,* the consumer magazine, young people under age experienced no difficulty in purchasing liquor. The *Which?* survey concluded, "Almost two-thirds of those of our teenagers who drank alcohol (including about half the 15-year-olds) said that every pub in their area would serve them with alcohol. The figures were about the same for pubs, off-licences and for clubs or discos . . . Even 15-year-olds seldom had much difficulty in obtaining alcohol from any source."[40] Liquor advertising aimed at capturing the young must have contributed to the vast extension of drinking among young teenage boys and girls.

A more sophisticated approach was made to young adults. For example, in 1976 it was announced that a new £250,000 TV and cinema campaign for Campari was being launched, aimed at getting young people to try a drink which was traditionally associated with the middle-age group. A spokesman for Findlater Matta, the agents for Campari in Britain, was reported as saying that the growth in popularity of Campari was particularly noticeable among the 25 to 34 aged drinkers.[41] It was to this age group that the Smirnoff Vodka advertisements were directed and some of the posters at London underground stations advertising this drink were so *risque* that protests from offended travellers seemed to have had an effect. At all events they were withdrawn and more discreet ones replaced them.

The Erroll Committee described the advertising of liquor as "a complicated and controversial subject." Certainly since the publication of the Erroll Report in 1972, though not necessarily as a direct consequence of what the Erroll Committee said, the advertising of liquor became a matter of widespread public concern. While the Erroll Committee thought it was inappropriate for them to become too closely involved in this matter they made one important observation. They had been struck, they said,

> *by certain recent trends in advertising, the desirability of which, in the general public interest, seems to us at least questionable. It now appears to be an accepted feature of advertising strategy to direct campaigns increasingly at young people. We do not think that it is particularly responsible for the industry to suggest to young people that drinking is in some way a pre-requisite of social success and acceptability – a suggestion which we think has been implicit in a number of recent television campaigns. These age groups are, perhaps, particularly susceptible on this score and we doubt whether current trends in advertising necessarily represent the most desirable ways of influencing their approach to drink. In our view, the brewing industry needs to recognise its social responsibilities particularly in relation to the appeals it makes to young people. We hope that the way these responsibilities are exercised will be kept under review by the Government Departments principally concerned.*[42]

A code of liquor advertising

The first official response to the obvious concern about the characteristics and effects of liquor advertising came from the Advertising Standards Authority in 1975, when a new code of advertising practice for the advertising of alcoholic drinks was issued (Appendix I). This declared that in exercising their freedom to advertise in the United Kingdom, the liquor advertisers had an obligation to ensure that their advertising was always socially responsible. The new code was in the nature of "ten commandments." It consisted of the kind of controls which responsible advertisers might be expected to welcome. These were that children should not be portrayed in drink advertisements, except in, for example, a family situation where they would normally be present, but would not be consuming alcohol. Advertisements should not encourage young people to drink and anyone shown should be obviously over eighteen. It should not be implied that not to drink was a failure to accept a challenge. There should be no emphasis on the stimulent or tranquillizing effects of any drink, nor should an impression be given that drinks were being offered for their intoxicating effect. It should not be suggested that drinking was beneficial for health, or for social or sexual success. Drink should not be associated with driving. The Code of Advertising Practice Committee has the responsibility for seeing that the standards are observed and any member of the public or a group or organization offended by an advertisement that seems to contravene the Code of Practice may appeal to the committee for judgement.

In 1978 the Independent Broadcasting Authority responded to pressure for more effective controls of liquor advertising on television and radio. A new code was adopted and came into force on 5th October 1978 (Appendix II). This was a comprehensive code which was welcomed by "watchdog" groups, but the trade and the advertising consultants were not so enthusiastic. Certainly it was much more rigorous than the Advertising Standards Authority Code of Practice. For instance, it prohibited advertisements directed towards young people and insisted that no person portrayed on television should seem to be younger than about twenty-five. Children might not be seen or heard on such advertisements. No personality commanding the loyalty of the young might be featured. The code, like that of the ASA, banned advertisements which implied that drinking was essential to social success, or that it encouraged sexual prowess. No encouragement was to be given to immoderate drinking and there must be no reference to buying rounds. Advertisements must not place undue emphasis on the strength of certain drinks, nor must they claim therapeutic value or give an impression that physical performance can be improved by drink. The association of drink with driving was expressly forbidden. No liquor advertisement could publicize a competition. Regular solitary drinking was not to be portrayed as acceptable.

These new codes were clear evidence that the public concern expressed about liquor advertising was not dismissed as the predictable reaction of temperance and moral reformers, whose views could be ignored because they represented a minority opinion. The severity of some of the controls embodied in these codes of practice, indicate how seriously those responsible for the oversight of standards regarded the public exposure of modern advertising techniques in creating an increasing demand for a product the consumption of which threatened so many aspects of society.

References

1. Royal Commission on Liquor Licensing Evidence, para. 20, 181–20, 182.
2. House of Lords Official Report, Thursday, 28th March 1935, Vol. 96. (H.M.S.O.) p. 429.
3. Lords debate op cit p. 434 – speech by Lord Rhayader.

4. Issued October 1933 by the Temperance Council of the Christian Churches from which quotations in this chapter are taken.
5. *Royal Commission on Licensing, England and Wales 1929–1931 Report* H.M.S.O. (1932) pp. 156–157.
6. *The Brewers' Journal* 15th July 1933, p. 344.
7. *The Brewing Trade Review* 1st January 1934 p. 36 ff.
8. *The Brewers' Journal* 15th March 1934 p. 129.
9. *The Brewers' Journal* 15th July 1933, p. 345, 15th August 1933, p. 404.
10. Op cit 15th July 1933 p. 345.
11. Op cit p. 345.
12. Op cit 15th August 1933 p. 404.
13. Op cit 15th August 1933 p. 404.
14. Op cit 15th December 1933 p. 623.
15. *Brewing Trade Review* 1st December 1935 p. 524.
16. On 25th March 1931 Ernest Winterton had applied to introduce an identical bill under the ten minutes rule but had not succeeded. See *Alliance News* April 1931 p. 44.
17. *Brewing Trade Review* 1st March 1935 pp. 134, 135.
18. March 1937 pp. 124, 125.
19. March 1937 p. 125.
20. 5th May 1938.
21. *Advertising Alcohol:* Advertising Inquiry Committee (1960) p. 20.
22. *Advertising in a Free Society* Arthur Seldon and Ralph Harris p. 123.
23. *Advertising Alcohol* p. 17.
24. *Advertising Alcohol* p. 15.
25. Op cit p. 17.
26. Op cit p. 29.
27. Op cit p. 29.
28. Op cit p. 31.
29. 2nd June 1950.
30. 2nd June 1950.
31. See *Alliance News* November/December 1950.
32. *Report on drink Advertising:* Advertising Inquiry Council (1964)
33. Op cit p. 2.
34. Op cit p. 2.
35. Published by the Christian Economic and Social Research Foundation.
36. *Advertising Alcohol* (1960).
37. Op cit p. 22.
38. *The Teenage consumer* Mark Abrams. LPE papers No. 5. July 1959 pp. 9–11.
39. *Morning Advertiser* 31st May 1960.
40. *Which?* July 1978 p. 383.
41. *Alliance News* July/August 1976 p. 9
42. *Report of the Departmental Committee on Liquor Licensing.* H.M.S.O. (1972) pp. 45, 46.

CHAPTER 14

THE TRADE

The retailing of liquor has a long and interesting history, but until the seventeenth century it was largely confined to ale. This was the earliest and most common alcoholic beverage sold in England. It was made as a rule from malted barley (though wheat was sometimes used) and water. This was then fermented with yeast. The term "beer" was used to describe a similar beverage which was imported from Europe. The one difference between this and ale was that beer was brewed with hops. Ale houses existed from before the time of King Edgar (959–975) who, when he came to the throne, issued a decree to limit their number. It is not our purpose to trace the entire history of the retailing of liquor which has been done in a convenient form by H. A. Monckton in *A history of the English public house.* Only a brief reference is required before we address ourselves to the progress and changes in the twentieth century.

Monckton provides a link between the earliest period and the beginning of what has become an extensive trade in various types of liquor. He writes, "Until the seventeenth century the ale-house keeper had little or no rivalry in the way of drinks with which to compete. While it is perfectly true that most families continued to brew for themselves and wine was becoming a little more easily available, the ale houses had a fairly clear field in which to operate. From the middle of the seventeenth century the spectre of uninhibited spirit consumption slowly began to materialize and within a century was to produce a situation in London which can fairly be described as a social disaster of horrible proportions. With the duty on beer rising all the time and no duty on spirits, the scene was set for one of the biggest orgies of over-indulgence our island history has ever known."[1] We have already noted the steps taken at various times to regularize and control the retailing of liquor. Notably the control was in the hands of local justices, and the traditional outlet for which a justices' licence was issued was the public house.

Emergence of "the Trade"

The emergence of "the Trade" was late in the history of drinking in Britain. Initially the brewing of ale was done on the premises by the publican, or more likely by his wife. It was during the nineteenth century that the "common brewer" emerged. Between 1840 and 1890 the number of brewing victuallers declined from 27,125 to 6,350.[2] At the same time, and earlier, there was a noticeable trend towards what has since been known as the "tied house" system. This is the system by which breweries own licensed premises to ensure that they are outlets for their own products. Monckton quotes an Excise return for 1816 which showed that out of a total of 48,000 licensed ale houses in England and Wales, 14,200 belonged to breweries, 10,800 to the occupiers and 22,700 to disinterested persons. Shortly after, in 1830, the Beerhouse Act was passed to divert people from excessive spirit drinking in fully-licensed houses. At this time there were 51,000 publicans' licences in England and Wales. As we have seen already,[3] during the first year of the Beerhouse Act over 24,000 beerhouse licences were issued. By the middle of the century there were 60,000 publicans' licences and 40,000 beerhouses licences. "The nineteenth century marked a rapid decline of private brewing simply because it was gradually becoming less economic to brew at home or on the estate. In round figures, private brewing accounted for about half the consumption at the beginning of the century, but by the end it had dwindled almost to nothing."[4] At the same time beer output increased from 14 million standard barrels in 1830 to 20 million standard barrels in 1860, and to 32 million standard barrels in 1890.

This process was accelerated by changes in brewing techniques, the application of science to production and preservation, and the development of transport. The concentration of brewing in the hands of a small number of large companies provided resources for the employment of scientists in laboratories to keep a check on quality and to advise on methods of production. Among the first to do this were Arthur Guinness, Allsopp and Ind Coope. An important contribution was made by Pasteur who in *Etudes sur le Vin* in 1860 showed that yeast was a living organism and that changes in its life pattern were responsible for fermentation. In 1876 in *Etudes sur la Biere,* he carried his analysis much further, and described the effect of infectious disease on the fermenting process.[5] This and other studies focused attention on the need to produce the right type of yeast for brewing. Work was also done on malt, which led to the development of new varieties of barley suitable for brewing. Out of these studies came the Laboratory Club in 1886 which, in 1890, became the Institute of Brewing. Inevitably the scientists addressed themselves to discovering the best methods of preserving beer, containing it and transporting it in peak condition to the retailers.

These factors all favoured big brewers. And mention of big brewers provides an opportunity to note the process of contraction so far as the number of brewers is concerned. In 1870, 28,679 "brewers' licences" were issued, in 1906, only 5,025. The nature of the change is illustrated in the following table:

	1880	**1906**
Brewers brewing under 10,000 barrels a year	18,538	4,463
Brewers brewing under 100,000 barrels a year	475	513
Brewers brewing under 500,000 barrels a year	23	41
Brewers brewing under 1,000,000 barrels a year	3	6
Brewers brewing over 1,000,000 barrels a year	1	2
Totals	**19,040**	**5,025**

The brew in 1906 was 35,278,990 barrels of 36 gallons each. Of this, 224 companies brewed 24,601,416 barrels or 69 per cent. Nearly twelve million barrels (or a third of the whole) were brewed by 26 companies. Commenting on these figures G. B. Wilson said, "The manufacture of malt liquors and the distribution of intoxicating liquors in England and Wales is now practically controlled by 381 companies, who own all tied houses."[6] As the number of brewers declined so those which were left increased in size. It was only such larger brewers which could finance the research and development and the installation of equipment which made the brewing and marketing of beer of high quality economically profitable.

Going "public"

Most prominent of all such brewers were Arthur Guinness. They had been brewers in Dublin for a hundred years before October 1886, when they became the first brewery to go "public" with a £6 million share issue which was over-subscribed many times.[7] By 1870 they were almost the only brewers left in Dublin, and by that time they had a large English trade. The firm became famous and prosperous. Other large breweries expanded and the issue of shares and the underwriting by finance houses indicated the confidence of investors in the industry. "Gradually more and more firms came on to the market; by 1888 shares to the value of £25 million had been issued, and in August 1888 a separate Stock Exchange list of brewery companies was made."[8] By 1890 there were more than two hundred breweries trading on this basis.[9] According to G. B. Wilson, by 1906 there were 381 such companies whose subscribed capital could be described thus, "Forty with subscribed capital of over one million: £100,533,000; 71 with five hundred thousand and over; £48,651,000; 72 with three hundred thousand and over: £26,955,000; 154 with one hundred thousand and over, £28,543,000: 44 with under one hundred thousand, £2,571,000. Total £207,253,000."[10]

Although these figures appear to be substantial, in fact they do not reflect the fall in the price of brewery shares which had been "continuous over a number of years", and which was the subject of an article by Sir Thomas Whittaker MP in the *Westminster Gazette*.[11] He produced a table of twenty-five brewery companies showing the price of their shares in 1898 and what they had fallen to by 1905. The following are examples taken from the table,

	1898	1905	Fall %
Allsopp Ord.	187	15	92
Bass and Co. 5% Pref.	156	112	28
Courage and Co. 5% Pref.	148	94	36
Ind Coope 4 ½ % Pref.	11 ⅛	1 ⅝	85
Ind Coope 4 ½ % Debs.	115 ½	63	45
Watney, Coombe and Co. Pref. Ord.	100	48	52

The decline which took place after 1905 was not so severe.

Whittaker thought the reasons why brewery shares had fallen in price were many. First, towards the end of the previous century, public houses had been bought at "preposterous figures", so that there was no possibility of them being remunerative. Besides, most companies were over capitalized. Many of them had made no adequate provision for writing down their inflated capital nor the excessively-high amounts at which their precarious licence values stood in their books. Whittaker commented, "The money which should have been devoted to that purpose was used to pay dividends on watered or wasted capital". Another, and different, reason was that people were drinking less. Drinking habits had changed. A large direct delivery trade in jars and bottles had been developed by many breweries which had cut back the more profitable sales in public houses. As a result, dividends had been reduced, and consequently the market value of the shares. The public had also begun to realize that the brewery boom of the last ten or fifteen years of the previous century had been grossly inflated and finally brewery securities had shared in the generally adverse conditions of the stock markets since the South African War.

The boom had been vigorously stimulated with information about the new issues and mergers, and invariably mentioned the important element of "property and assets", which, in fact, referred to licensed property. There was considerable activity in the acquisition of such property, not so much for its intrinsic value as for its marketing prospects. Some firms over-stretched themselves, others, led by shrewd management, established a position from which further expansion was assured. Arthur Guinness, for example, never looked back, though, in fact, they never owned their own public houses. The prosperity of the company was built on the quality of its products and its ability to sell nationwide.

But generally the boom was short-lived and decline set in towards the end of the nineteenth century and spanned the first decade of the twentieth century, with no signs of real recovery until 1913, when the loss of an overall majority by the Liberals in parliament and evidence that the temperance agitation had passed its peak, encouraged more optimistic expectations for the trade which encouraged another round of acquisitions of smaller brewers by bigger ones, and amalgamations between companies.

The war changes things

The outbreak of the First World War (1914–18) may be seen in retrospect as the beginning of one of the most far-reaching periods of change in the retailing of liquor. The emergency controls which were introduced have been dealt with in a separate chapter,[12] but the war had two other immediate effects on the trade. First there was a marked fall in output, and, second a considerable rise in prices due to higher duties and increases in costs of raw materials. With a Liberal government in power at the beginning of the war, the trade had faint hopes of any relief, but despite their fears, brewers, and especially the bigger ones, made profits. The economics of brewing at this time are dealt with by Vaizey.[13]

Immediately the war was over restrictions on output were relaxed and in July 1919 they were lifted altogether. Raw materials were short, notably barley and this led to an increase in price not only for the materials but for the product. Beer duty was also raised. However, output considerably increased, from 19 million bulk barrels in 1918 to 35 million bulk barrels in 1920. Profits also increased, but the post-war boom was shortlived. "By 1922 output had fallen to 30 million bulk barrels and by 1924 to 28 million bulk barrels".[14] This contraction, accompanied by changes in cost and marketing, further accelerated the trend towards concentration of brewing in a diminishing number of companies. There was another round of amalgamations with consequent closures of brewing plants. There were other important changes, too. Brewers sought to acquire or amalgamate with companies in control of licensed premises adjacent to their established plant or capable of incorporation into viable delivery services. Transport costs were now a factor of some importance, and the provision of vehicles especially suitable for the delivery of beer enabled the economic radius of some breweries to be extended. The rationalization of the trade meant that in many places licensed premises became redundant. There emerged a pattern of what Vaizey refers to as "regional" brewing companies, whose products were mainly sold in the licensed premises adjacent to their breweries and acquired by them to create a convenient economic unit.

"Throughout the early thirties this process continued. It was reinforced by the renewed depression after the economic revivial of the late 1920s. British output remained after 1924 reasonably steady at about 25 millions bulk barrels. In 1931 and 1932 it fell to 20 millions and in 1933 to 17 millions. The beer duty was raised in 1930 and again in 1931, so that the price of beer rose both relatively and absolutely. Those breweries operating in badly depressed areas suffered most."[15] Vaizey goes on to observe that the exception to the process of amalgamation and combination was Guinness, which also had its difficulties following the creation of the Irish Free State which raised particular problems for it. It was a Protestant company based in a mainly Roman Catholic country which had introduced its own independent excise and customs system. In 1932 there began a tariff war between England and Ireland, and being a big exporter to England, Guinness was caught in the cross-fire. In 1934 Guinness built a new brewery at Park Royal in north London. With the expansion of production in this new brewery, output in Ireland declined, but the prosperity of Guinness continued, partly because by this time its marketing was being backed by brilliantly conceived and executed advertising. The Brewers' Society had also launched its great advertising campaign to which extensive reference has been made elsewhere,[16] and by 1939 the brewing industry had recovered something of the stability and prosperity it had enjoyed in 1913.

New trends

It was in the period between the two world wars that other trends appeared which were to have far-reaching results after the Second World War and particularly during and since the 1960s.

It had been traditional for public houses to sell draught beer, that is, beer produced by brewers and delivered to the retailer in barrels which were stored in cellars and which needed experienced handling to ensure that it was served to the customer at the critical point of fermentation. The processes are described in detailed in a number of books of which *Dr Foster's book of beer* is one of the latest and which has the merit of being written for the general reader. With the development of modern methods of brewing, the barrels have been generally displaced by metal containers (kegs). These new containers ensure that the beer is uniformly the same and does not require a high degree of expertise on the part of the cellar-man.

However, the change which has had the most far-reaching implications for retailing liquor is bottling, which came in as the public demanded, for instance, their preferred national brew, or as more convenient from a "take home" point of view. Because of the cost of installing bottling machinery, only the larger brewers were able to respond effectively to this demand which, although apparent long before the development of supermarkets, was a portent of things to come. It was certainly one of the factors in the growth of off-licences which could sell only bottled liquor, whether, beer wine or spirits.

It is interesting to note that in Vaizey's *The Brewing Industry 1886–1951* first published in 1960, there is not a single reference to supermarkets whose off-licence sales are now a major factor in the retailing of liquor and whose development has been one of the major causes of the decline in the number of bona fide off-licences which, until this development, was as prominent a phenomenon as supermarkets which we shall be referring to separately when we come to consider more recent changes in marketing liquor. In 1900 there were 18,000 off-licences and by 1950 there were 32,000.

A fact which can be anticipated with some confidence, is that as bottled beer took over from draught beer, so canned beer has become a threat to bottled beer, which was not apparent when cans appeared before the Second World War. After the war new-type cans were introduced following the American pattern, the American and British scenes being different. In America there were no "pubs" and there was no system of returning empty bottles. In Britain at that time most drinking was done at the public house and there was no massive demand for take-home liquor. Moreover, when beer was purchased in bottles they were returnable. "As bottles completed about twenty return trips to customers before becoming broken or chipped, the replacement and washing costs placed a comparitively small extra charge upon the beer."[17] Cans were non-returnable and so their total cost was an immediate charge on the retail price of the beer, unlike the deposit on the bottle which was returned to the customer. In 1969 Monckton judged that "canned beer is moving steadily, if slowly, forward".[18] Since then the pace has quickened and the development of purchasing liquor at supermarkets has created a demand for a convenient form of take-home packaging. The brewers have responded with four- or six-can packs which can be readily taken from the shelves, taken home with no greater difficulty than a packet of breakfast cereal, and stored in the "fridge", now to be found in most homes where supplies of liquor are held.

Before considering other retail outlets, it must be said that the traditional public house has been for several centuries the main point of sale of liquor to the public. The public house has evolved from three types of premises which existed about a thousand years ago. These were the "ale house", the "tavern" and the "inn". They each had a separate function. The ale house was a shop selling ale on the premises for consumption on the premises. The inn likewise sold ale, but for travellers rather than "locals", and the tavern sold wine only. Although the public house is in a state of constant change, its basic characteristics are those of the original ale house. Here the drinking went on in the kitchen which became a meeting place for local residents. As the facilities were extended to other parts of the house traditions were established which are still part of the character of public houses. For example, the public bar retains the basic features of the original kitchen, the beer is usually cheaper, the furnishings are generally plain and working people do not feel they have to dress up to be there. It is generally in the public bar where the facilities for games are provided. One of the reasons why many public houses have more expansive facilities is that they may have been inns which, after coach travel ceased, no longer had a function to fulfil for travellers and so became public houses. Here the bars would be more ostentatious. Thus public houses which set out to cater for the whole community developed "public bars" and "saloon" or "lounge" bars for different types of customers.

This is not the only strand in the pattern of development, for the gin palaces also had their impact. "Gin palaces are very important in the evolution of the pub because they were the first custom-built drinking places. They are famous for their rich decorations, and their elaborate use of brass fittings, etched glass and mirrors, and mahogany carving; all this was designed to entice the customer from the dismal street, and to persuade him to buy gin because sales were falling with increasing taxation. But they were important for another reason, for the gin palaces were the first establishments deliberately to incorporate a variety of bars."[19] These bars were really partitioned areas of a central serving bar.

There is a tendency for people to idealize the English public house, to think of it as a small inviting building, whose white-washed walls and hanging baskets of geraniums and lobelia are common features everywhere. Inside they expect to find an open fire, copper warming pans and horse brasses adorning the walls, and black oak chairs and tables. To go with the traditional image of the English pub is a type-cast landlord who acts as a kind of focus for friendship in the community. There are, no doubt, public houses which epitomize the ideal. In particular there are the purpose-built public houses, which are invariably stereotyped with the architectural vogue of the times when they were built. This means that many public houses built in the 1930s are almost indistinguishable from the new post offices and council offices built at that time. No doubt there was public pressure which demanded that public houses should be simply functional. The trend in recent times has been for architects either to imitate the distant past and create mock Tudor, or to produce futuristic designs. Since most public houses of long standing are required to remain structurally unchanged, it is the interiors which have been transformed. What Roger Protz in *Pulling a fast one* calls "trendy young architects" have been let loose on the modernization of public houses. "The regular users of street corner locals find to their horror that their pub has been redesigned as a large pineapple, a sputnik or a wild west saloon to attract the gin-and-tonic and lager-and-lime trade. Public bars are ripped out and replaced by lounges with soft lights, soft carpets, wet-look mock leather and several pennies on the price of a pint".[20] Less desirable than some attempts at modernization have been the blatant attempts to attract large numbers of young people to discos and other forms of participant entertainment, often with insufficient oversight to ensure that under-age drinking laws are observed.

Threats to the public house

What we have been describing are the threats from within to the typical English pub. The more serious threats have come from other establishments and methods of retailing. The first major threat came from the registered club. The Working Men's Club and Institute Union, which is the principal federation of such establishments, was formed in 1862 by the Revd Henry Solly, and it is interesting to note that the club union movement began as a temperance enterprise. With the growing popularity of such clubs the pressure for the provision of alcoholic drinks increased. And so the club, which was open only to members, became an alternative to the public house. Because of its controlled membership it was thought that the restrictions imposed on public houses need not apply. Despite pledges from governments contemplating comprehensive licensing legislation that they would "deal with the clubs", they continue to enjoy a privileged freedom compared with public houses. An important sector of the club scene are the prestigious clubs, particularly in the West End of London, which have so far claimed successfully that the club is an extension of the homes of the members. Here it is argued liquor is not sold as a commercial commodity, but is supplied for the convenience of the members. The impossibility of distinguishing in law between these types of clubs and the "working men's clubs" has meant that all clubs have been accorded the same privileges. The 1902 Licensing Act made the registration of clubs supplying alcoholic liquor compulsory. However, apart from laying down certain conditions under which registration could be withdrawn, the act failed to do anything effective to "deal with the clubs". The 1961 Licensing Act established two categories of clubs, (a) Licensed clubs which differ only slightly from public houses and are run for the profit of the owner; and (b) registered clubs which are run for the benefit of the members and are controlled by them. Since there are no restrictions on the presence of children in clubs they frequently serve as social centres for families.

One of the features of the trade in the twentieth century has been the decline in the number of public houses and the growth in the number of clubs. In England and Wales in 1900 there were 102,189 full on-licences which represented a proportion of 31.69 per 10,000 of the population. The comparable figures for 1978 were 66,057 and 13.45 per 10,000 of the population. Between 1901 and 1978 the population of England and Wales rose from 32,528,000 to 49,117,000[21] which makes the comparable figures between public houses and clubs the more striking. The period of most dramatic decline in the number of public houses was between 1900 and 1910, by which time the number of full on-licences was 91,247. The slower rate of decline after 1910 can be seen in the following table:

1920	82,739
1930	77,335
1940	73,365
1950	73,483
1960	69,184
1970	64,702

It is not simply in the relative numbers of clubs and public houses that the threat is evident. As the club movement grew it became plain that federations of clubs could enter competitively into brewing their own beer.

The Northern Clubs' Federation Brewery began as a co-operative venture by eleven clubs who, in May 1919, bought a small brewery in Alnwick in Northumberland. This proved unsuitable, and after brewing occasionally in other breweries, they bought another brewery in Newcastle. This expanded rapidly, so that by 1930, when they bought another brewery at Hanover Square, Newcastle, they were brewing 50,000 barrels yearly, and in 1939, 70,000 barrels. This newly-acquired brewery was extended considerably and modernized, and their local trade with clubs was substantially expanded. In fact it now supplies clubs as far away as St. Austell. Clubs in Coventry also decided they would have more satisfactory service from N.C.F.B. than the Midlands breweries with which they had been trading.[22]

This was an experience typical of the six other club-breweries founded in industrial areas.[23] There were two consequences of clubs manufacturing their own beers, one was that it could be sold cheaper than recognized brands in the clubs, and the other was that the clubs movement benefited from the profits which usually accrued to the brewers.

A second major threat to the public house was the development of the off-licence, though many public houses had their own off-sales department. The original off-licences, as distinct from those of the modern supermarkets, often began as wine and spirit shops. When the people's drinking habits changed and there was more drinking at home, bottled beer came into fashion. The brewers were quick to seize upon these changes and began to buy up off-licences, creating them as tied-outlets. Such off-licences were advantageous from the owners point of view because they were not subject to such severe controls as were full on-licences; moreover, the extra facilities required in the public-house trade were not needed. Following the 1961 Licensing Act and the lifting of resale price maintenance on liquor sales, the traditional off-licence itself received a threat from which it seems unlikely to recover. This was from the supermarkets off-licence. Since the 1960s supermarkets have changed the shopping habits of the majority of people, some of the first supermarket chains to apply for off-licences arguing that they were simply concerned with the convenience of the customer who wished to take home the odd bottle of wine with the groceries. Two references as recent as 1979 indicate how modest and misleading were such arguments. In his annual statement to shareholders, Leslie Porter, head of Tesco supermarkets said the company had almost 400 off-licence branches. He said that with Tesco selling nearly 120 million cans of beer a year, which was equal to 60 million pints, the drinks side of their business had made a valuable contribution to the group's profits which in the year to 24th February 1979 amounted to £37,641,000. Total sales of the group amounted to £1,235 million. He said Tesco's competitive prices particularly appealed to women who were becoming increasingly responsible for the purchases of liquor for the family.[24] The other instance of increasing sales of liquor through supermarkets came from the Co-op, who reported in 1979 that in twenty years their drinks group based in Manchester had seen its turnover grow from nothing to £100 million a year. At their plant at Irlam, a Manchester suburb, was installed one of the most modern chilling and processing plants in Britain, where two-and-a-half million gallons of wine and spirit are bottled annually and distributed to over three thousand retail outlets in Britain. When the Co-op began to bottle in 1964 there were about one thousand off-licences, by 1979 there were three times that number, not all supermarkets. Their aim is to increase their 9 per cent share of the grocery table-wine market to over fifteen per cent by 1985.[25]

Campaign for Real Ale

What the future holds for the smaller brewers has become a matter of concern to an intriguing pressure group – the Campaign for Real Ale (CAMRA). In 1971 four journalists from England visited Ireland. They were so impressed by the quality of the local beers that they returned to England determined to do something to improve the quality of English beer. The products of the six big breweries in England lacked individuality, they said. The method of brewing in a few large modern breweries scattered around the country produced a gaseous, characterless drink which could not be called beer in any true sense. The four journalists gathered a few friends and formed CAMRA. Within two years they had hundreds of supporters. The membership, which included an annual subscription of £4 a year, rose to 30,000 and then settled back to about 20,000 with a small full-time staff to administer it and produce a journal and other publications. One of these *The Penguin Guide to Real Draught Ale* is quite manifestly a campaigning book, but it contains a great amount of factual information.[26] Of particular value is the considerable digest of information about local and regional brewers who are commended for keeping alive the craft of making distinctive beer. There is also a summary of the interests of the "big six" brewers.[27]

The "big six"

The "big six" emerged out of a decade or more of mergers and takeovers which was heralded by Charles Clore's unsuccessful bid of £21 million in 1959 in an attempted takeover of Watneys. In 1972 Maxwell Joseph tried and there followed a series of bids of increasing magnitude. "One hundred and fifteen days after the original bid was made, Maxwell Joseph was able to declare that he had gained control of Watneys. The price had risen to £420 million during the bidding, exactly twenty times the price that Charles Clore had offered thirteen years beforehand."[28]

It was in the 1960s that the giants began to grow. Hutt points out that in 1960 there was no such thing as a national brewery in the style of Allied Breweries or Bass-Charrington. There were nationally-known brews, but these were generally distributed through the free trade rather than tied houses.[29] An indication of the extent to which the original companies expanded by mergers is given in a table provided by Hutt.[30] In 1960 the six original companies owned 16,600 public houses. By 1972 these companies, vastly expanded, owned 39,000 public houses. The methods of growth varied. Allied Breweries, now the biggest drinks group in Europe, was formed in 1961 by the merger of Ind Coope, Ansell and Tetley Walker. Bass and Charrington had both engaged in big takeovers before they came together in 1961. Courage, the third of the "big six" was later than its rivals in establishing a nationwide chain of outlets. It was throughout the 1960s that Watneys built up its strength by acquiring other companies. Whitbread's methods were somewhat different. Ten years before the 1960s they were gathering small breweries into a special relationship, by taking a stake in their equities and putting two directors on the boards to offer advice and act as a brake on takeover bids from other quarters. It was not a great step to securing complete control which happened in the 1960s. The final brewery of the "big six" is Scottish and Newcastle which did not engage in the takeover scramble, but sought to expand through the free trade.[31]

In their report *Beer: a report on the supply of beer (1969)* the Monopolies Commission described the extent to which the brewers had expanded their control of the wine and spirit trade. A major wines and spirits supplier was quoted as saying to the commission, "Before the 1939–1945 war most brewery-owned houses were tied only for the company's products which were mostly beers. We as a company had dealt direct with many hundred and thousands of public houses for wines and spirits supplies for a great number of years."[32] The Monopolies Commission explained that with the easing of restrictions on supplies in the 1950s "most brewers began to expand their own wine and spirits departments". They did so in two main directions. First, they began bulk buying of wine and bottling, often with the registration of their own brand name. Second, they acquired "wholly or substantially" well-known wines and spirits businesses. For example, Grants of St. James's and Victoria Wines had become subsidiaries of Allied Breweries Limited. Similarly Bass-Charrington, through its subsidiary Bass-Charrington Vintners, controlled the marketing of well-known brands. The Monopolies Commission reported that this process had continued with Watney Mann in 1968 acquiring a 38 per cent interest in International Distillers and Vintners Limited. In the same year Allied Breweries acquired Showerings, Vine Products and Whiteways Limited. This merger brought to the Allied Breweries subsidiary Grants of St James's such products as Babycham perry, Whiteways, Coates and Gaymers cider, Harvey's sherries and table-wines and Britvic fruit juices of the Showerings' group, "and thereby created the largest wines and spirits business in Europe".[33] The control of sales of wine and spirits by the brewers has not extended to large-scale wine production and distilling of spirits, though there has been some expansion into these areas, the principal trend being to the production of "house brands".[34]

The grip the brewers have on the wine and spirits trade especially through the tied-house system, is deeply resented by tenants. "We received a greater volume of complaint about the tie on wines and spirits than on other aspects and those who criticised urged strongly that the tie should be abolished", the Monopolies Commission reported.[35] "Tenants, trade associations and others complained about restrictions on brands of wines and spirits that tenants of brewery-owned premises could sell. Some of these complaints were concerned with the landlord's refusal to allow tenants to stock certain brands of wines and spirits, but more with the restriction of choice resulting from the brewers' promotion through their wholesale prices and discount structure and through other means, of 'house brands'."[36] The brewers' increasing control of the wines and spirits trade also affected the wholesalers and the manufacturers. They told the Monopolies Commission that "the independent brand owners were finding that their brands were being frozen out of distribution by the brewers"; because of the large ownership of retail outlets by the brewers, independent brand owners were limited in their ability to launch new products.[37] Hawkins and Pass, in their book *The Brewing Industry* challenged the criticisms made of the structure of the brewing industry by the Price and Monopolies Commissions' Reports. Because their book was published after the manuscript of this one had reached its final stage, it was not possible to discuss their findings. Students of the subject will find the work of Hawkins and Pass well-researched and exceedingly interesting because they view the industry as economists and not, as have most other writers, as social historians.[38]

Trade organisation

The brewers are exceedingly well organized. The Brewers' Society was formed in 1904 as an amalgamation of three existing bodies, the oldest of which was the Country Brewers' Society established in 1822. The other two were the London Brewers' Association and the Burton Brewers Association. The society is administered by a council which consists of a chairman, vice-chairman, nine vice-presidents who have served as chairman, and one or more representatives of each independent brewing company according to the output of barrels per year. The principal committee is the Executive which receives reports from the other committees and is concerned with matters affecting the policy of the industry. A survey committee acts as a forward-looking policy committee. There are also law and technical committees. Brewers own three-quarters of the public houses and the Estates Committee of the society considers and advises on all matters relating to brewing and licensed property. It has a wide brief, being concerned with licensing planning, valuation, compulsory purchase, building, fire regulations and rating. Two other functions of the society may be mentioned. There is a fund which, at Birmingham School of Malting and Brewing and at the Heriot-Watt College at Edinburgh, provides scholarships and post-graduate awards to future potential brewers. Through its research committee the society collaborates with the Institute of Brewing, and is responsible for the disbursement of large sums of money for work at the Brewing Industry Research Foundation at Nutfield, Surrey.[39]

There is a Wine and Spirit Association, but it has neither the facilities nor the resources of the Brewers' Society. So far as whisky is concerned the dominant element in the structure of the industry is the Distillers Company Limited which was formed in 1877. It was composed of six Scottish Lowland grain distilleries with a nominal capital of £2,000,000. Three years later shares were offered to the public. At the time the company was formed Scotch whisky was just beginning to be known outside Scotland. Until the middle of the nineteenth century each of the whiskies on the market was the product of one distillery only. The blending of whiskies began in the 1860s. This led to the production of distinctive brands marketed under proprietory labels. By the end of the century Scotch whisky was being exported. Government restrictions during the 1914–18 war accelerated the process of integration in the industry, which culminated in the "Big Amalgamation" in 1925 when Buchanan-Dewar, Distillers Company Limited and John Walker and Sons came together. Expansion followed, and so did further acquisitions. Now the Distillers Company Limited (D.C.L.) is by far the largest producer and exporter of Scotch whiskies, with each individual company in the group responsible for the sale and promotion of its own brands. D.C.L. companies do not own any retail outlets. Sales in England and Wales are made to wholesalers, including brewery companies who, as we have seen, own most of the retail outlets for the sale of wines and spirits except those in supermarkets. In Scotland there is still a trade with licensed grocers and with the owners of free public houses. D.C.L. also have interests in the production of gin and vodka. There are plants and companies in many countries. Besides its main liquor products the company has a Food Group and a Yeast and Food Division and since 1928 has developed the industrial use of carbon-dioxide gas as a by-product of the fermentation process.

Two main bodies represent those engaged in the retailing of liquor. The National Union of Licensed Victuallers represents the licensees of public houses, and the managers are represented by the National Association of Licensed House Managers which is a trade union. The origins of such associations is particularly interesting, the first appearing to be the Friendly Society of Licensed Victuallers formed in 1794 when the members combined to provide relief in the form of small weekly allowances to distressed members of the trade. The *Morning Advertiser* was founded at the same time to further these charitable purposes. The old Friendly Society obtained a Charter of Incorporation in 1836 and has since been known as the Incorporated Society of Licensed Victuallers, which, besides its original purpose, with additional subscriptions, maintained the Licensed Victuallers School, first in London and now in Slough. No part of the income of the Incorporated Society, including the profits of the *Morning Advertiser,* was used for protective purposes. This still obtains.

It was not until 1833 that the Licensed Victuallers' Protection Society of London was formed. Its influence was not great, and when the 1872 Licensing Act seemed to pose a threat to the trade, licensed victuallers formed local protection societies to operate in specific areas. The subsequent organization of trade protection owed most to Charles Walker, himself a publican, and well known in the trade. He saw the threat to the trade of the trends of public opinion and of the efforts of the temperance organizations. Charles Walker realized that the lack of effective organization among members of the trade would leave them no match for the well-organized campaigns of the temperance party. He proposed the formation of a central board to take the place of the Licensed Victuallers Protection Society. The old body resented the proposal. Eventually, however, the Licensed Victuallers' Central Protection Society of London was formed. Charles Walker saw his vision fully realized in 1892 when the Central Board, as it came to be known, was fully established and he was appointed its first chairman. Offices were taken in Westminster and the local associations were reorganized to conform strictly to parliamentary constituency boundaries. Soon after its formation a weekly journal, *Licensing World* was launched in the interests of "protection". Of course it was quite independent of the *Morning Advertiser,* and unlike that journal ceased publication.[40] The Central Board's activities were confined to London, the comparable organization for the provinces in England and Wales was the Licensed Victuallers' National Defence League. Eventually the National Federation of Licensed Victuallers was formed to represent the provincial associations. In 1976 the Central Board and the N.F.L.V. united to form the National Union of Licensed Victuallers.

References

1. *A history of the English public-house* H. A. Monckton. The Bodley Head (1969) p. 54.
2. Op cit p. 87.
3. See p. 5.
4. Op cit p. 89.
5. *The Brewing Industry 1886–1951* John Vaizey. Pitman (1960) p. 4.
6. *Alliance News* 16th January 1908 p. 39. Article by G. B. Wilson reproduced from the *Shields Daily Gazette* 11th January 1908.
7. Vaizey op cit p. 8.
8. Vaizey op cit p. 9.
9. *Dr Foster's book of beer* Terence Foster. Adam and Charles Black (1979) p. 79.
10. *Alliance News* 10th January 1908 p. 39.
11. Sir Thomas Whittaker MP in *Westminster Gazette* 16th March 1908.
12. See pp. 47–61.
13. Op cit pp. 20 ff.
14. Vaizey op cit p. 26.
15 Vaizey op cit p. 30.
16 See p. 193.
17. Monckton op cit p. 131.
18. Op cit p. 131.
19. Foster op cit p. 73.
20. *Pulling a fast one: What the brewers have done to your beer* Roger Protz. Pluto Press (1978) p. 14.
21. *The Liquor Licensing Statistics for England and Wales.*
22. *The death of the English Pub* Christopher Hutt. Hutchinson (1973) p. 85.
23. Vaizey op cit p. 34.
24. *Alliance News* September–October 1979 p. 12.
25. *Alliance News* September–October 1979 p. 12.
26. *The Penguin Guide to Real Draught Beer* Michael Dunn. Penguin Handbooks (1979).
27. Op cit pp. 152–186.
28. Hutt op cit p. 58.
29. Hutt op cit p. 60.
30. Hutt op cit p. 60.
31. Hutt op cit p. 58 ff.
32. *Beer: A report on the supply of beer* H.M.S.O. (1969) p. 20.
33. Op cit p. 21.
34. Op cit pp. 22, 23 and 101.
35. Op cit p. 61.
36. Op cit p. 61.
37. Op cit p. 62.
38. *The Brewing Industry* K. H. Hawkins and C. L. Pass. Heinemann (1979).
39. *Alcohol: its consumption and control* Thompson Brake p. 23.
40. *Alliance News* 15th July 1909 p. 444.

CHAPTER 15

THE PURPOSE OF LICENSING LEGISLATION

In the course of the preceding chapters we have referred to some of the principal legislative measures taken to deal with various aspects of the alcohol problem. Because legislation has been regarded as one of the major controls in dealing with the sale and consumption of liquor, we believe some consideration should be given to the underlying principles of liquor licensing law. We conclude this chapter with references to the most recent licensing acts which form the basis of licensing administration as we approach the remaining two decades of the twentieth century. This should mean that contemporary responses to the alcohol problem, which is the subject of the final chapter, can be seen not only in relation to history but also to the principles of licensing law.

There are four main objects of licensing legislation: (a) to provide reasonable, controlled conditions under which alcoholic drink may be sold and consumed; (b) to protect the public from the abuse of the consumption of liquor; (c) to act as a control of the excessive use of alcohol in society and to protect the public from exploitation by the commercial elements in the retailing of liquor; and, (d) to relate licensing to the administration of law in areas of personal and social conduct affected by drinking.

(a) It has to be accepted that drinking alcoholic beverages is a legitimate activity, that is to say it is lawful. Unlike most other narcotics, alcohol is not proscribed by law for social purposes. One of the important functions of liquor legislation, therefore, is to ensure that the trade is free to operate and that people have adequate facilities for drinking. The licensing justices have the responsibility of ensuring that within their districts the facilities are reasonable and controlled according to the law. They also have the responsibility of exercising discipline over both the retailer and the consumer.

The history of licensing in Britain shows that there have been periods when these aspects of licensing law have been more satisfactory in the public interest than at others. Periods of what may be called "relaxed licensing" have been periods of drunkenness and disorder. For example, we saw that the Beerhouse Act of 1830 was followed by such drunkenness that in 1834 a select committee of the House of Commons was set up to report on the prevailing state of drunkenness in the nation,[1] and their report was a damning indictment of what was virtually a free-for-all in the retailing of beer.

Their recommendations for dealing with the problem were of two types, legislative and social, but the government was slow in introducing effective legislation. Some of what may be called the environmental recommendations were implemented, such as the provision of public walks and gardens, open spaces for sports and athletics, libraries, museums and reading rooms, all free from provisions for alcoholic drinks. It was not until 1869 that any restrictive legislation was introduced and even this was less than satisfactory. What is not in doubt is that the Beerhouse Act of 1830 is an example of the kind of legislation that results in a massive escalation of personal and social problems arising from the excessive availability of liquor.

The 1961 Licensing Act, which is summarized later in this chapter,[2] is another and recent example of the kind of relaxed licensing to which we refer. This act increased the number of retail outlets for liquor, and in particular made possible the provision of off-licences in supermarkets, this last provision probably accounting for the larger proportion of the statistics for drinking offences, especially among the young, and also for the higher incidence of alcoholism, especially among women. The proliferation of such off-licences coincided with another factor which has to be taken into account. This was the abolishing of resale price maintenance on liquor in 1966. Since then, consumption of wines and spirits has greatly increased and so has the incidence of various conditions and offences induced by alcohol. The period has been dealt with separately and it is cited here as an example supporting the contention that liberalizing licensing law generally leads to an increase in the dimensions of the problems arising from a greater consumption of alcohol. In the decade 1964 to 1974 the number of on-licensed premises increased from 74,012 to 80,977 while the number of off-licensed premises increased from 25,838 to 30,556. The number of registered clubs rose in the same decade from 21,010 to 24,665. In the same period the number of pedestrian drunkenness offences increased from 76,842 to 103,203; and drink/driving convictions increased from 7,363 to 59,267 (but this figures takes account of offences under the Road Safety Act 1967 which incorporated the offence of driving with excess alcohol in the blood).

It is also true that when restrictions are extremely severe the law is evaded and there are excesses other than drinking. For example, in 1728 an attempt was made to check spirit drinking by licensing and higher duties, but the law was repealed after four years because it was being evaded. In 1736 the Gin Act placed heavy duty on spirits, in the belief that it would put gin beyond the reach of the people. Once again, the act was evaded, and even prosecutions did not curb illicit trading.

It is often argued that prohibition in America failed because of its severity. There is substantial truth in this argument, although the benefits of prohibition have often been ignored and in public health and public order they were impressive. It was the evasion of the law which resulted in protection rackets and illicit sales. Evidently there are always people to be found who, for the sake of personal gain, will exploit the alcohol habit even to the extent of breaking the law. So then, the control of this problem is a matter of balance, and can be achieved only with the consent of the people.

(b) The second object of licensing legislation is to protect the public from the abuse of the consumption of liquor. The reaction of many people to proposed laws for the protection of the public is that they will infringe personal liberty. As we have already mentioned, such objections greeted the introduction of speed limits for motor vehicles, pedestrian crossings, one-way streets, parking meters and, of course, the breathalyser. Licensing laws have also been criticized as infringements of personal liberty. It is argued that adults should be free to regulate their own consumption of liquor and their drinking habits. Unfortunately, experience over hundreds of years in Britain, and in most other countries, has shown that liquor cannot be treated as a normal food product and left to unfettered individual choice. Alcohol, because it is a narcotic, modifies the behaviour of those who consume it, and usually the behaviour deteriorates in direct proportion to the potency and amount of liquor consumed. Its effect when taken in moderate quantities is to interfere with the performance of mechanical skills, to inhibit self-criticism and control, and to dull the senses. Taken in large quantities it reduces capacity for work, lowers resistance to disease, and frequently leads to foolish and criminal behaviour. Persistent use of alcohol may lead to addiction.

Licensing laws are designed to exert controls on the availability of liquor so that its consumption remains within bounds. Thus licensing magistrates have been able to regulate the number of licensed premises on the basis of need, to determine the nature of the licensed premises by requiring plans to be submitted, to enforce such statutory requirements as permitted hours, to co-operate with the police in ensuring that young persons are not served with liquor in the bars of public houses. They also have the power to impose conditions with the granting of licences to minimize abuse. Thus the role of the magistrates is to impose such restraints within the law as they consider necessary in the public interest. This system has an important aspect. While legislation is passed by parliament, its administration is in the hands of local magistrates. They are people who can relate their licensing administration to local conditions they know well, as a result of their experience in the courts. The propensity to commit offences is clearly aggravated by the consumption of alcohol. The frequency of some offences in particular areas may be related to the numbers and types of licensed premises within those areas. In considering new applications, or the renewal of licences, the magistrates are able to take into account other factors in their experience.

(c) A third object of licensing legislation is to act as a control of the excessive use of alcohol in society and to protect the public from exploitation by the commercial element in the retailing of liquor. Licensing law provides a defined framework within which liquor may be sold and consumed. From time to time pleas have been made for the virtual removal of the framework. During the second reading debate in the House of Commons on a bill which passed into law as the Alehouse Act 1828, the view was powerfully advocated that there should be no system of licensing. The liquor trade, like every other, should be free. Even Sir Robert Peel admitted that the throwing open of the trade was good, but he advised caution because of the risks involved. Another member, R. A. Slaney described liquor as "the second necessity of life", and he thought that the general principle, that the demand of goods ought to regulate the number of vendors, should be applied to the liquor trade as well as to every other. G. B. Wilson commented, "The struggle of 1828–30 illustrates the prevalence of opinion, that everyone ought to be free to use his capital and talents as he pleased, and that the interests of the consumer were best safeguarded by unrestricted competition."[3]

Wilson pointed out that this view was held by the excise authorities, as well as by the extreme free-traders. In the *Nineteenth Report of the Excise Enquiry 1836,* it was stated, "In the first place, according to right principles of trade and taxation, the price of a licence and the forms of granting it, being fixed by law, it should be in the power of everyone to obtain such a licence as a matter of right, on making application in the form prescribed by law and paying the amount of the specified duty, whether the licence be for the sale of spirits or for the sale of tea or any other excisable article; and, in the one case more than the other, the exercise of such right ought not to be checked by interference on the part of the magistrates or any other authority superadded to that of the excise."[4] In fact, the commissioners went further. They challenged the principle that had operated in licensing legislation since the act of 1552 which had granted absolute discretionary powers to the justices. They dismissed somewhat contemptuously the view that because of their local knowledge the magistrates were "peculiarly fitted to judge on the question whether a public house is required in the neighbourhood proposed". They believed that unrestricted competition in any branch of trade produced results which were entirely satisfactory. Their views did not prevail, and the 1552 Act has formed the basis of licensing administration until the present time.

It was, therefore, surprising to find the plea for unrestrictive competition appearing in a new form as recently as 1969. It was in this year that the Monopolies Commission issued its report on the supply of beer, with special reference to the tied house.[5] Since we have dealt with the Monopolies Commission report in a previous chapter it is only necessary here to recall that the principal recommendation was that "the present licensing system should be substantially relaxed, the general objective being to permit the sale of alcoholic drinks, for on or off consumption, by any retailer whose character and premises satisfy certain minimum standards" and "without a system of licensing controlled by justices".

Without the framework of restrictive legislation the manufacture and sale of liquor would be subject only to market forces. With the development of aggressive advertising and pursuasive promotion techniques a free-for-all could have personal and social consequences of appalling dimensions. It is unlikely, after four hundred years of experience in licensing administration, that so drastic a step as lifting all restrictions would be contemplated.

(d) A fourth purpose of liquor licensing is to relate licensing to the administration of the law in areas of personal and social conduct affected by drinking. In recent years this aspect of licensing has acquired great prominence. This is because scientific research has shown, with greater precision than formerly, how the consumption of alcohol modifies human health and behaviour. Statistical evidence, too, confirms the conclusion reached by scientists that the consumption of alcohol modifies human behaviour to such a degree that it is reflected, for instance, in road accidents and various driving offences. The Road Safety Act 1967, which created the offence of driving or being in charge of a motor vehicle with a blood/alcohol level over a prescribed limit, also acknowledged that scientific tests were sufficiently reliable for their results to be used in evidence.[6]

Until recently, there has been insufficient data to determine the relation between the consumption of alcohol and offences other than those connected with driving. In their annual reports chief constables frequently blame drinking for such offences as violence and vandalism. Statistics on this aspect of law and order are not easy to gather. That they can be gathered for statistical purposes has been shown by an experiment carried out under the direction of the Chief Constable of Bedfordshire (Anthony Armstrong). He arranged for the magistrates' courts at Luton and Dunstable to be monitored for a defined period in 1975, when 1,220 cases were analysed for reference to alcohol. The method adopted was for police cadets to ask police officers presenting cases at the courts to say whether in their opinion offenders had been drinking at a material time before the alleged offences were committed. Nearly half the men charged with offences to do with theft had taken some alcohol beforehand, and more than half had done so in cases of dangerous or offensive behaviour. Worst affected were youths of sixteen and seventeen and men between thirty and thirty-nine. The report concluded that if the data secured at Luton and Dunstable were applicable to England and Wales as a whole, 660,000 offences would have been committed in 1975 under some influence of alcohol consumed beforehand, whereas only 165,000 showed up in statistics.[7]

Thus the magistrates are in a particularly crucial position to relate licensing administration to other matters of law and order in their districts. A remarkable example of the extent to which the action of licensing magistrates can influence public behaviour is described by Sidney and Beatrice Webb in their book *The History of Liquor Licensing in England Principally from 1700 to 1830.* This concerned the adoption in 1786–87 by county and borough benches of a policy of restriction and regulation which, in a systematic form, lasted for only about six years. By such devices as early closing, the refusal of new licences, the withdrawal of licences from badly-conducted houses, the closing of what they regarded as surplus houses in various localities, and the introduction of a system of local option or veto, the magistrates effected a reduction of consumption which was reflected in an improvement of manners and morals. Other actions taken in many counties were to prohibit gaming, skittles and various forms of animal baitings at public houses and to ensure more vigilant oversight of public houses by constables. The Webbs believed that the effect of these restrictions lasted for a whole generation. They concluded,

> *We think that any impartial student of the contemporary records will be driven to the inference that the limitation of the opportunities for disorderly drinking between 1787 and 1825 outside the metropolis was at any rate an important contributory cause of the remarkable advance in "respectability" made by the English working-man during the first two decades of the nineteenth century.*[8]

While it is true that licensing magistrates have a major role in the administration of licensing law, they are limited by the law itself. When the law is severely restrictive they have no power to relax its provisions. Equally, when the law is permissive, they are unable to introduce restrictive measures not provided for in the legislation. Some recent judgments and recommendations have pre-empted actions which might have been taken by magistrates. For instance, until a Home Office instruction was issued, following the Valentine Report in 1971, chief constables arranged for regular police surveillance of public houses. After the new instructions police had access to public houses only if they suspected that the law was being broken. Police and magistrates felt inhibited from ensuring regular visits to public houses, and licensees believed that the neglect of police supervision was a major factor in the increase of violence on their premises and of assaults on licensees and their staffs. In January 1977 a Private Member's Bill, introduced by Sir Bernard Braine, was passed. This amended Section 186 of the Licensing Act 1964 and so restored to police unrestricted right of entry to licensed premises.

Another factor which limits the control that magistrates can exercise is the proliferation of licences. The determination of licensing justices to limit the number of licensed premises was illustrated in 1902 by the notable example of the justices of Farnham. It is of such note that no historical survey of licensing administration in the twentieth century would be complete without a reference to it. The congestion of licences had been brought to the attention of the Farnham justices by the county justices. A committee formed to collect information found that in a town with a population of 6,200 there were forty-five licensed houses, that is one public house for every twenty-four male adults in the town. The Farnham proposal was to introduce a ratio of one licensed house for every 155 adult persons. The action of the Farnham justices in refusing to renew some licences on the basis of this ratio was challenged by licensees who lost their licenses. On 8th May 1902 in the King's Bench Division of the High Court of Justice the case "The King v. the Licensing justices of Farnham" came before the Divisional Court. The issue was whether a rule obtained commanding the justices to hold an adjourned licensing session, was valid, and whether in the circumstances the justices could adjudicate. It was argued that because the justices themselves had given notice of the adjourned session they were debarred from acting. The Divisional Court upheld the action of the Farnham justices. Nine licensees whose application for licences had been refused by the justices appealed to the Court of Appeal, but this court upheld the judgment of the Divisional Court.

It was an important judgment because it encouraged licensing justices in other places to follow the example of those at Farnham, who had refused to renew nine of the forty-five licences in their district, not for disorderly conduct or any other intrinsic reason, but because in their judgment, they were not necessary in the public interest.[9] Thus the discretion of justices in granting licences on the basis of need was strengthened by the outcome of the Farnham case.

There was strong reaction from the licensed trade and pressure was put on the Unionist government to introduce new legislation. The response of the government was the Licensing Act 1904, popularly known as the

"Balfour Act", the object of which was to amend the law "in respect to the extinction of licences and the grant of new licences." Its main provision, as we have seen,[10] was to guard against existing on-licences being taken away without compensation. In 1910 the Licensing (Consolidation) Act mainly reproduced existing licensing law in a simplified form. However, *Paterson's Licensing Acts* pointed out that in one important respect the act appeared to have altered the existing law. "A new definition of 'renewal' meant that the grant of a licence in respect of any premises could no longer be treated as a grant by way of renewal unless a similar licence was actually in force in respect of the premises at the date of application, or was in force at the date of the general annual licensing meeting in the previous year".[11] Previously, at however remote a time a licence had been held for a set of premises, the grant of a similar licence in respect of those premises was reckoned as a renewal and not as the grant of a new licence. Thus the discretion of the justices was further strengthened and the consideration of "need" was not challenged or eroded until the Licensing Act 1961.

For the sake of completeness there must be a reference to the Second World War and after. The war certainly created special circumstances, but the existing laws were thought to be adequate so far as the retailing and consuming of liquor were concerned. However, because so many licensed premises were either destroyed or severely damaged during the war, and because shortage of materials and manpower made it impossible for repairs and rebuilding to be carried out immediately, extraordinary measures had to be taken. In 1942, the Finance Act "provided machinery by which the licences of such premises might be suspended (so as to avoid the payment of duty and the necessity for annual renewal) and revived at a future date".[12] Since many urban areas suffered such severe damage that restoration to their former state was neither possible nor desirable, their future had to be planned comprehensively. Public buildings of all kinds were destroyed and their future location became the subject of "planning". Public houses fell into this category, and so, towards the end of the war, the Home Secretary set up a departmental committee to advise on the restoration of devastated public houses. The recommendations of this committee were incorporated into the Licensing Planning (Temporary Provisions) Act 1945, which gave the Home Secretary power to declare any such devastated area to be a licensing planning area and to direct that licensing planning committees should be set up. These were to be composed of representatives of the licensing justices and the local planning authorities. Their function was to control the development of the licensed premises in their area. In 1946 an amending act was passed which provided greater flexibility in licensing planning without seriously affecting the provisions of the original act.

After the war, and before the Licensing Act 1949, there were a number of enactments in Finance Acts and other measures which affected licensing administration. However, these were not important compared with the 1949 act, which was the most comprehensive licensing act of the first half of the twentieth century. In summary, it extended state management to new towns, made new provisions in respect of state management districts, changed the law relating to licensing justices and confirming authorities, provided for the payment of allowances to members of licensing courts and courts of appeal in Scotland, amended the law regarding permitted hours and made further provisions regarding refreshment houses and wine and spirit dealers. It prohibited the employment of persons under eighteen in bars, it amended the Licensing Planning (Temporary Provisions) Act 1945 and 1946 with regard to the suspension of justices' licences, and provided for the application of the licensing laws to the Isles of Scilly.

Part I of the act reflected a major social change in the life of Britain, that is the development of new towns. Certain areas had been designated sites for new towns, and under the Licensing Act 1949, these became state management districts. In such districts the Home Secretary was empowered to provide and maintain hotels, inns and public houses, restaurants and cafés, even if they did not sell alcoholic drink. Under the same powers entertainment of various kinds could be provided in such places. Beer could be brewed and provisions made for maintenance, storage and transport facilities required in connection with these various activities. This did not mean that the Home Office was free from ordinary licensing restrictions; managers of state premises were subject to the licensing laws just as licensees elsewhere. In each new town an advisory committee would be set up by the local development corporation to prepare plans and recommendations as to the number, size and siting of all premises concerned with the selling of intoxicants in new towns. The Home Secretary's consent was required for the opening of clubs in the new towns. It was not intended that the advisory committee should ensure uniformity. For example, in some areas it might be decided that existing licensed premises should remain independent, while in others all such premises would come under state management.

Part II of the act introduced certain changes in the composition and powers of local licensing authorities. Under the 1910 Licensing Act the whole body of justices in a division were the licensing justices for the petty sessional division of a county or for metropolitan boroughs. In county boroughs these were licensing committees, and the new act extended their arrangement to the counties. These divisional licensing committees were restricted to membership of not less than five and, not more than fifteen justices. All justices with any connection with the trade were barred from serving on licensing committees. Any justice holding shares in companies associated with the trade were required to declare their interest in the event of them being appointed to licensing committees, and the justices appointing them had to satisfy themselves that the declared interest was so small as not to constitute a threat to the integrity of the committee.

There were a number of miscellaneous provisions. These included the grant of special hours certificates in such parts of the Metropolis as were specified by the Secretary of State. As soon as the act received the Royal Assent the Secretary of State made the Licensing (Metropolitan Special Hours Area) Order (S. I. 1949 No. 1482), which applied to an area in Central London. Included in the act were regulations governing the applications for special hours certificates, the effect of which was to extend permitted hours on weekdays to 12.30 p.m. to 3 p.m. and 6.30 p.m. to 2 a.m. (except Saturday when midnight was substituted for 2 a.m.). Certificates were confined to premises which had a music and dancing licence. The act also included regulations concerning bottle parties in London which were organized for gain. These must cease at 11 p.m., although they could apply for registration as clubs and so become eligible for special hours certificates.

Some important changes in the operation of excise licences were also effected. Hitherto a person holding a dealer's licence permitting the sale of wine and spirits in wholesale quantities, could obtain additional retail wine and spirit licences without the sanction of licensing justices. The intention of this provision was to enable a wholesale trader to supply his trade customers with wines and spirits in less quantities than permitted under a wholesale licence. It also enabled retail businesses for the sale of wines and spirits in retail quantities to be opened without the sanction of the licensing justices. The new act introduced stricter controls which confined sales under such circumstances (a) to persons holding wholesale or retail licences; (b) to a mess or registered club; (c) for delivery outside Great Britain; (d) to a person employed by a licensee. In future all sales to the public in retail quantities required a retail licence obtained with the sanction of the licensing justices.

The act further protected young people employed on licensed premises. No young person under eighteen could be employed in any bar at a time when it was open for sale and consumption of alcoholic drinks. This did not apply to a young person passing through the bar, for example a hotel page boy conveying a message.

At various times provisions were included in acts whose titles gave no indication that they were at all concerned with licensing matters, so that, as *Paterson's Licensing Acts* observed, "By this time . . . the licensing laws had become spread over a considerable number of separate enactments".[13] To meet this difficulty the Licensing Act 1953 consolidated the law as it then stood, at the same time opportunity being taken to include some minor amendments. Readers are directed to the relevant paragraphs in *Paterson's Licensing Acts* for details of these numerous and varied amendments.[14]

The Licensing Act 1961 was the first general revision of the licensing law for forty years. It was followed in 1964 by a consolidating measure which incorporated without substantial alteration, the unrepealed provisions of the Licensing Act 1953, the Licensing (Seamen's Canteens) Act 1954, the Licensing (Airports) Act 1956, the Licensing Act 1961 and some minor provisions of other statutes relating to licensing matters. This consolidating act is the present licensing law, and the following is a summary of its main provisions based on the summary contained in *Alcohol: its consumption and control*.[15]

In Britain liquor may be sold only through licensed outlets. The licensing authority is the licensing committee of the magistrates in a petty sessional division. Appeals against decisions of the magistrates lie to the crown court. There are two main types of licences: a justices' on-licence which authorizes the sale of intoxicating liquor for consumption on or off the premises; and an off-licence which authorizes sale for consumption off the premises. The situation is complicated by various other provisions within these main categories. For practical purposes the following are the main types of licence in operation:

1. **A full on-licence.** This is granted to premises such as public houses, where intoxicants are sold for consumption by the public on or off the premises. The licence may either allow the sale of intoxicating liquor of all descriptions or a more limited range.
2. **Off-licence** This applies to premises where liquor is the principal commodity sold to the public, or, as in the case of supermarkets where special provision is made for the sale of liquor in association with other commodities. In all cases consumption must be off the premises.
3. **Restaurant licence.** This was a new type of licence provided in the Licensing Act 1961. It is granted to premises where main meals are provided at midday or in the evening or both. It is subject to the condition that drink may be sold only to persons taking a meal and for consumption as an ancillary to a meal.
4. **Residential licence.** This licence was introduced to enable premises, such as hotels, to serve liquor to persons for whom board and lodging is provided for reward. Board must include breakfast and at least one other main meal. Only persons so accommodated, or their guests, may be served for consumption on the premises.
5. **Residential and restaurant licence.** This licence applies to premises used for both purposes described in 3 and 4 above and allows similar sales.
6. **Occasional licence.** A licence may be granted to the holder of an off-licence to enable him to sell liquor temporarily at some place other than his own premises (e.g. sports meetings, dances or fetes).

There is one other main category of licensed premises, the clubs. These are divided into two types.

1. **Proprietory Clubs**
   The Erroll Report described these as "clubs in which the premises and the stock belong to a proprietor or proprietors". If the stock belongs to the proprietor, a "sale" takes place when a member orders and pays for a drink. Thus, these types of clubs have to be licensed in the same way as ordinary on-licensed premises.
2. **Members' Clubs.** In the case of "members" clubs, all the property, including the stock of liquor, belongs to the members jointly, and when a member obtains liquor, even on payment, the position is that a "supply" rather than a sale takes place. As no sale takes place, no licence is required. Instead, Part II of the act of 1964 applies a separate procedure to those clubs in which liquor is supplied to members or guests. Members' clubs have to apply for a registration certificate which, in effect, authorizes the supply of liquor on the premises. Registration certificates are granted by magistrates' courts rather than by licensing justices. To qualify for registration, a members' club has to meet certain conditions. The club has to be established in good faith and the supply of liquor must be so managed that profits or commission arising out of that activity do not accrue to individuals. There are also requirements relating to the minimum number of members and the period of nomination for membership. Registered members' clubs are not subject to "permitted hours" in the same way as other full on-licensed premises; the provisions of the 1964 Act relating to children do not apply; and the police may enter club premises only on the issue of a warrant by a magistrate.

Permitted hours

The principal provisions concerning hours are that on weekdays (other than Good Friday and Christmas Day) the total number of hours during which full on-licensed premises may be open must not exceed nine hours (ending at 10.30 p.m.) or nine-and-a-half hours (ending at 11 p.m.) in any day; that they must not begin before 10 a.m.; and that they must be broken by a single period of not less than two hours in the afternoon. On Sundays, Good Fridays and Christmas Days the hours are 12 noon to 2 p.m. and 7 p.m. to 10.30 p.m. A ten-minute drinking-up time is added to on-licensed premises, while in restaurants this is extended to half an hour. Off-licences' permitted hours on weekdays are 8.30 a.m. to 10.30 p.m. with no break. On Sundays their permitted hours are the same as for on-licences.

The justices have power to grant variations of hours. There are three ways in which they can extend the hours on a regular basis: (a) a supper hour certificate which adds one hour to the permitted evening hours in restaurants and can extend by one hour the first part of permitted hours for the day; (b) an extended hours order which extends permitted hours to 1 a.m. in premises offering both meals and musical entertainment; and (c) a special hours certificate which extends the permitted hours to 2 a.m. (3 a.m. in the metropolis) for premises in respect of which there is a public music and dancing licence in force and where the sale of liquor is ancillary to the music and dancing and to the provision of substantial refreshments.

Children and licensed premises

The law seeks to protect children from familiarity with and indulgence in the drinking of intoxicating liquor. It is an offence to give a child under five years of age any alcoholic liquor. Children under fourteen are not allowed in the bar of licensed premises during permitted hours. The Licensing Act defines a bar as a place exclusively or mainly used for the sale and consumption of intoxicating liquor. Railway refreshment rooms and similar ancillary provisions are exempt. The only categories of children to whom these provisions do not apply are the children of licensees, children resident in the premises and children passing through the bar. Persons under eighteen are not allowed to buy liquor anywhere on licensed premises. There are two exceptions. Persons over sixteen can buy beer, porter, cider and perry for consumption at a meal not served at a bar; and persons under sixteen, though they cannot drink at a bar, can drink elsewhere on licensed premises. Eighteen is a crucial age in licensing law. The following offences are related to this age threshold; (a) it is an offence for a licensee knowingly to sell drink to persons under eighteen or to allow them to drink in a bar; (b) it is an offence for anyone to buy a drink in a bar for someone under eighteen; (c) it is an offence for persons under eighteen themselves to buy intoxicating liquor or to consume it in a bar.

References

1. See p. 5.
2. See p. 229 ff.
3. *Alcohol and the Nation* Wilson p. 103.
4. Ouoted in Wilson op cit p. 103.
5. See p. 136 ff.

6. For a consideration of this act see p. 144 ff.
7. *Alcohol and Crime,* Christian Economic and Social Research Foundation (1976).
8. *History of Licensing in England principally from 1700 to 1830.* Sidney and Beatrice Webb (1903) pp. 83, 84 (Longman's Green & Co.).
9. Wilson op cit p. 110.
10. See p. 24.
11. *Paterson's Licensing Acts* (1977) p. 11.
12. Op cit p. 16.
13. Op cit p. 20.
14. Op cit p. 21.
15. *Alcohol: its consumption and control;* G. Thompson Brake (1976) p. 5–8.

CHAPTER 16

CONTEMPORARY RESPONSES

At the conclusion of this historical survey it is necessary to pause and reflect upon the factors which may determine the course which will be taken in the future in the consumption and control of alcohol. In Britain the habit of drinking intoxicants emerged centuries ago. The types of liquor have changed and the preferences of drinkers have changed, too. Methods of brewing and distilling remained remarkably constant until recent times, when the scientists and technicians introduced new techniques. Although the traditional English public houses remain, their character has been threatened by modern marketing men and architects. More important has been the proliferation of other retail outlets, especially in the supermarket off-licences. CAMRA (Campaign for Real Ale), dedicated as it is to the recovery and retention of individually produced brews dispensed at traditional public houses, is one response to modern trends. However, it is doubtful whether there will ever be a widespread recovery of what some people would call "the simple drinking habits" of the British people. The drink trade is firmly in the hands of the brewers who, as we have seen, control not only most of the public houses and off-licences, but the production and marketing of almost every type of liquor. The brewers' share of the market is now being challenged by the involvement of big supermarket chains. Thus a new type of monopoly is emerging, which is not concerned with the "tied" house system, but with the control of other retail outlets. The slight shrinkage in the number of outlets controlled by the brewers will not worry them while their products are being sold, albeit through outlets controlled by others. In the present situation it is not surprising to find licensees of public houses apprehensive about their future and critical of the brewers. Their anxieties are understandable now that about half the liquor consumed is bought at supermarkets. The proliferation of clubs and wine bars pose other threats to traditional outlets.

The factor of availability

If the total volume of liquor sold remained constant it could be argued that the major changes were in marketing methods. The facts are not so simple. Consumption levels have increased in recent years and continue to do so. However, the most disturbing aspect is that now half the liquor consumed is purchased at outlets which lack the controls required of public houses. In most supermarkets liquor is taken straight from the racks like any other commodity. It is rare for purchases to be supervised by experienced staff. The girls at the check-outs are there simply to ensure that goods are paid for. This lax system is open to abuse. It is too late to impose a ban on the sale of liquor in supermarkets, but if for no other reason than to ensure fair competition, some restrictions ought to be imposed. Consideration should be given to safeguards such as confining the sale of liquor to self-contained areas separate from the rest of the store. Sales should be over the counter with experienced staff in charge. There is also a case for some restriction of hours when such off-licences would be open. In view of the past unfulfilled intentions of governments to "deal with the clubs" the prospect of the introduction of more effective controls in this area is not bright. Nevertheless, those with a sincere concern for the maintenance of "reasonable controlled conditions" will not be content until some of the anomalies are removed. The development of wine bars creates a particular problem now that the consideration of "need" is largely removed from the powers of the justices. They have little option but to grant facilities, often near other licensed premises, and with the prospect that at a future time application may be made for extended facilities for such premises. It is doubtful whether any government in the foreseeable future will introduce major licensing reform legislation, and so it will rest with the licensing justices to exercise to the full their powers of restraint and control in the public interest. It would certainly assist them if a measure was introduced which gave them similar discretion to impose conditions on off-licences which they have over full on-licences.

This is a suitable point at which to refer to a comparitively new outlet for the sale of liquor in Britain. This is the provision of duty-free liquor, which has now assumed proportions far in excess of the convenience it was designed to provide. Duty-free allowances date back to at least the early part of the nineteenth century. In 1820 travellers were permitted to bring into the country alcohol, perfume and cigarettes as part of the necessary requirements for a long journey. With the increase in travel the first attempt to rationalize the position was taken by the United Nations in 1954. A convention in New York produced recommendations relating to the scales of duty-free allowances. This document is known as the 1954 New York Convention on Tourism.[1] The United Kingdom is a signatory and the provisions were brought into force in Britain in 1957. The regulations were framed for people visiting other countries and were not intended to apply to people returning to their own country from abroad.[2] The British Customs' regulations state clearly "persons under seventeen are not entitled to tobacco and drink allowances". In the E.E.C. countries the age is fifteen. "The United Kingdom is thought to be the only country in Europe not operating the 15-year age limit and is technically in breach of EEC regulations".[3] The expansive duty-free shops at airports give some indication of the growth of a "point of sale" which began as a convenience for travellers and has become a considerable outlet not only for liquor but for other merchandise.

The proliferation of retail outlets can be seen to have a causal relationship to an increase in the incidence of alcoholism and other drink-related offences if at the same time there has been a rise in consumption. What seems beyond doubt now is that the incidence of alcoholism has a direct relation to per capita average consumption. Since 1961 there has also been an increase in the number and types of retail outlets. It is only in recent years that there has been an acceptance of the relation between consumption and social consequences, and thus with the factor of availability. This may result in a greater emphasis on the prevention of alcoholism rather than on its treatment. Swinson and Eaves summarize this conclusion, "In the prevention of alcoholism, the main aims should be to reduce the total amount drunk at any time and to have strict controls on drunkenness. The ways in which these aims might be achieved include the use of legislation, education, taxation and advertising. In other words, quite apart from any directly therapeutic approach a massive "social engineering" campaign would be required and at present society is only beginning to accept that there is any need for this."[4]

The temperance response

Clearly society has not yet found an effective way of preventing alcoholism and other consequences of excessive drinking. The first response to the problem was the emergence of the temperance societies. The first of these were composed of people who took a pledge to abstain from spirituous liquors. It was later, in the 1830s, that "total abstinence" societies arose. The scope of this present study does not require an account of the origins of the various societies which collectively made up the Temperance Movement. What has been done is to record, where it was relevant, the involvement of the temperance forces at particular times during this century. As we have progressed through this century it has been evident that their influence, once so powerful, has declined. Most of the hundreds of local temperance societies which existed at one time have perished. However, some of the famous national organizations can still be traced through the London telephone directory. The United Kingdom Alliance, the United Kingdom Band of Hope Union and the National British Women's Total Abstinence Union have London headquarters. The temperance Council of the Christian Churches was wound up in 1979, to appear in a new form as the Churches Council on Alcohol and Drugs. The leaders of these organizations still have a sense of destiny, but they lack financial resources, young leadership and the back-up of large memberships. And yet, no account of the history of drinking and its consequences in either the nineteenth or twentieth centuries could be written without according a prominent place to the Temperance Movement.

The future of one or two of these organizations was secured by the foresight of those who purchased sites and erected buildings which have provided continuous sources of income. The most notable of these is Alliance House, Caxton Street, Westminster. In 1853, as we have seen, the United Kingdom Alliance was formed to campaign for prohibition by the will of the people. This organization became the focus of power and influence for the temperance cause in parliament. A parliamentary agent was employed who became a familiar figure in the lobby at Westminster. Beside a small headquarters staff there were district superintendents or agents throughout the country. Tens of thousands of subscriptions ensured a regular income and legacies built up capital. Its close ties with the Liberal Party and non-conformity meant that it was affected by their numerical decline, and the First World War deprived it of young men to lead it. The few who returned to their district superintendencies were required to spend much of their time collecting their own salaries by way of subscriptions. Only half a dozen or so were at their posts at the end of the Second World

War, and now there are none at all. There is a general secretary, but he is the only full-time officer. The reported membership is about seven hundred, and since their subscriptions are the only source of income apart from interest on about £30,000 of invested funds, the resources are limited. The organization is admininstered by an executive which is elected annually by the members at the annual meeting. Because of its past reputation the views of the UKA are still listened to with respect when matters of licensing legislation are before parliament.

Another organization which fulfils a political role is the National Temperance Federation which, as its name implies, is an association of various temperance bodies. Its rules lay down that the N.T.F. shall take such action as has the support of its constituent bodies. The most notable action in recent years was to respond to an invitation to act as the co-ordinating body to represent the views of temperance societies to the Erroll Committee. When there was an all-party parliamentary temperance group, this was serviced by the National Temperance Federation. Its officers are honorary.

In 1942 the United Kingdom Temperance Alliance Limited was formed under the Companies Act 1929, limited by guarantee and having no share capital, and being subject to the provisions of the Charities Acts. In 1940 a site had been purchased at Caxton Street, Westminster on which was built a six-storey office block. The site and the building cost less than £70,000, but today its value is in excess of £1 million. In 1942, Alliance House Westminster Limited, the company which acquired the site and erected the building, went into voluntary liquidation. The building then became the property of the United Kingdom Temperance Alliance Limited, the Memorandum of Association of which provided for it "to take over as a going concern all the educational and charitable work of the unincorporated body", that is the United Kingdom Alliance, except for its political activities. The company was also charged with promoting the principles of temperance and total abstinence, and to "promote the moral, religious and physical welfare of the community". The United Kingdom Alliance has generally been confused about its relationship with the company. Legal opinion has maintained the complete independence of the two bodies, the one being concerned with political action and the other precluded from such action by its status as a charity. The effect of this distinction is that the company is unable to give financial assistance of any kind to the UKA.

Deployment of assets

The projects for which the United Kingdom Temperance Alliance Limited makes substantial grants lie within the fields of research, education and publications. The Christian Economic and Social Research Foundation was formed as a Charity in 1966. From its inception it has received grants from the U.K.T.A. Limited. In 1975 the company established a library and research centre at Alliance House which is serviced by the foundation. For over twenty-five years the Christian Economic and Social Research Foundation has specialized in monitoring various aspects arising from the consumption of alcohol. Its purpose is set out in its constitution which states that it is "an educational body set up to undertake objective research into the social and economic conditions affecting the individual and society in Britain, having regard not only to the material factors, but also to those moral and spiritual values which form part of the tradition of the British people". The method of the foundation has been to publish statistical and other evidence with the minimum of comment and without value judgements. Each year it publishes a report on drink offences from the annual reports of chief constables. It has also undertaken research into specific areas relating to alcohol, and into matters lying outside that relationship. The foundation gave evidence to the Erroll Committee. In 1975 it accepted an invitation to send an expert witness to give evidence to the Royal Commission on Liquor in New Zealand and was gratified when its two main recommendations were embodied in the Royal Commission's own recommendations. These were that off-licences should not be granted to supermarkets and that a government-sponsored Liquor Advisory Council should be set up, and we have earlier noted that both recommendations were implemented. The objectivity and integrity of the work of the foundation has enabled it for many years to enjoy grant-aid from the Rowntree Social Service Trust.

The educational body to which the United Kingdom Temperance Alliance Limited contributes £50,000 a year is the Teachers' Advisory Council on Alcohol and Drug Education. This, too, is an educational charity which receives grants from other bodies and generates income itself by arranging courses for teachers and other educationists and by the sale of publications and audio and visual aids. TACADE, as it is generally known, was formed in 1969. Initially its work was largely among pupils at school. Now, however, it confines its work to teachers. The emphasis of its philosophy has also changed. Whereas it began with a factually-based approach to alcohol and drug education is has seen the importance of developing in children decision-making skills. TACADE is based at Manchester where there is a resources centre and a qualified resources officer. Three full-time directors are employed with secretarial back-up staff. TACADE frequently works in association with the Health Education Council, and played a prominent part in the government-sponsored campaigns to combat alcoholism in the North East.

In the field of publications the principal project of the United Kingdom Temperance Alliance Limited is *Alliance News.* This was founded in 1854 by the UKA as a weekly newspaper and sold at one penny. Its sub-title was "A journal of moral and social reform", but this was later changed to a journal "for the suppression of the liquor traffic". The change of title represented a change of editorial policy and coincided with the campaigning methods of the temperance societies when they isolated the alcohol problem from other social issues and believed the destruction of the liquor trade should be their primary objective. In 1969 when the United Kingdom Temperance Alliance Limited became the proprietors and publishers of *Alliance News* the original sub-title was restored. Since then the editorial policy has conformed to the charity status of the company. It is now published as a "quality" bi-monthly magazine embodying an editorial policy which puts the alcohol problem into a broad social context. Whereas for the greater part of its life *Alliance News* was read almost exclusively by people in the "temperance movement", it is now increasing its readership among people who meet the alcohol problem in the course of their work as medical practitioners, psychiatrists, social workers, probation officers, police and magistrates.

The ability of the UKTA Limited to respond to contemporary initiatives rests upon the considerable capital asset of Alliance House and the income from tenancies of office accommodation. The income bears no relation to the resources of "the trade", but in terms of what can be effectively used it is significant. No other temperance-based organization has similar resources. Closest to it comes the United Kingdom Band of Hope Union whose capital asset is Hope House, Great Peter Street, Westminster, a leasehold property which is considerably smaller than Alliance House and so its letting potential is less. However, the income enables some initiatives to be taken in three specific areas, which are lectures in schools, temperance knowledge examinations and publications. Recently strip-cartoon material has become a feature of the publications. Its work is directed, as it has always been, towards children. The first Band of Hope is reckoned to have been formed in 1847 and at the peak of its growth in the early part of the twentieth century there were about 3,500,000 children enrolled in membership, all having signed a pledge to abstain from drinking alcohol. Few local Bands of Hope remain, probably fifty or sixty, and where possible these are grouped in county unions which since about 1860 have retained their autonomy. The organization still has some appeal, especially through the annual ceremonies of crowning Band of Hope Queens.

The only other national "property owning" temperance organization, as distinct from temperance-based friendly societies and insurance companies, is the National British Women's Total Abstinence Union. This was founded in 1876 at Newcastle-upon-Tyne. Its headquarters are at Rosalind Carlisle House, Dawson Place, London, W2, from which a small income is received from rented flats. In 1893 the first year for which figures are available, it had a membership of 34,800, but in common with all temperance organizations it has suffered a catastrophic decline so that the membership reported 80 years later in 1973 was about seven thousand. The only other national temperance organization whose primary object is to promote the principles of temperance and total abstinence is the international Order of Good Templars. This organization had its origin in the United States of America. Here the Sons of Temperance, another organization to which reference will be made, had a children's branch called the Cadets of Temperance. As the children grew older an intermediate branch was formed for young people. This was called The Knights of Jericho and was organized in lodges with an initiation ceremony and special ritual. In 1850 the lodge at Oneida County had a meeting at which members of the city lodge at Utica were present. At this meeting it was decided to change the name from The Knights of Jericho to The Order of Good Templars. Two years later an internal disagreement in the organization led to the formation of the Independent Order of Good Templars and the former organization gradually disappeared. In 1868 Joseph Malins, a prominent temperance leader in England, founded the first British branch at Birmingham. The name was changed in 1902 to the International Order of Good Templars. The organization has experienced a similar numerical decline in Britain as have other temperance societies. The lodges which remain are small and the adherence to the use of regalia and rituals does not seem to attract younger people. The organization owns a printing works in Birmingham, but its committee structure is not geared to business management in the competitive world of print. Nevertheless, the quality of its work is of a high standard and the works attract considerable business from the Birmingham Corporation.

The churches' involvement

The involvement of the churches in the temperance cause would require a separate study. Joseph Livesey and those who signed the total abstinence pledge in Preston in 1832 were members of Christian churches, but at that time there was not a strong temperance sentiment generally in the churches. However, by the 1870s it had become the major social concern and the major denominations formed their own temperance societies. No co-ordinating organization was formed, but the churches gave strong support to the initiatives taken by the United Kingdom Alliance. During the 1914–18 war dissension appeared in the temperance movement, first over the acceptance of an invitation by the Wesleyan Methodist leader, the Revd Henry Carter, to join the Liquor Control Board on which a liquor lord had been invited to serve. Second, proposals for public ownership of the liquor trade created division. On this issue the UKA was opposed to it, but Henry Carter and many churchmen favoured it. This division of view was one reason for the formation of the Temperance Council of the Christian Churches in 1915. Because of its representative character and the leadership it attracted, the T.C.C.C. became a powerful influence in all matters of temperance advocacy and reform. This influence declined when some of the major denominations set up departments which incorporated temperance as only one among many moral and social issues on their agenda. The term "temperance" disappeared from the titles of the departments, which adopted such descriptions as "Christian Citizenship" and more recently "Social Responsibility". The churches' support of the T.C.C.C. waned and, as we have noted, it was wound up in 1979 to be replaced by the Churches Council on Alcohol and Drugs. The churches' financial support of the new body was greater than it had been for the T.C.C.C., but even so the maximum contribution by any denomination for the first year was £250. Only a grant of over £3,000 per annum for five years from the United Kingdom Temperance Alliance Limited made possible the appointment of a full-time secretary. Charity status may enable other trusts to contribute, but the churches themselves will have to decide whether this new body is to fulfil a truly representative role on their behalf.

Other enterprises

There have been, and there remain, enterprises founded on total abstinence principles. Notably there are two temperance friendly societies, the Sons of Temperance which received its charter as the National Division of Great Britain and Ireland in 1855 and the Independent Order of Rechabites founded in 1835. These have not only survived but continue to operate very successfully. Before the inception of the Welfare State these, in common with many other friendly societies, offered modest social security benefits. They now offer certain facilities to their members which supplement statutory social security and they are able to negotiate various insurances and mortgages. There was until recent years a temperance building society whose directors were required to renew their total abstinence pledge annually. Controversy surrounded the change of the name to Gateway Building Society in 1974, when at the same time the renewal of the pledge by the directors was no longer required. In 1959 the Ansvar Insurance Company of Sweden, which offers policies to total abstainers, established a subsidiary in Britain which for a small company has registered impressive growth. The promotion of non-alcoholic drinks by mail-order was begun by the Reading Temperance Society under the name of Amethyst drinks. More recently a commercial company, Leisure Drinks Limited, has been established. This is a wholesale company and markets its range through normal trade outlets.

These enterprises seem small when compared with some of the famous companies founded and expanded by such teetotallers in engineering as the Crossley Brothers (gas engines), John Colville (boilers), James Campbell (tunnelling), Alexander Finaly (bridges), Priestman Brothers (oil engines), Robinson Souttar (tramways), Benjamin Whitworth (mining), Thomas Alva Edison (telephones, etc), I. C. Johnson (Portland cement), Joseph Lucas (cycle lamps) and Sir Hiram Maxim (electric lamps). Many of the founders of the railway companies in Britain were Quakers and teetotallers. In food manufacturing and catering some of the best known firms, many still in business, had teetotal founders, such as Carrs (Carlisle), Huntley's (Reading), Jacobs (Dublin), Palmers (Reading) and Meads (Leeds) who were biscuit manufacturers. In the manufacture of such products as cocoa, tea, jam and other basic foodstuffs there are household names which fall within the same category, such as Cadbury (chocolates) Fry (chocolates), Rowntrees (sweets), Chivers (jellies), Hartley (jam), Horniman (tea), Harris (bacon), Neave (food), Symington (soup), Mackintosh (toffee), Rank (flour), Tolmer (cheese) and Watson (Skipper Sardines). Thomas Cook the travel agents trace their origin back to a founder who began by arranging trips for young abstainers. A more complete list was published in *Alliance News* April 1922 and republished as a pamphlet.

Pausing to reflect upon the permanent effects of temperance advocacy in this century it has to be said that they have been negligible. This is not to say that such advocacy at no time in the twentieth century was effective. It is clear from a historical survey of the period from 1900, that up to the First World War the temperance sentiment in Britain was strong. Indeed it was in the 1930s that Sir Edgar Sanders observed that the public houses were frequented only by old men. A conclusion reached by the Royal Commission 1929–1931 was that there was no serious drinking problem among young people. The temperance societies, and notably the Band of Hope, had helped to raise a generation of people for whom drinking intoxicants and going into public houses were disreputable habits.

A great change has come since the end of the Second World War. The temperance organizations in numerical terms have almost disappeared. The nation's per capita consumption is rising and for comparable figures for offences connected with drinking one has to go back one hundred years. There are few signs yet that people have become so appalled by the disastrous personal and social consequences of drinking that they are ready to embrace the temperance sentiment. The temperance reformers, who led the massive demonstrations of the early years of the twentieth century, believed they had virtually destroyed both the drinking habit and the vested interests which thrived on it. The ultimate decline of their cause is a phenomenon of social history for which there is no single explanation.

The "disease concept"

What has to be said is that although the temperance societies *per se* have declined, there has been a reponse which in many ways reflects their intentions. The object of temperance societies was to enable people to abandon the drink habit. Their method was to educate people as to the nature and effects of alcohol and on the basis of the facts to persuade them to become total abstainers. Because many of these societies had close ties with the churches, and chiefly non-conformist churches, there was frequently a moral appeal as well as one of expediency. For a number of reasons the moral appeal lost favour with the British people, and not simply in relation to alcohol. Nevertheless, the problem of excessive drinking persisted and another motivation had to be found to persuade people to abstain, and what emerged in the twentieth century was the "disease concept" of alcoholism. Whereas alcoholics tend to react strongly against a moral appeal, they seem prepared to accept the concept that they are sick. It is on this basis that almost everything has been done for the alcoholic since the end of the Second World War.

One of the earliest and most notable responses arising from the disease concept was Alcoholics Anonymous. This began in the U.S.A. and established itself in Britain in 1947. The thousands of men and women who have been helped to sobriety by A. A. resent any implication that they belong to a temperance society, and yet the purpose is the same, to achieve sobriety. The method is based on what are called "The Twelve Steps of Alcoholics Anonymous" and "The Twelve Traditions". Insistent as they are that alcoholism is a "disease", members who adopt the "twelve steps" find themselves acknowledging their powerlessness over alcohol, and the need to make "a searching and fearless moral inventory" of themselves, and admit to themselves and others their wrongs, and rely upon God as they understand him to restore them to sanity. They are encouraged to improve their conscious contact with God through prayer and meditation. The final "step" reads, "Having had a spiritual awakening as a result of these steps, we tried to carry this message to alcoholics and to practise these principles in all our affairs".

Essential to the practice of A.A. is the group meeting. Here those who meet are on first-name terms only, anonymity is of the essence of the method. At group meetings, which are usually held weekly, the members share their drinking experiences and their recovery progress in the group. There has been a striking increase in the number of groups in recent years. Between 1974 and 1976 in England and Wales the number increased from 451 to 619.[5]

Alcoholics Anonymous is not the only response arising from the acceptance of the disease concept. The emergence of councils on alcoholism is another and increasingly important development. The originator of the treatment of alcoholism in Britain is generally reckoned to be Dr Lincoln Williams. After visiting the United States in 1947 he returned resolved that in future he would treat alcoholics only. While in the States he met Marty Mann, the founder of the National Council on Alcoholism in New York, and this prompted him to establish a Council on Alcoholism in Britain.

Another important pioneer was Dr Max Glatt who, at Warlingham Park Hospital, became interested in the problem of alcoholism. In 1952 he started an experimental group for alcoholics which led to the establishment by the National Health Service in the 1960s of the Alcoholic Treatment Centres. In 1956 the Joseph Rowntree Social Service Trust set up a steering group on alcoholism, and then in 1962 the National Council on Alcoholism was formed.[6] Those who remember its tentative beginnings, and who have seen it develop into a nationwide network of about thirty regional councils, must sometimes marvel that so much has been achieved. The importance of this work is recognized by government, and substantial assistance is given by the Department of Health and Social Security. In 1978–79 the grant from the D.H.S.S. was £147,000.[7] Grants are received from other sources. The Brewers' Society contributes £8,000 per annum and in 1978 the United Kingdom Temperance Alliance Limited pledged £8,000 per annum for three years to enable the N.C.A. to appoint an industrial officer.

Recently the N.C.A. and two other bodies receiving grants from the D.H.S.S. became joint tenants of offices at Grosvenor Crescent. The two other bodies were the Medical Council on Alcoholism and the Federation of Alcoholic Rehabilitation Establishments. The Medical Council, like the N.C.A., had an inauspicious beginning. It was formed in 1967 by a small group of persons interested in the medical aspects of the alcohol problem who each made a modest financial contribution towards such basic expenses as postages. Hopefully, a classified advertisement was put in *The Times.* It brought an unexpected response from a charity based in Scotland which, after considering the objects of the new council, offered a grant of £30,000 per annum. Since then the council has attracted other funds. The Brewers' Society contributes £25,000 per annum and in addition to a grant of £14,450 from the D.H.S.S. the accounts for 1978–79 showed a covenanted income of £10,000 from the Distillers Company. The Medical Council initiates and encourages research, informs the medical profession on new developments in the treatment of alcoholism and produces the *British Journal on Alcohol and Alcoholism* which is published quarterly.

Independent of the M.C.A. and indeed from any other organization, is the British Doctors' Group. This was founded in 1973 in London when two general practitioners began to meet to discuss problems relating to their recovery from alcoholism. They were joined by others and monthly meetings were held. In 1977 the group was extended to include dental surgeons. A family group for the relations and friends of alcoholics was formed. Because a monthly meeting is not sufficient to sustain recovery, the group has established links with Alcoholics Anonymous and with such bodies as ACCEPT. Valuable experience has come from contact with similar groups in the U.S.A. "Like our colleagues in the U.S.A. we are firmly committed to total abstinence, i.e. abstinence from alcohol and all mood-changing drugs, also believing that this must be the primary goal for treatment. In our experience those who use our group together with A.A. (or other supporting groups) maintain good sobriety with a high degree of success. As a group we have yet to learn of a single case of a successful return to 'controlled' drinking. All such attempts have sooner or later ended in failure. Sadly, some of our members have died in the terminal phases of chronic alcoholism still believing they could 'control' their drinking, and four have committed suicide."[8] However, the recovery rate among doctors seems to be encouraging. "In a recent survey of the results of treatment of doctors in a N.H.S. Alcohol and Drug Dependency Centre over a period of 10 years, 66 per cent of the doctors have achieved sobriety and are working in their full professional capacity."[9]

The Federation of Alcoholic Rehabilitation Establishments (FARE) was founded in 1974. Its objectives are described as "To serve as a national focal point for all activities related to the provision of residential and day-care facilities for people with alcohol-related problems; to work on behalf of management and staff, presenting their views as appropriate to government and local authorities; to campaign when necessary and generally encourage better co-ordination and increased availability of facilities throughout the country."[10] FARE is concerned primarily with residential and day-care facilities, but there is a wide range of services available to alcoholics.

As already noted the National Health Service founded alcoholism treatment units. Nationally, the number of beds available in these units in 1979 was about seven hundred. In addition, detoxification services are provided at some psychiatric hospitals and at psychiatric departments in general hospitals. In Manchester and Leeds, experimental detoxification units were established to which police might take drunkenness offenders instead of putting them in the cells at the police station. Hostels are usually residential rehabilitation houses for homeless people, but in the category there are those with drinking problems. Day centres, too, care for homeless people, but centres exclusively for homeless alcoholics are few. Various other experimental centres have been opened, but taken together, facilities are inadequate to deal with the scale of the problem. The conclusion reached by a FARE working party was, "In our view co-operation and co-ordination will not only draw the best from existing services but will demonstrate clearly the gaps which in so many places, still exist."[11] FARE is largely funded by a grant from the D.H.S.S. which for the financial year 1978–79 was £45,000 plus £901 for fieldwork expenses. The only other income was £1,445 from the sale of publications and £638 from membership fees.

Although the disease concept of alcoholism has been the basis for the treatment of alcoholics, its validity has been questioned. Jellinek is most frequently quoted in connection with this theory. In 1960 he published a book which had great influence. This was *The disease concept of Alcoholism*.[12] In this he propounded his formula that the number of deaths reported to be due to cirrhosis of the liver could be used as the basis for calculating the number of alcoholics in the general population. In their book *Alcoholism and Addiction*, Swinson and Eaves commented that the accuracy of the findings based on this formula were open to question from various aspects.[13] Taking account of all reliable surveys the conclusion to be drawn is that in England and Wales the total number of alcoholics is between 200,000 and 400,000. If these figures were taken as a minimum, then Swinson and Eaves concluded that figures of 350,000 to 500,000 "appear to be fairly reasonable"![14] So far as Scotland and Ireland are concerned, the same authors quoted a survey of alcoholism in Scotland (1971) on the basis of which it could be stated that "the prevalence of alcoholism in Scotland is higher than in England and Wales".[15] In Ireland alcoholism is a major problem. Swinson and Eaves quoted the findings of a survey by Walsh in 1969, which showed that the rate of first admissions to hospitals for alcoholism is 24.5 per 100,000 of the total population, "which is surpassed only by France."[16] Much more work has been done to ascertain whether physiological factors lie behind alcoholism. The conclusion of Swinson and Eaves is that "despite a tremendous amount of work, it has not yet been shown that alcoholics differ from non-alcoholics in any physiological sense before the development of alcoholism."[17] This means that other reasons must be found in justification of the disease concept, and there are those who doubt whether it is a concept which has sufficient validity to justify Lincoln William's conclusion that "alcoholism is primarily a medical problem".[18]

Early in 1979 the *British Medical Journal* published an article by Professor R. E. Kendall of the University Department of Psychiatry, Royal Edinburgh Hospital in which he cast serious doubts on the disease concept.[19] "Its success owed more to humanitarian sentiments and disenchantment with the efficiency of moral exhortations than to any evidence that alcoholism exhibited the defining characteristics of disease in general but even so, that success was ultimately almost complete. For the past twenty years the "disease concept" has been everyone's official dogma, with medical organizations, alcoholics themselves, and well-meaning people speaking on their behalf, all urging governments and employers to accept and act on its implications."[20] Professor Kendall referred to some of these implications. For instance, alcoholics must not be blamed or punished, they are sick, and this means they must be accepted for treatment and rehabilitation. When the condition continues to spread unchecked, everyone assumes that the problem is one for the medical profession to solve. He acknowledged that some benefits had arisen from the acceptance of this concept. Public attitudes to alcoholics had changed. They were regarded more humanely than at one time. "Unfortunately, our new knowledge is making it increasingly clear that most of the assumptions of the 'disease concept' are unjustified and act as a barrier to a more intelligent and effective approach to the problem", he concluded. He discussed in some detail the work of Ledermann* who claimed that there is a fixed relation between average and excessive consumption.[21] Although some of Ledermann's statistical assumptions had been rightly criticized, Kendall believed Ledermann was right "in suggesting that the proportion of a population drinking excesssively is largely determined by the average consumption of that population". Kendall observed, "The reason for this probably lies in the social nature of most drinking. When, for whatever reason, a person's consumption rises, his behaviour towards others also changes. He is more likely to offer a drink to friends visiting him or to buy another round of drinks at a public house. As a result, his friends' consumption rises and because they feel obliged to repay the debt there are further repercussions affecting other people as well. In addition, changed drinking habits that spread in this way ultimately lead to changes in social attitudes to drinking and in the availability of commerical outlets, which in turn have further effects on consumption." When trends were ominous, Professor Kendall believed that instead of working on assumptions, there should be a serious re-examination of them to see whether the assumption that medical treatment was the answer to alcoholism was valid. The drinking habits of a population were more likely to be affected by changes in legislation and alteration in price. "Changes in legislation and in general economic conditions have probably been the major cause of the dramatic increases in consumption that have taken place throughout the world in the past 25 years."

We refer to Professor Kendall's opinions because they represent one of the first serious challenges to the concept on which the identification, presentation and treatment of alcoholics are based. If he proves to be right, then it will be necessary to see whether the application of economic and legislative controls in the past did, in fact, affect the level of consumption and the incidence of predictable personal and social consequences and whether such controls are valid for all times.

Health education

The assumption that alcoholism is primarily a medical problem has persuaded government to regard it as a public-health matter and not as one of law and order. While public drunkenness remains an offence, the identification and treatment of alcoholism does not come within the purview of the law. The responsibility for this aspect of the alcohol problem does not rest with the Home Office, but with the Department of Health and Social Security. This department is well-informed on the nature and extent of alcoholism and is sensitive to the need for on-going research, treatment facilities and education. It appears equally aware of the need for preventive measures. The variety of agencies receiving grants from the D.H.S.S. is an indication of the concern the department has to encourage research facilities and treatment and rehabilitation centres. On 5th December 1979, Sir George Young, a minister at the D.H.S.S., gave the following list of voluntary organizations receiving grants and the amounts given in 1978–79. The list was given in response to a parliamentary question.

* *A French scientist who developed a controversial formula for determining the distribution of alcohol consumption in a given community.*

GRANTS TOWARDS THE SETTING UP AND RUNNING OF HOSTELS*

	£
Alcoholics Recovery Projects	24,312
Allen House Trust, Bognor Regis	5,388
Aquarius	27,795
Avon Council on Alcoholism	12.382
Birmingham Diocesan Council for Social Aid	9,882
Bow Mission	32,201
Camden Alcoholics Support Association	28,258
Church Army (final claim not yet received)	—
Coventry Cyrenians	3,673
Devon Council on Alcoholism	6,752
Hostel, Maidstone Council of Churches	2,903
Hampshire Association for the Care and Resettlement of Offenders	7,040
Hastings Hostel Ltd, Leicester	9,894
Helping Hand Organisation	74,845
Homeless Action and Accommodation Ltd	3,885
Oxford and District Council on Alcoholism	8,063
Petrus Community	20,005
Royal London Aid Society	9,400
Salvation Army	30,075
St. Anne's Shelter and Housing Action Ltd, Leeds	30,664
Society of St. Dismas, Southampton	19,365
Scunthorpe Committee on Alcoholism	1,639
South East London Consortium	26,000
Spelthorne St. Mary, Harpenden	4,540
Spitalfields Crypt Association	18,179
Stonham Housing Association	14,834
Thamesdown and North Wiltshire Council on Alcoholism	8,344
Wayback Foundation, Plymouth	7,472
West London Cyrenians	1,808
Westminster Advisory Centre on Alcoholism	125
OTHER	
Alcohol Education Centre	50,000
Alcoholic Recovery Project	11,000
Aquarius Resource Centre	14,219
Federation of Alcoholic Rehabilitation Establishments	46,265
Helping Hand Organisation	24,300
Helping Hand Organisation/Bedford Advice Centre	10,400
Medical Council on Alcoholism	14,450
National Council on Alcoholism	147,000
Norfolk Council on Alcoholism	24,000
South-East London Consortium	13,000
St. Botolph's	3,500

The total grants paid to voluntary organizations to provide hostels for alcoholics, including homeless alcoholics since April 1974 are as follows:

	Capital £	Revenue £	Total £
1974–75	132,505	88,035	220,540
1975–76	199,903	102,934	302,837
1976–77	270,883	188,033	458,916
1977–78	205,060	263,219	468,279
1978–79	145,524	318,116	463,640
1979–80†	150.000	350,000	500.000
Totals	**1,103,875**	**1,310,337**	**2,414,212**

*Since Sir George Young made this statement, the government has announced its intention to phase out such government grants and to place the responsibility of funding such facilities upon the local authorities and voluntary bodies.

†Estimated.

The acceptance of alcoholism as a public health problem has led to the inference that there must be a health education programme directed at prevention. As we have seen, the first syllabus for use in schools was produced in 1909 and there have been many published since.[22] Almost without exception these were based on the "factual" approach. They were designed to present children with the facts about the nature and effects of alcohol. The assumption was that given the facts, children would decide either to abstain or adopt strict limits to their consumption when they grew up.

It is now widely accepted that the factual approach has not achieved the aim in view, and other bases have been sought for an effective health education programme. The Health Education Council itself devotes staff and resources to the creation of such a programme, not just for children but for the community as a whole. We have already referred to two bodies which have emerged in recent years specifically to initiate alcohol education. These are the Teachers' Advisory Council on Alcohol and Drug Education and the Alcohol Education Centre.[23] We have described their approaches, which have merit, but the central issue is not how sound is the theory, but how solid are the results. In the report of the Central Health Services Council for 1978, there was evidence of a difference of views about the role of education in the prevention of alcohol abuse. The Standing Nursing and Midwifery Advisory Committee said that "a continuing programme of education was generally preferable to statutory controls". However, some of the members of the Central Council itself argued that "health education against alcoholism was largely ineffective".[24] These two views are shared by others, and so the conflict needs to be resolved. There are some authorities in the field who think that all such education only confirms people in their established attitudes to drinking.

Having noted the doubts now being cast on the "disease concept" on which the treatment of alcoholism has been based, is it now to be noted that alcohol education may not be the ultimate basis for prevention?

Drink in industry

A neglected area of research has been the relation of drinking and accidents and efficiency at work. In view of the very considerable research which has established a relation between the consumption of alcohol and road accidents, it is surprising that so little has been done in the industrial field. Textbooks on industrial psychology, for example, give scant attention, if any, to alcohol.

In 1977 the United Kingdom Temperance Alliance Limited funded research at the Polytechnic of Wales into the relationship of drinking to industrial accidents. The work, which was monitored by the Christian Economic and Social Research Foundation, was undertaken by Argyropoulon-Grisanon supervised by Dr Peter Hawkins, head of the Social Studies Department at the polytechnic. Grisanon examined the accident statistics at three different firms in South Wales as the first stage of a more ambitious research project. Accidents were classified as to type and then plotted in relation to the hourly periods of shifts when they occurred.

Grisanon found that the "three different plants, each with a different technology, and therefore different in hazards, all showed basically the same pattern of accidents".[25] In two plants the highest incidence of accidents was found in the first two hours of a new shift. In the third, a laboratory, there were not as many accidents and there was not a shift system extending over 24 hours, but most accidents occurred in the two hours following the lunch break. Grisanon studied various possible explanations of the phenomenon of accidents happening with greater frequency at specific times, but concluded that it was the consumption of alcohol which was responsible for the increased rate of accidents rather than any other factor. To test the validity of this conclusion Grisanon set up in the laboratory an 'L'-shaped corridor in which to simulate what he had found to be the most accident prone situation in both a paper-mill and a rubber-factory. The walls of the corridor were sensitized so that any contact was automatically recorded. Twenty-four subjects took part in the test, twelve were assigned to group A and twelve to group B, this assignment being worked out randomly. Within each group, six subjects received a placebo drink first and then alcohol, and the other six were given alcohol first and the placebo second to counterbalance any order effects. Subjects in group A received 1.5 millilitres of alcohol per kilogram of body weight, and subjects in group B were given 3.0 millilitres of alcohol per kilogram of body weight. A small group of two was used as a control and did not receive any alcohol.

After receiving the placebo, two subjects at a time were asked to carry a roll, supplied by the factories concerned, through the corridor. Similarly after they had received alcohol. The subjects wore sensitized overalls so that any contacts made with the walls of the corridor were recorded. Using all three groups, it was expected that the control group would record least "accidents" and that the number of "accidents" would increase with the intake of alcohol, which proved to be the case. Consumption of alcohol led to at least four to five times the number of "accidents" which increased with larger amounts of alcohol. It is expected that these studies will be extended to other industrial situations, and a further study is now being undertaken to relate the findings of Grisanon to attitudes to drinking by people at work.

References

1. Command Paper 9475 Miscellaneous No. 7 (1955).
2. The present position in the United Kingdom is regulated by statutory instrument 1968 No. 1558 as amended by S.I. 1972 No. 1770. These statutory instruments in general reflect the U.K. obligations in the E.E.C. which are set out in the combined text of E.E.C. directives 69/169 of 28th May 1969 and 72/30 of 12th June 1972 (covering Excise Duty and V.A.T.), Regulations 1554/69 of July 1969 (covering C.C.T. duty) and Regulation 1818/75 of 10th July 1975 (covering CAP).
3. See article by Kenneth Lawton *Alliance News* March-April 1978 p. 3.
4. *Alcoholism and Addiction* R. P. Swinson and Derek Eaves. Macdonald and Evans (1978) p. 275.
5. *Talking out of alcoholism* David Robinson. Croom Helm, London (1979) p. 25.
6. *16th Annual Report of the National Council on Alcoholism (1978–79)* p. 5 ff.
7. See table p. 246.
8. *British Journal on Alcohol and Alcoholism* Vol. 15, p. 15.
9. Op cit p. 16.
10. See 6th Annual report of FARE 1978–79 p. 1.

11. Op cit p. 23.
12. *The Disease Concept of Alcoholism* E. M. Jellinek, Hillhouse Press, New Haven, Connecticut (1960).
13. Readers are referred to Swinson and Eaves' discussion of the Jellinek formula for their specific criticisms.
14. Op cit p. 21.
15. Op cit p. 21.
16. Op cit p. 22.
17. Op cit p. 102.
18. *Alcoholism: A manual for students and practitioners.* Lincoln Williams. E. and S. Livingstone (1956) p. vi.
19. *British Medical Journal.* 10th February 1979 p. 367.
20. Op cit p. 367.
21. *Alcool, Alcoolisme, Alcoolisation.* Institut National d'Etudes Demographiques, Travaux et Documents, Cahier No. 29, Paris, Presses Universitaires de France (1956).
22. See Chapter "Children and Drink" p. 182.
23. See p. 188.
24. Central Health Services Council Report for year ended 31st December 1978. House of Commons Paper 205 (H.M.S.O.).
25. *Effects of alcohol on the performance of some industrial tasks.* M. A. Argyropoulon-Grisanon, PhD Thesis 1980 (Unpublished but deposited at the library of the Christian Economic and Social Research Foundation).

PART II

CHAPTER 17

DRUNKENNESS: THE FIRST FORTY YEARS, 1900–39

The first forty years of the twentieth century are best discussed in terms of two quite different social and demographic situations separated by the World War of 1914–18 which was largely responsible for the change in the social environment. Drunkenness is a reflection of the exuberance of either a whole society or a portion of it. Normally, only a very small proportion of the alcohol-consuming population is either so immature or so over-indulgent as to behave in such a way as draw down the penalties for anti-social activity. It follows that the offences of drunkenness (proceedings, prior to 1939; an over-statement of some 10 per cent when compared with the later figures) are akin to the chart at the foot of a patient's bed in that they emphasize the departures from the steady state of the organism. In a real social sense, excesses in the prevalent tend to be noticed by police and public to a greater extent than idiosyncratic behaviour when the particular kind of behaviour is not generally regarded as a potential threat to the safety of property or the persons in the local community.

From 1900 to 1914, the twentieth century must be regarded as a simple extension of the late nineteenth; the same social and economic problems were rampant. The attitudes towards alcohol on the part of reformers and indulgers remained the same. So far as the reformers were concerned, the damage to the family and the children caused by excessive consumption by the fathers or the mothers was so great and so common that the need for bringing about a reduction in the numbers of parents falling into that category continued as urgent as it had been for generations before. So far as the age and class groups most prone to excessive indulgence were concerned, the habit of heavy indulgence continued to be socially acceptable, at least within the social class and age groups in which the indulgent moved.

The Great War changed much. Probably the most important result was the removal from the "marrying ages" of at least one-third of the eligible males, with no change in the numbers of females in the, younger, comparable age-group. After the burst of marriages in 1919 and 1920 as the survivors from the armies overseas came back, the formation of potential new familiies suffered a severe set-back. Not only that, but the numbers of bachelors, always a reservoir of potential drunken offenders, in the younger age groups were reduced. The girls could not afford to be as particular in picking a husband as they had been when the numbers of potential partners were more or less equal. It is, of course, important to bear in mind that, even with conscription, most men did not join in the actual hostilities, so that the unmarried state was unusual among women. There was also the obvious distress of the war-widows, socially and economically, to underline its unattractiveness.

The trends in drunkenness

Before going further into the quite complicated social differences between the periods before and after 1914–18, it is desirable to look at the actual trends in the number of proceedings taken against persons for drunkenness in Scotland and in England and Wales. Chart I illustrates the changes from 1900 to 1935. The figures for 1936 and onwards are increasingly subject to the influence of war and the preparations for war so that their inclusions might give rise to misunderstanding of the generality of the picture. It is important to realize that the Scottish data on the chart is, in effect, multiplied ten times in the visual scale, the numbers plotted being hundreds rather than the thousands used in the case of England and Wales. This is not unfair to Scotland; the population of England and Wales has generally been about ten times that of Scotland, so that the visual situation is reflective of the relative incidence of drunkenness in the two nations.

In the case of England and Wales, the line fluctuates slightly about the 200,000 cases level with a fall from 1904 to 1910 and a compensating rise from then to 1914. As will be seen from the later analysis, this fluctuation is to a large part associated with the slump in shipbuilding and railway construction and the recovery when the naval building, to keep up with the German move towards parity, became increasingly important. As the drunkenness in Scotland is more concentrated on the heavy industrial areas around the Clyde, this volatility is even more pronounced. Thus, Scotland exhibits a sharp decline in 1903, when the figures south of the border shown an increase. The "boom" in 1906–8 was also one bringing work to the coalmining and shipbuilding sectors.

In both countries, the fall in the numbers of proceedings over the war years is precipitous, and calls for no particular comment. The same reflection of the shortages in the civilian sector will be apparent in the data for the 1939–46 period.

The early indication of a return to pre-war "normality" proved to be wrong. The shipbuilding boom of 1919–20 was shortlived and was followed by the slump of 1921, from which there has been no real recovery. Once again, the effect of the boom in the basic industries is more apparent in Scotland than it is in England and Wales. The Scottish proceedings rise to 80 per cent of the 1914 boom peak, while those in England and Wales barely achieve 50 per cent of the pre-war levels.

After 1922, both nations settled down to levels of about a half of those holding before 1914, but with a gently-sloping-downward tendency, to be made temporarily steeper as the great depression of 1929–33 began to have its full effect. There are fluctuations to be seen but they are of small amplitude as compared with those occurring twenty years before. It is clear that a profound change has taken placed in the incidence of drunkenness, as indicated by the totals of proceedings.

Differences in the experience in respect of the sexes

Chart II displays the data in respect of persons. While there is an underlying tendency for the fluctuations to be reflected in the trends of proceedings against both sexes, the trends themselves are not the same. Even before the First World War, there was a tendency for the number of proceedings taken against women to fall away, in the face of a rising population. This was more pronounced in England and Wales than it was in Scotland, as the smaller charts overleaf make clear. Separate charts are given for Scotland and for England and Wales, but they are displayed opposite each other to facilitate comparison.

CHART I

Proceedings against persons in England and Wales, and Scotland, 1900-35

SCALE England & Wales, thousands of proceedings. Scotland, hundreds of proceedings.

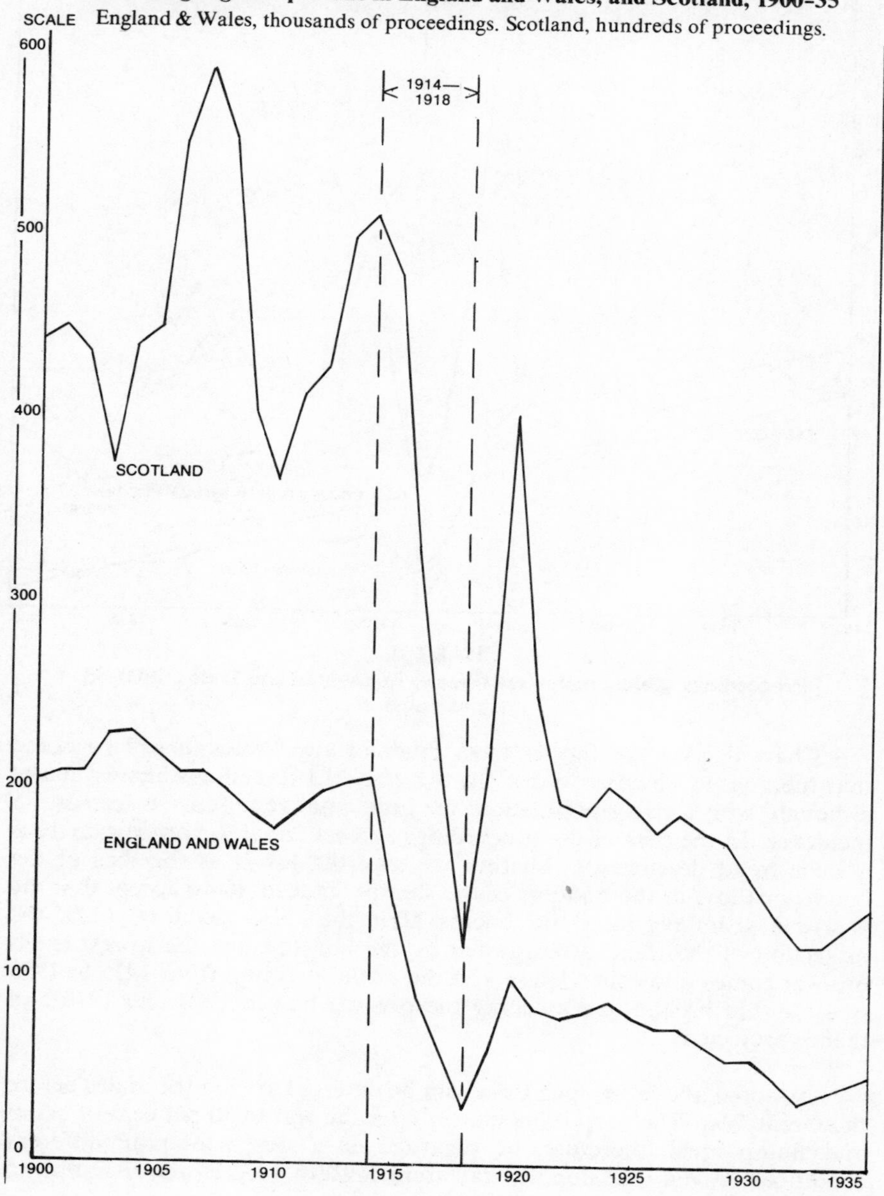

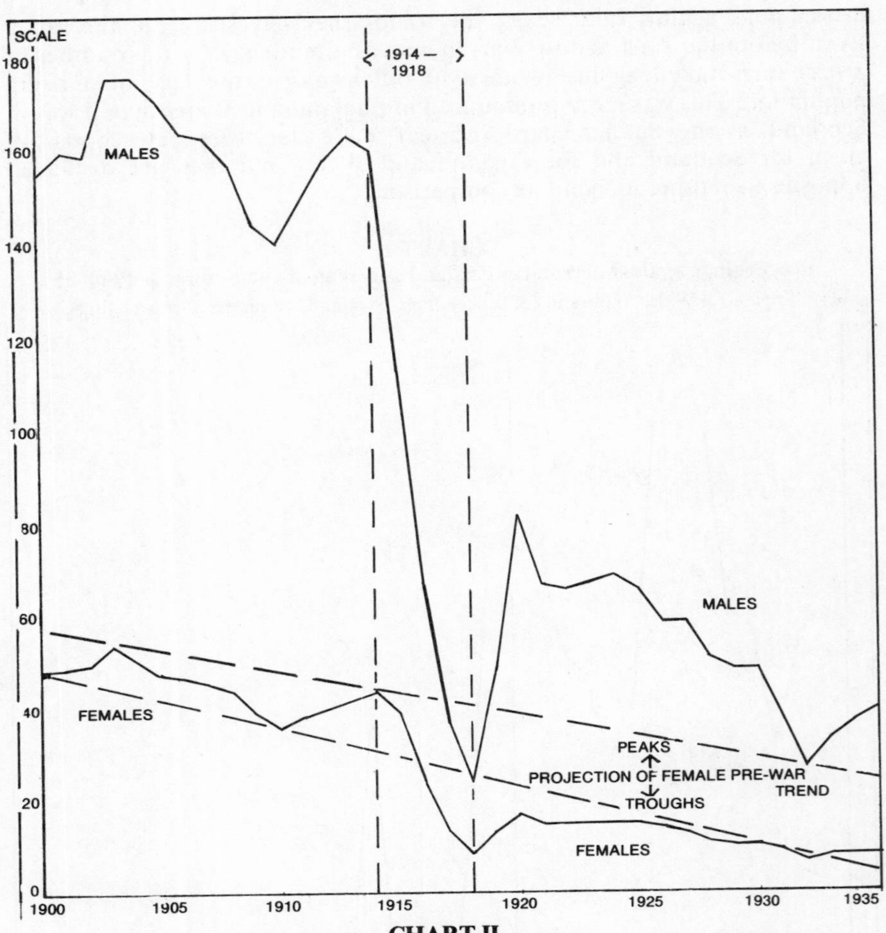

CHART II
Proceedings against males and females in England and Wales, 1900–35
(thousands)

Chart II gives the figures from England and Wales. It will be noted that there is no obvious "trend" in the case of proceedings against males although, with a rising population, the horizontal represents a decrease in incidence. In the case of the proceedings against females, however, there is a clear trend downwards, whether we take the levels at the tops of the booms or those at the bottoms of the slumps. Indeed, if we accept that the post-war years produced no booms after the false dawn of 1920, the projection of the trend as suggested by the line through the lowest levels pre-war comes into coincidence with the actual readings from 1925 to 1933 (see the thin broken line touching the pre-war line at 1900 and 1910 and thence projected).

As noted above, no such trend can be detected among the males before the Great War. The drop immediately after the war to 50 per cent of boom and slump must, therefore, be regarded as a step into quite different conditions. Given that step, the fall from 1920 to 1932 is not dissimilar to the fall from the boom of 1904 to the nadir of 1910. So far as England and Wales are concerned, we need to look for explanations for the step in the incidence of drunkenness among males, and we can afford to treat the situation among the women as being to a large extent the continuation of influences already apparent at the beginning of the century.

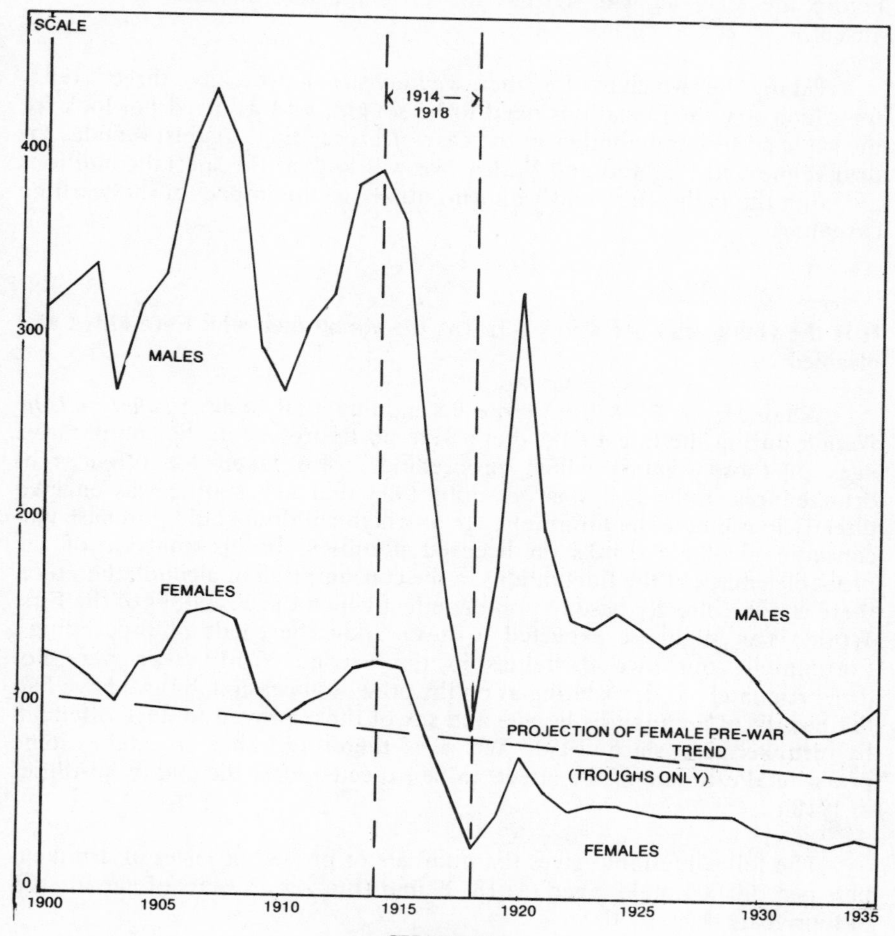

CHART III
Proceedings against males and females in Scotland, 1900–35
(hundreds)

Chart III, above, compares the history of proceedings for offences of drunkenness in Scotland. Having seen the situation as it affected women in England and Wales, it is instructive to draw in the same projection of the line across the "bottoms" of the slumps in 1903 and 1910 into the 1920–35 period. It is clear that the same coincidence with trend does not occur; rather there is a step.

The fact that this step (about 50 per cent) is not as great as the "step" in the case of proceedings against males in Scotland, which fell to some one-third of pre-1914 levels, is to some extent a reflection of the slight downward trend that was just visible in the pre-war years. The figures for males display the high degree of volatility that we noted for "persons" until 1922; thereafter, there is rather less fluctuation than occurs in England and Wales. The Scottish basic industries did not show any recovery until just before the 1939–46 war so that the pre-requisites for fluctuation were absent.

Taking the two charts together, we may say that we have three "steps" for which some explanations need to be sought, and we need not look for the same sort of explanation in the case of proceedings against females for drunkenness in England and Wales. We will look at the special conditions affecting the males first, and we turn initially to the impact of the wartime casualties.

It is the young who get drunk – it was the young men who were killed and disabled

When Dr G. B. Wilson wrote his monumental book *Alcohol and the Nation* during the late 1930s, there were no figures upon the comparative ages of those against whom proceedings were taken for offences of drunkenness. Indeed, it was not until 1923 that any statute was enacted directly to regulate the minimum age at which children could purchase and consume alcoholic drinks on licensed premises. In his analyses of the probable causes of the fluctuations in the consumption of alcohol, therefore, there is none directly based upon the effect which the casualties of the First World War might be expected to have upon the totals of proceedings. Fortunately, our own casualties in the Second World War were not proportionately as devastating as on the previous occasion, but we have had the benefit of an analysis by age and sex of those proved to have offended by drunkenness since 1956. We are, therefore, able to make some provisional estimate of the effects to be expected after the end of hostilities in 1918.

The following table gives the numbers of proved offences of drunkenness per 100,000 males aged (a) 18–29 and (b) over 29 years of age in each of four years since 1956.

Proved offences of drunkenness per 100,000 males (England and Wales)

	1956	1961	1971	1976
18–29 years	544	678	705	792
30 years and older	299	358	387	434
Incidence under 30 as per cent of incidence 30 years and over	182%	189%	182%	182%

In other words, since records permit of the analysis, the incidence of drunkenness among the young has remained about twice that among the mature.

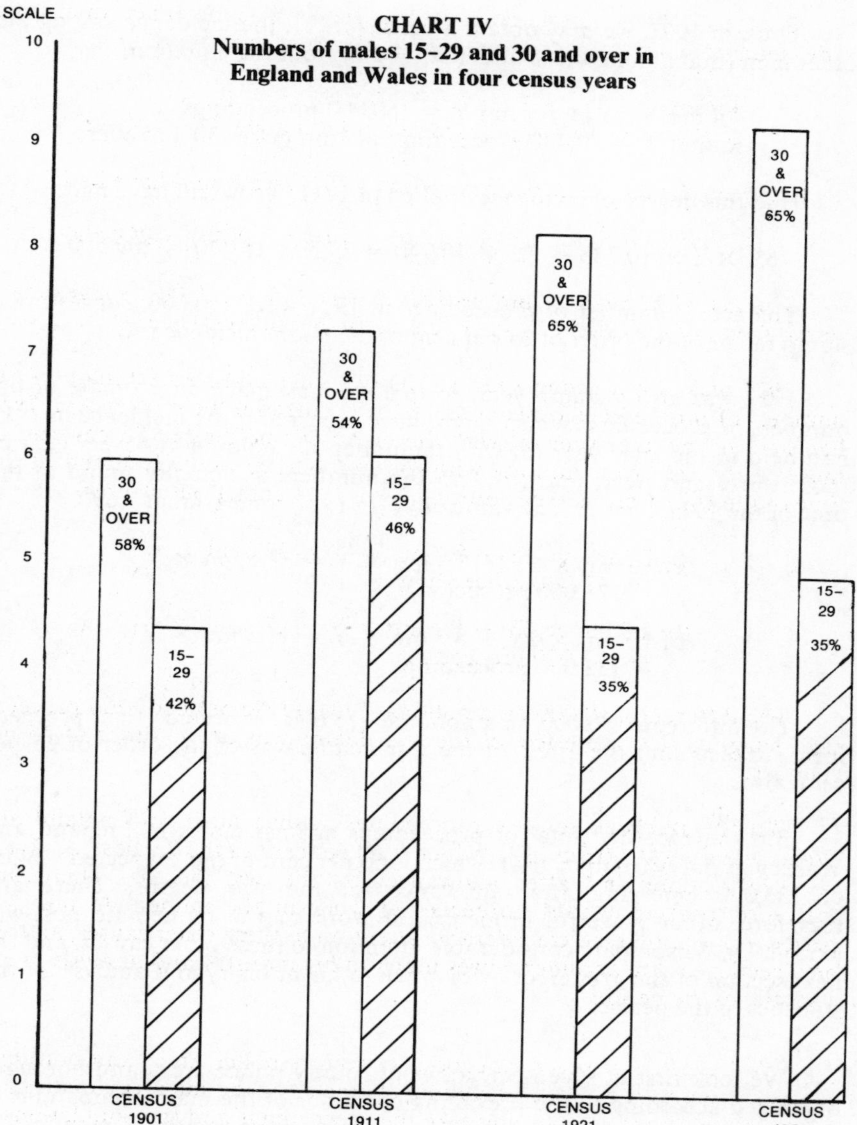

Chart IV shows how the numbers of males aged under and over thirty varied in the four census years of 1901, 1911, 1921 and 1931. The effect of the wartime deaths among the young is apparent. The trends in Chart IV prior to the outbreak of war suggest that male drinking habits did not change very much except under the influence of boom and slump in the heavy industries. Assuming the incidence among those aged 15–29 in those census years to be twice that among the older men (there was no bar on youthful drinking; youths become drunk on smaller quantities of alcohol than those of greater weight in later years), we can first obtain an indication of the effect upon incidence of boom and slump in the heavy industries.

Thus, in 1901, we may obtain a value for 'Y', the incidence among the older men (that among those under 30 = 2Y) from the equation:

$$4.4 \text{ mn} \times 2Y + 6.1 \text{ mn } Y = 160{,}000 \text{ proceedings}$$
$$\text{so that } Y = 10{,}740 \text{ proceedings per mn males 30 and over.}$$

Had this degree of incidence applied in 1911, we would have had:

$$6.1 \times 2 \times 10{,}740 + 7.3 \times 10{,}740 = 19.5 \times 10{,}740 = 209{,}500$$

The actual number of proceedings in 1911 were 150,000, suggesting a slump factor of the order of 25 per cent of the boom incidence.

1921 was also a slump year, so that we may make an estimate of the numbers of proceedings which might have occurred if the incidence in 1911 had held in the later year (a) with the under-30s holding at 85 per cent of those thirty and over; and (b) with the numbers as actually found at the time of the 1921 Census. The value of 'Y' in 1911 comes out at 7,690.

$$\text{(a) } 7.3 \text{ mn} \times 2Y + 8.3 \text{ mn} \times Y = 22.5 \text{ mn} \times Y = 173{,}000 \text{ proceedings;}$$

$$\text{(b) } 4.5 \text{ mn} \times 2Y + 8.3 \text{ mn} \times Y = 17.3 \text{ mn} \times Y = 133{,}000 \text{ proceedings.}$$

The difference, 40,000 on a notional 173,000 "expected" total proceedings, suggests that the effect of the war deaths was of the order of 25 per cent, also.

But the recorded total of proceedings against males in England and Wales was only 80,000 in 1921, which is 60 per cent of the "expected" figure of 133,000 emerging after allowance for the war deaths. There are, therefore, other powerful influences at work in the immediate post-war period. Dr Wilson paid considerable attention to these other causes, and the next section of the argument owes much to his industry and analysis of the statistics of the period.

We look first at seven categories of county police areas and boroughs organized according to the prevailing character of the main occupations of the inhabitants or visitants, and take the proceedings and the populations at each of the four census years, 1901, 1911, 1921 and 1931.

Proceedings per 10,000 population in combined authorities

Category of Police Authority Area	**1901**	**1911**	**1921**	**1931**
Seaports	96.3	99.1	48.6	22.2
Mining counties	114.8	61.6	22.4	8.4
London, City and Metropolitan	80.0	86.5	39.6	23.9
Manufacturing towns	61.7	50.4	26.3	13.5
Pleasure towns and seaside resorts	35.8	27.1	8.4	9.2
Agricultural counties	24.1	15.9	4.4	4.4
London: Home Counties	27.2	15.8	3.8	2.9

We see in the table how the influences already mentioned of boom and slump, different in their timing in Scotland from that in England and Wales, affected different kinds of localities in 1901 and 1911. The seaports through which the imported foods and raw materials came into the country, not much affected in terms of the number of vessels by the end-products of manufacturing, show an increase in the incidence of proceedings, an increase also to be seen in the case of the Greater London area, itself a seaport of world importance at this time. The drop in the incidence in the group of police districts comprising the manufacturing towns is apparent, at some 20 per cent of the boom incidence, but it is a small decline compared with the fall in the mining counties (46 per cent) and in the agricultural areas both near to and far from London (rather under 40 per cent). The pleasure towns and seaside resorts occupy a middle position, with a fall in incidence of 25 per cent.

When we compare 1921 with 1911, we are comparing across two slump years, but we are also faced with the differential effect of the war deaths. Even so close to the end of hostilities, it is dangerous to read the figures too simply, especially when, as in the present instance, the data are in terms of persons, but it is broadly true that the effect of the reservations under conscription, as well as the delayed effects of the volunteer system early in the war, was to bring about a greater relative concentration of war deaths in those localities not predominantly of an industrial, manufacturing or seaport character. In the table, the lowest three categories show decreases in incidence of the order of 70 per cent and more; the upper four categories, decreases of the order of 45 per cent (mining counties 64 per cent).

By contrast, in the movements between 1921 and 1931, it is the industrial areas and the seaports which show the greatest reductions in the rate of incidence. The agricultural counties stay at the low rates established at the beginning of the decade, while the pleasure resorts actually record an increase in the incidence of drunkenness. The seaports and the manufacturing towns, including London, exhibit decreases of the order of 50 per cent as against 1921, while the mining counties show an incidence of only about one-third of the immediate post-war period.

Before we proceed to analyse more deeply, there is another table to be culled from Dr Wilson's book which sheds the same kind of light upon the situation, but from a slightly different angle. In the table which follows, the proceedings per 10,000 persons in the populations at the four census years are again used, but this time with the groupings more geographically inclined, and comprising twelve large areas in England and Wales.

Some parts of this table are illustrated on Chart V on page 262. The main solid line traces the changes in the overall incidence in England and Wales, and the lighter solid line the figures for London and the Metropolitan Police district. Three sets of broken lines represent, respectively, those parts of the country which were particularly dependent upon what came to be termed the "exposed" occupations – coalmining and shipbuilding in the North East, cotton in Lancashire and Cheshire, and coalmining and the

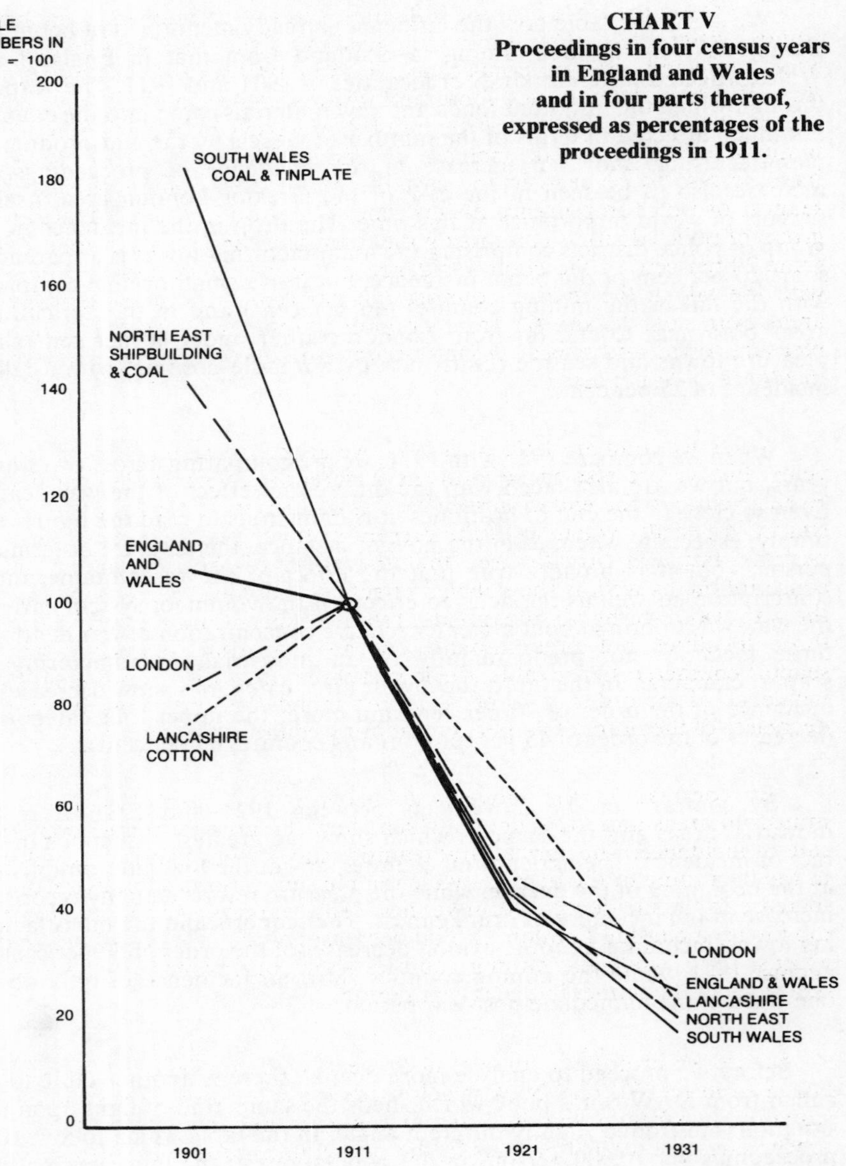

CHART V
Proceedings in four census years in England and Wales and in four parts thereof, expressed as percentages of the proceedings in 1911.

manufacture of tinplate in South Wales. The effect of slump in the heavy industries in the pre-war decade contrasts with the rising incidence in the cotton areas and in London. The fall after the end of the war is common to all, except that in 1921 South Wales was still "enjoying" a relatively higher incidence of proceedings than the other areas charted. By 1931, South Wales was among the lowest incidences.

There was one great difference between slumps before and after the First World War, at least so far as Great Britain was concerned. Prior to the war, boom and slump had alternated with a regularity that gave birth to the

Proceedings per 10,000 population in the census years

Region	1901	1911	1921	1931
Northern Counties	133	87	37	16
Lancashire and Cheshire	73	65	32	13
Yorkshire	63	52	20	11
Midlands	50	40	12	9
South Wales and Monmouth	123	51	19	8
Metropolitan Police District and City	80	89	41	25
Nearer Home Counties	34	18	5	7
Outer Home Counties	24	20	4	6
East Anglia	27	31	10	8
Oxfordshire and the Welsh Marches	46	27	8	5
South and South West of England	31	21	7	6
Rest of Wales	59	41	16	10
England and Wales as a whole	65	54	23	12

theory of "trade cycles" in explanation. Each boom and each slump was of short duration. That ceased to be the case in the United Kingdom after the war. The depression which started in 1921 went on and on, until it merged with the world-wide slump of 1929–32. This had an important effect upon the ability of those who habitually consumed large quantities of beer (whether or not accompanied by "chasers" of whisky as in Scotland) to maintain the habit when their incomes were reduced. It was the custom in those areas where heavy consumption was accompanied by frequent periods of reduced activity, seasonal or induced by recession in output, to accord established patrons of public houses extended credit – the money due being "put on the slate" for later settlement. When the period of lowered income became extended and the income reduced to the very low levels represented by the "dole", this practice clearly could not be sustained. Already, by late 1921, it was apparent that in the cotton and shipbuilding areas the old pattern was not going to be repeated.

With some reservations which will become apparent as we go on to discuss the period between 1921 and 1931, and extending to the immediate pre-war years, we may conclude that the changes between 1911 and 1921 are attributable to the war deaths and the post-war slump especially in the latter's relative concentration on the steel-using industries and the mines serving these and the cotton areas in the North West where the consumption of alcohol was particularly high and coupled with bouts of really excessive drinking.

We may now turn to the reservations, which concern the effects of the spread of quite different social customs from London to most of the provinces as the decade wore on.

Not because it was the most important, but because it began before the outbreak of hostilities and because it underlies the gradual reduction in the incidence of proceedings against women between 1901 and 1911, we must note the increase in the employment of women in commerce and industry, and especially in the trade and office work in London and some of the other commercial centres. The first noticeable effect is the growth of establishments offering lunchtime refreshment to the women who could not return to their own homes in the midday break, and who often had no facilities for eating sandwiches and the like at their places of work. Even at that time, it was not respectable for unaccompanied women to frequent public houses; the places where for centuries the men in offices and shops had gone for refreshment when they could not go home for it.

CHART VI
Numbers of on-licensed premises in England and Wales, and Scotland in four census years.
England and Wales: thousands. Scotland: hundreds.

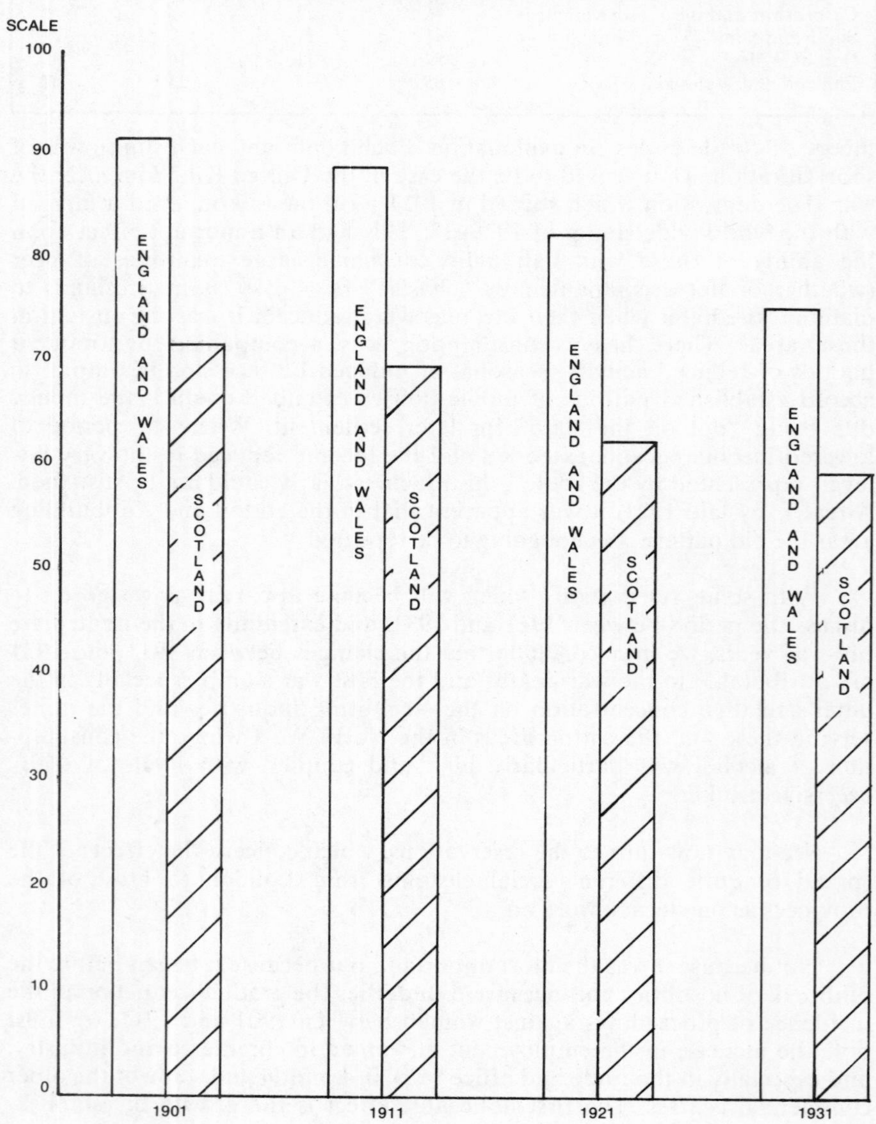

The "tea-shop" began to expand in the commercial centres before the war and the considerable increase in the employment opportunities for women which occurred after the war, and which were expanded by the dearth of young men, led to something of an explosion in the early twenties. This was the era of Lyons, ABC, Express Dairies and the like, and Lyons' "Nippies" became a household word, and, of course, made even more popular that type of employment for young women. This was to make accessible, and even more convenient than the public houses, a place where the male office worker could get his lunch more cheaply than in the pub, especially when the price of beer was compared with the price of a cup of tea. From their establishment as noontime resorts, the tea-rooms went on to make a feature of tea, itself, and then took over as the place of resort after office-hours, especially for the young men and women taking time to meet and court before catching the rising number of suburban trains and trams which were reaching out further and further from the centre of the cities. The tea-shop, therefore, took away some of the previously natural growth of patrons of the public house, and those in the very ages most prone to inebriety out of inexperience with strong or over-much drink. Before leaving the topic of competition for the pub, we need to note the equally explosive expansion of the "milk-bar" under the sponsorship of the Milk Marketing Board from about 1928 onwards. These snack bars were even cheaper than the tea-shops – a factor of importance to the young at all times – but they also permitted of quicker ingestion of the light meal, leaving more time out of the hour available from the office for other pursuits. Even more than the tea-shops, these milk-bars remained open late into the evening, and became an almost complete subsitute for the public house in the central urban areas. Taken together, these outlets for the non-alcoholic beverages meant that no young woman needed to go near a public house and, as was to be expected, the presence of young women in such places of refreshment drew young men away from the pubs in the evening, too.

Not only did the pub come to suffer competition from places of refreshment; both the pub and the music hall – a pub with music for the most part – become the victims of the rapidly growing numbers of cinemas, first in the centres of the larger towns and then in small towns and the suburbs of the big ones. The music hall had an unsavoury reputation for turning out large numbers of noisy, inebriated patrons after the late sessions; the cinemas, seldom possessing any bar licence at all, turned out even larger numbers of sober young men and women from the "last house" and the change on the streets was especially noticeable. Growing in numbers at the same time, but somewhat more restricted in their appeal, were the dance halls. Many of these did have licensed bars, but the presence of the young women who were their mainstay had a limiting effect upon the amount of liquor taken aboard by their eventual dancing partners, and the exercise and the ministrations of the supervising staff were normally sufficient to ensure an equally sober if rather more noisy exodus when the late sessions were over.

While the opportunities of spending time and money in the evening at places other than the pubs and music halls were increasing, so were the opportunities of spending money generally which might have gone on drink for lack of more exciting avenues of expenditure.

More ways of betting and watching evening sport

The opportunities of betting before the 1914–18 War were largely confined to placing bets with bookmakers at local public houses and, by runners, at their houses during the day. There was an evening trade, but the police made it a *sub-rosa* affair. The introduction of greyhound racing in local stadia, with most of the races run by floodlight after working hours, created a much more immediate betting situation, and there is plenty of evidence that many of those who would otherwise have been in music halls and public houses were to be found at the tracks. There the betting was no more profitable for the punter than it had been in the more traditional *milieux,* but, at least, the loser had the satisfaction of seeing how his choice had performed. There was also so many more opportunities of placing bets, and that, in the end, meant even less to spend on beer and spirits.

After 1928, it is safe to say that the "Football Pools" had arrived. While Wednesday evening was the time sacrosanct for the completion of the weekly "forecast", the money that had to be set aside for repaying the "credit" with the coupon for the next week came out of the wage-earner's pocket, and not out of the housekeeping. Since it takes quite a lot of money to get sufficiently drunk to attract the attention of the police, the result of this enforced saving was further to dampen down the numbers of proceedings.

Expenditure upon the motor-car was a feature of the early- and mid-thirties, rather than the decade after 1921, so far as the young were concerned, but that delay did not apply to the motor cycle. The early motor cyclist had been rather an adventurous solitary, but the perfection of the machine under the pressures of wartime use meant that very serviceable motor cycles were available for the young at quite cheap prices from 1919 onwards. The early, and continuing, popularity of pedal cycling meant that there was no dearth of young men qualified to ride cycles, even if prone to exceed that qualification on the rather powerful machines which were most popular with the young. Once again, what had been spent on the machine, its upkeep, modification, embellishment and fuelling, was no longer available to spend upon drink.

Buying a home and furnishing it

So far we have been dealing with the personal expenditure patterns of the single person, and the married man spending upon himself. The decade after the first World War saw a new interest in the home by the young married man. Perhaps it would be more correct to say that a habit of the lower-middle classes came to be within the scope of the upper and middle working class and, in some areas of the country, of even the lowest paid.

The interest took three forms which transferred money from more personal spending to spending upon the home. Whether the home was being bought or rented, it became customary to furnish much of it with new equipment, such as beds, drawing-room suites, tables, etc., while the cooking arrangements often required the renting or purchase of gas or electric ovens. There came into increasing existence the establishments eager to help in these endeavours by providing the rather larger sums at credit than the working classes had hitherto been able to command. Hire-purchase, although often abused by both suppliers and customers, nevertheless brought new comfort and pride into the home, and with its weekly instalments to be met, further restricted the money available for drink.

Again, whether the house was rented or being bought, most of the new housing was set in places where a fair amount of ground was available for a flower and vegetable garden. A vegetable garden can be a producer of savings in the household budget, but it requires the investment of both time and money by the man in the house, while the benefit is felt in monetary terms by the woman and that, at a later season.

With the migration of younger people from the depressed areas of the north east and north west of England, and from South Wales, to London and the more prosperous Midlands, there arose a demand for new housing and, with the taking up of employment by the new migrants, an ability to pay rather more than the rentals that such housing would normally command. Further, the arrangements previously made by the building societies for relief of income tax upon the interest on loans for house purchase for the benefit of their pre-war members proved to be attractive to the new family formers and the migrants alike. A large number of speculative builders became active in the suburbs of the main centres of growth in and around London and in the Midlands, so that the choice open to the newly-married became wide. Eventually, by the early thirties, the choice of houses in the £500 to £700 bracket had become considerable and, with interest rates at the low levels of that time, the level of income necessary to acquire a new house proportionately lowered.

The two kinds of instalment and seasonal investment of disposable income already mentioned, applied in full measure to the buyers of these new houses and siphoned off much that might earlier have been spent upon excessive drinking.

Fewer public houses meant less convenient access to drink

The numbers of licensed houses in both England and Wales and Scotland had been declining for some time even before 1900, and the decline continued up to 1914 in the face of a rising population, and a rise in the disposable income of the working classes. The decade from 1911 to 1921 witnessed a greater fall in both Scotland and south of the border, but the numbers did not fall quite as much in the next ten years. However, the rather slower rate of decline tends to mask a real change in the situation after the war.

Up to the migrations from 1925 onwards, the closing of public houses had not meant much difference in the accessibility of houses of refreshment.

There were, in most densely-populated areas, more than enough such pubs, so that the closure of any one meant the transfer of custom to another in the near neighbourhood, and (often the incentive for the closure) rather better utilization of the resources of the remaining licensed houses. After 1925, this was not necessarily the case. Not only was there a depopulation of many of the most densely-inhabited areas in the depressed areas, so that the patronage for all the local pubs fell off, but the migrating potential patrons were ever more frequently housed in the newer suburbs of the more prosperous Midlands and London.

The provision of public houses in such developing areas is always at a rate slower than the increase in the numbers of houses, partly as a result of the reluctance of the local licensing magistrates to grant new licences, partly as a result of the objections of licensees in the neighbourhood, but mainly because the brewers who will be investing in the new facilities have long come to know that the propensity to consume liquor at local public-houses is slow to grow, what with the demands upon the purses of the new house-owners and the greater attractions of established houses in the central parts of the towns and cities. To some extent, the expectation of slow growth in turnover at such new public houses is self-justifying, in that the reluctance of the brewers to invest ahead of the demand means that the mobile demand is expressed elsewhere, and will later prove difficult to transfer back to the new local amenity.

To the other influences converging towards a tendency for the young to spend less upon intoxicating liquor, at least in the more prosperous regions of England and Wales, we may therefore add a diminution in the ease of access to public-houses, so that some falling away of the incidence of proceedings for drunkenness between 1921 and 1931 is only to be expected. It is, however, very difficult on the statistics available for the period, to say where and to what extent the different influences played a part. Indeed, given the spread of national newspapers and other media, modes of behaviour appropriate to the Metropolis and its suburbs were frequently taken up in the provinces in circumstances of quite a different nature, but, once established, produced the environment in which they became appropriate, even in the worst of the depressed areas.

Consumption decreases less than proceedings in general

As will be seen from Chart VII, opposite, the consumption of beer did not decline at the same rate as the numbers of proceedings between 1900 and 1921 in either Scotland or England and Wales, but from 1921 to 1931 the rate of fall is roughly the same as that of drunkenness. On the other hand, there is a dramatic drop in the actual amount of spirits consumed in Scotland between each of the census years, a fall paralleled in England and Wales up to 1921, but not thereafter. The consumption of wine cannot be allocated as between the two nations, and there is an upsurge from 1921 to 1931, mainly brought about by the inroads of the cheaper and taxation-favoured wines from the British Empire.

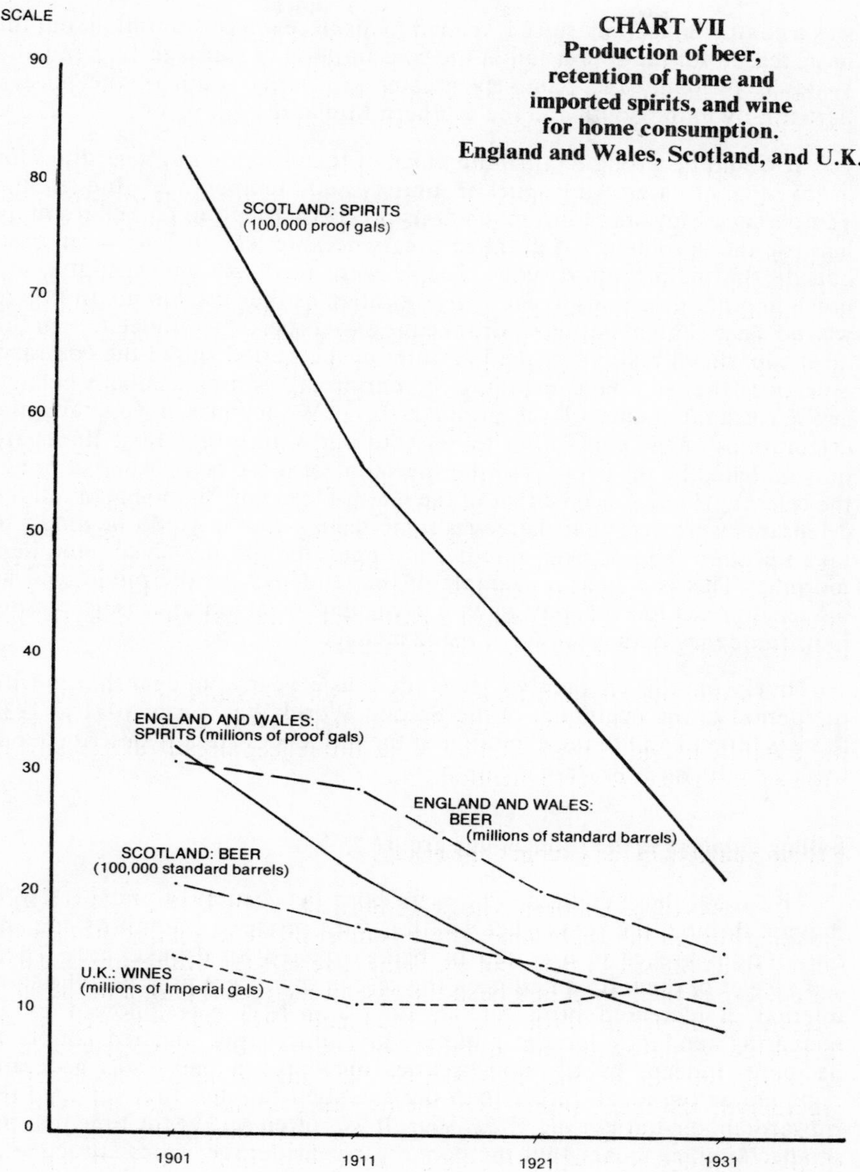

CHART VII
Production of beer, retention of home and imported spirits, and wine for home consumption. England and Wales, Scotland, and U.K.

The literature of the time is much taken up with the growing importance of the cocktail, a form of consumption of alcohol originating from America and often dispensed at so-called American bars. It is possible that this fashion accounts for the resistance of spirits consumption in England and Wales to the influences which led to the great reduction in consumption in Scotland, but too much weight cannot be given to what was, at its height, a habit confined to a small part of the middle and upper classes. The growth in the popularity of sherry among women of most classes, especially as the cheaper Empire sherries achieved full distribution, was a contra-indication, since it tended to displace gin consumption, but the basic reason for the slower fall in the consumption of spirits in England and Wales is probably the relatively greater prosperity south of the border, particularly in the South and the southern Midlands.

It would be wrong to attribute much of the decrease in proceedings for drunkenness to a growing spirit of sobriety and "temperance". Indeed, the Temperance Movement lost much of its pre-1914 attention potential simply because the "problem" of drunken excess became less obvious — at least, outside the main seaport areas. People were too busy and spending too much in other directions to get "tight" as often as they used to do. But there was no clear condemnation of drunkenness as a social evil. Indeed, even the most superficial reading of the literature of the period shows the contrary. Sowing of the wild oats, including the purloining of a policeman's helmet, are a constant theme of the popular P. G. Wodehouse novels, and the celebrations of the crews after the Oxford and Cambridge Boat Races are only matched by the exploits of the spectators of those races, whether or not the celebrants had graced either of the seats of learning. By no means all the celebrants were arrested: there was some feeling that it would be unfair to take up more than a token number to appear before the "beak" the next morning. This is a special example of the tendency for the public and its officers to react less severely when a particular social nuisance is decreasing in its frequency than when it is a rising menace.

In closing this chapter, we leave the census years and deal shortly with the period to the beginning of the Second World War. From 1931 to 1938 there is little to add to the evolution of the influences already described, but two new influences deserve mention.

Falling numbers in the younger age groups

By 1934, those children who were born between 1914 and 1918 were moving through the years when youth is most prone to commit its one and only serious breach in decorum by being arrested for drunkenness. There were fewer of them than had been the case in the recent past, and the short interval of increased birth rate in 1920 and 1921 was followed by an increasing tendancy for the numbers of children per married couple to decrease. Indeed, by the mid-twenties the "pigeon pair" was generally regarded as the ideal, rather than the extended families that survived the Edwardian age but not the Great War. It was often said at the time that the smaller families meant that the home was considerably more attractive to the father than it had been with large families and an increasing difficulty in hiring the servants with which to cope. Insofar as this was the case, here is another influence tending towards sobriety. The entry of radio into the home may be held to be yet another influence tending in the same direction.

Suburbs mean long travel to and from the home and empty city centres

The other new influence, at least in the cities (where most of the offences occur in practice), was the extension of the housing of the inhabitants into the surrounding countryside. In the provinces the exodus in the evening was largely accomplished by tram and bus. In London the Metropolitan Railway opened up an area equivalent to the size of the whole of London some decades earlier. The radial lines of the Underground were also extended to produce a comparable extension in other directions, and the Southern Railway came in to "colonize" south of the Thames. The actual travelling times in the vehicles were not often much more than half an hour, but the journey from office to train and from train to home made up the greater part of an hour, and was very tiring in the rush hours in the evening. The thought of a return to "enjoy" what the centre of the city had to offer was seldom agreeable. If the suburbanite had stayed on in town to see a film or a play, the early ending of the train and bus services, and the numbers going on them, was a potent sanction against staying longer and "painting the town red". Suburbanites were sober people with good practical reason.

CHAPTER 18

DIFFERENCES BETWEEN SCOTLAND, ENGLAND AND WALES

Great Britain is a single economic community despite the differences in laws, social habits and, it is said, temperaments north and south of the border. The more influential occurrences during the war and its aftermath will have visible effects in both countries, albeit with differing amplitudes and timing. It would be tiresome to rehearse these influences in any great detail, but it will assist in brevity if some are mentioned in advance of the exposition of the history of drunkenness in Scotland, and in England and Wales.

As will be seen from the second and third graphs which are used to illustrate this chapter, it is the fluctuations in the per capita consumption of spirits which appear to exert the greatest influence on the number of offences of drunkenness; though this has been less evident among females than among males until recently. This is not, of course, to say that beer drinkers do not get drunk – they do, and in great numbers. But there is a fine, John Bull-ish steadiness about inebriated beer drinkers. As youngsters, they are probably as prone to intoxication on beer as they are on spirits, out of sheer ignorance and inexperience. As they grow older and stouter, it takes substantially more beer to produce the same results. Inebriety requires either steady, silent drinking or the stimulus of some grand occasion for consuming the remarkably large amounts of water necessary to achieve a degree of intoxication sufficient to attract the attention of the police. Such grand occasions are not frequent, but they do recur, and the victims go on to sustain the statistics.

No such heroic endurance is needed to get tight on spirits. It is just as expensive, but the amount consumed is smaller, and so is the time needed by the dedicated drinker. As will become apparent in the discussion, the individual who habitually drinks spirits rather than beer will appear before the magistrates more often. It follows that the national statistics of drunkenness will reflect the consumption of spirits more strongly than they will the consumption of beer. More spirits does not mean more occasions to celebrate, any more than more beer does; but more spirits, given the same number of occasions and near-occasions, will produce more inebriety.

With this in mind, it is clear that the rise of some 30 per cent in the per capita consumption of beer at the end of the war need not be expected to counterbalance the effects of the 25 per cent reduction in the per capita consumption of spirits (as against that in 1937 and 1938, in both cases). Nor did it, after all allowances are made for the absence of men in the services. Male drunkenness in Scotland was, even in 1949, only one-third of what it had been in 1937; this was a much sharper reduction than that in England and Wales, where the 1949 figure was 75 per cent of that for 1937. Very broadly, the experience among women was proportionately similar.

From 1949 to 1956 the per capita consumption of spirits climbed slowly and hesitantly back to the pre-war levels, while that of beer sank equally slowly to rather below that experienced in 1938. The recovery of spirits, and the relative decline of beer, was accompanied by a doubling of the number of arrests for drunkenness among males in both Scotland and England and Wales – but by no significant alteration in the offences by females anywhere.

TABLE IA

The common background of consumption per head of beer, spirits and wine in the United Kingdom, with consumption per head in 1937 taken as datum = 100.

Year	Index per capita consumption of Beer	Spirits	Wine
1937	100	100	100
1938	105	100	100
1939	106	92	97
1940	108	100	95
1941	110	88	84
1942	126	88	43
1943	123	81	22
1944	126	81	19
1945	130	73	19
1946	137	76	27
1947	122	81	46
1948	125	81	59
1949	112	73	46
1950	106	81	51
1951	102	92	59
1952	102	77	62
1953	101	81	59
1954	100	88	62
1955	97	92	70
1956	99	100	76
1957	99	104	81
1958	98	112	84
1959	95	112	84
1960	103	115	97
1961	105	127	111
1962	108	127	114
1963	108	131	119
1964	110	142	135
1965	111	150	146
1966	112	131	143
1967	115	138	149
1968	115	150	176
1969	117	138	178
1970	121	138	165
1971	126	154	189
1972	130	173	214
1973	131	192	251
1974	140	250	322
1975	140	254	305

The situation after 1956 became more complicated. Table IA gives the annual per capita consumption of beer, spirits and wine for each year from 1937 to 1975, expressed as index numbers with the per capita consumption in 1937 being represented by 100 in each case. It will be seen that the consumption of beer, per capita, fell slightly until 1959, and then rose slowly until 1966, accelerating quite uncharacteristically thereafter. The per capita consumption of wine was, absolutely, low in 1937, but post-war indulgence did not even achieve the 1937 levels until 1961. There was a rise to 143 per cent of the 1937 level by 1966, to be followed by more than a doubling of this in the eight years to 1974.

The consumption of spirits was affected by the gradual release to the home market of whisky first put down in 1949. To some extent, these new supplies of mature whisky displaced the rum and gin which had been the more important substitutes under whisky rationing. But they were additional supplies, and the eventual effect was an increase in spirits consumption overall of some 30 per cent with a short-lived peak of 50 per cent increase in 1964 and 1965.

CHART IA

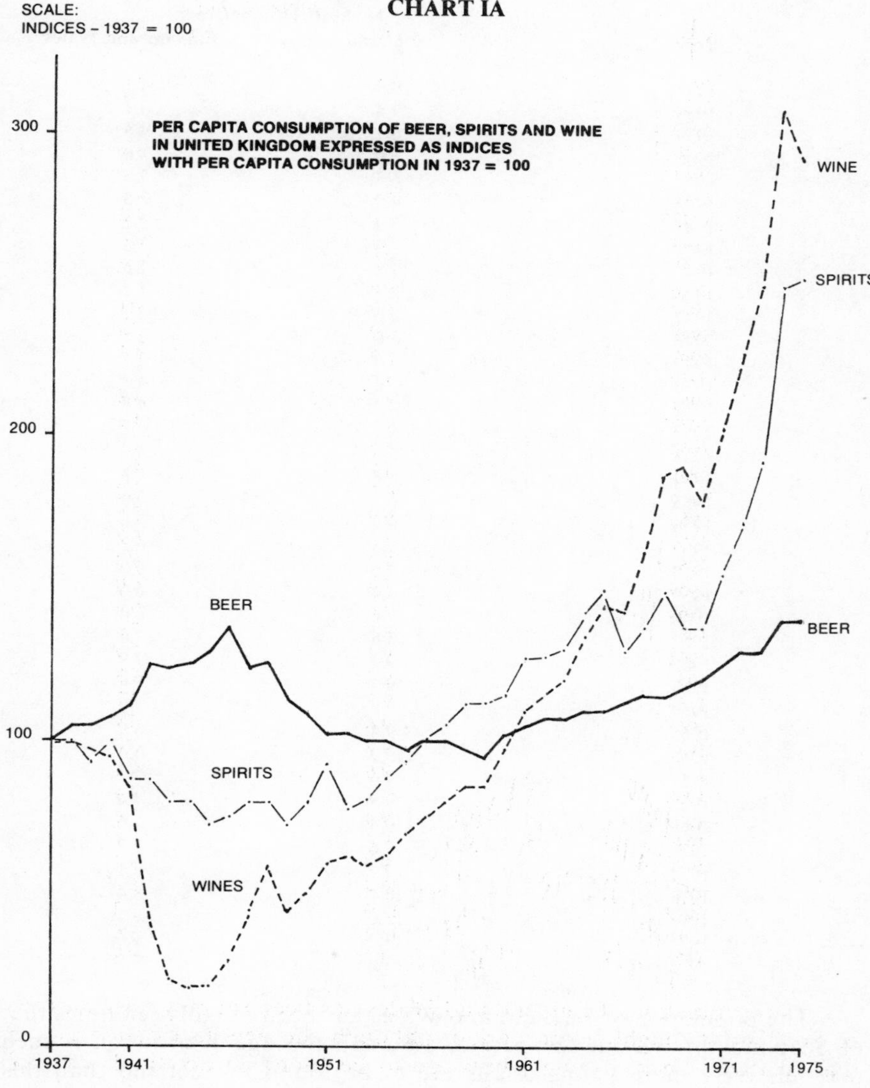

The figures in Table IA are expressed graphically in Chart IA. It will be seen that, as in the case of wine, there was a doubling of the annual per capita consumption of spirits between 1966 and 1975. In both cases, the increases are contemporary with the appearance and multiplication of off-licensed departments in supermarkets, advertising wines and spirits (and, later canned beer) at cut prices. Both the use of wines and spirits as inducements for new customers, and the higher incidence of value added tax on beer bought by the glass, were bound to lead to a shift in the pattern of consumption which is apparent on the chart.

TABLE IB

Convictions of drunkenness, all males, in Scotland (thousands), and England and Wales (tens of thousands), 1937 to 1975.

	Male Drunkenness	
Year	**Scotland**	**England and Wales**
1937	9.9	4.1
1938	9.4	4.1
1939	10.1	4.6
1940	9.0	4.0
1941	6.8	3.5
1942	4.2	2.3
1943	3.3	2.2
1944	2.2	1.8
1945	1.8	1.6
1946	2.3	1.7
1947	3.0	2.1
1948	3.0	2.8
1949	3.4	3.1
1950	3.8	4.3
1951	4.4	4.8
1952	4.9	4.9
1953	5.6	4.9
1954	5.8	4.8
1955	6.3	5.0
1956	6.9	5.6
1957	7.5	6.2
1958	7.0	6.0
1959	7.4	6.0
1960	7.6	6.4
1961	8.8	7.0
1962	9.1	7.9
1963	9.7	7.8
1964	9.8	7.2
1965	9.4	6.9
1966	9.7	6.6
1967	9.6	7.1
1968	9.9	7.4
1969	9.4	7.6
1970	9.6	7.7
1971	9.7	8.1
1972	10.4	8.4
1973	12.0	9.3
1974	13.2	9.6
1975	13.2	9.7

The population of England and Wales has been roughly ten times that of Scotland throughout the period, although the age-distribution is such that relatively more young adults are to be found in Scotland than this would indicate. For the present, however, the actual convictions for drunkenness among all males, if expressed in terms of thousands for Scotland and in tens of thousands for England and Wales, do give a sound indication of the incidence of proved offences in the two countries.

Objection to such comparison is frequently made because it is said that what policemen regard as "being drunk" is largely a variable and subjective value-judgement. This can well be the case, but broken windows and obstreperous or comatose men are awkwardly factual whatever the police district or the nationality. Further, when one is concerned with movements of large numbers over time, and of comparisons of such movements, as we have in the table and the illustrative graph below, the maintenance of sustained departures, as against the play of random influences, as a result of official attitudes becomes impossible to conceive.

CHART IB

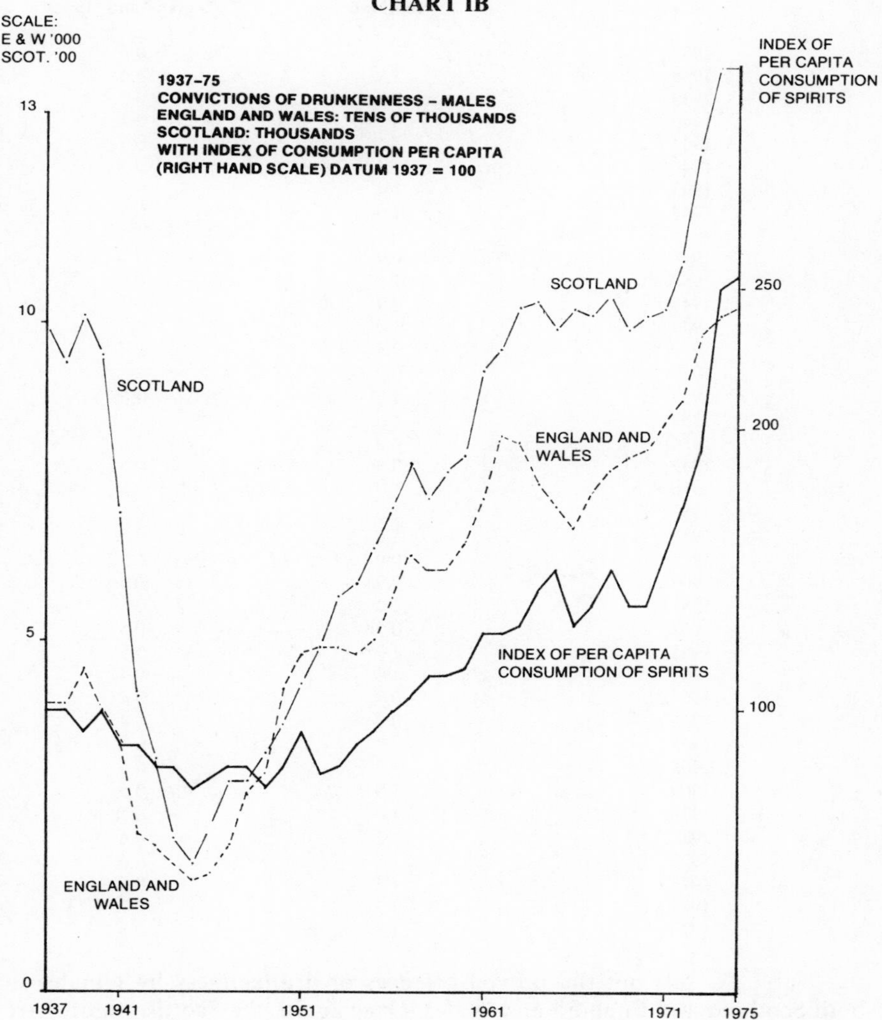

As the graph shows, a change of massive dimensions occurred between 1937 and 1950. Not only was male drunkenness substantially lowered – but the incidence of offences in Scotland, more than twice that in England and Wales in 1937, was roughly equal in 1950. The incidence in both countries rose with the increased consumption of spirits until the late 1960s, that for Scotland rather more rapidly than in England and Wales. It was not, however, until 1971 that a 50 per cent greater incidence was registered, and that was contemporary with the doubling of the annual per capita consumption of spirits in the United Kingdom.

TABLE IC

Convictions of drunkenness, all females, in Scotland (thousands), and England and Wales (tens of thousands), 1937 to 1975.

Year	Female Drunkenness Scotland	England and Wales
1937	3.1	0.6
1938	2.9	0.6
1939	2.9	0.7
1940	2.5	0.7
1941	2.0	0.6
1942	1.4	0.5
1943	1.4	0.5
1944	1.0	0.5
1945	0.7	0.4
1946	0.9	0.4
1947	1.0	0.4
1948	0.9	0.5
1949	1.0	0.5
1950	0.9	0.5
1951	0.9	0.5
1952	1.0	0.5
1953	1.0	0.5
1954	1.0	0.5
1955	0.9	0.5
1956	1.0	0.5
1957	1.0	0.5
1958	1.0	0.5
1959	0.9	0.5
1960	0.9	0.4
1961	1.0	0.5
1962	0.9	0.5
1963	1.0	0.5
1964	1.0	0.4
1965	0.9	0.4
1966	0.9	0.4
1967	0.9	0.4
1968	1.0	0.5
1969	1.0	0.5
1970	1.0	0.5
1971	1.2	0.6
1972	1.3	0.6
1973	1.5	0.6
1974	1.5	0.7
1975	1.8	0.8

Table IC sets out the proved offences of drunkenness by females in both Scotland and England and Wales. Once again, the Scottish figures are expressed as thousands and those in England and Wales as tens of thousands. Thus, in 1937, 3,100 offences by women in Scotland compare with 6,000 offences by women in England and Wales. The relative incidence is five to one, incomparably worse than the pre-war position among men on either side of the border.

Contrary, again, to the experience among male offenders, while the absolute incidence in both countries fell sharply, the relative incidence did not close up so quickly, so that recovery from war restrictions still found Scottish females twice as likely to be guilty of drunkenness as their English counterparts.

CHART IC

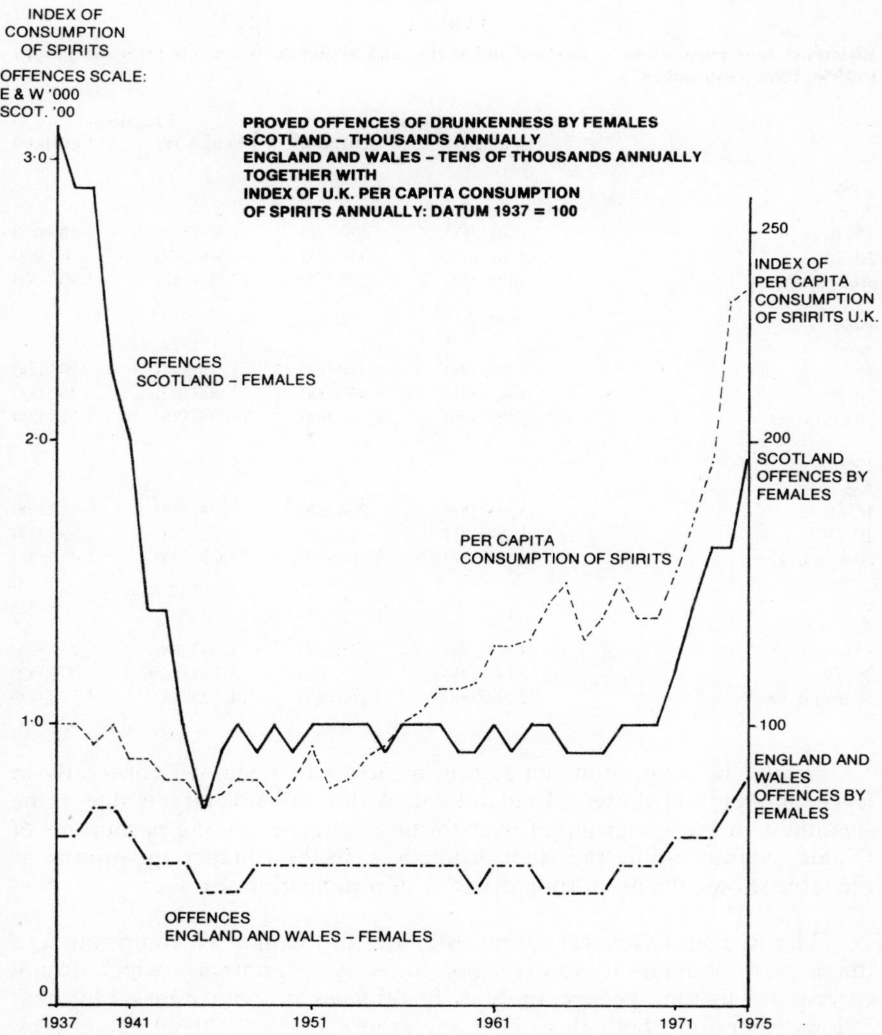

As Chart IC, illustrating the figures in Table IC, shows, there was not the same reaction to the increasing supplies and consumption of spirits among women. With a slightly rising total population, the incidence of drunkenness among both Scottish and English females must be taken as going down from 1950 to 1966.

The change thereafter was comparatively slight in England and Wales – for females of all ages. This has certainly not been the case in Scotland where the numbers of offences and, with stagnating population, the incidence of offences, has doubled.

So much for the broad picture, interesting enough in its differences. When the analysis goes deeper – into age and sex groups – differences multiply.

TABLE II

Estimated June populations of England and Wales, and Scotland, by sex and three age groups in 1956, 1960, 1966 and 1975.

	Males		Females	
	E. and W.	Scotland	E. and W.	Scotland
1956				
Age				
15–19	1,400,000	170,000	1,400,000	190,000
20–29	2,900,000	340,000	2,900,000	360,000
30 and over	12,000,000	1,290,000	13,900,000	1,500,000
1960				
Age				
15–19	1,600,000	190,000	1,500,000	190,000
20–29	2,900,000	330,000	2,900,000	350,000
30 and over	12,200,000	1,300,000	14,200,000	1,510,000
1966				
Age				
15–19	1,900,000	200,000	1,800,000	210,000
20–29	3,200,000	320,000	3,100,000	330,000
30 and over	12,600,000	1,260,000	14,400,000	1,470,000
1975				
Age				
15–19	1,800,000	220,000	1,700,000	210,000
20–29	3,600,000	370,000	3,300,000	370,000
30 and over	12,700,000	1,260,000	14,700,000	1,500,000

While the total adult population in Scotland remained constantly at levels one-tenth of those in England and Wales, this was largely due to the steadiness in the age-group of over-thirties, with the varying porportons of females countervailing the other differences. In the younger age-groups, as the table shows, the proportion differed, as it did within sexes.

The Registrar General's June Estimates of the age/sex composition of the *de facto* population are expressed in five-year groupings which do not correspond to the age/sex analyses of offences of drunkenness. In what follows, therefore, both the 15–19 age-groups and the 20–29 age-groups, have been used as guides rather than exact determinants of the ratio of Scottish population to that of England and Wales in the age/sex groups of:

Males aged under 21:	Scottish population 1/8th England and Wales
Females aged under 21:	Scottish population 1/8th England and Wales
Males aged 21–29:	Scottish population 1/9th England and Wales
Females aged 21–29:	Scottish population 1/9th England and Wales
Males aged 30 and over:	Scottish population 1/10th England and Wales
Females aged 30 and over:	Scottish population 1/10th England and Wales

These proportions are applied in the following tables.

TABLE III

Proved offences of drunkenness by males aged under twenty-one in Scotland and in England and Wales, together with estimates of offences in Scotland if the population in the age/sex group were the same size as that in England and Wales, that is, × 8.

Year	Total offences in England and Wales	Scotland	Scotland × eight
1956	5127	347	2776
1957	5905	438	3504
1958	6029	464	3712
1959	6299	536	4288
1960	7579	553	4424
1961	8733	657	5256
1962	9096	645	5160
1963	8924	635	5080
1964	9037	800	6400
1965	9712	798	6384
1966	9677	961	7688
1967	10710	989	7912
1968	11602	1002	8016
1969	12295	903	7224
1970	13095	1026	8208
1971	13462	1071	8568
1972	14088	1097	8776
1973	17383	1325	10600
1974	18937	1412	11295
1975	18828	1420	11360

Table III gives the actual number of proved offences of drunkenness by males aged under twenty-one in England and Wales and in Scotland for the twenty years since 1956 during which the Home Office statistics distinguish between males and females. The Scottish Office data makes the distinction earlier, but comparisons cannot safely be extended backwards into the previous years.

The third column repeats the Scottish data, but as multiplied by eight. The population of males aged under twenty-one in Scotland has fluctuated around one-eighth of that in England and Wales over the period, as the approximating data in Table II indicates. There are two elements militating against too great a nicety in calculating the inter-country proportions. The first is the fact that drunkenness amongst the under eighteens is not reliably reflected in the convictions *per se;* there are a number of charges which can be preferred in lieu of drunkenness and police forces, who are properly concerned to guide the young offender to moderation, vary in the extent to which they use the alternatives. The second is the approximate nature of the estimates made by the Registrar General in the inter-censal years. Nevertheless, as there is no reason to suppose systematic biases to increase or decrease as these influences affect Scotland on the one hand, and England and Wales on the other, multiplication of the Scottish totals by eight allows a more facile comparison of the fluctuations in incidence.

CHART II

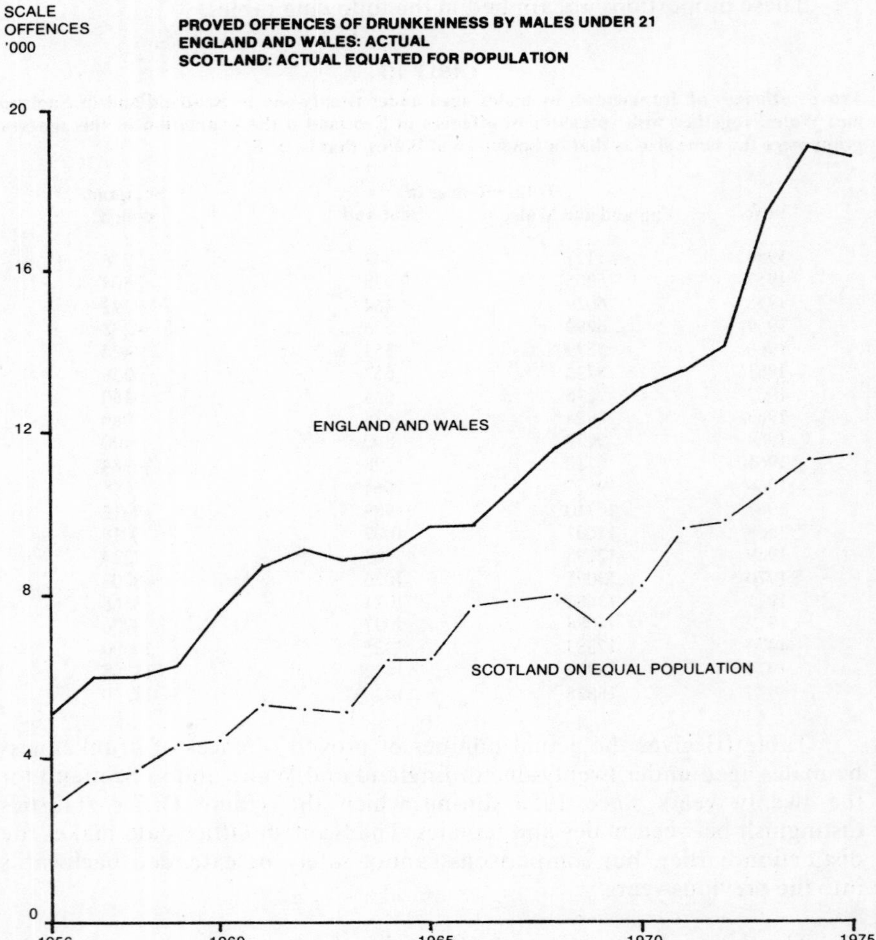

Chart II shows how the actual numbers of offences in England and Wales compare with the figures derived by multiplying the actual offences in Scotland by eight, so as to equate the approximate incidences. It will be seen that the incidence of offences of drunkenness per mille of males aged under twenty-one is consistently lower than that in England and Wales. The difference is not a steady one – the Scottish incidences in the 1950s were about one-half those of England and Wales, but they rose to just on 80 per cent in 1966, falling back to 63 per cent in 1970 and to 60 per cent in 1975. Both curves are levelling off in 1974 and 1975.

It is not generally realized that this lower tendency to be arrested for offences of drunkenness is a characteristic of Scottish youths. Before further comments can be made usefully, the behaviour of the other age/sex groupings needs to be studied.

TABLE IV

Proved offences of drunkenness by males aged twenty-one but under thirty in Scotland and in England and Wales, together with estimates of offences in Scotland if the population of the age/sex group were the same size as that in England and Wales, that is, × 9.

Year	Total offences in England and Wales	Total offences in Scotland	Scotland × nine
1956	14239	1223	11007
1957	15165	1410	12690
1958	14338	1272	11448
1959	14098	1336	12024
1960	15307	1319	11871
1961	16883	1584	14256
1962	18918	1464	13176
1963	17937	1705	15345
1964	16549	1658	14922
1965	16254	1633	14697
1966	15527	1637	14733
1967	16324	1646	14814
1968	17666	1647	14823
1969	17709	1493	13437
1970	18166	1479	13311
1971	19178	1409	12681
1972	19193	1503	13527
1973	21657	1737	15633
1974	22998	1870	16830
1975	23729	1927	17343

While there are not the same uncertainties about the way in which police officers will deal with persons who are simply drunk over the age of twenty-one – there being no alternatives such as purchasing under age, etc – there remains the continuing tendency for recorded offences of drunkenness significantly to understate the prevalence when more serious crimes are committed at the same time. It is not known how the matter is dealt with in Scotland – the law is such that direct and prolonged experience of its working is necessary before comparisons can safely be made – but in England and Wales the need to establish *mens rea* (a clear intention) in the committal of crime means that the police are loth to volunteer the excuse of "incapacity" where this is not inescapably established by fact.

In the table, therefore, the multiplication of the actual Scottish figures by nine is a reflection of the relative populations. It is possible, if there is substantial depression of the actual occurrences in the recorded offences in England and Wales, that the multiple should be eight, rather than nine. While, however, this would affect the general level, it is extremely unlikely that the relative variations over time would be influenced by practice south of the border. It is equally true that the generally lower per mille incidence in the age-group is most unlikely to give a false impression.

CHART III

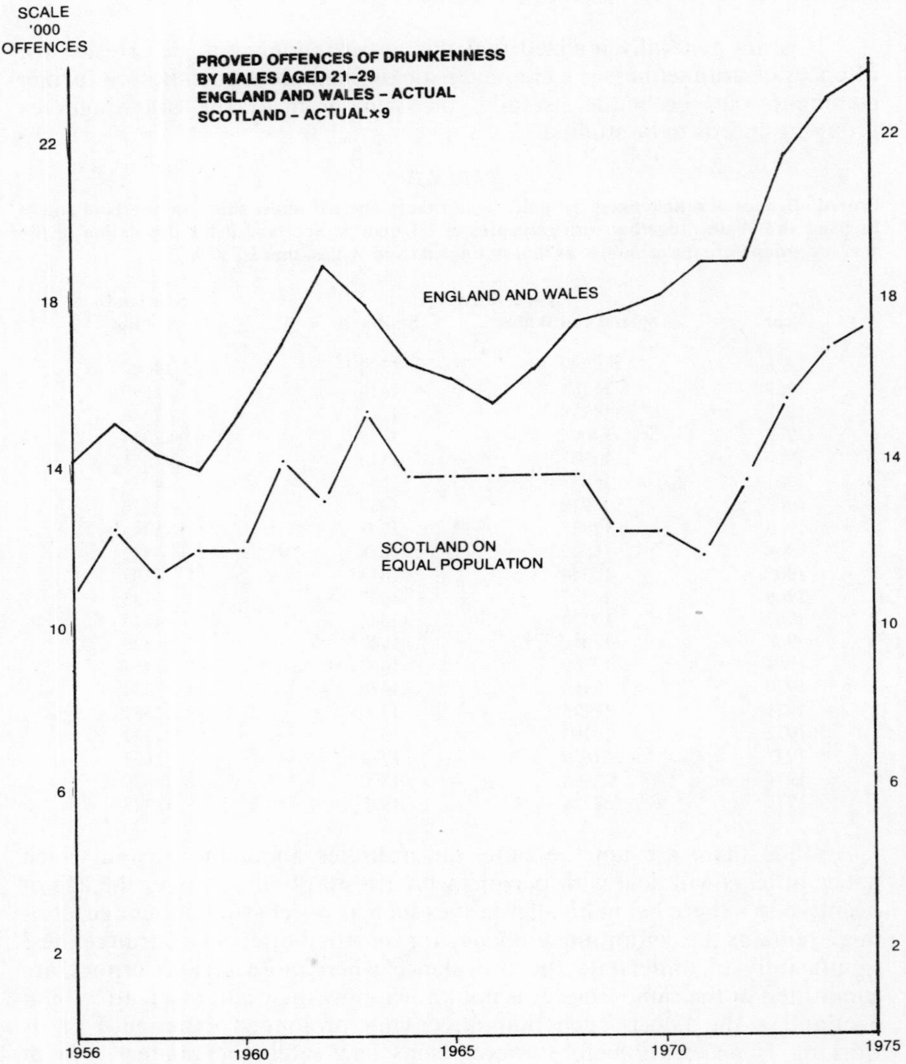

There are a number of points of interest in the graph. The generally lower incidence per mille population at risk has already been mentioned. There is also a remarkable steadiness in the total number of Scottish offences until 1972 or 1973, consistent with unvarying incidence in a more or less static population. By contrast, the incidence in England and Wales is not only rising (the population in the age/sex group does rise, but not by over 50 per cent) but is subject to substantial fluctuations – sudden increases around 1962 (the vodka syndrome) and 1972 (the cut-price licensed supermarkets), and the sharp decrease from 1962 to 1966, when the population of the age/sex group was in fact falling only slightly.

The picture of a more temperate and more stable Scottish youth is maintained.

TABLE V

Proved offences of drunkenness by males aged thirty and over in Scotland and in England and Wales, together with estimates of offences in Scotland if the population of the age/sex group were the same size as that in England and Wales, that is, × 10.

Year	Total offences in England and Wales	Total offences in Scotland	Scotland × ten
1956	36207	5329	53290
1957	40990	5662	56620
1958	38849	5261	52610
1959	40288	5538	55380
1960	40675	6289	62890
1961	44375	6516	65160
1962	51185	6975	69750
1963	51367	7491	74910
1964	46819	7364	73640
1965	43125	7013	70130
1966	41264	7110	71100
1967	44133	6981	69810
1968	44958	7283	72830
1969	45271	6974	69740
1970	45847	7087	70870
1971	48366	7258	72580
1972	50887	7767	77670
1973	53934	8969	89690
1974	54359	9907	99070
1975	53833	9856	98560

As the table shows, the situation among males aged thirty and over is radically different. The column showing the actual Scottish figures multiplied by ten is rather more reliably comparable with the actual figures for England and Wales. This is because the inter-censal estimates have proved to be reasonably close to the position established by the actual censuses than has sometimes been the case with the younger age groups, and also because there is no need for estimating the deduction to be made, for, e.g. the twenty-year-olds.

It will be seen later that it is of the greatest importance to bear in mind that the data refers to "offences" and not to persons. This is always an important point to remember in dealing with single years, but here, as will emerge from later tables, the matter has relevance over a number of years.

One possible interpretation of the table, in comparison with the two preceding tables, is that it is the Scotsmen who were born well before the war who are the real drunkards. This will not bear examination; the tables show clearly that the comparative incidence of offences, 47 per cent higher in Scotland than in England and Wales in 1956, has risen as the twenty years elapsed until it is over 80 per cent higher in 1975. Whatever the cause for the remarkable change, it is an influence that goes on affecting the behaviour of Scotsmen as they grow older, generation after generation.

CHART IV

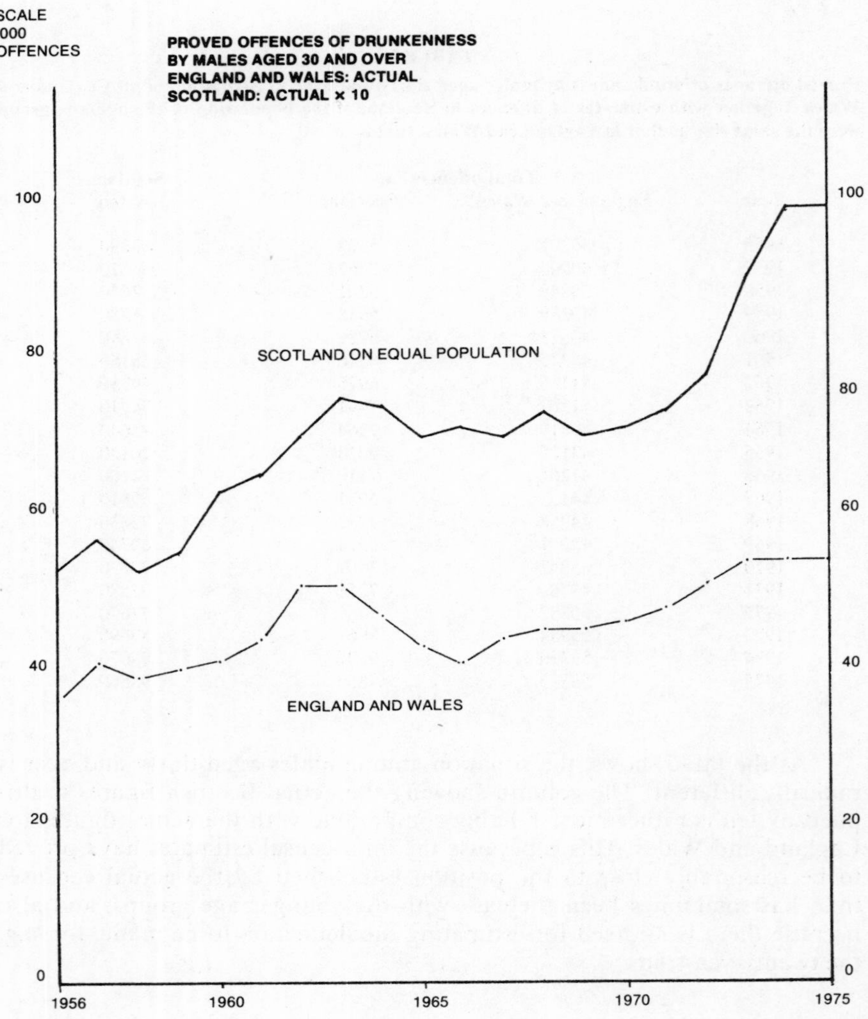

The chart, illustrating the figures in Table V, brings out another contrast with the behaviour of Scottish males aged under thirty. It will be remembered that the line depicting offences was noticeably smoother than that for the same age/sex group in England and Wales. The picture above shows the same sort of fluctuation between 1956 and 1972 – after which the Scots take off on their own for a couple of years. Previously, both the Scots and the English had reacted to the de-rationing of whisky after 1956 and, later, to the sudden growth in the popularity of vodka; the Scottish figures, influenced by the New Year celebrations rather than Christmas Eve, are lagged one calendar year.

It will be convenient to defer analysis of the surge from 1971 to 1974 until drunkenness among women has been discussed.

TABLE VI

Proved offences of drunkenness by females aged under twenty-one in Scotland and in England and Wales, together with estimates of offences in Scotland if the population in the age/sex group were the same size as that in England and Wales, that is, × 8.

Year	Total offences in England and Wales	Scotland	Scotland × eight
1956	258	28	242
1957	290	19	152
1958	268	27	216
1959	278	22	176
1960	303	22	176
1961	345	25	200
1962	311	29	232
1963	317	41	328
1964	287	33	264
1965	284	42	336
1966	297	58	464
1967	377	57	456
1968	427	83	664
1969	438	56	448
1970	589	112	896
1971	705	143	1144
1972	775	165	1320
1973	995	168	1344
1974	1213	170	1360
1975	1209	185	1480

As mentioned earlier, the approximate comparative incidence of offences of drunkenness among females aged under twenty-one is best observed when the actual figures for Scotland are multiplied by eight and then related directly to those recorded for England and Wales.

The same reservations about the data in both countries have to be made as were mentioned in the case of youths aged under twenty-one. Not only is the population "open-ended" in that we do not know with certainty at what age it is sensible to assume a more-than-rare propensity to indulge immoderately among young girls. There is also the tendency for girls in groups of young people to be protected by their escorts, and the social habits of the past twenty years have made it easy for the latter practically to carry their inert companions without attracting even a passing glance. However, observation in both countries does not suggest any great deviance in following the evolving patterns of behaviour, so that the *relative* trends and fluctuations in the figures for Scotland and for England and Wales are unlikely to be misleading as to the variation in actual drinking behaviour.

Probably the most striking contrast between the tables affecting girls and youths is the near-equality in per mille incidence across the border in the former case, and the greater moderation of Scottish youths.

CHART V

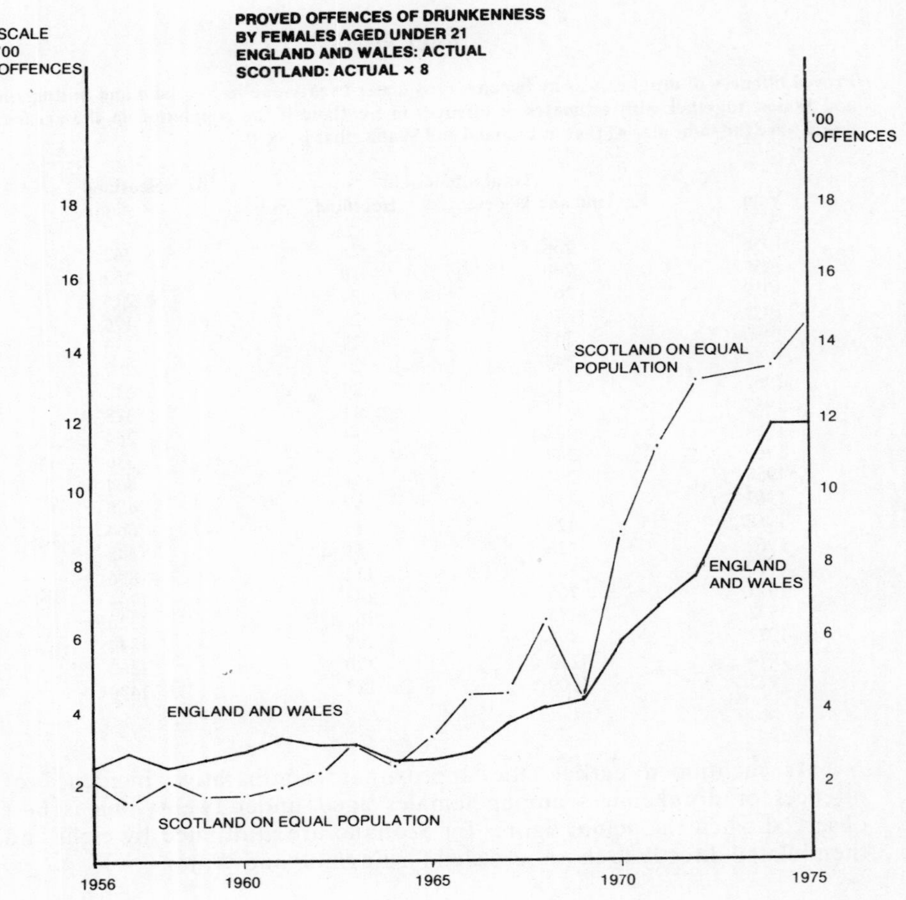

This near-quality "across the borders" is, in fact, only maintained for ten years from 1956 to 1965. As the graph shows clearly, from 1966 onwards not only is the incidence of drunken offences per mille population of females aged under twenty-one sometimes twice that south of the border, but the deterioration is "led" by the Socttish young women some two years ahead of those in England and Wales. Though it is by no means certain that the lag applies to female drunkenness to the extent that it does for men, the effect of celebration of the New Year rather than Christmas would suggest an even greater "lead".

However, the figures are actually small, and the age limits of the population group at risk so nebulous at the younger end, that it is best to seek confirmatory evidence.

TABLE VII

Proved offences of drunkenness by females aged twenty-one but under thirty in Scotland and in England and Wales, together with estimates of offences in Scotland if the population of the age/sex group were the same size as that in England and Wales, that is, × 9.

Year	Total offences in England and Wales	Scotland	Scotland × nine
1956	716	85	765
1957	760	89	801
1958	698	117	1053
1959	608	108	972
1960	588	101	909
1961	643	90	810
1962	652	88	792
1963	630	89	801
1964	609	100	900
1965	533	88	792
1966	503	98	882
1967	642	112	1008
1968	657	122	1098
1969	685	118	1062
1970	817	128	1152
1971	984	164	1476
1972	1152	157	1413
1973	1207	182	1638
1974	1398	167	1503
1975	1762	191	1719

In order to facilitate comparison with the English figures, the table contains a column in which the number of actual offences by women aged twenty-one but under thirty in Scotland are multiplied by nine.

While the "escort" effect described earlier will apply equally strongly in this age-group, there is not the same uncertainty as to the extent to which actual offences of drunkenness are diverted to less censorious titles such as "consuming under the permitted age", etc. Equally, the sizes of the populations at risk are more precisely delineated. Anyone over eighteen can be charged with drunkenness; the proportions of the Registrar-General's estimates of the population aged 20–29, inclusive, which need to be deducted to allow for the strictly twenty-year-olds are not difficult to assess, and do not differ greatly as between the two countries.

The table is interesting in that, starting with near-equality of incidence, and ending with the same near-equation in 1975, in all other years the numbers per mille females at risk is consistently and substantially higher in Scotland than it is in England and Wales. This is again in sharp contrast to the situation found among men of the same age-group, where the line representing Scottish incidence was consistently below that of offences in England and Wales. The chart brings out other interesting differences.

CHART VI

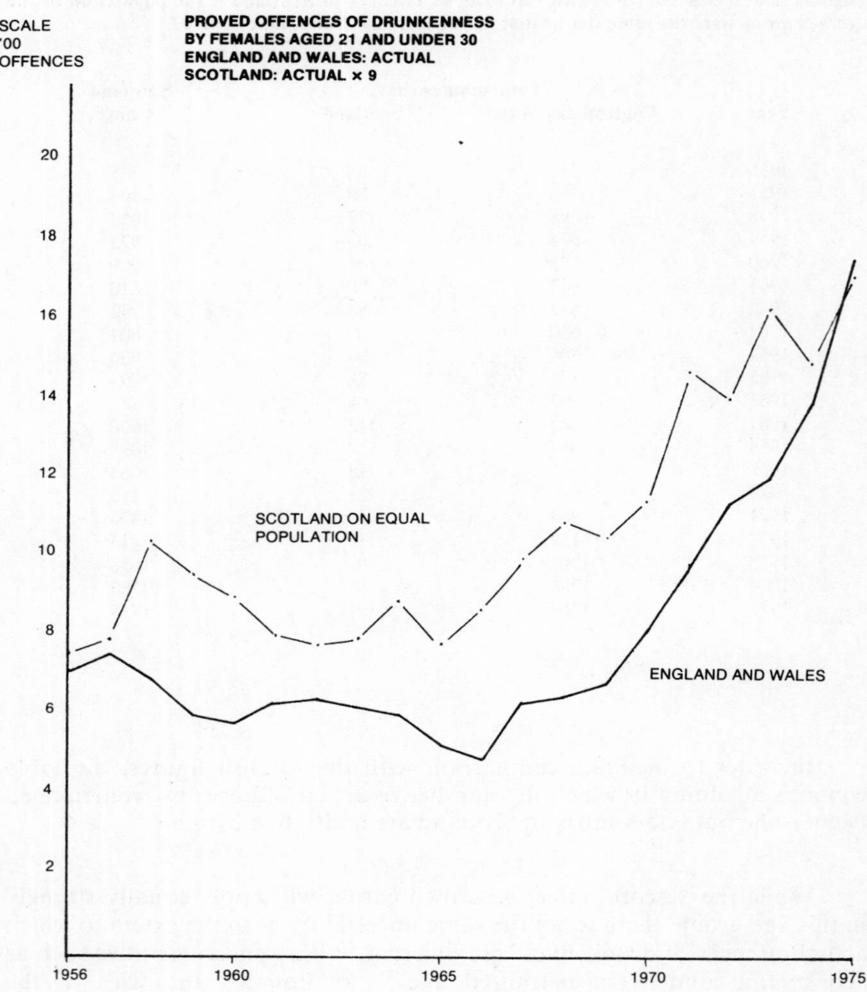

The incidence among Scottish women aged 21–29 shows a reaction to the derationing of whisky in the late 1950s which is absent in the English data. There is, now, some evidence of the one-year lag deriving from Hogmanay, but this ceases to show on the chart after 1965. From 1966 onward, it is the Scottish offences which "lead" those of England and Wales in the doubling of the former and the trebling of the latter by 1975. This is, again, in the sharpest contrast with the fluctuations and trends which we have noted in the case of young Scottish men aged 21–29.

Clearly, it is desirable to review the performance of the older women and, if possible, to bring together the similarities and differences with a view to seeking the causes thereof.

TABLES VIII

Proved offences of drunkeness by females aged thirty and over in Scotland and England and Wales, together with estimates of offences in Scotland if the population of the age/sex group were the same size as that in England and Wales, that is, × 10.

Year	Total offences in England and Wales	Scotland	Scotland × ten
1956	3635	852	8520
1957	3910	907	9070
1958	3876	851	8510
1959	3616	780	7800
1960	3357	776	7760
1961	3715	841	8410
1962	3830	795	7950
1963	3832	857	8570
1964	3541	813	8130
1965	3072	806	8060
1966	3231	754	7540
1967	3358	705	7050
1968	3760	800	8000
1969	3907	733	7330
1970	3896	762	7620
1971	4040	853	8530
1972	4103	975	9750
1973	4098	1135	11350
1974	4298	1157	11570
1975	4601	1420	14200

The numbers of women aged thirty and over in Scotland have held steady at around a million and a half throughout the period. In England and Wales the comparable population has risen from fourteen millions to just under fifteen millions in the twenty years. In the table above, the third column showing the actual numbers of offences attributable to the age/sex group multiplied by ten somewhat overstates the Scottish incidence up to about 1966, but is more-or-less comparable with the figures for England and Wales thereafter.

It is clear that the incidence of drunken offences committed by women aged thirty and over is very much higher in Scotland than it is, and has been, in England and Wales. Reference back to Table V shows that the relative deterioration is greater, although not by an order of magnitude, than was found to be the case among Scottish males in the same age-group at least until 1970. After that year, the incidence among the older Scottish women not only doubles in numbers but moves from being twice the incidence in England and Wales to being well over three times the frequency per mille population at risk.

The change is not as clearly apparent in the tables as it is in the next chart, which illustrates the table.

CHART VII

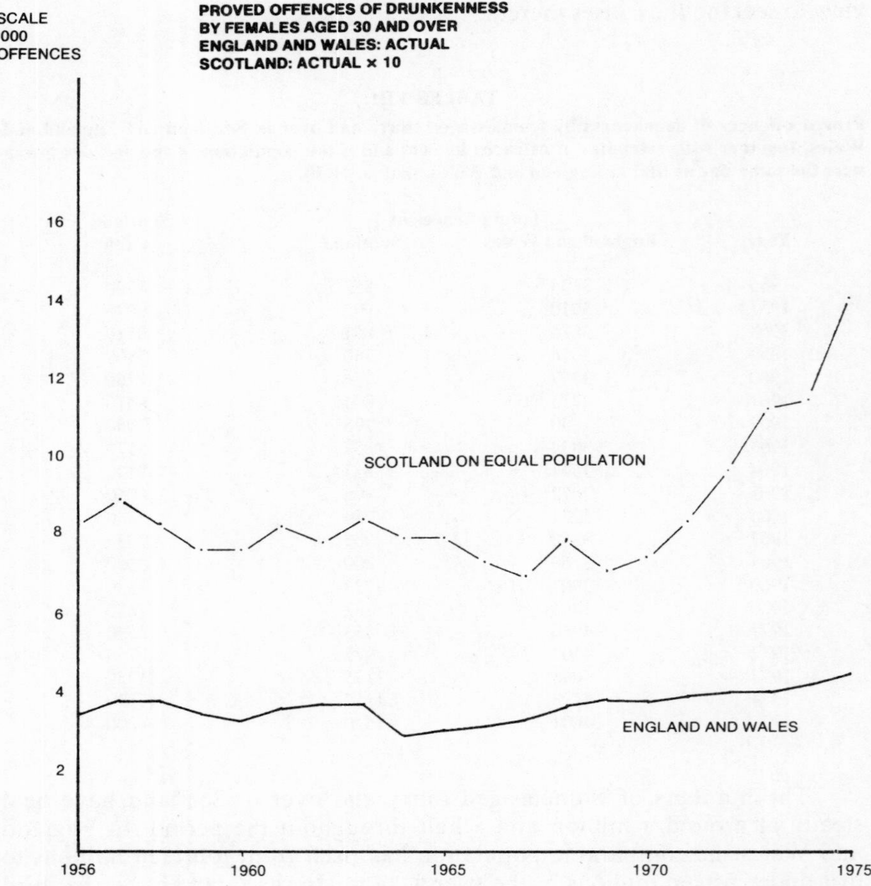

In Chart VI, illustrating the figures of Table VII, the general trend of the incidence in Scotland is clearly seen to parallel the steadiness in England and Wales, at about twice the frequency, for the first fifteen years of the period for which comparable age/sex data are available. If allowance is made for the slight over-statement of the Scottish incidence in comparison with England and Wales, due to rising numbers in England and stagnation of population in Scotland, the parallelism becomes even more strongly established. This steadiness makes the leaping figures after 1970 all the more dramatically out of historical context – to an even greater degree than with Scottish males of the same ages.

Before going on to analyse in greater detail the long-established and probably long continuing differences in the character of Scottish and English drunkenness generally, it is clearly desirable to identify the cause for the sudden jumps in incidence in some, only, of the age/sex groups after 1970, and if possible, to discount this in the historical context.

The following box-diagram summarizes the seriousness of the impacts by age/sex groups in Scotland as against England and Wales.

Females aged under-21	*Females aged 21–29*	*Males aged 30 and over*	*Females aged 30 and over*
Scotland: Very sharp deterioration	Scotland: Very sharp deterioration	Scotland: Very sharp deterioration	Scotland: Very sharp deterioration
England and Wales Very sharp deterioration	England and Wales Very sharp deterioration	England and Wales: No deterioration	England and Wales: No deterioration

Males aged under-21

Scotland:	Sharp deterioration
England and Wales:	Some deterioration

Males aged 21–29

Scotland:	Some deterioration
England and Wales:	No deterioration

In the box-diagram, the seriousness of the impact of the infuence which suddenly affects long-established behaviour patterns is arranged so as to diminish from the top and left of the diagram to the bottom and right – where the impact is so slight as to be indescernible. As the contrast is most pronounced in England and Wales, analysis can best start there, reference being made to the Scottish data to check on the plausibility of the inferences.

Briefly, the English data show that the impact, at least up to and including 1975, was confined to age and sex groups not frequently found in public houses of the "basic" type. From this, it may be concluded that the intoxicating element came from off-licensed premises, and, having regard to the nature of their sales, from bottled alcohol (at that time). This, of course, fits in well with the known proliferation of off-licensed departments in supermarkets – easily secured under the 1961 Licensing Act, and amenable to promotion in the general interest of the supermarkets as soon as the distillers and the importers of wine decided not to defend resale price maintenance in the courts, as the 1964 Act required them to do. Once most large supermarkets had installed off-licensed departments, price-cutting and heavy advertising became necessary to justify the otherwise wholly-uneconomic allocation of shelf-space by increasing the numbers of general buyers moving through the stores. Since men are poor patrons, the advertising and display concentrated upon wines and spirits – until the increased acceptance of canned beer made it possible to market half-dozen packs for consumption in the home. It has been established beyond question that supervision of the sale of alcohol in supermarkets is not comparable with that exercised by publicans, which explains the aberration in the male pattern in England and Wales found in the under twenty-one age-group. The sharp deterioration among younger females derives simply from the novel provision of a point of access to alcohol which was dominated by women and practically free from men during the daylight hours of the working week. Many surveys have shown that women are averse to entering pubs on their own.

If this analysis is applied to the rather different condition in Scotland – a preference for whisky rather than beer, and the prevalence of public houses more akin to those in Eire and Ulster in their lack of amenity than to the general English pub – the relevance becomes apparent. The increase among men and women aged thirty and over is one to be expected from any thrifty people when an article in general demand becomes much cheaper at one type of outlet than it has been, and continues to be, in the traditional source of supply. The fall in cost was, indeed, substantial, being occasioned by:

(a) purchase in a bottle rather than glass;

(b) price-cutting of the bottle supply;

(c) V.A.T. on the cut-price bottle only as against V.A.T. on the "glass plus pub overhead and service on-cost."

Given the same amount of money to spend on alcoholic beverage, addicts and/or heavy drinkers would tend to consume more when the cost decreased, and the offences of drunkenness would reflect this higher consumption.

The Scottish reaction among the older drinkers differed from that in England and Wales, therefore, mainly because bottles of wines and spirits could be sold at cut prices by off-licensed departments of supermarkets in the early years after the ending of resale price maintenance, while the demand for canned beer was too small to justify the same stocking, display and price-cutting tactics. Now that the demand for canned beer has improved, more supermarkets are stocking and advertising them but – in packs of six cans – they are not so conducive to *ad-hoc* over-indulgence as the bottle, without a place to go to drink the contents slowly and in comfort.

We may therefore, return to the consideration of the long-established differences between Scottish and English drunkenness – the lower incidence of offences per annum among males aged under thirty; the equality of incidence among females aged under twenty-one; and the substantially higher incidence of *offences per annum* among all the other age/sex groups in Scotland.

Before doing so, however, it is useful to establish that the propensity exists in the oldest age-group, "thirty and over", being a wide category. Scottish data differ in presentation from the Home Office but, for the years 1956 to 1970, inclusive, the data are comparable for men and women aged sixty and over. The actual number of offences are given in Table IX and Chart VIII which follows, illustrates these figures – but with the Scottish figures multiplied ten-fold to allow for the differences in the numbers at risk in the two countries. The similarity in principle with the tables and graphs dealing with thirty-and-over groups is obvious. The phenomenon is general.

TABLE IX

Proved offences of drunkenness by males and females aged sixty and over, Scotland, and England and Wales, 1956–70.

	Males		Females	
Year	**Scotland**	**England and Wales**	**Scotland**	**England and Wales**
1956	894	3461	215	721
1957	925	4004	224	777
1958	805	3742	185	849
1959	878	3749	195	780
1960	986	3891	199	701
1961	1139	4240	243	714
1962	1227	4973	198	659
1963	1250	4944	207	686
1964	1171	4562	192	613
1965	1138	4090	178	537
1966	1074	4265	147	504
1967	1068	4883	110	606
1968	1100	4868	148	710
1969	1007	4996	124	692
1970	1027	4801	123	772

If we start with the numerically more important topic of drunkenness among males, we have the progression of Scottish drunkenness, as compared with that in England and Wales of:

In the age group 15 to 20 inclusive, 60 per cent of E. & W. offences.
In the age group 21 to 29 inclusive, 75 per cent of E. & W. offences.
In the age group of 30 and over, 180 per cent of E. & W. offences.

Since it is unrealistic to suppose that men get less able "to carry their drink" in a general sense as they get older (alcoholics, imbibing alcohol during virtually all waking hours, are seldom "drunk" in the sense of being obstreperous, incapable or comatose – rather it is a persistent twilight of relatively inefficient "managing to get by"), the explanation is likely to be found in the more frequent occurrence of occasions of voluntary over-indulgence. This, of course, could be the pattern among all drinkers, but the evidence set out below suggests that it is rather a persistently small proportion of each year's recruits to alcoholic drinking which accounts for the phenomenon.

The data are not analysed by the Scottish Office by sexes, and it is clear that the annual figures are mostly made up of males. Further, common experience suggests that "First Offenders" are likely to be aged under thirty to an overwhelming degree.

CHART VIII

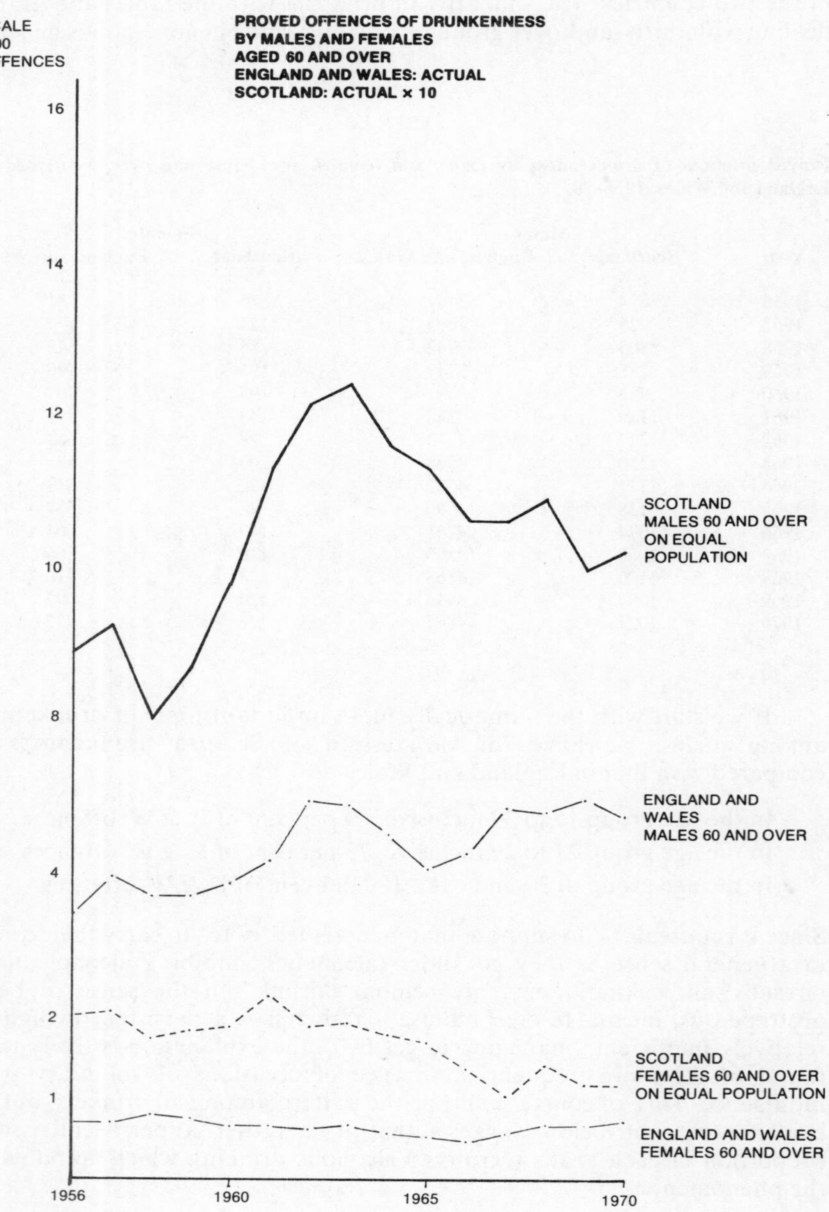
SCALE
'000
OFFENCES
PROVED OFFENCES OF DRUNKENNESS
BY MALES AND FEMALES
AGED 60 AND OVER
ENGLAND AND WALES: ACTUAL
SCOTLAND: ACTUAL × 10
16
14
12
10
8
4
2
1
SCOTLAND
MALES 60 AND OVER
ON EQUAL
POPULATION
ENGLAND AND
WALES
MALES 60 AND OVER
SCOTLAND
FEMALES 60 AND OVER
ON EQUAL POPULATION
ENGLAND AND WALES
FEMALES 60 AND OVER
1956
1960
1965
1970

TABLE X

SCOTLAND. Offences of drunkenness proved against persons analysed by first offences and by persons who, at the commission of the offence of drunkenness, had (a) two, three or four previous offences of any kind, or (b) had more numerous previous convictions.

Year	First Offenders	2, 3 or 4 Previous Convictions	More Numerous Previous Convictions
1953	3053	1158	2355
1954	3225	1236	2318
1955	3447	1400	2389
1956	3808	1537	2519
1957	4216	1725	2583
1958	3904	1619	2469
1959	3970	1711	2639
1960	4162	1682	2676
1961	4558	1992	3163
1962	4914	2018	3064
1963	5314	2135	3350
1964	4926	2162	3690
1965	5002	2015	3363
1966	5074	1974	3572
1967	5063	1867	3560
1968	5182	2017	3738
1969	5046	1785	3496
1970	5464	1611	3519
1971	5382	1743	3773
1972	5684	1727	4253
1973	6379	2145	4992
1974	6457	2455	5771
1975	7154	2114	5731

Chart IX illustrates the figures in the table. Comparison with Chart II will confirm that the fluctuations and trend (since 1956) of the line for first offenders is practically a replica of that for offences by males aged under twenty-one in Scotland.

That no great proportion of first offenders go on to repeat the offence (or any offences, for the data after the first offence are not confined to drunkenness) is borne out by the lower, and flatter, curve for persons accused in a particular year of drunkenness who are found to have had one, two or three previous convictions. Thus, if 20 per cent of first offenders during an average year in the 1960s went on to commit one more offence; 15 per cent to commit two; and 10 per cent to commit three other offences (of which one, only, need be that of drunkenness), the figures in the second column would, on average, be nearly one-third larger than they are. A *fortiori,* for the column of figures for four to over ten previous convictions for offences, the latest of them being drunkenness.

It is not, of course, suggested that some men who were convicted of an offence of drunkenness in youth are never victims of over-indulgence again much later in life. This must occur, but it will occur as a random element in the data for England and Wales. It cannot account for the near-double incidence of drunkenness among Scottish males aged thirty or over; nor for the fact that offences in the mid-1970s by persons with more than three previous convictions come near to outstripping the contribution by first offenders each year.

CHART IX

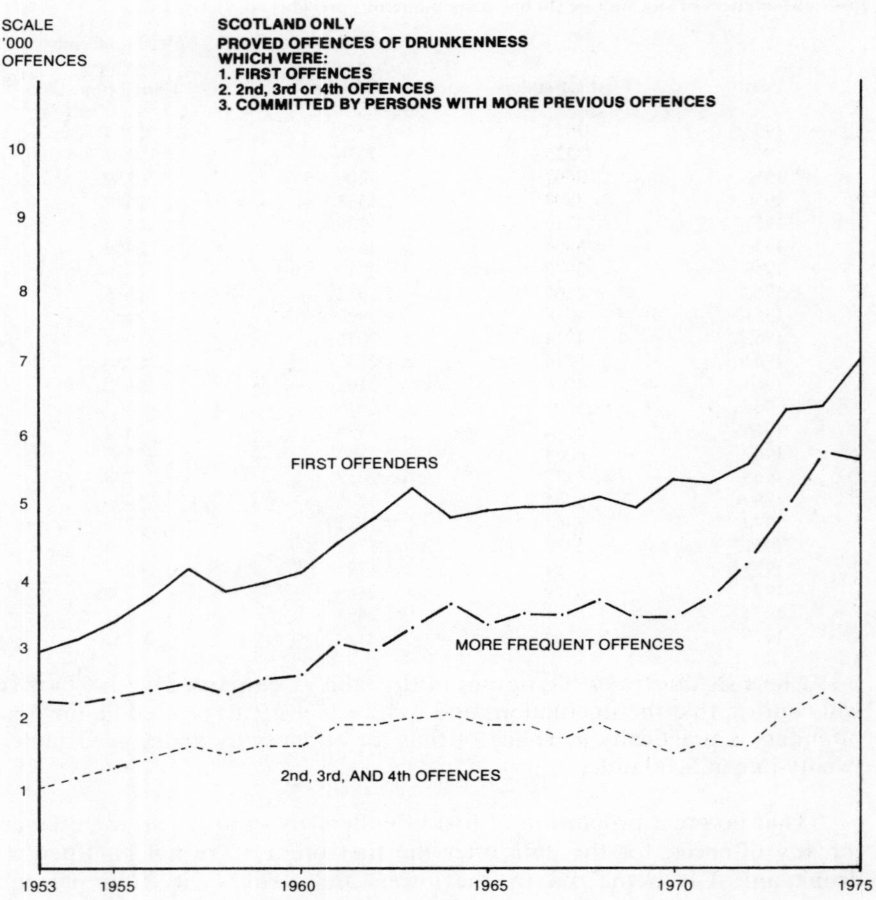

The only robust explanation is that each new crop of recruits to over-indulgence in Scotland contributes a small addition to increase the number of drinkers who will over-indulge again, and in most cases, again quite frequently.

The same general explanation applies in part to the progression of drunkenness of Scottish females as compared with that of England and Wales:

In the age group 15 to 20 inclusive, 150 per cent of E. & W. offences
In the age group 21 to 29 inclusive, 150 per cent of E. & W. offences
In the age group over-thirties, 250 per cent of E. & W. offences.

The repetition of offences by a small proportion of each year's recruitment of females convicted of drunkenness for the first time is needed to produce the arithmetic. But there is also the higher level of relative incidence at which this process operates in all-phases. Since it is known that the general preference of English women is also for wines and short spiritous drinks rather than beer, the explanation must lie elsewhere. Admittedly limited observation suggests a combination of circumstances – fewer dance/disco halls; fewer and smaller groups of male escorts; and the relative lack of public houses offering seating and related amenities.

While there are pockets of repeating drunkards in England and Wales, it is not as general as in Scotland. Chief constables mention the matter from time to time in their annual reports to the police authorities and the licensing magistrates, and a survey of such reports points to the existence of local concentrations rather than a widespread incidence even in the larger urban areas.

Two "statistical" checks on the truth of this supposition can be made. The first makes use of data from the 127 police districts which covered England and Wales until the mid-1960s. Age and sex analyses are available between 1956 and 1963 for all these police districts, providing a gross total of 1,016 police district/years. The Scottish data suggests that "repeating" is an increasing proportion of total offences as age advances. The following is, therefore, based on offences proved against males and females aged sixty and over between 1956 and 1963.

Taking males first, analysis shows that during 176 police district years (or 17 per cent of the total) there were fewer than three offences committed by males aged sixty and over. There is little room for "repeaters" in this category. There is only limited scope when the offences in the police districts are limited to fewer than eight cases per annum (three to seven offences) or all or most of the eight-year span. 584 police district years (or 58 per cent of the total) were of this character. this means that only in 32 police districts out of 127 were there more than seven offences in each of the eight years. Substantial numbers of "repeaters" are likely to be found only in a quarter of the police districts as constituted in 1963 and not necessarily in all of these.

The data on females are even more definite. 816 police district years (or 80 per cent of the total) recorded fewer than three offences committed by females aged sixty and over. A further 168 police district/years (or 17 per cent of the total) had fewer than eight cases for all or nearly all of the eight years involved. This left only four police districts with eight or more offences recorded each year between 1956 and 1963 – 3 per cent of the total.

Indigent "repeaters" and others finding it difficult to get service in public houses used to have recourse to methylated spirits, and, until 1970, Home Office statistics included the numbers found guilty of drunkenness after consuming denatured alcohol. Since 1970, the indigent have been able to buy cheap wines at the off-licensed departments of supermarkets (often "lacing" the wine or cider with gin) and those unwelcome at public houses have had a new source of supply. The following table shows that the numbers of offences were never large, and decreased steadily after 1950.

Year	Persons	Males	Females
1949	604	N.A.	N.A.
1950	670	N.A.	N.A.
1951	588	N.A.	N.A.
1952	569	N.A.	N.A.
1953	461	N.A.	N.A.
1954	396	388	8
1955	309	302	7
1956	228	216	12
1957	252	245	7
1958	224	223	1
1959	192	189	3
1960	152	151	1
1961	126	122	4
1962	139	137	2
1963	107	106	1
1964	116	113	3
1965	85	83	2
1966	73	70	3
1967	73	73	
1968	70	70	
1969	47	46	1
1970	40	38	2

(Series discontinued by Home Office)

Drunken motorists

The introduction of the breathalyser in 1967 completely altered the basis for statistics on drunken driving, so that no useful purpose is served by treating the post-war years as a whole, or in attempting comparison with pre-war experience. The following table, and the chart illustrating the figures, is therefore confined to the period 1968–1975 inclusive.

TABLE XI

Proceedings against motorists for all offences related to drunken driving since the introduction of the "Breathalyser" in 1967.

Year	Total proceedings in Scotland	England and Wales
1968	5597	22746
1969	7036	29427
1970	8413	31834
1971	9781	46028
1972	10158	55590
1973	11565	65248
1974	12201	66774
1975	11685	70394

No reliable information exists on the relative numbers of licensed drivers in Scotland and in England and Wales on the use made of vehicles, or on the degree to which offences occur "over the border" respectively.

CHART X

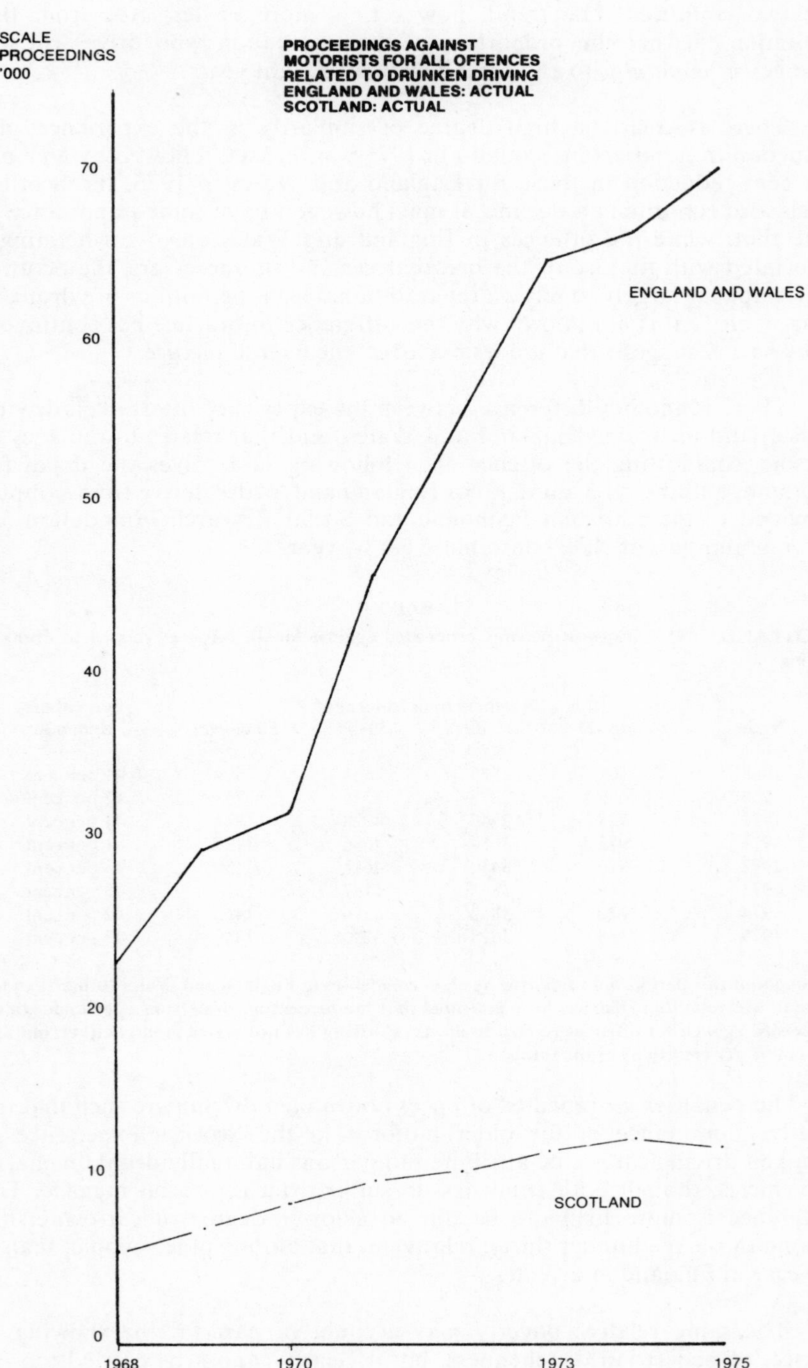
SCALE
PROCEEDINGS
'000
PROCEEDINGS AGAINST
MOTORISTS FOR ALL OFFENCES
RELATED TO DRUNKEN DRIVING
ENGLAND AND WALES: ACTUAL
SCOTLAND: ACTUAL
70
60
50
40
30
20
10
0
ENGLAND AND WALES
SCOTLAND
1968
1970
1973
1975

Chart X uses one scale to illustrate the figures, since we cannot assume that the numbers of offences depend upon the gross population of the two countries. The trend, however, is more or less free from this limitation, in that the proportion of the population who drive will not change, *differentially*, to any great degree over eight years.

There is clearly a high degree of similarity in the experience; the reduction in numbers in Scotland in 1975 was, in fact, followed by an eight per cent reduction in those for England and Wales in 1976, the Scottish totals also continuing a decline. It may, however, be of some importance to note that, while the offences in England and Wales are overwhelmingly associated with the use of the breathalyser and its successors, the Scottish police appear largely to rely on the traditional legal definitions of "drunk in charge, etc.". It is not known why this difference in practice has continued, but Chart X suggests that it does not affect the overall picture.

There is another difference between the experience of drunken driving in Scotland as against England and Wales, and that relates to the ages of persons committing the offence. The following table gives the detail for Scotland, and the relevant data for England and Wales derive from samples provided to the Christian Economic and Social Research Foundation, by varying numbers of chief constables year by year.

TABLE XII

SCOTLAND ONLY: Ages of persons proceeded against for all offences related to drunken driving.

Year	Numbers of persons aged Under-21	21–29	30–49	50 & over	Percentage Under-30
1968	507	1825	2666	599	41 per cent
1969	679	2278	3326	753	42 per cent
1970	728	2746	4028	911	41 per cent
1971	912	3054	4686	1127	41 per cent
1972	976	3410	4613	1159	43 per cent
1973	1169	3835	5187	1374	43 per cent
1974	1220	3852	5576	1453	42 per cent
1975	1368	3623	5236	1449	43 per cent

Throughout this period, data reported by chief constables in England and Wales (other than the London Metropolitan District) have indicated that the percentage of persons aged under thirty proceeded against for offences related to drunken driving has not varied greatly either, but at a level of 51 per cent to 53 of the totals.

The penalties for repeated offences of drunken driving are such that the relative dominance of the older motorist in the Scottish experience of drunken driving cannot be attributed to persons habitually drunk in charge of vehicles, though both countries do suffer from the social menace. The difference is more likely to be due to a lower degree of car-ownership among those aged under thirty, relative to that among older people, than is the case in England and Wales.

The same relative poverty may account in part for the showing in respect of pedestrian drunkenness, but it clearly cannot be carried too far because of the contrary picture presented by women aged under twenty-one and aged 21–29. It is more consistent with the generality of the comparison to conclude that Scottish youths and young men do not get offensively drunk as often or as generally as do their contemporaries south of the border.

The Scottish data by police authorities are not analysed in the kind of detail discussed above.

CHAPTER 19

PEDESTRIAN DRUNKENNESS IN ENGLAND AND WALES, 1937–73

This chapter is concerned with the convictions for drunkenness of pedestrians in the whole of England and Wales over a period of forty years which covered a world war and a higher degree of immigration than had been experienced in the country before. The data are confined to pedestrians for two mains reasons. The first is that the numbers of pedestrians at risk is at all times related to the population of adults and near adults at any one time; the numbers of drivers is never so well delimited. The second reason for leaving out consideration of drunken drivers is that the means of detecting a drunken driver changed radically after 1966, so that there is a break in continuity which is missing in the case of those arrested on foot. England and Wales is treated as a single whole because the tables which form the largest part of this volume are in the detail of the police districts as they existed at various times in the period; and, while it will be seen that this kind of detail is the minimum that is necessary to avoid quite false conclusions being drawn from the statistics, the mass is such that only by re-assembly can the wood be seen for the trees. Finally, the history is analytical because it is necessary to demonstrate that the "trees" cannot be assembled into any pattern without having regard to the peculiarities inherent in regions, seasons, ages and sexes which this chapter sets out to illustrate.

But there were broad influences to which all the people and the localities reacted and it will be useful to take an equally broad look at the totals for men and for women as they fluctuated from year to year for England and Wales as a whole. The columnar diagram overleaf sets out to do this by taking, on the left hand, the numbers of offences of drunkenness proved against women in 1937 as a vertical datum line, plotting the subsequent annual totals as hundreds so that they lie on one side or the other of this datum. Bearing in mind that the population of England and Wales was greater in 1976 than in 1937, it will be clear that such a treatment tends to overstate the incidence as time goes on; but over any short stretch of years the difference so caused is immaterial and there are many more important differences between 1937 and 1976 at either end. To help the eye to gather the wide view of the fluctuations, shading is used to emphasize both where the line lies and how far and in what direction it has veered away from the datum of the 1937 level. The same treatment is used on the right hand for the proved convictions of drunkenness among men, the datum in 1937 being, of course, much larger in terms of numbers, so that the change in shading takes place around the figure of 40,000 as against the 600 in the case of women. Even with this effect of scale, however, the band that is needed to contain the data for men is two-thirds wider than that needed for the women. It is some sort of comment on the special nature of

DIAGRAM I

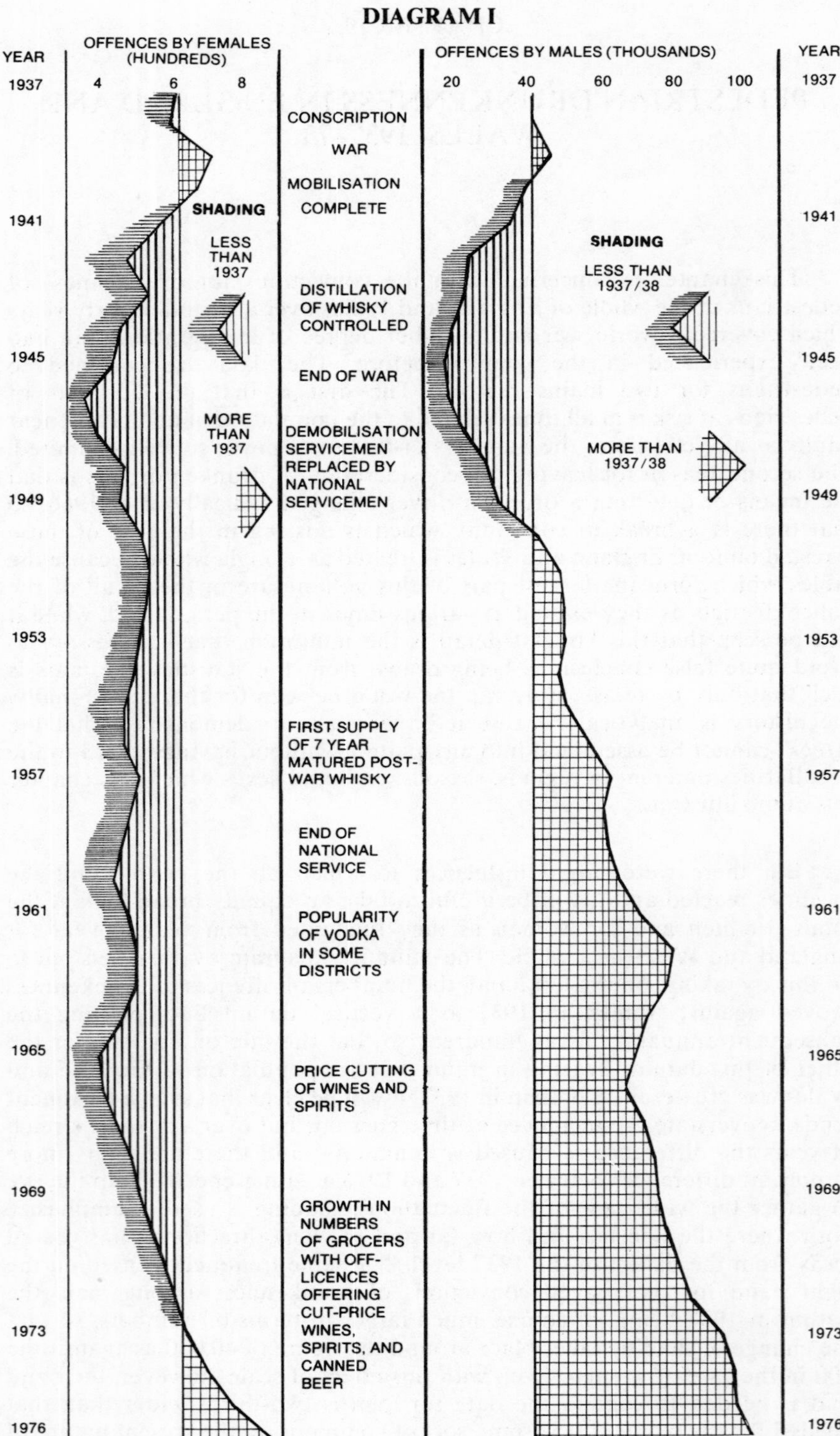

YEAR
OFFENCES BY FEMALES (HUNDREDS)
4
6
8
OFFENCES BY MALES (THOUSANDS)
20
40
60
80
100
YEAR
1937
CONSCRIPTION
WAR
MOBILISATION
COMPLETE
SHADING
1941
LESS THAN 1937
DISTILLATION OF WHISKY CONTROLLED
SHADING
LESS THAN 1937/38
1945
END OF WAR
MORE THAN 1937
DEMOBILISATION SERVICEMEN REPLACED BY NATIONAL SERVICEMEN
MORE THAN 1937/38
1949
1953
FIRST SUPPLY OF 7 YEAR MATURED POST-WAR WHISKY
1957
END OF NATIONAL SERVICE
1961
POPULARITY OF VODKA IN SOME DISTRICTS
1965
PRICE CUTTING OF WINES AND SPIRITS
1969
GROWTH IN NUMBERS OF GROCERS WITH OFF-LICENCES OFFERING CUT-PRICE WINES, SPIRITS, AND CANNED BEER
1973
1976

the period of forty years under review to say that this particular relationship does not survive 1977.

So far as the convictions of women are concerned, it will be seen that the first two years of the war saw a considerable increase. This is attributable to the mobilization of the forces, indigenous and from the Empire. From 1941, there is an even more substantial drop. Much of the drunkenness of women in the inter-war years was a phenomenon of the centres of the large metropolitan areas, as was prostitution. The bombing of these central areas destroyed the locale, and, while there was some re-surgence in 1943 as the intensive bombing stopped, it was short-lived. The centres were a long time being reinstated and, with the effect of the lower birthrates of the inter-war years becoming increasingly dominant in the age-groups most liable, the numbers of proved offences per annum remained approximately twenty per cent below the pre-war level until 1967. It will be noticed that this is later than one would expect if age were the only factor. The post-war "bulge" was over twenty years of age by that time and nearly twenty-five by the time the increase in proved offences came near to the 1937 figure. There is little doubt that it was the new kind of off-licence that brought about the change. Once these off-licensed shops within the supermarkets were prevalent, many women had easier access to liquor than they had ever had before – close to the groceries that they had to buy weekly and with the weekly housekeeping money also at hand. It was not long before the not-yet-married women found that the outlets were open to them, too; the years after the end of this review show how the age of conviction responded.

So far as the proved offences by men are concerned, it is necessary to dismiss the years from 1940 to 1950 as being irrelevant to the consideration of civilian drunkenness. Not only were most of the age-groups most prone to arrest then in the armed services and, to a large extent, absent from the country, but there were other servicemen with money to spend on their leaves in what was to them "overseas"; though it needs to be borne in mind that their own military police frequently took over the arrested personnel.

From 1953 to 1955 there is little for comment; the incidence was slightly higher than just before the war but not dissimilar to that holding around 1930. There was a surge in offences in 1956 and 1957; the analysis of age-groups affected is indicative that it was the release of Scotch whisky from rationing in the home market which underlay the increase. Many drinkers of gin and rum, the prevalent substitutes for the whisky, were not accustomed to the more mature spirit and behaved as if they were much younger and less experienced. Some five years later, vodka caught many more "experienced drinkers" – not surprising in view of its peculiar qualities as a drink. However, experience "taught" once more and the numbers of male offences fell again sharply until 1967. From then on, the tale has been one of steadily rising convictions and, once more, it is to the off-licensed departments of the supermarkets, with advertising of cut-prices and easy access in units of purchase much larger than was or is usual in public houses, that one must look for the cause. So much for the broad picture; we now turn to the detail underlying it.

Seasonal characteristics: 1953–1973 in overlapping 5-year periods

We start with an analysis based upon the four seasons because we have the data in terms of persons (it was 1956 before the Home Office made available the ages of offenders) and in terms of the quantities of beer, wines and spirits released from bond for consumption in the United Kingdom. It will be appreciated that some uncertainty is introduced by comparing the releases of alcoholic liquor for the United Kingdom with the offences in England and Wales alone. However, as will be seen from the first of the five-year summary charts opposite, there is little or no visible relationship between the quantities released and the number of proved offences in each quarter. One further general comment is necessary before we turn to the actual experience. Offences of pedestrian drunkenness tend to be dealt with both summarily and promptly; the releases of liquor from bond takes place some time before the alcohol is consumed by the customers. It would be misleading to plot the two sets of figures crudely in respect of the months to which they refer as published. In general, beer tends to move into consumption faster than wines or spirits, but there are increasing signs that this is not always true, especially in respect of canned beer sold through supermarkets. On the other hand, there is a tendency for drunkenness to overlap the end of the year, so that December and January are often one unbroken season of over-indulgence, at least until "twelfth night". We have, therefore, adopted the device of starting our "seasons" with an overlap in calendar terms; that is, December, January and February form the first season of the offences of drunkenness, followed by March, April and May (which has the advantage of always including the Easter holiday), and so on. We have labelled these on the diagrams as winter, spring, summer and autumn so as to emphasize the broadness which we have introduced. To allow for the delays in delivery to the retail outlets, the time for which the goods lie in stock at those outlets, and the further hiatus around Christmas and the New Year between the purchase by the public in advance of seasonal parties and its consumption, our "winter" of releases, consists of October, November and December; our "spring" of January, February and March; and so on.

1953–1957

The diagram plots the variations in the quantities of beer, wines and spirits, separately for each of our "seasons", released in each of the five years 1953–57, inclusive, against the numbers of offences of drunkenness proved in the relevant set of months comprising the same "seasons". The intoxicating effect of the beer and the spirits as plotted are broadly comparable; that of the wines is about one-third of this. It will be apparent that the trends of the offences over the five years is not the same in each season. In winter and spring, the numbers of offences decrease from 1953 to 1955, and then rise sharply to 1957; in the summers, the numbers of offences rise slowly at first, but join the two preceding seasons in the acceleration thereafter. By contrast, the figures for the autumns can best be described as fluctuating slightly about a gentle rise. Further, within each season there is little or no correlation between the changes in the quantities

DIAGRAM II
Comparitive trends of offences and quantities released by Customs and Excise 1953-57

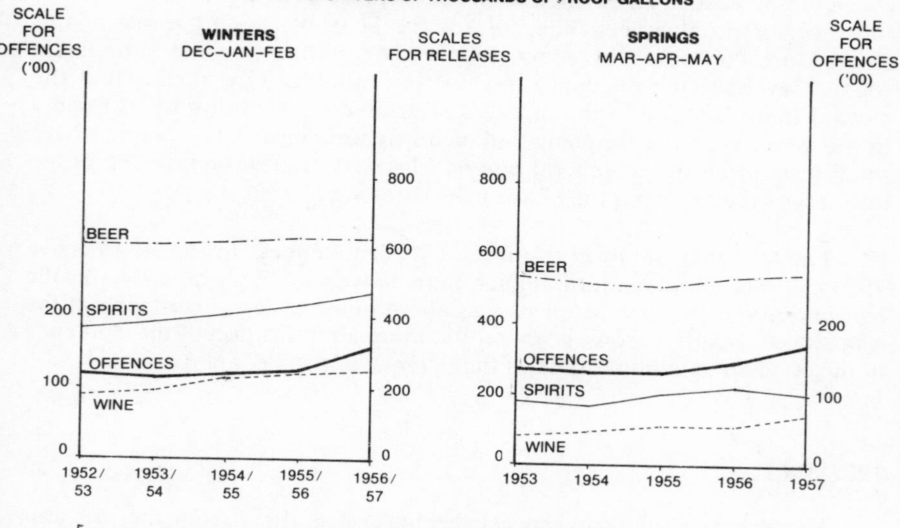

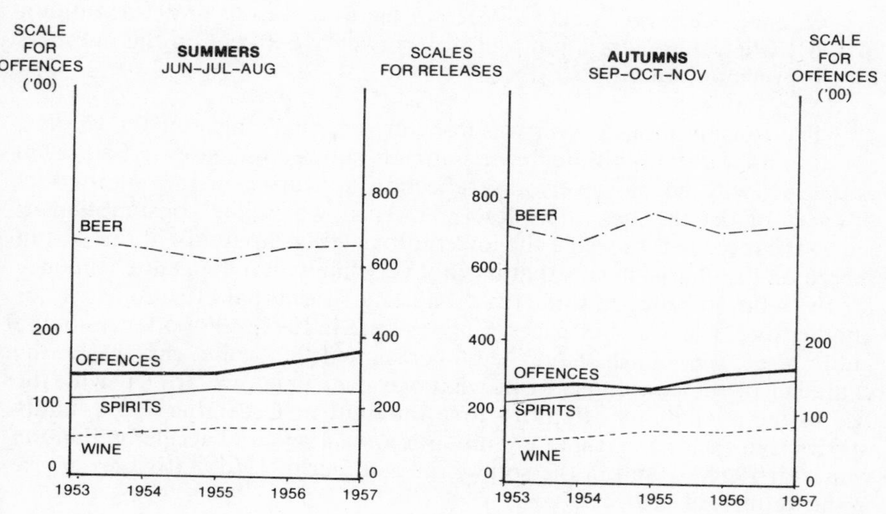

available for consumption of any of the categories of alcohol and those in the numbers of offences.

This is not surprising when it is remembered that there have not been as many as 200,000 proved offences of drunkenness, pedestrian and motorist, in England and Wales in any year since before the First World War. With something of the order of twenty million persons taking alcohol at least more than occasionally, somewhat less than one in a hundred over-indulge to such an extent and in such a place as to lay themselves open to arrest for drunkenness. The bulk of the beer, wines and spirits in this country are consumed by sober people – or, if they are not sufficiently sober, they have the residual sense to stay indoors. That means that the alcohol that gives rise to the offences of drunkenness, and more especially to the changes in the frequency of such offences, must be consumed by a small proportion of the general body of drinkers, and those must be prone to emerge outdoors after they have been drinking.

The fact that the level of offences of drunkenness in the summers of 1953–57 was about a third higher than it was in the winters while the consumption of wines and spirits was about one-half less, beer being at the same level in both seasons, is, therefore, more an indication of the clemency of the open air in summer than of the potency of the alcoholic drink.

1957–1961

The diagram opposite repeats the figures for 1957 from the previous chart and goes on to show the variations in both offences of drunkenness and the consumption of beer, wines and spirits until the beginning of 1962.

Offences were very steady in each of the four seasons until the autumn of 1961, when there was a jump of nearly twenty per cent on the numbers for the previous autumn.

The consumption of beer was more or less steady also for the winters, springs and autumns, although the summers showed increases in both 1960 and 1961, without, however, any reflection appearing in the numbers of offences of drunkenness. The lower levels at which the consumption of wines are recorded, as well a the lower intoxicating capability of the unit of record on the charts, means that it is not very likely that the gentle tendency for the amount released to increase had any substantial effect one way or another on the levels of offences. Since the rise in the level of offences in the autumn of 1961 must have been occasioned by some change in the character of the consumers or in what was consumed, we are left with the rise in the availability of spirits, first apparent in December 1959, mildly apparent in the spring, summer and autumn of 1960, and accelerated in the winter of 1960/61 and in the spring and summer of 1961, with a lesser rise in the autumn of 1961.

The interest lies in the next set of years, and the diagram illustrating the experience follows overleaf.

DIAGRAM III
Comparitive trends of offences and quantities released by Customs and Excise 1957–61

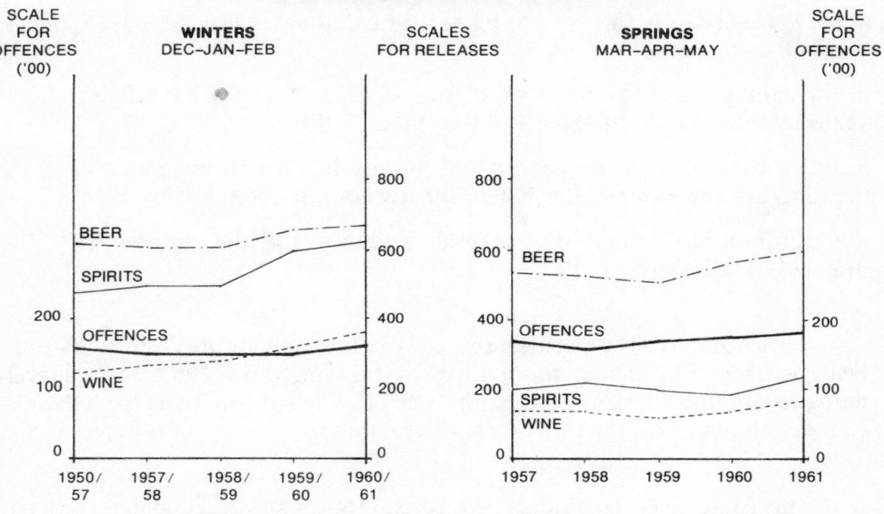

[RELEASES ARE FOR THE FIRST MONTH OF THE PERIOD AND FOR THE TWO PRECEDING MONTHS TO ALLOW FOR DISTRIBUTION]

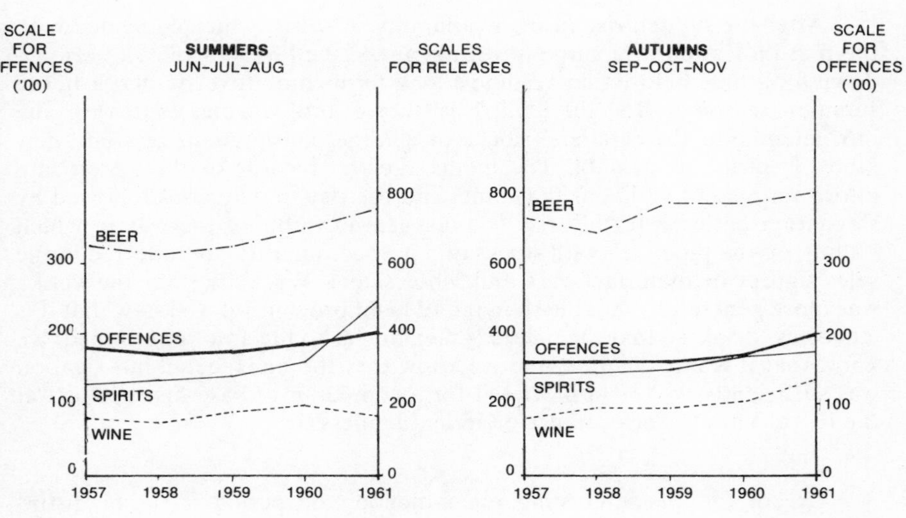

1961–1965

Once again the diagram repeats the last year of the preceding set of years and goes on to show the data for the next four years. Taking the levels of the proved offences of drunkenness first;

In the winter season, they rise from December 1960 to December 1961 and again to December 1962, then fall away again;

in the spring season, they rise to Easter 1962 and again to Easter 1963, then fall away again;

in the summer season, they rise to August 1962, but they have fallen again by the summer of 1963, and they go on falling;

in the autumn season, we have noted the rise in 1961 from 1960, and the diagram shows a smaller rise in the autumn of 1962, but by 1963,

the autumn has joined the general tendency for the number of offences to fall away.

If we compare the performance of the lines illustrating the release of beer, we see that except for a drop in the spring of 1963, the general tendency is upward throughout the period. Clearly, there is no obvious connection here with the short-term fluctuation in the level of offences.

The same may be said of the consumption of wines which, indeed, shows the largest increases after the level of offences has started to fall, in all of the four seasons.

After the sudden rise in the availability of spirits which coincided with the first indication of a surge in drunkenness, the levels of releases also go down for a time before they resume a long-term climb (except, that is in the summer seasons). But the "blip" is there, and is consistent with the movement into the retailers' stocks of a large consignment of some new kind of spirituous alcohol. The media are the record for the advertising effort put behind vodka at that time, and the rise in deliveries followed by stagnation before a further rise is a classical example of the way in which "filling up the pipeline" with stocks of a new commodity are reflected in the sales figures of manufacturers and wholesalers. We know that the vodka was more generally available than it had been previously; we know that it is a tasteless drink, so that the palate is no guide as to the amount imbibed; we know that it is intoxicating; and we know that the unexpected intoxication was sufficiently widely appreciated for a comedian to base his short act at the Royal Variety Performance on its suddenness.

Except for this interesting phenomenon, the period is rather distinguished by a tendency for the level of drunkenness to fall while the consumption of all three types of alcoholic drinks is increasing. It was a time of some optimism among those interested in temperance.

DIAGRAM IV
Comparitive trends of offences and quantities released by Customs and Excise 1961-65

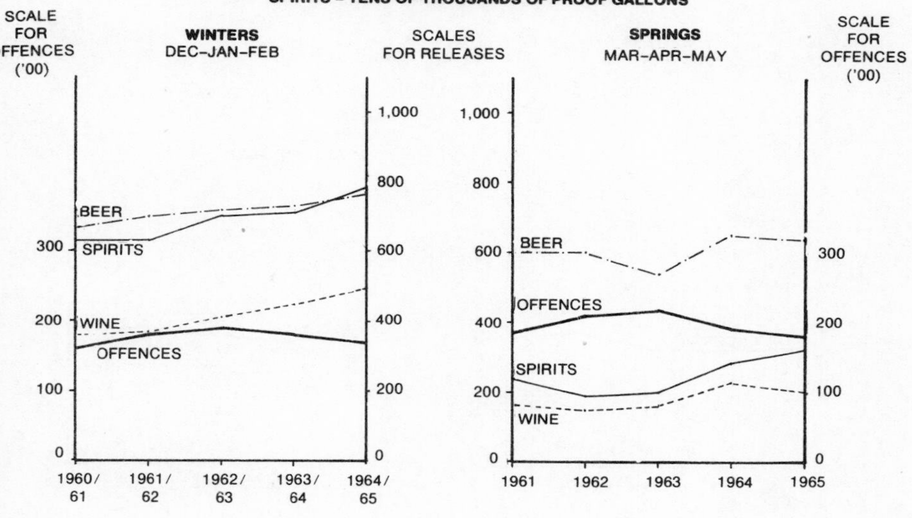

[RELEASES ARE FOR THE FIRST MONTH OF THE PERIOD AND FOR THE TWO PRECEDING MONTHS TO ALLOW FOR DISTRIBUTION]

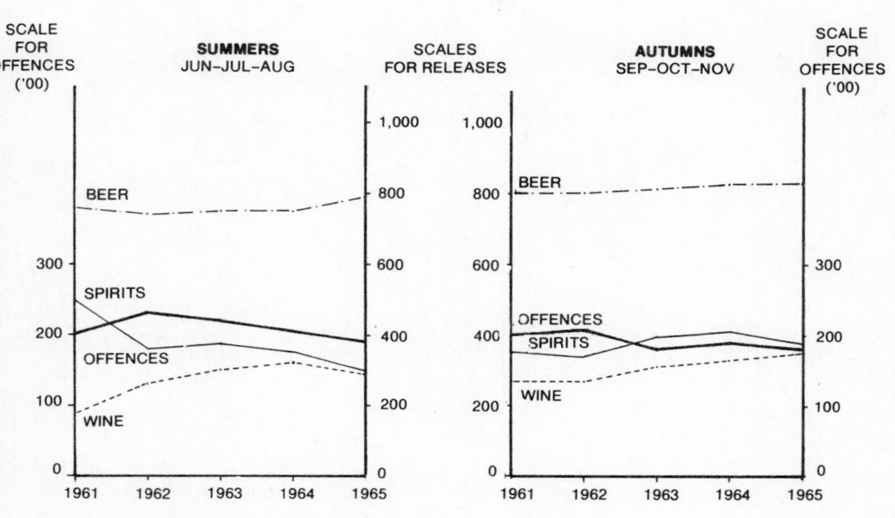

DIAGRAM V
Comparitive trends of offences and quantities released by Customs and Excise 1965–69

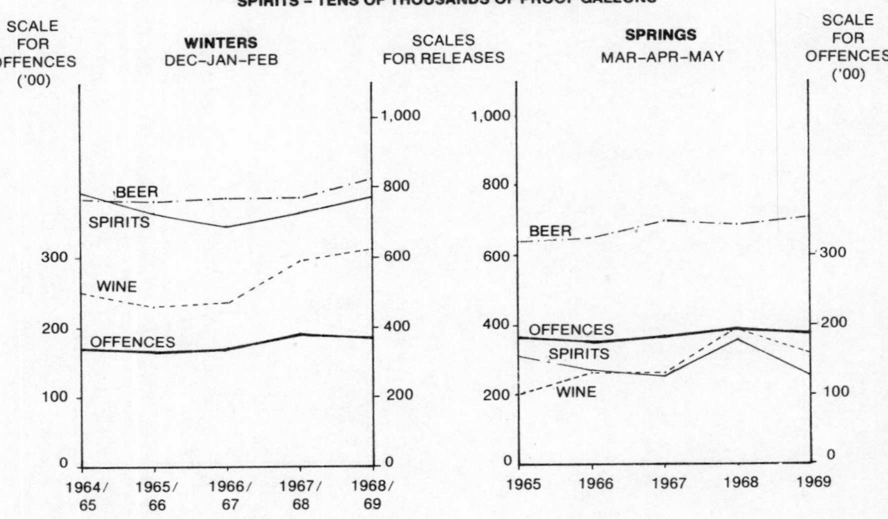

[RELEASES ARE FOR THE FIRST MONTH OF THE PERIOD AND FOR THE TWO PRECEDING MONTHS TO ALLOW FOR DISTRIBUTION]

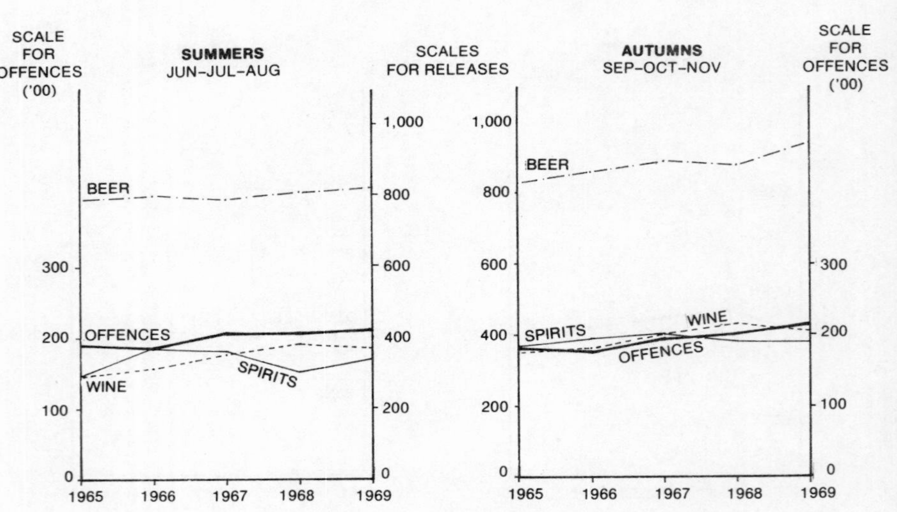

1965–1969

The diagram on the opposite page sets out the behaviour of all our indices over the next and partially-overlapping period of five years. It is again an era of more or less stagnation in the numbers of offences of drunkenness, although these now run at about twenty thousand per quarter as against the 15,000 with which we started the review in the early 1950s. Amongst the alcoholic beverages the gentle rise in the consumption of beer goes on, with the autumn moving forward more rapidly than the other three seasons. If, once more, we glance back at the earlier diagrams, we see that in doing so the season is re-establishing the lead it enjoyed at the beginning of our review.

It is difficult to discover any trend in the consumption of either wines or spirits. The spirits are more or less maintaining the levels to which they returned after the presumed "vodka stocking-up of the trade". In the three non-winter seasons, the trend in the consumption of wines is hesitantly upward, but in the important three winter months there is a setback in the Christmas/New Year period of 1965–66. This is followed by a remarkable increase of over a third in the next two seasons so that the 1967/68 festive season achieves a total of consumption three times that registered in 1953/54.

But none of this has any effect upon the numbers of offences of drunkenness, so that we are driven back to the conclusion of some pages ago: the numbers of persons arrested for drunkenness does not depend at all directly upon the amount of alcoholic beverage moving into general consumption. It is important to look back at the diagrams illustrating the experience of the seventeen years from 1953 and see how generally true this statement is of the whole period, because we are about to turn to a period when it would seem that something quite different is occurring. It is therefore once again desirable to stress that, with offences of drunkenness of only some 80,000 cases proved against pedestrians, the bulk of the citizens do not get drunk sufficiently and in such places that the police have to take them into custody. It is at all times a small proportion of the totality of drinkers who "get into the statistics".

1969–1973

The diagrams on the page overleaf are very different from those for the earlier five-year periods. Before we discuss them in detail, it is important to remember that the increase in the licensed sections or departments of supermarkets did not come immediately after the decision by the distillers and the bottlers of the main brands of wine not to continue with the practice of denying supplies to any retailer who sold their branded products at less than the prices set by the original sellers. It was necessary for the supermarkets first to satisfy the local magistrates that their premises were suitable for the sale of alcoholic beverages for consumption off the premises, and in most cases, though not all, this meant some substantial internal changes in the fittings of the shops. The figures for the releases

DIAGRAM VI
Comparitive trends of offences and quantities released by Customs and Excise 1969–73

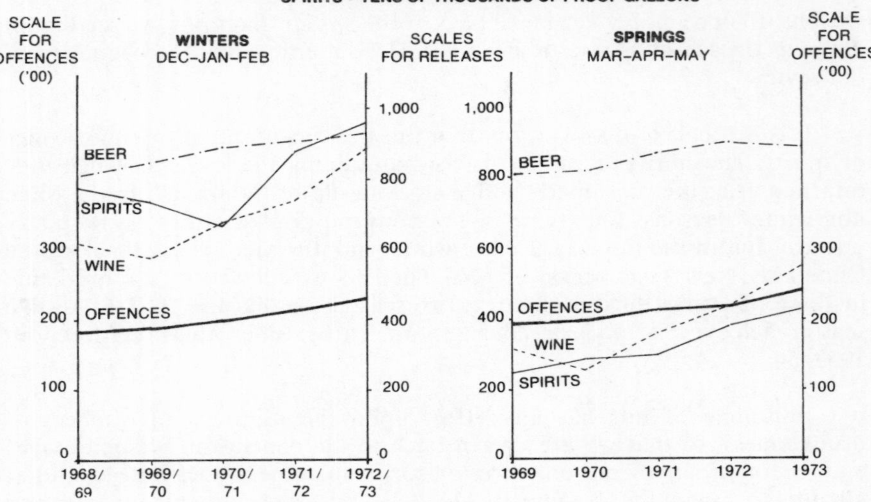

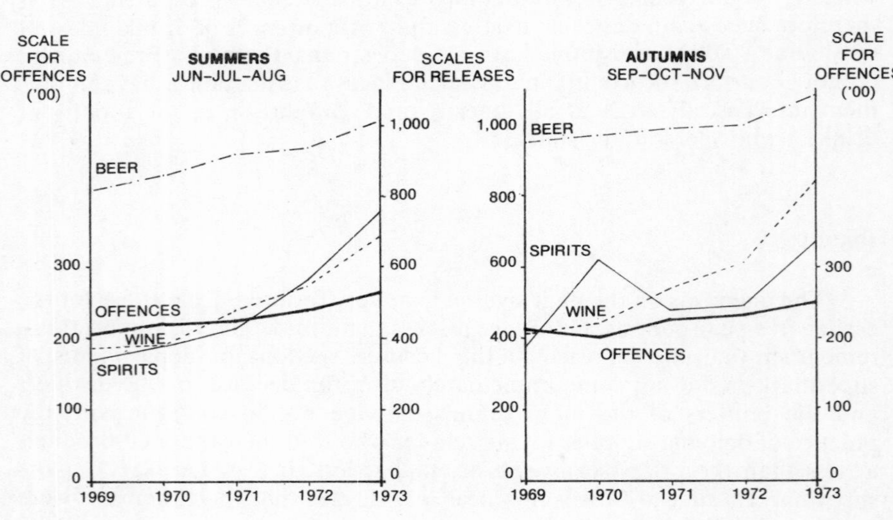

from bond of wines and of spirits show that the large stocking-up of the new off-licences did not take place until after 1970.

The change in the character of the outlets for alcoholic drinks is best seen in the rise in the quantities of spirits and wines, both absolutely and relative to beer, which were consumed after 1970. A substantial part of the higher releases went to form the stocks-in-trade of the supermarkets with the new off-licensed departments, but it is clear that the rise was a continuing one, so that the supermarkets were actually selling more spirits and wines than the public houses with their attached off-licence shops had been able to dispose of.

The offences of drunkenness were also rising but not steadily. The pictures presented by the four "seasons" show differences in the progress, although all four register a change from around twenty thousand offences each year at the beginning of the period to a figure of around twenty-five thousand during 1973. This 25 per cent increase in some four years followed upon a period when the totals of offences were, if anything, inclined to diminish.

The winter seasons show a steady rise in offences from the Christmas of 1968 to that of 1972. This steadiness contrasts with the fall and rise in the quantity of spirits that was released from bond in time for the retail purchases in the seasons; and with the smaller fall and much greater increase in the releases of wines. The amount of beer moving into consumption went up more steadily, achieving record dimensions by the end of 1972.

Offences in the spring seasons were a little slower in growth, but displayed the same steadiness as the winter figures. Releases of spirits were also much steadier in their growth than in the previous case, and the total increase was also rather less. Wines went down in 1970, as they had in the winter seasons, but thereafter the increase was in all senses comparable with that in winter. The releases of beer increased but with some uncertainty at the beginning and end of the period.

It is when we look at the summer "seasons" that the most remarkable change in the character of the "mix" of alcoholic drinks released for consumption is seen. For nearly twenty years, beer had been the completely dominant alcoholic drink in the summer; now it was surpassed in "intoxicating capability" by the wines and spirits taken together, and this change was almost compressed into the two years of 1972 and 1973. It was at the same time that the numbers of offences rose from 22,000 in three months to 26,500.

In looking at the diagram for the autumn "seasons" it is necessary to make allowance for the possibility that the sharp rise in the releases of spirits in, actually, July, August and September of 1970 was caused by some fiscal event and accounted in part for the untypical decline in releases during October, November and December of the same year (see the diagram for winter and its discussion, above). Offences show a slower rate of increase than any of the other three seasons, despite the quantity of beer reaching record levels by 1973. Again, the "pipe-line" effect needs to be borne in mind.

The monthly statistics of offences of drunkenness upon which the previous pages and diagrams have been based did not distinguish the ages or sexes of those convicted of the offence. In order to see better which kind of drinkers it was that caused the ups and downs in the totals of offences, we have to be content with annual figures; and that, only from 1956 onward.

The ages of females convicted of drunkenness – 1956–1961

As the fluctuations in the number of offences by females were different from those recorded against males, it will be less confusing if this analysis is made separately as between the sexes, taking each in turn from 1956 to 1973 in three stages each of six calendar years. The first set of six years consists of 1956 through 1961. Although the official statistics are given for ages under eighteen for most of the years, it is by no means certain that the same proportions of girls found to be drunk under the permitted age for purchasing intoxicating liquor were always charged with the offence of drunkenness. There is the alternative charge of purchasing under-age. That alternative is not available as soon as the girl reaches the age of eighteen, and this gives a "purity" to the statistics of offences at and over that age.

All the diagrams that follow will take the form of that appearing opposite, with separate small diagrams for each of four age-groups – 18–20, inclusive; 21–29, inclusive; 30–59 inclusive; and 60 years of age and over. The annual totals of offences will be charted on each diagram, but the scales will be chosen so that the lines joining up the annual figures will tend to occupy roughly the same levels in each of the four squares. Thus, the offences by females aged 18–20; 21–29; and 60 and over are in units of ten, while the scale for women aged 30–59 (a span of thirty years) gives the number of hundreds of offences.

We have already seen that the amount of beer, wines and spirits released from bond for consumption in the United Kingdom appears to have little bearing on the changes in trend of the figures of offences – the much larger releases in the winter seasons coincided with actually smaller numbers of offences than those in most of the summer seasons. Nevertheless, the practice has been adopted of including in the bottom left-hand square diagram a set of three lines which show how the annual total of releases moved over the period.

Turning now to what the diagrams indicate, we see that all four of the squares show a rise in the number of offences between 1956 and 1957. This is followed by a sharp fall in the numbers of offences by girls aged 18–20, and by women 21–29; by a less pronounced fall to 1958 by women aged 30–59; and by an actual further rise among the oldest women. There is then steadiness or further decrease until 1960, after which the downward trend is reversed – sharply in the cases of women aged 21–29, and aged 30–59. While the numbers of women convicted of drunkenness is small compared

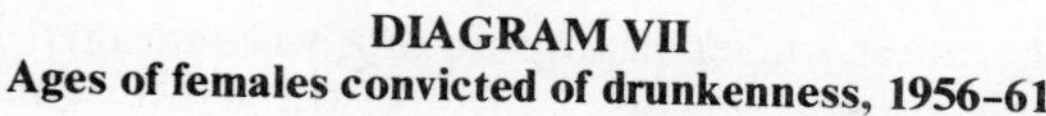

DIAGRAM VII
Ages of females convicted of drunkenness, 1956-61

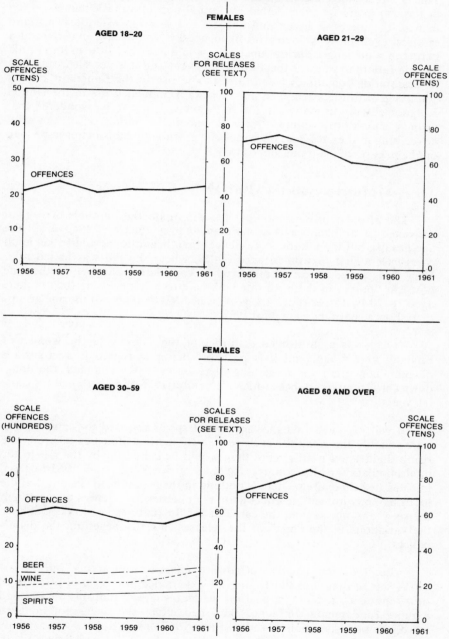

with the numbers of offences by men, it would appear that the de-rationing of matured whisky in 1956 and 1957 had some effect in all the age-groups, the effect being rather longer-lasting among women aged sixty and over. This is a plausible conclusion. Since most of the whisky that was available in the war years was channelled by formal and informal channels to the men in the forces at home and abroad and those in essential work and services, even those women who liked whisky would have experienced a period of some length during which they would have had little of it to drink. The de-rationing was, for them, quite an event and it is not surprising that its celebration sometimes led to arrest. The rise in the figures in 1961 is connected with the attempt to make vodka a popular drink in the United Kingdom. Being in many ways akin to gin, it is not to be wondered that women should be willing to try it under the influence of powerful advertising in the press and on posters. The denouement is better to be seen on the next set of diagrams, opposite.

The ages of females convicted - 1962–1967

The effect of the promotion of vodka upon the numbers of women convicted of drunkenness was maintained over 1962 and 1963 in all the age-groups, but the numbers of offences then began to fall until 1966 in all cases except that of women aged 30–59, where the fall was halted after 1965. It is to be borne in mind, when considering the figures that the post-war "bulge" in the birth rate had the effect of increasing the numbers aged 18–20 by 15 per cent each year from 1960 to 1966. All the age groups then show a sharp increase until 1967.

Vodka was a short-lived disturber of the sobriety of the women of England and Wales, and it is probably better to regard it as a surface phenomenon than as something that importantly changed the long, downward trend in offences which set in after 1956 and continued for some ten years.

It will be noted that the amounts of spirits released for consumption were roughly the same for each year in the period. Releases of beer were rising slightly but hardly more than would be called for by the rise in the total population of the country. Releases of wines rose from 1963 to 1965, but steadied thereafter. There is nothing in these figures to suggest that the totals had any immediate effect upon the numbers of offences by women in the six years; once again, the cause of the fluctuations has to be sought in the variations in the "mix" of the releases; novelty begetting the disturbances.

After 1967, another type of novelty makes its appearance and the last of the sets of diagrams illustrating the experience in respect of offences of drunkenness by females, appearing overleaf, suggests that this novelty had a more fundamental influence than had either the release of matured whisky or the promotion of vodka. From 1967 onwards there was a steady increase in the numbers of supermarkets with off-licensed departments, offering women a convenient access to intoxicating liquor such as they had never enjoyed before.

DIAGRAM VIII
Ages of females convicted of drunkenness, 1962–67

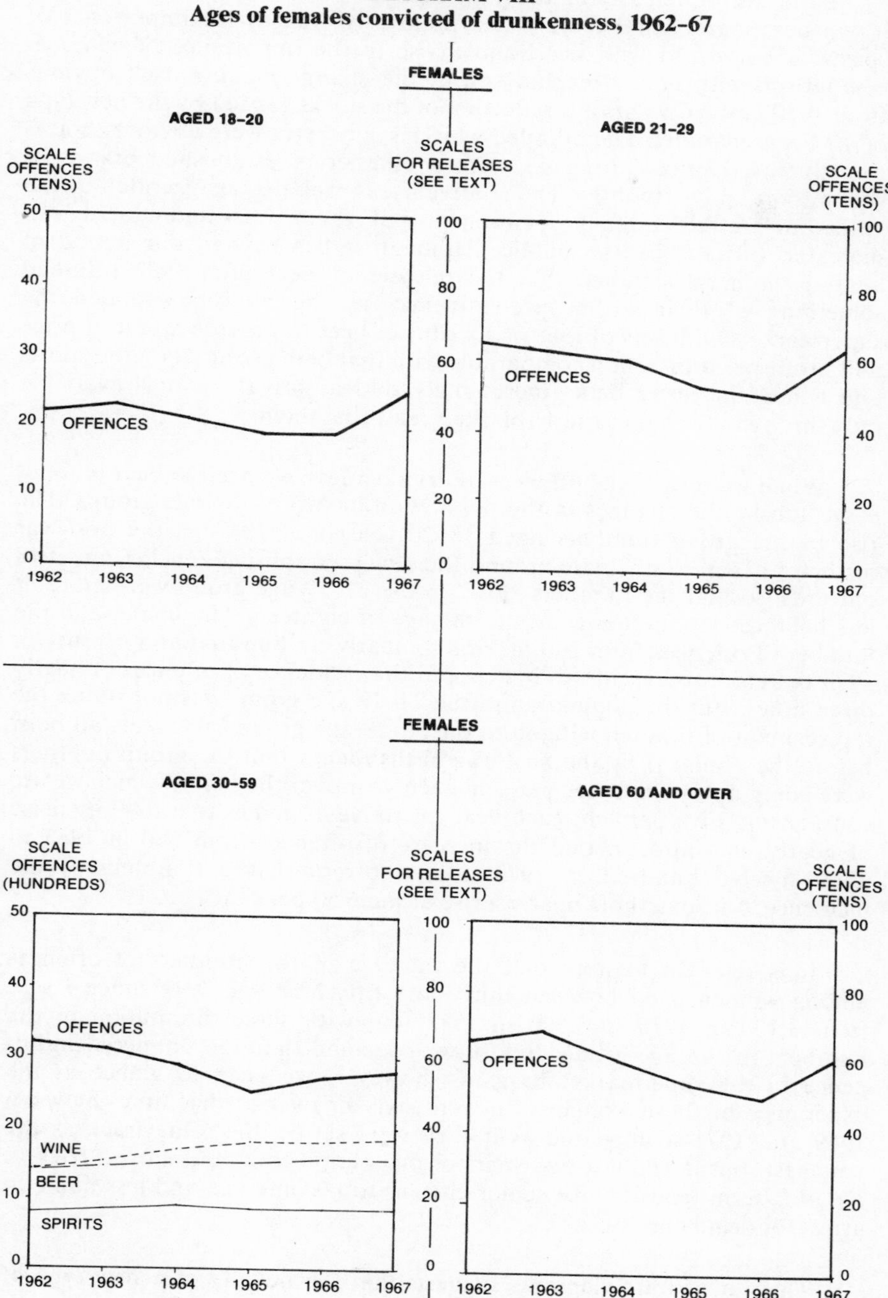

The ages of females convicted - 1968–1973

So far as the releases of alcoholic liquors to consumption is concerned, it will be apparent that there was a progressive rise in the importance of spirits as compared with beer, and a rise in the importance of wines in comparison with both beer and spirits, the change making itself obvious from 1970 onwards. This is a reflection of the stocks carried by the new type of off-licensed outlet. The branded whiskies, gins, etc., were obvious choices for advertised price-cutting, as were a number of established brands of sherry, port and vermouths. The relative rise is probably exaggerated by the "pipe-line" effect already mentioned, but there was undoubtedly an increased off-take by the public. Although it lies beyond our period of analysis, it may be noted that the releases of beer after 1973 resumed something of their earlier pre-eminence, as the brewers supplied the supermarkets with sets of four or six cans of beer to provide a unit of price and profit per transaction comparable with that being secured on the spirits and wines, the latter being increasingly sold as private brands available only through the chain of supermarkets featuring them.

When we turn to the offences of drunkenness, we need to bear in mind some substantial changes in the population in two of the age-groups. The rise in the group numbers aged 18–20 ceased in 1967 as the post-war birthrate began to fluctuate around the newly established levels from 1948 onwards, so that the numbers "lost" to the 21–19 age-group were more or less balanced by the newcomes to the age of eighteen. The increase in the number of offences from 260 in 1968 to nearly six hundred and seventy in 1973 therefore represents an increase in the incidence of offences of nearly three times. But the population in the 21–29 age-group was not static; the replacement of those moving in to the 30–59 age-group each year (all born before the "bulge") by the post-war births meant that the group numbers were going up by some five per cent each year over the period which we are considering. Five per cent each year for six years comes to a total increase of nearly one-third, so that the increase of offences from 650 in 1968 to about twelve hundred in 1973 does not represent a doubling of the incidence, but something nearer a rise of some 50 per cent.

It is relevant to note that the increase in the numbers of offences among women aged between thirty and fifty-nine was very much less – from 3,100 in 1970 to 3,500 in 1973, but with some diminution in the numbers in the age-group. Before we conclude that age tempered indulgence in the supermarket bargains, however, we need to glance at the experience of those women who were sixty or over at that time. Between 1969 and 1971 it appeared as if they were set on the same track as the youngest, but in the last two years of our period the trend moved back to the long-term tendency for senior citizens to become less and less liable to arrest for drunkenness.

This set of four diagrams suggests that the novelty of a new type of alcoholic drink ceases to have an influence upon the arrests for drunkenness just as quickly in the 1970s as it did in the two previous decades, but there is much more doubt that the appearance of a new and convenient type of

DIAGRAM IX
Ages of females convicted of drunkenness, 1968-73

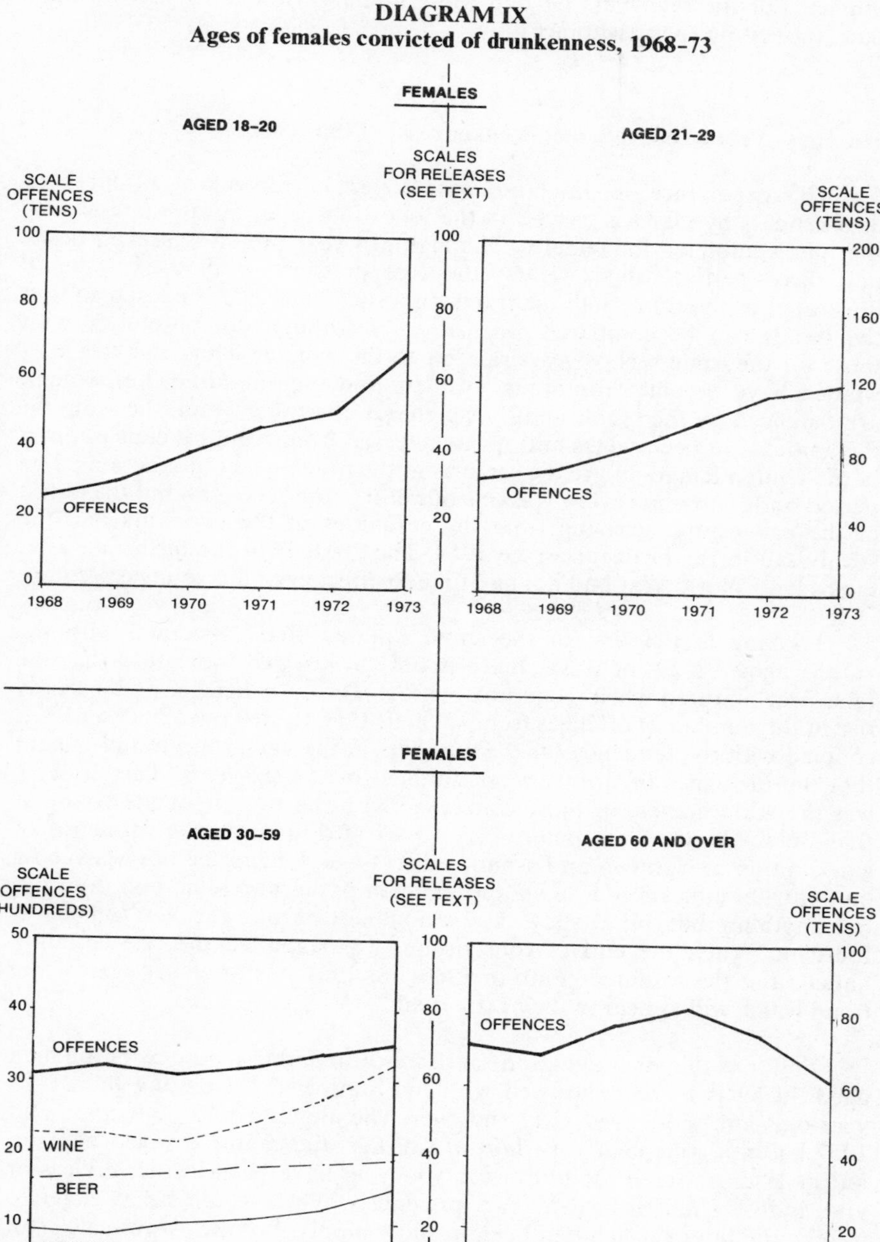

access to all kinds of alcoholic liquor will have a similarly short-lived impact. For the few years beyond those under review for which we have data, there is no such assurance.

The ages of males convicted of drunkenness - 1956-1961

The experience in England and Wales in respect of offences of drunkenness by males is treated in the following pages in the same way as that just completed for females. The eighteen-year period is broken down into three periods of six years; the first of these - 1956–61 - being illustrated in the four small diagrams opposite. The scale is chosen so that the trends can be compared *proportionately* though not absolutely with those for the same sets of years relating to the women. Thus, the "tens" of women have become "hundreds" of men, and the "hundreds" of women are balanced by the "thousands" of men. On the other hand, the scale for the amounts of beer, wines and spirits released from bond for consumption in the United Kingdom are the same as in the previous set of diagrams. The period under present review was one of falling numbers in all but the oldest of the age-groups, deriving from the casualties of the two wars and the steady fall in the birth-rate since 1914. The "bulge" in the birth-rate after the Second World War had not had time to affect even the youngest group.

Looking at the first of the small squares, that concerned with the youths aged 18–20 inclusive, there is only a vestigial indication that the release of matured whisky had much effect. On the other hand, the steady rise in the number of offences from 4,000 in 1956 to well over 7,000 in 1961, coupled with the tendency for the numbers in the age-group to fall, meant that the incidence of drunkenness doubled in the six years. This, indeed, was the main anxiety of those concerned with the welfare of the young at that time. Much of the deterioration was attributed to the influence of conscription at eighteen-and-a-half years of age. Unless the boy was going on to higher education or to an apprenticeship, there were no opportunities for anything but blind-alley occupations for those who left school at fourteen. When the end of conscription was signalled the rise certainly halted, and the resumed climb in 1960 and 1961 has to be set against the trend which will appear in the next period.

So far as the other age-groups are concerned, the steadiness of the men aged 30–59 is to be contrasted with the jump in 1957 among the 21–29 year-olds and those aged sixty and over. The men aged 30–59 in 1956 and 1957 had not gone nearly as short of whisky, after matured stocks had run out in 1942, as those too old or too young to have been in the services or vital industry ten to fifteen years previously. They would be as eager to imbibe the liquor which had been in short supply, but they would also still be "experienced whisky drinkers", which the men in the other two groups would not be when the supplies were released.

There is the evidence of a repetition of this kind of inexperience at the end of the period, when vodka was being promoted in many parts of the country in 1961 and 1962, taking advantage of the willingness of the

DIAGRAM X
Ages of males convicted of drunkenness, 1956–61

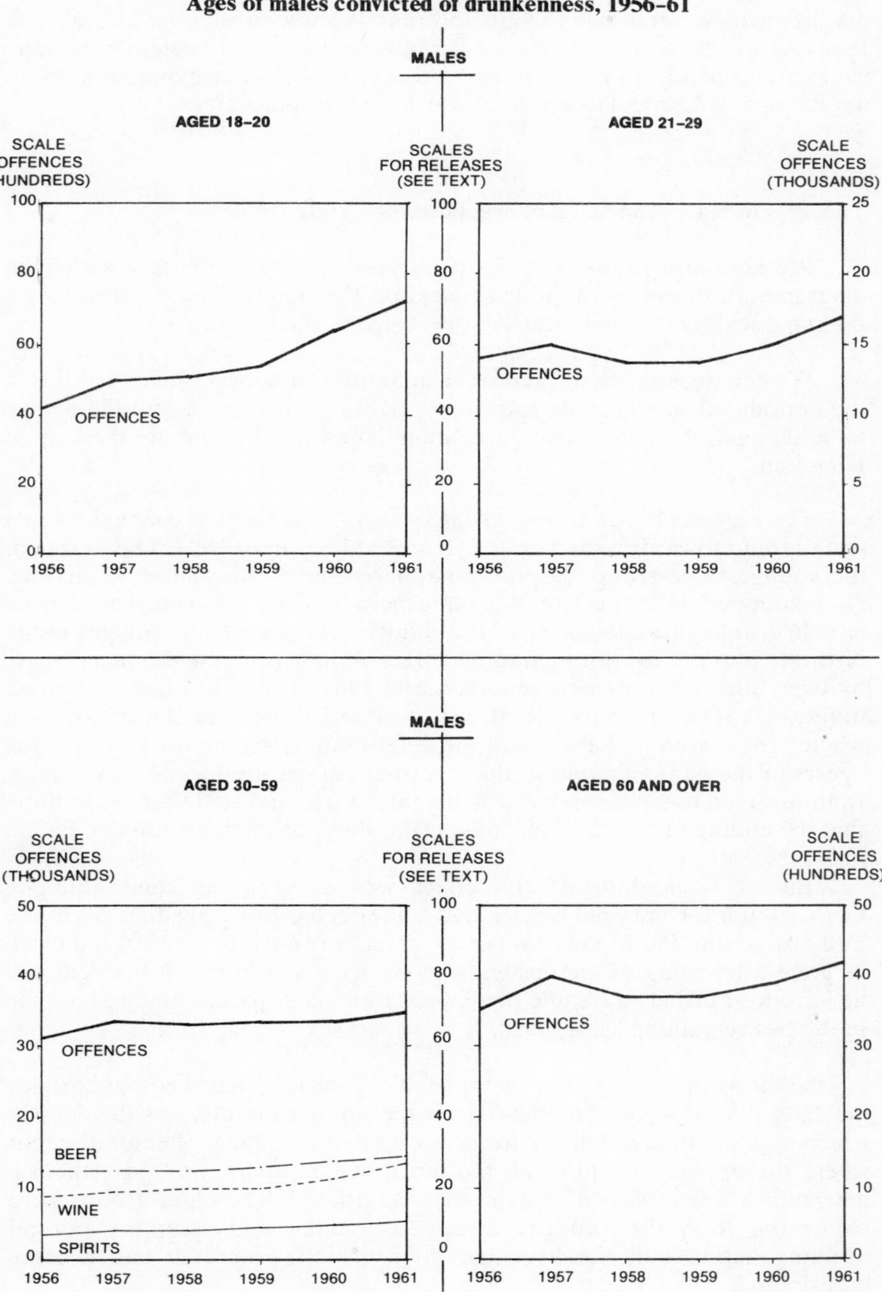

Russian political leaders of that time to visit the West and move among the people. There is no sign of a rise in offences in 1961 among men aged 30–59, but the same age-groups that proved sensitive to the novelty of matured whisky after a diet of gin and rum do show substantial increases in 1961. As will be clear from the lines showing the trend of releases of beer, wines and spirits from bond, in the bottom left-hand square diagram, it was not the quantities available in total which were responsible.

The ages of males convicted of drunkenness - 1962–1967

We now turn to the next set of six years. The experience is set out in diagrammatic form in the four squares on the opposite page, drawn with the same scales as were used for the 1956–61 period.

We can dismiss the influences of quantity summarily, since the lines in the bottom left-hand square show only slight upward trends and these have to be set against a gently-rising total population of adult men in the United Kingdom.

The biggest change is from rising or steady numbers of convictions to a strong trend towards reduction in offences at least until 1967. This is true of the youngest age-group, despite the apparent level movement of the line. As mentioned in respect of the same period when we were considering female drunkenness, the entry of the children of the post-war "bulge" in the birthrate into this age-group had the effect of increasing the numbers at risk by over forty per cent between 1964 and 1967. The "flat" line, therefore, indicates a drop in incidence of well over one-third over the period as a whole. Those who had attributed the deterioration among the young to the "years of the gap" inherent in the deferment of call-up for national service from fourteen to eighteen-and-a-half years of age had some reason to think that the ending of conscription could claim the credit for the improvement.

But it is doubtful if the effect was as great as some thought. Conscription for national service had not affected those aged 30–59 in the mid-60s yet the fall in the number of offences from 1963 to 1966 indicated as great a lowering of the incidence as we have attributed to the youngest age-group. Further, the same downward trend is apparent among the men in the two remaining age-groups.

So far as the young are concerned, it is probable that the popularity of the "groups", of whom The Beatles are the prime example, was the novelty which took the impressionistic fringe away from the places of entertainment where the opportunity to drink too much was frequent, and gave them a new and different way of proving their adulthood. The older groups were recovering from the "novelty effects" of vodka and resuming normal drinking habits with the beverages to which they were or had become accustomed.

In 1967 we see a reversal of the short-lived trend downward. It is most marked in the oldest age-group and least obvious among men aged 21–29

DIAGRAM XI
Ages of males convicted of drunkenness, 1962–67

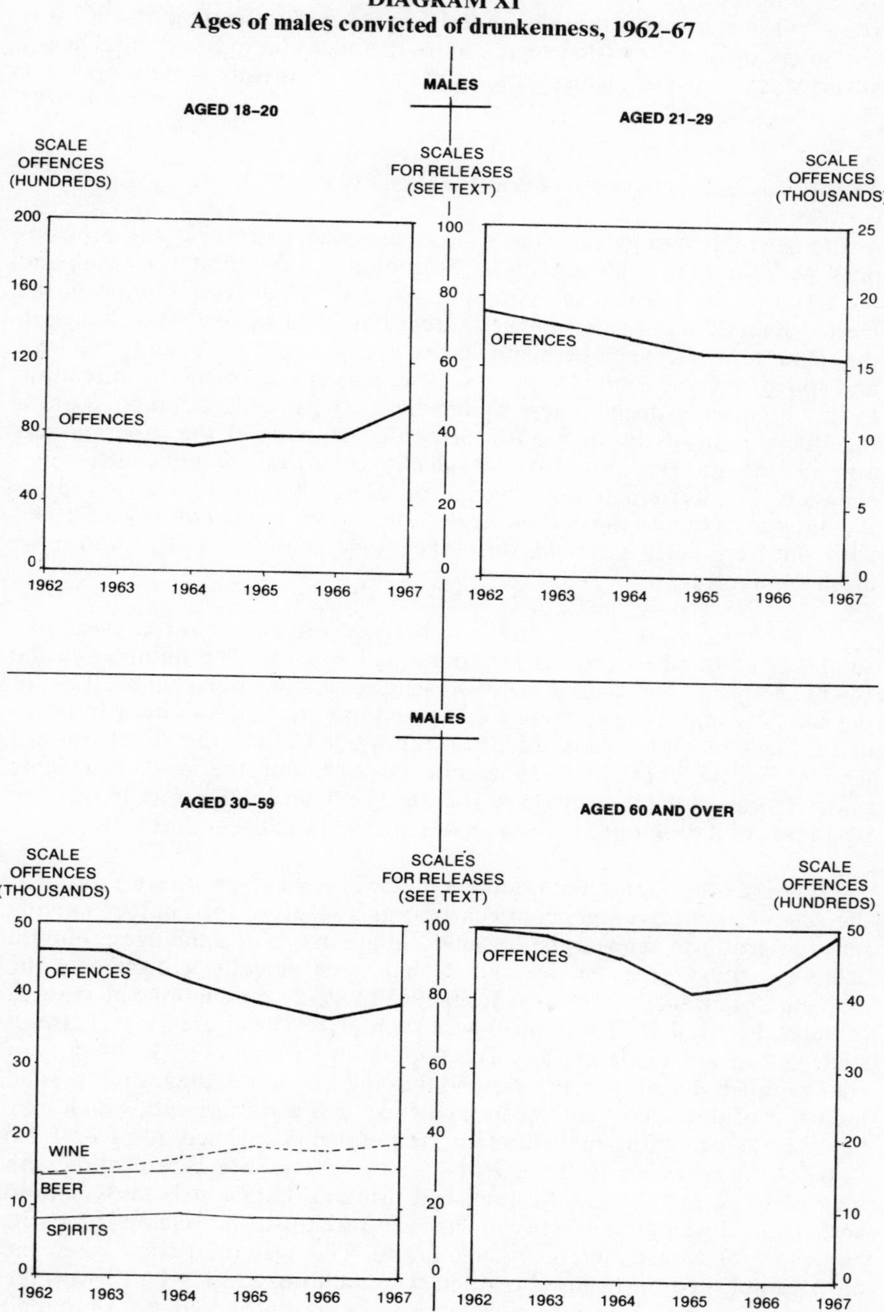

in 1967. We have been over the proximate cause of the change – the increase in the numbers of off-licensed departments among the supermarkets – but it is probable that the underlying reason for the jump in 1967 was not more off-licences (they come into the next period) but the heavy advertising of cut-price whisky and spirits by those already in business.

The ages of males convicted of drunkenness – 1968–1973

The set of diagrams opposite follow the same pattern as the previous ones, with the four small squares each devoted to a different age-group and the trend of the releases of beer, spirits and wines to consumption in the United Kingdom indicated in the bottom left-hand square. The change in the relationship between beer and spirits, and between wines and both beer and spirits, was mentioned when the same period was discussed in relation to the offences of drunkenness by females. It represents a combination of the stocking-up of the new off-licensed departments of the supermarkets and of the growing purchase of alcoholic drinks through such retail channels. The introduction of "packs" of canned beer will go far to redress the imbalance before the end of the decade, but we are only now concerned with the very early years of this innovatory channel of distribution of alcoholic beverages.

The lines representing the numbers of offences have a deceptive similarity of trend in each of the four small squares. The numbers in the 18–20 age-group had ceased to grow each year as the "bulge" moved out of the category, and latterly there was some diminution in numbers. In terms of the incidence of arrests for drunkenness, therefore, the slight upward tendency from 1968 to 1971 is not far out, but the next two years under-represent the increase in incidence. The deterioration was, in fact, the beginning of a prolonged worsening among the 18–20 year olds.

On the other hand, the numbers in the 21–29 age-group were rising at the rate of about five per cent each year as a result of the "bulge" moving into the group to replace the lessening numbers leaving the age-group on achieving thirty years of age. Thus, there was actually a decline in the incidence of offences every year from 1968 to 1972, although the increase in offences between 1972 and 1973 was such as to constitute an increase of some size in the incidence, too. The population of men aged 30–59 did not change much during the six years, so that the line in the diagram is a good indicator of the rate of change in incidence. It is a rising trend, which may be taken as beginning in 1970, with the numbers convicted going up from 41,000 to over 47,000 in three years. Given that we are here dealing with men of some maturity and established drinking habits, it is fairly safe to accept the close parallel between the rising trend in the releases of spirits and those of convictions in the age-group. This was the period when the older-established off-licensed retailers were fighting a losing battle with the supermarkets, and both sets of retailers were cutting the prices of branded spirits to a degree that has not been equalled once the issue of the battle became clear. Such an effective reduction in the price of spirits was conducive to greater indulgence, and the age-group most attached to spirits

DIAGRAM XII
Ages of males convicted of drunkenness, 1968–73

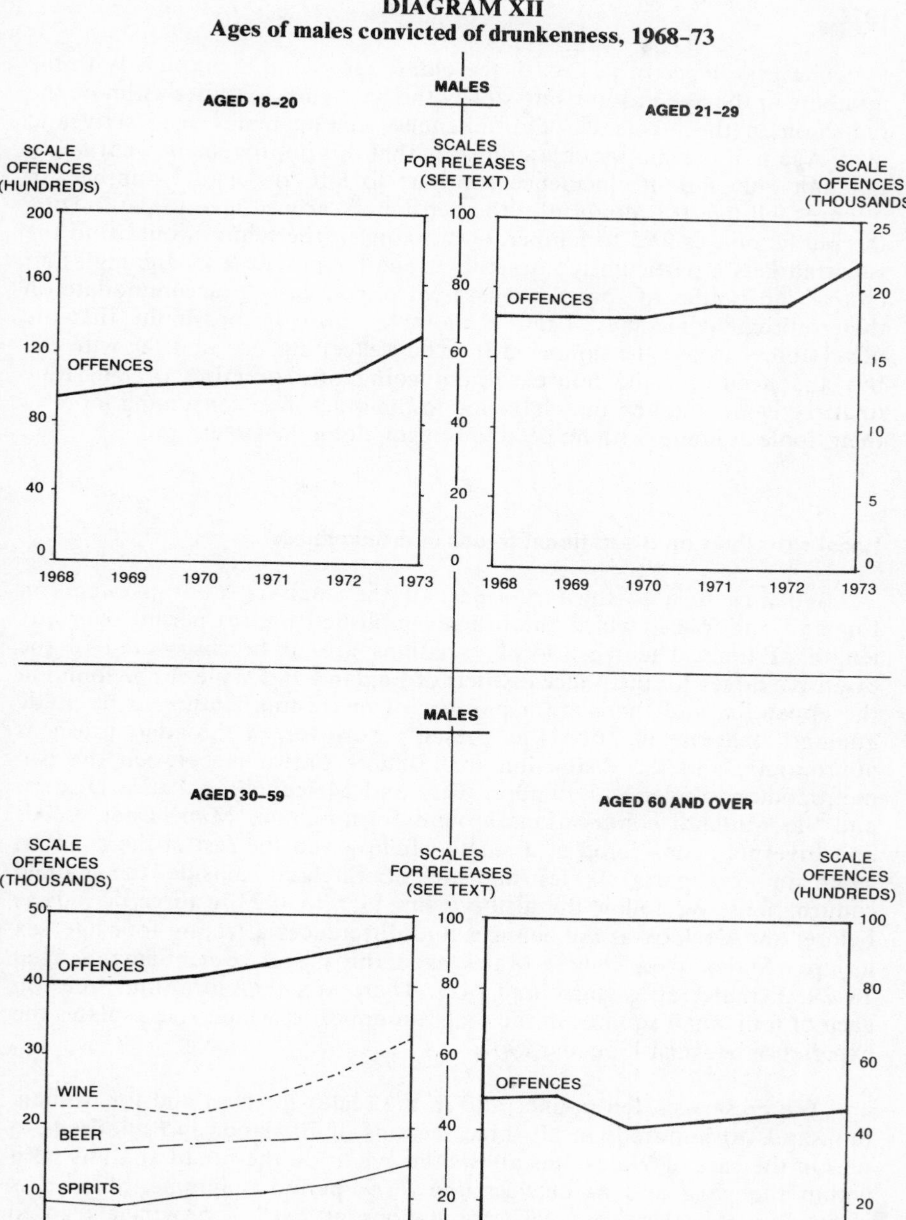

showed the greatest reaction. It is a matter of later history that the incidence of offences did not go on increasing at anything like the same rate after 1974.

The experience in respect of the oldest age-group is simpler. With the numbers in the age-group rising slowly the line tends to under-estimate the reduction in the incidence of drunkenness among males aged sixty and over. Again, it is a matter of later history that this improvement went on, so that not only did the incidence continue to fall; the actual numbers of offences fell too. It is doubtful if the pensioners, accustomed to patronizing the public houses and to temperate drinking in the home, would find the supermarkets a particularly attractive venue for purchase, or the high unit cost of full bottles of spirits, even at cut prices, easy to accommodate on their retirement incomes. There is, however, also the possibility that the novel ability to put the liquor on the "housekeeping", so that the wife can buy the needs for the house without going into premises of long-time unattractiveness to her, may have led to the older men consuming more of their tipple at home, with no need to stagger along the streets.

Local variations on the national trends of drunkenness

We now turn to the last aspect of the analysis of drunkenness in England and Wales which the official published figures permit over any length of time. The truly local variations are to be discovered in the extensive tables for the police districts of England and Wales to be found in the appendix, and there are a number of interesting studies to be made amongst that detail. For the present, however, a broader brush is appropriate, and the distinction that is here drawn is between the two metropolitan congeries – London, City and Metropolitan Police District; and the Midland conurbations around Birmingham, Manchester, Leeds and Liverpool considered as a single whole – and the rest of the country, again in two parts, Wales and all of England outside the named conurbations. We follow the history from 1956 to 1973 in three periods as before, and we look at the changes and differences affecting four age/sex groups: Males aged 18–29; Males aged thirty and over; Females aged 18–29; Females aged thirty and over. There are, therefore, four lines on each of four small squares in the diagram opposite, which encapsulates the experience between 1956 and 1961.

We preserve a ten-to-one ratio in the scales for men and for women, thousands to hundreds in all three sections of England, and hundreds to tens in the case of Wales. this allows the eye to do the broad analysis both within the page and as between the three period diagrams. Since it is impossible to assess the real "populations at risk" – provincials go to London to get drunk; countrymen go to the Midlands conurbations in much the same way; while the urban concentrations pour out into the country and to the seaside at weekends and for holidays, equally bent on enjoyment – the comparisons should be limited to the different patterns of male and female offences and the age distributions. Thus, in the diagram, opposite, for the period 1956–61, London is manifestly different from all

DIAGRAM XIII
Regional variations in drunkenness, 1956–61

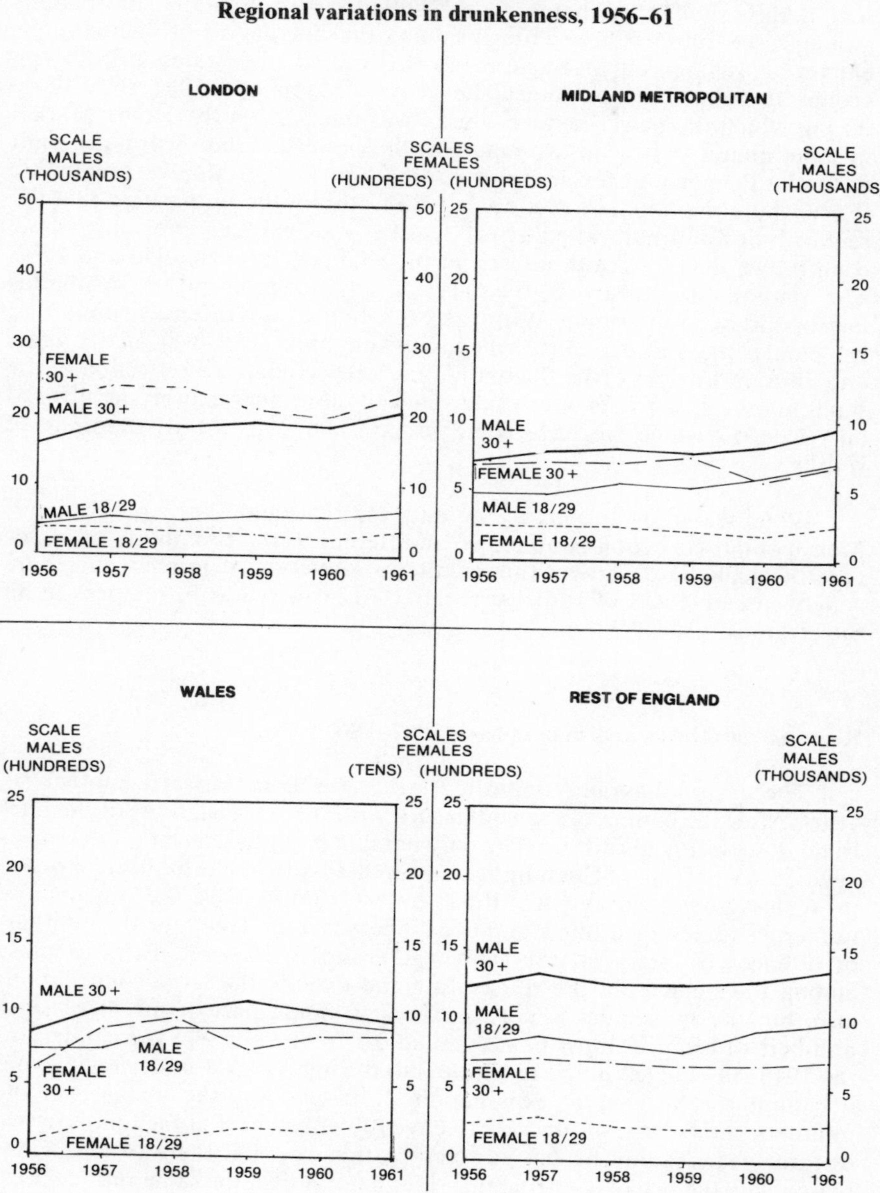

the other regions in that the middle-aged female is dominant over the other age/sex groups, whereas the middle-aged male is relatively more important in the Midland metropolitan police districts (taken together) than in London, and so is the male aged 18–29. The pattern for Wales is remarkably similar to that for the Midland metropolitan conurbations although the numbers are so much smaller that the degree of fluctuation is enhanced. In the rest of England, at this period, the males in both age groups dominate the position. The years of 1956 and 1957 were those during which the newly-mature whisky was released on the Home Market in some quantity. It is unfortunate that the published data will not permit us to plot the age and sex grouping earlier than 1956, so that we are unable to see where the initial impact was greatest. But on the supposition that the removal of informal rationing of whisky was gradual over the whole country, we may look with interest at the changes between 1956 and 1957. The remarkable feature is the lack of any reaction in the Midlands metropolitan conurbations. With the exception of the offences committed by females aged under thirty which run smoothly level over all six years and all four "regions" (the fluctuation in Wales could be a reflection of the small numbers of events in any one year) all other lines exhibit the upward kink in 1957 which we have come to associate with the de-rationing of whisky.

When we go on to look at the data for 1960 and 1961, the Midlands Metropolitan collection is no longer indifferent to the promotion of a new type of alcoholic beverage. Indeed, the introduction of greater and more widely-spread stocks of vodka was reflected in increases in offences in all the "regions" except Wales.

Regional variations in drunkenness – 1962–1967

The set of diagrams opposite carries the story forward another six years. After the ending of the vodka surge in 1963 or 1964, most of the lines trend downwards until 1967. The only notable exception is that of the males aged 18–29 in Wales. The numbers of offences attributed to this age-group in Wales grow to be greater than those committed by the much more numerous males aged thirty and over. There is a tendency for the numbers of offences by males in the same age-group to rise, relatively to those among their elders, in the rest of England outside the large conurbations also, but the movement is not as dramatic. Some part of the increase in numbers of offences must be accounted for by the entry of the children of the 1946–48 "bulge" in the birthrate into the age bracket under review, but it cannot be the general explanation. Not only was the increase in the numbers in this large group slow to have full effect, so that the jumps in two or three years cannot be caused solely in this way, but there is no obvious reason why the urban conurbations should not reflect the same influences.

This was a relatively quiet period in the span of thirty-seven years which we are analysing and it is possible that the improvement visible in all the localities and in all the age/sex groups would have continued if, in 1967, there had not been the impetus which eventually led to the supermarkets

DIAGRAM XIV
Regional variations in drunkenness, 1962–67

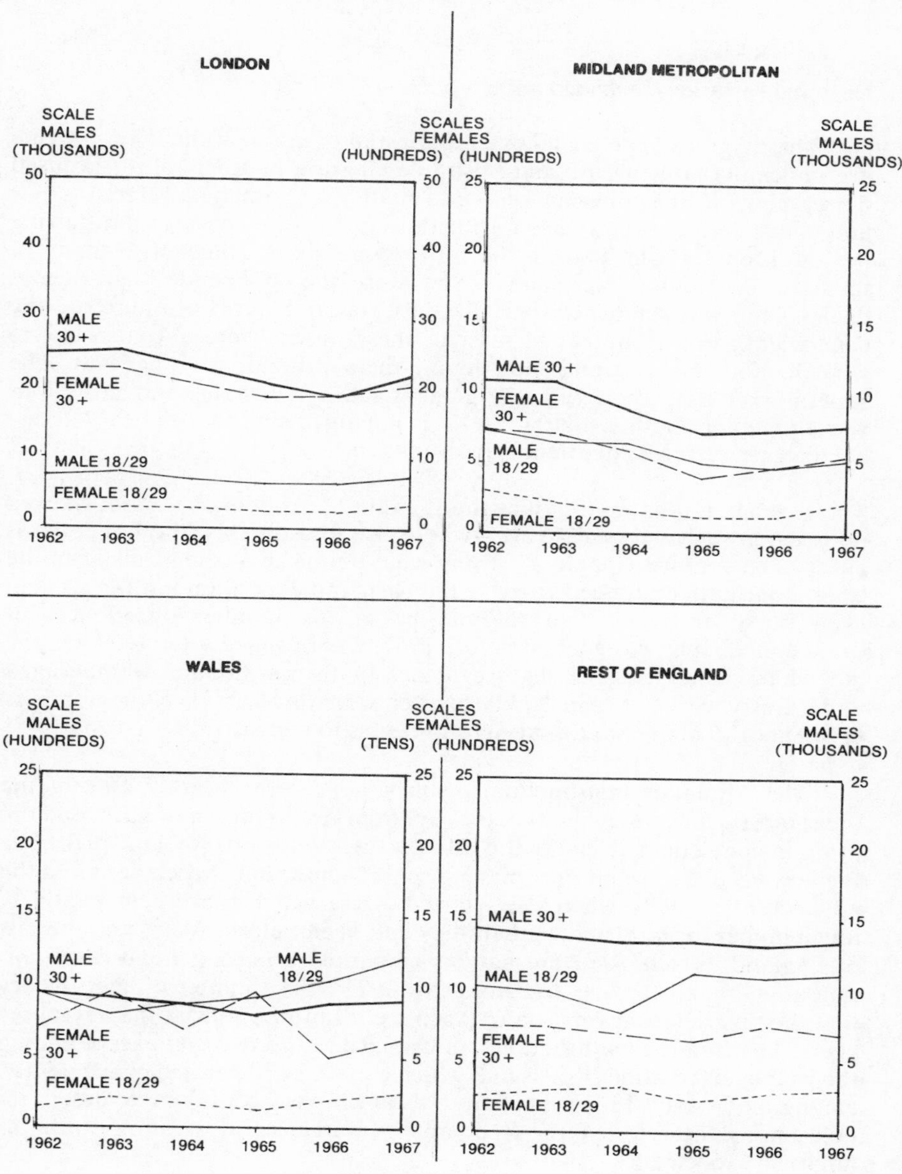

entering forcefully into the field of retailing alcoholic liquor. The impact of the novel access to alcoholic drink was not the same in all our "regions"; but we have to turn to the next set of six years to see this clearly. 1967 witnessed only some sharp price-cutting by the few off-licences held by grocery organizations.

Regional variations in drunkenness – 1968–1973

The diagram opposite takes us to the end of our analysis. The six years are under the growing influence of the increasing numbers of off-licensed departments in the supermarkets. Essentially, such retailers offered a new and convenient access to alcohol for those who were chary of patronizing the traditional public houses, the off-licensed shops attached to many of them or the "Wine Merchants" who were the independent off-licence dealers, and who tended to specialize in wines and spirits of interest to the cognoscenti. For a number of reasons, these outlets were not attractive to women, and many young men found them difficult to cope with. The supermarket concerned with the general sale of groceries and provisions was altogether another matter, and it is not surprising that the easy access led to sharp increases in offences in drunkenness.

It is again illuminating that the London Metropolitan District showed no reaction such as is visible everywhere else. Presumably, the Londoner is and has been quite capable of getting what liquor he or she wants from the traditional outlets. Indeed there is the clear indication among the women aged thirty and over that the decline in the number of offences of drunkenness, that was general before 1967, was resumed after 1969. On the other hand, there is some slight evidence that some London women aged under thirty were not quite so blasé; after years of quiescence, the numbers of offences attributed to this age group begins to increase in 1970.

The Midlands metropolitan conurbations were naturally one of the areas most quickly exploited by the supermarkets in their new garb, and the jump in convictions is marked in all age/sex groups in 1969 and 1970. The females aged thirty and over, having set off somewhat earlier, resumed the advance after 1970, when they started a rise which took them relatively much higher in the "league" than they had been before. Wales and the rest of England outside the conurbations embarked upon a general deterioration affecting all the age/sex groups by 1971. It is a matter of later history that the deterioration went on to reach record proportions in the next three years. The London conurbation still displayed little reaction except among the women aged under thirty and, which cannot be illustrated conveniently, among males aged 18–20. There has also been very considerable deterioration among those too young to be able to purchase intoxicating drinks, as might be expected.

The kind of differential changes which have occurred in our four "regions" over the past nineteen years to 1973 is brought out by the following table which shows the percentages of convictions for drunkenness in England and Wales as a whole arising in London, in the Midlands

DIAGRAM XV
Regional variations in drunkenness, 1968–73

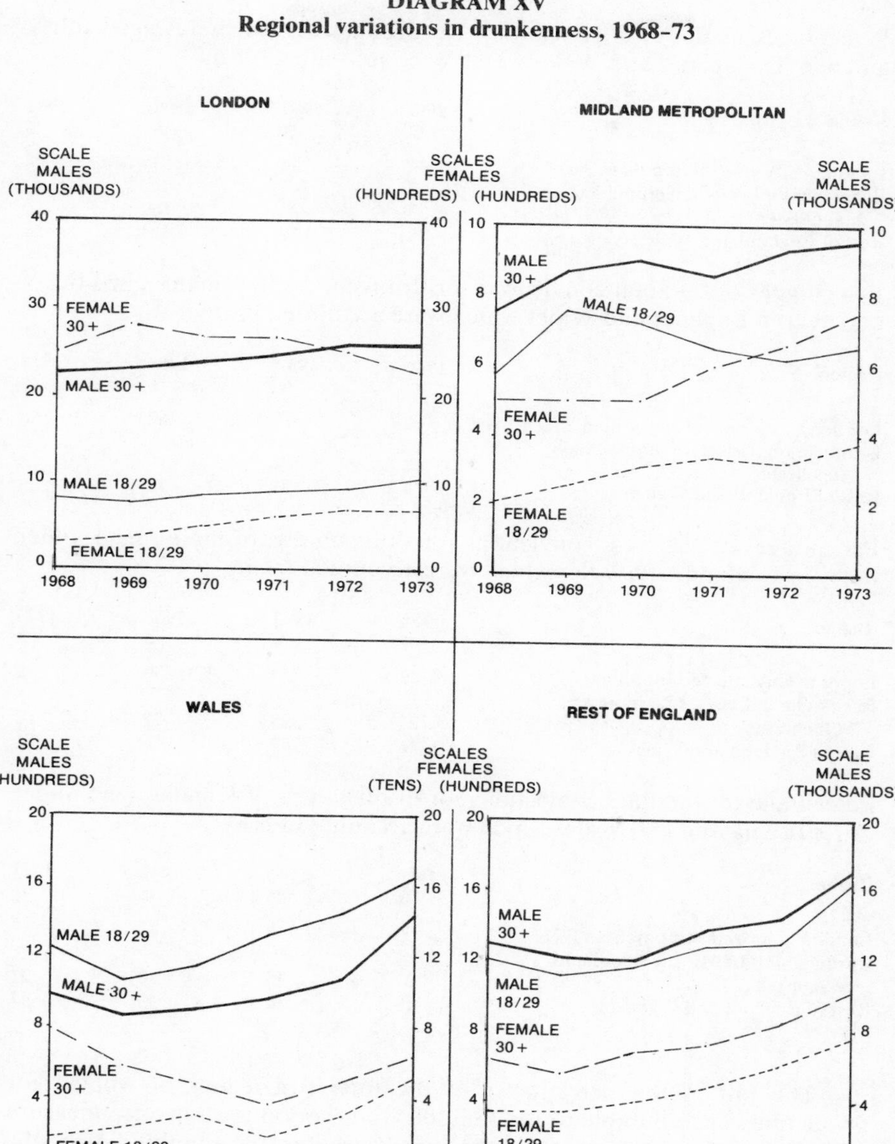

metropolitan areas, and in the rest of England and Wales in each of four years from the beginning to the end of the period of analysis. There are, in effect, four sub-tables, each treating of one of the age and sex categories.

Percentages of the total convictions for drunkenness of males aged thirty and over in England and Wales which were accounted for by:

Region	**1956** %	**1962** %	**1968** %	**1973** %
London, City and Metropolitan P.D.	44	48	53	48
Birmingham, Leeds, Liverpool and Manchester	20	23	16	17
Rest of England and Wales	36	29	31	35

Percentages of the total convictions for drunkenness of females aged thirty and over in England and Wales which were accounted for by:

Region	**1956** %	**1962** %	**1968** %	**1973** %
London, City and Metropolitan P.D.	60	61	68	56
Birmingham, Leeds, Liverpool and Manchester	17	19	13	18
Rest of England and Wales	23	20	19	26

Percentages of the total convictions for drunkenness of males aged under thirty in England and Wales which were accounted for by:

Region	**1956** %	**1962** %	**1968** %	**1973** %
London, City and Metropolitan P.D.	27	29	30	29
Birmingham, Leeds, Liverpool and Manchester	27	29	22	20
Rest of England and Wales	46	42	48	51

Percentages of the total convictions for drunkenness of females aged under thirty in England and Wales which were accounted for by:

Region	**1956** %	**1962** %	**1968** %	**1973** %
London, City and Metropolitan P.D.	50	35	40	32
Birmingham, Leeds, Liverpool and Manchester	31	35	20	21
Rest of England and Wales	19	30	40	47

The fall in the percentages of the total convictions of women for drunkenness attributable to the London conurbation is an inverse measure of the increasing importance of the supermarket in the supply of alcoholic drinks to women between 1968 and 1973, in other parts of the country.

We may summarize the conclusions to be drawn from this analysis of the history of drunkenness in England and Wales through and after the Second World War by saying that an increase in the amount of alcoholic liquor available for consumption is not a sufficient condition for an increase in drunkenness. If there is a change in the "mix" of the supply, then there is likely to be a short-lived deterioration, probably until the bulk of the drinkers get used to the new potion or return to what they used to drink before. When, however, there is a new channel of distribution opened so that access is made easier to some or all the age and sex groups, then there will be deterioration among some age and sex groups, and this deterioration will be serious and continuing if the channel is widespread so that most of the population is open to its influence.

On the more reassuring side it is also clear that most of the drinkers of alcoholic beverages in England and Wales take what they like when they want it and do not become a nuisance or a terror to their neighbours; and that the young seem to become more sober as they age in much the same way as their counterparts did ten, fifteen and twenty years ago.

CHAPTER 20

DRUNKENNESS IN GREAT BRITAIN, 1973–79

The year 1973 marked the end of a twenty-year period of gently-rising living standards, low unemployment, cheap petrol and inflation at a rate of less than five per cent per annum, compounded. In 1974 and, again, in 1977, disposable incomes failed to keep pace with the cost of living. In 1972 the numbers of wholly-unemployed were just over 800,000; by 1977 the figure had risen to 1,450,000. In 1972 4-star petrol was 36p per gallon; in 1977 it was 77p and in 1979 around 120p per gallon. Between 1972 and 1979 the rate of inflation was rather over 14 per cent per annum, compounded. There were some substantial fluctuations in the amount of personal income at the disposal of consumers.

The following table gives the estimates made by the Central Statistical Office of the amount of money, in real terms (in this case at constant 1970 prices) available after payment of taxes, national insurance, etc. available each quarter since 1969 in thousands of millions of pounds sterling. The Central Statistical Office has made corrections for seasonal factors, so that the figures can be taken as they stand.

Total disposable income per quarter,
£'000 million at constant 1970 prices, seasonally corrected

Year	Quarter	£th.mn.	Year	Quarter	£th.mn.	Year	Quarter	£th.mn.
1969	I	8.4	1973	I	9.9	1977	I	10.2
	II	8.3		II	10.2		II	10.0
	III	8.4		III	10.2		III	10.1
	IV	8.5		IV	10.2		IV	10.5
1970	I	8.4	1974	I	10.1	1978	I	10.4
	II	8.7		II	10.0		II	10.8
	III	8.8		III	10.4		III	11.0
	IV	8.7		IV	10.5		IV	11.2
1971	I	8.8	1975	I	10.6	1979	I	11.2
	II	8.8		II	10.3		II	11.1
	III	8.9		III	10.3		III	11.1
	IV	9.1		IV	10.2		IV	11.1*
1972	I	9.1	1976	I	10.5			
	II	9.6		II	10.2			
	III	9.5		III	10.5			
	IV	9.9		IV	10.3			

* Provisional

The figures do not appear to vary by much, but it must be remembered that a change from 10.5 to 10.0 represents a fall of £500,000,000 and the disposable income has to meet fixed charges like rent, rates and the interest upon the mortgage. Further, a level trend on a global basis may conceal substantial changes in some parts of the country and for some categories of consumers. Thus, the coal strike of early 1974 and the resultant 3-day week affected Scotland, North-East England and the Birmingham area more than they did the rest of Great Britain. The exceptionally hard winter weather early in 1979 practically stopped the construction industry for some weeks but affected few other workers.

Such a change in social and economic circumstances should be reflected in the statistics of drunkenness and, as the table following shows, this was the case. The table is divided in two; the first part shows the offences of drunkenness proved against pedestrians separately for Scotland and England with Wales, the second part does the same for the *proceedings* against motorists for offences to do with drink and drugs. As in the earlier chapter dealing with the differences between England with Wales and Scotland the figures for the former are in terms of thousands and those for Scotland in hundreds – approximately reflecting the ratio of populations.

	Offences of drunkenness proved		**Proceedings against motorists**	
Year	**England and Wales thousands**	**Scotland hundreds**	**England and Wales thousands**	**Scotland hundreds**
1970	82	106	32	97
1971	87	109	46	113
1972	90	117	56	116
1973	99	135	65	131
1974	103*	147	67*	145
1975	104	150**	70	140**
1976	109	142	63	117
1977	109	123†	53	106†
1978	107	126	65	125
1979	115††	130††	73††	130††

Notes:

* Local authority and police district boundaries altered in England and Wales causing some alteration in recording procedures.

** Local authority and police district boundaries altered in Scotland again causing some alteration in recording procedures.

† Permitted hours on weekdays extended by two hours and a number of restrictions on Sunday drinking removed, in Scotland only.

†† Estimates by the Christian Economic and Social Research Foundation based on statistics supplied by chief constables – incomplete data.

It will be convenient to describe and discuss the changes made to the permitted hours in Scotland at the beginning of 1977 before turning to an examination of the other detail in the tables above. The impact of the local government changes was small at national levels, although it was enough to make other regional comparisons difficult or impossible.

Departmental Committee on Scottish Licensing Law

At the same time as the Home Office set up the Erroll Committee, the Scottish Office asked a departmental committee chaired by Dr Christopher Clayson:

> *To review the liquor licensing law of Scotland and to make recommendations on what changes, if any, might be made in the public interest; and to report.*

As seen in earlier chapters, nothing was done about the recommendations of the Erroll Committee during the seventies. It was otherwise with the

Clayson Committee. This is not surprising. The English law had been altered twice during the sixties and the changes had hardly had time to be evaluated. Apart from the Guest Committee (1958) which only dealt with four aspects of the licensing law in Scotland, the Clayson Committee was the first general review since 1929. That Royal Commission, under the chairmanship of Lord Mackay, was unable to reach complete agreement and, in 1931, submitted a majority and a minority report. In the event, none of the recommendations was implemented. Meantime, wide differences had emerged in the laws on either side of the border.

Many of the recommendations, therefore, concerned official procedures, licensing courts, courts of appeal and the like. Some of these were of a specifically Scottish controversial nature; especially the proposal that licensing courts should be replaced by tribunals appointed by district councils and consisting of district councillors. Most such, even if adopted, would take time to affect the general situation, and a discussion would be out of place in this review. But the retention of the age limited and the extension of the permitted hours so as to run from 11 a.m. to 11 p.m. throughout Scotland (to prevent motorists driving from the earlier to the later closing districts) as well as a general permission to open on Sunday are cleary relevant. Of these, the only alterations relate to opening hours, and the Scottish Office acted on the recommendations with unusual rapidity, so that the recommendations made in 1973 were law at the opening of 1977.

We need not concern ourselves with the changes in the Sunday regulations. As in Wales, the population wishing to drink on Sundays had long ago found ways to satisfy their thirsts without running foul of the law. It was a different matter with the extension of drinking hours during the weekdays. The police had been in favour of later closing because it had some effect in pushing the drunken motorists out of the earlier evening traffic to times when not only were there fewer cars about and fewer pedestrians on the streets, so that the risk of accidents might be expected to be reduced, but the erratic driver would be easier to spot and to overtake.

It is doubtful if we shall ever know whether the expectations of the police have been realized because of the change in driving which resulted from the petrol shortages and the rising prices of petrol. The combination is such as to make comparisons based upon road accidents at different times of the day between 1977 and 1978 and, say, 1975 and 1976, hazardous in the extreme.

But some of the protagonists of the extended hours went so far as to claim that the longer hours available for drinking had resulted in a sharp reduction in offences of drunkenness, both pedestrian and among motorists. This would have been a truly remarkable result, gainsaying all that had been accepted in the past. However, as the table at the beginning of this chapter will have made abundantly clear, nothing of the sort happened.

So far as pedestrians are concerned, the offences of drunkenness reached a peak of approximately 15,000 in 1975 and fell sharply to 14,200 in 1976, against a small but continuing rise in England and Wales. There was a further fall to 12,300 after the extension of hours in 1977, while the English total was unchanged. But, in 1978 and 1979 the Scottish figures resumed their climb while the numbers of drunkenness convictions south of the border were falling. The case is at best "not proven" in respect of pedestrians.

It is almost certainly disproved in the case of proceedings against motorists for offences to do with drink and drugs. The peak of such proceedings in Scotland occurred in 1974, and there was a fall to 14,000 in 1975. There was a further sharp reduction in 1976, before the extension of hours, to 11,700. In 1977, the figure fell further to 10,600 but the rise in 1978, to 12,500 was greater than the fall hailed by those claiming the unusual benefit from extended hours of drinking. It does not help to cry in the almost parellel movement in the statistics in England and Wales. There was no change in hours there. But the fall from 63,000 in 1976 to 53,000 in 1977, a matter of 16 per cent is proportionately greater than that from 11,700 to 10,600, a matter of some 10 per cent. The rises in both countries in 1978 and 1979 are of the same order of magnitude and, in any case, we shall see that the English figures are subject to some artificial, or, rather, special Christmas influences in these last two years which bring about an unusual increase in the following year's statistics.

Regretfully, we must conclude that the millenium has not come in Scotland. Just as we have seen that easier access to drink means more rather than less drunkenness, so we must conclude that longer time in which to drink is more likely to result in more drunkenness, whatever may have been the benefits in the reduction in accidents brought about by intoxicated drivers leaving pubs and clubs later in the evening.

The influence of fluctuations in the standard of living and of the price and availability of petrol

In a period of economic pressures combined with sharply-rising prices for petrol, it is to the fluctuations in the numbers of offences committed by motorists that we should look first. The numbers of pedestrian drunkards may even be increased by motorists taking to their feet and still over-indulging.

The earlier table shows an abrupt stop in the long climb – in 1975 in Scotland and in 1976 in England and Wales – with two successive years of actual decline. We have already noted that Scotland suffered more from the coal strike and the three-day weeks of 1974 than did England and Wales taken as a whole. The table at the opening of this chapter shows that the global total of personal disposable incomes fell early in 1974, recovered for some months, and then fell gradually to a nadir in the second quarter of 1977. The fall, and the subsequent rise, in the numbers of proceedings against motorists is in complete accord with the existence of a direct connection between disposable income and the numbers of drunken motorists.

We can take the matter further. In the *26th Annual Review of Chief Constables' Reports, Great Britain, 1978,* published by the Christian Economic and Social Research Foundation, there is an essay on the relationship between unemployment and drinking/driving offences in England and Wales. The comparison is between 1977 and 1978. Police districts, outside the Metropolitan Police District, were grouped into three tables on the basis of the degree of unemployment in them in 1978. There was also calculated the percentage change in unemployment between 1977 and 1978, and the percentage change in drinking/driving offences between the same two years. In the 41 Police Districts making up the three tables there were a total of 48,164 offences in 1978, as against 43,609 in 1977; an overall average increase of 11 per cent. In the ten police districts with more than seven per cent unemployment in 1978 the increase was only 6.2 per cent. In the 17 police districts with levels of unemployment over five per cent but under seven per cent the increase in driving offences was 11 per cent; the average for the non-metropolitan police districts as a whole. In the 14 police districts enjoying the lowest levels of unemployment, the increase in drink/drive offences was 14 per cent. A subsidiary table includes seven police districts in which there had been an important increase in the numbers unemployed in 1978 as against 1977; here the increase in drink/drive offences was only 2.3 per cent.

Where there was improvement, it seems to have taken the form of a drop in the amount of alcohol consumed by the individual drivers in most cases. This would seem such a commonsensical expectation that it must be viewed with suspicion. There are, in fact, a number of supporting pieces of evidence. The first lies in the changes in the percentages of those asked by the police for samples of breath which proved positive. The table that follows gives the numbers of requests for samples of breath made in each year from 1970 to 1978 in England and Wales and the percentage of these, each year, which proved positive.

Year	Numbers of requests for samples of breath from motorists	Percentages positive
1970	73,000	56%
1971	97,000	62%
1972	120,000	62%
1973	132,000	62%
1974	124,000	60%
1975	134,000	58%
1976	134,000	48%
1977	131,000	45%
1978	142,000	47%

The breath sample is an indication of the amount of alcohol ingested in the relevant previous period. The police who asked for the samples come from 43 different police forces; it is quite impossible that the standards of driving or other behaviour which led these officers to ask for samples could have been influenced administratively to produce the results listed above – indeed, for the reductions to take place for administrative reasons, the police would have had to be taken off other work to seek out "unlikely" candidates. We shall come to mention a later aspect of police administrative activity which does affect the figures, but this is a special case and carries its own justification.

The more acceptable explanation is that motorists emerging from pubs and clubs at the same times and places and encountering circumstances which gave the police reason for asking for samples of breath had, on average, not consumed quite as much alcohol in 1976, 1977 and 1978 as similar motorists had done between 1971 and 1974 when the standard of living and the amount of personal disposable income was rising.

The second piece of supporting evidence comes from an extension of the same statistics. The Home Office has recently come to publish data on the numbers of motorists, convicted of drunken driving, whose blood alcohol is in excess of specified levels. For our purpose, it is sufficient to take the proportions of such guilty motorists who had less than 151 milligrams of alcohol per 100 millilitres of blood in each year from 1974 to 1978. The official statistics do not allow a breakdown of the numbers of really heavy drinkers among the convicted motorists, but a fall in the percentages of "less heavy-drinkers", when the total numbers of drunken motorists is also falling, is consistent with the presence of a core of hard drinkers in the motoring population and a diminution in the numbers of lighter drinkers consuming enough to take them over the 80 mg. threshold – that is to say, such a tendency would be another facet of the fall in the percentages positive among those asked for breath samples.

Motorists with blood counts under 151 mg. alcohol per 100 ml. blood as percentages of all motorists with blood counts over 80 mg.

1974	1975	1976	1977	1978	1979
47%	46%	45%	43%	42%	N.A.

This piece of evidence is further reinforced by the rather complicated data set out in the chart on the opposite page. This takes the data given by the Home Office in respect of the numbers of convicted motorists in 1976, 1977 and 1978 by ages within each of the four categories of concentrations of alcohol in the blood, and expresses them as four sets of three columns (each column giving the numbers in the specified year) in each of four age-groups.

We can see at a glance how each age-group of light, medium, heavy and very heavy drinkers reacted to the drop in the standard of living that took place in 1977 after the improvement in 1976 and before the later improvement in 1978 (see the first table in this chapter).

Among the heaviest drinkers, the drop in numbers in 1977 is clear in all age-groups except for the persons aged under twenty-one. Among the heavy drinkers, the same is the case except that the errant age-group is now that aged forty and over. All the age-groups among the medium drinkers show some drop in 1977. The light excess drinkers display a more mixed picture, which could be the combined result of some potential offenders not crossing the 80 mg. threshold in 1977, and some who did offend having drunk less than their comparable offenders did in 1976 and 1978.

DIAGRAM XVI
Numbers of convicted motorists in 1976, 1977 and 1978 by concentrations of alcohol in the blood by four age groups

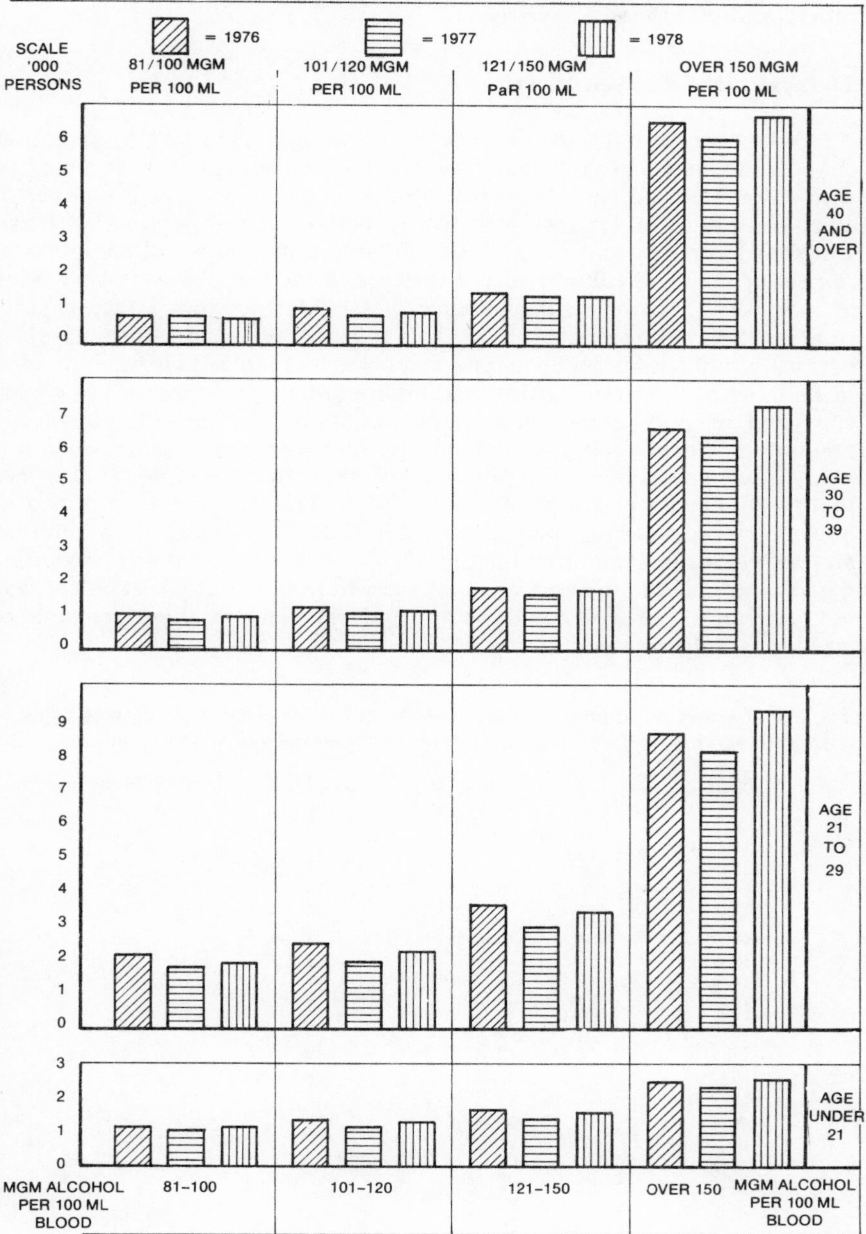

Taking the three pieces of evidence together, it does seem reasonable to conclude that motorists having less to spend when inflation gets ahead of earnings and the amount of disposable income falls in real terms will be constrained to spend somewhat less on drink as well as on the other items of consumption. Less spent on drink means either fewer drinking occasions or a reduction of the alcohol consumed on average on each such occasion. Either, or both in some combination, will produce the kind of effects on the official statistics that we have seen.

The ages of the drunken drivers

When we were discussing the experience from 1937 to 1973 in earlier chapters we were unable to make comment upon the ages of those motorists who committed offences to do with drink or drugs. A varying number of chief constables in England and Wales had been co-operating with the Christian Economic and Social Research Foundation in providing figures in respect of their individual police districts, and the samples were very large in most years. However, the absence of the Metropolitan Police District from all the samples made it hazardous to apply the results of the samples nationally until some independent check was available. This was provided in 1976, when the Home Office first published the age analysis of motorists convicted of drunkenness and for whom there was information of the amount of alcohol found in the blood. The figures emerging from this analysis were in such close conformity with those in the sample for that year that the full series of sample estimates from 1962 may now be given. It is, however, necessary to enter the caveat that the sample data refer to *proceedings* against motorists for all such offences, whereas the Home Office data do not include the ages of motorists whose blood-alcohol content was not determined. There could be an age bias among those refusing to provide samples of blood or urine.

The age distribution of motorists proceeded against for offences to do with drink or drugs in varying numbers of police districts in England and Wales by percentages

Year	Aged less than 21	Aged 21–29	Aged 30 and over
	%	%	%
1962	6	26	68
1963	6	27	67
1964	6	26	68
1965	7	28	65
1966	6	29	65
1967*	8	31	61
1968**	10	39	51
1969	10	37	53
1970	11	38	51
1971	12	39	49
1972	12	38	50
1973	13	40	47
1974†	13	39	48
1975††	16	38	46
1976	13	39	48
1977	Sampling interrupted		
1978	14	38	48
1979	14	38	48 (provisional)

* Breathalyser came into use in October 1967; not all police districts were able to use them at once.
** First full year of the breathalyser in practice.
† Boundaries of most police districts altered with effect from April 1974
†† First full year of new police districts.

Before looking at the Home Office data, it is desirable to comment on the remarkable change in the age composition of the samples after the full implementation of the 1967 Act. There was a sharp fall in the numbers of offenders as apprehension of the consequences of the positive readings on the breathalyser became widespread but the comment of the police at the time was that the young did not seem to be unduly worried – the middle-aged undoubtedly were. The data bear this impression out, although it must be remembered that a number of the "motorists" aged under twenty-one were youths of under eighteen who were riding in "borrowed" cars; their inebriation could well have been the proximate cause of their being in the cars at all.

We may now compare the distribution by ages among those motorists who were both convicted of drunken driving and for whom the alcohol content of the blood was known. They cover three years.

Motorists convicted of drunken driving (England and Wales)

	Aged under 21		Aged 21–29		Aged 30 and over	
Year	**Numbers**	**% age**	**Numbers**	**% age**	**Numbers**	**% age**
1976	4133	13	12133	37	16447	50
1977	3695	12	11014	37	15481	51
1978	4128	12	12606	37	17142	51

Taking both sets of figures it would seem safe to conclude that about one-half of motorists in England and Wales who are arrested and convicted for offences to do with drink or drugs are aged under thirty. There are no data on the age distribution of drivers, so that comparative incidences cannot be calculated.

The situation in Scotland would appear to be slightly different, with the young accounting for rather less of the totals.

Age of motorists involved in drink/driving offences (Scotland)

	Aged under 21		Aged 21–29		Aged 30 and over	
Year	**Numbers**	**% age**	**Numbers**	**% age**	**Numbers**	**% age**
1973	1169	10	3835	33	6561	57
1974	1320	10	3852	32	7029	58
1975	1378	12	3623	31	6684	57
1976	1084	11	3101	32	5436	57
1977	995	12	2678	31	5018	57
1978	Age distribution data not available					

As we have seen in the case of pedestrian drunkenness, the lower numbers and proportions of the younger persons would seem to be a continuing element in the Scottish statistics. We shall be looking at the pedestrian figures for the 1973–79 period later in this chapter.

Before we do so, there is a development affecting the statistics of drunken driving which needs to be mentioned. It will have been seen from the table giving the percentages of breath samples which were positive that the numbers of requests for samples in England and Wales were steady between 1975 and 1977, inclusive, at just over 130,000 per annum. A change has taken place since then. The following table sets out the numbers of requests for samples made by the police in England and Wales in each of the four seasons from 1973 to 1978. Because of the tendency for drunken driving to straddle the year-end, the "seasons" have been adjusted, so that the year starts with February, March and April, and ends with November and December, with January of the following year.

Numbers of requests for breath samples by police in England and Wales in each of the three-month periods specified

Period	1973	1974	1975	1976	1977	1978
Feb, Mar, April	32500	30400	32700	33200	31800	31400
May, June, July	33000	30200	32200	31900	32200	34800
Aug, Sep, October	32300	30600	33900	33400	32000	35400
Nov, Dec, January	34700	32300	36200	35200	35400	40000

The jump of some fifteen per cent in the 1978/79 Christmas–New Year quarter was to some extent the reflection of a change in policy on the part of a few large police districts; a change initiated as a result of the sharply-growing numbers of fatal and serious-injury accidents taking place over the winter holiday period and some careful analyses of the circumstances surrounding such accidents. A growing proportion were found to be associated with a degree of intoxication in one or more of the drivers concerned. There was also a growing number of "hit-and-run" accidents which the police came to think were also a reflection of a state of insobriety on the part of the drivers – if the driver could defer reporting the accident he would run less risk of losing his driving licence as the alcohol in his blood diminished with the passage of time.

A number of chief constables, therefore, decided that the public interest would be best served by mounting, and advertising the mounting, of an intense drive against drunken driving during the Christmas and New Year party period. It would appear to have been sufficiently beneficial in most of the areas in which it was tried in 1978 for the numbers of police districts doing the same thing in 1979 to be about twice that in the previous year. If the system continues, the numbers of convicted motorists will be bound to rise, and any simple comparison with previous years will be misleading.

Drunken pedestrians

There is a possibility that in the periods of petrol shortages persons who would otherwise have gone for a drink in their cars and so not have been at risk of arrest as pedestrian drunks, came and went on their own feet. It is therefore desirable to treat drunkenness among women first. It is known from the samples collected by the Christian Economic and Social Research Foundation that comparatively few women are offenders as drivers and the possible "transfer" can therefore be ignored.

The previous chapter described how the rise of off-licence departments in supermarkets had opened up novel ways for women desiring to purchase alcoholic drinks, and how the numbers of women arrested for drunkenness had increased. As the table which follows shows, the same process went on over the opening years of the period under present review.

Numbers of females found guilty of drunkenness

Year	England and Wales (hundreds)			Scotland (tens)		
	Under 21	21–29	30 and over	Under 21	21–29	30 and over
1973	10	12	41	17	18	114
1974	12	14	43	17	17	116
1975	12	18	46	19	19	142
1976	15	20	52	14	22	125
1977	15	19	50	13	23	117
1978	14	21	49	15	22	113
1979*	14	22	48	15	22	114

*Estimate based on sample of chief constables' reports received by the Christian Economic and Social Research Foundation (incomplete data).

The highest figures were reached in Scotland during 1975 and there followed a sharp fall in 1976 and a smaller one in 1977; thereafter the trend is more uncertain. In England and Wales the peak was a year later and the fall slower but continuing through 1978. These movements are in accord with the changes in the standard of living in the two countries, the boost in spending power coming from the settlement of the miners' strike proving shortlived in the consequent growth in redundances and unemployment. In England and Wales, it was the general inflation of prices above the controlled rises in wages and salaries in 1977 that caused the reduction in real spendable incomes.

It remains only to say that the patterns of comparative drunkenness as between the two countries show some signs of change from those noted for earlier years. Taking the ten-to-one ratio of populations into account, it would appear that the incidence of drunkenness among women aged under thirty, 50 per cent higher in Scotland in 1973, had moved to near parity by 1979, more as a result of deterioration in England and Wales than betterment in Scotland.

We now turn to drunkenness among males. The following table performs the same office as the previous, and the ten-to-one ratio is preserved but with the figures ten times as great.

Numbers of males found guilty of drunkenness

Year	England and Wales (thousands)			Scotland (hundreds)		
	Under 21	21–29	30 and over	Under 21	21–29	30 and over
1973	17	22	54	13	17	90
1974	19	23	54	14	19	99
1975	19	24	54	14	19	99
1976	20	24	55	13	18	94
1977	21	24	55	12	15	82
1978	21	24	53	12	15	84
1979*	23	27	57	12	16	85

*Estimate based on sample of chief constables' reports received by the Christian Economic and Social Research Foundation (incomplete data).

As in the case of women the highest figures in Scotland were recorded in 1975 while those in England and Wales did not peak until two years later. This lag may be some reflection of the change in habits of some motorists – the number of proceedings against motorists for drink/drive offences fell from 70,000 in 1975 to 53,000 in 1977, though there was a sharp recovery in 1978. There is no reason to suppose that such transfer from motor to feet would have much of an age bias, so that comparison between the two countries is not prevented.

When such comparison is made, the same ratios as were noticed throughout the post-war years are visible. The males under the age of thirty in England and Wales are still about 50 per cent more likely to be found guilty of drunkenness as their contemporaries in Scotland; while the reverse is true on average among men aged thirty and over. In this general connection it is worth noting that only 25 per cent of the male population of England and Wales is aged between fifteen and thirty, as against 28 per cent in Scotland, so that the relative incidence in the former is even greater. There is not quite the same proportional distortion among males aged over thirty, but the effect is again to widen the differences in incidences.

The period under present review has added one general truth to the set of axioms which seem to hold for drinking habits in Great Britain. The 1950s confirmed that the introduction of an unaccustomed form of drink of strong alcoholic content led to an increase in drunkenness, but the effect was not prolonged. The 1960s showed that the provision of easier access to alcoholic drinks (in the supermarkets) led to increasing drunkenness among those most benefiting from the new outlets. They also seemed to show that those drinks which became relatively cheaper would take volume away from the relatively more expensive, but this apparently sound piece of economics could not be established beyond doubt because of the confounding of the relative cheapening with the new easier access for women. The 1970s however, have given some comfort to the economist in that it is reasonably clear that less money available to spend on marginal consumption does lead to less being spent on drink.

What of the future? There is a development which could cause a great change in the drinking habits of both countries, in part beneficial for the public interest and in part damaging. It is only during the last two years of our present period of study that large volumes of beer have been sold in cans through the off-licence departments of the supermarkets, but the volume is growing steadily. Far more is being sold than can be consumed in holes and corners by teenagers too immature to "pass" in pubs. The trolleys coming down the car parks from the supermarkets are being wheeled by men and by women of all ages and, increasingly, by the young married, and the trolley bottoms are solid with the foursomes of cans of lager, ale and beer in the quadruple plastic rings. That beer is going to be consumed in the home, domestically and in neighbourly parties. Moreover, it is now a cheaper way to buy beer than in glasses at the pub. Three years ago, the average pint in the pub was 10 per cent cheaper than the equivalent in cans at the supermarket; at the beginning of 1980 the situation had been reversed, and the indications and the economics suggest that the gap will widen further.

If the beer is drunk in the home, it will not be drunk in the pub by the same men. If the trend goes far enough, the patronage at the pubs will become distorted from its present age distribution in that the married men will stay at home and the customers will be fewer, older and younger. Pubs are classic examples of outlets with inflexible overheads. Reduced patronage will mean either closing down, or charging more – and doing something to justify the higher charges. That something can only be entertainment of some kind or another – disco, amateur music hall, and the like. Very few new pubs of the traditional design are being built – discos, with licenses are accounting for the small rise in the total of pubs and clubs – four per cent since 1973 in England and Wales. Compare this with the 25 per cent increase in off-licences and the 33 per cent increase in restaurant licences of all sorts.

Drinking in the home, with or without neighbours, will tend to drive out the teenagers in the family and they will gravitate, as they already do, on the discos. Drinking in the home means less cars on the road. More in the discos, if recent experience is any guide, means a further increase in violence in the areas where the discos must be situated if they are to attract the custom.

SECTION I

STATISTICAL TABLES, 1900–37

TABLE I 1

LIQUOR CONSUMPTION

Great Britain and All Ireland, 1900–22
Great Britain and Northern Ireland only, 1923–35

Gross (to nearest thousand – millions in case of beer) *Per Head* (gallons – "proof" in case of spirits)

Year	Spirits, proof gallons Home	Imp'ted	Total	Wine, gallons	Beer, millions standard gallons, average	Spirits Home	Imp'ted	Total	Wine	Beer, England and Wales only, average
1900	37125	8764	45889	15816	1299	0.91	0.21	1.12	0.38	31.6
1901	36372	8838	45210	15202	1278	0.88	0.21	1.09	0.37	30.8
1902	35340	8739	44078	15281	1269	0.84	0.21	1.05	0.36	30.2
1903	33738	8147	41886	13872	1258	0.80	0.19	0.99	0.33	29.7
1904	33610	7122	40732	11935	1232	0.79	0.17	0.96	0.28	28.8
1905	32599	6733	39332	11891	1197	0.76	0.16	0.92	0.28	27.7
1906	32261	7002	39264	12278	1221	0.75	0.16	0.91	0.28	28.2
1907	32674	7308	39983	12282	1216	0.74	0.17	0.91	0.28	27.8
1908	31413	6666	38079	11293	1186	0.71	0.15	0.86	0.26	26.9
1909	25460	5604	31063	11399	1163	0.57	0.13	0.70	0.26	26.1
1910	24047	5219	29266	12672	1184	0.53	0.12	0.65	0.28	26.3
1911	25241	5446	30687	11218	1235	0.56	0.12	0.68	0.25	27.2
1912	25153	5374	30527	11230	1223	0.55	0.12	0.67	0.25	26.9
1913	26164	5629	31794	11368	1272	0.57	0.13	0.70	0.25	27.8
1914	25941	5720	31660	10630	1230	0.56	0.13	0.69	0.23	26.7
1915	28378	6624	35002	10175	1049	0.62	0.14	0.76	0.22	22.8
1916	22503	5642	28144	9910	960	0.49	0.12	0.61	0.22	20.8
1917	13213	5321	18534	7099	581	0.29	0.12	0.41	0.15	12.6
1918	11415	3692	15108	11317	460	0.25	0.08	0.33	0.25	10.0
1919	16092	5606	21699	19174	783	0.36	0.13	0.49	0.43	17.5
1920	16699	5426	22125	15054	969	0.36	0.11	0.47	0.32	20.8
1921	15028	3504	18532	11175	877	0.32	0.07	0.39	0.24	18.6
1922	14286	2617	16903	12549	754	0.30	0.06	0.36	0.26	15.9
1923	12237	2229	14466	13461	747	0.27	0.05	0.32	0.30	16.5
1924	11880	2265	14144	15334	789	0.26	0.05	0.31	0.34	17.6
1925	11631	2147	13777	16071	795	0.26	0.05	0.31	0.36	17.6
1926	10765	1828	12593	16786	762	0.24	0.04	0.28	0.37	16.9
1927	10799	1749	12547	16909	754	0.24	0.04	0.28	0.37	16.6
1928	10412	1655	12067	13467	738	0.23	0.04	0.27	0.30	16.2
1929	10360	1677	12037	14394	735	0.23	0.04	0.27	0.32	16.1
1930	9558	1418	10975	13721	719	0.21	0.03	0.24	0.30	15.7
1931	8867	1330	10198	13709	629	0.19	0.03	0.22	0.30	13.6
1932	8114	1145	9259	12490	509	0.18	0.02	0.20	0.27	11.0
1933	8247	1181	9428	13131	550	0.18	0.03	0.21	0.28	11.8
1934	8116	1130	9245	14208	595	0.17	0.02	0.19	0.30	12.7
1935	8137	1115	9252	14754	623	0.17	0.02	0.19	0.31	13.3

TABLE I 2

BRITISH SPIRITS, 1900-36

Quantities distilled and charged for consumption and exported

Thousands of proof gallons

Year ending March 31	Quantities distilled				Quantities charged for consumption			
	Eng.	Scot.	Ire.	U.K.	Eng.	Scot.	Ire.	U.K.
1900	12967	31798	14481	59246	25623	8380	4713	38717
1901	12603	30196	14222	57021	24994	7471	4238	36704
1902	12439	29973	12781	55192	22827	7115	3807	33749
1903	11296	26008	12441	49744	23357	7399	4009	34765
1904	11695	27111	13011	51817	22975	7192	3936	34103
1905	12157	25185	11798	49140	22661	6759	3738	33158
1906	12751	23813	12651	49214	22140	6711	3636	32487
1907	13425	24840	12053	50318	22027	6852	3633	32511
1908	13328	22797	11654	47778	21916	6956	3635	32507
1909	12930	24408	12192	49530	21827	6661	3563	32051
1910	10763	22309	10759	43831	14537	4559	2351	21446
1911	11422	20021	9724	41167	17485	5053	2776	25314
1912	12339	23630	9748	45717	17106	5539	2729	25374
1913	12702	24115	9876	46693	16935	5709	2643	25286
1914	13900	28024	9879	51802	17891	6173	2731	26795
1915	12891	26999	10249	50140	18834	6107	2871	27811
1916	11555	26741	10839	49135	19666	6108	3176	28949
1917	10445	28182	13201	51828	12849	3912	2035	18796
1918	9966	14767	12408	37141	6646	2448	1230	10325
1919	3438	13200	11077	27714	8107	2445	1338	11890
1920	3929	22542	13587	40058	12548	3546	1731	17826
1921	7123	29296	11129	47548	10759	3355	1350	15463
1922	5252	24588	6758	36598	10107	3068	1372*	14546
1923	6565	27096	2477	36137	9723	2757	379	12859
1924	7365	27424	2534	37323	9942	2641	314	12897
1925	8211	27436	2382	38028	9473	2532	281	12287
1926	9758	26027	1975	37759	9350	2454	251	12055
1927	10614	16532	177	27323	8398	2099	215	10712
1928	12392	18988	Included	31380	9135	2314	229	11678
1929	14278	20512	under	34790	8869	2180	223	11272
1930	18756	20907	England	39663	8303	2122	205	10630
1931	18423	15831		34254	8039	1959	191	10189
1932	19141	9232		28373	7011	1684	159	8855
1933	22178	5926		28104	7187	1483	152	8821
1934	30364	13174		43538	7098	1342	148	8588
1935	30683	16869		47551	6660	1543	141	8344
1936	35340	20252		55591	7184	1623	163	8970

*Northern Ireland only from 1922.

Source: Inland Revenue Reports (Financial Years).

TABLE I 3

SPIRITS IN STOCK, PRODUCTION, AND DISTRIBUTION OF HOME-MADE SPIRITS

Thousands of proof gallons

Year ending March 31	In warehouse on March 31 previous	Distilled	Total	Potable retained for consumption	Exports	Fortifying-wines or ships' stores	Arts and manufactures	Methylated	Deficiencies allowed	Total	Balance in warehouse
1911	157220	41167	198387	25314	10339	230	546	6681	4262	47371	151016
1912	151016	45717	196733	25374	9960	226	584	7349	5139	48632	148101
1913	148101	46693	194794	25286	9984	234	658	7257	4548	47968	146826
1914	146826	51802	198628	26795	10407	313	723	7719	4718	50674	147954
1915	147954	50140	198094	27811	9666	261	694	7500	4473	50405	147689
1916	147689	49135	196824	28949	9186	545	1165	9540	6503	55888	140936
1917	140936	51828	192764	18796	8575	695	13411	8538	4999	55015	137750
1918	137750	37141	174890	10325	5132	1153	25297	8194	3642	53743	121148
1919	121148	27714	148862	11890	3023	857	9472	6276	2444	33962	114900
1920	114900	40058	154958	17826	4662	608	496	4957	4484	33034	121924
1921	122539	47548	170087	15463	8000	410	555	4214	4102	32743	137344
1922	137344	36598	173942	14546	5707	270	403	5022	3783	29732	144210
1923	128625	36137	167120	13143	6017	321	598	6459	3707	30243	136877
1923	*2358										
1924	136877	37323	174200	12897	8032	412	668	7027	3152	32188	142011
1925	142243	38028	180272	12287	8433	587	696	7600	2923	32526	147746
1926	147802	37759	185561	12055	6983	377	732	8721	3134	32001	153560
1927	153593	27323	180916	10712	6688	330	592	8778	2635	29735	151181
1928	151209	31380	182590	11678	7552	359	757	9136	3185	32667	149924
1929	149960	34790	184749	11272	7381	340	1297	9950	2848	33090	151660
1930	151737	40669	192406	10630	8247	338	4482	11176	2868	37741	154665
1931	154811	35423	190234	10189	6232	266	6284	10299	3336	36606	153628
1932	153655	30447	184102	8855	5779	264	8473	9979	2664	36015	148087
1933	148098	31036	179134	8821	5542	227	11238	10966	2536	39331	139802
1934	139823	47185	187008	8588	5409	265	20639	12369	3214	50484	136524
1935	136590	51839	188429	8344	5898	309	19007	14831	3394	51783	136646

*I.F.S.

TABLE I 4
IMPORTED SPIRITS
Imports and Home Consumption

Thousands of Proof Gallons

Year	Imports				Home Consumption			
	Brandy	Rum	Other	Total	Brandy	Rum	Other	Total
1900	2,596	6,239	2,014	10,849	2,620	4,461	1,683	8,764
1901	3,082	6,719	2,617	12,418	2,512	4,386	1,940	8,838
1902	2,301	8,211	3,750	14,262	2,353	4,285	2,100	8,739
1903	2138	5501	2463	10102	2205	3982	1960	8147
1904	2048	4719	1003	7770	2175	4052	895	7122
1905	2638	4216	794	7648	2079	3973	681	6733
1906	1874	5214	1020	8108	2080	4051	871	7002
1907	2344	5512	1053	8909	2069	4328	912	7308
1908	1732	5286	817	7835	1960	4018	688	6666
1909	1419	5871	1118	8408	1550	3202	852	5604
1910	1413	4714	1264	7391	1457	2807	956	5219
1911	1435	4834	1203	7472	1561	2978	907	5446
1912	1376	3991	1049	6416	1455	3119	800	5374
1913	1490	4709	953	7152	1504	3320	805	5629
1914	1536	5672	1012	8220	1463	3581	675	5720
1915	2188	10484	1250	13922	1520	4512	591	6624
1916	2366	9958	2095	14419	1606	3354	682	5642
1917	1683	4562	435	6680	1519	3301	502	5321
1918	1502	2808	896	5206	1477	2027	188	3692
1919	2369	9266	2142	13777	1886	3162	559	5606
1920	1329	3882	1665	6876	1329	3123	974	5426
1921	393	4429	554	5376	880	2030	594	3504
1922	377	1526	553	2456	716	1542	358	2617
1923	493	639	1364	2496	676	1242	311	2229
1924	504	1381	1745	3630	672	1204	389	2265
1925	532	2027	1402	3961	634	1142	371	2147
1926	546	1269	1072	2887	591	911	326	1828
1927	453	2099	1291	3843	570	879	299	1749
1928	487	2269	1597	4353	542	805	307	1655
1929	510	1542	1140	3152	540	828	309	1677
1930	456	1752	741	2949	487	650	282	1418
1931	463	1491	532	2486	461	606	263	1330
1932	364	1079	374	1799	396	519	229	1146
1933	437	1559	326	2322	411	535	234	1181
1934	438	1724	403	2565	402	496	232	1130
1935	507	1475	365	2347	395	490	231	1115

TABLE I 5
FOREIGN WINES IMPORTED, 1900–35
Thousands of Imperial Gallons

Year	Cape	Austra-lasia	France	Portu-gal	Mad-eira	Spain	Ger-many	Hol-land	Italy	Other	Total
1900	8	822	5383	3862	71	4574	542	843	379	320	16804
1901	5	737	5518	3909	53	4185	569	878	348	342	16546
1902	4	991	5257	3952	69	4121	585	878	345	228	16430
1903	7	573	5102	3445	68	3498	573	951	313	181	14711
1904	3	648	3716	2896	54	2999	515	952	293	281	12347
1905	15	865	3787	2984	44	3186	435	880	283	252	12731
1906	4	627	4020	3736	56	2885	430	839	267	239	13103
1907	6	794	4098	3227	62	3357	420	754	251	210	13179
1908	8	665	3545	3070	42	2987	366	652	262	280	11877
1909	3	868	3647	2978	33	3252	819	25	294	415	12334
1910	3	796	3966	3795	39	3262	954	54	309	557	13735
1911	3	963	3458	3202	40	3172	907	77	286	462	12570
1912	4	671	3634	3303	41	2780	265	755	243	495	12191
1913	2	624	3052	3609	48	3133	895	58	321	591	12333
1914	3	641	2614	3902	42	2861	531	43	309	531	11477
1915	2	712	2291	3971	18	3293		9	344	515	11155
1916	7	503	2183	6108	55	3300			301	503	12960
1917	4	290	1617	2578	34	1775			174	225	6697
1918		176	3953	6660		1575				792	13156
1919	16	448	5032	12458	356	5423	33	1	648	837	25252
1920	26	903	4677	5740	100	3378	143	9	428	2331	17735
1921	48	542	1836	4593	82	1892	69	4	322	145	9533
1922	33	533	2282	6389	45	2283	159	10	359	186	12279
1923	65	707	2772	6374	48	2358	133	9	486	285	13237
1924	104	824	3195	9303	48	3168	206	5	542	256	17651
1925	62	1028	3184	8501	54	3643	306	9	680	300	17767
1926	116	1757	3541	7845	67	3453	282	15	648	252	17976
1927	245	4225	3175	6488	55	3114	308	13	665	238	18526
1928	288	1739	2846	5012	39	2515	238	8	712	247	13644
1929	455	2093	2805	5944	42	2684	264	13	707	233	15240
1930	558	1895	2443	5091	38	2604	231		724	255	13839
1931	789	2270	2219	5217	28	2977	269		664	272	14705
1932	724	3025	1423	3671	25	2399	216		620	316	12419
1933	1169	3421	1642	3943	36	3187	275		583	347	14603
1934	1149	2743	1728	4107	42	3482	319		615	343	14528
1935	1191	3321	1916	4294	35	3858	371		717	383	16,086

TABLE I 6

FOREIGN WINES RETAINED FOR CONSUMPTION, 1905–37

Thousands of Gallons

Year	France	Portugal	Spain	British South Africa	Australia	Other Countries	All Countries
1905	3621	2821	2894			2611	11947
1906	3813	3220	2801			2497	12331
1907	3969	3071	2854			2444	12338
1908	3503	2865	2753		730	1495	11346
1909	3514	2789	2836		777	1533	11449
1910	3796	3454	2949		780	1740	12719
1911	3097	2973	2758		811	1634	11273
1912	3165	3005	2795		721	1598	11284
1913	2814	3181	2881		749	1787	11421
1914	2430	3452	2695		651	1447	10681
1915	2039	3656	2990		627	1863	10175
1916	1866	4264	2569		555	656	9910
1917	1412	3301	1663		343	380	7099
1918	3452	4946	2017		248	654	11317
1919	4964	9307	3226		470	1207	19174
1920	4163	6089	3247		594	1555	15054
1921	1980	5440	2270		653	1485	11175
1922	2291	6375	2404		612	1479	12549
1923	2675	6730	2411		629	1016	13461
1924	2910	7992	2753		611	1069	15335
1925	3002	7898	3088	216	782	1085	16071
1926	3206	7600	3244	230	1414	1093	16787
1927	3106	6879	3218	252	2302	1152	16909
1928	2693	5005	2254	330	2158	1027	13467
1929	2676	5710	2220	315	2339	1134	14394
1930	2409	5065	2440	522	2121	1164	13721
1931	2166	4729	2590	647	2389	1188	13709
1932	1586	3923	2512	756	2626	1087	12490
1933	1587	3913	2716	982	2801	1132	13131
1934	1718	4004	3069	1065	3165	1187	14208
1935	1862	3947	3308	1187	3153	1297	14754
1936	2142	4162	3669	1222	3323	1161	15679
1937	2142	4297	3673	1336	3417	1326	16191

TABLE I 7
BEER PRODUCTION 1900–36
Thousands of Standard Barrels

Year	England	Scotland	Ireland	U.K.
1900	31474	2112	3083	36669
1901	30791	2116	3232	36140
1902	30638	1965	3250	35853
1903	30258	1888	3392	35838
1904	29726	1825	3262	34812
1905	28886	1771	3197	33854
1906	29288	1840	3400	34528
1907	29174	1806	3459	34438
1908	28447	1752	3338	33537
1909	27665	1721	3514	32901
1910	28048	1750	3672	33470
1911	29080	1858	3961	34899
1912	28751	1845	4039	34635
1913	29741	1970	4240	35951
1914	28695	1858	4197	34750
1915	24361	1549	3765	29675
1916	22411	1484	3577	27472
1917	13575	894	2085	16552
1918	10781	717	1513	13012
1919	18394	1360	2308	22063
1920	22525	1652	3226	27403
1921	20400	1438	2850	24688
1922	17563	1203	2503	21269
1923	18667	1294	*1146	19966
1924	19301	1431	1570	20732
1925	19439	1425	1625	20863
1926	18834	1300	1482	20133
1927	18537	1365	1449	19901
1928	18232	1365	1354	19597
1929	18016	1419	1459	19435
1930	17465	1346	1594	18811
1931	15256	1121	1437	16377
1932	12330	918	1202	13248
1933	13336	1002	1232	14339
1934	14433	1089	1315	15521
1935	15075	1179	1365	16254
1936	15502	1236	1381	16738

* From 1923 imports from Irish Free State and are not included in "total". The figures for Northern Ireland are officially included in those of England.

TABLE I 8
BREWING MATERIALS, 1900–35
Thousands of Hundredweights

Year	Malt	Hops Net, including Imports	Sugar etc.	Rice, Maize etc.
1900	21508	527	2980	1202
1901	21297	742	2859	1326
1902	20922	648	2825	1392
1903	20594	629	2875	1372
1904	19996	602	2887	1388
1905	19491	557	2747	1349
1906	19637	571	2842	1258
1907	19570	571	2859	1257
1908	19153	562	2883	1279
1909	18633	548	2891	1257
1910	18776	551	2910	1294
1911	19409	574	3011	1337
1912	19368	549	3068	1419
1913	19647	562	3280	1611
1914	19736	559	3280	1567
1915	16663	467	2679	1236
1916	15633	450	2400	1344
1917	10750	329	1614	801
1918	8350	263	890	234
1919	11171	368	1532	351
1920	15796	503	2135	1023
1921	14751	454	1874	980
1922	12445	399	1622	810
1923	10769	329	1599	804
1924	11298	350	1700	846
1925	11478	363	1864	908
1926	10972	355	1833	827
1927	10704	338	1817	823
1928	10548	331	1838	825
1929	10394	320	1817	797
1930	10106	307	1835	763
1931	9142	277	1698	689
1932	7128	220	1377	533
1933	7252	223	1380	521
1934	8007	234	1543	548
1935	8456	249	1632	588

N.B. – The Hop figures of 1900 and 1901 are the estimate production, less exports, and the net imports.

TABLE I 9
ON-LICENCES (ENGLAND AND WALES), 1855–1935

	1855	1875	1886	1896	1906	1915	1925	1935	Decrease 1855–1935	Persons per licence 1855	Persons per licence 1935
England (ex Monmouth)											
Bedford	997	935	995	987	987	885	802	758	239	125	291
Berks	1242	1341	1303	1261	1266	1171	1110	1086	156	137	287
Bucks	1320	1379	1336	1304	1290	1163	1085	1040	280	125	261
Cambridge	1643	1532	1477	1450	1415	1239	1116	1040	603	113	212
Cheshire	2553	2680	2626	2580	2506	2183	2021	1862	691	178	584
Cornwall	1155	945	834	758	756	687	624	595	560	309	531
Cumberland	1325	1255	1251	1190	1127	979	825	786	539	147	335
Derby	1943	2078	1987	1987	2022	1823	1723	1654	289	152	454
Devon	2847	2683	2257	2283	2257	2047	1875	1794	1053	199	409
Dorset	841	851	846	825	802	734	726	699	142	219	342
Durham	2788	2908	2925	2834	2768	2391	2264	2035	753	140	730
Essex	1959	2404	2508	2356	2287	2009	1948	1928	31	187	975
Gloucester	2174	3298	2833	2751	2602	2311	2135	1972	202	211	401
Hereford	535	620	552	536	514	480	463	442	93	215	253
Herts	1550	1633	1462	1545	1540	1382	1269	1188	362	108	387
Hunts	612	458	586	561	518	447	362	317	295	105	177
Kent	3567	4293	3282	3516	3543	3114	2923	2925	642	173	465
Lancashire	13004	13576	13003	12601	11754	9686	8920	8207	4797	156	614
Leicester	1322	1421	956	1400	1374	1218	1140	1079	243	174	502
Lincoln	2034	2022	1999	1937	1912	1763	1663	1627	407	200	384
London }			8582	7966	7521	6410	5853	5428	902	255	936
Middlesex }	7407	7666	1279	1277	1249	1102	1067	1077			
Norfolk	2734	2751	2760	2684	2638	2355	2184	2023	711	162	248
Northampton	1244	1278	1363	1332	1346	1159	1043	980	264	170	369
Northumberland	1540	1776	1628	1508	1421	1252	1128	1021	519	197	741
Notts	1308	1487	1533	1526	1464	1298	1192	1140	168	206	625
Oxen	1241	1303	1012	1131	1076	981	949	911	330	137	230
Rutland	129	125	121	119	118	111	108	97	32	178	179
Salop	1483	1362	1216	1164	1139	1041	952	897	586	155	272

TABLE I 9 – *continued*

	1855	1875	1886	1896	1906	1915	1925	1935	Decrease 1855–1935	Persons per Licence 1855	Persons per Licence 1935
England (ex Monmouth)											
Somerset	3073	2045	1853	1818	1808	1647	1559	1494	1579	144	315
Southampton	2708	3396	3259	3238	3156	2774	2585	2461	247	149	448
Stafford	4363	5357	4821	4694	4840	4119	3856	3557	806	139	403
Suffolk	1596	1698	1670	1672	1657	1466	1356	1290	306	211	311
Surrey	2801	3731	1503	1630	1586	1444	1429	1410	1391	245	978
Sussex	1613	2147	2169	2161	2101	1891	1799	1760	+147	209	437
Warwick	3204	3125	3160	3116	2882	2574	2302	2087	1117	148	734
Westmorland	361	281	279	261	257	223	214	201	160	161	325
Wiltshire	1042	1006	989	965	988	924	900	890	152	244	341
Worcester	1992	2068	1872	1833	1800	1513	1430	1325	667	139	317
Yorks, E.R. }		1118	1030	1018	1001	876	806	748 }			
Yorks, N.R. }	9191	1516	1588	1532	1462	1303	1246	1177 }	2039	196	613
Yorks, W.R. }		7406	7190	7149	6906	6088	5688	5227 }			
England	94441	100954	96550	94508	91656	80263	74640	70235	24206	177	532
Wales and Monmouth											
Monmouth	1308	1182	1092	1117	1103	979	936	873	435	120	498
Glamorgan	1924	2419	2210	2267	2278	1982	1826	1671	253	120	734
Rest of Wales	4634	4791	4396	4063	3857	3402	3018	2749	1885	166	339
Wales	7866	8392	7698	7447	7238	6363	5780	5293	2573	148	490
England and Wales	102307	109346	103593	101903	98894	86626	80420	75528	26779	185	529
Persons per licence	185	223	251	285	329	416	471	529			
Acres per licence	365	341	359	366	370	431	464	494			

* Figures for 1855 — Parliamentary Papers, 1856, LV.
Figures for 1886 } Figures for 1896 } — Royal Commission on Licensing Laws, 1899, Vol. 8.
Figures for 1906 onwards. — Licensing Statistics.

TABLE I 10

LICENSED PREMISES (SCOTLAND), 1886–1936

	Hotels and Inns				Public Houses				Licensed Grocers etc.				Total Licences			
	1886	1906	1916	1936	1886	1906	1916	1936	1886	1906	1916	1936	1886	1906	1916	1936
Aberdeen County	104	93	96	90	96	38	30	27	177	102	95	84	377	233	221	201
Aberdeen	29	17	15	14	101	113	113	113	249	200	173	152	379	330	301	279
Other Burghs	11	15	10	11	19	26	22	12	49	41	24	15	79	82	56	38
Argyll County	80	93	98	85	14	16	26	7	8	12	24	9	102	121	148	101
Burghs	24	32	19	24	33	35	22	24	13	32	12	28	70	99	53	76
Ayr County	126	99	95	88	280	267	246	176	201	136	124	77	607	502	465	341
Burghs	35	27	20	26	152	169	163	144	117	108	92	76	304	304	275	246
Banff County	49	35	36	40	33	20	18	21	68	43	32	37	150	98	86	98
Burghs	7	7	8	3	10	18	18	4	19	15	13	3	36	40	39	10
Berwick County	48	40	39	36	10	13	14	10	41	33	29	22	99	86	82	68
Bute County	19	17	16	14	5	4	6	5	3	3	4	3	27	24	26	22
Burghs	6	6	6	7	21	19	19	18	18	15	12	9	45	40	37	34
Caithness County	23	18	17	16	29	14	7	4	16	8	6	2	68	40	30	22
Burghs	3	6	6		6	14	12		7	13	11		16	33	29	
Clackmannan County	10	13	13	13	44	43	42	33	44	48	46	33	98	104	101	79
Dumbarton County	13	15	13	20	90	62	57	45	33	17	15	10	136	94	85	75
Burghs	1	3	3	2	21	72	73	56	3	15	14	10	25	90	90	68
Dumfries County	37	39	36	28	11	10	8	6	28	32	27	14	76	81	71	48
Burghs	31	24	11	12	50	35	29	33	33	20	13	14	114	79	53	59
Mid Lothian County	11	12	11	13	87	62	62	39	118	95	86	48	216	169	159	100
Edinburgh	44	30	23	24	327	310	292	416	451	414	332	389	822	754	647	829
Other Burghs	8	10	10	4	168	168	156	34	173	196	156	26	349	375	322	64
Moray County	25	22	21	22	15	18	16	8	56	39	37	30	96	79	74	60
Burghs	18	14	14	12	7	10	11	11	60	42	31	29	85	66	56	52
Fife County	45	71	69	72	132	166	140	113	164	192	150	108	341	429	359	293
Burghs	46	40	43	41	142	133	149	155	263	200	192	157	451	473	384	353
Angus County	26	34	33	31	42	20	15	12	38	30	26	20	106	84	74	63
Dundee	8	6	6	6	229	212	212	205	221	198	186	130	458	416	404	341
Other Burghs	29	26	25	26	102	96	77	74	141	133	90	60	272	255	192	160
East Lothian County	14	27	26	28	16	26	23	23	38	59	52	43	68	112	101	94
Burghs	13	5	4	4	19	7	6	5	43	19	16	9	75	31	26	18

TABLE I 10 – *continued*

Inverness County	86	81	68	70	9	15	11	12	21	12	13	12	116	108	92	94
Inverness	14	17	12	12	34	33	30	28	42	44	36	28	90	94	78	68
Kincardine County	32	33	34	39	30	22	18	11	40	28	25	27	102	83	77	77
Kinross County	16	12	12	12	6	8	7	7	16	12	10	9	38	32	29	28
Kirkcudbright County	40	38	36	37	27	28	19	8	33	21	16	10	100	87	71	55
Lanark County	48	41	37	43	554	331	304	244	326	143	119	79	928	515	460	366
Glasgow	20	17	15	13	1465	1330	1359	1138	261	304	321	254	1746	1651	1695	1405
Other Burghs	20	17	15	11	302	458	314	241	118	191	96	56	440	666	425	308
West Lothian County	12	13	13	19	53	41	41	45	52	32	27	28	117	86	81	92
Burghs	7	10	9	5	20	43	41	29	26	36	30	12	53	89	80	46
Nairn County	6	5	4	7	4	5	5	3	12	8	7	7	22	18	16	17
Orkney County	15	19	16	13	7	5	3		9	10	8	5	31	34	27	18
Peebles County	8	7	8	9			1		8	10	8	7	16	17	17	16
Burghs	5	5	6	6	3	3	2	3	17	14	11	6	25	22	19	15
Perth County	126	122	121	122	62	59	52	42	71	77	62	52	259	258	235	216
Burghs	24	12	13	11	43	45	43	41	40	41	37	33	107	98	93	85
Renfrew County	20	12	7	6	244	86	66	40	79	23	16	8	343	121	89	54
Greenock	8	5	4	3	168	128	112	66	33	29	28	15	209	162	144	84
Paisley	2	3	2	1	161	135	127	107	40	32	32	24	203	170	161	132
Other Burghs	1	1	1	5	59	118	82	80	11	24	17	15	71	143	100	100
Ross and Cromarty	80	89	77	63	36	22	16	15	31	24	16	11	147	135	109	89
Roxburgh County	23	24	23	21	17	19	20	19	41	42	37	26	81	85	80	66
Burghs	17	9	5	5	15	23	26	22	37	20	19	16	69	52	50	43
Selkirk County	4	5	5	6	2	1	1	1					6	6	6	7
Burghs	7	7	7	7	9	11	11	10	38	35	34	25	54	53	52	42
Stirling County	45	38	35	34	131	87	78	70	100	65	55	37	276	190	168	141
Burghs	16	16	14	9	91	116	108	76	79	79	70	47	186	211	192	132
Sutherland County	30	28	26	30	3	2	2	4	3	3	3	4	36	33	31	38
Wigtown County	33	45	43	39	23	27	18	16	4	6	5	4	60	78	66	59
Burghs	27	14	13	7	23	17	14	10	7	5	5	6	57	36	32	23
Zetland County	7	9	10	1	8	8	9	1	27	22	18	4	42	39	37	6
	1742	**1650**	**1533**	**1478**	**5920**	**5442**	**5024**	**4222**	**4515**	**3903**	**3301**	**2514**	**12177**	**10995**	**9858**	**8214**

	1886	**1906**	**1916**	**1936**
Grand Total	**12,177**	**10,995**	**9,858**	**8,214**
Spirits	**11,617**	**10,619**	**9,596**	**7,980**
Other	**560**	**376**	**262**	**234**

TABLE I 11

REGISTERED CLUBS (ENGLAND AND WALES)

	England						Wales				Working Men's Clubs and Institute Union	
Year	No. of Clubs	Proportion per 10,000 Population	Proceedings	Convictions	Struck off	Pro-ceedings	C'victions	Struck off	Club Duty £	No. of clubs	Member-ship, thousands
1887	1982	0.71								328	
1896	3655	0.18								531	224
1904	6371	1.89								1002	356
1905	6589	1.94	71	23	56	6	1	6		1041	376
1906	6721	1.96	46	19	34	7	1	7		1105	403
1907	6907	1.99	80	43	67	14	11	11		1195	428
1908	7133	2.03	65	32	50	2	2	2		1273	454
1909	7323	2.07	80	33	63	1		1		1322	453
1910	7536	2.11	111	32	89	3		3		1373	416
1911	7912	2.19	131	27	114	1		1		1445	444
1912	8209	2.25	123	36	109	75	3	70	53719	1513	487
1913	8457	2.29	152	41	129	6	2	6	59814	1558	507
1914	8738	2.35	135	43	107	5	2	3	59554	1613	489
1915	8902	2,39	250	64	192	5	2	4	70557	1638	491
1916	8520	2.28	254	110	136	15	8	8	80383	1638	520
1917	8167	2.19	191	90	84	13	11	1	98910	1645	521
1918	7972	2.14	89	41	42	3	2		107901	1666	689
1919	8049	2.24	100	43	45	4	3		235759	1764	854
1920	8994	2,39	207	104	71	9	7	1	367958	2007	994
1921	9924	2.62	176	74	87	11	4	5	365831	2207	1008
1922	10663	2.79	163	58	109	9	4	5	208426	2336	947
1923	11126	2.90	165	92	102	8		8	158041	2412	888
1924	11471	2.96	125	476	79	4		4	164525	2447	894
1925	11780	3.03	135	594	88	9	21	8	163136	1470	903
1926	12138	3.11	196	514	123	4	1	3	161487	2512	907
1927	12481	3.18	224	745	166	11		11	164075	2544	893
1928	12775	3.24	182	668	135	26	26	23	160811	2599	899
1929	13132	3.32	218	630	140	17	26	13	165876	2626	918
1930	13526	3.42	241	793	163	24	42	21	166125	2660	914
1931	13947	3.49	390	855	236	27	56	19	158869	2692	883
1932	14377	3.58	479	913	397	25	51	20	157734	1706	863
1933	15010	3.72	458	1238	374	15	33	6	148593	2692	848
1934	15298	3.78	292	1498	191	9	86	6	152693	2675	858
1935	15657	3.85	355	1986	222	7	67	4	168233	2719	906

* Club duty returns relate to the calendar year preceding the close of the financial year in which the duty is charged, and are so allocated in the Table.

TABLE I 12

EXCISE LICENCES TO MAKERS OF ALCOHOLIC LIQUORS, 1900-36

Year ending March 31	Common Brewers				Distillers and Rectifiers				Brewers not for Sale			Sweets Revenue Act, 1906			
	Eng.	Scot.	Ire.	U.K.	Eng.	Scot.	Ire.	U.K.	Eng.	Scot.	G.B.	Eng.	Scot.	Ire.	U.K.
1900	6270	136	41	6447	268	200	59	527	12607	127	12734				
1901	5937	132	41	6110	286	200	57	543	12296	114	12410				
1902	5736	126	36	5898	272	196	56	524	11772	100	11872				
1903	5533	122	37	5692	252	193	56	501	11665	87	11752		Sweets,		
1904	5340	117	38	5495	256	195	54	505	11275	84	11359		Revenue Act, 1906		
1905	5164	111	36	5211	264	191	51	506	9863	67	9930	Eng.	Scot.	Ire.	U.K.
1906	5001	108	33	5142	254	187	52	493	9266	56	9322				
1907	4846	108	31	4985	257	195	50	502	8840	49	8889	119	9	15	143
1908	4674	104	30	4808	261	188	48	497	8438	43	8481	136	13	23	172
1909	4539	98	30	4667	256	188	48	492	7530	38	7568	127	9	22	158
1910	4390	92	30	4512	241	185	46	472	6980	26	7006	110	9	22	141
1911	4212	88	29	4329	212	184	42	438	6833	22	6855	104	8	26	138
1912	4074	81	29	4184	212	177	41	430	5953	20	5973	101	8	23	132
1913	3833	79	29	3941	224	180	41	445	4992	17	5009	97	10	20	127
1914	3643	75	28	3746	213	179	41	433	4522	15	4537	97	9	18	124
1915	3458	71	27	3556	220	175	41	436	4728	13	4741	89	9	18	116
1916	3273	70	27	3370	222	173	41	436	5982	9	5991	91	9	18	118
1917	3141	67	26	3234	222	171	39	432	5207	10	5217	84	8	18	110
1918	3060	66	25	3151	219	169	39	427	1598	4	1602	71	8	18	97
1919	2968	64	25	3057	226	161	38	425	1876	3	1879	73	8	17	98
1920	2826	63	25	2914	270	161	38	469	2998	1	2999	87	9	18	114
1921	2587	60	23	2670	277	162	37	476	6174		6174	91	7	17	115
1922	2403	59	22	2484	260	160	37	457	7069		7069	101	7	17	125
1923	2238	58	2	2298	247	156	*12	415	8028	40	8068	89	7		96
1924	1089	57	2	2148	254	151	12	417	9423	409	9832	90	6		96
1925	1938	56	2	1996	252	159	12	423	8991	476	9467	87	6		93
1926	1789	54	1	1844	252	153	12	417	10869	618	11487	95	6		101
1927	1670	51	1	1722	246	150	11	407	11427	751	12178	96	7		103
1928	1550	49	1	1599	245	145	11	401	12257	842	13099	102	10		112
1929	1453	49		1502	237	145	11	393	11878	1044	12922	110	9		119
1930	1372	46		1418	241	136	11	388	11437	1076	12513	111	9		120
1931	1295	45		1340	231	134	10	375	11462	1088	12550	116	7		123
1932	1241	45		1286	235	129	10	374	10033	1106	11139	108	8		116
1933	1196	43		1239	221	126	10	357	10141	1135	11276	101	8		109
1934	1153	44		1197	215	123	8	346	9549	1197	10746	117	10		127
1935	1102	42		1144	217	124	10	341	8906	1264	10170	107	7		114
1936	1060	43		1103	204	121	9	334	8502	1265	9767	111	8		119

* From 1923 figures are for Northern Ireland only.

TABLE I 13

EXCISE LICENCES, RETAIL (ENGLAND AND WALES), 1911-36

Year ending March 31	Spirits inc. beer, wine		Beer, Cider and Perry		Cider and Perry		Wine and Sweets		Sweets		Passenger Boats	Restaurant Cars	Occasional Licences	Year
	On	Off	On	Off	On	Off	On	Off	On	Off				
1911	61063	8551	28358	17901	20	44	2672	10588	188	307	296	1053	14649	1911
1912	63732	8492	27837	18104	20	51	2857	10711	161	289	251	552	15009	1912
1913	63086	8324	27192	18023	19	44	2682	10699	150	278	244	545	14178	1913
1914	61928	8229	26517	17929	20	43	2631	10593	144	264	191	516	14045	1914
1915	61228	8089	26368	17774	18	50	2505	10416	138	257	187	624	8949	1915
1916	60406	7912	26900	17642	18	50	2473	10199	124	242	78	551	3784	1916
1917	60813	7818	27209	17518	18	47	2500	10080	120	228	61	332	2353	1917
1918	60153	7663	25333	17318	20	48	2450	9899	112	210	53	248	1534	1918
1919	59642	7604	24663	17231	19	46	2438	9852	107	193	42	380	1140	1919
1920	59236	7709	24808	17230	19	43	2477	9937	109	182	94	599	4621	1920
1921	59008	7716	23722	17209	19	47	2490	10030	105	182	100	570	7080	1921
1922	58875	7774	23201	17160	18	51	2535	10210	104	179	96	579	7925	1922
1923	58733	7943	22886	17194	18	58	2611	10494	105	180	152	591	9282	1923
1924	55907	7912	22092	16778	18	73	2551	10507	101	179	130	537	9958	1924
1925	60077	8301	22926	17448	22	87	2741	11069	102	176	161	852	11340	1925
1926	58218	8408	22161	17171	21	126	2766	11190	99	175	168	809	12962	1926
1927	57273	8455	21699	17121	22	177	2728	11275	94	167	131	853	13560	1927
1928	58014	8698	21532	17163	21	213	2878	11559	89	169	173	872	14657	1928
1929	57425	8753	21130	17116	21	248	2961	11672	86	158	184	911	14953	1929
1930	57486	8844	20941	17077	20	344	3098	11804	84	162	130	1037	15635	1930
1931	57284	8884	20703	17053	20	386	3165	11853	78	168	193	1038	17326	1931
1932	55947	8796	20142	17006	21	443	3197	11766	73	155	154	1055	18460	1932
1933	56801	8873	19965	17058	20	449	3277	11952	70	152	144	1108	20189	1933
1934	56960	8901	19813	17043	24	516	3380	12030	68	152	187	1141	21979	1934
1935	56794	9064	19516	17033	22	540	3560	12213	66	151	143	1107	24131	1935
1936	56477	9204	19232	17028	22	569	3702	12512	65	157	203	1163	27097	1936

N.B. – Certain (small) arrears of licences are not included in the figures for "off" licences from 1912–21 inclusive in this table.

TABLE I 14

EXCISE LICENCES, RETAIL (SCOTLAND), 1911-36

Year ending March 31	Spirits inc. beer, wine		Beer, Cider and Perry		Cider and Perry		Wine and Sweets		Sweets		Passenger Boats	Restaurant Cars	Occasional Licences	Year
	On	Off	On	Off	On	Off	On	Off	On	Off				
1911	6764	3511	192	3593		2	23	3313	1	3	167	14	2136	1911
1912	6699	3359	173	3441		2	20	3166	1	4	173	14	2251	1912
1913	6685	3353	171	3426		2	20	3165	1	3	174	16	2166	1913
1914	6686	3329	161	3401		2	20	3143	1	3	171	17	2163	1914
1915	6640	3272	193	3346		4	20	3108	1	3	166	17	1409	1915
1916	6560	3216	292	3289		4	21	3063	1	3	89	9	806	1916
1917	6459	3106	462	3161		3	22	2974	1	3	74	9	478	1917
1918	6332	2964	352	3022		3	19	2848	1	2	61		369	1918
1919	6239	2897	247	2955		3	18	2801	1	2	53		253	1919
1920	6254	2906	259	2966		4	17	2830	1	2	93	6	693	1920
1921	6070	2913	170	2958		4	17	2840	1	2	104	8	1085	1921
1922	5953	2784	165	2845		4	16	2725	1	1	89	8	1334	1922
1923	5933	2784	144	2821		5	14	2710	1	1	95	11	1481	1923
1924	5904	2728	135	2783		8	15	2679	1		96	12	1559	1924
1925	5872	2692	137	2750		12	15	2644	1	1	97	15	1651	1925
1926	5871	2648	137	2716		22	14	2614			96	15	1827	1926
1927	5882	2612	148	2682		27	15	2583			93		1908	1927
1928	5874	2571	124	2642		28	14	2551		2	93		1907	1928
1929	5844	2546	133	2618		31	14	2532		1	88		2073	1929
1930	5855	2509	134	2582		29	12	2506		2	88		2029	1930
1931	5822	2485	124	2551		33	14	2486		3	93		2075	1931
1932	5796	2443	119	2513		29	12	2445		3	89		1970	1932
1933	5766	2407	109	2485		26	11	2411		4	89		2167	1933
1934	5737	2377	114	2462		31	10	2387		4	90		2225	1934
1935	5704	2352	104	2444		36	9	2369		5	92		2352	1935
1936	5689	2320	97	2412		37	11	2342		5	94		2685	1936

TABLE I 15

REVENUE FROM THE MANUFACTURE, IMPORT AND SALE OF ALCOHOLIC LIQUORS IN THE UNITED KINGDOM, 1900–36

Thousands of Pounds

	Taxes on Liquor						Taxes on Licences				
Year	Spirits	Beer	Cider	Sweets	Wine	Total	Makers	Dealers	Retailers etc.	Total	Grand Total
1900	25436	12364			1730	39530	15	258	1883	2156	41686
1901	15112	13964			1488	40564	15	262	1904	2181	42745
1902	23282	13741			1450	38473	14	264	1934	2212	40685
1903	23988	13730			1524	39242	14	263	1940	2217	41459
1904	23329	13483			1336	38149	14	258	1962	2234	40383
1905	22132	13123			1186	36442	14	257	1959	2230	38672
1906	21659	13006			1176	35842	13	252	1923	2188	38030
1907	21961	13095			1238	36295	12	249	1953	2214	38509
1908	21839	13140			1177	36156	12	246	1935	2193	38349
1909	21417	12714			1121	35252	11	241	1923	2175	37427
1910	17858	12554			1123	31535	11	233	1992	2236	33771
1911	23049	12790			1236	37075	798	154	5871	6823	43898
1912	22727	13356			1088	37171	426	128	4114	4668	41839
1913	22599	13227			1110	36936	427	127	4041	4595	41531
1914	23976	13655			1152	38783	438	125	3951	4514	43297
1915	25275	15881			1004	42160	442	123	3759	4326	46486
1916	26839	33770			1078	61687	376	119	3025	3520	65207
1917	18014	31573	70		888	50545	355	116	3032	3503	54048
1918	10597	19109	144		781	30631	251	90	2088	2429	33060
1919	24242	25423	134		1409	51208	183	30	1060	1273	52481
1920	58804	71278	60		2235	132377	247	39	1210	1496	133873
1921	71035	123406	84		2913	197438	350	93	3477	3920	201358
1922	62819	121865	90		2751	187525	329	127	4118	4574	192099
1923	53648	92298	110		3052	149108	253	115	3818	4186	153294
1924	54037	81702	19		3369	139127	249	115	3944	4308	143435
1925	51054	81988			3752	136794	265	114	4279	4658	141452
1926	49928	82520			3746	136194	273	116	4163	4552	140746
1927	43553	84370			4329	132252	265	115	4116	4496	136748
1928	47367	83636		119	4149	135271	256	114	4254	4624	139895
1929	45668	76115		202	4248	126233	254	115	4201	4570	130803
1930	42599	77357		210	4881	125047	251	113	4223	4587	129634
1931	40639	75857		203	4096	120795	251	111	4220	4583	125378
1932	34926	75422		208	3802	114358	228	105	4289	4622	118980
1933	34499	73768		242	3755	112264	185	104	4239	4528	116792
1934	33453	59025		290	4142	96910	174	103	4113	4390	101298
1935	32363	58859		327	4397	95946	190	102	4097	4389	100335
1936	34917	60936		398	4633	100884	202	103	4054	4359	105243

TABLE I 16

NATIONAL DRINK BILLS 1910–35

Nearest million in quantities and cost etc.

U.K.	Spirits: Proof gals.	Spirits: Price £ s. d.	Spirits: Cost £	Spirits: Tax. £	Bulk Beer	Bulk: Price £ s. d.	Bulk: Cost £	Bulk: Tax. £	Foreign Wines: Gals	Foreign Wines: Price £ s. d.	Foreign Wines: Cost £	Foreign Wines: Tax. £	Other Liquors Cost	Grand Cost £	Total Taxation (inc. Lic. Duty etc.)	Tax % of Cost	Cost per Head £ s. d.
1910	29.3	1 11 6	46.2	21.7	33.9	2 18 0	98.5	12.7	12.7	18 0	11.5	1.3	1.5	157.6	40.3	25.5	3 9 3
1911	30.7	1 11 6	48.4	22.6	35.8	2 17 6	102.7	13.3	11.3	18 0	10.2	1.1	1.5	162.8	41.7	25.6	3 11 10
1912	30.6	1 11 6	48.2	22.5	35.7	2 17 0	101.7	13.1	11.3	18 0	10.2	1.1	1.5	161.6	41.3	25.5	3 10 9
1913	31.8	1 11 6	50.2	23.4	36.8	2 17 0	104.7	13.6	11.4	18 0	10.3	1.1	1.5	166.7	42.6	25.5	3 12 5
1914	31.7	1 11 6	49.9	23.3	35.7	2 18 0	103.4	12.7	10.7	18 0	9.6	1.1	1.5	164.5	41.4	25.1	3 10 10
1915	35.0	1 11 6	55.2	26.2	31.0	3 15 0	116.1	32.3	10.2	18 0	9.2	1.0	1.5	182.0	63.0	34.6	3 18 11
1916	28.2	2 2 0	59.1	21.2	29.9	4 10 0	134.3	32.1	10.0	18 0	9.0	1.0	1.5	204.0	57.8	28.3	4 8 6
1917	18.5	4 4 0	78.0	13.8	21.1	8 2 0	170.5	21.8	7.1	1 5 0	9.0	0.7	1.5	259.0	38.9	15.0	5 12 6
1918	15.1	5 10 0	83.2	20.8	21.9	7 4 0	158.1	22.4	11.3	1 8 0	15.9	1.2	1.5	259.3	45.7	17.6	5 13 0
1919	21.7	5 10 0	119.5	48.5	32.3	7 4 0	232.7	57.3	19.2	1 15 0	33.7	2.2	1.5	386.6	109.5	28.3	8 8 0
1920	22.1	6 10 0	144.0	71.1	35.0	8 8 0	294.2	113.0	15.2	2 0 0	30.3	2.9	1.3	469.7	191.0	40.6	10 0 0
1921	18.6	6 10 0	120.8	66.3	31.4	8 8 0	263.7	126.0	11.2	1 10 0	16.9	2.7	1.5	403.0	199.7	49.5	8 10 0
1922	16.9	6 10 0	110.2	60.0	26.6	8 8 0	223.5	107.7	12.1	1 10 0	18.9	3.1	1.6	354.2	175.1	49.4	7 9 0
G.B.																	
1923	14.3	6 10 0	93.0	52.1	*25.9	7 9 8	193.5	84.7	13.0	1 10 0	19.5	3.2	1.5	307.5	144.3	46.9	7 2 0
1924	14.3	6 10 0	93.2	51.9	27.6	7 4 0	198.4	80.3	15.2	1 10 0	22.7	3.7	1.5	316.0	140.6	44.5	7 5 0
1925	14.0	6 10 0	91.1	50.5	27.6	7 4 0	198.9	83.1	15.8	1 10 0	23.8	3.8	1.5	315.3	142.0	45.0	7 4 0
1926	12.9	6 10 0	83.6	46.2	26.6	7 4 0	191.5	84.5	16.5	1 10 0	24.7	3.9	1.5	301.3	139.2	46.2	6 17 0
1927	12.9	6 10 0	83.7	46.1	26.2	7 4 0	188.6	82.3	16.6	1 10 0	24.9	4.6	1.5	298.8	137.6	46.2	6 15 3
1928	12.4	6 10 0	80.5	44.3	25.8	7 4 0	185.8	80.3	13.3	1 10 0	19.9	4.2	2.0	288.2	133.8	46.4	6 9 10
1929	12.4	6 10 0	80.6	44.1	25.7	7 4 0	185.0	76.0	14.1	1 10 0	21.2	4.8	2.0	288.8	129.7	44.9	6 9 9
1930	11.3	6 10 0	73.3	39.2	25.3	7 4 0	182.1	75.7	13.4	1 10 0	20.2	4.4	2.0	277.5	124.1	44.7	6 4 0
1931	10.5	6 10 0	68.5	36.4	22.5	7 10 0	168.7	72.9	13.4	1 10 0	20.1	4.4	2.0	259.4	118.7	45.7	5 15 0
1932	9.6	6 10 0	62.4	33.8	19.2	7 16 0	149.7	76.2	12.3	1 10 0	18.4	4.0	2.0	232.5	118.5	51.0	5 3 0
1933	9.8	6 10 0	63.6	34.3	20.3	6 18 0	139.9	62.0	12.9	1 10 0	19.4	4.4	2.0	224.8	105.2	46.8	4 19 4
1934	9.6	6 10 0	62.2	32.7	21.6	6 12 0	142.9	57.4	14.0	1 10 0	20.9	5.0	3.0	229.0	99.7	43.5	5 1 0
1935	9.6	6 10 0	62.2	32.7	22.7	6 12 0	149.9	60.0	14.5	1 10 0	21.7	4.9	4.0	237.7	102.1	42.9	5 4 3

* Prices varied during the year.

TABLE I 17

ALCOHOL MORTALITY IN ENGLAND AND WALES: QUINQUENNIAL PERIODS

Years	Total Deaths certified as Alcoholism, D.T., etc.				Total Deaths certified as Cirrhosis of Liver				Total Deaths			
	M	F	Persons	Rate per Million	M	F	Persons	Rate per Million	M	F	Persons	Rate per Million
1880–4	4070	1968	6038	46	8657	6738	15395	117	12727	8706	21433	163
1885–9	4616	2569	7185	52	9541	7422	16963	122	14157	9991	24148	174
1890–4	6309	3770	10079	69	10110	7760	17870	121	16419	11530	27949	190
1895–9	7296	4669	11965	77	11229	8956	20185	130	18525	13625	32150	207
1900–4	8385	6076	14461	88	11601	9299	20900	127	19986	15375	35361	214
1905–9	6076	4225	10301	59	10461	8511	18972	109	16537	12736	29273	169
1910–4	5059	3570	8629	47	9688	7412	17100	94	14747	10982	25729	141
1915–9	2431	1545	3976	23	6932	4178	11110	64	9363	5723	15086	87
1920–4	1691	655	2346	12	5923	3038	8961	47	7614	3693	11307	59
1925–9	1578	767	2345	12	6009	3231	9240	47	7587	3998	11585	59
1930–5	1329	692	2021	8	5687	2956	8643	36	7016	3648	10664	44

TABLE I 18

ALCOHOL MORTALITY IN SCOTLAND: QUINQUENNIAL PERIODS

Years	Total Deaths certified as Alcoholism, D.T., etc.				Total Deaths certified as Cirrhosis of Liver				Total Deaths			
	M	F	Persons	Rate per Million	M	F	Persons	Rate per Million	M	F	Persons	Rate per Million
1880–4	739	420	1159	62	525	352	877	46	1,264	772	2036	108
1885–9	645	376	1021	52	563	420	983	50	1208	796	2004	102
1890–4	735	344	1079	53	638	448	1086	53	1373	792	2165	106
1895–9	665	418	1083	50	654	403	1057	49	1319	821	2140	99
1900–4	891	535	1426	63	722	436	1158	51	1613	971	2584	115
1905–9	698	437	1135	49	698	472	1170	50	1396	909	2305	99
1910–4	538	322	860	36	776	465	1241	52	1314	787	2101	89
1915–9	359	227	586	24	569	356	925	39	928	583	1511	63
1920–4	302	124	426	18	517	287	804	33	819	411	1230	50
1925–9	194	65	259	11	560	261	821	34	754	326	1080	44
1930–5	129	43	172	6	594	327	921	31	723	370	1093	37

TABLE I 19

ALCOHOL MORTALITY IN IRELAND: QUINQUENNIAL PERIODS

Years	Total Deaths certified as Alcoholism, D.T., etc.				Total Deaths certified as Cirrhosis of Liver				Total Deaths			
	M	F	Persons	Rate per Million	M	F	Persons	Rate per Million	M	F	Persons	Rate per Million
1880–4	643	115	758	30	642	313	955	38	1285	428	1713	68
1885–9	597	119	716	29	786	428	1214	50	1383	547	1930	79
1890–4	615	114	729	31	797	435	1232	53	1412	549	1961	84
1895–9	675	159	834	37	870	492	1362	60	1545	651	2196	97
1900–4	761	208	969	44	973	555	1528	69	1734	763	2497	113
1905–9	772	173	945	43	1049	614	1663	76	1821	787	2608	119
1910–4	546	83	629	29	940	465	1405	64	1486	548	2034	93
1915–9	255	34	289	13	670	327	1998	46	926	361	1287	59
1920–4	136	24	160	7	479	178	657	31	615	202	817	38
1925–9	89	13	102	5	449	189	638	30	538	202	740	35
1930–5	75	9	84	4	431	193	624	24	506	202	708	28

TABLE I 20

DRUNKENNESS PROCEEDINGS (ENGLAND AND WALES)

Criminal Statistics, 1900–05; Licensing Statistics, 1906–35

Arranged in Areas (thousands)

Areas:
1. Cumberland, Durham, Northumberland, Westmorland.
2. Cheshire and Lancashire.
3. Yorkshire.
4. Derby, Leicester, Northants, Notts, Stafford, Warwick.
5. Galmorgan, Monmouth.
6. Metropolitan Police Area.
7. Kent, Herts, Essex, Surrey (outside Metropolitan Police Area).
8. Bedford, Berks, Bucks, Sussex.
9. Cambridge, Hunts, Lincoln, Norfolk, Rutland, Suffolk.
10. Glos, Hereford, Oxon, Salop, Worcester.
11. Cornwall, Devon, Dorset, Somerset, Hants, Wilts.
12. Rest of Wales.

Year	1	2	3	4	5	6	7	8	9	10	11	12	Total
1900	27.5	35.3	22.2	19.6	12.5	53.8	5.7	2.8	4.5	7.3	8.6	4.6	204349
1901	28.3	38.2	22.7	20.7	14.2	52.6	5.5	2.9	4.4	7.4	8.4	5.0	210429
1902	26.4	39.1	23.2	20.8	13.4	53.7	5.3	3.5	5.0	6.8	8.0	5.0	209980
1903	24.4	43.5	27.0	21.4	14.7	62.7	5.7	2.9	5.6	6.8	8.8	6.0	230247
1904	24.2	41.2	26.7	21.5	14.3	63.9	5.7	3.6	5.3	6.6	8.8	5.6	227467
Average	**26.2**	**39.5**	**24.4**	**20.8**	**13.8**	**57.3**	**5.6**	**3.1**	**5.0**	**7.0**	**8.5**	**5.2**	**216494**
1905	24.4	41.4	26.0	20.3	11.6	62.0	5.4	3.3	5.6	6.1	8.0	5.2	219335
1906	27.4	44.6	24.8	20.5	8.9	60.6	4.9	3.2	5.6	6.1	7.4	4.7	218414
1907	27.1	46.7	25.2	21.2	9.5	55.4	4.8	3.3	6.0	6.1	7.7	4.5	217517
1908	25.6	44.1	24.6	19.6	9.6	54.6	4.3	3.0	6.0	5.7	7.8	4.6	209691
1909	22.2	38.6	22.2	18.1	9.0	52.6	3.9	2.6	5.2	5.0	6.9	3.9	190495
Average	**25.3**	**43.1**	**24.6**	**19.9**	**9.7**	**57.0**	**4.7**	**3.1**	**5.7**	**5.8**	**7.7**	**4.6**	**211090**
1910	18.9	35.9	20.8	17.1	7.7	58.2	3.6	2.5	5.3	4.6	6.2	3.6	184463
1911	20.8	37.3	20.6	18.2	7.7	65.5	3.5	2.7	5.3	4.5	6.3	3.7	195935
1912	20.4	41.7	20.0	19.1	9.8	69.4	3.9	2.5	5.6	4.3	6.8	3.7	207368
1913	20.5	43.3	20.2	20.0	10.1	74.6	3.5	2.4	5.1	4.1	5.8	3.6	213188
1914	21.1	41.3	20.6	18.3	8.5	77.9	3.7	1.8	4.9	3.9	6.1	3.8	212350
Average	**20.3**	**39.9**	**20.4**	**18.5**	**8.7**	**69.1**	**3.6**	**2.4**	**5.2**	**4.4**	**6.2**	**3.7**	**202661**
1915	15.3	39.7	15.8	11.9	5.5	60.2	3.2	1.2	2.9	2.8	5.5	2.6	157168
1916	11.5	20.5	8.8	4.6	4.0	35.1	1.9	0.7	1.9	1.9	2.9	1.8	94289
1917	6.4	10.3	5.0	2.7	2.3	19.4	0.8	0.5	0.9	1.2	1.6	1.1	52427
1918	4.9	6.3	2.7	2.0	1.2	11.7	0.5	1.0	0.7	0.6	1.1	0.6	32703
1919	8.6	12.5	5.6	3.7	2.8	24.1	1.1	1.0	1.3	0.9	1.8	1.2	64495
Average	**9.3**	**17.9**	**7.6**	**5.0**	**3.2**	**30.1**	**1.5**	**0.9**	**1.5**	**1.5**	**2.6**	**1.5**	**80216**
1920	14.0	22.4	10.6	7.1	4.8	33.6	1.3	1.0	2.4	1.6	2.8	1.9	103632
1921	9.4	19.2	8.2	5.8	3.2	30.5	1.1	0.6	1.8	1.4	2.2	1.5	85,166
1922	7.0	17.6	8.4	5.8	3.1	34.5	0.9	0.8	1.6	1.1	2.1	1.5	84,257
1923	7.6	15.6	8.9	7.6	3.7	33.5	1.0	0.8	1.5	1.1	2.0	1.9	85082
1924	8.4	16.0	9.5	8.6	3.2	33.4	1.0	0.9	1.5	1.2	1.9	2.0	87511
Average	**9.3**	**18.2**	**9.1**	**7.0**	**3.6**	**33.1**	**1.1**	**0.8**	**1.6**	**1.3**	**2.2**	**1.6**	**89130**
1925	7.0	16.7	8.8	7.7	2.8	33.3	1.1	1.0	1.5	1.1	2.1	1.7	84578
1926	4.7	16.0	7.4	5.5	1.9	32.4	1.1	1.0	1.4	1.1	2.1	1.3	75787
1927	5.4	13.4	8.2	6.4	2.2	30.5	1.1	1.0	1.4	1.2	2.3	1.3	74303
1928	4.8	11.1	6.9	5.9	1.8	26.4	1.0	1.0	1.2	1.0	2.0	1.2	64331
1929	4.8	10.3	6.5	5.6	1.9	23.9	1.1	1.0	1.2	1.1	2.1	1.2	60728
Average	**5.3**	**13.5**	**7.6**	**6.2**	**2.1**	**29.3**	**1.1**	**1.0**	**1.3**	**1.1**	**2.1**	**1.3**	**71945**
1930	5.1	9.9	6.3	5.6	1.8	24.6	1.2	1.1	1.3	1.0	2.2	1.2	61455
1931	4.1	8.0	4.7	4.6	1.3	20.1	1.7	0.9	1.5	0.9	1.8	0.9	49029
1932	2.5	6.6	3.2	2.8	1.0	14.4	0.5	1.0	0.7	0.7	1.5	0.6	35407
1933	3.4	7.6	3.9	3.9	1.3	17.1	0.6	0.9	0.8	0.8	1.5	0.7	42492
1934	3.8	8.4	4.5	4.5	1.3	17.5	0.7	0.9	0.8	0.8	1.5	0.8	46293
1935	3.9	9.8	4.8	5.0	1.3	19.3	0.8	1.1	1.0	0.9	1.5	0.7	50032
Average	**3.8**	**8.4**	**4.6**	**4.4**	**1.3**	**18.8**	**0.9**	**1.0**	**1.0**	**0.8**	**1.7**	**0.8**	**47350**

TABLE I 21
DRUNKENNESS PROCEEDINGS (SCOTLAND), 1900–35 and number per 10,000 population

Year	Male	Female	Persons	Proceed-ings per 10,000 Pop.	Year	Male	Female	Persons	Proceed-ings per 10,000 Pop.
1900	31462	12813	44275	99.8	1918	9168	2395	11563	24.0
1901	32672	12495	45167	100.8	1919	17722	4250	21972	45.6
1902	32006	11515	43521	96.6	1920	32843	7598	40441	83.1
1903	27094	10147	37241	82.1	1921	19787	5611	25398	52.2
1904	31820	12290	44110	96.4	1922	15029	4678	19707	40.4
1905	33507	12651	46158	100.5	1923	14475	5018	19493	40.0
1906	40321	15131	55452	120.0	1924	15316	5124	20440	42.0
1907	43490	15440	58930	126.7	1925	14567	4928	19495	40.1
1908	40498	14617	55115	117.7	1926	13407	4477	17884	36.8
1909	29748	10835	40583	86.2	1927	14429	4385	18814	38.8
1910	27150	9654	36804	77.7	1928	13769	4302	18071	37.3
1911	30932	10263	41195	86.7	1929	13207	4270	17477	36.1
1912	32355	10739	43094	90.0	1930	11770	3757	15527	32.2
1913	38443	11773	50216	106.2	1931	9856	3549	13405	27.7
1914	39306	11859	51165	107.8	1932	9045	3244	12289	25.2
1915	36438	11739	48177	101.0	1933	9072	3127	12199	24.8
1916	24388	8713	33101	71.1	1934	9500	3321	12821	26.0
1917	14922	5568	20490	42.6	1935	10634	3167	13801	27.8

SECTION II

STATISTICAL TABLES, 1937–52

TABLE II 1

LICENSED PREMISES (ENGLAND AND WALES, AND SCOTLAND), 1937–52

	England and Wales					Scotland				
Year	**Full All Drinks**	**On-licences Beer/ Wine**	**Regist. Clubs**	**Off-Licences**	**Total**	**Public Houses**	**Hotels**	**Regist. Clubs**	**Off-Licences**	**Total**
1937	56233	18093	16563	22109	112998	4214	1491	687	2475	8867
1938	56173	17747	16951	22052	112923	4203	1506	700	2435	8844
1939	56112	17460	17362	21995	112929	4177	1524	695	2404	8800
1940	56047	17318	16463	21884	111712					
1941	56961	17249	15864	21756	110830	4125	1509	661	2281	8576
1942	55901	17191	15682	21653	110427	4101	1501	649	2247	8498
1943	55868	17137	15732	21628	110365	4098	1502	651	2214	8465
1944	55856	17109	15678	21610	110253	4105	1498	657	2218	8478
1945	55875	17085	15590	21599	110149	4080	1506	681	2188	8455
1946	56009	17017	16496	21693	111215	4084	1565	740	2204	8593
1947	56305	16927	17470	21848	112550	4103	1646	773	2257	8779
1948	56850	16534	18370	22025	113779	4111	1690	834	2313	8948
1949	58140	15282	18962	22218	114602	4115	1709	884	2342	9050
1950	59054	14429	19221	23532	161236	4118	1740	912	2366	9136
1951	59757	13664	19511	23669	116601	4123	1768	944	2380	9215
1952	60333	13035	19903	23717	116988	4111	1770	966	2387	9234

TABLE II 2

EXCISE AND CUSTOMS REVENUE FROM ALCOHOLIC DRINK (UNITED KINGDOM), 1937–

£ millions

	Beer		Wine		Spirits		
Year	**UK**	**Imports**	**UK**	**Imports**	**UK**	**Imports**	**Duty Receipts in Total**
1937	57.3	5.4	0.5	5.1	31.4	4.8	104.5
1938	61.2	4.5	0.5	5.0	31.1	4.8	107.1
1939	62.4	3.2	0.5	4.8	30.9	4.7	106.5
1940	75.2	3.6	0.9	5.7	34.5	6.2	126.1
1941	133.5	5.6	1.6	7.8	33.9	11.6	194.0
1942	157.3	7.3	1.1	3.8	31.0	15.7	216.2
1943	209.6	8.0	1.7	2.4	49.4	18.2	289.3
1944	263.2	6.4	2.1	2.3	59.6	17.2	350.8
1945	278.9	8.9	2.0	2.5	50.1	13.5	355.9
1946	295.3	10.8	2.2	5.0	51.2	16.9	381.4
1947	250.4	9.4	2.2	10.8	51.6	24.9	349.3
1948	264.1	9.9	3.4	15.6	40.7	42.7	376.4
1949	294.7	12.6	3.8	15.7	46.7	44.1	417.6
1950	263.1	13.7	2.8	16.1	58.7	39.6	394.0
1951	249.1	13.0	3.2	18.1	75.8	38.7	397.9
1952	248.2	12.7	3.3	17.5	67.1	29.9	378.7

TABLE II 3

CONSUMPTION OF BEER AND WINE (UNITED KINGDOM), 1937-52

Year	Beer	Imported Wines Heavy	Imported Wines Light	Imported Wines Sparkling	British Wines	Total Wines
	mn bulk bbls	thousand gallons			thousand gallons	
1937	24	11709	3950	679	5690	22028
1938	25	11516	3623	628	6144	21910
1939	25	11602	3062	561	6418	21645
1940	26	11353	2572	388	6916	21228
1941	27	10392	1730	232	6408	18763
1942	30	4623	752	75	3957	9407
1943	30	1705	264	29	3100	5098
1944	31	1166	508	13	2898	4585
1945	32	1400	227	11	2735	4373
1946	34	2723	464	92	2921	6200
1947	30	5282	1837	329	2998	10445
1948	31	7098	2145	383	3899	13525
1949	28	5718	1282	497	2961	10458
1950	27	5939	1667	476	3662	11754
1951	26	6439	2684	560	4450	14133
1952	26	6078	3234	519	4672	14503

TABLE II 4

CONSUMPTION OF SPIRITS BY TYPES (UNITED KINGDOM), 1937-52

thousand proof gallons

Year	UK Produce	Rum	Imported Brandy	Liqueurs	Total
1937	9289	581	430	277	10578
1938	9239	583	411	290	10552
1939	8697	581	411	265	9955
1940	9094	786	478	277	10635
1941	7156	1063	396	870	9484
1942	6518	1855	212	901	9485
1943	7299	1459	131	452	9340
1944	7615	1290	86	242	9234
1945	6452	1344	57	176	8029
1946	6541	1697	124	204	8565
1947	6510	2479	305	243	9537
1948	4719	3822	340	610	9491
1949	4383	2783	568	658	8393
1950	5518	2133	626	902	9179
1951	7129	2061	740	835	10766
1952	6306	1450	631	690	9077

TABLE II 5

CONSUMPTION OF BEER, SPIRITS AND WINE (UNITED KINGDOM), 1937–52

per head in pints

Year	Beer	Spirits	Wine
1937	144	2.6	3.7
1938	151	2.6	3.7
1939	152	2.4	3.6
1940	156	2.6	3.5
1941	159	2.3	3.1
1942	182	2.3	1.6
1943	177	2.1	0.8
1944	181	2.1	0.7
1945	187	1.9	0.7
1946	197	2.0	1.0
1947	176	2.1	1.7
1948	180	2.1	2.2
1949	161	1.9	1.7
1950	153	2.1	1.9
1951	147	2.4	2.2
1952	147	2.0	2.3

TABLE II 6

CONVICTIONS FOR DRUNKENNESS (ENGLAND AND WALES, AND SCOTLAND), 1937–52

	England and Wales				Scotland			
Year	Total	Male	Female	Per 10,000 pop.	Total	Male	Female	Per 10,000 pop.
1937	46757	40587	6170	11.4	13468	9936	3136	27.0
1938	46603	40589	6014	11.3	12610	9396	2873	25.3
1939	52929	45846	7083	12.8	13362	10123	2899	26.7
1940	46998	40287	6711	11.2	11723	8999	2457	23.1
1941	40964	35359	5605	9.8	9018	6815	1959	17.5
1942	27435	22772	4663	6.5	5697	4188	1373	11.0
1943	27363	22069	5294	6.5	4796	3272	1405	9.2
1944	22628	18125	4503	5.3	3236	2203	950	6.2
1945	20669	16375	4294	4.8	2563	1759	738	4.9
1946	20545	17090	3455	4.8	3247	2268	890	6.3
1947	25170	21354	3816	5.8	4107	3045	977	8.0
1948	32871	28305	4566	7.6	3957	2996	875	7.7
1949	35733	31278	4455	8.2	4497	3421	982	8.7
1950	47717	42642	5075	10.8	4862	3847	911	9.4
1951	53676	48335	5341	12.2	5366	4434	932	10.5
1952	53888	48694	5194	12.3	5880	4929	951	11.5

SECTION III

STATISTICAL TABLES, 1953–75

TABLE III 1 CONSUMPTION OF BEER AND WINE (UNITED KINGDOM)

Year	Beer mn bulk bbls	Imported Wines Heavy	Light	Sparkling	British Wines	Total Wines
		thousands gallons				
1953	25	5639	3158	394	4411	13602
1954	25	6101	3556	427	4537	14621
1955	25	6531	4787	465	5075	16858
1956	25	6769	5404	500	5489	18162
1957	25	6794	6354	518	5750	19407
1958	25	6611	7320	580	5438	19948
1959	25	7028	7035	571	5636	20270
1960	27	7580	8333	685	6827	23424
1961	27	9024	9501	808	7794	27126
1962	29	9333	10513	827	7319	27992
1963	28	10044	11078	902	7810	29834
1964	29	11024	13609	1110	8330	34074
1965	30	11427	14702	1275	9570	36974
1966	30	11012	15055	1287	9183	36536
1967	31	10695	16281	1394	9111	37481
1968	32	12898	19639	1901	10270	44708
1969	32	12414	20070	1627	11440	45551
1970	33	11678	19144	1719	10100	42641
1971	35	13367	22058	1991	11000	48416
1972	36	14814	26710	2291	11621	55436
1973	37	16476	32877	2824	12643	64821
1974	39	19331	45163	3396	15629	83519
1975	39	17434	42538	2638	16762	79372

TABLE III 2 CONSUMPTION OF SPIRITS BY TYPES (UNITED KINGDOM)

thousands of proof gallons

Year	UK Produce		Rum	Imported Brandy	Liqueurs		Total
1953	7028		1472	617	607		9725
1954	7633		1359	613	498		10103
1955	8488		1352	651	471		10962
1956	9193		1449	692	486		11820
1957	9625		1418	761	546		12349
1958	10009		1440	737	548		12734
					Liqueurs	Other	
1959	10125		1350	764	293	243	12775
1960	10924		1336	839	321	296	13716
1961	12094		1487	950	368	459	15358
	Mature	Immature					
1962	7662	4362	1453	977	367	453	15273
1963	8077	4257	1572	1124	369	543	15942
1964	8990	4882	1649	1352	423	435	17729
1965	9589	4728	1698	1387	471	804	18677
1966	8687	4542	1527	1254	448	282	16740
1967	8971	4639	1505	1316	448	199	17079
1968	9772	4879	1676	1528	488	264	18607
1969	9288	4091	1561	1385	439	383	17146
1970	9566	4145	1665	1337	398	457	17567
1971	10374	4656	2014	1666	460	480	19549
1972	11486	4890	2270	1939	541	559	21685
1973	12777	5141	2681	2290	675	872	24434
1974	16267	7756	3644	2815	1010	531	32023
1975	16907	8039	3462	2486	1074	450	32418

TABLE III 3 CONSUMPTION OF BEER, SPIRITS AND WINE (UNITED KINGDOM)
per head in pints

Year	Beer	Spirits	Wine
1953	145	2.1	2.2
1954	144	2.3	2.3
1955	140	2.4	2.6
1956	143	2.6	2.8
1957	143	2.7	3.0
1958	142	2.9	3.1
1959	137	2.9	3.1
1960	148	3.0	3.6
1961	151	3.3	4.1
1962	156	3.3	4.2
1963	156	3.4	4.4
1964	158	3.7	5.0
1965	160	3.9	5.4
1966	161	3.4	5.3
1967	165	3.6	5.6
1968	165	3.9	6.5
1969	168	3.6	6.6
1970	174	3.6	6.1
1971	181	4.0	7.0
1972	187	4.5	7.9
1973	189	5.0	9.3
1974	202	6.5	11.9
1975	201	6.6	11.3

TABLE III 4 CONSUMERS' EXPENDITURE AT CURRENT PRICES (UNITED KINGDOM)
£ millions

Year	Expenditure All Items	Beer	Expenditure on Wines and Spirits	
1953	11402	529	288	
1954	12091	513	309	
1955	13038	536	334	
1956	13744	553	351	
1957	14509	581	365	
1958	15296	575	374	
1959	16117	563	366	
1960	16933	576	396	
1961	17835	635	451	
		Beer	**Spirits**	**Wines etc.**
1962	18923	687	350	125
1963	20118	717	355	160
1964	21477	792	406	192
1965	22845	882	420	197
1966	24211	951	453	222
1967	25428	1021	471	247
1968	27338	1067	519	284
1969	29102	1201	520	308
1970	31644	1355	611	333
1971	35165	1526	670	397
1972	39716	1662	777	471
1973	45044	1807	1004	604
1974	51832	2071	1140	715
1975	63373	2679	1392	831

TABLE III 5
EXCISE AND CUSTOMS REVENUE FROM ALCOHOLIC DRINK (UNITED KINGDOM), 1953–75. £ million

Year	Beer UK	Beer Import	Wine UK	Wine Import	Spirits UK	Spirits Import	Duty Receipts in Total
1953	243.4	12.6	3.0	16.2	74.6	28.7	378.5
1954	242.0	13.3	3.0	17.7	81.1	26.3	383.4
1955	237.5	13.6	3.3	19.6	90.1	26.3	390.4
1956	243.7	14.8	3.5	20.6	97.5	27.9	408.0
1957	245.5	15.5	3.6	21.3	102.1	29.0	417.0
1958	246.1	15.1	3.3	21.6	106.1	29.0	421.2
1959	238.7	14.6	3.2	18.3	107.3	28.2	410.3
1960	206.2	12.6	3.8	20.3	115.7	29.7	388.3
1961	210.1	12.1	4.2	17.8	128.1	34.8	407.1
1962	233.5	13.3	4.1	20.0	135.5	37.1	443.5
1963	241.4	12.8	4.5	21.3	143.6	42.2	465.8
1964	249.9	13.4	4.8	24.5	161.4	45.1	499.1
1965	284.4	14.7	6.2	28.9	184.5	56.1	574.8
1966	323.6	16.6	7.6	34.4	194.0	51.5	627.6
1967	355.2	18.6	8.3	37.7	213.6	54.9	688.3
1968	370.3	19.9	10.0	46.9	236.8	64.0	747.9
1969	385.0	20.8	13.0	54.5	237.2	67.1	777.6
1970	427.7	22.8	15.7	64.9	259.0	73.1	863.2
1971	442.0	25.0	17.9	74.9	283.8	87.7	931.3
1972	453.9	28.9	19.1	87.3	308.9	100.4	998.5
1973	463.4	28.3	20.8	103.1	336.6	122.4	1074.5
1974	343.2	21.9	13.9	80.7	371.0	123.4	954.1
1975	427.4	23.2	23.2	105.7	426.6	128.2	1134.3

TABLE III 6
RATES OF EXCISE DUTY ON BEER, WINES AND SPIRITS (UNITED KINGDOM), 1948–73

Date of Budget	Beer £ per Barrel 1030°	Beer £ per Barrel 1055°	Wines £ per Gallon Light	Wines £ per Gallon Heavy	Spirits £ per Gallon Proof
April 1948	9.94	18.22	1.25	2.50	10.54
April 1949	8.89	17.17	0.65	2.50	no change
April 1950	7.77	16.05	no change		no change
April 1958	no change		0.65	1.90	no change
April 1959	5.59	13.87	no change		no change
April 1960	no change		0.65	1.30	no change
July 1961	6.15	15.26	0.72	1.43	11.60
April 1962	no change		0.70	1.38	no change
April 1964	7.35	16.46	0.78	1.50	12.88
April 1965	8.55	17.66	0.93	1.83	14.60
July 1966	9.41	19.43	1.02	2.01	16.06
April 1967	9.43	19.43	1.01	1.96	16.06
March 1968	no change		1.16	2.26	17.14
November 1968	10.38	21.38	1.28	2.71	18.85
April 1969	no change		1.61	2.71	no change
April 1973 Adjustments for Value Added Tax	6.90	14.15	0.88	1.98	15.45
July 1973	no change		0.85	1.88	no change
March 1974	9.36	17.16	1.37	2.32	17.01
April 1975	13.68	25.08	2.68	3.55	22.09

TABLE III 7

LICENSED PREMISES (ENGLAND AND WALES), 1953–75

Year	Full On-Licences All Drinks	Full On-Licences Beer/Wine	Restricted On-Licences based on 1961 Licensing Act Rest-aurant	Resi-dential	Com-bined	Licensed Clubs	Regist'd Clubs	Off-Licences	Totals
1953	60869	12351					20348	23810	117378
1954	61265	11708					20772	23863	117608
1955	60670	10574					21164	23548	115596
1956	61087	9788					21438	23531	115844
1957	61471	8882					21988	23517	115858
1958	61762	8151					22567	23530	116010
1959	62039	7416					23232	23571	116258
1960	63682	5502					23773	23670	116627
1961	64570	4366					24418	23934	117288
1962	65615	2422	1318	350	942	1153	21459	24644	118103
1963	65627	1823	2130	709	1180	1940	20663	25258	119330
1964	65483	1448	2841	837	1358	2040	21010	25838	120855
1965	65353	1217	3520	963	1506	2193	21405	26352	122509
1966	65353	1020	4127	1087	1650	2318	21872	26590	124017
1967	65042	874	4590	1191	1769	2377	22368	26702	124913
1968	64827	714	5160	1365	1917	2438	22705	26906	126032
1969	64448	600	5739	1504	2055	2488	23176	27434	127444
1970	64211	491	6438	1685	2190	2511	23521	27910	128957
1971	63640	447	7100	1804	2324	2563	23985	28166	130029
1972	63351	381	7860	1988	2489	2659	24368	28808	131904
1973	63534	344	8664	2230	2598	2702	24593	29710	134375
1974	63467	360	9176	2354	2711	2849	24625	30502	136044
1975	64261	353	9599	2532	2763	2802	24931	31644	138885

TABLE III 8

MONTHLY TOTALS OF PROVED OFFENCES OF DRUNKENNESS (ENGLAND AND WALES), 1953–74

Year	Jan.	Feb.	Mar.	Apr.	May	Jun.	Jul.	Aug.	Sep.	Oct.	Nov.	Dec.
1953	3910	3587	4722	4339	4570	4517	4917	5079	4409	4462	4393	4669
1954	3518	3285	4254	4332	4646	4638	5025	4967	4565	4671	4728	4648
1955	3586	3521	4155	4596	4621	4375	4909	5392	4705	4623	4581	5146
1956	4121	3583	4789	4657	5239	5111	5777	5440	5305	5645	4746	5769
1957	5098	4717	5626	5564	5782	5586	6348	5927	5462	5551	5384	5957
1958	4763	4670	5124	5203	5622	5671	5870	5837	5723	5413	5277	5885
1959	4543	4365	5506	5494	5686	5741	5996	5946	5505	5453	5393	5559
1960	4684	4666	5619	5687	5979	5599	6308	6590	5536	5976	5645	5820
1961	5129	4935	5815	5903	6625	6171	7121	6766	6710	6897	6244	6378
1962	6292	5535	6439	7094	7151	7440	8185	7595	6638	7491	6803	7329
1963	6124	5781	7199	7267	7155	6483	7878	7401	7241	6897	7024	6557
1964	6347	5872	6329	6447	6527	7137	6736	6681	6189	6204	6258	6115
1965	5877	5235	6268	6930	6110	6209	6448	6522	6032	6154	5880	6315
1966	5458	5112	6122	5887	5804	6231	6113	5967	5948	6155	5825	5877
1967	5926	4985	6062	5493	6716	6531	7097	7103	6537	6693	6127	6274
1968	6687	5708	6033	6531	6723	6521	7527	6776	6651	7102	6429	6382
1969	6846	5124	6214	6221	6791	6924	7315	7010	7216	7776	6317	6748
1970	6812	5763	6193	6782	7052	6878	7817	7470	7224	6759	6428	7196
1971	6925	5956	7067	7168	7179	7246	7683	7651	7720	7588	7187	7365
1972	7575	6276	6963	7047	7733	7628	7969	8180	7315	8144	7633	7735
1973	8591	6965	8062	7786	8571	8413	9104	8622	7989	8963	8225	7983
1974	9199	7066	8016	8966	8993	8473	9615	8907	8884	8665	8189	8230

The Home Office ceased to publish monthly totals after the Annual Report for 1974.

TABLE III 9

THREE-MONTHLY TOTALS OF PROVED OFFENCES OF DRUNKENNESS (ENGLAND AND WALES), 1953–74 (in '000s)

Year	Winter Dec./Feb.	Spring Mar./May	Summer Jun./Aug.	Autumn Sep./Nov.
1953	12.2	13.6	14.5	13.3
1954	11.5	13.2	14.6	14.0
1955	11.8	13.4	14.7	13.9
1956	12.9	14.7	16.3	15.7
1957	15.6	17.0	17.9	16.4
1958	15.4	15.9	17.4	16.4
1959	14.8	16.7	17.7	16.4
1960	14.9	17.3	18.5	17.2
1961	15.9	18.3	20.1	19.9
1962	18.2	20.7	23.2	20.9
1963	19.2	21.6	21.8	18.2
1964	18.8	19.3	20.6	18.7
1965	17.2	18.3	19.2	18.1
1966	16.9	17.8	18.3	17.9
1967	16.8	18.3	20.7	19.4
1968	18.7	19.3	20.8	20.2
1969	18.4	19.2	21.2	21.3
1970	19.3	20.0	22.2	20.4
1971	20.1	21.4	22.6	22.5
1972	21.2	21.7	23.8	23.1
1973	23.3	24.4	26.1	25.2
1974	24.2	26.0	27.0	25.7

Monthly data not published by the Home Office after the Annual Report for 1974.

TABLE III 10
DRUNKENNESS OFFENCES, MOTORING OFFENCES AND LICENCES, (ENGLAND AND WALES), 1953-63

	1953	**1954**	**1955**	**1956**	**1957**	**1958**	**1959**	**1960**	**1961**	**1962**	**1963**
Population '000	**44090**					**45109**					**47023**
Proved Offences—Drunkenness											
Males											
Under 18	x	x	669	880	938	941	949	1460	1535	1435	1402
18 and under 21	3096	3502	3748	4247	4967	5088	5350	6419	7198	7661	7118
21 and under 30	13884	13686	13835	14239	15165	14338	14098	15307	16883	18918	17455
30 and under 60	32232	31977	31991	32746	36968	36107	36539	36784	40135	46212	45605
60 and over	4362	4112	3967	3461	4004	3742	3749	3891	4240	4873	4848
All ages	**48539**	**48377**	**49654**	**55573**	**62042**	**60216**	**60685**	**63861**	**69991**	**79199**	**76428**
Females											
Under 18			(Included in	53	49	59	59	87	118	88	83
18 and under 21			the number	205	241	209	219	216	227	223	222
21 and under 30			of persons	716	760	698	608	588	643	652	616
30 and under 60			by ages	2914	3133	3027	2836	2656	3001	3171	3091
60 and over			given above)	721	777	849	780	701	714	659	644
All ages	**5035**	**4900**	**4556**	**4609**	**4960**	**4842**	**4502**	**4248**	**4703**	**4793**	**4656**
All Proved Offences	**53574**	**53277**	**54210**	**60182**	**67002**	**65058**	**65187**	**68109**	**74694**	**83992**	**81084**
Motoring Offences											
Proceedings for:											
(a) Previously Convicted											
Unfit to drive											
Driving, undue alcohol											
Fail provide specimen											
(b) No Prev. Conviction											
Unfit to drive					3851	4098	4617	5417	6110	6786	7348
Driving, undue alcohol											
Fail provide spec.											
In charge and:											
Unfit to drive					803	968	1098	1389	1435	1689	1928
Undue alcohol											
Fail provide spec.											
Failure to provide breath specimen											
Total: All Proceedings	**3257**	**3608**	**3867**	**4456**	**4654**	**5066**	**5715**	**6806**	**7545**	**8475**	**9276**
Licensed Premises											
Public Houses:											
Full	60869					61762					65627
Beer and Cider	12130					7987					1748
Wine or Cider	221					164					75
Restaurant Licence											2128
Residential Licence											709
Above Combined											1180
Licensed Clubs											1938
Total On Licences	**73220**					**69913**					**73409**
Off Licences	**23818**					**23530**					**25258**
Total On/Off Licences	**97032**					**93443**					**98667**
Registered Clubs	**20348**					**22567**					**20663**
Total Licences & Clubs	**117380**					**116010**					**119330**

TABLE III 11
DRUNKENNESS OFFENCES, MOTORING OFFENCES AND LICENCES, 1953-63
BEDFORDSHIRE POLICE DISTRICT

	1953	1954	1955	1956	1957	1958	1959	1960	1961	1962	1963
Population '000	**320**					**344**					**404**
Proved Offences—											
Drunkenness											
Males											
Under 18	x	x	2	4	6	1	3	7	4	8	6
18 and under 21	9	7	17	23	38	28	28	34	45	36	35
21 and under 30	49	41	81	103	103	95	110	98	127	130	102
30 and under 60	114	119	148	217	151	190	208	218	276	286	275
60 and over	7	7	10	9	11	12	17	18	8	17	20
All ages	**174**	**169**	**254**	**356**	**309**	**326**	**366**	**375**	**460**	**477**	**438**
Females											
Under 18			(Included in	1			1	1	2		1
18 and under 21			the number				1	1	5	1	2
21 and under 30			of persons	2	7	3	4	3	6	5	13
30 and under 60			by ages	4	4	6	6	3	7	7	6
60 and over			given above)	1					2	1	2
All ages	**5**	**5**	**4**	**8**	**11**	**9**	**12**	**8**	**22**	**14**	**24**
All Proved Offences	**179**	**174**	**258**	**364**	**320**	**335**	**378**	**383**	**482**	**491**	**462**
Motoring Offences											
Proceedings for:											
(a) Previously Convicted											
Unfit to drive											
Driving, undue alcohol											
Fail provide specimen											
(b) No Prev. Conviction											
Unfit to drive					40	39	31	54	72	50	50
Driving, undue alcohol											
Fail provide spec.											
In charge and:											
Unfit to drive					4	3	5	10	16	15	22
Undue alcohol											
Fail provide spec.											
Failure to provide breath specimen											
Total: All Proceedings	**19**	**23**	**31**	**46**	**44**	**42**	**36**	**64**	**88**	**65**	**72**
Licensed Premises											
Public Houses:											
Full	607					668					676
Beer and Cider	145					53					12
Wine or Cider	1					2					2
Restaurant Licence											10
Residential Licence											1
Above Combined											1
Licensed Clubs											6
Total On Licences	**753**					**723**					**708**
Off Licences	**110**					**113**					**144**
Total On/Off Licences	**863**					**836**					**852**
Registered Clubs	**154**					**165**					**149**
Total Licences & Clubs	**1017**					**1001**					**1001**

TABLE III 12
DRUNKENNESS OFFENCES, MOTORING OFFENCES AND LICENCES, 1953-63
BERKSHIRE POLICE DISTRICT

	1953	1954	1955	1956	1957	1958	1959	1960	1961	1962	1963
Population '000	**310**					**364**					**417**
Proved Offences—Drunkenness											
Males											
Under 18	x	x	1	3	5	3	5	4	7	3	4
18 and under 21	3	4	6	10	15	14	12	17	10	17	20
21 and under 30	35	19	23	29	16	28	22	26	22	32	54
30 and under 60	52	42	52	44	62	71	59	67	64	110	103
60 and over	2	3	12	6	5	1	7	3	8	11	10
All ages	**93**	**63**	**91**	**92**	**103**	**117**	**105**	**117**	**111**	**173**	**191**
Females											
Under 18		(Included in the number of persons by ages given above)		1			1	1			1
18 and under 21				1		1	1			1	
21 and under 30				2	1			2			1
30 and under 60				3	2	1	1	2	2	5	7
60 and over											1
All ages	**2**	**5**	**3**	**7**	**3**	**2**	**3**	**5**	**2**	**6**	**10**
All Proved Offences	**95**	**68**	**94**	**99**	**106**	**119**	**108**	**122**	**113**	**179**	**201**
Motoring Offences											
Proceedings for:											
(a) Previously Convicted											
Unfit to drive											
Driving, undue alcohol											
Fail provide specimen											
(b) No Prev. Conviction											
Unfit to drive					32	24	28	34	31	30	38
Driving, undue alcohol											
Fail provide spec.											
In charge and:											
Unfit to drive					3	14	7	9	16	12	12
Undue alcohol											
Fail provide spec.											
Failure to provide breath specimen											
Total: All Proceedings	**14**	**18**	**33**	**36**	**35**	**38**	**35**	**43**	**47**	**42**	**50**
Licensed Premises											
Public Houses:											
Full	721					757					794
Beer and Cider	165					75					10
Wine or Cider	2					1					
Restaurant Licence											16
Residential Licence											2
Above Combined											5
Licensed Clubs											9
Total On Licences	**888**					**833**					**836**
Off Licences	**139**					**141**					**175**
Total On/Off Licences	**1027**					**974**					**1011**
Registered Clubs	**219**					**240**					**224**
Total Licences & Clubs	**1246**					**1214**					**1235**

TABLE III 13
DRUNKENNESS OFFENCES, MOTORING OFFENCES AND LICENCES, 1953-63
READING POLICE DISTRICT

	1953	1954	1955	1956	1957	1958	1959	1960	1961	1962	1963
Population '000	**118**					**118**					**121**
Proved Offences—											
Drunkenness											
Males											
Under 18	x	x	2	1		4		2		4	3
18 and under 21	4	6	10	7	5	6	12	9	19	15	8
21 and under 30	20	25	23	34	15	11	27	52	81	84	83
30 and under 60	65	86	82	89	108	79	96	105	201	206	219
60 and over	4	7	2	7	9	5	9	7	17	17	8
All ages	**86**	**122**	**115**	**138**	**137**	**105**	**144**	**175**	**318**	**326**	**321**
Females											
Under 18		(Included in			2				1		
18 and under 21		the number			2			2			
21 and under 30		of persons			1				1	1	
30 and under 60		by ages		5	3	1	6	3	1	1	2
60 and over		given above)		1							
All ages	**7**	**2**	**4**	**6**	**8**	**1**	**6**	**5**	**3**	**2**	**2**
All Proved Offences	**93**	**124**	**119**	**144**	**145**	**106**	**150**	**180**	**321**	**328**	**323**
Motoring Offences											
Proceedings for:											
(a) Previously Convicted											
Unfit to drive											
Driving, undue alcohol											
Fail provide specimen											
(b) No Prev. Conviction											
Unfit to drive					13	12	9	16	19	24	15
Driving, undue alcohol											
Fail provide spec.											
In charge and:											
Unfit to drive								1	3	12	6
Undue alcohol											
Fail provide spec.											
Failure to provide breath specimen											
Total: All Proceedings	**13**	**9**	**11**	**12**	**13**	**12**	**9**	**17**	**22**	**36**	**21**
Licensed Premises											
Public Houses:											
Full	128					142					154
Beer and Cider	41					26					2
Wine or Cider											
Restaurant Licence											5
Residential Licence											
Above Combined											1
Licensed Clubs											1
Total On Licences	**169**					**168**					**163**
Off Licences	**60**					**63**					**70**
Total On/Off Licences	**235**					**231**					**233**
Registered Clubs	**53**					**53**					**45**
Total Licences & Clubs	**288**					**284**					**278**

TABLE III 14
DRUNKENNESS OFFENCES, MOTORING OFFENCES AND LICENCES, 1953-63
BUCKINGHAMSHIRE POLICE DISTRICT

	1953	1954	1955	1956	1957	1958	1959	1960	1961	1962	1963
Population '000	**398**					**441**					**516**
Proved Offences— Drunkenness											
Males											
Under 18	x	x	2	2	2	4	1	3	3		5
18 and under 21	10	12	7	12	10	10	16	28	13	15	21
21 and under 30	22	30	26	25	27	18	46	79	50	53	71
30 and under 60	76	82	67	70	81	74	99	122	102	118	109
60 and over	7	8	5	1	5	4	4	8	9	2	12
All ages	**109**	**124**	**105**	**110**	**125**	**110**	**166**	**240**	**177**	**188**	**218**
Females											
Under 18		(Included in				1			1	1	1
18 and under 21		the number			2					1	2
21 and under 30		of persons			1		1		1	1	
30 and under 60		by ages		2		6	5	3	2	5	8
60 and over		given above)					2				
All ages	**6**	**8**	**2**	**2**	**3**	**7**	**8**	**3**	**4**	**8**	**11**
All Proved Offences	**115**	**132**	**107**	**112**	**128**	**117**	**174**	**243**	**181**	**196**	**229**
Motoring Offences											
Proceedings for:											
(a) Previously Convicted											
Unfit to drive											
Driving, undue alcohol											
Fail provide specimen											
(b) No Prev. Conviction											
Unfit to drive					24	39	41	39	30	48	61
Driving, undue alcohol											
Fail provide spec.											
In charge and:											
Unfit to drive					5	3	13	9	5	15	18
Undue alcohol											
Fail provide spec.											
Failure to provide breath specimen											
Total: All Proceedings	**23**	**31**	**27**	**33**	**29**	**42**	**54**	**48**	**35**	**63**	**79**
Licensed Premises											
Public Houses:											
Full	776					792					861
Beer and Cider	208					143					22
Wine or Cider											
Restaurant Licence											18
Residential Licence											2
Above Combined											3
Licensed Clubs											11
Total On Licences	**984**					**935**					**917**
Off Licences	**133**					**129**					**150**
Total On/Off Licences	**1117**					**1064**					**1067**
Registered Clubs	**232**					**259**					**261**
Total Licences & Clubs	**1349**					**1323**					**1328**

TABLE III 15
DRUNKENNESS OFFENCES, MOTORING OFFENCES AND LICENCES, 1953-63
CAMBRIDGESHIRE POLICE DISTRICT

	1953	1954	1955	1956	1957	1958	1959	1960	1961	1962	1963
Population '000	**86**					**183 (with City)**					**195**
Proved Offences—											
Drunkenness											
Males											
Under 18	x	x				1					
18 and under 21				2			2		1	2	1
21 and under 30		1		1	1		2	1	1	4	
30 and under 60		1	1		1	1	1	1	2		1
60 and over				2		1	1				
All ages		**2**	**1**	**5**	**2**	**3**	**6**	**2**	**4**	**6**	**2**
Females											
Under 18		(Included in									
18 and under 21		the number									
21 and under 30		of persons									
30 and under 60		by ages				1					
60 and over		given above)									
All ages						**1**					
All Proved Offences		**2**	**1**	**5**	**2**	**4**	**6**	**2**	**4**	**6**	**2**
Motoring Offences											
Proceedings for:											
(a) Previously Convicted											
Unfit to drive											
Driving, undue alcohol											
Fail provide specimen											
(b) No Prev. Conviction											
Unfit to drive					8	4	6	4	6	3	10
Driving, undue alcohol											
Fail provide spec.											
In charge and:											
Unfit to drive						1	4	2		6	4
Undue alcohol											
Fail provide spec.											
Failure to provide breath specimen											
Total: All Proceedings	**7**	**5**	**10**	**9**	**8**	**5**	**10**	**6**	**6**	**9**	**14**
Licensed Premises											
Public Houses:											
Full	283 (with City, 447)					465 (with City)					452
Beer and Cider	120 (with City, 136)					61 (with City)					10
Wine or Cider											
Restaurant Licence											9
Residential Licence											
Above Combined											
Licensed Clubs											2
Total On Licences	**403 (with City, 583)**					**526**					**473**
Off Licences	**17 (with City, 82)**					**84**					**96**
Total On/Off Licences	**420 (with City, 665)**					**610**					**569**
Registered Clubs	**37 (with City, 106)**					**109**					**101**
Total Licences & Clubs	**457 (with City, 771)**					**719**					**670**

TABLE III 16
DRUNKENNESS OFFENCES, MOTORING OFFENCES AND LICENCES, 1953–63
CAMBRIDGE CITY POLICE DISTRICT

	1953	1954	1955	1956	1957	1958	1959	1960	1961	1962	1963
Population '000	**91**	**(included in Cambridgeshire)**									
Proved Offences—											
Drunkenness											
Males											
Under 18	x	x							1		
18 and under 21		1	1	2	3	1		2	3	2	1
21 and under 30	10	3	8	6	12	5	7	5	2	2	3
30 and under 60	17	16	17	22	16	31	35	48	19	22	21
60 and over	1	2	6	5	11	2	7	10	3	1	
All ages	**25**	**17**	**32**	**35**	**42**	**39**	**49**	**65**	**28**	**27**	**25**
Females											
Under 18		(Included in the number of persons by ages given above)		1			1				
18 and under 21											
21 and under 30							3	1		1	
30 and under 60				2	2		1				
60 and over				1							
All ages	**3**	**5**		**4**	**2**		**5**	**1**		**1**	
All Proved Offences	**28**	**22**	**32**	**39**	**44**	**39**	**54**	**66**	**28**	**28**	**25**
Motoring Offences											
Proceedings for:											
(a) Previously Convicted											
Unfit to drive											
Driving, undue alcohol											
Fail provide specimen											
(b) No Prev. Conviction											
Unfit to drive											
Driving, undue alcohol					11	10	8	6	6	6	12
Fail provide spec.											
In charge and:											
Unfit to drive											
Undue alcohol					2	1	2	3	5	1	2
Fail provide spec.											
Failure to provide breath specimen											
Total: All Proceedings	**6**	**6**	**9**	**7**	**13**	**11**	**10**	**9**	**11**	**7**	**14**
Licensed Premises											
Public Houses:											
Full	(for details in 1953, see Cambridgeshire; City premises included with Cambridgeshire in 1958 and 1963)										
Beer and Cider											
Wine or Cider											
Restaurant Licence											
Residential Licence											
Above Combined											
Licensed Clubs											
Total On Licences											
Off Licences											
Total On/Off Licences											
Registered Clubs											
Total Licences & Clubs											

TABLE III 17
DRUNKENNESS OFFENCES, MOTORING OFFENCES AND LICENCES, 1953–63
ISLE-OF-ELY POLICE DISTRICT

	1953	1954	1955	1956	1957	1958	1959	1960	1961	1962	1963
Population '000	**88**					**89**					**90**
Proved Offences—											
Drunkenness											
Males											
Under 18	x	x	2			1		2	4	2	5
18 and under 21	2	3	2	1	5	2	4	2	9	5	16
21 and under 30	6	10	5	4	4	5	7	7	15	13	7
30 and under 60	12	13	5	15	19	14	13	7	11	18	9
60 and over	4	3	5	2	4		2	1		1	4
All ages	**22**	**29**	**18**	**22**	**32**	**22**	**26**	**19**	**39**	**39**	**41**
Females											
Under 18		(Included in							1	1	
18 and under 21		the number					1	1			
21 and under 30		of persons				1					
30 and under 60		by ages			1	1	2		1	4	
60 and over		given above)									
All ages	**2**		**1**		**1**	**2**	**3**	**1**	**2**	**5**	
All Proved Offences	**24**	**29**	**19**	**22**	**33**	**24**	**29**	**20**	**41**	**44**	**41**
Motoring Offences											
Proceedings for:											
(a) Previously Convicted											
Unfit to drive											
Driving, undue alcohol											
Fail provide specimen											
(b) No Prev. Conviction											
Unfit to drive					11	7	8	4	10	6	10
Driving, undue alcohol											
Fail provide spec.											
In charge and:											
Unfit to drive						2	1	2	1	1	8
Undue alcohol											
Fail provide spec.											
Failure to provide breath specimen											
Total: All Proceedings	**1**	**5**	**4**	**10**	**11**	**9**	**9**	**6**	**11**	**7**	**18**
Licensed Premises											
Public Houses:											
Full	271					273					263
Beer and Cider	93					44					12
Wine or Cider	7										
Restaurant Licence											3
Residential Licence											
Above Combined											
Licensed Clubs											
Total On Licences	**371**					**317**					**278**
Off Licences	**38**					**37**					**42**
Total On/Off Licences	**409**					**354**					**320**
Registered Clubs	**45**					**51**					**55**
Total Licences & Clubs	**454**					**405**					**375**

TABLE III 18
DRUNKENNESS OFFENCES, MOTORING OFFENCES AND LICENCES, 1953-63
CHESHIRE POLICE DISTRICT

	1953	1954	1955	1956	1957	1958	1959	1960	1961	1962	1963
Population '000	**880**					**928**					**961**
Proved Offences—											
Drunkenness											
Males											
Under 18	x	x	11	6	4	8	7	13	21	11	17
18 and under 21	17	19	19	29	25	28	39	56	56	77	64
21 and under 30	101	55	84	68	70	54	45	72	80	86	106
30 and under 60	112	141	129	100	82	106	112	152	101	106	115
60 and over	12	8	12	7	9	12	11	15	9	8	4
All ages	**228**	**213**	**244**	**210**	**190**	**208**	**214**	**308**	**267**	**288**	**306**
Females											
Under 18		(Included in				1	1				
18 and under 21		the number			5	1	4	2	2	1	3
21 and under 30		of persons		1	1	1		2	3		3
30 and under 60		by ages		8	2	4	3	6	4	5	4
60 and over		given above)			1	3		2			
All ages	**14**	**10**	**11**	**9**	**9**	**10**	**8**	**12**	**9**	**6**	**10**
All Proved Offences	**242**	**223**	**255**	**219**	**199**	**218**	**222**	**320**	**276**	**294**	**316**
Motoring Offences											
Proceedings for:											
(a) Previously Convicted											
Unfit to drive											
Driving, undue alcohol											
Fail provide specimen											
(b) No Prev. Conviction											
Unfit to drive					31	35	50	51	48	73	58
Driving, undue alcohol											
Fail provide spec.											
In charge and:											
Unfit to drive					16	10	22	18	8	17	13
Undue alcohol											
Fail provide spec.											
Failure to provide breath specimen											
Total: All Proceedings	**63**	**69**	**68**	**73**	**47**	**45**	**72**	**69**	**56**	**90**	**71**
Licensed Premises											
Public Houses:											
Full	1108					1063					1194
Beer and Cider	253					173					31
Wine or Cider	9					6					4
Restaurant Licence											31
Residential Licence											2
Above Combined											14
Licensed Clubs											19
Total On Licences	**1370**					**1232**					**1295**
Off Licences	**431**					**409**					**467**
Total On/Off Licences	**1801**					**1641**					**1762**
Registered Clubs	**511**					**454**					**469**
Total Licences & Clubs	**2312**					**2095**					**2231**

TABLE III 19
DRUNKENNESS OFFENCES, MOTORING OFFENCES AND LICENCES, 1953-63
BIRKENHEAD POLICE DISTRICT

	1953	1954	1955	1956	1957	1958	1959	1960	1961	1962	1963
Population '000	**142**					**143**					**144**
Proved Offences—											
Drunkenness											
Males											
Under 18	x	x	6	8	4	7	7	8	7	2	9
18 and under 21	17	23	25	29	29	33	17	38	39	33	32
21 and under 30	76	64	70	86	64	52	45	53	53	46	51
30 and under 60	156	123	107	111	147	123	95	134	94	118	102
60 and over	12	16	13	19	21	19	16	7	12	9	6
All ages	**251**	**219**	**217**	**253**	**265**	**234**	**180**	**240**	**205**	**208**	**200**
Females											
Under 18		(Included in				1			2	2	
18 and under 21		the number		1	1	3	1		1	1	1
21 and under 30		of persons			1	1	1	1	4	1	1
30 and under 60		by ages		1	3	4	7	2	5	2	9
60 and over		given above)		2	2	1	2	1		1	2
All ages	**10**	**7**	**4**	**4**	**7**	**10**	**11**	**4**	**12**	**7**	**13**
All Proved Offences	**261**	**226**	**221**	**257**	**272**	**244**	**191**	**244**	**217**	**215**	**213**
Motoring Offences											
Proceedings for:											
(a) Previously Convicted											
Unfit to drive											
Driving, undue alcohol											
Fail provide specimen											
(b) No Prev. Conviction											
Unfit to drive					14	20	30	26	31	23	26
Driving, undue alcohol											
Fail provide spec.											
In charge and:											
Unfit to drive							3	2	3	2	5
Undue alcohol											
Fail provide spec.											
Failure to provide breath specimen											
Total: All Proceedings	**11**	**15**	**24**	**19**	**14**	**20**	**33**	**28**	**34**	**25**	**31**
Licensed Premises											
Public Houses:											
Full	135					132					155
Beer and Cider	36					29					1
Wine or Cider											
Restaurant Licence											3
Residential Licence											
Above Combined											
Licensed Clubs											8
Total On Licences	**171**					**161**					**167**
Off Licences	**58**					**58**					**56**
Total On/Off Licences	**229**					**219**					**223**
Registered Clubs	**43**					**46**					**48**
Total Licences & Clubs	**272**					**265**					**271**

TABLE III 20
DRUNKENNESS OFFENCES, MOTORING OFFENCES AND LICENCES, 1953-63
STOCKPORT POLICE DISTRICT

	1953	1954	1955	1956	1957	1958	1959	1960	1961	1962	1963
Population '000	**141**					**141**					**143**
Proved Offences—Drunkenness											
Males											
Under 18	x	x	1	3	1	6	1	5	1		4
18 and under 21	6	8	6	12	11	10	13	32	14	8	16
21 and under 30	25	38	29	43	30	17	28	34	27	26	30
30 and under 60	57	48	63	60	64	41	55	50	28	41	44
60 and over	10	13	3	6	12	4	9	13	6	7	8
All ages	**95**	**102**	**92**	**124**	**118**	**78**	**106**	**134**	**76**	**82**	**102**
Females											
Under 18		(Included in									
18 and under 21		the number		2						1	2
21 and under 30		of persons		1				1			
30 and under 60		by ages		5	4	2	1	5	3	3	5
60 and over		given above)			1			1	1	1	
All ages	**3**	**5**	**10**	**8**	**5**	**2**	**1**	**7**	**4**	**5**	**7**
All Proved Offences	**98**	**107**	**102**	**132**	**123**	**80**	**107**	**141**	**80**	**87**	**109**
Motoring Offences											
Proceedings for:											
(a) Previously Convicted											
Unfit to drive											
Driving, undue alcohol											
Fail provide specimen											
(b) No Prev. Conviction											
Unfit to drive					13	15	17	18	25	16	15
Driving, undue alcohol											
Fail provide spec.											
In charge and:											
Unfit to drive					2	1	7	9	2	7	7
Undue alcohol											
Fail provide spec.											
Failure to provide breath specimen											
Total: All Proceedings	**14**	**14**	**16**	**15**	**15**	**16**	**24**	**27**	**27**	**23**	**22**
Licensed Premises											
Public Houses:											
Full	128					128					156
Beer and Cider	60					53					21
Wine or Cider						1					
Restaurant Licence											1
Residential Licence											1
Above Combined											3
Licensed Clubs											7
Total On Licences	**188**					**182**					**189**
Off Licences	**91**					**95**					**94**
Total On/Off Licences	**279**					**277**					**283**
Registered Clubs	**35**					**65**					**64**
Total Licences & Clubs	**314**					**342**					**347**

TABLE III 21
DRUNKENNESS OFFENCES, MOTORING OFFENCES AND LICENCES, 1953–63
WALLASEY POLICE DISTRICT

	1953	1954	1955	1956	1957	1958	1959	1960	1961	1962	1963
Population '000	**102**					**103**					**103**
Proved Offences— Drunkenness											
Males											
Under 18	x	x	2	4	4	2	5	19	5	6	12
18 and under 21	11	9	12	14	16	18	11	25	17	44	26
21 and under 30	22	27	28	36	18	25	8	18	25	33	18
30 and under 60	29	20	20	26	19	20	24	19	29	31	19
60 and over	5	3			1	2	1	1	1	1	1
All ages	**63**	**59**	**60**	**80**	**58**	**67**	**49**	**82**	**77**	**115**	**76**
Females											
Under 18		(Included in		1	1		1				
18 and under 21		the number		3	2		1				
21 and under 30		of persons			1	1	1			1	
30 and under 60		by ages		1	2	1	3				1
60 and over		given above)		1		1					
All ages	**4**		**2**	**6**	**6**	**4**	**6**			**1**	**1**
All Proved Offences	**67**	**59**	**62**	**86**	**64**	**71**	**55**	**82**	**77**	**116**	**77**
Motoring Offences											
Proceedings for:											
(a) Previously Convicted											
Unfit to drive											
Driving, undue alcohol											
Fail provide specimen											
(b) No Prev. Conviction											
Unfit to drive					5	5	5	4	8	4	12
Driving, undue alcohol											
Fail provide spec.											
In charge and:											
Unfit to drive						5	3	2	5	4	4
Undue alcohol											
Fail provide spec.											
Failure to provide breath specimen											
Total: All Proceedings	**7**		**5**	**4**	**5**	**10**	**8**	**6**	**13**	**8**	**16**
Licensed Premises											
Public Houses:											
Full	65					66					72
Beer and Cider	7					6					
Wine or Cider											
Restaurant Licence											2
Residential Licence											2
Above Combined											2
Licensed Clubs											4
Total On Licences	**72**					**72**					**82**
Off Licences	**37**					**37**					**38**
Total On/Off Licences	**109**					**109**					**120**
Registered Clubs	**37**					**46**					**46**
Total Licences & Clubs	**146**					**155**					**166**

TABLE III 22
DRUNKENNESS OFFENCES, MOTORING OFFENCES AND LICENCES, 1953-63
CORNWALL POLICE DISTRICT

	1953	1954	1955	1956	1957	1958	1959	1960	1961	1962	1963
Population '000	**343**					**339**					**343**
Proved Offences—											
Drunkenness											
Males											
Under 18	x	x		2		3		6		1	4
18 and under 21	6	10	6	13	6	3	9	11	14	7	4
21 and under 30	24	28	14	16	18	12	18	18	30	21	21
30 and under 60	24	27	39	28	29	21	38	38	40	41	49
60 and over	7	11	4	2	4	1	3	6	1	5	5
All ages	**67**	**75**	**57**	**61**	**57**	**40**	**68**	**79**	**85**	**75**	**85**
Females											
Under 18			(Included in	1							
18 and under 21			the number			1	1				
21 and under 30			of persons								
30 and under 60			by ages	1	2	2	1	2		2	2
60 and over			given above)								
All ages	**4**	**1**	**6**	**2**	**2**	**3**	**2**	**2**		**2**	**2**
All Proved Offences	**71**	**76**	**63**	**63**	**59**	**43**	**70**	**81**	**85**	**77**	**87**
Motoring Offences											
Proceedings for:											
(a) Previously Convicted											
Unfit to drive											
Driving, undue alcohol											
Fail provide specimen											
(b) No Prev. Conviction											
Unfit to drive					32	34	48	38	40	53	62
Driving, undue alcohol											
Fail provide spec.											
In charge and:											
Unfit to drive					3			9	11	13	22
Undue alcohol											
Fail provide spec.											
Failure to provide breath specimen											
Total: All Proceedings	**30**	**36**	**39**	**30**	**35**	**34**	**48**	**47**	**51**	**66**	**84**
Licensed Premises											
Public Houses:											
Full	653					672					682
Beer and Cider	28					11					2
Wine or Cider	2					4					2
Restaurant Licence											49
Residential Licence											70
Above Combined											159
Licensed Clubs											64
Total On Licences	**683**					**687**					**1028**
Off Licences	**79**					**80**					**123**
Total On/Off Licences	**762**					**767**					**1151**
Registered Clubs	**155**					**225**					**145**
Total Licences & Clubs	**917**					**992**					**1296**

TABLE III 23
DRUNKENNESS OFFENCES, MOTORING OFFENCES AND LICENCES, 1953–63
CUMBERLAND POLICE DISTRICT

	1953	1954	1955	1956	1957	1958	1959	1960	1961	1962	1963
Population '000	**216**					**218**					**225**
Proved Offences—											
Drunkenness											
Males											
Under 18	x	x	1	1	4	1	6	3	3	7	14
18 and under 21	5	6	7	7	9	9	13	26	31	26	42
21 and under 30	27	36	46	43	46	35	28	37	39	48	57
30 and under 60	43	43	50	58	54	56	41	34	41	43	54
60 and over	5	5	4	6	3	5	3	6	2	5	6
All ages	**79**	**84**	**103**	**115**	**116**	**106**	**91**	**106**	**116**	**129**	**173**
Females											
Under 18		(Included in			1			3		1	1
18 and under 21		the number									
21 and under 30		of persons		2		1	1	2			1
30 and under 60		by ages		2	3	3			4	2	
60 and over		given above)		3	1	3	1	1	3		3
All ages	**1**	**6**	**5**	**7**	**5**	**7**	**2**	**6**	**7**	**3**	**2**
All Proved Offences	**80**	**90**	**108**	**122**	**121**	**113**	**93**	**112**	**123**	**132**	**178**
Motoring Offences											
Proceedings for:											
(a) Previously Convicted											
Unfit to drive											
Driving, undue alcohol											
Fail provide specimen											
(b) No Prev. Conviction											
Unfit to drive					27	35	26	39	28	33	41
Driving, undue alcohol											
Fail provide spec.											
In charge and:											
Unfit to drive					13	8	11	9	14	14	9
Undue alcohol											
Fail provide spec.											
Failure to provide breath specimen											
Total: All Proceedings	**19**	**21**	**29**	**33**	**40**	**43**	**37**	**48**	**42**	**47**	**50**
Licensed Premises											
Public Houses:											
Full	652					664					640
Beer and Cider	34					27					10
Wine or Cider											
Restaurant Licence											14
Residential Licence											4
Above Combined											21
Licensed Clubs											1
Total On Licences	**686**					**671**					**690**
Off Licences	**57**					**58**					**67**
Total On/Off Licences	**743**					**729**					**757**
Registered Clubs	**85**					**112**					**124**
Total Licences & Clubs	**828**					**841**					**881**

TABLE III 24
DRUNKENNESS OFFENCES, MOTORING OFFENCES AND LICENCES, 1953-63
CARLISLE POLICE DISTRICT

	1953	1954	1955	1956	1957	1958	1959	1960	1961	1962	1963
Population '000	**58**					**69**					**71**
Proved Offences—Drunkenness											
Males											
Under 18	x	x							2		
18 and under 21	1	2	7	2	5	1	4	6	4	17	5
21 and under 30	7	8	10	12	8	10	5	12	5	40	44
30 and under 60	37	20	24	28	23	23	20	26	16	58	66
60 and over	5	4	8	5	4	4	4	1	2	13	10
All ages	**46**	**32**	**45**	**47**	**40**	**38**	**33**	**45**	**29**	**128**	**125**
Females											
Under 18		(Included in								1	
18 and under 21		the number									
21 and under 30		of persons						1		1	
30 and under 60		by ages		2	1		1		2	2	7
60 and over		given above)				1					
All ages	**4**	**2**	**4**	**2**	**1**	**1**	**1**	**1**	**2**	**4**	**7**
All Proved Offences	**50**	**34**	**49**	**49**	**41**	**39**	**34**	**46**	**31**	**132**	**132**
Motoring Offences											
Proceedings for:											
(a) Previously Convicted											
Unfit to drive											
Driving, undue alcohol											
Fail provide specimen											
(b) No Prev. Conviction											
Unfit to drive					14	12	14	23	10	28	36
Driving, undue alcohol											
Fail provide spec.											
In charge and:											
Unfit to drive							5	3	4	8	4
Undue alcohol											
Fail provide spec.											
Failure to provide breath specimen											
Total: All Proceedings	7	15	4	16	14	12	19	26	14	36	40
Licensed Premises											
Public Houses:											
Full	60					60					59
Beer and Cider											
Wine or Cider											
Restaurant Licence											5
Residential Licence											
Above Combined											2
Licensed Clubs											
Total On Licences	**60**					**60**					**66**
Off Licences	**1**					**4**					**5**
Total On/Off Licences	**61**					**64**					**71**
Registered Clubs	**14**					**17**					**39**
Total Licences & Clubs	**75**					**81**					**110**

TABLE III 25
DRUNKENNESS OFFENCES, MOTORING OFFENCES AND LICENCES, 1953–63
DERBYSHIRE POLICE DISTRICT

	1953	1954	1955	1956	1957	1958	1959	1960	1961	1962	1963
Population '000	**702**					**725**					**766**
Proved Offences—Drunkenness											
Males											
Under 18	x	x	7	2	9	6	7	5	8	2	11
18 and under 21	10	11	7	13	21	27	39	40	23	44	27
21 and under 30	49	75	53	48	72	66	47	52	36	52	50
30 and under 60	131	120	97	91	107	126	108	83	61	91	72
60 and over	15	16	10	8	8	15	5	8	14	8	10
All ages	**201**	**212**	**177**	**162**	**217**	**240**	**206**	**188**	**142**	**197**	**170**
Females											
Under 18		(Included in		1			1	2			
18 and under 21		the number			1			1			
21 and under 30		of persons			1			2			1
30 and under 60		by ages		4	5	7	5	6	5	2	9
60 and over		given above)				1					
All ages	**4**	**10**	**2**	**5**	**7**	**8**	**6**	**11**	**5**	**2**	**10**
All Proved Offences	**205**	**222**	**179**	**167**	**224**	**248**	**212**	**199**	**147**	**199**	**180**
Motoring Offences											
Proceedings for:											
(a) Previously Convicted											
Unfit to drive											
Driving, undue alcohol											
Fail provide specimen											
(b) No Prev. Conviction											
Unfit to drive					58	55	58	61	70	51	67
Driving, undue alcohol											
Fail provide spec.											
In charge and:											
Unfit to drive					5	5	12	21	22	21	20
Undue alcohol											
Fail provide spec.											
Failure to provide breath specimen											
Total: All Proceedings	**43**	**63**	**61**	**53**	**63**	**60**	**70**	**82**	**92**	**72**	**87**
Licensed Premises											
Public Houses:											
Full	1219					1255					1325
Beer and Cider	164					115					27
Wine or Cider	5					4					1
Restaurant Licence											12
Residential Licence											3
Above Combined											1
Licensed Clubs											19
Total On Licences	**1388**					**1374**					**1388**
Off Licences	**452**					**459**					**519**
Total On/Off Licences	**1840**					**1833**					**1907**
Registered Clubs	**331**					**345**					**343**
Total Licences & Clubs	**2171**					**2178**					**2250**

TABLE III 26
DRUNKENNESS OFFENCES, MOTORING OFFENCES AND LICENCES, 1953-63
DERBY CITY POLICE DISTRICT

	1953	1954	1955	1956	1957	1958	1959	1960	1961	1962	1963
Population '000	**139**					**134**					**132**
Proved Offences—Drunkenness											
Males											
Under 18	x	x	2			2	2	1	3	4	1
18 and under 21	13	4	6	7	8	16	13	14	10	11	13
21 and under 30	47	36	42	40	54	79	59	75	54	43	44
30 and under 60	207	153	115	169	223	172	174	244	179	243	178
60 and over	20	30	9	8	19	19	20	29	21	27	23
All ages	**277**	**201**	**166**	**224**	**304**	**288**	**268**	**363**	**367**	**328**	**259**
Females											
Under 18		(Included in						1			
18 and under 21		the number						1			
21 and under 30		of persons		2	2	3	1	2	1	5	1
30 and under 60		by ages		2	3	4	9	1	5	13	9
60 and over		given above)		1	1	3		3	2	2	
All ages	**10**	**5**	**8**	**5**	**6**	**10**	**10**	**8**	**8**	**20**	**10**
All Proved Offences	**287**	**206**	**174**	**229**	**310**	**298**	**278**	**371**	**275**	**348**	**269**
Motoring Offences											
Proceedings for:											
(a) Previously Convicted											
Unfit to drive											
Driving, undue alcohol											
Fail provide specimen											
(b) No Prev. Conviction											
Unfit to drive					15	16	16	22	22	48	25
Driving, undue alcohol											
Fail provide spec.											
In charge and:											
Unfit to drive					2	4	8	9	11	5	10
Undue alcohol											
Fail provide spec.											
Failure to provide breath specimen											
Total: All Proceedings	**8**	**9**	**17**	**21**	**17**	**20**	**24**	**31**	**33**	**53**	**35**
Licensed Premises											
Public Houses:											
Full	213					220					225
Beer and Cider	21					21					6
Wine or Cider											
Restaurant Licence											6
Residential Licence											
Above Combined											
Licensed Clubs											2
Total On Licences	**234**					**241**					**239**
Off Licences	**136**					**136**					**139**
Total On/Off Licences	**370**					**377**					**378**
Registered Clubs	**86**					**81**					**73**
Total Licences & Clubs	**456**					**458**					**451**

TABLE III 27
DRUNKENNESS OFFENCES, MOTORING OFFENCES AND LICENCES, 1953–63
DEVONSHIRE POLICE DISTRICT

	1953	1954	1955	1956	1957	1958	1959	1960	1961	1962	1963
Population '000	**510**					**518**					**543**
Proved Offences—Drunkenness											
Males											
Under 18	x	x		1	1	1		1	4	3	3
18 and under 21	5	6	6	8	14	6	14	14	7	15	23
21 and under 30	15	26	19	21	26	29	24	15	12	22	33
30 and under 60	91	89	55	77	78	70	64	65	63	85	142
60 and over	11	8	4	14	12	16	7	8	6	11	15
All ages	**115**	**112**	**81**	**121**	**131**	**122**	**109**	**103**	**92**	**136**	**216**
Females											
Under 18			(Included in						2	1	
18 and under 21			the number		1						1
21 and under 30			of persons							1	
30 and under 60			by ages	4	1	4	2	2		3	2
60 and over			given above)	1	1						1
All ages	**7**	**7**	**3**	**5**	**3**	**4**	**2**	**2**	**2**	**5**	**4**
All Proved Offences	**122**	**129**	**84**	**126**	**134**	**126**	**111**	**105**	**94**	**141**	**220**
Motoring Offences											
Proceedings for:											
(a) Previously Convicted											
Unfit to drive											
Driving, undue alcohol											
Fail provide specimen											
(b) No Prev. Conviction											
Unfit to drive					33	36	47	33	52	59	81
Driving, undue alcohol											
Fail provide spec.											
In charge and:											
Unfit to drive					5	3	3	13	6	7	10
Undue alcohol											
Fail provide spec.											
Failure to provide breath specimen											
Total: All Proceedings	**43**	**45**	**33**	**34**	**38**	**39**	**50**	**46**	**58**	**66**	**91**
Licensed Premises											
Public Houses:											
Full	1236					1270					1289
Beer and Cider	81					35					6
Wine or Cider	4					2					1
Restaurant Licence											22
Residential Licence											29
Above Combined											114
Licensed Clubs											75
Total On Licences	**1321**					**1307**					**1585**
Off Licences	**183**					**184**					**243**
Total On/Off Licences	**1504**					**1491**					**1828**
Registered Clubs	**269**					**348**					**279**
Total Licences & Clubs	**1773**					**1839**					**2107**

TABLE III 28
DRUNKENNESS OFFENCES, MOTORING OFFENCES AND LICENCES, 1953–63
EXETER POLICE DISTRICT

	1953	1954	1955	1956	1957	1958	1959	1960	1961	1962	1963
Population '000	**77**					**77**					**80**
Proved Offences—Drunkenness											
Males											
Under 18	x	x						2	1	3	1
18 and under 21	1		2	4	2	1	4	1	6	9	1
21 and under 30	6	12	10	6	10	5	11	8	8	8	11
30 and under 60	25	28	22	17	15	28	30	39	40	33	42
60 and over	2	3	4	3	8	5	1	3	8	10	8
All ages	**31**	**43**	**36**	**30**	**35**	**39**	**46**	**53**	**63**	**63**	**63**
Females											
Under 18		(Included in							1	1	
18 and under 21		the number				1					1
21 and under 30		of persons									
30 and under 60		by ages		3	7		6	3	5	1	3
60 and over		given above)			1			1			
All ages	**3**		**2**	**3**	**8**	**1**	**6**	**4**	**6**	**2**	**4**
All Proved Offences	**34**	**43**	**38**	**33**	**43**	**40**	**52**	**57**	**69**	**65**	**67**
Motoring Offences											
Proceedings for:											
(a) Previously Convicted											
Unfit to drive											
Driving, undue alcohol											
Fail provide specimen											
(b) No Prev. Conviction											
Unfit to drive					8	14	12	13	9	14	14
Driving, undue alcohol											
Fail provide spec.											
In charge and:											
Unfit to drive							1	2			1
Undue alcohol											
Fail provide spec.											
Failure to provide breath specimen											
Total: All Proceedings	**4**	**5**	**7**	**6**	**8**	**14**	**13**	**15**	**9**	**14**	**15**
Licensed Premises											
Public Houses:											
Full	113					98					94
Beer and Cider	6					1					
Wine or Cider											
Restaurant Licence											9
Residential Licence											3
Above Combined											
Licensed Clubs											
Total On Licences	**119**					**99**					**106**
Off Licences	**48**					**50**					**56**
Total On/Off Licences	**167**					**149**					**162**
Registered Clubs	**37**					**38**					**41**
Total Licences & Clubs	**204**					**187**					**203**

TABLE III 29
DRUNKENNESS OFFENCES, MOTORING OFFENCES AND LICENCES, 1953–63 PLYMOUTH POLICE DISTRICT

	1953	1954	1955	1956	1957	1958	1959	1960	1961	1962	1963
Population '000	**221**					**216**					**210**
Proved Offences—Drunkenness											
Males											
Under 18	x	x	1	2	3	1	2	4	3	2	5
18 and under 21	5	12	9	8	17	18	25	23	22	25	16
21 and under 30	29	44	43	33	43	42	42	44	67	55	42
30 and under 60	118	129	127	173	154	166	135	207	244	190	165
60 and over	22	29	20	35	17	34	14	42	49	31	28
All ages	**161**	**192**	**189**	**251**	**234**	**261**	**218**	**320**	**385**	**303**	**256**
Females											
Under 18	(Included in the number of persons by ages given above)				1			2		1	1
18 and under 21				2	4	4		6		6	2
21 and under 30				8	10	3	3	2	5	2	2
30 and under 60				4	4	14	16	8	7	3	5
60 and over				1		1	2	1	3	5	
All ages	**13**	**22**	**11**	**15**	**19**	**22**	**21**	**19**	**15**	**17**	**10**
All Proved Offences	**174**	**214**	**200**	**266**	**253**	**283**	**239**	**339**	**400**	**320**	**266**
Motoring Offences											
Proceedings for:											
(a) Previously Convicted											
Unfit to drive											
Driving, undue alcohol											
Fail provide specimen											
(b) No Prev. Conviction											
Unfit to drive					29	40	38	52	67	68	69
Driving, undue alcohol											
Fail provide spec.											
In charge and:											
Unfit to drive					8	11	13	18	18	7	12
Undue alcohol											
Fail provide spec.											
Failure to provide breath specimen											
Total: All Proceedings	**36**	**34**	**34**	**47**	**37**	**51**	**51**	**70**	**85**	**75**	**81**
Licensed Premises											
Public Houses:											
Full	253					210					232
Beer and Cider	100					48					7
Wine or Cider											
Restaurant Licence											15
Residential Licence											
Above Combined											1
Licensed Clubs											
Total On Licences	**353**					**258**					**255**
Off Licences	**76**					**70**					**69**
Total On/Off Licences	**429**					**328**					**324**
Registered Clubs	**73**					**79**					**84**
Total Licences & Clubs	**502**					**407**					**408**

TABLE III 30
DRUNKENNESS OFFENCES, MOTORING OFFENCES AND LICENCES, 1953-63
DORSETSHIRE POLICE DISTRICT

	1953	1954	1955	1956	1957	1958	1959	1960	1961	1962	1963
Population '000	**299**					**304**					**322**
Proved Offences—Drunkenness											
Males											
Under 18	x	x	2	4	6	3	5	2	7	5	9
18 and under 21	18	16	13	25	22	21	26	26	23	33	27
21 and under 30	40	33	37	28	29	60	28	41	41	40	42
30 and under 60	103	114	123	107	131	111	101	77	106	118	137
60 and over	20	21	27	16	18	24	18	17	13	10	11
All ages	**177**	**170**	**193**	**180**	**206**	**219**	**178**	**163**	**190**	**206**	**226**
Females											
Under 18		(Included in						1			
18 and under 21		the number		1	2			1	1	1	
21 and under 30		of persons					1	2	2	1	1
30 and under 60		by ages		9	4	2	3	1	2	3	3
60 and over		given above)			2			2	2		
All ages	**4**	**14**	**9**	**10**	**8**	**2**	**4**	**7**	**7**	**5**	**2**
All Proved Offences	**181**	**184**	**202**	**190**	**214**	**221**	**182**	**170**	**197**	**211**	**228**
Motoring Offences											
Proceedings for:											
(a) Previously Convicted											
Unfit to drive											
Driving, undue alcohol											
Fail provide specimen											
(b) No Prev. Conviction											
Unfit to drive					18	36	36	32	28	34	23
Driving, undue alcohol											
Fail provide spec.											
In charge and:											
Unfit to drive					2		5	7	9	19	20
Undue alcohol											
Fail provide spec.											
Failure to provide breath specimen											
Total: All Proceedings	**20**	**24**	**17**	**19**	**20**	**36**	**41**	**39**	**37**	**53**	**43**
Licensed Premises											
Public Houses:											
Full	624					647					662
Beer and Cider	78					40					7
Wine or Cider											
Restaurant Licence											28
Residential Licence											13
Above Combined											25
Licensed Clubs											24
Total On Licences	**702**					**687**					**759**
Off Licences	**125**					**130**					**153**
Total On/Off Licences	**827**					**817**					**912**
Registered Clubs	**163**					**195**					**155**
Total Licences & Clubs	**990**					**1012**					**1067**

TABLE III 31
DRUNKENNESS OFFENCES, MOTORING OFFENCES AND LICENCES, 1953–63 DURHAM POLICE DISTRICT

	1953	1954	1955	1956	1957	1958	1959	1960	1961	1962	1963
Population '000	**1062**					**1093**					**1132**
Proved Offences—											
Drunkenness											
Males											
Under 18	x	x	15	53	50	46	41	45	66	47	53
18 and under 21	207	188	218	196	286	269	246	251	266	200	228
21 and under 30	583	526	519	534	584	522	456	439	429	431	342
30 and under 60	723	751	719	794	867	769	696	631	730	641	502
60 and over	55	58	52	57	57	39	61	58	71	56	39
All ages	**1522**	**1472**	**1480**	**1634**	**1824**	**1645**	**1500**	**1424**	**1562**	**1375**	**1164**
Females											
Under 18			(Included in	1		1	3	2	1	4	4
18 and under 21			the number	1	3	1	1	1	4	1	3
21 and under 30			of persons	5	8	8	8	8	6	3	9
30 and under 60			by ages	25	22	21	9	14	13	23	12
60 and over			given above)	4	6	2		2	4		2
All ages	**46**	**51**	**43**	**36**	**39**	**33**	**21**	**27**	**28**	**31**	**30**
All Proved Offences	**1568**	**1523**	**1523**	**1670**	**1863**	**1678**	**1521**	**1451**	**1590**	**1406**	**1194**
Motoring Offences											
Proceedings for:											
(a) Previously Convicted											
Unfit to drive											
Driving, undue alcohol											
Fail provide specimen											
(b) No Prev. Conviction											
Unfit to drive					154	167	183	226	257	261	225
Driving, undue alcohol											
Fail provide spec.											
In charge and:											
Unfit to drive					28	50	22	24	19	53	39
Undue alcohol											
Fail provide spec.											
Failure to provide breath specimen											
Total: All Proceedings	**92**	**91**	**95**	**117**	**182**	**217**	**205**	**250**	**276**	**314**	**264**
Licensed Premises											
Public Houses:											
Full	1371					1367					1332
Beer and Cider	121					93					25
Wine or Cider	3					1					
Restaurant Licence											17
Residential Licence											1
Above Combined											5
Licensed Clubs											9
Total On Licences	**1495**					**1461**					**1389**
Off Licences	**471**					**523**					**606**
Total On/Off Licences	**1966**					**1984**					**1995**
Registered Clubs	**549**					**604**					**620**
Total Licences & Clubs	**2515**					**2588**					**2615**

TABLE III 32
DRUNKENNESS OFFENCES, MOTORING OFFENCES AND LICENCES, 1953–63
GATESHEAD POLICE DISTRICT

	1953	1954	1955	1956	1957	1958	1959	1960	1961	1962	1963
Population '000	**114**					**110**					**103**
Proved Offences—Drunkenness											
Males											
Under 18	x	x	13	9	11	8	9	22	5	12	9
18 and under 21	24	20	46	60	41	69	77	89	76	81	57
21 and under 30	104	109	132	149	141	122	99	151	151	147	71
30 and under 60	159	184	177	216	222	194	146	165	202	186	151
60 and over	14	23	10	18	15	12	15	18	13	13	10
All ages	**287**	**324**	**373**	**452**	**430**	**405**	**346**	**445**	**447**	**439**	**300**
Females											
Under 18	(Included in the number of persons by ages given above)								1		
18 and under 21				2	1			1			1
21 and under 30				4	1		1	1		1	1
30 and under 60				6	5	3	1	6	2	1	3
60 and over				1	1						
All ages	**14**	**12**	**5**	**13**	**8**	**3**	**2**	**8**	**3**	**2**	**5**
All Proved Offences	**301**	**336**	**378**	**465**	**438**	**408**	**348**	**453**	**450**	**441**	**305**
Motoring Offences											
Proceedings for:											
(a) Previously Convicted											
Unfit to drive											
Driving, undue alcohol											
Fail provide specimen											
(b) No Prev. Conviction											
Unfit to drive					37	46	38	42	46	45	42
Driving, undue alcohol											
Fail provide spec.											
In charge and:											
Unfit to drive					3	15	7	5	12	7	10
Undue alcohol											
Fail provide spec.											
Failure to provide breath specimen											
Total: All Proceedings	**17**	**13**	**24**	**34**	**40**	**61**	**45**	**47**	**58**	**52**	**52**
Licensed Premises											
Public Houses:											
Full	102					102					100
Beer and Cider	11					10					
Wine or Cider											
Restaurant Licence											2
Residential Licence											
Above Combined											
Licensed Clubs											
Total On Licences	**113**					**112**					**102**
Off Licences	**61**					**62**					**64**
Total On/Off Licences	**174**					**174**					**166**
Registered Clubs	**45**					**47**					**35**
Total Licences & Clubs	**219**					**221**					**201**

TABLE III 33
DRUNKENNESS OFFENCES, MOTORING OFFENCES AND LICENCES, 1953–63
SOUTHSHIELDS POLICE DISTRICT

	1953	1954	1955	1956	1957	1958	1959	1960	1961	1962	1963
Population '000	**107**					**109**					**109**
Proved Offences—Drunkenness											
Males											
Under 18	x	x	5	7	13	1	3	6	6	5	10
18 and under 21	20	13	18	21	42	17	18	21	20	28	33
21 and under 30	69	52	64	59	78	44	27	54	43	50	52
30 and under 60	94	101	93	108	98	81	95	76	96	111	108
60 and over	5	5	6	3	4	5	5	6	11	7	11
All ages	**173**	**168**	**173**	**198**	**235**	**148**	**148**	**163**	**176**	**201**	**214**
Females											
Under 18		(Included in					1		1		
18 and under 21		the number		2	1	1	3	2		1	
21 and under 30		of persons		2	5		2	3	5	3	
30 and under 60		by ages		10	4	6	4	2	2	11	10
60 and over		given above)				1					
All ages	**15**	**3**	**13**	**14**	**10**	**8**	**10**	**7**	**8**	**15**	**10**
All Proved Offences	**188**	**171**	**186**	**212**	**245**	**156**	**158**	**170**	**184**	**216**	**224**
Motoring Offences											
Proceedings for:											
(a) Previously Convicted											
Unfit to drive											
Driving, undue alcohol											
Fail provide specimen											
(b) No Prev. Conviction											
Unfit to drive					18	10	21	22	21	24	22
Driving, undue alcohol											
Fail provide spec.											
In charge and:											
Unfit to drive					6	6	6	7	2	2	3
Undue alcohol											
Fail provide spec.											
Failure to provide breath specimen											
Total: All Proceedings	**5**	**8**	**10**	**17**	**24**	**16**	**27**	**29**	**23**	**26**	**25**
Licensed Premises											
Public Houses:											
Full	97					90					87
Beer and Cider	25					17					6
Wine or Cider											
Restaurant Licence											
Residential Licence											6
Above Combined											
Licensed Clubs											
Total On Licences	**122**					**107**					**99**
Off Licences	**92**					**88**					**78**
Total On/Off Licences	**214**					**195**					**177**
Registered Clubs	**34**					**40**					**40**
Total Licences & Clubs	**248**					**235**					**217**

TABLE III 34
DRUNKENNESS OFFENCES, MOTORING OFFENCES AND LICENCES, 1953-63
SUNDERLAND POLICE DISTRICT

	1953	1954	1955	1956	1957	1958	1959	1960	1961	1962	1963
Population '000	**181**					**185**					**190**
Proved Offences—											
Drunkenness											
Males											
Under 18	x	x	1	2	5	3	3	12	3	4	4
18 and under 21	17	13	9	14	24	16	13	38	26	39	39
21 and under 30	61	66	40	31	64	57	40	61	67	80	69
30 and under 60	70	61	49	57	95	60	58	69	99	95	78
60 and over	8	7	10	3	9	4	7	8	5	5	8
All ages	**145**	**140**	**105**	**107**	**197**	**140**	**121**	**188**	**200**	**223**	**198**
Females											
Under 18			(Included in								
18 and under 21			the number	1	1					1	1
21 and under 30			of persons	2	1				1	4	
30 and under 60			by ages	5	5	4	3	6	3	2	
60 and over			given above)	1	1	1					1
All ages	**11**	**7**	**4**	**9**	**8**	**5**	**3**	**6**	**4**	**7**	**2**
All Proved Offences	**156**	**147**	**109**	**116**	**205**	**145**	**124**	**194**	**204**	**230**	**200**
Motoring Offences											
Proceedings for:											
(a) Previously Convicted											
Unfit to drive											
Driving, undue alcohol											
Fail provide specimen											
(b) No Prev. Conviction											
Unfit to drive					12	12	10	17	13	13	14
Driving, undue alcohol											
Fail provide spec.											
In charge and:											
Unfit to drive					1	3	2	2	7	4	4
Undue alcohol											
Fail provide spec.											
Failure to provide breath specimen											
Total: All Proceedings	**17**	**10**	**5**	**11**	**13**	**15**	**12**	**19**	**20**	**17**	**18**
Licensed Premises											
Public Houses:											
Full	150					144					136
Beer and Cider	61					55					28
Wine or Cider											
Restaurant Licence											4
Residential Licence											
Above Combined											
Licensed Clubs											1
Total On Licences	**211**					**199**					**169**
Off Licences	**158**					**157**					**159**
Total On/Off Licences	**369**					**356**					**328**
Registered Clubs	**20**					**39**					**42**
Total Licences & Clubs	**389**					**395**					**370**

TABLE III 35
DRUNKENNESS OFFENCES, MOTORING OFFENCES AND LICENCES, 1953-63
ESSEX POLICE DISTRICT

	1953	1954	1955	1956	1957	1958	1959	1960	1961	1962	1963
Population '000	**1644**					**1783**					**1918**
Proved Offences—											
Drunkenness											
Males											
Under 18	x	x	4	5	14	6	10	13	15	12	7
18 and under 21	10	16	24	27	18	29	41	24	39	44	32
21 and under 30	35	49	56	42	50	52	62	53	61	73	72
30 and under 60	93	110	100	102	127	106	132	123	125	161	152
60 and over	14	16	17	21	18	7	15	11	23	25	21
All ages	**144**	**180**	**184**	**200**	**227**	**200**	**260**	**224**	**263**	**315**	**284**
Females											
Under 18		(Included in		3	1			2		2	
18 and under 21		the number					1			1	
21 and under 30		of persons		1	3		1	1	5		3
30 and under 60		by ages		4	6	7	9	9	6	4	5
60 and over		given above)		4		2	1	4	4		1
All ages	**8**	**11**	**17**	**12**	**10**	**9**	**12**	**16**	**15**	**7**	**9**
All Proved Offences	**152**	**191**	**201**	**212**	**237**	**209**	**272**	**240**	**278**	**322**	**293**
Motoring Offences											
Proceedings for:											
(a) Previously Convicted											
Unfit to drive											
Driving, undue alcohol											
Fail provide specimen											
(b) No Prev. Conviction											
Unfit to drive					90	70	72	112	128	138	105
Driving, undue alcohol											
Fail provide spec.											
In charge and:											
Unfit to drive					9	5	14	13	11	10	21
Undue alcohol											
Fail provide spec.											
Failure to provide breath specimen											
Total: All Proceedings	**34**	**30**	**45**	**68**	**99**	**75**	**86**	**125**	**139**	**148**	**126**
Licensed Premises											
Public Houses:											
Full	1405					1528					1643
Beer and Cider	267					151					16
Wine or Cider	1					2					4
Restaurant Licence											45
Residential Licence											8
Above Combined											22
Licensed Clubs											83
Total On Licences	**1673**					**1681**					**1821**
Off Licences	**512**					**533**					**586**
Total On/Off Licences	**2185**					**2214**					**2407**
Registered Clubs	**511**					**589**					**570**
Total Licences & Clubs	**2696**					**2803**					**2977**

TABLE III 36
DRUNKENNESS OFFENCES, MOTORING OFFENCES AND LICENCES, 1953–63
SOUTHEND ON SEA POLICE DISTRICT

	1953	1954	1955	1956	1957	1958	1959	1960	1961	1962	1963
Population '000	**153**					**158**					**166**
Proved Offences— Drunkenness											
Males											
Under 18	x	x	2	8	3		3	5	6	4	7
18 and under 21	7	5	11	7	15	14	18	6	6	9	17
21 and under 30	20	15	29	22	20	27	20	11	23	28	24
30 and under 60	52	41	28	47	29	40	31	37	43	53	57
60 and over	18	10	7	7	2	3	2	1	4		7
All ages	**81**	**53**	**69**	**91**	**69**	**84**	**74**	**60**	**82**	**94**	**122**
Females											
Under 18		(Included in					1				1
18 and under 21		the number		1		1	2			1	
21 and under 30		of persons		1	1		1				1
30 and under 60		by ages		10	5	8	5	5	5	4	3
60 and over		given above)		5	5	2	1	1	2	1	2
All ages	**16**	**18**	**8**	**17**	**11**	**11**	**10**	**6**	**7**	**6**	**7**
All Proved Offences	**97**	**71**	**77**	**108**	**80**	**95**	**84**	**66**	**89**	**100**	**129**
Motoring Offences											
Proceedings for:											
(a) Previously Convicted											
Unfit to drive											
Driving, undue alcohol											
Fail provide specimen											
(b) No Prev. Conviction											
Unfit to drive					15	13	10	20	15	24	23
Driving, undue alcohol											
Fail provide spec.											
In charge and:											
Unfit to drive					3	7	2	2	4	3	4
Undue alcohol											
Fail provide spec.											
Failure to provide breath specimen											
Total: All Proceedings	**3**	**6**	**18**	**18**	**18**	**20**	**12**	**22**	**19**	**27**	**27**
Licensed Premises											
Public Houses:											
Full	65					63					65
Beer and Cider	2					1					1
Wine or Cider	1					1					
Restaurant Licence											1
Residential Licence											6
Above Combined											4
Licensed Clubs											5
Total On Licences	**68**					**65**					**92**
Off Licences	**55**					**57**					**61**
Total On/Off Licences	**123**					**122**					**153**
Registered Clubs	**55**					**51**					**47**
Total Licences & Clubs	**178**					**173**					**200**

TABLE III 37
DRUNKENNESS OFFENCES, MOTORING OFFENCES AND LICENCES, 1953–63
GLOUCESTERSHIRE POLICE DISTRICT

	1953	1954	1955	1956	1957	1958	1959	1960	1961	1962	1963
Population '000	**506**					**535**					**590**
Proved Offences—Drunkenness											
Males											
Under 18	x	x	4	1	4	4	3	6	7	3	8
18 and under 21	17	9	14	13	7	14	5	15	15	23	24
21 and under 30	78	44	52	49	37	45	38	43	48	47	34
30 and under 60	135	110	127	127	140	144	133	138	149	164	162
60 and over	14	17	17	14	20	20	16	9	13	22	30
All ages	**228**	**172**	**210**	**204**	**208**	**227**	**195**	**211**	**232**	**259**	**258**
Females											
Under 18		(Included in			3				4		1
18 and under 21		the number		1	2	1	2		1		
21 and under 30		of persons		2		1	1	2	2		1
30 and under 60		by ages		1	2	7	11	8	3	2	8
60 and over		given above)		3		1	1			1	1
All ages	**16**	**8**	**4**	**7**	**7**	**10**	**15**	**10**	**10**	**3**	**11**
All Proved Offences	**244**	**180**	**214**	**211**	**215**	**237**	**210**	**221**	**242**	**262**	**269**
Motoring Offences											
Proceedings for:											
(a) Previously Convicted											
Unfit to drive											
Driving, undue alcohol											
Fail provide specimen											
(b) No Prev. Conviction											
Unfit to drive					47	36	44	49	47	52	56
Driving, undue alcohol											
Fail provide spec.											
In charge and:											
Unfit to drive					13	12	16	22	13	16	25
Undue alcohol											
Fail provide spec.											
Failure to provide breath specimen											
Total: All Proceedings	**38**	**41**	**55**	**85**	**60**	**48**	**60**	**71**	**60**	**68**	**81**
Licensed Premises											
Public Houses:											
Full	922					977					1132
Beer and Cider	301					209					21
Wine or Cider	4					4					4
Restaurant Licence											25
Residential Licence											4
Above Combined											19
Licensed Clubs											32
Total On Licences	**1227**					**1190**					**1242**
Off Licences	**260**					**272**					**328**
Total On/Off Licences	**1487**					**1462**					**1570**
Registered Clubs	**216**					**255**					**233**
Total Licences & Clubs	**1703**					**1717**					**1803**

TABLE III 38
DRUNKENNESS OFFENCES, MOTORING OFFENCES AND LICENCES, 1953-63
BRISTOL POLICE DISTRICT

	1953	1954	1955	1956	1957	1958	1959	1960	1961	1962	1963
Population '000	**444**					**438**					**434**
Proved Offences—Drunkenness											
Males											
Under 18	x	x	1		3	2	2	6	4	2	4
18 and under 21	5	1	3	2	4	9	8	12	13	22	14
21 and under 30	21	15	23	23	17	18	13	29	42	47	19
30 and under 60	62	45	37	58	65	51	87	92	91	91	79
60 and over	10	10	9	10	13	12	9	25	12	15	6
All ages	**94**	**96**	**71**	**93**	**102**	**92**	**119**	**164**	**162**	**177**	**122**
Females											
Under 18	(Included in the number of persons by ages given above)						1				
18 and under 21								1	1		
21 and under 30					2	2	1	2		4	1
30 and under 60				4	3	4	4	12	4	2	3
60 and over				1			2		1		
All ages	**4**	**5**	**2**	**5**	**5**	**6**	**8**	**15**	**6**	**6**	**4**
All Proved Offences	**98**	**71**	**73**	**98**	**107**	**98**	**127**	**179**	**168**	**183**	**126**
Motoring Offences											
Proceedings for:											
(a) Previously Convicted											
Unfit to drive											
Driving, undue alcohol											
Fail provide specimen											
(b) No Prev. Conviction											
Unfit to drive					24	14	14	29	18	21	22
Driving, undue alcohol											
Fail provide spec.											
In charge and:											
Unfit to drive					1	4	3	8	5	16	9
Undue alcohol											
Fail provide spec.											
Failure to provide breath specimen											
Total: All Proceedings	**13**	**6**	**12**	**15**	**25**	**18**	**17**	**37**	**23**	**37**	**41**
Licensed Premises											
Public Houses:											
Full	382					356					482
Beer and Cider	283					196					34
Wine or Cider											
Restaurant Licence											9
Residential Licence											1
Above Combined											2
Licensed Clubs											8
Total On Licences	**665**					**552**					**546**
Off Licences	**326**					**278**					**253**
Total On/Off Licences	**991**					**830**					**799**
Registered Clubs	**99**					**115**					**118**
Total Licences & Clubs	**1090**					**945**					**917**

TABLE III 39
DRUNKENNESS OFFENCES, MOTORING OFFENCES AND LICENCES, 1953–63
HAMPSHIRE AND ISLE OF WIGHT POLICE DISTRICT

	1953	1954	1955	1956	1957	1958	1959	1960	1961	1962	1963
Population '000	**769**					**826**					**917**
Proved Offences—Drunkenness											
Males											
Under 18	x	x	2	3	3	6	3	5	7	6	8
18 and under 21	26	28	15	26	30	43	39	45	20	36	55
21 and under 30	44	37	47	50	43	50	61	74	60	66	73
30 and under 60	121	119	114	107	136	133	93	101	116	138	173
60 and over	14	16	13	11	14	19	14	16	14	18	12
All ages	**203**	**195**	**187**	**197**	**226**	**251**	**210**	**241**	**217**	**264**	**321**
Females											
Under 18		(Included in		1		1			1	1	
18 and under 21		the number		1				2		1	1
21 and under 30		of persons				3	1		2		2
30 and under 60		by ages		5	4	5	3	3	2	8	3
60 and over		given above)			1	1	2		1	1	1
All ages	**2**	**5**	**4**	**7**	**5**	**10**	**6**	**5**	**6**	**11**	**7**
All Proved Offences	**205**	**200**	**191**	**204**	**231**	**261**	**216**	**246**	**223**	**275**	**328**
Motoring Offences											
Proceedings for:											
(a) Previously Convicted											
Unfit to drive											
Driving, undue alcohol											
Fail provide specimen											
(b) No Prev. Conviction											
Unfit to drive					47	72	75	66	72	73	95
Driving, undue alcohol											
Fail provide spec.											
In charge and:											
Unfit to drive					10	11	4	17	11	27	36
Undue alcohol											
Fail provide spec.											
Failure to provide breath specimen											
Total: All Proceedings	**65**	**52**	**40**	**67**	**57**	**83**	**79**	**83**	**83**	**100**	**131**
Licensed Premises											
Public Houses:											
Full	1363					1421					1488
Beer and Cider	185					91					6
Wine or Cider	1					1					
Restaurant Licence											40
Residential Licence											81
Above Combined											58
Licensed Clubs											81
Total On Licences	**1549**					**1513**					**1754**
Off Licences	**384**					**388**					**476**
Total On/Off Licences	**1933**					**1901**					**2230**
Registered Clubs	**434**					**481**					**408**
Total Licences & Clubs	**2367**					**2382**					**2638**

TABLE III 40
DRUNKENNESS OFFENCES, MOTORING OFFENCES AND LICENCES, 1953-63
BOURNEMOUTH POLICE DISTRICT

	1953	1954	1955	1956	1957	1958	1959	1960	1961	1962	1963
Population '000	**131**					**144**					**151**
Proved Offences—Drunkenness											
Males											
Under 18	x	x	1					2	2	3	
18 and under 21	2	2			3	4	6	13	7	3	4
21 and under 30	10	10	7	5	13	8	9	18	8	9	19
30 and under 60	56	50	46	55	78	97	88	102	109	135	155
60 and over	4	5	5	5	5	4	6	10	26	25	22
All ages	**58**	**61**	**61**	**65**	**99**	**113**	**109**	**145**	**152**	**175**	**200**
Females											
Under 18		(Included in the number of persons by ages given above)									
18 and under 21				1				2			1
21 and under 30					1				1		
30 and under 60				5	10	5	9	7	7	2	6
60 and over				1		2	3			1	5
All ages	**4**	**6**	**8**	**7**	**11**	**7**	**12**	**9**	**8**	**3**	**12**
All Proved Offences	**72**	**67**	**59**	**72**	**110**	**120**	**121**	**154**	**160**	**178**	**212**
Motoring Offences											
Proceedings for:											
(a) Previously Convicted											
Unfit to drive											
Driving, undue alcohol											
Fail provide specimen											
(b) No Prev. Conviction											
Unfit to drive											
Driving, undue alcohol					17	6	5	6	6	8	10
Fail provide spec.											
In charge and:											
Unfit to drive											
Undue alcohol					3	6	5	3	8	3	7
Fail provide spec.											
Failure to provide breath specimen											
Total: All Proceedings	**7**	**10**	**15**	**7**	**20**	**12**	**10**	**9**	**14**	**11**	**17**
Licensed Premises											
Public Houses:											
Full	72					77					80
Beer and Cider	1					2					
Wine or Cider											
Restaurant Licence											24
Residential Licence											28
Above Combined											51
Licensed Clubs											7
Total On Licences	**73**					**79**					**190**
Off Licences	**80**					**79**					**85**
Total On/Off Licences	**153**					**158**					**275**
Registered Clubs	**62**					**85**					**54**
Total Licences & Clubs	**215**					**243**					**329**

TABLE III 41
DRUNKENNESS OFFENCES, MOTORING OFFENCES AND LICENCES, 1953–63 PORTSMOUTH POLICE DISTRICT

	1953	1954	1955	1956	1957	1958	1959	1960	1961	1962	1963
Population '000	**246**					**223**					**225**
Proved Offences—Drunkenness											
Males											
Under 18	x	x	3	3	18	12	13	11	7	6	4
18 and under 21	68	95	84	114	176	113	36	39	46	47	31
21 and under 30	189	232	204	173	278	139	62	69	89	80	95
30 and under 60	180	200	154	170	216	206	155	168	179	210	213
60 and over	43	31	31	24	35	24	46	34	36	38	38
All ages	**449**	**532**	**458**	**484**	**723**	**494**	**312**	**321**	**357**	**381**	**381**
Females											
Under 18		(Included in		2		1	1		1	4	2
18 and under 21		the number		5	2	6	13	7	4	9	
21 and under 30		of persons		5	8	8	15	8	7	11	9
30 and under 60		by ages		15	14	19	31	17	24	25	23
60 and over		given above)		1	3	2	6	3	6	8	9
All ages	**31**	**26**	**18**	**28**	**27**	**36**	**66**	**35**	**42**	**57**	**43**
All Proved Offences	**480**	**558**	**476**	**512**	**750**	**530**	**378**	**356**	**399**	**438**	**424**
Motoring Offences											
Proceedings for:											
(a) Previously Convicted											
Unfit to drive											
Driving, undue alcohol											
Fail provide specimen											
(b) No Prev. Conviction											
Unfit to drive					36	40	62	65	43	45	72
Driving, undue alcohol											
Fail provide spec.											
In charge and:											
Unfit to drive					1	12	13	12	11	15	13
Undue alcohol											
Fail provide spec.											
Failure to provide breath specimen											
Total: All Proceedings	**34**	**34**	**41**	**43**	**37**	**52**	**75**	**77**	**54**	**60**	**85**
Licensed Premises											
Public Houses:											
Full	333					344					386
Beer and Cider	192					66					3
Wine or Cider											
Restaurant Licence											16
Residential Licence											1
Above Combined											6
Licensed Clubs											20
Total On Licences	**525**					**410**					**432**
Off Licences	**183**					**150**					**144**
Total On/Off Licences	**708**					**560**					**576**
Registered Clubs	**81**					**93**					**69**
Total Licences & Clubs	**789**					**653**					**645**

TABLE III 42
DRUNKENNESS OFFENCES, MOTORING OFFENCES AND LICENCES, 1953-63
SOUTHAMPTON POLICE DISTRICT

	1953	1954	1955	1956	1957	1958	1959	1960	1961	1962	1963
Population '000	**177**					**199**					**207**
Proved Offences—Drunkenness											
Males											
Under 18	x	x	1	1	6	3	1	8	5	10	12
18 and under 21	28	32	24	17	24	43	44	40	66	79	54
21 and under 30	104	106	84	88	82	127	138	148	137	206	160
30 and under 60	222	210	145	138	175	237	251	283	353	434	367
60 and over	14	12	8	9	15	17	23	43	43	40	38
All ages	**344**	**345**	**242**	**253**	**302**	**427**	**457**	**522**	**604**	**769**	**631**
Females											
Under 18	(Included in the number of persons by ages given above)			2				1			
18 and under 21				1		1		1	3	3	
21 and under 30				1	3	6	3	2	6	2	2
30 and under 60				12	18	20	17	17	28	17	14
60 and over				4	2	1	1	2		2	5
All ages	**24**	**15**	**20**	**20**	**23**	**28**	**21**	**23**	**37**	**24**	**21**
All Proved Offences	**368**	**360**	**262**	**273**	**325**	**455**	**478**	**545**	**641**	**793**	**652**
Motoring Offences											
Proceedings for:											
(a) Previously Convicted											
Unfit to drive											
Driving, undue alcohol											
Fail provide specimen											
(b) No Prev. Conviction											
Unfit to drive					25	38	35	29	34	43	38
Driving, undue alcohol											
Fail provide spec.											
In charge and:											
Unfit to drive					6	9	13	12	13	18	7
Undue alcohol											
Fail provide spec.											
Failure to provide breath specimen											
Total: All Proceedings	**21**	**25**	**23**	**37**	**31**	**47**	**48**	**41**	**47**	**61**	**45**
Licensed Premises											
Public Houses:											
Full	234					252					289
Beer and Cider	114					50					11
Wine or Cider											
Restaurant Licence											11
Residential Licence											
Above Combined											4
Licensed Clubs											9
Total On Licences	**348**					**302**					**324**
Off Licences	**103**					**99**					**109**
Total On/Off Licences	**451**					**401**					**433**
Registered Clubs	**69**					**85**					**111**
Total Licences & Clubs	**520**					**486**					**544**

TABLE III 43
DRUNKENNESS OFFENCES, MOTORING OFFENCES AND LICENCES, 1953-63 HEREFORDSHIRE POLICE DISTRICT

	1953	1954	1955	1956	1957	1958	1959	1960	1961	1962	1963
Population '000	**128**					**128**					**134**
Proved Offences—Drunkenness											
Males											
Under 18	x	x	2		2	2	2		3	7	3
18 and under 21	3	6	8	7	9	7	7	11	8	5	25
21 and under 30	26	18	27	22	15	28	22	14	22	13	26
30 and under 60	55	27	43	38	40	52	53	50	38	36	42
60 and over	5	2	3	5	5	9	6	3	3	4	5
All ages	**84**	**51**	**78**	**72**	**71**	**98**	**90**	**78**	**74**	**65**	**101**
Females											
Under 18		(Included in									
18 and under 21		the number			1						
21 and under 30		of persons		1			2	1			
30 and under 60		by ages		2	3	1	1		1		3
60 and over		given above)		1	1			1		1	1
All ages	**5**	**2**	**5**	**4**	**5**	**1**	**3**	**2**	**1**	**1**	**4**
All Proved Offences	**89**	**53**	**83**	**76**	**76**	**99**	**93**	**80**	**75**	**66**	**105**
Motoring Offences											
Proceedings for:											
(a) Previously Convicted											
Unfit to drive											
Driving, undue alcohol											
Fail provide specimen											
(b) No Prev. Conviction											
Unfit to drive					21	26	23	19	39	27	29
Driving, undue alcohol											
Fail provide spec.											
In charge and:											
Unfit to drive					4	3	4	3	1	5	5
Undue alcohol											
Fail provide spec.											
Failure to provide breath specimen											
Total: All Proceedings	**28**	**35**	**22**	**21**	**25**	**29**	**27**	**22**	**40**	**32**	**34**
Licensed Premises											
Public Houses:											
Full	352					354					393
Beer and Cider	73					53					7
Wine or Cider	2					2					
Restaurant Licence											9
Residential Licence											1
Above Combined											10
Licensed Clubs											6
Total On Licences	**427**					**409**					**426**
Off Licences	**61**					**62**					**82**
Total On/Off Licences	**488**					**471**					**508**
Registered Clubs	**57**					**62**					**47**
Total Licences & Clubs	**545**					**533**					**555**

TABLE III 44
DRUNKENNESS OFFENCES, MOTORING OFFENCES AND LICENCES, 1953–63
HERTFORDSHIRE (beyond M.P.D.) POLICE DISTRICT

	1953	1954	1955	1956	1957	1958	1959	1960	1961	1962	1963
Population '000	**652**					**761**					**874**
Proved Offences—Drunkenness											
Males											
Under 18	x	x		6	4	1	7	6	2	2	11
18 and under 21	12	6	11	10	8	10	19	17	11	21	21
21 and under 30	54	32	30	39	39	61	50	48	48	37	61
30 and under 60	103	120	70	96	103	96	146	135	102	84	85
60 and over	11	7	12	15	10	8	8	1	5	11	10
All ages	**171**	**160**	**117**	**166**	**164**	**176**	**230**	**207**	**168**	**155**	**188**
Females											
Under 18	(Included in			2				1	1		1
18 and under 21	the number			1	2			1	1	1	
21 and under 30	of persons				1						
30 and under 60	by ages			9	1	2	6	1	5		1
60 and over	given above)			2	3	1			1	1	2
All ages	**9**	**5**	**6**	**14**	**7**	**3**	**6**	**3**	**8**	**2**	**4**
All Proved Offences	**180**	**165**	**123**	**180**	**171**	**179**	**236**	**210**	**176**	**157**	**192**
Motoring Offences											
Proceedings for:											
(a) Previously Convicted											
Unfit to drive											
Driving, undue alcohol											
Fail provide specimen											
(b) No Prev. Conviction											
Unfit to drive					55	51	48	40	42	39	55
Driving, undue alcohol											
Fail provide spec.											
In charge and:											
Unfit to drive					3	1	19	10	6	25	13
Undue alcohol											
Fail provide spec.											
Failure to provide breath specimen											
Total: All Proceedings	**24**	**31**	**27**	**53**	**58**	**52**	**67**	**50**	**48**	**64**	**68**
Licensed Premises											
Public Houses:											
Full	915					1001					1043
Beer and Cider	291					162					37
Wine or Cider	1										
Restaurant Licence											21
Residential Licence											
Above Combined											9
Licensed Clubs											15
Total On Licences	**1207**					**1163**					**1125**
Off Licences	**221**					**244**					**285**
Total On/Off Licences	**1428**					**1407**					**1410**
Registered Clubs	**338**					**399**					**431**
Total Licences & Clubs	**1766**					**1806**					**1841**

TABLE III 45
DRUNKENNESS OFFENCES, MOTORING OFFENCES AND LICENCES, 1953–63
HUNTINGDONSHIRE POLICE DISTRICT

	1953	1954	1955	1956	1957	1958	1959	1960	1961	1962	1963
Population '000	**71**					**79**					**88**
Proved Offences— Drunkenness											
Males											
Under 18	x	x	1	1			1	2	3	2	2
18 and under 21	2	2	3	4		1	6	5	8	8	10
21 and under 30	6	6	21	30	7	9	5	6	12	5	5
30 and under 60	33	28	45	50	17	20	16	16	18	18	12
60 and over	1	5	6	2	3	6	2	4	1	1	1
All ages	**42**	**40**	**76**	**87**	**27**	**36**	**30**	**33**	**42**	**34**	**30**
Females											
Under 18	(Included in the number of persons by ages given above)										
18 and under 21				1	1				1		1
21 and under 30										1	1
30 and under 60						1			1		
60 and over											
All ages		**1**		**1**	**1**	**1**			**2**	**1**	**2**
All Proved Offences	**42**	**41**	**76**	**88**	**28**	**37**	**30**	**33**	**44**	**35**	**32**
Motoring Offences											
Proceedings for:											
(a) Previously Convicted											
Unfit to drive											
Driving, undue alcohol											
Fail provide specimen											
(b) No Prev. Conviction											
Unfit to drive					22	12	18	13	26	28	22
Driving, undue alcohol											
Fail provide spec.											
In charge and:											
Unfit to drive					2	3	3	7	4	3	6
Undue alcohol											
Fail provide spec.											
Failure to provide breath specimen											
Total: All Proceedings	**8**	**10**	**13**	**21**	**24**	**15**	**21**	**20**	**20**	**31**	**28**
Licensed Premises											
Public Houses:											
Full	231					232					222
Beer and Cider	45					17					6
Wine or Cider											
Restaurant Licence											
Residential Licence											
Above Combined											1
Licensed Clubs											
Total On Licences	**276**					**249**					**229**
Off Licences	**34**					**34**					**34**
Total On/Off Licences	**310**					**283**					**263**
Registered Clubs	**25**					**26**					**35**
Total Licences & Clubs	**335**					**309**					**298**

TABLE III 46
DRUNKENNESS OFFENCES, MOTORING OFFENCES AND LICENCES, 1953-63
KENT POLICE DISTRICT

	1953	1954	1955	1956	1957	1958	1959	1960	1961	1962	1963
Population '000	**1588**					**1654**					**1748**
Proved Offences—Drunkenness											
Males											
Under 18	x	x	10	3	6	7	4	11	16	16	18
18 and under 21	21	25	31	24	44	71	39	50	55	43	50
21 and under 30	94	75	68	73	56	93	78	74	110	106	98
30 and under 60	135	98	85	77	99	166	168	156	144	177	183
60 and over	8	10	22	6	14	13	18	13	21	21	10
All ages	**240**	**195**	**207**	**183**	**219**	**350**	**307**	**304**	**346**	**363**	**359**
Females											
Under 18		(Included in			3	2		2			
18 and under 21		the number		1	1	5	6	1		4	
21 and under 30		of persons		1	5	3	5	6		2	5
30 and under 60		by ages		10	5	12	9	11	7	5	5
60 and over		given above)		3	6	2	5		1	7	3
All ages	**18**	**13**	**9**	**15**	**20**	**24**	**25**	**20**	**8**	**18**	**13**
All Proved Offences	**258**	**208**	**216**	**198**	**239**	**374**	**332**	**324**	**354**	**381**	**372**
Motoring Offences											
Proceedings for:											
(a) Previously Convicted											
Unfit to drive											
Driving, undue alcohol											
Fail provide specimen											
(b) No Prev. Conviction											
Unfit to drive					77	58	54	69	71	86	105
Driving, undue alcohol											
Fail provide spec.											
In charge and:											
Unfit to drive					8	20	36	23	21	28	27
Undue alcohol											
Fail provide spec.											
Failure to provide breath specimen											
Total: All Proceedings	**40**	**58**	**75**	**67**	**85**	**78**	**90**	**92**	**92**	**114**	**132**
Licensed Premises											
Public Houses:											
Full	2567					2615					2700
Beer and Cider	356					193					32
Wine or Cider	12					10					1
Restaurant Licence											109
Residential Licence											111
Above Combined											56
Licensed Clubs											108
Total On Licences	**2935**					**2818**					**3117**
Off Licences	**701**					**706**					**755**
Total On/Off Licences	**3636**					**3524**					**3872**
Registered Clubs	**863**					**942**					**764**
Total Licences & Clubs	**4499**					**4466**					**4634**

TABLE III 47

DRUNKENNESS OFFENCES, MOTORING OFFENCES AND LICENCES, 1953–63
LANCASHIRE POLICE DISTRICT

	1953	1954	1955	1956	1957	1958	1959	1960	1961	1962	1963
Population '000	**2102**					**2187**					**2330**
Proved Offences—											
Drunkenness											
Males											
Under 18	x	x	39	36	57	53	44	79	103	99	95
18 and under 21	87	128	145	164	267	193	276	339	371	342	390
21 and under 30	297	349	391	403	471	445	374	492	503	527	587
30 and under 60	628	681	348	703	779	800	735	736	819	889	846
60 and over	59	59	59	62	61	67	69	78	89	81	79
All ages	**1042**	**1181**	**1246**	**1368**	**1635**	**1558**	**1498**	**1724**	**1885**	**1938**	**1997**
Females											
Under 18		(Included in		2	2	3	2	2	6	6	8
18 and under 21		the number			6	4	7	2	8	3	5
21 and under 30		of persons		7	7	9	7	5	5	7	7
30 and under 60		by ages		19	22	24	24	31	30	19	20
60 and over		given above)		7	10	3	8	6	6	3	7
All ages	**29**	**36**	**36**	**35**	**47**	**43**	**48**	**46**	**55**	**38**	**47**
All Proved Offences	**1071**	**1217**	**1282**	**1403**	**1682**	**1601**	**1546**	**1770**	**1940**	**1976**	**2044**
Motoring Offences											
Proceedings for:											
(a) Previously Convicted											
Unfit to drive											
Driving, undue alcohol											
Fail provide specimen											
(b) No Prev. Conviction											
Unfit to drive					209	255	221	325	335	381	296
Driving, undue alcohol											
Fail provide spec.											
In charge and:											
Unfit to drive					42	40	46	55	64	50	68
Undue alcohol											
Fail provide spec.											
Failure to provide breath specimen											
Total: All Proceedings	**129**	**184**	**183**	**223**	**251**	**295**	**267**	**380**	**399**	**431**	**364**
Licensed Premises											
Public Houses:											
Full	2305					2388					2827
Beer and Cider	690					529					82
Wine or Cider	16					12					2
Restaurant Licence											51
Residential Licence											13
Above Combined											25
Licensed Clubs											62
Total On Licences	**3011**					**2929**					**3062**
Off Licences	**1182**					**1197**					**1302**
Total On/Off Licences	**4193**					**4126**					**4364**
Registered Clubs	**1202**					**1244**					**1146**
Total Licences & Clubs	**5395**					**5360**					**5510**

TABLE III 48
DRUNKENNESS OFFENCES, MOTORING OFFENCES AND LICENCES, 1953-63
BARROW IN FURNESS POLICE DISTRICT

	1953	1954	1955	1956	1957	1958	1959	1960	1961	1962	1963
Population '000	**66**					**64**					**65**
Proved Offences—Drunkenness											
Males											
Under 18	x	x	1	4		3	3	5	3	4	3
18 and under 21	2	5	1	4	5	3	9	16	12	19	17
21 and under 30	17	22	15	15	16	26	13	30	19	17	16
30 and under 60	34	40	23	43	39	59	31	51	47	28	24
60 and over	10	3	5	5	3	8	6	3	4	1	3
All ages	**60**	**69**	**44**	**71**	**63**	**99**	**62**	**105**	**85**	**69**	**63**
Females											
Under 18		(Included in the number of persons by ages given above)									
18 and under 21						3					
21 and under 30											
30 and under 60				2	2		3		1	1	
60 and over				1					3	1	
All ages	**3**	**1**	**1**	**3**	**2**	**3**	**3**		**4**	**2**	
All Proved Offences	**63**	**70**	**45**	**74**	**65**	**102**	**65**	**105**	**89**	**71**	**63**
Motoring Offences											
Proceedings for:											
(a) Previously Convicted											
Unfit to drive											
Driving, undue alcohol											
Fail provide specimen											
(b) No Prev. Conviction											
Unfit to drive					9	6	9	11	6	10	6
Driving, undue alcohol											
Fail provide spec.											
In charge and:											
Unfit to drive									1	3	3
Undue alcohol											
Fail provide spec.											
Failure to provide breath specimen											
Total: All Proceedings	**4**	**2**	**3**	**5**	**9**	**6**	**9**	**11**	**7**	**13**	**9**
Licensed Premises											
Public Houses:											
Full	66					69					81
Beer and Cider	17					12					
Wine or Cider											
Restaurant Licence											3
Residential Licence											
Above Combined											1
Licensed Clubs											1
Total On Licences	**83**					**81**					**86**
Off Licences	**69**					**61**					**57**
Total On/Off Licences	**152**					**142**					**143**
Registered Clubs	**36**					**36**					**36**
Total Licences & Clubs	**188**					**178**					**179**

TABLE III 49

DRUNKENNESS OFFENCES, MOTORING OFFENCES AND LICENCES, 1953–63 BLACKBURN POLICE DISTRICT

	1953	1954	1955	1956	1957	1958	1959	1960	1961	1962	1963
Population '000	**100**					**106**					**105**
Proved Offences— Drunkenness											
Males											
Under 18	x	x	3	6	2	4	6	5	9	4	2
18 and under 21	8	14	17	20	24	29	28	18	30	29	22
21 and under 30	26	42	43	51	55	43	45	41	57	56	66
30 and under 60	62	66	83	105	133	112	109	87	102	124	129
60 and over	8	9	6	8	11	6	11	5	14	12	10
All ages	**95**	**117**	**138**	**190**	**225**	**194**	**199**	**156**	**212**	**225**	**229**
Females											
Under 18	(Included in the number of persons by ages given above)									1	1
18 and under 21				6	2	1					2
21 and under 30				3	12	4	3	2	2	2	1
30 and under 60				5	10	4	5	6	3	15	2
60 and over									2	1	
All ages	**9**	**14**	**14**	**14**	**24**	**9**	**8**	**8**	**7**	**19**	**6**
All Proved Offences	**104**	**131**	**152**	**204**	**249**	**203**	**207**	**164**	**219**	**244**	**235**
Motoring Offences											
Proceedings for:											
(a) Previously Convicted											
Unfit to drive											
Driving, undue alcohol											
Fail provide specimen											
(b) No Prev. Conviction											
Unfit to drive					17	9	12	17	21	20	26
Driving, undue alcohol											
Fail provide spec.											
In charge and:											
Unfit to drive					4	4	3	3	2	13	7
Undue alcohol											
Fail provide spec.											
Failure to provide breath specimen											
Total: All Proceedings	**10**	**8**	**10**	**33**	**21**	**13**	**15**	**20**	**23**	**33**	**33**
Licensed Premises											
Public Houses:											
Full	209					202					212
Beer and Cider	29					25					4
Wine or Cider	1					1					1
Restaurant Licence											4
Residential Licence											
Above Combined											1
Licensed Clubs											1
Total On Licences	**239**					**228**					**223**
Off Licences	**51**					**54**					**62**
Total On/Off Licences	**290**					**282**					**285**
Registered Clubs	**47**					**43**					**35**
Total Licences & Clubs	**337**					**325**					**320**

TABLE III 50
DRUNKENNESS OFFENCES, MOTORING OFFENCES AND LICENCES, 1953-63
BLACKPOOL POLICE DISTRICT

	1953	1954	1955	1956	1957	1958	1959	1960	1961	1962	1963
Population '000	**147**					**144**					**151**
Proved Offences—Drunkenness											
Males											
Under 18	x	x	8	6	8	8	19	13	32	9	11
18 and under 21	35	11	28	23	17	35	46	40	59	45	45
21 and under 30	47	27	39	44	25	38	35	39	72	44	53
30 and under 60	67	80	73	67	62	46	67	77	97	103	88
60 and over	16	12	8	3	2	6	6	4	3	9	11
All ages	**144**	**108**	**135**	**143**	**114**	**133**	**173**	**173**	**263**	**210**	**208**
Females											
Under 18		(Included in the number of persons by ages given above)				2		1	3		
18 and under 21				5		1	3	3	3	1	3
21 and under 30					1	1		1	5	7	5
30 and under 60				12	9	12	20	9	20	17	28
60 and over				2	6	5	1	2	1	3	7
All ages	**21**	**22**	**21**	**19**	**16**	**21**	**24**	**16**	**32**	**28**	**38**
All Proved Offences	**165**	**130**	**156**	**162**	**130**	**154**	**197**	**189**	**295**	**238**	**246**
Motoring Offences											
Proceedings for:											
(a) Previously Convicted											
Unfit to drive											
Driving, undue alcohol											
Fail provide specimen											
(b) No Prev. Conviction											
Unfit to drive					7	14	20	26	31	9	21
Driving, undue alcohol											
Fail provide spec.											
In charge and:											
Unfit to drive					4	4	3	4		3	9
Undue alcohol											
Fail provide spec.											
Failure to provide breath specimen											
Total: All Proceedings	**14**	**10**	**18**	**6**	**11**	**18**	**23**	**30**	**31**	**12**	**30**
Licensed Premises											
Public Houses:											
Full	110					119					131
Beer and Cider	9					6					2
Wine or Cider											
Restaurant Licence											9
Residential Licence											53
Above Combined											42
Licensed Clubs											12
Total On Licences	**119**					**125**					**249**
Off Licences	**81**					**83**					**97**
Total On/Off Licences	**200**					**208**					**346**
Registered Clubs	**58**					**62**					**56**
Total Licences & Clubs	**258**					**270**					**402**

TABLE III 51
DRUNKENNESS OFFENCES, MOTORING OFFENCES AND LICENCES, 1953–63
BOLTON POLICE DISTRICT

	1953	1954	1955	1956	1957	1958	1959	1960	1961	1962	1963
Population '000	**165**					**162**					**160**
Proved Offences—											
Drunkenness											
Males											
Under 18	x	x	2	3	4	2	1	4	7	10	13
18 and under 21	15	6	14	16	16	12	19	18	12	22	26
21 and under 30	37	44	50	36	37	42	29	31	49	50	43
30 and under 60	101	85	77	84	80	81	72	67	56	79	81
60 and over	17	12	14	9	10	10	6	8	9	13	11
All ages	**156**	**138**	**149**	**148**	**147**	**147**	**127**	**128**	**133**	**174**	**174**
Females											
Under 18		(Included in							2		1
18 and under 21		the number			2						2
21 and under 30		of persons		2		3		2	1	2	
30 and under 60		by ages		17	6	12	4	5	3	9	8
60 and over		given above)		1	5	1	1		2	1	1
All ages	**14**	**9**	**8**	**20**	**13**	**16**	**5**	**7**	**8**	**12**	**12**
All Proved Offences	**170**	**147**	**157**	**168**	**160**	**163**	**132**	**135**	**141**	**186**	**186**
Motoring Offences											
Proceedings for:											
(a) Previously Convicted											
Unfit to drive											
Driving, undue alcohol											
Fail provide specimen											
(b) No Prev. Conviction											
Unfit to drive					23	12	21	24	16	17	21
Driving, undue alcohol											
Fail provide spec.											
In charge and:											
Unfit to drive					7	10	3	8	9	9	9
Undue alcohol											
Fail provide spec.											
Failure to provide breath specimen											
Total: All Proceedings	**18**	**12**	**18**	**17**	**30**	**22**	**24**	**32**	**25**	**26**	**30**
Licensed Premises											
Public Houses:											
Full	135					138					201
Beer and Cider	145					132					48
Wine or Cider	5					4					3
Restaurant Licence											4
Residential Licence											
Above Combined											
Licensed Clubs											
Total On Licences	**285**					**274**					**256**
Off Licences	**169**					**164**					**171**
Total On/Off Licences	**454**					**438**					**427**
Registered Clubs	**67**					**65**					**60**
Total Licences & Clubs	**521**					**503**					**487**

TABLE III 52
DRUNKENNESS OFFENCES, MOTORING OFFENCES AND LICENCES, 1953-63
BOOTLE POLICE DISTRICT

	1953	1954	1955	1956	1957	1958	1959	1960	1961	1962	1963
Population '000	**76**					**82**					**83**
Proved Offences—Drunkenness											
Males											
Under 18	x	x	5	15	3	4	3	3	6	4	2
18 and under 21	27	17	12	29	15	19	15	4	18	23	23
21 and under 30	60	48	33	38	25	30	37	22	20	24	18
30 and under 60	73	61	45	64	33	35	33	32	35	47	31
60 and over	15	2	1	4	2	2	3	4	5	6	2
All ages	**166**	**125**	**92**	**150**	**78**	**90**	**91**	**65**	**84**	**104**	**76**
Females											
Under 18		(Included in the number of persons by ages given above)							1		
18 and under 21				3	4	2			1		
21 and under 30				1		2			1		1
30 and under 60				2	1	1	4	2	1	2	2
60 and over				2				1	1		
All ages	**9**	**3**	**4**	**8**	**5**	**5**	**4**	**3**	**5**	**2**	**3**
All Proved Offences	**175**	**128**	**96**	**158**	**83**	**95**	**95**	**68**	**89**	**106**	**79**
Motoring Offences											
Proceedings for:											
(a) Previously Convicted											
Unfit to drive											
Driving, undue alcohol											
Fail provide specimen											
(b) No Prev. Conviction											
Unfit to drive					6	4	4	10	10	6	7
Driving, undue alcohol											
Fail provide spec.											
In charge and:											
Unfit to drive					1						1
Undue alcohol											
Fail provide spec.											
Failure to provide breath specimen											
Total: All Proceedings	**3**	**3**	**11**	**7**	**7**	**4**	**4**	**10**	**10**	**6**	**8**
Licensed Premises											
Public Houses:											
Full	49					48					49
Beer and Cider	1										
Wine or Cider											
Restaurant Licence											2
Residential Licence											
Above Combined											
Licensed Clubs											
Total On Licences	**50**					**48**					**51**
Off Licences	**13**					**12**					**17**
Total On/Off Licences	**63**					**60**					**68**
Registered Clubs	**24**					**25**					**26**
Total Licences & Clubs	**87**					**85**					**94**

TABLE III 53
DRUNKENNESS OFFENCES, MOTORING OFFENCES AND LICENCES, 1953-63
BURNLEY POLICE DISTRICT

	1953	1954	1955	1956	1957	1958	1959	1960	1961	1962	1963
Population '000	**83**					**81**					**80**
Proved Offences—Drunkenness											
Males											
Under 18	x	x	2	1	1	1	1	1			
18 and under 21	9	6	2	5	3	8	6	6	2	7	6
21 and under 30	31	17	19	17	19	17	18	13	20	16	9
30 and under 60	48	38	32	45	30	33	35	20	29	16	24
60 and over	4	7	9	3	5	4	2	2	1	5	
All ages	**87**	**68**	**63**	**71**	**58**	**63**	**62**	**42**	**52**	**44**	**39**
Females											
Under 18		(Included in				2					
18 and under 21		the number			1						1
21 and under 30		of persons		1					2	1	
30 and under 60		by ages		3	1	1	1	2	2	4	4
60 and over		given above)				1		1			
All ages	**5**		**1**	**4**	**2**	**4**	**1**	**3**	**4**	**5**	**5**
All Proved Offences	**92**	**68**	**64**	**75**	**60**	**67**	**63**	**45**	**56**	**49**	**44**
Motoring Offences											
Proceedings for:											
(a) Previously Convicted											
Unfit to drive											
Driving, undue alcohol											
Fail provide specimen											
(b) No Prev. Conviction											
Unfit to drive					17	11	18	17	26	20	14
Driving, undue alcohol											
Fail provide spec.											
In charge and:											
Unfit to drive					5	1	2	1		1	6
Undue alcohol											
Fail provide spec.											
Failure to provide breath specimen											
Total: All Proceedings	**17**	**11**	**12**	**15**	**22**	**12**	**20**	**18**	**26**	**21**	**20**
Licensed Premises											
Public Houses:											
Full	81					93					114
Beer and Cider	53					31					
Wine or Cider	1										
Restaurant Licence											1
Residential Licence											
Above Combined											2
Licensed Clubs											1
Total On Licences	**135**					**124**					**118**
Off Licences	**92**					**93**					**98**
Total On/Off Licences	**227**					**217**					**216**
Registered Clubs	**37**					**40**					**43**
Total Licences & Clubs	**264**					**257**					**259**

TABLE III 54
DRUNKENNESS OFFENCES, MOTORING OFFENCES AND LICENCES, 1953-63
LIVERPOOL POLICE DISTRICT

	1953	1954	1955	1956	1957	1958	1959	1960	1961	1962	1963
Population '000	**790**					**762**					**740**
Proved Offences—Drunkenness											
Males											
Under 18	x	x	42	142	115	149	139	257	287	241	182
18 and under 21	353	352	420	443	598	618	635	957	1148	1125	845
21 and under 30	1123	861	857	1013	1216	1392	1506	1673	2279	2186	1681
30 and under 60	1951	1633	1574	1970	2147	2668	2681	2916	3892	4185	3806
60 and over	293	207	192	196	194	231	252	263	356	443	489
All ages	**3296**	**2763**	**2776**	**3764**	**4270**	**5058**	**5231**	**6066**	**7962**	**8180**	**7003**
Females											
Under 18			(Included in	7	3	9	5	11	15	12	12
18 and under 21			the number	30	21	29	34	26	35	45	25
21 and under 30			of persons	63	70	93	66	57	71	77	51
30 and under 60			by ages	169	198	198	226	134	206	234	184
60 and over			given above)	66	69	57	85	65	59	47	45
All ages	**424**	**290**	**309**	**335**	**361**	**386**	**416**	**293**	**386**	**415**	**317**
All Proved Offences	**3720**	**3053**	**3085**	**4099**	**4631**	**5444**	**5647**	**6359**	**8348**	**8595**	**7320**
Motoring Offences											
Proceedings for:											
(a) Previously Convicted											
Unfit to drive											
Driving, undue alcohol											
Fail provide specimen											
(b) No Prev. Conviction											
Unfit to drive					56	66	88	92	134	148	140
Driving, undue alcohol											
Fail provide spec.											
In charge and:											
Unfit to drive					17	17	33	43	37	41	61
Undue alcohol											
Fail provide spec.											
Failure to provide breath specimen											
Total: All Proceedings	**57**	**65**	**45**	**92**	**73**	**83**	**121**	**135**	**171**	**189**	**201**
Licensed Premises											
Public Houses:											
Full	1132					1072					1056
Beer and Cider	39					25					3
Wine or Cider	1					1					
Restaurant Licence											13
Residential Licence											1
Above Combined											3
Licensed Clubs											46
Total On Licences	**1172**					**1098**					**1122**
Off Licences	**164**					**161**					**165**
Total On/Off Licences	**1336**					**1259**					**1287**
Registered Clubs	**187**					**251**					**239**
Total Licences & Clubs	**1523**					**1510**					**1526**

TABLE III 55
DRUNKENNESS OFFENCES, MOTORING OFFENCES AND LICENCES, 1953–63 MANCHESTER POLICE DISTRICT

	1953	**1954**	**1955**	**1956**	**1957**	**1958**	**1959**	**1960**	**1961**	**1962**	**1963**
Population '000	**702**					**677**					**655**
Proved Offences—Drunkenness											
Males											
Under 18	x	x	24	34	56	51	69	73	58	76	88
18 and under 21	138	204	129	162	204	219	239	325	336	394	391
21 and under 30	669	619	586	563	567	601	593	653	665	968	939
30 and under 60	1203	1223	1094	1001	1163	1293	1343	1384	1343	1737	1936
60 and over	193	172	174	81	113	123	108	125	107	127	143
All ages	**1854**	**1894**	**1721**	**1841**	**2103**	**2287**	**2352**	**2560**	**2509**	**3302**	**3497**
Females											
Under 18		(Included in			1	1	5	6	4	2	3
18 and under 21		the number		10	7	14	11	13	7	14	20
21 and under 30		of persons		49	75	54	55	38	39	50	53
30 and under 60		by ages		140	128	131	130	111	138	141	158
60 and over		given above)		41	34	51	53	44	45	38	36
All ages	**349**	**324**	**286**	**240**	**245**	**251**	**254**	**212**	**233**	**245**	**270**
All Proved Offences	**2203**	**2218**	**2007**	**2081**	**2348**	**2538**	**2606**	**2772**	**2742**	**3547**	**3767**
Motoring Offences											
Proceedings for:											
(a) Previously Convicted											
Unfit to drive											
Driving, undue alcohol											
Fail provide specimen											
(b) No Prev. Conviction											
Unfit to drive					113	142	171	218	320	329	372
Driving, undue alcohol											
Fail provide spec.											
In charge and:											
Unfit to drive					50	62	72	71	89	84	105
Undue alcohol											
Fail provide spec.											
Failure to provide breath specimen											
Total: All Proceedings	**110**	**128**	**110**	**128**	**163**	**204**	**243**	**289**	**409**	**413**	**477**
Licensed Premises											
Public Houses:											
Full	487					501					846
Beer and Cider	607					538					136
Wine or Cider	1					1					1
Restaurant Licence											27
Residential Licence											7
Above Combined											5
Licensed Clubs											72
Total On Licences	**1095**					**1040**					**1094**
Off Licences	**641**					**621**					**608**
Total On/Off Licences	**1736**					**1661**					**1702**
Registered Clubs	**207**					**277**					**230**
Total Licences & Clubs	**1943**					**1938**					**1932**

TABLE III 56
DRUNKENNESS OFFENCES, MOTORING OFFENCES AND LICENCES, 1953-63
OLDHAM POLICE DISTRICT

	1953	1954	1955	1956	1957	1958	1959	1960	1961	1962	1963
Population '000	**119**					**118**					**114**
Proved Offences—Drunkenness											
Males											
Under 18	x	x	4	5	12	11	4	7	8	11	5
18 and under 21	14	24	13	36	28	35	28	40	36	38	44
21 and under 30	59	67	61	72	56	67	57	65	49	71	64
30 and under 60	98	101	87	92	84	105	78	74	88	106	89
60 and over	13	14	6	9	7	7	1	7	6	14	12
All ages	**176**	**189**	**162**	**214**	**187**	**225**	**168**	**193**	**187**	**240**	**214**
Females											
Under 18		(Included in the number of persons by ages given above)					2	1	1		1
18 and under 21				2	1	2	4	3	1		3
21 and under 30				1	4	1	4		1	2	2
30 and under 60				4	1	5	5	9	2	7	6
60 and over				3		3	1	3	3	2	5
All ages	**8**	**17**	**9**	**10**	**6**	**11**	**16**	**16**	**7**	**11**	**17**
All Proved Offences	**184**	**206**	**171**	**224**	**193**	**236**	**184**	**209**	**194**	**251**	**231**
Motoring Offences											
Proceedings for:											
(a) Previously Convicted											
Unfit to drive											
Driving, undue alcohol											
Fail provide specimen											
(b) No Prev. Conviction											
Unfit to drive					16	12	8	15	19	26	23
Driving, undue alcohol											
Fail provide spec.											
In charge and:											
Unfit to drive							2	3		2	4
Undue alcohol											
Fail provide spec.											
Failure to provide breath specimen											
Total: All Proceedings	**26**	**15**	**13**	**27**	**16**	**12**	**10**	**18**	**19**	**28**	**27**
Licensed Premises											
Public Houses:											
Full	161					171					229
Beer and Cider	103					90					19
Wine or Cider											
Restaurant Licence											3
Residential Licence											1
Above Combined											
Licensed Clubs											4
Total On Licences	**264**					**261**					**256**
Off Licences	**119**					**124**					**129**
Total On/Off Licences	**383**					**385**					**385**
Registered Clubs	**51**					**47**					**46**
Total Licences & Clubs	**434**					**432**					**431**

TABLE III 57
DRUNKENNESS OFFENCES, MOTORING OFFENCES AND LICENCES, 1953-63
PRESTON POLICE DISTRICT

	1953	**1954**	**1955**	**1956**	**1957**	**1958**	**1959**	**1960**	**1961**	**1962**	**1963**
Population '000	**119**					**115**					**112**
Proved Offences—											
Drunkenness											
Males											
Under 18	x	x				2	4	1	2	10	13
18 and under 21	8	5	6	9	9	14	22	33	52	88	86
21 and under 30	16	22	20	33	17	40	43	60	69	119	134
30 and under 60	51	23	31	50	56	57	65	82	102	171	157
60 and over	7	12	5	5	3	5	1	5	7	15	17
All ages	**73**	**46**	**57**	**97**	**85**	**118**	**139**	**181**	**232**	**403**	**407**
Females											
Under 18		(Included in							1		1
18 and under 21		the number		1	2	2	2		1	5	2
21 and under 30		of persons		3	2	5	1	4	4	3	3
30 and under 60		by ages		1	3	4	3	9	4	10	14
60 and over		given above)		5	2		3		3	1	2
All ages	**9**	**16**	**5**	**10**	**9**	**11**	**9**	**13**	**13**	**19**	**22**
All Proved Offences	**82**	**62**	**62**	**107**	**94**	**129**	**148**	**194**	**245**	**422**	**429**
Motoring Offences											
Proceedings for:											
(a) Previously Convicted											
Unfit to drive											
Driving, undue alcohol											
Fail provide specimen											
(b) No Prev. Conviction											
Unfit to drive					11	16	14	33	40	25	29
Driving, undue alcohol											
Fail provide spec.											
In charge and:											
Unfit to drive					1	3	13	11	14	6	4
Undue alcohol											
Fail provide spec.											
Failure to provide breath specimen											
Total: All Proceedings	**3**	**7**	**4**	**21**	**12**	**19**	**27**	**44**	**54**	**31**	**33**
Licensed Premises											
Public Houses:											
Full	178					180					215
Beer and Cider	61					54					7
Wine or Cider											
Restaurant Licence											3
Residential Licence											
Above Combined											1
Licensed Clubs											3
Total On Licences	**239**					**234**					**229**
Off Licences	**84**					**83**					**86**
Total On/Off Licences	**323**					**317**					**315**
Registered Clubs	**52**					**56**					**53**
Total Licences & Clubs	**375**					**373**					**368**

TABLE III 58
DRUNKENNESS OFFENCES, MOTORING OFFENCES AND LICENCES, 1953–63
ROCHDALE POLICE DISTRICT

	1953	1954	1955	1956	1957	1958	1959	1960	1961	1962	1963
Population '000	**86**					**85**					**86**
Proved Offences— Drunkenness											
Males											
Under 18	x	x	1			1	1	1	9	6	1
18 and under 21	4	5	3	5	2	8	10	4	14	5	8
21 and under 30	20	21	26	15	18	20	17	21	33	26	16
30 and under 60	59	46	76	43	52	63	76	72	80	74	64
60 and over	11	10	10	4	8	8	9	6	11	6	7
All ages	**86**	**76**	**110**	**67**	**80**	**100**	**113**	**104**	**147**	**117**	**96**
Females											
Under 18		(Included in the number of persons by ages given above)						1		1	1
18 and under 21				3	1	1			1	2	1
21 and under 30						4	4		1	3	
30 and under 60				3	2	2	3	4	3		
60 and over					1	2		2	4	1	5
All ages	**8**	**6**	**6**	**6**	**4**	**9**	**7**	**7**	**9**	**7**	**7**
All Proved Offences	**94**	**82**	**116**	**73**	**84**	**109**	**120**	**111**	**156**	**124**	**103**
Motoring Offences											
Proceedings for:											
(a) Previously Convicted											
Unfit to drive											
Driving, undue alcohol											
Fail provide specimen											
(b) No Prev. Conviction											
Unfit to drive					3	3	13	8	9	9	6
Driving, undue alcohol											
Fail provide spec.											
In charge and:											
Unfit to drive					2	1	2	3	1	1	1
Undue alcohol											
Fail provide spec.											
Failure to provide breath specimen											
Total: All Proceedings	**6**	**8**	**5**	**4**	**5**	**4**	**15**	**11**	**10**	**10**	**7**
Licensed Premises											
Public Houses:											
Full	130					133					161
Beer and Cider	55					44					11
Wine or Cider	1					1					
Restaurant Licence											
Residential Licence											
Above Combined											
Licensed Clubs											
Total On Licences	**186**					**178**					**172**
Off Licences	**88**					**88**					**87**
Total On/Off Licences	**274**					**266**					**259**
Registered Clubs	**53**					**51**					**53**
Total Licences & Clubs	**327**					**317**					**312**

TABLE III 59
DRUNKENNESS OFFENCES, MOTORING OFFENCES AND LICENCES, 1953–63
ST. HELENS POLICE DISTRICT

	1953	1954	1955	1956	1957	1958	1959	1960	1961	1962	1963
Population '000	**108**					**111**					**107**
Proved Offences—Drunkenness											
Males											
Under 18	x	x	1	5	5	4	1	4	2	1	5
18 and under 21	1	7	3	11	5	6	5	2	11	11	19
21 and under 30	13	16	19	36	21	10	12	5	21	8	31
30 and under 60	25	43	37	42	34	29	38	24	26	21	30
60 and over	4	3	4	3	10	4	5	1	4	2	2
All ages	**41**	**66**	**63**	**97**	**75**	**53**	**61**	**36**	**64**	**43**	**87**
Females											
Under 18		(Included in				1					
18 and under 21		the number									2
21 and under 30		of persons					1				1
30 and under 60		by ages			1		2				1
60 and over		given above)		2		1	1				1
All ages	**2**	**3**	**1**	**2**	**1**	**2**	**4**				**5**
All Proved Offences	**43**	**69**	**64**	**99**	**76**	**55**	**65**	**36**	**64**	**43**	**92**
Motoring Offences											
Proceedings for:											
(a) Previously Convicted											
Unfit to drive											
Driving, undue alcohol											
Fail provide specimen											
(b) No Prev. Conviction											
Unfit to drive					3	2	6	10	5	11	6
Driving, undue alcohol											
Fail provide spec.											
In charge and:											
Unfit to drive					3	1	4	2	3	1	3
Undue alcohol											
Fail provide spec.											
Failure to provide breath specimen											
Total: All Proceedings	**2**	**3**	**3**	**7**	**6**	**3**	**10**	**12**	**8**	**12**	**9**
Licensed Premises											
Public Houses:											
Full	118					121					131
Beer and Cider	20					16					7
Wine or Cider											
Restaurant Licence											2
Residential Licence											
Above Combined											
Licensed Clubs											
Total On Licences	**138**					**137**					**140**
Off Licences	**25**					**25**					**30**
Total On/Off Licences	**163**					**162**					**170**
Registered Clubs	**45**					**53**					**58**
Total Licences & Clubs	**208**					**215**					**228**

TABLE III 60
DRUNKENNESS OFFENCES, MOTORING OFFENCES AND LICENCES, 1953–63
SALFORD POLICE DISTRICT

	1953	1954	1955	1956	1957	1958	1959	1960	1961	1962	1963
Population '000	**174**					**164**					**153**
Proved Offences—Drunkenness											
Males											
Under 18	x	x	35	23	25	25	30	50	37	11	26
18 and under 21	57	89	101	84	90	82	93	146	147	114	121
21 and under 30	200	187	200	252	181	206	157	232	231	205	198
30 and under 60	313	313	342	435	423	428	378	397	377	334	330
60 and over	29	23	44	40	36	37	21	19	24	21	25
All ages	**551**	**558**	**666**	**834**	**755**	**778**	**679**	**844**	**816**	**685**	**700**
Females											
Under 18		(Included in			1	1			5	1	
18 and under 21		the number		4	3		1	1	2	3	6
21 and under 30		of persons		15	5	3	6	3	11	5	5
30 and under 60		by ages		23	30	17	30	21	18	18	20
60 and over		given above)		3	7	12	10	14	9	4	2
All ages	**48**	**54**	**56**	**45**	**46**	**33**	**47**	**39**	**45**	**31**	**33**
All Proved Offences	**599**	**612**	**722**	**879**	**801**	**811**	**726**	**883**	**861**	**716**	**733**
Motoring Offences											
Proceedings for:											
(a) Previously Convicted											
Unfit to drive											
Driving, undue alcohol											
Fail provide specimen											
(b) No Prev. Conviction											
Unfit to drive					46	54	64	87	114	89	109
Driving, undue alcohol											
Fail provide spec.											
In charge and:											
Unfit to drive					15	10	11	10	19	16	23
Undue alcohol											
Fail provide spec.											
Failure to provide breath specimen											
Total: All Proceedings	**30**	**44**	**58**	**63**	**61**	**64**	**75**	**97**	**133**	**105**	**132**
Licensed Premises											
Public Houses:											
Full	105					99					199
Beer and Cider	208					197					71
Wine or Cider											
Restaurant Licence											1
Residential Licence											1
Above Combined											
Licensed Clubs											2
Total On Licences	**313**					**296**					**274**
Off Licences	**373**					**336**					**310**
Total On/Off Licences	**686**					**632**					**584**
Registered Clubs	**43**					**46**					**48**
Total Licences & Clubs	**729**					**678**					**632**

TABLE III 61
DRUNKENNESS OFFENCES, MOTORING OFFENCES AND LICENCES, 1953–63 SOUTHPORT POLICE DISTRICT

	1953	1954	1955	1956	1957	1958	1959	1960	1961	1962	1963
Population '000	**82**					**82**					**80**
Proved Offences— Drunkenness											
Males											
Under 18	x	x		1					1		1
18 and under 21	7	7	5	3	3	4	2	2	5	1	
21 and under 30	10	8	2	6	11	3	3	8	6	4	11
30 and under 60	10	14	16	16	9	5	19	7	13	17	19
60 and over	3	4	1	2	1	2	2			2	2
All ages	**28**	**28**	**21**	**28**	**24**	**14**	**26**	**17**	**25**	**24**	**33**
Females											
Under 18		(Included in									
18 and under 21		the number									
21 and under 30		of persons			1					1	
30 and under 60		by ages		3	2	1				1	1
60 and over		given above)						1			
All ages	**2**	**5**	**3**	**3**	**3**	**1**		**1**		**2**	**1**
All Proved Offences	**30**	**33**	**24**	**31**	**27**	**15**	**26**	**18**	**25**	**26**	**34**
Motoring Offences											
Proceedings for:											
(a) Previously Convicted											
Unfit to drive											
Driving, undue alcohol											
Fail provide specimen											
(b) No Prev. Conviction											
Unfit to drive					4	2	2	1	7	2	3
Driving, undue alcohol											
Fail provide spec.											
In charge and:											
Unfit to drive					1	1	1	3	2	4	2
Undue alcohol											
Fail provide spec.											
Failure to provide breath specimen											
Total: All Proceedings	**7**	**3**	**3**	**10**	**5**	**3**	**3**	**4**	**9**	**6**	**5**
Licensed Premises											
Public Houses:											
Full	44					46					48
Beer and Cider	7					3					
Wine or Cider											
Restaurant Licence											7
Residential Licence											8
Above Combined											3
Licensed Clubs											1
Total On Licences	**51**					**49**					**67**
Off Licences	**58**					**55**					**55**
Total On/Off Licences	**109**					**104**					**122**
Registered Clubs	**64**					**43**					**57**
Total Licences & Clubs	**173**					**147**					**179**

TABLE III 62
DRUNKENNESS OFFENCES, MOTORING OFFENCES AND LICENCES, 1953-63
WARRINGTON POLICE DISTRICT

	1953	1954	1955	1956	1957	1958	1959	1960	1961	1962	1963
Population '000	**80**					**79**					**76**
Proved Offences—Drunkenness											
Males											
Under 18	x	x	2	3		3	1	2	1		2
18 and under 21	7	6	5	3	9	11	5	4	5	7	7
21 and under 30	24	26	20	22	27	20	16	12	17	13	16
30 and under 60	32	51	42	44	83	52	64	77	59	68	54
60 and over	7	6	6	3	12	1	9	3	7	6	10
All ages	**63**	**84**	**70**	**75**	**131**	**87**	**95**	**98**	**89**	**94**	**89**
Females											
Under 18		(Included in the number of persons by ages given above)									1
18 and under 21				3		2	2				2
21 and under 30				2		2	1				1
30 and under 60					4	2	1		1	2	2
60 and over				1				1			
All ages	**7**	**5**	**5**	**6**	**4**	**6**	**4**	**1**	**1**	**2**	**6**
All Proved Offences	**70**	**89**	**75**	**81**	**135**	**93**	**99**	**99**	**90**	**96**	**95**
Motoring Offences											
Proceedings for:											
(a) Previously Convicted											
Unfit to drive											
Driving, undue alcohol											
Fail provide specimen											
(b) No Prev. Conviction											
Unfit to drive					22	13	11	8	6	5	10
Driving, undue alcohol											
Fail provide spec.											
In charge and:											
Unfit to drive					4	6	1	5	7	5	1
Undue alcohol											
Fail provide spec.											
Failure to provide breath specimen											
Total: All Proceedings	**5**	**11**	**19**	**22**	**26**	**19**	**12**	**13**	**13**	**10**	**11**
Licensed Premises											
Public Houses:											
Full	70					72					84
Beer and Cider	21					17					7
Wine or Cider											
Restaurant Licence											3
Residential Licence											
Above Combined											
Licensed Clubs											
Total On Licences	**91**					**89**					**94**
Off Licences	**72**					**72**					**72**
Total On/Off Licences	**163**					**161**					**166**
Registered Clubs	**51**					**49**					**44**
Total Licences & Clubs	**214**					**210**					**210**

TABLE III 63
DRUNKENNESS OFFENCES, MOTORING OFFENCES AND LICENCES, 1953-63
WIGAN POLICE DISTRICT

	1953	1954	1955	1956	1957	1958	1959	1960	1961	1962	1963
Population '000	**83**					**81**					**79**
Proved Offences— Drunkenness											
Males											
Under 18	x	x	2		1		1		3		1
18 and under 21	4	2	5	3	4	2	5	3	14	9	4
21 and under 30	17	20	20	24	27	18	14	11	19	18	8
30 and under 60	49	41	46	50	57	50	23	31	38	23	27
60 and over	5	4	5	7	9	8	7	2	3	5	4
All ages	**69**	**63**	**75**	**84**	**98**	**78**	**50**	**47**	**77**	**55**	**44**
Females											
Under 18		(Included in									
18 and under 21		the number				1				1	
21 and under 30		of persons			1					1	
30 and under 60		by ages		2	2	1	2	3	2	6	1
60 and over		given above)			2				1		
All ages	**6**	**4**	**3**	**2**	**5**	**2**	**2**	**3**	**3**	**8**	**1**
All Proved Offences	**75**	**67**	**78**	**86**	**103**	**80**	**52**	**50**	**80**	**63**	**45**
Motoring Offences											
Proceedings for:											
(a) Previously Convicted											
Unfit to drive											
Driving, undue alcohol											
Fail provide specimen											
(b) No Prev. Conviction											
Unfit to drive					6	1	5	2	9	3	10
Driving, undue alcohol											
Fail provide spec.											
In charge and:											
Unfit to drive							2		2	2	5
Undue alcohol											
Fail provide spec.											
Failure to provide breath specimen											
Total: All Proceedings	**8**	**8**	**14**	**8**	**6**	**1**	**7**	**2**	**11**	**5**	**15**
Licensed Premises											
Public Houses:											
Full	120					122					128
Beer and Cider	31					23					12
Wine or Cider	1										
Restaurant Licence											2
Residential Licence											
Above Combined											
Licensed Clubs											
Total On Licences	**152**					**145**					**142**
Off Licences	**55**					**56**					**58**
Total On/Off Licences	**207**					**201**					**200**
Registered Clubs	**46**					**52**					**51**
Total Licences & Clubs	**253**					**253**					**251**

TABLE III 64
DRUNKENNESS OFFENCES, MOTORING OFFENCES AND LICENCES, 1953-63
LEICESTERSHIRE AND RUTLAND POLICE DISTRICT

	1953	1954	1955	1956	1957	1958	1959	1960	1961	1962	1963
Population '000	**374**					**381**					**452**
Proved Offences—Drunkenness											
Males											
Under 18	x	x	3	2		1	1	3	4	3	
18 and under 21	2	8	4	8	7	11	5	9	6	9	8
21 and under 30	16	5	14	38	21	17	22	12	20	18	14
30 and under 60	41	43	48	47	28	20	38	26	26	27	35
60 and over	6	2	6	1	3	5	6		4	5	2
All ages	**61**	**57**	**75**	**96**	**59**	**54**	**72**	**50**	**60**	**62**	**59**
Females											
Under 18		(Included in the number of persons by ages given above)									
18 and under 21											
21 and under 30						3	2		2		
30 and under 60					2	1	1	1		3	2
60 and over					1						2
All ages	**4**	**1**			**3**	**4**	**3**	**1**	**2**	**3**	**4**
All Proved Offences	**65**	**58**	**75**	**96**	**62**	**58**	**75**	**51**	**62**	**65**	**63**
Motoring Offences											
Proceedings for:											
(a) Previously Convicted											
Unfit to drive											
Driving, undue alcohol											
Fail provide specimen											
(b) No Prev. Conviction											
Unfit to drive					11	9	10	19	22	12	28
Driving, undue alcohol											
Fail provide spec.											
In charge and:											
Unfit to drive					7	5	2	9	9	6	7
Undue alcohol											
Fail provide spec.											
Failure to provide breath specimen											
Total: All Proceedings	**16**	**22**	**11**	**13**	**18**	**14**	**12**	**28**	**31**	**18**	**35**
Licensed Premises											
Public Houses:											
Full	788					716					809
Beer and Cider	60					31					4
Wine or Cider											
Restaurant Licence											12
Residential Licence											
Above Combined											5
Licensed Clubs											6
Total On Licences	**848**					**747**					**836**
Off Licences	**279**					**269**					**319**
Total On/Off Licences	**1127**					**1016**					**1155**
Registered Clubs	**183**					**199**					**216**
Total Licences & Clubs	**1310**					**1215**					**1371**

TABLE III 65
DRUNKENNESS OFFENCES, MOTORING OFFENCES AND LICENCES, 1953–63
CITY OF LEICESTER POLICE DISTRICT

	1953	1954	1955	1956	1957	1958	1959	1960	1961	1962	1963
Population '000	**287**					**278**					**270**
Proved Offences—											
Drunkenness											
Males											
Under 18	x	x	4	2	5		3	6	8	1	3
18 and under 21	5	8	6	4	18	8	22	12	27	12	21
21 and under 30	36	40	42	36	46	44	50	37	43	49	44
30 and under 60	99	99	118	126	104	111	143	149	156	159	150
60 and over	19	15	18	10	16	22	32	38	31	27	20
All ages	**151**	**150**	**174**	**178**	**189**	**185**	**250**	**242**	**265**	**248**	**238**
Females											
Under 18			(Included in							1	2
18 and under 21			the number	1	1					2	1
21 and under 30			of persons	2	4	1			2	1	4
30 and under 60			by ages	9	6	6	12	4	3	8	13
60 and over			given above)	2	5	4		2	1	4	7
All ages	**8**	**12**	**14**	**14**	**16**	**11**	**12**	**6**	**6**	**16**	**27**
All Proved Offences	**159**	**162**	**188**	**192**	**205**	**196**	**262**	**248**	**271**	**264**	**265**
Motoring Offences											
Proceedings for:											
(a) Previously Convicted											
Unfit to drive											
Driving, undue alcohol											
Fail provide specimen											
(b) No Prev. Conviction											
Unfit to drive					7	14	17	17	25	21	31
Driving, undue alcohol											
Fail provide spec.											
In charge and:											
Unfit to drive								2	12	9	6
Undue alcohol											
Fail provide spec.											
Failure to provide breath specimen											
Total: All Proceedings	**11**	**14**	**18**	**9**	**7**	**14**	**17**	**19**	**37**	**30**	**37**
Licensed Premises											
Public Houses:											
Full	232					235					235
Beer and Cider	50					30					4
Wine or Cider	2					2					2
Restaurant Licence											15
Residential Licence											2
Above Combined											2
Licensed Clubs											4
Total On Licences	**284**					**267**					**264**
Off Licences	**359**					**337**					**307**
Total On/Off Licences	**643**					**604**					**571**
Registered Clubs	**89**					**94**					**98**
Total Licences & Clubs	**732**					**698**					**669**

TABLE III 66
DRUNKENNESS OFFENCES, MOTORING OFFENCES AND LICENCES, 1953–63
LINCOLNSHIRE (HOLLAND) POLICE DISTRICT

	1953	1954	1955	1956	1957	1958	1959	1960	1961	1962	1963
Population '000	**101**					**103**					**105**
Proved Offences—Drunkenness											
Males											
Under 18	x	x			1			4	1	3	
18 and under 21	1	2		2	5	2		3	7	8	8
21 and under 30	10	8	16	6	8	9	8	7	8	9	4
30 and under 60	29	28	29	24	26	42	29	28	31	32	39
60 and over	4	3	6	5	1	3	2	5	1	2	3
All ages	**44**	**41**	**50**	**37**	**41**	**56**	**39**	**47**	**48**	**54**	**54**
Females											
Under 18		(Included in the number of persons by ages given above)									
18 and under 21					1				1		
21 and under 30					1						
30 and under 60											1
60 and over											
All ages			**1**		**2**				**1**		**1**
All Proved Offences	**44**	**41**	**51**	**37**	**43**	**56**	**39**	**47**	**49**	**54**	**55**
Motoring Offences											
Proceedings for:											
(a) Previously Convicted											
Unfit to drive											
Driving, undue alcohol											
Fail provide specimen											
(b) No Prev. Conviction											
*Unfit to drive					46	42	36	43	42	36	33
Driving, undue alcohol											
Fail provide spec.											
In charge and:											
*Unfit to drive					12	4	7	17	11	15	20
Undue alcohol											
Fail provide spec.											
Failure to provide breath specimen											
***Total: All Proceedings**	**45**	**27**	**41**	**48**	**58**	**46**	**43**	**60**	**53**	**51**	**53**
Licensed Premises											
Public Houses:											
Full	299					290					284
Beer and Cider	91					35					3
Wine or Cider											
Restaurant Licence											4
Residential Licence											
Above Combined											
Licensed Clubs											4
Total On Licences	**390**					**325**					**295**
Off Licences	**46**					**51**					**59**
Total On/Off Licences	**436**					**376**					**354**
Registered Clubs	**47**					**53**					**58**
Total Licences & Clubs	**483**					**429**					**416**

*All Lincolnshire

TABLE III 67
DRUNKENNESS OFFENCES, MOTORING OFFENCES AND LICENCES, 1953–63
LINCOLNSHIRE (KESTEVEN) POLICE DISTRICT

	1953	1954	1955	1956	1957	1958	1959	1960	1961	1962	1963
Population '000	**133**					**134**					**142**
Proved Offences—Drunkenness											
Males											
Under 18	x	x					2		1		1
18 and under 21	2	3	2	1	3	5	3	6	8	1	5
21 and under 30	11	13	7	7	11	4	2	3	11	4	8
30 and under 60	51	26	35	63	30	18	31	22	25	23	18
60 and over	2	7	11	4	2	4	3	1	1		5
All ages	**66**	**49**	**55**	**75**	**46**	**31**	**41**	**32**	**46**	**28**	**37**
Females											
Under 18	(Included in										
18 and under 21	the number										
21 and under 30	of persons					1					
30 and under 60	by ages			1			1		2		1
60 and over	given above)			1							
All ages				**2**		**1**	**1**		**2**		**1**
All Proved Offences	**66**	**49**	**55**	**77**	**46**	**32**	**42**	**32**	**48**	**28**	**38**
Motoring Offences											
Proceedings for:											
(a) Previously Convicted											
Unfit to drive	See LINCOLNSHIRE (HOLLAND)										
Driving, undue alcohol											
Fail provide specimen											
(b) No Prev. Conviction											
Unfit to drive											
Driving, undue alcohol											
Fail provide spec.											
In charge and:											
Unfit to drive											
Undue alcohol											
Fail provide spec.											
Failure to provide breath specimen											
Total: All Proceedings	See LINCOLNSHIRE (HOLLAND)										
Licensed Premises											
Public Houses:											
Full	379					359					310
Beer and Cider	53					20					6
Wine or Cider											
Restaurant Licence											9
Residential Licence											
Above Combined											1
Licensed Clubs											1
Total On Licences	**432**					**379**					**327**
Off Licences	**49**					**50**					**57**
Total On/Off Licences	**481**					**429**					**384**
Registered Clubs	**59**					**63**					**67**
Total Licences & Clubs	**540**					**492**					**451**

TABLE III 68
DRUNKENNESS OFFENCES, MOTORING OFFENCES AND LICENCES, 1953-63
LINCOLNSHIRE (LINDSEY) POLICE DISTRICT

	1953	1954	1955	1956	1957	1958	1959	1960	1961	1962	1963
Population '000	**312**					**320**					**344**
Proved Offences—											
Drunkenness											
Males											
Under 18	x	x		7	8	5	5	7	15	10	5
18 and under 21	10	15	11	15	18	19	24	35	38	57	24
21 and under 30	45	63	34	52	63	41	61	43	49	73	53
30 and under 60	103	83	83	122	104	91	96	112	129	147	115
60 and over	5	10	3	6	11	10	7	11	7	8	3
All ages	**161**	**163**	**128**	**202**	**204**	**166**	**193**	**208**	**238**	**295**	**200**
Females											
Under 18		(Included in								1	1
18 and under 21		the number								1	
21 and under 30		of persons				1		2		1	5
30 and under 60		by ages		4	5	2	3	10	4	4	1
60 and over		given above)		1		1	3	1			
All ages	**2**	**8**	**3**	**5**	**5**	**4**	**6**	**13**	**4**	**7**	**7**
All Proved Offences	**163**	**171**	**131**	**207**	**209**	**170**	**199**	**221**	**242**	**302**	**207**
Motoring Offences											
Proceedings for:											
(a) Previously Convicted											
Unfit to drive						See LINCOLNSHIRE (HOLLAND)					
Driving, undue alcohol											
Fail provide specimen											
(b) No Prev. Conviction											
Unfit to drive											
Driving, undue alcohol											
Fail provide spec.											
In charge and:											
Unfit to drive											
Undue alcohol											
Fail provide spec.											
Failure to provide breath specimen											
Total: All Proceedings						See LINCOLNSHIRE (HOLLAND)					
Licensed Premises											
Public Houses:											
Full	517					514					571
Beer and Cider	69					34					1
Wine or Cider	4					4					
Restaurant Licence											26
Residential Licence											4
Above Combined											10
Licensed Clubs											5
Total On Licences	**590**					**552**					**617**
Off Licences	**140**					**151**					**175**
Total On/Off Licences	**730**					**703**					**792**
Registered Clubs	**134**					**164**					**158**
Total Licences & Clubs	**864**					**867**					**950**

TABLE III 69
DRUNKENNESS OFFENCES, MOTORING OFFENCES AND LICENCES, 1953–63
GRIMSBY POLICE DISTRICT

	1953	1954	1955	1956	1957	1958	1959	1960	1961	1962	1963
Population '000	**93**					**96**					**96**
Proved Offences—Drunkenness											
Males											
Under 18	x	x	3	8	4	7	9	15	7	13	19
18 and under 21	25	15	26	14	15	22	32	25	28	35	28
21 and under 30	92	64	58	96	71	73	67	64	62	59	81
30 and under 60	129	136	109	192	157	142	128	157	193	168	155
60 and over	18	17	9	4	11	5	5	13	7	3	11
All ages	**251**	**222**	**196**	**314**	**258**	**249**	**241**	**174**	**297**	**278**	**294**
Females											
Under 18		(Included in		2	1					1	3
18 and under 21		the number		2			1				1
21 and under 30		of persons		2	1		3	2	2		1
30 and under 60		by ages		8	7	9	1	8	8	2	5
60 and over		given above)					2		1	1	
All ages	**13**	**10**	**9**	**14**	**9**	**9**	**7**	**10**	**11**	**4**	**10**
All Proved Offences	**264**	**232**	**205**	**328**	**267**	**258**	**248**	**184**	**308**	**282**	**304**
Motoring Offences											
Proceedings for:											
(a) Previously Convicted											
Unfit to drive											
Driving, undue alcohol											
Fail provide specimen											
(b) No Prev. Conviction											
Unfit to drive					9	15	23	17	19	21	14
Driving, undue alcohol											
Fail provide spec.											
In charge and:											
Unfit to drive					4	3	1		2	8	3
Undue alcohol											
Fail provide spec.											
Failure to provide breath specimen											
Total: All Proceedings	**7**	**6**	**7**	**10**	**13**	**18**	**24**	**17**	**21**	**29**	**17**
Licensed Premises											
Public Houses:											
Full	46					42					58
Beer and Cider	29					20					
Wine or Cider											
Restaurant Licence											4
Residential Licence											
Above Combined											1
Licensed Clubs											
Total On Licences	**75**					**62**					**63**
Off Licences	**64**					**58**					**57**
Total On/Off Licences	**139**					**120**					**120**
Registered Clubs	**54**					**57**					**57**
Total Licences & Clubs	**193**					**177**					**177**

TABLE III 70
DRUNKENNESS OFFENCES, MOTORING OFFENCES AND LICENCES, 1953-63
CITY OF LINCOLN POLICE DISTRICT

	1953	1954	1955	1956	1957	1958	1959	1960	1961	1962	1963
Population '000	**70**					**72**					**77**
Proved Offences—Drunkenness											
Males											
Under 18	x	x	1	3			1			1	
18 and under 21	2	1	1	1	2	6	8	15	9	6	5
21 and under 30	9	14	16	10	14	13	22	18	14	26	12
30 and under 60	32	35	35	31	20	28	28	25	21	21	16
60 and over	2	1	3	9	1	4	2	3	2	1	2
All ages	**45**	**51**	**53**	**54**	**37**	**51**	**61**	**61**	**46**	**55**	**35**
Females											
Under 18		(Included in									1
18 and under 21		the number									
21 and under 30		of persons									
30 and under 60		by ages		2			3				
60 and over		given above)									
All ages			**3**	**2**			**3**				**1**
All Proved Offences	**45**	**51**	**56**	**56**	**37**	**51**	**64**	**61**	**46**	**55**	**36**
Motoring Offences											
Proceedings for:											
(a) Previously Convicted											
Unfit to drive											
Driving, undue alcohol											
Fail provide specimen											
(b) No Prev. Conviction											
Unfit to drive					2	4	3	3	5	6	5
Driving, undue alcohol											
Fail provide spec.											
In charge and:											
Unfit to drive							2		3		
Undue alcohol											
Fail provide spec.											
Failure to provide breath specimen											
Total: All Proceedings	**2**	**7**	**5**	**4**	**2**	**4**	**5**	**3**	**8**	**6**	**5**
Licensed Premises											
Public Houses:											
Full	94					98					98
Beer and Cider	9					5					
Wine or Cider											
Restaurant Licence											1
Residential Licence											
Above Combined											2
Licensed Clubs											1
Total On Licences	**103**					**103**					**102**
Off Licences	**73**					**71**					**72**
Total On/Off Licences	**176**					**174**					**174**
Registered Clubs	**29**					**31**					**34**
Total Licences & Clubs	**205**					**205**					**208**

TABLE III 71
DRUNKENNESS OFFENCES, MOTORING OFFENCES AND LICENCES, 1953–63
CITY OF LONDON POLICE DISTRICT

	1953	1954	1955	1956	1957	1958	1959	1960	1961	1962	1963
Population '000	**5**					**5**					**5**
Proved Offences—											
Drunkenness											
Males											
Under 18	x	x	1			1			1	1	3
18 and under 21	3	5	3	3	2	2	2	4	3	4	7
21 and under 30	17	7	10	19	24	8	14	6	17	21	29
30 and under 60	96	80	99	113	126	109	126	104	134	140	157
60 and over	18	24	18	18	11	14	18	22	24	22	19
All ages	**121**	**100**	**121**	**153**	**163**	**134**	**160**	**136**	**179**	**188**	**215**
Females											
Under 18		(Included in									
18 and under 21		the number									
21 and under 30		of persons		1	3		1	1	2	1	1
30 and under 60		by ages		8	14	8	12	7	10	14	14
60 and over		given above)		2	3	7	6	2	6	5	5
All ages	**13**	**16**	**10**	**11**	**20**	**15**	**19**	**10**	**18**	**20**	**20**
All Proved Offences	**134**	**116**	**131**	**164**	**183**	**149**	**179**	**146**	**197**	**208**	**235**
Motoring Offences											
Proceedings for:											
(a) Previously Convicted											
Unfit to drive											
Driving, undue alcohol											
Fail provide specimen											
(b) No Prev. Conviction											
Unfit to drive					8	13	11	14	9	21	21
Driving, undue alcohol											
Fail provide spec.											
In charge and:											
Unfit to drive					4	5	4	3	6	4	9
Undue alcohol											
Fail provide spec.											
Failure to provide breath specimen											
Total: All Proceedings	**5**	**8**	**10**	**5**	**12**	**18**	**15**	**17**	**15**	**25**	**30**
Licensed Premises											
Public Houses:											
Full	297					212					217
Beer and Cider	19					10					5
Wine or Cider											
Restaurant Licence											14
Residential Licence											
Above Combined											
Licensed Clubs											19
Total On Licences	**316**					**222**					**255**
Off Licences	**119**					**95**					**93**
Total On/Off Licences	**435**					**317**					**348**
Registered Clubs	**102**					**117**					**84**
Total Licences & Clubs	**537**					**434**					**432**

TABLE III 72
DRUNKENNESS OFFENCES, MOTORING OFFENCES AND LICENCES, 1953-63
METROPOLITAN POLICE DISTRICT

	1953	1954	1955	1956	1957	1958	1959	1960	1961	1962	1963
Population '000	**6105**					**5993**					**5932**
Proved Offences—Drunkenness											
Males											
Under 18	x	x	81	123	125	105	121	169	156	171	168
18 and under 21	475	619	647	731	877	825	924	960	1177	1496	1450
21 and under 30	3527	3587	3545	3925	4786	4357	4723	4693	5248	6238	6323
30 and under 60	12761	13078	13627	14057	16867	16232	16950	16507	18072	22021	22069
60 and over	2079	2037	2003	1795	2112	1941	1871	1959	2131	2724	2676
All ages	**16132**	**16563**	**17327**	**20631**	**24767**	**23460**	**24589**	**24288**	**26784**	**32650**	**33226**
Females											
Under 18			(Included in	5	16	10	15	20	25	8	14
18 and under 21			the number	51	63	51	55	71	74	52	48
21 and under 30			of persons	366	343	335	285	265	275	258	253
30 and under 60			by ages	1749	1892	1804	1639	1617	1840	1880	1862
60 and over			given above)	443	495	565	462	412	399	378	380
All ages	**2710**	**2758**	**2576**	**2614**	**2809**	**2765**	**2456**	**2385**	**2613**	**2576**	**2557**
All Proved Offences	**18842**	**19321**	**19903**	**23245**	**27576**	**26225**	**27045**	**26673**	**29397**	**35226**	**35783**
Motoring Offences											
Proceedings for:											
(a) Previously Convicted											
Unfit to drive											
Driving, undue alcohol											
Fail provide specimen											
(b) No Prev. Conviction											
Unfit to drive					559	673	876	991	1184	1706	1952
Driving, undue alcohol											
Fail provide spec.											
In charge and:											
Unfit to drive					126	160	212	245	260	377	457
Undue alcohol											
Fail provide spec.											
Failure to provide breath specimen											
Total: All Proceedings	**516**	**581**	**551**	**697**	**685**	**833**	**1088**	**1236**	**1444**	**2083**	**2409**
Licensed Premises											
Public Houses:											
Full	5762					5349					5499
Beer and Cider	1041					598					120
Wine or Cider	51					28					10
Restaurant Licence											477
Residential Licence											17
Above Combined											50
Licensed Clubs											397
Total On Licences	**6854**					**5975**					**6370**
Off Licences	**3048**					**2804**					**2799**
Total On/Off Licences	**9902**					**8779**					**9169**
Registered Clubs	**2326**					**2580**					**1794**
Total Licences & Clubs	**12228**					**11359**					**10963**

TABLE III 73
DRUNKENNESS OFFENCES, MOTORING OFFENCES AND LICENCES, 1953–63
MONMOUTHSHIRE POLICE DISTRICT

	1953	1954	1955	1956	1957	1958	1959	1960	1961	1962	1963
Population '000	**319**					**328**					**343**
Proved Offences—											
Drunkenness											
Males											
Under 18	x	x	1	3	2	9	2	7	9	9	8
18 and under 21	5	15	13	21	15	16	18	26	28	31	26
21 and under 30	36	27	32	37	31	40	36	32	35	30	49
30 and under 60	52	41	53	53	45	53	39	45	47	44	32
60 and over	5	5	5	7	4	4	3	4	4	2	2
All ages	**96**	**80**	**104**	**121**	**97**	**122**	**98**	**114**	**123**	**116**	**117**
Females											
Under 18		(Included in								2	
18 and under 21		the number			1						
21 and under 30		of persons		3		1				1	
30 and under 60		by ages		5	2			2			1
60 and over		given above)				1					
All ages	**2**	**8**		**8**	**3**	**2**		**2**		**3**	**1**
All Proved Offences	**98**	**88**	**104**	**129**	**100**	**124**	**98**	**116**	**123**	**119**	**118**
Motoring Offences											
Proceedings for:											
(a) Previously Convicted											
Unfit to drive											
Driving, undue alcohol											
Fail provide specimen											
(b) No Prev. Conviction											
Unfit to drive					36	33	16	29	29	35	37
Driving, undue alcohol											
Fail provide spec.											
In charge and:											
Unfit to drive					7	11	2	8	10	5	10
Undue alcohol											
Fail provide spec.											
Failure to provide breath specimen											
Total: All Proceedings	**30**	**34**	**46**	**38**	**43**	**44**	**18**	**37**	**39**	**40**	**47**
Licensed Premises											
Public Houses:											
Full	550					558					601
Beer and Cider	121					87					12
Wine or Cider						2					2
Restaurant Licence											5
Residential Licence											
Above Combined											2
Licensed Clubs											7
Total On Licences	**671**					**647**					**629**
Off Licences	**83**					**93**					**120**
Total On/Off Licences	**754**					**740**					**749**
Registered Clubs	**208**					**222**					**222**
Total Licences & Clubs	**962**					**962**					**971**

TABLE III 74
DRUNKENNESS OFFENCES, MOTORING OFFENCES AND LICENCES, 1953–63
NEWPORT (MONMOUTHSHIRE) POLICE DISTRICT

	1953	1954	1955	1956	1957	1958	1959	1960	1961	1962	1963
Population '000	**105**					**104**					**109**
Proved Offences—Drunkenness											
Males											
Under 18	x	x	1	4	6	1	3	2	2	7	2
18 and under 21	19	16	19	17	19	10	10	25	15	19	15
21 and under 30	60	53	53	56	56	52	44	63	64	60	31
30 and under 60	114	140	114	143	141	149	160	248	214	141	127
60 and over	16	31	19	21	16	14	12	11	10	4	8
All ages	**197**	**228**	**196**	**241**	**238**	**226**	**229**	**349**	**305**	**231**	**183**
Females											
Under 18	(Included in the number of persons by ages given above)			1							
18 and under 21						2			1	1	4
21 and under 30				1		1	1	1			
30 and under 60				2	6	5	7	5	7	4	
60 and over					1	1				4	1
All ages	**12**	**12**	**10**	**4**	**7**	**9**	**8**	**6**	**8**	**9**	**5**
All Proved Offences	**209**	**240**	**206**	**245**	**245**	**235**	**237**	**355**	**313**	**240**	**188**
Motoring Offences											
Proceedings for:											
(a) Previously Convicted											
Unfit to drive											
Driving, undue alcohol											
Fail provide specimen											
(b) No Prev. Conviction											
Unfit to drive					13	9	13	12	14	12	17
Driving, undue alcohol											
Fail provide spec.											
In charge and:											
Unfit to drive					7	3	3	8	5	6	2
Undue alcohol											
Fail provide spec.											
Failure to provide breath specimen											
Total: All Proceedings	**6**	**8**	**13**	**9**	**20**	**12**	**16**	**20**	**19**	**18**	**19**
Licensed Premises											
Public Houses:											
Full	93					98					116
Beer and Cider	26					20					2
Wine or Cider											
Restaurant Licence											1
Residential Licence											
Above Combined											3
Licensed Clubs											
Total On Licences	**119**					**118**					**122**
Off Licences	**32**					**32**					**50**
Total On/Off Licences	**151**					**150**					**172**
Registered Clubs	**68**					**74**					**65**
Total Licences & Clubs	**219**					**224**					**237**

TABLE III 75
DRUNKENNESS OFFENCES, MOTORING OFFENCES AND LICENCES, 1953-63 NORFOLK POLICE DISTRICT

	1953	1954	1955	1956	1957	1958	1959	1960	1961	1962	1963
Population '000	**375**					**387**					**397**
Proved Offences—											
Drunkenness											
Males											
Under 18	x	x	2		1		1	2	7	1	5
18 and under 21	18	4	9	10	16	10	6	8	6	12	11
21 and under 30	24	25	23	22	17	29	16	17	12	12	9
30 and under 60	43	28	40	35	38	55	46	22	31	22	34
60 and over	12	7	9		3	9	6	2	7	7	3
All ages	**93**	**59**	**79**	**67**	**75**	**103**	**75**	**51**	**63**	**54**	**62**
Females											
Under 18		(Included in		1	1	1			2		1
18 and under 21		the number		1					1		1
21 and under 30		of persons		1	1	1	1			1	1
30 and under 60		by ages		1	1	1	1	1		3	1
60 and over		given above)								1	
All ages	**4**	**5**	**4**	**4**	**3**	**3**	**2**	**1**	**3**	**5**	**4**
All Proved Offences	**97**	**64**	**83**	**71**	**78**	**106**	**77**	**52**	**66**	**59**	**66**
Motoring Offences											
Proceedings for:											
(a) Previously Convicted											
Unfit to drive											
Driving, undue alcohol											
Fail provide specimen											
(b) No Prev. Conviction											
Unfit to drive					16	18	19	22	22	24	18
Driving, undue alcohol											
Fail provide spec.											
In charge and:											
Unfit to drive					1	4	3	14	11	7	11
Undue alcohol											
Fail provide spec.											
Failure to provide breath specimen											
Total: All Proceedings	**10**	**17**	**19**	**19**	**17**	**22**	**22**	**36**	**33**	**31**	**29**
Licensed Premises											
Public Houses:											
Full	1182					1161					1118
Beer and Cider	184					115					39
Wine or Cider	1					1					1
Restaurant Licence											17
Residential Licence											5
Above Combined											16
Licensed Clubs											14
Total On Licences	**1367**					**1277**					**1210**
Off Licences	**105**					**113**					**117**
Total On/Off Licences	**1472**					**1390**					**1327**
Registered Clubs	**153**					**165**					**137**
Total Licences & Clubs	**1625**					**1555**					**1464**

TABLE III 76
DRUNKENNESS OFFENCES, MOTORING OFFENCES AND LICENCES, 1953-63
GREAT YARMOUTH POLICE DISTRICT

	1953	1954	1955	1956	1957	1958	1959	1960	1961	1962	1963
Population '000	**51**					**51**					**53**
Proved Offences—Drunkenness											
Males											
Under 18	x	x	2			3	2	4	5		2
18 and under 21	7	11	12	6	12	15	17	3	4	10	7
21 and under 30	7	13	23	10	15	22	8	8	4	10	15
30 and under 60	17	20	30	24	24	9	29	16	12	18	18
60 and over	2	2	1	3	4	2	4	4	3	1	1
All ages	**31**	**45**	**68**	**43**	**55**	**51**	**60**	**35**	**28**	**39**	**33**
Females											
Under 18		(Included in the number of persons by ages given above)									
18 and under 21				1				1			2
21 and under 30											
30 and under 60				2	2	1	2				
60 and over											
All ages	**2**	**1**		**3**	**2**	**1**	**2**	**1**			**2**
All Proved Offences	**33**	**46**	**68**	**46**	**57**	**52**	**62**	**36**	**28**	**39**	**35**
Motoring Offences											
Proceedings for:											
(a) Previously Convicted											
Unfit to drive											
Driving, undue alcohol											
Fail provide specimen											
(b) No Prev. Conviction											
Unfit to drive					6	2	5		3	3	
Driving, undue alcohol											
Fail provide spec.											
In charge and:											
Unfit to drive						2		2	1	1	1
Undue alcohol											
Fail provide spec.											
Failure to provide breath specimen											
Total: All Proceedings	**1**	**5**	**5**	**5**	**6**	**4**	**5**	**2**	**4**	**4**	**1**
Licensed Premises											
Public Houses:											
Full	151					152					170
Beer and Cider	36					19					5
Wine or Cider											
Restaurant Licence											8
Residential Licence											80
Above Combined											16
Licensed Clubs											8
Total On Licences	**187**					**171**					**287**
Off Licences	**20**					**18**					**22**
Total On/Off Licences	**207**					**189**					**309**
Registered Clubs	**14**					**40**					**12**
Total Licences & Clubs	**221**					**229**					**321**

TABLE III 77
DRUNKENNESS OFFENCES, MOTORING OFFENCES AND LICENCES, 1953–63
NORWICH POLICE DISTRICT

	1953	1954	1955	1956	1957	1958	1959	1960	1961	1962	1963
Population '000	**121**					**119**					**119**
Proved Offences—											
Drunkenness											
Males											
Under 18	x	x	2	1			1	2	2	1	
18 and under 21	3	1	6	3	4	3	6	2	3	6	5
21 and under 30	4	12	12	8	3	8	7	4	9	7	6
30 and under 60	28	15	20	18	23	21	18	13	19	19	14
60 and over	4	4	2	3	2	6	4	2	6	13	6
All ages	**36**	**30**	**37**	**33**	**32**	**38**	**36**	**23**	**39**	**46**	**31**
Females											
Under 18		(Included in			1						
18 and under 21		the number			1				1	2	1
21 and under 30		of persons		1	1	2		1			
30 and under 60		by ages			2	1		1			
60 and over		given above)									
All ages	**3**	**2**	**5**	**1**	**5**	**3**		**2**	**1**	**2**	**1**
All Proved Offences	**39**	**32**	**42**	**34**	**37**	**41**	**36**	**25**	**40**	**48**	**32**
Motoring Offences											
Proceedings for:											
(a) Previously Convicted											
Unfit to drive											
Driving, undue alcohol											
Fail provide specimen											
(b) No Prev. Conviction											
Unfit to drive					4	10	10	8	7	10	7
Driving, undue alcohol											
Fail provide spec.											
In charge and:											
Unfit to drive					2	5	2	5	3	1	1
Undue alcohol											
Fail provide spec.											
Failure to provide breath specimen											
Total: All Proceedings	**4**	**4**	**9**	**2**	**6**	**15**	**12**	**13**	**10**	**11**	**8**
Licensed Premises											
Public Houses:											
Full	367					337					309
Beer and Cider	12					9					1
Wine or Cider	1					1					
Restaurant Licence											6
Residential Licence											
Above Combined											2
Licensed Clubs											3
Total On Licences	**380**					**347**					**321**
Off Licences	**35**					**34**					**37**
Total On/Off Licences	**415**					**381**					**358**
Registered Clubs	**40**					**45**					**33**
Total Licences & Clubs	**455**					**426**					**391**

TABLE III 78
DRUNKENNESS OFFENCES, MOTORING OFFENCES AND LICENCES, 1953-63
NORTHAMPTONSHIRE POLICE DISTRICT

	1953	1954	1955	1956	1957	1958	1959	1960	1961	1962	1963
Population '000	**263**					**284**					**306**
Proved Offences—											
Drunkenness											
Males											
Under 18	x	x	4		2	1	2	4	1	3	2
18 and under 21	7	4	4	2	4	9	8	8	10	16	3
21 and under 30	16	22	21	16	17	18	18	23	27	28	19
30 and under 60	39	58	52	54	51	53	52	38	73	68	45
60 and over	7	6	7	10	9	7	15	5	11	8	2
All ages	**65**	**86**	**82**	**82**	**83**	**88**	**95**	**78**	**122**	**123**	**77**
Females											
Under 18		(Included in the number of persons by ages given above)		1				1			
18 and under 21							1	2	2		
21 and under 30				1				3			1
30 and under 60				1	2	5	4	4	5	2	3
60 and over					1	1				1	
All ages	**4**	**4**	**6**	**3**	**3**	**6**	**5**	**10**	**7**	**3**	**4**
All Proved Offences	**69**	**90**	**88**	**85**	**86**	**94**	**100**	**88**	**129**	**126**	**81**
Motoring Offences											
Proceedings for:											
(a) Previously Convicted											
Unfit to drive											
Driving, undue alcohol											
Fail provide specimen											
(b) No Prev. Conviction											
Unfit to drive					12	15	22	29	29	30	26
Driving, undue alcohol											
Fail provide spec.											
In charge and:											
Unfit to drive					4	6	4	10	5	8	16
Undue alcohol											
Fail provide spec.											
Failure to provide breath specimen											
Total: All Proceedings	**18**	**22**	**29**	**35**	**16**	**21**	**26**	**39**	**34**	**38**	**42**
Licensed Premises											
Public Houses:											
Full	573					565					524
Beer and Cider	77					27					4
Wine or Cider	2					1					
Restaurant Licence											8
Residential Licence											
Above Combined											4
Licensed Clubs											20
Total On Licences	**652**					**593**					**560**
Off Licences	**265**					**259**					**268**
Total On/Off Licences	**917**					**852**					**828**
Registered Clubs	**136**					**141**					**151**
Total Licences & Clubs	**1053**					**993**					**979**

TABLE III 79
DRUNKENNESS OFFENCES, MOTORING OFFENCES AND LICENCES, 1953-63
NORTHAMPTON BOROUGH POLICE DISTRICT

	1953	1954	1955	1956	1957	1958	1959	1960	1961	1962	1963
Population '000	**104**					**101**					**105**
Proved Offences—Drunkenness											
Males											
Under 18	x	x		1				2	3	1	
18 and under 21	4	7	6	5	2	2		1	1	3	5
21 and under 30	11	29	25	23	13	8	15	16	14	14	10
30 and under 60	46	42	51	54	41	55	46	42	35	30	25
60 and over	3	6	2	5	8	5	6	5	6	2	2
All ages	**61**	**75**	**79**	**88**	**64**	**70**	**67**	**66**	**59**	**50**	**42**
Females											
Under 18		(Included in							1		
18 and under 21		the number			2		1	1			
21 and under 30		of persons		1		1	1			1	
30 and under 60		by ages			4	1	2		1	1	
60 and over		given above)							1	1	
All ages	**3**	**9**	**5**	**1**	**6**	**2**	**4**	**1**	**3**	**3**	
All Proved Offences	**64**	**84**	**84**	**89**	**70**	**72**	**71**	**67**	**62**	**53**	**42**
Motoring Offences											
Proceedings for:											
(a) Previously Convicted											
Unfit to drive											
Driving, undue alcohol											
Fail provide specimen											
(b) No Prev. Conviction											
Unfit to drive					9	12	14	8	15	20	7
Driving, undue alcohol											
Fail provide spec.											
In charge and:											
Unfit to drive					1	4	1	1	6	6	1
Undue alcohol											
Fail provide spec.											
Failure to provide breath specimen											
Total: All Proceedings	**3**	**4**	**6**	**11**	**10**	**16**	**15**	**9**	**21**	**26**	**8**
Licensed Premises											
Public Houses:											
Full	80					107					111
Beer and Cider	87					32					6
Wine or Cider	2					2					2
Restaurant Licence											6
Residential Licence											
Above Combined											
Licensed Clubs											2
Total On Licences	**169**					**141**					**127**
Off Licences	**183**					**175**					**148**
Total On/Off Licences	**352**					**316**					**275**
Registered Clubs	**36**					**38**					**44**
Total Licences & Clubs	**388**					**354**					**319**

TABLE III 80
DRUNKENNESS OFFENCES, MOTORING OFFENCES AND LICENCES, 1953-63
PETERBOROUGH POLICE DISTRICT

	1953	1954	1955	1956	1957	1958	1959	1960	1961	1962	1963
Population '000	**64**					**69**					**78**
Proved Offences—Drunkenness											
Males											
Under 18	x	x		1		1	1	4	1	1	
18 and under 21	1	1	4	3	3	5	7	14	10	5	4
21 and under 30	22	14	12	18	20	15	28	38	18	17	21
30 and under 60	38	30	21	48	61	70	71	89	63	52	60
60 and over	5	1	2		8	2	6	4	2	5	5
All ages	**66**	**46**	**37**	**70**	**92**	**93**	**113**	**149**	**94**	**80**	**90**
Females											
Under 18	(Included in							1			
18 and under 21	the number				1			1			
21 and under 30	of persons				1						
30 and under 60	by ages							1	1	2	
60 and over	given above)				1						
All ages			**2**		**3**			**3**	**1**	**2**	
All Proved Offences	**66**	**46**	**39**	**70**	**95**	**93**	**113**	**152**	**95**	**82**	**90**
Motoring Offences											
Proceedings for:											
(a) Previously Convicted											
Unfit to drive											
Driving, undue alcohol											
Fail provide specimen											
(b) No Prev. Conviction											
Unfit to drive					14	14	7	7	14	8	12
Driving, undue alcohol											
Fail provide spec.											
In charge and:											
Unfit to drive					1	3	2	1	3		4
Undue alcohol											
Fail provide spec.											
Failure to provide breath specimen											
Total: All Proceedings	**5**	**6**	**7**	**11**	**15**	**17**	**9**	**8**	**17**	**8**	**16**
Licensed Premises											
Public Houses:											
Full	121					120					118
Beer and Cider	8					4					
Wine or Cider											
Restaurant Licence											3
Residential Licence											
Above Combined											
Licensed Clubs											3
Total On Licences	**129**					**124**					**124**
Off Licences	**51**					**49**					**52**
Total On/Off Licences	**180**					**173**					**176**
Registered Clubs	**31**					**32**					**29**
Total Licences & Clubs	**211**					**205**					**205**

TABLE III 81
DRUNKENNESS OFFENCES, MOTORING OFFENCES AND LICENCES, 1953–63
NORTHUMBERLAND POLICE DISTRICT

	1953	1954	1955	1956	1957	1958	1959	1960	1961	1962	1963
Population '000	**441**					**470**					**491**
Proved Offences—Drunkenness											
Males											
Under 18	x	x	13	22	10	19	11	19	31	26	16
18 and under 21	57	64	71	75	75	76	84	87	74	132	114
21 and under 30	207	188	190	193	198	199	178	141	166	207	157
30 and under 60	337	303	293	310	443	362	324	296	286	332	340
60 and over	36	26	18	30	18	14	16	21	15	26	25
All ages	**602**	**556**	**563**	**630**	**744**	**670**	**613**	**564**	**572**	**723**	**652**
Females											
Under 18		(Included in		2	1	1	1				
18 and under 21		the number			6	3		1		3	2
21 and under 30		of persons		3	1	6	1	7	1	10	3
30 and under 60		by ages		23	26	24	17	13	20	15	15
60 and over		given above)		1	3		1	1	4	4	1
All ages	**35**	**25**	**22**	**29**	**37**	**34**	**20**	**22**	**25**	**32**	**21**
All Proved Offences	**637**	**581**	**585**	**659**	**781**	**704**	**633**	**586**	**597**	**755**	**673**
Motoring Offences											
Proceedings for:											
(a) Previously Convicted											
Unfit to drive											
Driving, undue alcohol											
Fail provide specimen											
(b) No Prev. Conviction											
Unfit to drive					57	54	72	71	108	83	68
Driving, undue alcohol											
Fail provide spec.											
In charge and:											
Unfit to drive					2	14	15	25	17	16	11
Undue alcohol											
Fail provide spec.											
Failure to provide breath specimen											
Total: All Proceedings	**54**	**52**	**53**	**66**	**59**	**68**	**87**	**96**	**125**	**99**	**79**
Licensed Premises											
Public Houses:											
Full	529					538					553
Beer and Cider	25					16					1
Wine or Cider											
Restaurant Licence											8
Residential Licence											3
Above Combined											7
Licensed Clubs											11
Total On Licences	**554**					**554**					**583**
Off Licences	**130**					**155**					**217**
Total On/Off Licences	**684**					**709**					**800**
Registered Clubs	**213**					**253**					**265**
Total Licences & Clubs	**897**					**962**					**1065**

TABLE III 82
DRUNKENNESS OFFENCES, MOTORING OFFENCES AND LICENCES, 1953-63
NEWCASTLE-UPON-TYNE POLICE DISTRICT

	1953	1954	1955	1956	1957	1958	1959	1960	1961	1962	1963
Population '000	**290**					**272**					**263**
Proved Offences—Drunkenness											
Males											
Under 18	x	x	24	14	18	23	18	36	53	49	60
18 and under 21	71	82	73	102	82	115	112	172	258	224	245
21 and under 30	457	423	318	318	317	265	250	353	484	522	453
30 and under 60	927	867	697	533	606	601	567	631	787	918	769
60 and over	62	61	69	55	45	45	64	54	82	69	52
All ages	**1397**	**1323**	**1073**	**1022**	**1068**	**1049**	**1011**	**1246**	**1664**	**1782**	**1579**
Females											
Under 18			(Included in			4		1	2		
18 and under 21			the number	2	8		3		9	5	6
21 and under 30			of persons	7	9	12	10	11	15	9	28
30 and under 60			by ages	48	47	38	39	41	49	50	43
60 and over			given above)	6	4	4	9	7	2	13	11
All ages	**120**	**110**	**108**	**63**	**68**	**58**	**61**	**60**	**77**	**77**	**88**
All Proved Offences	**1517**	**1433**	**1181**	**1085**	**1136**	**1107**	**1072**	**1306**	**1741**	**1859**	**1667**
Motoring Offences											
Proceedings for:											
(a) Previously Convicted											
Unfit to drive											
Driving, undue alcohol											
Fail provide specimen											
(b) No Prev. Conviction											
Unfit to drive					29	40	36	66	80	76	58
Driving, undue alcohol											
Fail provide spec.											
In charge and:											
Unfit to drive					8	14	6	17	11	4	14
Undue alcohol											
Fail provide spec.											
Failure to provide breath specimen											
Total: All Proceedings	**36**	**34**	**39**	**27**	**37**	**54**	**42**	**83**	**91**	**80**	**72**
Licensed Premises											
Public Houses:											
Full	276					279					276
Beer and Cider	31					21					7
Wine or Cider						1					
Restaurant Licence											14
Residential Licence											1
Above Combined											3
Licensed Clubs											8
Total On Licences	**307**					**301**					**309**
Off Licences	**159**					**160**					**179**
Total On/Off Licences	**466**					**461**					**488**
Registered Clubs	**152**					**174**					**142**
Total Licences & Clubs	**618**					**635**					**630**

TABLE III 83
DRUNKENNESS OFFENCES, MOTORING OFFENCES AND LICENCES, 1953–63
TYNEMOUTH POLICE DISTRICT

	1953	1954	1955	1956	1957	1958	1959	1960	1961	1962	1963
Population '000	**67**					**69**					**72**
Proved Offences—Drunkenness											
Males											
Under 18	x	x		5	5	3	4	10	3	6	6
18 and under 21	14	19	23	22	19	17	10	24	28	38	19
21 and under 30	15	60	61	60	51	56	33	46	55	61	48
30 and under 60	99	82	131	115	128	95	83	122	115	94	84
60 and over	4	2	4	3	4	1	6	3	3	10	2
All ages	**163**	**153**	**196**	**205**	**207**	**172**	**136**	**205**	**204**	**209**	**159**
Females											
Under 18		(Included in		2		1				2	
18 and under 21		the number				1	1	2	2	1	
21 and under 30		of persons		9	17	10	3	8	9	6	8
30 and under 60		by ages		11	16	13	8	10	18	16	10
60 and over		given above)				2					
All ages	**13**	**10**	**23**	**22**	**33**	**27**	**12**	**20**	**29**	**25**	**18**
All Proved Offences	**176**	**163**	**219**	**227**	**240**	**199**	**148**	**225**	**231**	**234**	**177**
Motoring Offences											
Proceedings for:											
(a) Previously Convicted											
Unfit to drive											
Driving, undue alcohol											
Fail provide specimen											
(b) No Prev. Conviction											
Unfit to drive					12	14	7	16	15	11	27
Driving, undue alcohol											
Fail provide spec.											
In charge and:											
Unfit to drive					2	3	2		6	1	1
Undue alcohol											
Fail provide spec.											
Failure to provide breath specimen											
Total: All Proceedings	**10**	**18**	**23**	**11**	**14**	**17**	**9**	**16**	**21**	**12**	**28**
Licensed Premises											
Public Houses:											
Full	95					95					95
Beer and Cider	9					7					3
Wine or Cider											
Restaurant Licence											
Residential Licence											1
Above Combined											
Licensed Clubs											2
Total On Licences	**104**					**102**					**101**
Off Licences	**42**					**46**					**61**
Total On/Off Licences	**146**					**148**					**162**
Registered Clubs	**32**					**33**					**42**
Total Licences & Clubs	**178**					**181**					**204**

TABLE III 84
DRUNKENNESS OFFENCES, MOTORING OFFENCES AND LICENCES, 1953-63
NOTTINGHAMSHIRE POLICE DISTRICT

	1953	1954	1955	1956	1957	1958	1959	1960	1961	1962	1963
Population '000	**541**					**570**					**611**
Proved Offences—Drunkenness											
Males											
Under 18	x	x	3	1	1		2		4	6	6
18 and under 21	3	11	9	7	19	15	10	15	15	10	10
21 and under 30	29	21	22	25	34	27	29	23	20	17	27
30 and under 60	56	49	63	41	58	53	45	37	42	55	49
60 and over	4	5	3	4	3	3	4	5	3	2	2
All ages	**91**	**83**	**98**	**78**	**115**	**98**	**90**	**80**	**84**	**90**	**94**
Females											
Under 18		(Included in the number of persons by ages given above)									
18 and under 21				1				1			2
21 and under 30							1				1
30 and under 60					2	3		1		1	3
60 and over											
All ages	**1**	**3**	**2**	**1**	**2**	**3**	**1**	**2**		**1**	**6**
All Proved Offences	**92**	**86**	**100**	**79**	**117**	**101**	**91**	**82**	**84**	**91**	**100**
Motoring Offences											
Proceedings for:											
(a) Previously Convicted											
Unfit to drive											
Driving, undue alcohol											
Fail provide specimen											
(b) No Prev. Conviction											
Unfit to drive					29	29	43	34	32	35	34
Driving, undue alcohol											
Fail provide spec.											
In charge and:											
Unfit to drive					2	1	4	7	8	4	4
Undue alcohol											
Fail provide spec.											
Failure to provide breath specimen											
Total: All Proceedings	**32**	**25**	**30**	**27**	**31**	**30**	**47**	**41**	**40**	**39**	**38**
Licensed Premises											
Public Houses:											
Full	688					710					733
Beer and Cider	27					20					8
Wine or Cider	3					2					1
Restaurant Licence											14
Residential Licence											1
Above Combined											3
Licensed Clubs											16
Total On Licences	**718**					**732**					**766**
Off Licences	**304**					**313**					**359**
Total On/Off Licences	**1022**					**1045**					**1135**
Registered Clubs	**268**					**282**					**260**
Total Licences & Clubs	**1290**					**1327**					**1395**

TABLE III 85
DRUNKENNESS OFFENCES, MOTORING OFFENCES AND LICENCES, 1953–63
NOTTINGHAM BOROUGH POLICE DISTRICT

	1953	**1954**	**1955**	**1956**	**1957**	**1958**	**1959**	**1960**	**1961**	**1962**	**1963**
Population '000	**312**					**313**					**315**
Proved Offences—											
Drunkenness											
Males											
Under 18	x	x			3	6		1	2	3	4
18 and under 21	21	16	18	12	20	9	11	14	21	21	22
21 and under 30	111	91	81	66	73	64	50	52	34	43	37
30 and under 60	170	196	176	143	148	176	126	143	122	152	115
60 and over	21	29	26	12	22	26	24	28	28	23	20
All ages	**296**	**305**	**265**	**233**	**266**	**281**	**211**	**238**	**207**	**242**	**198**
Females											
Under 18		(Included in				1				1	3
18 and under 21		the number		2	2	2	1		1	1	2
21 and under 30		of persons		8	4	1	1	2	6	2	1
30 and under 60		by ages		8	9	11	4	11	7	17	11
60 and over		given above)		2	4		1		1		5
All ages	**27**	**27**	**36**	**20**	**19**	**15**	**7**	**13**	**15**	**21**	**22**
All Proved Offences	**323**	**332**	**301**	**253**	**285**	**296**	**218**	**251**	**222**	**263**	**220**
Motoring Offences											
Proceedings for:											
(a) Previously Convicted											
Unfit to drive											
Driving, undue alcohol											
Fail provide specimen											
(b) No Prev. Conviction											
Unfit to drive					18	9	14	12	1		15
Driving, undue alcohol											
Fail provide spec.											
In charge and:											
Unfit to drive					4	4	5	18	30	26	5
Undue alcohol											
Fail provide spec.											
Failure to provide breath specimen											
Total: All Proceedings	**21**	**21**	**37**	**24**	**22**	**13**	**19**	**30**	**31**	**26**	**20**
Licensed Premises											
Public Houses:											
Full	358					364					387
Beer and Cider	37					28					7
Wine or Cider											
Restaurant Licence											10
Residential Licence											1
Above Combined											2
Licensed Clubs											14
Total On Licences	**395**					**392**					**421**
Off Licences	**414**					**408**					**408**
Total On/Off Licences	**809**					**800**					**829**
Registered Clubs	**81**					**82**					**72**
Total Licences & Clubs	**890**					**882**					**901**

TABLE III 86
DRUNKENNESS OFFENCES, MOTORING OFFENCES AND LICENCES, 1953-63
OXFORDSHIRE POLICE DISTRICT

	1953	1954	1955	1956	1957	1958	1959	1960	1961	1962	1963
Population '000	**189**					**194**					**217**
Proved Offences—Drunkenness											
Males											
Under 18	x	x	1			1	1	3	1	2	1
18 and under 21	7	6	6	4	2	8	8	2	6	10	9
21 and under 30	22	12	7	10	17	11	15	16	10	17	21
30 and under 60	46	31	32	40	32	34	52	40	51	25	29
60 and over	3	5	4	3	3	2	1	4	12		6
All ages	**74**	**51**	**45**	**57**	**54**	**56**	**77**	**65**	**80**	**54**	**66**
Females											
Under 18	(Included in the number of persons by ages given above)			1							
18 and under 21				1				2		1	1
21 and under 30				1	2	1			1	2	1
30 and under 60				1	1					2	1
60 and over							2				
All ages	**4**	**3**	**5**	**4**	**3**	**1**	**2**	**2**	**1**	**5**	**3**
All Proved Offences	**78**	**54**	**50**	**61**	**57**	**57**	**79**	**67**	**81**	**59**	**69**
Motoring Offences											
Proceedings for:											
(a) Previously Convicted											
Unfit to drive											
Driving, undue alcohol											
Fail provide specimen											
(b) No Prev. Conviction											
Unfit to drive					12	16	15	34	26	21	28
Driving, undue alcohol											
Fail provide spec.											
In charge and:											
Unfit to drive					11		6	1		1	4
Undue alcohol											
Fail provide spec.											
Failure to provide breath specimen											
Total: All Proceedings	**17**	**13**	**17**	**19**	**23**	**16**	**21**	**35**	**26**	**22**	**32**
Licensed Premises											
Public Houses:											
Full	574					594					659
Beer and Cider	143					93					9
Wine or Cider											
Restaurant Licence											6
Residential Licence											2
Above Combined											1
Licensed Clubs											2
Total On Licences	**717**					**687**					**679**
Off Licences	**70**					**73**					**96**
Total On/Off Licences	**787**					**760**					**767**
Registered Clubs	**75**					**86**					**96**
Total Licences & Clubs	**862**					**846**					**863**

TABLE III 87
DRUNKENNESS OFFENCES, MOTORING OFFENCES AND LICENCES, 1953–63
CITY OF OXFORD POLICE DISTRICT

	1953	1954	1955	1956	1957	1958	1959	1960	1961	1962	1963
Population '000	**107**					**104**					**107**
Proved Offences—Drunkenness											
Males											
Under 18	x	x	2	2		1	2	1			
18 and under 21	7	6	8	1	4	8	4	2	3	1	2
21 and under 30	17	21	21	22	22	12	16	23	14	20	8
30 and under 60	37	39	34	34	52	52	35	41	37	42	37
60 and over	6	4	4		3	3	3	5	4	3	5
All ages	**65**	**66**	**60**	**59**	**81**	**76**	**60**	**72**	**58**	**66**	**50**
Females											
Under 18		(Included in						1			
18 and under 21		the number		1	5	1	1				
21 and under 30		of persons		3	2	2	1		1	1	1
30 and under 60		by ages		1	2	2	4	6	2	1	3
60 and over		given above)					1				
All ages	**2**	**4**	**9**	**5**	**9**	**5**	**7**	**7**	**3**	**2**	**4**
All Proved Offences	**67**	**70**	**69**	**64**	**90**	**81**	**67**	**79**	**61**	**68**	**54**
Motoring Offences											
Proceedings for:											
(a) Previously Convicted											
Unfit to drive											
Driving, undue alcohol											
Fail provide specimen											
(b) No Prev. Conviction											
Unfit to drive					11	16	18	14	16	17	26
Driving, undue alcohol											
Fail provide spec.											
In charge and:											
Unfit to drive								10	6	12	7
Undue alcohol											
Fail provide spec.											
Failure to provide breath specimen											
Total: All Proceedings	**21**	**8**	**10**	**11**	**11**	**16**	**18**	**24**	**22**	**29**	**33**
Licensed Premises											
Public Houses:											
Full	143					149					169
Beer and Cider	35					21					
Wine or Cider	5					6					5
Restaurant Licence											7
Residential Licence											
Above Combined											1
Licensed Clubs											1
Total On Licences	**183**					**176**					**183**
Off Licences	**61**					**60**					**73**
Total On/Off Licences	**244**					**236**					**256**
Registered Clubs	**66**					**102**					**74**
Total Licences & Clubs	**310**					**338**					**330**

TABLE III 88
DRUNKENNESS OFFENCES, MOTORING OFFENCES AND LICENCES, 1953-63
SHROPSHIRE POLICE DISTRICT

	1953	1954	1955	1956	1957	1958	1959	1960	1961	1962	1963
Population '000	**299**					**299**					**307**
Proved Offences—											
Drunkenness											
Males											
Under 18	x	x	1	2	1		3	4	7	7	4
18 and under 21	20	20	16	38	27	36	32	23	28	25	35
21 and under 30	70	58	36	56	51	36	36	34	42	30	59
30 and under 60	93	96	97	89	86	83	80	87	67	71	74
60 and over	15	10	16	11	17	13	12	13	18	11	11
All ages	**195**	**182**	**161**	**196**	**182**	**168**	**163**	**161**	**162**	**144**	**183**
Females											
Under 18		(Included in				1				1	
18 and under 21		the number					1				1
21 and under 30		of persons				1	1				1
30 and under 60		by ages		1	1	1	1	2			
60 and over		given above)		2		1		1	1		
All ages	**3**	**2**	**5**	**3**	**1**	**4**	**3**	**3**	**1**	**1**	**2**
All Proved Offences	**198**	**184**	**166**	**199**	**183**	**172**	**166**	**164**	**163**	**145**	**185**
Motoring Offences											
Proceedings for:											
(a) Previously Convicted											
Unfit to drive											
Driving, undue alcohol											
Fail provide specimen											
(b) No Prev. Conviction											
Unfit to drive					31	29	44	38	39	44	59
Driving, undue alcohol											
Fail provide spec.											
In charge and:											
Unfit to drive					13	17	7	11	24	16	16
Undue alcohol											
Fail provide spec.											
Failure to provide breath specimen											
Total: All Proceedings	**24**	**47**	**32**	**36**	**44**	**46**	**51**	**49**	**63**	**60**	**75**
Licensed Premises											
Public Houses:											
Full	761					771					826
Beer and Cider	105					77					8
Wine or Cider	7					5					1
Restaurant Licence											15
Residential Licence											
Above Combined											5
Licensed Clubs											7
Total On Licences	**873**					**853**					**862**
Off Licences	**119**					**122**					**143**
Total On/Off Licences	**992**					**975**					**1005**
Registered Clubs	**124**					**142**					**145**
Total Licences & Clubs	**1116**					**1117**					**1150**

TABLE III 89
DRUNKENNESS OFFENCES, MOTORING OFFENCES AND LICENCES, 1953-63
SOMERSET POLICE DISTRICT

	1953	1954	1955	1956	1957	1958	1959	1960	1961	1962	1963
Population '000	**483**					**497**					**533**
Proved Offences—Drunkenness											
Males											
Under 18	x	x	3	1	3	2	1	6	4	3	6
18 and under 21	6	5	12	14	14	21	17	18	19	17	19
21 and under 30	27	29	23	35	28	29	43	23	41	61	38
30 and under 60	110	143	69	90	83	112	117	96	96	111	114
60 and over	13	15	6	6	11	12	14	10	3	14	16
All ages	**154**	**185**	**109**	**146**	**139**	**176**	**192**	**153**	**163**	**206**	**193**
Females											
Under 18		(Included in the number of persons by ages given above)			1			3	1		
18 and under 21					1		1	2	1	1	1
21 and under 30							1		1		
30 and under 60				4	4	1	3	8	2	2	2
60 and over								1	1		
All ages	**2**	**7**	**4**	**4**	**6**	**1**	**5**	**14**	**6**	**3**	**3**
All Proved Offences	**156**	**192**	**113**	**150**	**145**	**177**	**197**	**167**	**169**	**209**	**196**
Motoring Offences											
Proceedings for:											
(a) Previously Convicted											
Unfit to drive											
Driving, undue alcohol											
Fail provide specimen											
(b) No Prev. Conviction											
Unfit to drive					23	35	34	34	36	41	49
Driving, undue alcohol											
Fail provide spec.											
In charge and:											
Unfit to drive					8	4	8	14	9	13	15
Undue alcohol											
Fail provide spec.											
Failure to provide breath specimen											
Total: All Proceedings	**22**	**30**	**22**	**35**	**31**	**39**	**42**	**48**	**45**	**54**	**64**
Licensed Premises											
Public Houses:											
Full	1022					1090					1169
Beer and Cider	296					172					37
Wine or Cider						1					
Restaurant Licence											34
Residential Licence											11
Above Combined											37
Licensed Clubs											17
Total On Licences	**1318**					**1263**					**1305**
Off Licences	**226**					**229**					**263**
Total On/Off Licences	**1544**					**1492**					**1568**
Registered Clubs	**235**					**271**					**245**
Total Licences & Clubs	**1779**					**1763**					**1813**

TABLE III 90
DRUNKENNESS OFFENCES, MOTORING OFFENCES AND LICENCES, 1953–63
BATH POLICE DISTRICT

	1953	1954	1955	1956	1957	1958	1959	1960	1961	1962	1963
Population '000	**79**					**80**					**83**
Proved Offences— Drunkenness											
Males											
Under 18	x	x	3	1	9		4	3	7	1	1
18 and under 21	1	4	14	6	17	6	14	15	12	19	10
21 and under 30	8	18	12	18	29	18	27	17	16	32	15
30 and under 60	47	49	57	44	58	38	54	45	54	43	33
60 and over	7	3	6	9	9	4	6	9	12	7	5
All ages	**61**	**73**	**88**	**78**	**122**	**66**	**105**	**89**	**101**	**102**	**64**
Females											
Under 18		(Included in the number of persons by ages given above)					3				
18 and under 21				2	1		1		1		
21 and under 30						1					
30 and under 60				3	1		2				
60 and over											
All ages	**2**	**1**	**4**	**5**	**2**	**1**	**6**		**1**		
All Proved Offences	**63**	**74**	**92**	**83**	**124**	**67**	**111**	**89**	**102**	**102**	**64**
Motoring Offences											
Proceedings for:											
(a) Previously Convicted											
Unfit to drive											
Driving, undue alcohol											
Fail provide specimen											
(b) No Prev. Conviction											
Unfit to drive					7	5	4	1	5	7	6
Driving, undue alcohol											
Fail provide spec.											
In charge and:											
Unfit to drive							1	4	3	2	
Undue alcohol											
Fail provide spec.											
Failure to provide breath specimen											
Total: All Proceedings	**7**	**1**	**7**	**3**	**7**	**5**	**5**	**5**	**8**	**9**	**6**
Licensed Premises											
Public Houses:											
Full	150					142					146
Beer and Cider	26					20					5
Wine or Cider											
Restaurant Licence											5
Residential Licence											
Above Combined											1
Licensed Clubs											
Total On Licences	**176**					**162**					**157**
Off Licences	**38**					**40**					**54**
Total On/Off Licences	**214**					**202**					**211**
Registered Clubs	**25**					**31**					**33**
Total Licences & Clubs	**239**					**233**					**244**

TABLE III 91

DRUNKENNESS OFFENCES, MOTORING OFFENCES AND LICENCES, 1953–63 STAFFORDSHIRE POLICE DISTRICT

	1953	1954	1955	1956	1957	1958	1959	1960	1961	1962	1963
Population '000	**1015**					**1148**					**1250**
Proved Offences—Drunkenness											
Males											
Under 18	x	x	14	12	14	19	24	25	26	34	20
18 and under 21	28	33	49	74	63	89	120	108	102	99	91
21 and under 30	169	155	179	213	219	183	148	209	198	226	232
30 and under 60	221	286	293	300	310	297	337	311	327	333	371
60 and over	18	18	16	16	27	21	25	22	33	22	27
All ages	**421**	**483**	**544**	**615**	**633**	**609**	**654**	**675**	**686**	**714**	**741**
Females											
Under 18		(Included in				1	1	1	2	1	1
18 and under 21		the number			1	1		1	1	1	2
21 and under 30		of persons		1	3	3	2	2	1	3	5
30 and under 60		by ages		10	4	12	5	4	7	7	5
60 and over		given above)				5	3	4	1		1
All ages	**15**	**9**	**7**	**11**	**8**	**22**	**11**	**12**	**12**	**12**	**14**
All Proved Offences	**436**	**492**	**551**	**626**	**641**	**631**	**665**	**687**	**698**	**726**	**755**
Motoring Offences											
Proceedings for:											
(a) Previously Convicted											
Unfit to drive											
Driving, undue alcohol											
Fail provide specimen											
(b) No Prev. Conviction											
Unfit to drive					61	69	78	80	109	106	105
Driving, undue alcohol											
Fail provide spec.											
In charge and:											
Unfit to drive					16	11	14	28	26	25	34
Undue alcohol											
Fail provide spec.											
Failure to provide breath specimen											
Total: All Proceedings	**63**	**63**	**72**	**96**	**77**	**80**	**92**	**108**	**135**	**131**	**139**
Licensed Premises											
Public Houses:											
Full	1887					1952					2100
Beer and Cider	452					318					82
Wine or Cider	15					12					4
Restaurant Licence											21
Residential Licence											1
Above Combined											
Licensed Clubs											20
Total On Licences	**2354**					**2282**					**2228**
Off Licences	**590**					**596**					**604**
Total On/Off Licences	**2944**					**2878**					**2832**
Registered Clubs	**606**					**660**					**653**
Total Licences & Clubs	**3550**					**3538**					**3485**

TABLE III 92
DRUNKENNESS OFFENCES, MOTORING OFFENCES AND LICENCES, 1953-63
STOKE-ON-TRENT POLICE DISTRICT

	1953	1954	1955	1956	1957	1958	1959	1960	1961	1962	1963
Population '000	**274**					**271**					**266**
Proved Offences—Drunkenness											
Males											
Under 18	x	x	2		2	4	4	7	5	8	8
18 and under 21	7	11	7	15	22	23	18	19	34	34	24
21 and under 30	68	49	42	40	47	50	43	46	54	61	48
30 and under 60	99	86	86	70	99	101	115	103	94	107	84
60 and over	12	6	7	4	6	8	8	10	5	10	9
All ages	**182**	**141**	**139**	**129**	**176**	**186**	**188**	**185**	**192**	**220**	**173**
Females											
Under 18		(Included in								2	
18 and under 21		the number		1					2		1
21 and under 30		of persons			1	1	1	2	2	2	1
30 and under 60		by ages		2	5	2		2	1	5	4
60 and over		given above)			1	1		1	1		1
All ages	**4**	**11**	**5**	**3**	**7**	**4**	**1**	**5**	**6**	**9**	**7**
All Proved Offences	**186**	**152**	**144**	**132**	**183**	**190**	**189**	**190**	**198**	**229**	**180**
Motoring Offences											
Proceedings for:											
(a) Previously Convicted											
Unfit to drive											
Driving, undue alcohol											
Fail provide specimen											
(b) No Prev. Conviction											
Unfit to drive					28	34	35	40	37	45	44
Driving, undue alcohol											
Fail provide spec.											
In charge and:											
Unfit to drive					9	7	7	11	7	9	6
Undue alcohol											
Fail provide spec.											
Failure to provide breath specimen											
Total: All Proceedings	**25**	**31**	**46**	**22**	**37**	**41**	**42**	**51**	**44**	**54**	**50**
Licensed Premises											
Public Houses:											
Full	228					253					367
Beer and Cider	296					230					73
Wine or Cider	7					5					1
Restaurant Licence											7
Residential Licence											
Above Combined											1
Licensed Clubs											1
Total On Licences	**531**					**488**					**450**
Off Licences	**227**					**206**					**183**
Total On/Off Licences	**758**					**694**					**633**
Registered Clubs	**73**					**82**					**83**
Total Licences & Clubs	**831**					**776**					**716**

TABLE III 93
DRUNKENNESS OFFENCES, MOTORING OFFENCES AND LICENCES, 1953–63
WALSALL POLICE DISTRICT

	1953	1954	1955	1956	1957	1958	1959	1960	1961	1962	1963
Population '000	**115**					**115**					**121**
Proved Offences—Drunkenness											
Males											
Under 18	x	x	3		2	3	2	6	5	4	7
18 and under 21	4	4	10	7	13	12	8	25	17	11	17
21 and under 30	31	32	38	44	48	29	22	32	29	53	30
30 and under 60	42	53	68	76	33	41	50	64	64	63	77
60 and over	3	3	2	5	3	4	2	5	4	2	6
All ages	**76**	**87**	**117**	**132**	**99**	**89**	**84**	**132**	**119**	**133**	**137**
Females	(Included in the number of persons by ages given above)										
Under 18				1							
18 and under 21				3	1						
21 and under 30				1	2	1		1	2	7	3
30 and under 60				8	9	12	9	7	3	3	1
60 and over								1		1	2
All ages	**4**	**5**	**4**	**13**	**12**	**13**	**9**	**9**	**5**	**11**	**6**
All Proved Offences	**80**	**92**	**121**	**145**	**111**	**102**	**93**	**141**	**124**	**144**	**143**
Motoring Offences											
Proceedings for:											
(a) Previously Convicted											
Unfit to drive											
Driving, undue alcohol											
Fail provide specimen											
(b) No Prev. Conviction											
Unfit to drive					5	8	4	7	18	13	11
Driving, undue alcohol											
Fail provide spec.											
In charge and:											
Unfit to drive								4	2	3	1
Undue alcohol											
Fail provide spec.											
Failure to provide breath specimen											
Total: All Proceedings	**8**	**4**	**10**	**10**	**5**	**8**	**4**	**11**	**20**	**16**	**12**
Licensed Premises											
Public Houses:											
Full	160					160					164
Beer and Cider	20					17					1
Wine or Cider											
Restaurant Licence											1
Residential Licence											
Above Combined											2
Licensed Clubs											4
Total On Licences	**180**					**177**					**172**
Off Licences	**48**					**49**					**55**
Total On/Off Licences	**228**					**226**					**227**
Registered Clubs	**54**					**62**					**47**
Total Licences & Clubs	**282**					**288**					**274**

TABLE III 94
DRUNKENNESS OFFENCES, MOTORING OFFENCES AND LICENCES, 1953-63
WOLVERHAMPTON POLICE DISTRICT

	1953	1954	1955	1956	1957	1958	1959	1960	1961	1962	1963
Population '000	**161**					**148**					**150**
Proved Offences—Drunkenness											
Males											
Under 18	x	x	2	1	1	1				1	
18 and under 21	4	8	7	10	3	4	2	6	5	5	5
21 and under 30	27	31	42	36	22	23	12	15	20	14	18
30 and under 60	54	66	76	59	54	37	50	39	54	37	42
60 and over	2	7	8	4	8	9	1	6	8	5	2
All ages	**85**	**110**	**129**	**110**	**88**	**74**	**65**	**66**	**87**	**62**	**65**
Females											
Under 18		(Included in						1			
18 and under 21		the number				1					2
21 and under 30		of persons			2	1	3	2		2	1
30 and under 60		by ages		5	4	2	2	4	3	4	5
60 and over		given above)			1		1				
All ages	**3**	**2**	**6**	**5**	**7**	**4**	**6**	**7**	**3**	**6**	**8**
All Proved Offences	**88**	**112**	**135**	**115**	**95**	**78**	**71**	**73**	**90**	**68**	**73**
Motoring Offences											
Proceedings for:											
(a) Previously Convicted											
Unfit to drive											
Driving, undue alcohol											
Fail provide specimen											
(b) No Prev. Conviction											
Unfit to drive					9	7	5	16	14	6	10
Driving, undue alcohol											
Fail provide spec.											
In charge and:											
Unfit to drive					6	2	3	2	5	2	
Undue alcohol											
Fail provide spec.											
Failure to provide breath specimen											
Total: All Proceedings	**14**	**15**	**10**	**14**	**15**	**9**	**8**	**18**	**19**	**8**	**10**
Licensed Premises											
Public Houses:											
Full	207					207					216
Beer and Cider	58					46					6
Wine or Cider											
Restaurant Licence											3
Residential Licence											1
Above Combined											
Licensed Clubs											2
Total On Licences	**265**					**253**					**228**
Off Licences	**91**					**91**					**92**
Total On/Off Licences	**356**					**344**					**320**
Registered Clubs	**77**					**76**					**73**
Total Licences & Clubs	**433**					**420**					**393**

TABLE III 95
DRUNKENNESS OFFENCES, MOTORING OFFENCES AND LICENCES, 1953–63
SUFFOLK (EAST) POLICE DISTRICT

	1953	1954	1955	1956	1957	1958	1959	1960	1961	1962	1963
Population '000	**219**					**223**					**238**
Proved Offences—Drunkenness											
Males											
Under 18	x	x	1		1	2	1	1	2	1	3
18 and under 21	1	3	3	2	8	11	14	6	10	9	21
21 and under 30	4	10	6	9	15	10	7	6	15	14	12
30 and under 60	18	20	12	17	14	8	17	13	11	24	42
60 and over	1	2	2	1	4	4	3	3	3	3	4
All ages	**23**	**30**	**22**	**29**	**42**	**35**	**42**	**29**	**41**	**51**	**82**
Females											
Under 18		(Included in the number of persons by ages given above)						1		1	1
18 and under 21											1
21 and under 30										1	2
30 and under 60						1		1	2		1
60 and over											1
All ages	**1**	**5**	**2**			**1**		**2**	**2**	**2**	**6**
All Proved Offences	**24**	**35**	**24**	**29**	**42**	**36**	**42**	**31**	**43**	**53**	**88**
Motoring Offences											
Proceedings for:											
(a) Previously Convicted											
Unfit to drive											
Driving, undue alcohol											
Fail provide specimen											
(b) No Prev. Conviction											
Unfit to drive					8	11	9	14	21	17	21
Driving, undue alcohol											
Fail provide spec.											
In charge and:											
Unfit to drive					10	3	7	5	7	5	6
Undue alcohol											
Fail provide spec.											
Failure to provide breath specimen											
Total: All Proceedings	**14**	**10**	**16**	**19**	**18**	**14**	**16**	**19**	**28**	**22**	**27**
Licensed Premises											
Public Houses:											
Full	505					518					585
Beer and Cider	131					86					13
Wine or Cider	5										1
Restaurant Licence											8
Residential Licence											1
Above Combined											10
Licensed Clubs											5
Total On Licences	**641**					**604**					**623**
Off Licences	**105**					**103**					**111**
Total On/Off Licences	**746**					**707**					**734**
Registered Clubs	**113**					**118**					**88**
Total Licences & Clubs	**859**					**825**					**822**

TABLE III 96
DRUNKENNESS OFFENCES, MOTORING OFFENCES AND LICENCES, 1953-63
IPSWICH POLICE DISTRICT

	1953	1954	1955	1956	1957	1958	1959	1960	1961	1962	1963
Population '000	**108**					**113**					**119**
Proved Offences—Drunkenness											
Males											
Under 18	x	x		1	2	3	2	3		3	1
18 and under 21	2	2	1	8	2	7	8	9	3	6	13
21 and under 30	22	7	10	19	9	14	15	12	15	16	22
30 and under 60	28	25	19	26	36	30	38	52	52	57	65
60 and over	5	7	3	1	4	3	2	3	4	5	5
All ages	**52**	**37**	**29**	**55**	**53**	**57**	**65**	**79**	**74**	**87**	**106**
Females											
Under 18		(Included in the number of persons by ages given above)			2						
18 and under 21					3		3				1
21 and under 30							1	1		3	4
30 and under 60				2		1	2	2	1	2	
60 and over					3		1	1			1
All ages	**5**	**4**	**4**	**2**	**8**	**1**	**7**	**4**	**1**	**5**	**6**
All Proved Offences	**57**	**41**	**33**	**57**	**61**	**58**	**72**	**83**	**75**	**92**	**112**
Motoring Offences											
Proceedings for:											
(a) Previously Convicted											
Unfit to drive											
Driving, undue alcohol											
Fail provide specimen											
(b) No Prev. Conviction											
Unfit to drive					6	8	15	20	23	20	34
Driving, undue alcohol											
Fail provide spec.											
In charge and:											
Unfit to drive					4	1	6	5	3	5	10
Undue alcohol											
Fail provide spec.											
Failure to provide breath specimen											
Total: All Proceedings	**4**	**4**	**11**	**3**	**10**	**9**	**21**	**25**	**26**	**25**	**44**
Licensed Premises											
Public Houses:											
Full	125					135					129
Beer and Cider	32					15					2
Wine or Cider											
Restaurant Licence											5
Residential Licence											
Above Combined											1
Licensed Clubs											3
Total On Licences	**157**					**150**					**140**
Off Licences	**54**					**55**					**56**
Total On/Off Licences	**211**					**205**					**196**
Registered Clubs	**50**					**58**					**50**
Total Licences & Clubs	**261**					**263**					**246**

TABLE III 97
DRUNKENNESS OFFENCES, MOTORING OFFENCES AND LICENCES, 1953–63 SUFFOLK (WEST) POLICE DISTRICT

	1953	1954	1955	1956	1957	1958	1959	1960	1961	1962	1963
Population '000	**126**					**127**					**138**
Proved Offences—Drunkenness											
Males											
Under 18	x	x	1		1	1		1	1	2	7
18 and under 21	5	9	7	4	7	6	7	4	6	7	8
21 and under 30	16	10	10	14	10	9	10	8	8	10	12
30 and under 60	39	25	20	12	21	19	20	6	12	9	21
60 and over	11	5	2	4	2	2	2	2	2	2	
All ages	**68**	**48**	**38**	**34**	**41**	**37**	**39**	**21**	**29**	**30**	**48**
Females											
Under 18	(Included in							1		1	1
18 and under 21	the number			2	4						
21 and under 30	of persons				2					1	
30 and under 60	by ages				1			1	3		1
60 and over	given above)										
All ages	**3**	**1**	**2**	**2**	**7**			**2**	**2**	**2**	**2**
All Proved Offences	**71**	**49**	**40**	**36**	**48**	**37**	**39**	**23**	**31**	**32**	**50**
Motoring Offences											
Proceedings for:											
(a) Previously Convicted											
Unfit to drive											
Driving, undue alcohol											
Fail provide specimen											
(b) No Prev. Conviction											
Unfit to drive					11	14	15	16	27	19	12
Driving, undue alcohol											
Fail provide spec.											
In charge and:											
Unfit to drive							1	5		4	4
Undue alcohol											
Fail provide spec.											
Failure to provide breath specimen											
Total: All Proceedings	**7**	**18**	**14**	**16**	**11**	**14**	**16**	**21**	**27**	**23**	**16**
Licensed Premises											
Public Houses:											
Full	364					374					397
Beer and Cider	89					67					24
Wine or Cider											
Restaurant Licence											6
Residential Licence											
Above Combined											2
Licensed Clubs											5
Total On Licences	**453**					**441**					**434**
Off Licences	**57**					**57**					**58**
Total On/Off Licences	**510**					**498**					**492**
Registered Clubs	**74**					**83**					**83**
Total Licences & Clubs	**584**					**581**					**575**

TABLE III 98
DRUNKENNESS OFFENCES, MOTORING OFFENCES AND LICENCES, 1953-63
SURREY POLICE DISTRICT

	1953	1954	1955	1956	1957	1958	1959	1960	1961	1962	1963
Population '000	**1250**					**1433**					**1502**
Proved Offences—											
Drunkenness											
Males											
Under 18	x	x	4	3	3	2	1	5	5	1	4
18 and under 21	6	5	11	14	11	7	10	15	14	17	16
21 and under 30	20	14	20	28	19	10	26	21	26	24	36
30 and under 60	47	45	64	52	48	73	72	46	77	87	90
60 and over	8	16	9	8	4	11	5	3	9	5	8
All ages	**77**	**77**	**102**	**105**	**85**	**103**	**114**	**90**	**131**	**134**	**154**
Females											
Under 18		(Included in the number of persons by ages given above)									
18 and under 21				2			1	1			1
21 and under 30					1			1		1	1
30 and under 60				3	10	6	2	2	1	1	1
60 and over				2					2	3	1
All ages	**4**	**3**	**6**	**7**	**11**	**6**	**3**	**4**	**3**	**5**	**4**
All Proved Offences	**81**	**80**	**108**	**112**	**96**	**109**	**117**	**94**	**134**	**139**	**158**
Motoring Offences											
Proceedings for:											
(a) Previously Convicted											
Unfit to drive											
Driving, undue alcohol											
Fail provide specimen											
(b) No Prev. Conviction											
Unfit to drive					47	39	61	53	62	78	101
Driving, undue alcohol											
Fail provide spec.											
In charge and:											
Unfit to drive					13	14	12	16	11	26	28
Undue alcohol											
Fail provide spec.											
Failure to provide breath specimen											
Total: All Proceedings	**46**	**39**	**46**	**44**	**60**	**53**	**73**	**69**	**73**	**104**	**129**
Licensed Premises											
Public Houses:											
Full	912					1162					1206
Beer and Cider	147					86					11
Wine or Cider						1					1
Restaurant Licence											61
Residential Licence											3
Above Combined											18
Licensed Clubs											40
Total On Licences	**1059**					**1249**					**1340**
Off Licences	**504**					**575**					**622**
Total On/Off Licences	**1563**					**1824**					**1962**
Registered Clubs	**695**					**798**					**792**
Total Licences & Clubs	**2258**					**2422**					**2754**

TABLE III 99
DRUNKENNESS OFFENCES, MOTORING OFFENCES AND LICENCES, 1953–63
SUSSEX (EAST) POLICE DISTRICT

	1953	1954	1955	1956	1957	1958	1959	1960	1961	1962	1963
Population '000	**335**					**355**					**388**
Proved Offences—Drunkenness											
Males											
Under 18	x	x		2	3	2	3		6	2	2
18 and under 21	4	2	6	5	9	9	8	11	10	9	13
21 and under 30	9	9	18	10	9	11	13	13	12	12	15
30 and under 60	22	19	23	23	22	23	47	39	34	33	41
60 and over	2	9	9	2	3	5	4	5	4	5	4
All ages	**32**	**33**	**54**	**42**	**46**	**50**	**75**	**68**	**66**	**61**	**75**
Females											
Under 18		(Included in						1	1	1	
18 and under 21		the number			1	1	1				
21 and under 30		of persons			1		1			1	
30 and under 60		by ages		4	3	6	10	6	1	2	7
60 and over		given above)			1		1	2	1	2	2
All ages	**5**	**6**	**2**	**4**	**6**	**7**	**13**	**9**	**3**	**6**	**9**
All Proved Offences	**37**	**39**	**56**	**46**	**52**	**57**	**88**	**77**	**69**	**67**	**84**
Motoring Offences											
Proceedings for:											
(a) Previously Convicted											
Unfit to drive											
Driving, undue alcohol											
Fail provide specimen											
(b) No Prev. Conviction											
Unfit to drive					19	21	27	23	29	25	35
Driving, undue alcohol											
Fail provide spec.											
In charge and:											
Unfit to drive					5	9	12	11	9	18	10
Undue alcohol											
Fail provide spec.											
Failure to provide breath specimen											
Total: All Proceedings	**22**	**26**	**21**	**25**	**24**	**30**	**39**	**34**	**38**	**43**	**45**
Licensed Premises											
Public Houses:											
Full	533					556					585
Beer and Cider	65					29					9
Wine or Cider	1					1					1
Restaurant Licence											24
Residential Licence											4
Above Combined											21
Licensed Clubs											32
Total On Licences	**599**					**586**					**676**
Off Licences	**225**					**232**					**263**
Total On/Off Licences	**824**					**818**					**939**
Registered Clubs	**218**					**222**					**160**
Total Licences & Clubs	**1042**					**1040**					**1099**

TABLE III 100
DRUNKENNESS OFFENCES, MOTORING OFFENCES AND LICENCES, 1953-63
BRIGHTON POLICE DISTRICT

	1953	1954	1955	1956	1957	1958	1959	1960	1961	1962	1963
Population '000	**157**					**160**					**163**
Proved Offences—Drunkenness											
Males											
Under 18	x	x	2	8	2	3	7	4	7	7	6
18 and under 21	7	7	9	16	14	15	23	28	24	27	29
21 and under 30	26	24	24	43	39	35	53	45	54	86	88
30 and under 60	90	111	89	76	113	130	171	161	192	308	242
60 and over	10	26	14	20	23	27	22	15	17	20	12
All ages	**97**	**130**	**126**	**163**	**191**	**210**	**276**	**253**	**294**	**448**	**377**
Females											
Under 18		(Included in								1	2
18 and under 21		the number		1	1	1	2	3		2	
21 and under 30		of persons		1	2		3	1	1	5	7
30 and under 60		by ages		9	18	25	25	17	30	38	33
60 and over		given above)		5	2	10	10	5	23	9	11
All ages	**36**	**38**	**12**	**16**	**23**	**36**	**40**	**26**	**54**	**54**	**53**
All Proved Offences	**133**	**168**	**138**	**179**	**214**	**246**	**316**	**279**	**348**	**502**	**430**
Motoring Offences											
Proceedings for:											
(a) Previously Convicted											
Unfit to drive											
Driving, undue alcohol											
Fail provide specimen											
(b) No Prev. Conviction											
Unfit to drive					3	17	13	15	34	37	36
Driving, undue alcohol											
Fail provide spec.											
In charge and:											
Unfit to drive							1	7	1	7	6
Undue alcohol											
Fail provide spec.											
Failure to provide breath specimen											
Total: All Proceedings	**10**	**5**	**5**	**7**	**3**	**17**	**14**	**22**	**35**	**44**	**42**
Licensed Premises											
Public Houses:											
Full	288					310					317
Beer and Cider	66					32					8
Wine or Cider	3					3					3
Restaurant Licence											26
Residential Licence											10
Above Combined											9
Licensed Clubs											17
Total On Licences	**357**					**345**					**390**
Off Licences	**84**					**84**					**93**
Total On/Off Licences	**441**					**429**					**483**
Registered Clubs	**63**					**65**					**47**
Total Licences & Clubs	**504**					**494**					**530**

TABLE III 101
DRUNKENNESS OFFENCES, MOTORING OFFENCES AND LICENCES, 1953–63 EASTBOURNE POLICE DISTRICT

	1953	1954	1955	1956	1957	1958	1959	1960	1961	1962	1963
Population '000	**57**					**58**					**62**
Proved Offences—Drunkenness											
Males											
Under 18	x	x									2
18 and under 21	1		3	2	1	1		1			4
21 and under 30	3	1	2	4	2	3	8		2	6	9
30 and under 60	26	15	22	21	27	17	25	23	25	19	22
60 and over	4	3	5	4	3	8	2	2	1	3	1
All ages	**32**	**16**	**30**	**31**	**33**	**29**	**35**	**26**	**28**	**28**	**38**
Females											
Under 18		(Included in						1			
18 and under 21		the number						2	1		
21 and under 30		of persons			1						
30 and under 60		by ages			1				1	4	
60 and over		given above)					1	1		1	2
All ages	**2**	**3**	**2**		**2**		**1**	**4**	**2**	**5**	**2**
All Proved Offences	**24**	**19**	**32**	**31**	**35**	**29**	**36**	**30**	**30**	**33**	**40**
Motoring Offences											
Proceedings for:											
(a) Previously Convicted											
Unfit to drive											
Driving, undue alcohol											
Fail provide specimen											
(b) No Prev. Conviction											
Unfit to drive					2	6	5	4	7	6	3
Driving, undue alcohol											
Fail provide spec.											
In charge and:											
Unfit to drive										3	2
Undue alcohol											
Fail provide spec.											
Failure to provide breath specimen											
Total: All Proceedings	**2**	**3**	**5**	**4**	**2**	**6**	**5**	**4**	**7**	**9**	**5**
Licensed Premises											
Public Houses:											
Full	69					77					92
Beer and Cider	9					4					1
Wine or Cider											
Restaurant Licence											10
Residential Licence											4
Above Combined											6
Licensed Clubs											6
Total On Licences	**78**					**81**					**119**
Off Licences	**49**					**45**					**45**
Total On/Off Licences	**127**					**126**					**164**
Registered Clubs	**31**					**40**					**34**
Total Licences & Clubs	**158**					**166**					**198**

TABLE III 102
DRUNKENNESS OFFENCES, MOTORING OFFENCES AND LICENCES, 1953-63
HASTINGS POLICE DISTRICT

	1953	1954	1955	1956	1957	1958	1959	1960	1961	1962	1963
Population '000	**65**					**64**					**67**
Proved Offences—Drunkenness											
Males											
Under 18	x	x		2		1				1	2
18 and under 21	3	4	5	4	2	7		6	6	9	5
21 and under 30		5	6	16	6	4	4	13	8	11	9
30 and under 60	11	22	22	14	16	18	20	10	19	17	30
60 and over	11	6	9	1	6		5	5	6	3	7
All ages	**19**	**33**	**34**	**37**	**30**	**30**	**29**	**34**	**39**	**41**	**53**
Females											
Under 18		(Included in the number of persons by ages given above)						1		1	
18 and under 21				1							
21 and under 30							1	1			
30 and under 60					4	1		2		1	5
60 and over						1	1	2	1	3	2
All ages	**6**	**4**	**8**	**1**	**4**	**2**	**2**	**6**	**1**	**5**	**7**
All Proved Offences	**25**	**37**	**42**	**38**	**34**	**32**	**31**	**40**	**40**	**46**	**60**
Motoring Offences											
Proceedings for:											
(a) Previously Convicted											
Unfit to drive											
Driving, undue alcohol											
Fail provide specimen											
(b) No Prev. Conviction											
Unfit to drive					1	1	7	6	10	9	14
Driving, undue alcohol											
Fail provide spec.											
In charge and:											
Unfit to drive						1	1				6
Undue alcohol											
Fail provide spec.											
Failure to provide breath specimen											
Total: All Proceedings	**2**	**2**	**7**	**4**	**1**	**2**	**8**	**6**	**10**	**9**	**20**
Licensed Premises											
Public Houses:											
Full	131					126					123
Beer and Cider	8					2					
Wine or Cider	3					2					2
Restaurant Licence											10
Residential Licence											4
Above Combined											6
Licensed Clubs											17
Total On Licences	**142**					**130**					**162**
Off Licences	**66**					**64**					**59**
Total On/Off Licences	**208**					**194**					**221**
Registered Clubs	**33**					**49**					**28**
Total Licences & Clubs	**241**					**242**					**249**

TABLE III 103
DRUNKENNESS OFFENCES, MOTORING OFFENCES AND LICENCES, 1953-63
SUSSEX (WEST) POLICE DISTRICT

	1953	1954	1955	1956	1957	1958	1959	1960	1961	1962	1963
Population '000	**329**					**383**					**426**
Proved Offences—											
Drunkenness											
Males											
Under 18	x	x	1	3	2	2		8	8	5	1
18 and under 21	2	9	2	2	8	9	21	18	12	12	10
21 and under 30	16	13	17	21	21	16	34	39	21	27	25
30 and under 60	35	34	42	36	42	33	60	51	76	71	72
60 and over	6	7	7	6	9	9	8	8	18	12	11
All ages	**54**	**59**	**65**	**68**	**82**	**69**	**123**	**124**	**135**	**127**	**119**
Females											
Under 18	(Included in the number of persons by ages given above)								1		
18 and under 21					1		1		1		1
21 and under 30							1	1			
30 and under 60				4	3	3	3	3	9	7	
60 and over						2	3	2	4	3	
All ages	**5**	**4**	**4**	**4**	**4**	**5**	**8**	**6**	**15**	**10**	**1**
All Proved Offences	**59**	**63**	**69**	**72**	**86**	**74**	**131**	**130**	**150**	**137**	**120**
Motoring Offences											
Proceedings for:											
(a) Previously Convicted											
Unfit to drive											
Driving, undue alcohol											
Fail provide specimen											
(b) No Prev. Conviction											
Unfit to drive					35	24	27	49	37	43	38
Driving, undue alcohol											
Fail provide spec.											
In charge and:											
Unfit to drive						6		11	12	17	23
Undue alcohol											
Fail provide spec.											
Failure to provide breath specimen											
Total: All Proceedings	**28**	**17**	**24**	**26**	**35**	**30**	**27**	**60**	**49**	**60**	**61**
Licensed Premises											
Public Houses:											
Full	547					585					617
Beer and Cider	80					40					9
Wine or Cider	2					2					2
Restaurant Licence											25
Residential Licence											8
Above Combined											23
Licensed Clubs											56
Total On Licences	**629**					**627**					**740**
Off Licences	**184**					**184**					**208**
Total On/Off Licences	**813**					**811**					**948**
Registered Clubs	**193**					**225**					**177**
Total Licences & Clubs	**1006**					**1036**					**1125**

TABLE III 104
DRUNKENNESS OFFENCES, MOTORING OFFENCES AND LICENCES, 1953-63
WARWICKSHIRE POLICE DISTRICT

	1953	1954	1955	1956	1957	1958	1959	1960	1961	1962	1963
Population '000	**449**					**563**					**647**
Proved Offences—Drunkenness											
Males											
Under 18	x	x	2	4	10	15	9	7	8	11	8
18 and under 21	34	15	22	·32	38	46	33	57	59	39	40
21 and under 30	88	75	78	65	57	93	76	119	85	72	57
30 and under 60	154	132	156	106	148	164	146	143	144	103	107
60 and over	15	12	17	11	10	12	10	17	7	12	12
All ages	**286**	**229**	**266**	**218**	**263**	**330**	**274**	**343**	**303**	**237**	**224**
Females											
Under 18	(Included in the number of persons by ages given above)								1	1	
18 and under 21							1		1		
21 and under 30					1						
30 and under 60				1	3	8	4	6	3	14	7
60 and over				1							
All ages	**5**	**5**	**9**	**2**	**4**	**8**	**5**	**6**	**5**	**15**	**7**
All Proved Offences	**291**	**234**	**275**	**220**	**267**	**338**	**279**	**349**	**308**	**252**	**231**
Motoring Offences											
Proceedings for:											
(a) Previously Convicted											
Unfit to drive											
Driving, undue alcohol											
Fail provide specimen											
(b) No Prev. Conviction											
Unfit to drive					39	38	30	46	51	64	84
Driving, undue alcohol											
Fail provide spec.											
In charge and:											
Unfit to drive					16	14	11	13	24	17	25
Undue alcohol											
Fail provide spec.											
Failure to provide breath specimen											
Total: All Proceedings	**81**	**48**	**45**	**58**	**55**	**52**	**41**	**59**	**75**	**81**	**109**
Licensed Premises											
Public Houses:											
Full	777					805					825
Beer and Cider	62					39					5
Wine or Cider											
Restaurant Licence											24
Residential Licence											1
Above Combined											9
Licensed Clubs											22
Total On Licences	**839**					**844**					**886**
Off Licences	**268**					**280**					**333**
Total On/Off Licences	**1107**					**1124**					**1219**
Registered Clubs	**369**					**421**					**423**
Total Licences & Clubs	**1476**					**1545**					**1642**

TABLE III 105
DRUNKENNESS OFFENCES, MOTORING OFFENCES AND LICENCES, 1953-63
BIRMINGHAM POLICE DISTRICT

	1953	1954	1955	1956	1957	1958	1959	1960	1961	1962	1963
Population '000	**1119**					**1095**					**1116**
Proved Offences—Drunkenness											
Males											
Under 18	x	x	43	41	60	49	51	60	71	57	42
18 and under 21	185	290	332	317	298	332	335	345	431	408	402
21 and under 30	1205	1555	1814	1360	1169	1070	906	978	1064	1180	1096
30 and under 60	2522	1441	2464	1998	1991	1882	1628	1633	1679	2152	2049
60 and over	208	166	153	109	138	91	119	83	99	123	96
All ages	**3936**	**4273**	**4635**	**3825**	**3656**	**3424**	**3039**	**3099**	**3344**	**3920**	**3685**
Females											
Under 18	(Included in the number of persons by ages given above)			1	2		2	2	1	4	1
18 and under 21				11	7	16	13	5	7	8	5
21 and under 30				47	31	28	19	27	48	36	17
30 and under 60				124	118	118	113	73	88	101	109
60 and over				14	11	8	7	2	6	8	3
All ages	**184**	**179**	**171**	**197**	**169**	**170**	**154**	**109**	**150**	**157**	**135**
All Proved Offences	**4120**	**4452**	**4806**	**4022**	**3825**	**3594**	**3193**	**3208**	**3494**	**4077**	**3820**
Motoring Offences											
Proceedings for:											
(a) Previously Convicted											
Unfit to drive											
Driving, undue alcohol											
Fail provide specimen											
(b) No Prev. Conviction											
Unfit to drive					126	135	143	146	164	156	189
Driving, undue alcohol											
Fail provide spec.											
In charge and:											
Unfit to drive					23	38	37	35	41	51	48
Undue alcohol											
Fail provide spec.											
Failure to provide breath specimen											
Total: All Proceedings	**47**	**98**	**114**	**121**	**149**	**173**	**180**	**181**	**205**	**207**	**237**
Licensed Premises											
Public Houses:											
Full	776					777					815
Beer and Cider	172					103					42
Wine or Cider											21
Restaurant Licence											1
Residential Licence											3
Above Combined											11
Licensed Clubs											
Total On Licences	**948**					**880**					**893**
Off Licences	**672**					**652**					**659**
Total On/Off Licences	**1620**					**1532**					**1552**
Registered Clubs	**456**					**497**					**398**
Total Licences & Clubs	**2076**					**2029**					**1950**

TABLE III 106
DRUNKENNESS OFFENCES, MOTORING OFFENCES AND LICENCES, 1953-63
COVENTRY POLICE DISTRICT

	1953	1954	1955	1956	1957	1958	1959	1960	1961	1962	1963
Population '000	**263**					**281**					**314**
Proved Offences— Drunkenness											
Males											
Under 18	x	x	4	3	1	4	5	12	13	22	10
18 and under 21	18	29	15	25	27	31	23	70	70	75	55
21 and under 30	194	197	165	156	144	116	115	149	162	162	142
30 and under 60	400	432	393	392	371	365	337	333	304	330	374
60 and over	40	21	23	23	15	23	34	20	21	30	16
All ages	**638**	**656**	**576**	**599**	**558**	**539**	**514**	**584**	**570**	**619**	**597**
Females											
Under 18		(Included in the number of persons by ages given above)				1	1	2			
18 and under 21					4		1	3	4	1	2
21 and under 30				3	3	1		2	4	2	4
30 and under 60				6	24	13	17	10	11	16	16
60 and over					1	2			6	3	5
All ages	**14**	**23**	**24**	**9**	**32**	**17**	**19**	**17**	**25**	**22**	**27**
All Proved Offences	**652**	**697**	**600**	**608**	**590**	**556**	**533**	**601**	**595**	**641**	**624**
Motoring Offences											
Proceedings for:											
(a) Previously Convicted											
Unfit to drive											
Driving, undue alcohol											
Fail provide specimen											
(b) No Prev. Conviction											
Unfit to drive					12	12	32	27	50	30	38
Driving, undue alcohol											
Fail provide spec.											
In charge and:											
Unfit to drive					5	4	1	4	5	11	17
Undue alcohol											
Fail provide spec.											
Failure to provide breath specimen											
Total: All Proceedings	**10**	**19**	**26**	**31**	**17**	**16**	**33**	**31**	**55**	**41**	**55**
Licensed Premises											
Public Houses:											
Full	241					234					234
Beer and Cider	3										
Wine or Cider											
Restaurant Licence											10
Residential Licence											1
Above Combined											
Licensed Clubs											6
Total On Licences	**244**					**234**					**251**
Off Licences	**128**					**140**					**150**
Total On/Off Licences	**372**					**374**					**401**
Registered Clubs	**124**					**136**					**139**
Total Licences & Clubs	**496**					**510**					**540**

TABLE III 107

DRUNKENNESS OFFENCES, MOTORING OFFENCES AND LICENCES, 1953–63 WESTMORLAND POLICE DISTRICT

	1953	1954	1955	1956	1957	1958	1959	1960	1961	1962	1963
Population '000	**67**					**66**					**67**
Proved Offences—Drunkenness											
Males											
Under 18	x	x	1	2	3		1	1		3	3
18 and under 21	2	5	4	1	5	2	4	2		8	11
21 and under 30	11	10	10	7	6	9	12	9	10	12	12
30 and under 60	13	18	3	15	12	8	11	19	9	8	23
60 and over	2	2	2		1	1	2	3		2	
All ages	**25**	**35**	**19**	**25**	**27**	**20**	**30**	**34**	**19**	**33**	**49**
Females											
Under 18		(Included in the number of persons by ages given above)									
18 and under 21						2					1
21 and under 30						1					
30 and under 60							2	2			3
60 and over											
All ages	**3**		**1**			**3**	**2**	**2**			**4**
All Proved Offences	**28**	**35**	**20**	**25**	**27**	**23**	**32**	**36**	**19**	**33**	**53**
Motoring Offences											
Proceedings for:											
(a) Previously Convicted											
Unfit to drive											
Driving, undue alcohol											
Fail provide specimen											
(b) No Prev. Conviction											
Unfit to drive					6	6	8	12	7	7	9
Driving, undue alcohol											
Fail provide spec.											
In charge and:											
Unfit to drive					3	6	3	2	5	3	5
Undue alcohol											
Fail provide spec.											
Failure to provide breath specimen											
Total: All Proceedings	**7**	**13**	**12**	**10**	**9**	**12**	**11**	**14**	**12**	**10**	**14**
Licensed Premises											
Public Houses:											
Full	187					192					198
Beer and Cider	13					7					1
Wine or Cider											
Restaurant Licence											5
Residential Licence											2
Above Combined											10
Licensed Clubs											8
Total On Licences	**200**					**199**					**224**
Off Licences	**26**					**26**					**32**
Total On/Off Licences	**226**					**225**					**256**
Registered Clubs	**20**					**28**					**29**
Total Licences & Clubs	**246**					**253**					**285**

TABLE III 108
DRUNKENNESS OFFENCES, MOTORING OFFENCES AND LICENCES, 1953-63
WILTSHIRE POLICE DISTRICT

	1953	1954	1955	1956	1957	1958	1959	1960	1961	1962	1963
Population '000	**391**					**406**					**447**
Proved Offences—Drunkenness											
Males											
Under 18	x	x	1	2	1	3			2	1	5
18 and under 21	2	17	17	15	12	15	22	17	15	12	19
21 and under 30	14	33	39	24	27	19	36	23	30	42	48
30 and under 60	49	49	71	72	53	52	53	33	47	76	87
60 and over	6	6	6	8	6	3	8	4	3	9	4
All ages	**63**	**94**	**127**	**121**	**99**	**92**	**119**	**77**	**97**	**140**	**163**
Females											
Under 18		(Included in the number of persons by ages given above)		1			1		1	2	
18 and under 21										1	4
21 and under 30				4	2	2	1		2	1	3
30 and under 60				4	5	1	3	3		6	3
60 and over				1							
All ages	**8**	**11**	**7**	**10**	**7**	**3**	**5**	**3**	**3**	**10**	**10**
All Proved Offences	**71**	**105**	**134**	**131**	**106**	**95**	**124**	**80**	**100**	**150**	**173**
Motoring Offences											
Proceedings for:											
(a) Previously Convicted											
Unfit to drive											
Driving, undue alcohol											
Fail provide specimen											
(b) No Prev. Conviction											
Unfit to drive					21	18	19	14	32	35	12
Driving, undue alcohol											
Fail provide spec.											
In charge and:											
Unfit to drive						7	9	7	7	13	7
Undue alcohol											
Fail provide spec.											
Failure to provide breath specimen											
Total: All Proceedings	**23**	**18**	**23**	**19**	**21**	**25**	**28**	**21**	**39**	**48**	**19**
Licensed Premises											
Public Houses:											
Full	757					788					820
Beer and Cider	124					64					5
Wine or Cider	1					1					
Restaurant Licence											19
Residential Licence											1
Above Combined											3
Licensed Clubs											3
Total On Licences	**882**					**853**					**857**
Off Licences	**161**					**168**					**194**
Total On/Off Licences	**1043**					**1021**					**1045**
Registered Clubs	**238**					**256**					**253**
Total Licences & Clubs	**1281**					**1277**					**1298**

TABLE III 109
DRUNKENNESS OFFENCES, MOTORING OFFENCES AND LICENCES, 1953-63
WORCESTERSHIRE POLICE DISTRICT

	1953	1954	1955	1956	1957	1958	1959	1960	1961	1962	1963
Population '000	**408**					**406**					**457**
Proved Offences—Drunkenness											
Males											
Under 18	x	x	1	3	2	10	6	4	4	8	10
18 and under 21	6	8	6	7	13	19	23	23	36	31	28
21 and under 30	28	34	31	31	28	23	39	35	52	41	58
30 and under 60	112	78	85	76	91	93	101	66	69	87	89
60 and over	17	16	10	7	13	15	13	12	8	7	14
All ages	**159**	**133**	**131**	**124**	**147**	**160**	**182**	**140**	**169**	**174**	**199**
Females											
Under 18		(Included in									
18 and under 21		the number			3			1		1	
21 and under 30		of persons		1	2	1	1	1		1	
30 and under 60		by ages		2	4	6	2	2	3	1	1
60 and over		given above)				1	1		2	3	2
All ages	**4**	**3**	**2**	**3**	**9**	**8**	**4**	**4**	**5**	**6**	**3**
All Proved Offences	**163**	**136**	**133**	**127**	**156**	**168**	**186**	**144**	**174**	**180**	**202**
Motoring Offences											
Proceedings for:											
(a) Previously Convicted											
Unfit to drive											
Driving, undue alcohol											
Fail provide specimen											
(b) No Prev. Conviction											
Unfit to drive					31	29	46	47	47	52	48
Driving, undue alcohol											
Fail provide spec.											
In charge and:											
Unfit to drive					4	2	6	5	12	9	12
Undue alcohol											
Fail provide spec.											
Failure to provide breath specimen											
Total: All Proceedings	**25**	**31**	**41**	**35**	**35**	**31**	**52**	**52**	**59**	**61**	**60**
Licensed Premises											
Public Houses:											
Full	801					819					861
Beer and Cider	114					84					18
Wine or Cider	4					5					3
Restaurant Licence											8
Residential Licence											2
Above Combined											12
Licensed Clubs											10
Total On Licences	**909**					**908**					**914**
Off Licences	**192**					**202**					**244**
Total On/Off Licences	**1111**					**1110**					**1158**
Registered Clubs	**272**					**317**					**301**
Total Licences & Clubs	**1383**					**1427**					**1459**

TABLE III 110

DRUNKENNESS OFFENCES, MOTORING OFFENCES AND LICENCES, 1953-63 DUDLEY POLICE DISTRICT

	1953	1954	1955	1956	1957	1958	1959	1960	1961	1962	1963
Population '000	**61**					**65**					**64**
Proved Offences—Drunkenness											
Males											
Under 18	x	x								1	
18 and under 21	5	5		3	5	1	5	4	3	3	3
21 and under 30	12	9	14	10	3	6	9	13	11	11	12
30 and under 60	29	15	15	14	14	20	20	27	23	33	27
60 and over	4	4	2	2	2	2	3	3	2		4
All ages	**44**	**31**	**29**	**29**	**24**	**29**	**37**	**47**	**39**	**48**	**46**
Females											
Under 18		(Included in the number of persons by ages given above)								1	
18 and under 21											
21 and under 30									1	1	
30 and under 60				1	1	4	4	6	2	1	
60 and over											
All ages	**6**	**2**	**2**	**1**	**1**	**4**	**4**	**6**	**3**	**3**	
All Proved Offences	**50**	**33**	**31**	**30**	**25**	**33**	**41**	**53**	**42**	**51**	**46**
Motoring Offences											
Proceedings for:											
(a) Previously Convicted											
Unfit to drive											
Driving, undue alcohol											
Fail provide specimen											
(b) No Prev. Conviction											
Unfit to drive					5	7	5	1	6	4	3
Driving, undue alcohol											
Fail provide spec.											
In charge and:											
Unfit to drive						1	2		1	3	2
Undue alcohol											
Fail provide spec.											
Failure to provide breath specimen											
Total: All Proceedings	**5**		**14**	**6**	**5**	**8**	**7**	**1**	**7**	**7**	**5**
Licensed Premises											
Public Houses:											
Full	162					160					155
Beer and Cider	19					12					5
Wine or Cider											
Restaurant Licence											1
Residential Licence											
Above Combined											
Licensed Clubs											2
Total On Licences	**181**					**172**					**163**
Off Licences	**24**					**26**					**28**
Total On/Off Licences	**205**					**198**					**191**
Registered Clubs	**30**					**30**					**27**
Total Licences & Clubs	**235**					**228**					**218**

TABLE III 111
DRUNKENNESS OFFENCES, MOTORING OFFENCES AND LICENCES, 1953–63
WORCESTER POLICE DISTRICT

	1953	1954	1955	1956	1957	1958	1959	1960	1961	1962	1963
Population '000	**63**					**64**					**67**
Proved Offences—Drunkenness											
Males											
Under 18	x	x		3			1	1	1	2	4
18 and under 21	3	5	2	4	1	4	4	4	10	10	13
21 and under 30	13	13	2	16	16	17	17	22	18	15	16
30 and under 60	49	61	40	37	27	44	48	55	49	72	48
60 and over	4	12	5	3	3	4	4	7	6	4	8
All ages	**66**	**86**	**43**	**63**	**47**	**69**	**74**	**89**	**84**	**103**	**89**
Females											
Under 18		(Included in the number of persons by ages given above)									
18 and under 21								1	1		
21 and under 30				1		1		1			
30 and under 60				4	6	3	6	2	2	5	9
60 and over						1			1	2	
All ages	**3**	**5**	**6**	**5**	**6**	**5**	**6**	**4**	**4**	**7**	**9**
All Proved Offences	**69**	**91**	**49**	**68**	**53**	**74**	**80**	**93**	**88**	**110**	**98**
Motoring Offences											
Proceedings for:											
(a) Previously Convicted											
Unfit to drive											
Driving, undue alcohol											
Fail provide specimen											
(b) No Prev. Conviction											
Unfit to drive					3	7	13	13	19	11	12
Driving, undue alcohol											
Fail provide spec.											
In charge and:											
Unfit to drive									1		7
Undue alcohol											
Fail provide spec.											
Failure to provide breath specimen											
Total: All Proceedings	**6**	**5**	**3**	**4**	**3**	**7**	**13**	**13**	**20**	**11**	**19**
Licensed Premises											
Public Houses:											
Full	151					152					143
Beer and Cider	5					3					
Wine or Cider	1					1					5
Restaurant Licence											
Residential Licence											
Above Combined											
Licensed Clubs											1
Total On Licences	**157**					**156**					**149**
Off Licences	**45**					**42**					**43**
Total On/Off Licences	**202**					**198**					**192**
Registered Clubs	**57**					**57**					**51**
Total Licences & Clubs	**259**					**255**					**243**

TABLE III 112
DRUNKENNESS OFFENCES, MOTORING OFFENCES AND LICENCES, 1953-63
YORKSHIRE, EAST RIDING POLICE DISTRICT

	1953	1954	1955	1956	1957	1958	1959	1960	1961	1962	1963
Population '000	**214**					**219**					**232**
Proved Offences—Drunkenness											
Males											
Under 18	x	x	1			2	1	3	3	3	
18 and under 21	1	9	3	4	6	6	14	13	8	13	6
21 and under 30	15	8	13	17	13	10	14	12	11	19	13
30 and under 60	12	17	16	21	21	22	25	20	26	16	14
60 and over	1	3	1	2	5	3	4	2	4	2	29
All ages	**28**	**34**	**34**	**44**	**45**	**43**	**58**	**50**	**52**	**53**	1
											63
Females											
Under 18		(Included in the number of persons by ages given above)				1		1			1
18 and under 21											
21 and under 30					1		1		1		
30 and under 60					2	1	1	1	2		1
60 and over											
All ages	**1**	**3**			**3**	**2**	**2**	**2**	**3**		**2**
All Proved Offences	**29**	**37**	**34**	**44**	**48**	**45**	**60**	**52**	**55**	**53**	**65**
Motoring Offences											
Proceedings for:											
(a) Previously Convicted											
Unfit to drive											
Driving, undue alcohol											
Fail provide specimen											
(b) No Prev. Conviction											
Unfit to drive					9	9	7	8	19	38	42
Driving, undue alcohol											
Fail provide spec.											
In charge and:											
Unfit to drive					2	5	6	2	5	4	8
Undue alcohol											
Fail provide spec.											
Failure to provide breath specimen											
Total: All Proceedings	**6**	**3**	**7**	**14**	**11**	**14**	**13**	**10**	**24**	**42**	**50**
Licensed Premises											
Public Houses:											
Full	430					431					448
Beer and Cider	20					13					2
Wine or Cider	1					1					
Restaurant Licence											11
Residential Licence											7
Above Combined											5
Licensed Clubs											16
Total On Licences	**451**					**445**					**489**
Off Licences	**71**					**68**					**84**
Total On/Off Licences	**522**					**513**					**573**
Registered Clubs	**87**					**90**					**85**
Total Licences & Clubs	**609**					**603**					**658**

TABLE III 113
DRUNKENNESS OFFENCES, MOTORING OFFENCES AND LICENCES, 1953–63
KINGSTON-UPON-HULL POLICE DISTRICT

	1953	1954	1955	1956	1957	1958	1959	1960	1961	1962	1963
Population '000	**299**					**301**					**301**
Proved Offences—											
Drunkenness											
Males											
Under 18	x	x	27	24	12	14	21	39	19	24	30
18 and under 21	76	78	92	80	93	60	81	71	85	67	92
21 and under 30	198	216	174	197	185	130	124	138	115	136	135
30 and under 60	317	379	371	309	332	273	269	209	250	262	265
60 and over	40	27	50	19	38	17	31	32	21	26	18
All ages	**572**	**642**	**654**	**629**	**660**	**494**	**526**	**489**	**490**	**515**	**540**
Females											
Under 18			(Included in	1	1	1	1	1	4		1
18 and under 21			the number	8	10	5	3	2	5	3	5
21 and under 30			of persons	4	3	3	1	9	9	3	8
30 and under 60			by ages	26	22	23	13	15	12	7	18
60 and over			given above)	12	2	2	4	7	5	1	5
All ages	**59**	**58**	**60**	**51**	**38**	**34**	**22**	**34**	**35**	**14**	**37**
All Proved Offences	**631**	**700**	**714**	**680**	**698**	**528**	**548**	**523**	**525**	**529**	**577**
Motoring Offences											
Proceedings for:											
(a) Previously Convicted											
Unfit to drive											
Driving, undue alcohol											
Fail provide specimen											
(b) No Prev. Conviction											
Unfit to drive					24	24	20	66	40	59	76
Driving, undue alcohol											
Fail provide spec.											
In charge and:											
Unfit to drive					15	2	5	7	12	12	24
Undue alcohol											
Fail provide spec.											
Failure to provide breath specimen											
Total: All Proceedings	**23**	**19**	**26**	**24**	**39**	**26**	**25**	**73**	**52**	**71**	**100**
Licensed Premises											
Public Houses:											
Full	204					194					230
Beer and Cider	65					44					5
Wine or Cider											
Restaurant Licence											11
Residential Licence											
Above Combined											1
Licensed Clubs											58
Total On Licences	**269**					**238**					**305**
Off Licences	**288**					**229**					**224**
Total On/Off Licences	**557**					**467**					**529**
Registered Clubs	**119**					**119**					**65**
Total Licences & Clubs	**676**					**586**					**594**

TABLE III 114
DRUNKENNESS OFFENCES, MOTORING OFFENCES AND LICENCES, 1953-63
YORKSHIRE, NORTH RIDING POLICE DISTRICT

	1953	1954	1955	1956	1957	1958	1959	1960	1961	1962	1963
Population '000	**378**					**388**					**413**
Proved Offences—Drunkenness											
Males											
Under 18	x	x	12	4	10	8	12	16	18	19	15
18 and under 21	36	44	33	73	62	40	54	88	88	98	93
21 and under 30	85	133	103	117	115	98	90	124	134	151	107
30 and under 60	118	94	102	121	146	97	125	108	131	115	122
60 and over	16	15	7	5	12	6	8	5	7	8	8
All ages	**244**	**276**	**255**	**320**	**345**	**249**	**289**	**341**	**378**	**391**	**345**
Females											
Under 18		(Included in the number of persons by ages given above)							2		1
18 and under 21								1	1	1	3
21 and under 30					1	1		3		1	1
30 and under 60				1	6	5	1	4	6	3	3
60 and over					1				2		1
All ages	**5**	**10**	**2**	**1**	**8**	**6**	**1**	**8**	**11**	**5**	**9**
All Proved Offences	**249**	**286**	**257**	**321**	**353**	**255**	**290**	**349**	**389**	**396**	**354**
Motoring Offences											
Proceedings for:											
(a) Previously Convicted											
Unfit to drive											
Driving, undue alcohol											
Fail provide specimen											
(b) No Prev. Conviction											
Unfit to drive					31	28	33	37	64	64	83
Driving, undue alcohol											
Fail provide spec.											
In charge and:											
Unfit to drive					7	15	11	25	27	28	25
Undue alcohol											
Fail provide spec.											
Failure to provide breath specimen											
Total: All Proceedings	**27**	**36**	**44**	**41**	**38**	**43**	**44**	**62**	**91**	**92**	**108**
Licensed Premises											
Public Houses:											
Full	846					850					865
Beer and Cider	22					15					2
Wine or Cider											
Restaurant Licence											17
Residential Licence											7
Above Combined											14
Licensed Clubs											8
Total On Licences	**868**					**865**					**913**
Off Licences	**185**					**182**					**228**
Total On/Off Licences	**1053**					**1047**					**1141**
Registered Clubs	**153**					**176**					**159**
Total Licences & Clubs	**1206**					**1223**					**1300**

TABLE III 115
DRUNKENNESS OFFENCES, MOTORING OFFENCES AND LICENCES, 1953-63
MIDDLESBOROUGH POLICE DISTRICT

	1953	1954	1955	1956	1957	1958	1959	1960	1961	1962	1963
Population '000	**148**					**153**					**158**
Proved Offences—											
Drunkenness											
Males											
Under 18	x	x	8	10	12	15	11	27	17	12	17
18 and under 21	56	35	46	45	65	74	48	80	87	80	91
21 and under 30	285	194	185	201	206	195	143	188	210	150	135
30 and under 60	399	277	295	315	332	283	308	340	346	349	324
60 and over	27	26	20	30	25	16	17	17	21	20	23
All ages	**718**	**483**	**523**	**601**	**640**	**583**	**527**	**652**	**681**	**611**	**590**
Females											
Under 18			(Included in								
18 and under 21			the number	1	2	3	5	5		2	4
21 and under 30			of persons	14	11	11	12	6	11	9	5
30 and under 60			by ages	32	25	20	13	16	15	33	23
60 and over			given above)	6	4	6	8	8	3	7	4
All ages	**49**	**49**	**31**	**53**	**42**	**40**	**38**	**35**	**29**	**51**	**36**
All Proved Offences	**767**	**532**	**554**	**654**	**682**	**623**	**565**	**687**	**710**	**662**	**626**
Motoring Offences											
Proceedings for:											
(a) Previously Convicted											
Unfit to drive											
Driving, undue alcohol											
Fail provide specimen											
(b) No Prev. Conviction											
Unfit to drive					17	24	25	33	35	30	38
Driving, undue alcohol											
Fail provide spec.											
In charge and:											
Unfit to drive								4	10	14	10
Undue alcohol											
Fail provide spec.											
Failure to provide breath specimen											
Total: All Proceedings	**28**	**33**	**28**	**14**	**17**	**24**	**25**	**37**	**45**	**44**	**48**
Licensed Premises											
Public Houses:											
Full	88					87					98
Beer and Cider	12					9					2
Wine or Cider											
Restaurant Licence											3
Residential Licence											
Above Combined											
Licensed Clubs											
Total On Licences	**100**					**96**					**103**
Off Licences	**82**					**78**					**84**
Total On/Off Licences	**182**					**174**					**187**
Registered Clubs	**57**					**60**					**60**
Total Licences & Clubs	**239**					**234**					**247**

TABLE III 116
DRUNKENNESS OFFENCES, MOTORING OFFENCES AND LICENCES, 1953-63
YORK POLICE DISTRICT

	1953	1954	1955	1956	1957	1958	1959	1960	1961	1962	1963
Population '000	**105**					**106**					**104**
Proved Offences—Drunkenness											
Males											
Under 18	x	x	2		1		1	4	3	1	7
18 and under 21	5	3	2	11	11	8	7	18	6	10	20
21 and under 30	18	29	11	20	21	9	24	23	15	20	38
30 and under 60	34	32	33	32	31	33	26	26	28	13	19
60 and over	4	4	3	2	2	2	2	3	5	4	3
All ages	**59**	**63**	**47**	**65**	**66**	**52**	**60**	**74**	**57**	**48**	**87**
Females											
Under 18		(Included in				1	2	1			
18 and under 21		the number						5	5		
21 and under 30		of persons				1				1	
30 and under 60		by ages			1	1	5	3	2		3
60 and over		given above)									1
All ages	**2**	**5**	**4**		**1**	**3**	**7**	**9**	**7**	**1**	**4**
All Proved Offences	**61**	**68**	**51**	**65**	**67**	**55**	**67**	**83**	**64**	**49**	**91**
Motoring Offences											
Proceedings for:											
(a) Previously Convicted											
Unfit to drive											
Driving, undue alcohol											
Fail provide specimen											
(b) No Prev. Conviction											
Unfit to drive					25	6	14	19	18	25	19
Driving, undue alcohol											
Fail provide spec.											
In charge and:											
Unfit to drive					10	3	10	7	1	4	10
Undue alcohol											
Fail provide spec.											
Failure to provide breath specimen											
Total: All Proceedings	**15**	**17**	**15**	**19**	**35**	**9**	**24**	**26**	**19**	**29**	**29**
Licensed Premises											
Public Houses:											
Full	154					149					149
Beer and Cider	13					10					1
Wine or Cider											
Restaurant Licence											4
Residential Licence											
Above Combined											4
Licensed Clubs											1
Total On Licences	**167**					**159**					**159**
Off Licences	**107**					**110**					**107**
Total On/Off Licences	**274**					**269**					**266**
Registered Clubs	**33**					**66**					**66**
Total Licences & Clubs	**307**					**335**					**332**

TABLE III 117
DRUNKENNESS OFFENCES, MOTORING OFFENCES AND LICENCES, 1953–63
YORKSHIRE, WEST RIDING POLICE DISTRICT

	1953	1954	1955	1956	1957	1958	1959	1960	1961	1962	1963
Population '000	**1593**					**1630**					**1696**
Proved Offences—											
Drunkenness											
Males											
Under 18	x	x	26	26	26	26	26	50	42	47	52
18 and under 21	93	99	95	112	126	154	129	192	203	213	199
21 and under 30	305	273	281	287	322	281	233	298	278	269	286
30 and under 60	437	419	389	396	523	428	396	402	367	315	358
60 and over	55	37	31	34	35	35	34	44	31	32	30
All ages	**857**	**800**	**798**	**855**	**1032**	**924**	**818**	**986**	**921**	**876**	**925**
Females											
Under 18		(Included in						1	5	5	2
18 and under 21		the number		1	1	2	4	2	1	3	3
21 and under 30		of persons		2	4	4	4	1	1	1	5
30 and under 60		by ages		18	12	12	18	12	7	11	8
60 and over		given above)				3	1	2	2	2	2
All ages	**33**	**28**	**24**	**21**	**17**	**21**	**27**	**18**	**16**	**22**	**20**
All Proved Offences	**890**	**828**	**822**	**876**	**1049**	**945**	**845**	**1004**	**937**	**898**	**945**
Motoring Offences											
Proceedings for:											
(a) Previously Convicted											
Unfit to drive											
Driving, undue alcohol											
Fail provide specimen											
(b) No Prev. Conviction											
Unfit to drive					141	139	139	180	161	148	202
Driving, undue alcohol											
Fail provide spec.											
In charge and:											
Unfit to drive					20	29	30	41	33	33	37
Undue alcohol											
Fail provide spec.											
Failure to provide breath specimen											
Total: All Proceedings	**125**	**150**	**118**	**152**	**161**	**168**	**169**	**221**	**194**	**181**	**239**
Licensed Premises											
Public Houses:											
Full	2098					2153					2346
Beer and Cider	330					256					53
Wine or Cider	2					2					1
Restaurant Licence											34
Residential Licence											2
Above Combined											13
Licensed Clubs											12
Total On Licences	**2430**					**2411**					**2461**
Off Licences	**922**					**920**					**1029**
Total On/Off Licences	**3352**					**3331**					**3490**
Registered Clubs	**1045**					**1065**					**1057**
Total Licences & Clubs	**4397**					**4396**					**4547**

TABLE III 118
DRUNKENNESS OFFENCES, MOTORING OFFENCES AND LICENCES, 1953-63
BARNSLEY POLICE DISTRICT

	1953	1954	1955	1956	1957	1958	1959	1960	1961	1962	1963
Population '000	**75**					**76**					**75**
Proved Offences—Drunkenness											
Males											
Under 18	x	x	2		2	4	2	3	2	3	5
18 and under 21	3	5	4	13	11	17	18	24	18	15	21
21 and under 30	25	26	26	34	45	56	52	31	24	34	30
30 and under 60	38	60	70	75	61	62	87	83	80	65	59
60 and over	4	10	3	5	5	8	9	9	2	5	6
All ages	**65**	**88**	**91**	**127**	**124**	**147**	**168**	**150**	**126**	**122**	**121**
Females											
Under 18		(Included in									
18 and under 21		the number			2	1	2		2	2	2
21 and under 30		of persons		1				1		5	
30 and under 60		by ages		9	7	5	2	16	13	14	24
60 and over		given above)		2	2	5	2	3	1	1	1
All ages	**5**	**13**	**14**	**12**	**11**	**11**	**6**	**20**	**16**	**22**	**27**
All Proved Offences	**70**	**101**	**105**	**139**	**135**	**158**	**174**	**170**	**142**	**144**	**148**
Motoring Offences											
Proceedings for:											
(a) Previously Convicted											
Unfit to drive											
Driving, undue alcohol											
Fail provide specimen											
(b) No Prev. Conviction											
Unfit to drive					11	18	13	4	14	15	25
Driving, undue alcohol											
Fail provide spec.											
In charge and:											
Unfit to drive					3	4	3	6	6	4	6
Undue alcohol											
Fail provide spec.											
Failure to provide breath specimen											
Total: All Proceedings	**11**	**14**	**16**	**18**	**14**	**22**	**16**	**10**	**20**	**19**	**31**
Licensed Premises											
Public Houses:											
Full	90					91					99
Beer and Cider	16					12					
Wine or Cider											
Restaurant Licence											1
Residential Licence											
Above Combined											
Licensed Clubs											
Total On Licences	**106**					**103**					**100**
Off Licences	**81**					**79**					**80**
Total On/Off Licences	**187**					**182**					**180**
Registered Clubs	**35**					**40**					**44**
Total Licences & Clubs	**222**					**222**					**224**

TABLE III 119
DRUNKENNESS OFFENCES, MOTORING OFFENCES AND LICENCES, 1953–63
BRADFORD POLICE DISTRICT

	1953	1954	1955	1956	1957	1958	1959	1960	1961	1962	1963
Population '000	**289**					**288**					**297**
Proved Offences—Drunkenness											
Males											
Under 18	x	x	7	10	2	1	3	12	2	15	10
18 and under 21	19	18	21	23	30	21	28	41	61	64	66
21 and under 30	138	141	161	117	154	110	118	176	206	231	209
30 and under 60	442	442	401	448	491	392	427	600	726	671	846
60 and over	81	68	53	50	53	37	44	60	60	43	72
All ages	**634**	**624**	**607**	**648**	**730**	**561**	**620**	**889**	**1055**	**1024**	**1203**
Females											
Under 18		(Included in					1		1	4	1
18 and under 21		the number		2	1	4	1	3	3	2	
21 and under 30		of persons		3	7	5		5	11	20	14
30 and under 60		by ages		21	24	32	28	25	34	48	55
60 and over		given above)		11	10	4	12	9	8	8	5
All ages	**46**	**45**	**36**	**37**	**42**	**45**	**42**	**42**	**57**	**82**	**75**
All Proved Offences	**680**	**669**	**643**	**685**	**772**	**606**	**662**	**931**	**1112**	**1106**	**1278**
Motoring Offences											
Proceedings for:											
(a) Previously Convicted											
Unfit to drive											
Driving, undue alcohol											
Fail provide specimen											
(b) No Prev. Conviction											
Unfit to drive					7	15	16	33	35	30	50
Driving, undue alcohol											
Fail provide spec.											
In charge and:											
Unfit to drive					6	9	17	16	19	18	14
Undue alcohol											
Fail provide spec.											
Failure to provide breath specimen											
Total: All Proceedings	**29**	**29**	**17**	**20**	**13**	**24**	**33**	**49**	**54**	**48**	**64**
Licensed Premises											
Public Houses:											
Full	266					283					348
Beer and Cider	136					109					25
Wine or Cider	1					1					1
Restaurant Licence											11
Residential Licence											1
Above Combined											2
Licensed Clubs											5
Total On Licences	**403**					**393**					**393**
Off Licences	**422**					**411**					**388**
Total On/Off Licences	**825**					**804**					**781**
Registered Clubs	**152**					**156**					**158**
Total Licences & Clubs	**977**					**960**					**939**

TABLE III 120
DRUNKENNESS OFFENCES, MOTORING OFFENCES AND LICENCES, 1953–63
DEWSBURY POLICE DISTRICT

	1953	1954	1955	1956	1957	1958	1959	1960	1961	1962	1963
Population '000	**53**					**53**					**54**
Proved Offences—Drunkenness											
Males											
Under 18	x	x	6	2	2	1	2			3	4
18 and under 21	6	8	2	18	8	6	1	7	3	5	10
21 and under 30	21	27	18	24	20	14	10	8	7	9	12
30 and under 60	21	33	26	26	21	18	16	14	18	16	20
60 and over	3	3	2	1	2	1	2	4		2	4
All ages	**50**	**70**	**52**	**71**	**53**	**40**	**31**	**33**	**28**	**35**	**50**
Females											
Under 18	(Included in the number of persons by ages given above)										
18 and under 21											
21 and under 30											1
30 and under 60						1	1	1	1		1
60 and over									1		
All ages	**1**	**1**	**2**			**1**	**1**	**1**	**2**		**2**
All Proved Offences	**51**	**71**	**54**	**71**	**53**	**41**	**32**	**34**	**30**	**35**	**52**
Motoring Offences											
Proceedings for:											
(a) Previously Convicted											
Unfit to drive											
Driving, undue alcohol											
Fail provide specimen											
(b) No Prev. Conviction											
Unfit to drive					4	19	12	17	14	11	20
Driving, undue alcohol											
Fail provide spec.											
In charge and:											
Unfit to drive					6	4	5	10	4	3	
Undue alcohol											
Fail provide spec.											
Failure to provide breath specimen											
Total: All Proceedings	**6**	**4**	**11**	**15**	**10**	**23**	**17**	**27**	**18**	**14**	**20**
Licensed Premises											
Public Houses:											
Full	66					67					67
Beer and Cider	25					21					13
Wine or Cider											
Restaurant Licence											3
Residential Licence											
Above Combined											
Licensed Clubs											
Total On Licences	**91**					**88**					**83**
Off Licences	**61**					**63**					**62**
Total On/Off Licences	**152**					**151**					**145**
Registered Clubs	**41**					**43**					**42**
Total Licences & Clubs	**193**					**194**					**187**

TABLE III 121

DRUNKENNESS OFFENCES, MOTORING OFFENCES AND LICENCES, 1953–63 DONCASTER POLICE DISTRICT

	1953	1954	1955	1956	1957	1958	1959	1960	1961	1962	1963
Population '000	**82**					**84**					**87**
Proved Offences—Drunkenness											
Males											
Under 18	x	x	3	1	3		3	1	2	1	4
18 and under 21	8	7	9	13	17	16	25	26	22	13	24
21 and under 30	63	47	51	61	58	57	28	55	49	73	53
30 and under 60	91	98	93	95	100	94	102	66	114	133	102
60 and over	15	9	8	3	13	6	6	8	6	10	10
All ages	**170**	**152**	**147**	**173**	**191**	**173**	**174**	**156**	**193**	**230**	**193**
Females											
Under 18		(Included in the number of persons by ages given above)								1	
18 and under 21									2		1
21 and under 30				7	1	1		1	1		2
30 and under 60				8	11	5	3	8	9	7	7
60 and over						2		2			
All ages	**7**	**9**	**17**	**15**	**12**	**8**	**3**	**11**	**12**	**8**	**10**
All Proved Offences	**177**	**161**	**164**	**188**	**203**	**181**	**177**	**167**	**205**	**238**	**203**
Motoring Offences											
Proceedings for:											
(a) Previously Convicted											
Unfit to drive											
Driving, undue alcohol											
Fail provide specimen											
(b) No Prev. Conviction											
Unfit to drive					12	8	6	13	9	16	12
Driving, undue alcohol											
Fail provide spec.											
In charge and:											
Unfit to drive					3	1	1	6	4	1	4
Undue alcohol											
Fail provide spec.											
Failure to provide breath specimen											
Total: All Proceedings	**11**	**11**	**8**	**12**	**15**	**9**	**7**	**19**	**13**	**17**	**16**
Licensed Premises											
Public Houses:											
Full	91					91					82
Beer and Cider	3					2					
Wine or Cider											
Restaurant Licence											9
Residential Licence											1
Above Combined											2
Licensed Clubs											1
Total On Licences	**94**					**93**					**95**
Off Licences	**75**					**76**					**74**
Total On/Off Licences	**169**					**169**					**169**
Registered Clubs	**26**					**36**					**40**
Total Licences & Clubs	**195**					**205**					**209**

TABLE III 122
DRUNKENNESS OFFENCES, MOTORING OFFENCES AND LICENCES, 1953–63
HALIFAX POLICE DISTRICT

	1953	1954	1955	1956	1957	1958	1959	1960	1961	1962	1963
Population '000	**97**					**95**					**96**
Proved Offences—Drunkenness											
Males											
Under 18	x	x	1	1	1	2	1	1		2	4
18 and under 21	1	4	1	8	1	10	1	2	2	3	4
21 and under 30	16	24	24	13	10	21	3	19	15	26	44
30 and under 60	59	81	89	77	38	37	40	42	53	75	109
60 and over	8	8	7	3	4	2	1	2	6	7	10
All ages	**74**	**114**	**118**	**102**	**54**	**72**	**46**	**66**	**76**	**113**	**171**
Females											
Under 18		(Included in the number of persons by ages given above)				1			1	2	
18 and under 21										1	
21 and under 30						1				4	2
30 and under 60				4	3	2	2	4	2	8	6
60 and over						1	2				
All ages	**10**	**3**	**2**	**4**	**3**	**5**	**4**	**4**	**3**	**15**	**8**
All Proved Offences	**84**	**117**	**120**	**106**	**57**	**77**	**50**	**70**	**79**	**128**	**179**
Motoring Offences											
Proceedings for:											
(a) Previously Convicted											
Unfit to drive											
Driving, undue alcohol											
Fail provide specimen											
(b) No Prev. Conviction											
Unfit to drive						6	9	12	12	7	7
Driving, undue alcohol											
Fail provide spec.											
In charge and:											
Unfit to drive								1	4	3	2
Undue alcohol											
Fail provide spec.											
Failure to provide breath specimen											
Total: All Proceedings	**2**	**6**	**8**	**1**		**6**	**9**	**13**	**16**	**10**	**9**
Licensed Premises											
Public Houses:											
Full	121					122					161
Beer and Cider	64					53					10
Wine or Cider											1
Restaurant Licence											4
Residential Licence											
Above Combined											2
Licensed Clubs											4
Total On Licences	**185**					**175**					**182**
Off Licences	**119**					**118**					**110**
Total On/Off Licences	**304**					**293**					**292**
Registered Clubs	**49**					**50**					**50**
Total Licences & Clubs	**353**					**343**					**342**

TABLE III 123
DRUNKENNESS OFFENCES, MOTORING OFFENCES AND LICENCES, 1953–63
HUDDERSFIELD POLICE DISTRICT

	1953	1954	1955	1956	1957	1958	1959	1960	1961	1962	1963
Population '000	**129**					**128**					**132**
Proved Offences—Drunkenness											
Males											
Under 18	x	x	2			2				1	3
18 and under 21	3		2	6	10	4	4	2	6	1	3
21 and under 30	14	6	10	12	11	11	15	13	15	7	9
30 and under 60	48	45	67	45	61	45	52	35	41	31	38
60 and over	7	5	7	5	7	7	5	6	3	6	2
All ages	**65**	**52**	**85**	**68**	**89**	**69**	**76**	**56**	**65**	**46**	**55**
Females											
Under 18			(Included in	1					2		
18 and under 21			the number	3							
21 and under 30			of persons	1			1				1
30 and under 60			by ages	1	2	2		1	1	3	5
60 and over			given above)		2		2				1
All ages	**7**	**4**	**3**	**6**	**4**	**2**	**3**	**1**	**3**	**3**	**7**
All Proved Offences	**72**	**56**	**88**	**74**	**93**	**71**	**79**	**57**	**68**	**49**	**62**
Motoring Offences											
Proceedings for:											
(a) Previously Convicted											
Unfit to drive											
Driving, undue alcohol											
Fail provide specimen											
(b) No Prev. Conviction											
Unfit to drive					15	10	20	31	29	26	11
Driving, undue alcohol											
Fail provide spec.											
In charge and:											
Unfit to drive					1	5	4	1	3	5	3
Undue alcohol											
Fail provide spec.											
Failure to provide breath specimen											
Total: All Proceedings	**8**	**20**	**9**	**7**	**16**	**15**	**24**	**32**	**32**	**31**	**14**
Licensed Premises											
Public Houses:											
Full	171					173					179
Beer and Cider	22					17					3
Wine or Cider	1					1					1
Restaurant Licence											7
Residential Licence											
Above Combined											
Licensed Clubs											
Total On Licences	**194**					**191**					**190**
Off Licences	**70**					**67**					**65**
Total On/Off Licences	**264**					**258**					**255**
Registered Clubs	**114**					**109**					**111**
Total Licences & Clubs	**378**					**367**					**366**

TABLE III 124
DRUNKENNESS OFFENCES, MOTORING OFFENCES AND LICENCES, 1953–63
LEEDS POLICE DISTRICT

	1953	1954	1955	1956	1957	1958	1959	1960	1961	1962	1963
Population '000	**506**					**512**					**514**
Proved Offences—Drunkenness											
Males											
Under 18	x	x	9	16	21	13	9	12	9	26	26
18 and under 21	80	76	79	81	97	94	115	90	115	122	181
21 and under 30	305	311	333	320	294	266	243	266	309	405	466
30 and under 60	658	671	727	749	844	686	633	644	720	888	1068
60 and over	99	96	96	101	130	107	74	89	96	113	156
All ages	**1065**	**1075**	**1165**	**1267**	**1386**	**1166**	**1074**	**1101**	**1249**	**1554**	**1897**
Females											
Under 18		(Included in the number of persons by ages given above)		1	2				1		2
18 and under 21				5	10	7	3	5	4	5	10
21 and under 30				10	14	12	15	29	10	13	25
30 and under 60				54	65	64	50	57	47	66	82
60 and over				10	18	9	12	11	17	28	19
All ages	**77**	**77**	**79**	**80**	**109**	**92**	**80**	**102**	**79**	**112**	**138**
All Proved Offences	**1142**	**1154**	**1244**	**1347**	**1495**	**1258**	**1154**	**1203**	**1328**	**1666**	**2035**
Motoring Offences											
Proceedings for:											
(a) Previously Convicted											
Unfit to drive											
Driving, undue alcohol											
Fail provide specimen											
(b) No Prev. Conviction											
Unfit to drive											
Driving, undue alcohol					92	86	78	94	102	106	124
Fail provide spec.											
In charge and:											
Unfit to drive											
Undue alcohol					19	13	28	31	19	21	39
Fail provide spec.											
Failure to provide breath specimen											
Total: All Proceedings	**65**	**77**	**76**	**100**	**111**	**99**	**106**	**125**	**121**	**127**	**163**
Licensed Premises											
Public Houses:											
Full	301					323					385
Beer and Cider	137					106					34
Wine or Cider	2					1					1
Restaurant Licence											17
Residential Licence											
Above Combined											2
Licensed Clubs											13
Total On Licences	**440**					**430**					**452**
Off Licences	**389**					**376**					**404**
Total On/Off Licences	**829**					**806**					**856**
Registered Clubs	**190**					**199**					**191**
Total Licences & Clubs	**1019**					**1005**					**1047**

TABLE III 125
DRUNKENNESS OFFENCES, MOTORING OFFENCES AND LICENCES, 1953–63 ROTHERHAM POLICE DISTRICT

	1953	1954	1955	1956	1957	1958	1959	1960	1961	1962	1963
Population '000	**82**					**84**					**87**
Proved Offences—											
Drunkenness											
Males											
Under 18	x	x	1	1		1	3	1	3		
18 and under 21	3	4	7	17	9	12	9	11	19	10	10
21 and under 30	18	20	16	26	35	30	34	17	24	39	35
30 and under 60	47	55	45	68	63	63	36	53	59	48	65
60 and over	7	7	6	5	4	2	3	4	3	3	3
All ages	**71**	**79**	**72**	**117**	**111**	**108**	**85**	**86**	**108**	**100**	**113**
Females											
Under 18	(Included in the number of persons by ages given above)										
18 and under 21											
21 and under 30					1			1	2		1
30 and under 60				3	4	1	1	3			
60 and over					1						
All ages	**4**	**7**	**3**	**3**	**6**	**1**	**1**	**4**	**2**		**1**
All Proved Offences	**75**	**86**	**75**	**120**	**117**	**109**	**86**	**90**	**110**	**100**	**114**
Motoring Offences											
Proceedings for:											
(a) Previously Convicted											
Unfit to drive											
Driving, undue alcohol											
Fail provide specimen											
(b) No Prev. Conviction											
Unfit to drive					11	12	11	7	15	24	15
Driving, undue alcohol											
Fail provide spec.											
In charge and:											
Unfit to drive					4	2	3	3	2		4
Undue alcohol											
Fail provide spec.											
Failure to provide breath specimen											
Total: All Proceedings	**7**	**6**	**13**	**23**	**15**	**14**	**14**	**10**	**17**	**24**	**19**
Licensed Premises											
Public Houses:											
Full	86					96					111
Beer and Cider	26					17					3
Wine or Cider											
Restaurant Licence											2
Residential Licence											
Above Combined											1
Licensed Clubs											2
Total On Licences	**112**					**113**					**119**
Off Licences	**66**					**64**					**64**
Total On/Off Licences	**178**					**177**					**183**
Registered Clubs	**23**					**24**					**25**
Total Licences & Clubs	**201**					**201**					**208**

TABLE III 126
DRUNKENNESS OFFENCES, MOTORING OFFENCES AND LICENCES, 1953-63
SHEFFIELD POLICE DISTRICT

	1953	1954	1955	1956	1957	1958	1959	1960	1961	1962	1963
Population '000	**508**					**499**					**495**
Proved Offences—Drunkenness											
Males											
Under 18	x	x	7	8	7	8	2	14	20	15	16
18 and under 21	24	19	23	42	33	43	42	71	68	126	163
21 and under 30	145	118	139	177	173	163	146	220	203	306	281
30 and under 60	300	269	362	398	474	396	405	537	482	390	679
60 and over	34	22	38	43	40	31	34	45	37	55	51
All ages	**465**	**411**	**543**	**668**	**727**	**641**	**629**	**887**	**810**	**1092**	**1200**
Females											
Under 18		(Included in the number of persons by ages given above)						1	1		
18 and under 21				1	6	7	5	1		3	4
21 and under 30				6	11	7	5	10	5	7	5
30 and under 60				14	14	13	14	28	43	23	33
60 and over				9	3	7	4	2	7	5	4
All ages	**38**	**17**	**26**	**30**	**34**	**34**	**28**	**42**	**56**	**38**	**46**
All Proved Offences	**503**	**428**	**569**	**698**	**761**	**675**	**657**	**929**	**866**	**1130**	**1246**
Motoring Offences											
Proceedings for:											
(a) Previously Convicted											
Unfit to drive											
Driving, undue alcohol											
Fail provide specimen											
(b) No Prev. Conviction											
Unfit to drive					27	25	25	33	29	52	74
Driving, undue alcohol											
Fail provide spec.											
In charge and:											
Unfit to drive					5	12	1	8	5	12	18
Undue alcohol											
Fail provide spec.											
Failure to provide breath specimen											
Total: All Proceedings	**35**	**28**	**38**	**51**	**32**	**37**	**26**	**41**	**34**	**64**	**92**
Licensed Premises											
Public Houses:											
Full	459					454					478
Beer and Cider	209					166					115
Wine or Cider	1					1					
Restaurant Licence											11
Residential Licence											
Above Combined											2
Licensed Clubs											1
Total On Licences	**669**					**621**					**607**
Off Licences	**522**					**476**					**440**
Total On/Off Licences	**1191**					**1097**					**1047**
Registered Clubs	**131**					**130**					**124**
Total Licences & Clubs	**1322**					**1227**					**1171**

TABLE III 127
DRUNKENNESS OFFENCES, MOTORING OFFENCES AND LICENCES, 1953–63
WAKEFIELD POLICE DISTRICT

	1953	1954	1955	1956	1957	1958	1959	1960	1961	1962	1963
Population '000	**60**					**60**					**60**
Proved Offences— Drunkenness											
Males											
Under 18	x	x		2	1	2		2	5		3
18 and under 21	3	1	1	10	10	4	8	11	26	13	32
21 and under 30	21	14	12	19	22	14	26	26	33	23	34
30 and under 60	30	37	43	31	29	22	21	35	36	32	32
60 and over	2	1	2	3	5	4	3	4	4	2	3
All ages	**53**	**49**	**54**	**65**	**67**	**46**	**58**	**78**	**104**	**70**	**104**
Females											
Under 18		(Included in								2	
18 and under 21		the number								1	
21 and under 30		of persons					1			2	
30 and under 60		by ages			3	1	3	2			
60 and over		given above)			1						
All ages	**3**	**4**	**4**		**4**	**1**	**4**	**2**		**5**	
All Proved Offences											
Motoring Offences											
Proceedings for:											
(a) Previously Convicted											
Unfit to drive											
Driving, undue alcohol											
Fail provide specimen											
(b) No Prev. Conviction											
Unfit to drive					4	3	7	10	8	10	14
Driving, undue alcohol											
Fail provide spec.											
In charge and:											
Unfit to drive					3	1	3		1	1	
Undue alcohol											
Fail provide spec.											
Failure to provide breath specimen											
Total: All Proceedings	**3**	**11**	**12**	**7**	**7**	**4**	**10**	**10**	**9**	**11**	**14**
Licensed Premises											
Public Houses:											
Full	111					111					108
Beer and Cider	14					9					3
Wine or Cider	3					1					
Restaurant Licence											3
Residential Licence											
Above Combined											2
Licensed Clubs											2
Total On Licences	**128**					**121**					**119**
Off Licences	**69**					**65**					**66**
Total On/Off Licences	**197**					**186**					**185**
Registered Clubs	**48**					**50**					**35**
Total Licences & Clubs	**245**					**236**					**220**

TABLE III 128

DRUNKENNESS OFFENCES, MOTORING OFFENCES AND LICENCES, 1953-63
CARMARTHENSHIRE & CARDIGANSHIRE POLICE DISTRICT

	1953	1954	1955	1956	1957	1958	1959	1960	1961	1962	1963
Population '000	**225**					**222**					**220**
Proved Offences—Drunkenness											
Males											
Under 18	x	x	7	5	6	4	6	10	13	6	6
18 and under 21	20	24	19	17	24	30	37	53	46	43	43
21 and under 30	61	65	49	52	61	77	109	99	87	72	48
30 and under 60	102	99	122	99	134	120	186	146	113	97	88
60 and over	7	18	14	8	15	16	15	4	9	10	6
All ages	**177**	**191**	**198**	**181**	**240**	**247**	**353**	**312**	**268**	**228**	**191**
Females											
Under 18			(Included in	1				1	2		
18 and under 21			the number		1	1		1	1		
21 and under 30			of persons	1	1	1		1		1	2
30 and under 60			by ages	4	6	11	7	4	6	5	5
60 and over			given above)	4	4	7	3	5	5	3	1
All ages	**13**	**15**	**13**	**10**	**12**	**20**	**10**	**12**	**14**	**9**	**8**
All Proved Offences	**190**	**206**	**211**	**191**	**252**	**247**	**363**	**324**	**282**	**237**	**199**
Motoring Offences											
Proceedings for:											
(a) Previously Convicted											
Unfit to drive											
Driving, undue alcohol											
Fail provide specimen											
(b) No Prev. Conviction											
Unfit to drive					36	39	44	55	35	56	40
Driving, undue alcohol											
Fail provide spec.											
In charge and:											
Unfit to drive						1	3	10	9	11	11
Undue alcohol											
Fail provide spec.											
Failure to provide breath specimen											
Total: All Proceedings	**27**	**40**	**30**	**33**	**36**	**40**	**47**	**65**	**44**	**67**	**51**
Licensed Premises											
Public Houses:											
Full	681					669					659
Beer and Cider	18					13					1
Wine or Cider											
Restaurant Licence											17
Residential Licence											4
Above Combined											11
Licensed Clubs											8
Total On Licences	**699**					**682**					**700**
Off Licences	**59**					**62**					**66**
Total On/Off Licences	**758**					**744**					**766**
Registered Clubs	**57**					**67**					**89**
Total Licences & Clubs	**815**					**811**					**855**

TABLE III 129
DRUNKENNESS OFFENCES, MOTORING OFFENCES AND LICENCES, 1953-63
DENBIGHSHIRE POLICE DISTRICT

	1953	1954	1955	1956	1957	1958	1959	1960	1961	1962	1963
Population '000	**170**					**170**					**175**
Proved Offences—Drunkenness											
Males											
Under 18	x	x		8			1	4	5	1	4
18 and under 21	7	4	10	14	8	17	9	14	16	24	19
21 and under 30	20	30	28	20	13	35	15	22	25	35	43
30 and under 60	17	31	32	29	35	32	33	34	56	77	76
60 and over	3	5	3	5	6	4	10	7	10	27	28
All ages	**43**	**65**	**72**	**76**	**62**	**88**	**68**	**81**	**112**	**164**	**170**
Females											
Under 18		(Included in						1			
18 and under 21		the number			1			1			
21 and under 30		of persons			1		1				
30 and under 60		by ages		2	1	4	2	4	1	8	2
60 and over		given above)			1		1	2	4		3
All ages	**4**	**5**	**1**	**2**	**4**	**4**	**4**	**8**	**5**	**8**	**5**
All Proved Offences	**47**	**70**	**73**	**78**	**66**	**92**	**72**	**89**	**117**	**172**	**175**
Motoring Offences											
Proceedings for:											
(a) Previously Convicted											
Unfit to drive											
Driving, undue alcohol											
Fail provide specimen											
(b) No Prev. Conviction											
Unfit to drive					18	15	21	22	17	26	26
Driving, undue alcohol											
Fail provide spec.											
In charge and:											
Unfit to drive					2	8	7	7	1	10	2
Undue alcohol											
Fail provide spec.											
Failure to provide breath specimen											
Total: All Proceedings	**5**	**15**	**13**	**24**	**20**	**23**	**28**	**29**	**18**	**36**	**28**
Licensed Premises											
Public Houses:											
Full	302					304					343
Beer and Cider	76					56					15
Wine or Cider											
Restaurant Licence											10
Residential Licence											4
Above Combined											5
Licensed Clubs											1
Total On Licences	**378**					**360**					**378**
Off Licences	**33**					**34**					**48**
Total On/Off Licences	**411**					**394**					**426**
Registered Clubs	**45**					**65**					**69**
Total Licences & Clubs	**466**					**459**					**495**

TABLE III 130
DRUNKENNESS OFFENCES, MOTORING OFFENCES AND LICENCES, 1953-63
FLINTSHIRE POLICE DISTRICT

	1953	1954	1955	1956	1957	1958	1959	1960	1961	1962	1963
Population '000	**145**					**147**					**152**
Proved Offences—Drunkenness											
Males											
Under 18	x	x	2	2	2	4	1	1		1	2
18 and under 21	3		7	9	8	25	11	3	5	2	6
21 and under 30	7	14	13	12	13	25	18	13	9	18	16
30 and under 60	17	20	27	16	17	22	13	11	13	17	18
60 and over	1		1		3	1			1	3	
All ages	**24**	**32**	**48**	**39**	**43**	**77**	**43**	**28**	**28**	**41**	**42**
Females											
Under 18		(Included in the number of persons by ages given above)		1		1					
18 and under 21					1						
21 and under 30											2
30 and under 60				2		3	2	2		1	
60 and over							1				
All ages	**4**	**2**	**2**	**3**	**1**	**4**	**3**	**2**		**1**	**2**
All Proved Offences	**28**	**34**	**50**	**42**	**44**	**81**	**46**	**30**	**28**	**42**	**44**
Motoring Offences											
Proceedings for:											
(a) Previously Convicted											
Unfit to drive											
Driving, undue alcohol											
Fail provide specimen											
(b) No Prev. Conviction											
Unfit to drive					16	17	25	20	24	17	15
Driving, undue alcohol											
Fail provide spec.											
In charge and:											
Unfit to drive					2	2	1	4	4	7	2
Undue alcohol											
Fail provide spec.											
Failure to provide breath specimen											
Total: All Proceedings	**11**	**20**	**27**	**32**	**18**	**19**	**26**	**24**	**28**	**24**	**17**
Licensed Premises											
Public Houses:											
Full	284					283					295
Beer and Cider	26					23					9
Wine or Cider											
Restaurant Licence											14
Residential Licence											2
Above Combined											7
Licensed Clubs											25
Total On Licences	**310**					**306**					**352**
Off Licences	**25**					**31**					**53**
Total On/Off Licences	**335**					**337**					**405**
Registered Clubs	**65**					**78**					**73**
Total Licences & Clubs	**400**					**415**					**478**

TABLE III 131

DRUNKENNESS OFFENCES, MOTORING OFFENCES AND LICENCES, 1953–63 GLAMORGANSHIRE POLICE DISTRICT

	1953	1954	1955	1956	1957	1958	1959	1960	1961	1962	1963
Population '000	**736**					**743**					**752**
Proved Offences—Drunkenness											
Males											
Under 18	x	x	13	14	16	28	20	16	22	28	33
18 and under 21	44	39	59	65	65	100	113	92	122	105	100
21 and under 30	146	127	145	123	155	152	157	152	139	149	105
30 and under 60	193	189	201	166	212	208	184	174	161	178	139
60 and over	15	7	6	6	10	10	9	7	14	10	13
All ages	**394**	**353**	**419**	**374**	**458**	**498**	**483**	**441**	**458**	**470**	**390**
Females											
Under 18		(Included in		1		1	1		1		1
18 and under 21		the number				2		1	2	2	1
21 and under 30		of persons		1	3	1	4	4	3	2	1
30 and under 60		by ages		5	6	6	8	3	7	5	7
60 and over		given above)		2	2			1			
All ages	**4**	**9**	**5**	**9**	**11**	**10**	**13**	**9**	**13**	**9**	**10**
All Proved Offences	**398**	**362**	**424**	**383**	**469**	**508**	**496**	**450**	**471**	**479**	**400**
Motoring Offences											
Proceedings for:											
(a) Previously Convicted											
Unfit to drive											
Driving, undue alcohol											
Fail provide specimen											
(b) No Prev. Conviction											
Unfit to drive					52	58	58	90	78	79	100
Driving, undue alcohol											
Fail provide spec.											
In charge and:											
Unfit to drive					6	9	3	6	20	18	21
Undue alcohol											
Fail provide spec.											
Failure to provide breath specimen											
Total: All Proceedings	**40**	**55**	**76**	**55**	**58**	**67**	**61**	**96**	**98**	**97**	**121**
Licensed Premises											
Public Houses:											
Full	909					924					970
Beer and Cider	66					47					1
Wine or Cider											
Restaurant Licence											30
Residential Licence											
Above Combined											5
Licensed Clubs											30
Total On Licences	**975**					**971**					**1036**
Off Licences	**184**					**210**					**270**
Total On/Off Licences	**1159**					**1181**					**1306**
Registered Clubs	**337**					**373**					**433**
Total Licences & Clubs	**1496**					**1554**					**1739**

TABLE III 132
DRUNKENNESS OFFENCES, MOTORING OFFENCES AND LICENCES, 1953-63
CARDIFF POLICE DISTRICT

	1953	1954	1955	1956	1957	1958	1959	1960	1961	1962	1963
Population '000	**247**					**253**					**261**
Proved Offences—Drunkenness											
Males											
Under 18	x	x	2	6	7	2	5	4	10	9	3
18 and under 21	25	22	18	28	34	32	26	29	31	21	28
21 and under 30	73	81	106	113	86	104	101	64	71	69	58
30 and under 60	245	242	228	203	242	282	265	245	220	193	221
60 and over	27	31	38	22	29	37	41	31	30	12	14
All ages	**339**	**341**	**359**	**372**	**398**	**457**	**438**	**373**	**362**	**304**	**324**
Females											
Under 18			(Included in	1			1	1	1	1	1
18 and under 21			the number	1	1	4	2	1	1	1	4
21 and under 30			of persons	5	9	1	5	1	3	6	1
30 and under 60			by ages	32	44	38	9	17	21	14	22
60 and over			given above)	3	9	10	17	26	18	17	30
All ages	**31**	**35**	**33**	**42**	**63**	**53**	**34**	**46**	**44**	**39**	**58**
All Proved Offences	**370**	**376**	**392**	**414**	**461**	**510**	**472**	**419**	**406**	**343**	**382**
Motoring Offences											
Proceedings for:											
(a) Previously Convicted											
Unfit to drive											
Driving, undue alcohol											
Fail provide specimen											
(b) No Prev. Conviction											
Unfit to drive					57	50	41	34	33	30	35
Driving, undue alcohol											
Fail provide spec.											
In charge and:											
Unfit to drive					15	15	15	11	13	8	10
Undue alcohol											
Fail provide spec.											
Failure to provide breath specimen											
Total: All Proceedings	**40**	**29**	**41**	**46**	**72**	**65**	**56**	**45**	**46**	**38**	**45**
Licensed Premises											
Public Houses:											
Full	199					206					212
Beer and Cider	12					2					
Wine or Cider	6					2					
Restaurant Licence											17
Residential Licence											
Above Combined											6
Licensed Clubs											31
Total On Licences	**217**					**210**					**266**
Off Licences	**77**					**81**					**109**
Total On/Off Licences	**294**					**291**					**375**
Registered Clubs	**77**					**95**					**74**
Total Licences & Clubs	**371**					**386**					**449**

TABLE III 133

DRUNKENNESS OFFENCES, MOTORING OFFENCES AND LICENCES, 1953-63 MERTHYR TYDVIL POLICE DISTRICT

	1953	1954	1955	1956	1957	1958	1959	1960	1961	1962	1963
Population '000	**60**					**59**					**59**
Proved Offences—Drunkenness											
Males											
Under 18	x	x	2	3	1		4	7	6	5	5
18 and under 21	4	11	7	5	14	16	29	27	23	17	29
21 and under 30	15	24	17	13	14	20	33	33	30	35	25
30 and under 60	43	56	25	24	31	48	32	49	30	32	21
60 and over	6	9	4	1	1	5	2	5	4		2
All ages	**64**	**96**	**54**	**46**	**61**	**89**	**100**	**121**	**93**	**89**	**82**
Females											
Under 18	(Included in the number of persons by ages given above)										
18 and under 21									1		
21 and under 30											1
30 and under 60				1	1	3	1	1	2	1	4
60 and over				1		2					4
All ages	**4**	**4**	**1**	**2**	**1**	**5**	**1**	**1**	**3**	**1**	**9**
All Proved Offences	**68**	**100**	**55**	**48**	**62**	**94**	**101**	**122**	**96**	**90**	**91**
Motoring Offences											
Proceedings for:											
(a) Previously Convicted											
Unfit to drive											
Driving, undue alcohol											
Fail provide specimen											
(b) No Prev. Conviction											
Unfit to drive					5	8	9	7	6	6	8
Driving, undue alcohol											
Fail provide spec.											
In charge and:											
Unfit to drive						2	1	2	2	1	1
Undue alcohol											
Fail provide spec.											
Failure to provide breath specimen											
Total: All Proceedings	**4**	**2**	**3**	**7**	**5**	**10**	**10**	**9**	**8**	**7**	**9**
Licensed Premises											
Public Houses:											
Full	124					118					118
Beer and Cider	18					16					4
Wine or Cider											
Restaurant Licence											
Residential Licence											
Above Combined											
Licensed Clubs											1
Total On Licences	**142**					**134**					**123**
Off Licences	**18**					**19**					**19**
Total On/Off Licences	**160**					**153**					**142**
Registered Clubs	**30**					**31**					**32**
Total Licences & Clubs	**190**					**184**					**174**

TABLE III 134
DRUNKENNESS OFFENCES, MOTORING OFFENCES AND LICENCES, 1953-63
SWANSEA POLICE DISTRICT

	1953	1954	1955	1956	1957	1958	1959	1960	1961	1962	1963
Population '000	**161**					**163**					**170**
Proved Offences—Drunkenness											
Males											
Under 18	x	x	8	11	11	9	11	10	8	7	11
18 and under 21	45	19	26	36	37	35	41	60	48	43	50
21 and under 30	97	68	95	111	122	75	77	103	86	112	81
30 and under 60	138	101	142	150	144	111	117	125	134	153	141
60 and over	17	15	23	6	15	10	12	15	20	19	26
All ages	**274**	**192**	**284**	**314**	**329**	**240**	**258**	**313**	**296**	**334**	**309**
Females											
Under 18	(Included in the number of persons by ages given above)			2	2	3	2				
18 and under 21					1		2	2	4	2	
21 and under 30				1	4		2	1	6	3	2
30 and under 60				1	10	7	10	6	12	8	5
60 and over				1	2	3	1	10	7	2	3
All ages	**23**	**11**	**10**	**5**	**19**	**13**	**17**	**19**	**29**	**15**	**10**
All Proved Offences	**297**	**203**	**294**	**319**	**348**	**253**	**275**	**332**	**325**	**349**	**319**
Motoring Offences											
Proceedings for:											
(a) Previously Convicted											
Unfit to drive											
Driving, undue alcohol											
Fail provide specimen											
(b) No Prev. Conviction											
Unfit to drive					14	17	17	21	24	30	36
Driving, undue alcohol											
Fail provide spec.											
In charge and:											
Unfit to drive					6	8	3	3	1	5	3
Undue alcohol											
Fail provide spec.											
Failure to provide breath specimen											
Total: All Proceedings	**11**	**13**	**9**	**16**	**20**	**25**	**20**	**24**	**25**	**35**	**39**
Licensed Premises											
Public Houses:											
Full	226					201					215
Beer and Cider	25					18					2
Wine or Cider											
Restaurant Licence											14
Residential Licence											2
Above Combined											2
Licensed Clubs											6
Total On Licences	**251**					**219**					**241**
Off Licences	**40**					**43**					**46**
Total On/Off Licences	**291**					**262**					**287**
Registered Clubs	**54**					**58**					**60**
Total Licences & Clubs	**345**					**320**					**347**

TABLE III 135

DRUNKENNESS OFFENCES, MOTORING OFFENCES AND LICENCES, 1953–63 GWYNEDD POLICE DISTRICT

	1953	1954	1955	1956	1957	1958	1959	1960	1961	1962	1963
Population '000	**173**					**174**					**172**
Proved Offences—Drunkenness											
Males											
Under 18	x	x	4			4		9	12	6	7
18 and under 21	11	10	13	11	10	26	12	29	32	37	29
21 and under 30	27	44	38	39	37	53	44	54	47	63	50
30 and under 60	40	54	26	42	52	50	57	57	43	57	47
60 and over	4	13	4	4	4	4	1	1	3		1
All ages	**77**	**112**	**82**	**96**	**103**	**137**	**114**	**150**	**137**	**163**	**134**
Females											
Under 18		(Included in				2			1		2
18 and under 21		the number		1		2		2			
21 and under 30		of persons		1		1	3	1		1	3
30 and under 60		by ages		2	2	2	3	1	3	2	8
60 and over		given above)			2	1				1	1
All ages	**5**	**9**	**3**	**4**	**4**	**8**	**6**	**4**	**4**	**4**	**14**
All Proved Offences	**82**	**121**	**85**	**100**	**107**	**145**	**120**	**154**	**141**	**167**	**148**
Motoring Offences											
Proceedings for:											
(a) Previously Convicted											
Unfit to drive											
Driving, undue alcohol											
Fail provide specimen											
(b) No Prev. Conviction											
Unfit to drive					23	23	25	34	43	50	39
Driving, undue alcohol											
Fail provide spec.											
In charge and:											
Unfit to drive						9	8	10	20	12	15
Undue alcohol											
Fail provide spec.											
Failure to provide breath specimen											
Total: All Proceedings	**20**	**31**	**36**	**35**	**23**	**32**	**33**	**44**	**63**	**62**	**54**
Licensed Premises											
Public Houses:											
Full	346					345					350
Beer and Cider	4					3					
Wine or Cider											
Restaurant Licence											20
Residential Licence											36
Above Combined											45
Licensed Clubs											15
Total On Licences	**350**					**348**					**466**
Off Licences	**45**					**46**					**55**
Total On/Off Licences	**395**					**394**					**521**
Registered Clubs	**62**					**102**					**79**
Total Licences & Clubs	**457**					**496**					**600**

TABLE III 136
DRUNKENNESS OFFENCES, MOTORING OFFENCES AND LICENCES, 1953-63
MID-WALES POLICE DISTRICT

	1953	1954	1955	1956	1957	1958	1959	1960	1961	1962	1963
Population '000	**162**					**160**					**155**
Proved Offences—Drunkenness											
Males											
Under 18	x	x		1		1	1	1	1	1	2
18 and under 21	2	6	13	8	11	10	7	7	6	9	7
21 and under 30	21	14	18	22	16	15	10	10	14	13	13
30 and under 60	44	41	23	20	33	24	18	15	13	10	10
60 and over	5	5	4	7	4	6	2	3	1		2
All ages	**66**	**65**	**56**	**58**	**64**	**56**	**38**	**36**	**35**	**33**	**34**
Females											
Under 18		(Included in									
18 and under 21		the number									
21 and under 30		of persons									
30 and under 60		by ages		1	1			1			
60 and over		given above)							1		
All ages	**6**	**1**	**2**	**1**	**1**			**1**	**1**		
All Proved Offences	**72**	**66**	**58**	**59**	**65**	**56**	**38**	**37**	**36**	**33**	**34**
Motoring Offences											
Proceedings for:											
(a) Previously Convicted											
Unfit to drive											
Driving, undue alcohol											
Fail provide specimen											
(b) No Prev. Conviction											
Unfit to drive					20	18	23	15	16	13	18
Driving, undue alcohol											
Fail provide spec.											
In charge and:											
Unfit to drive								3	5	8	5
Undue alcohol											
Fail provide spec.											
Failure to provide breath specimen											
Total: All Proceedings	**20**	**12**	**13**	**18**	**20**	**18**	**23**	**18**	**21**	**21**	**23**
Licensed Premises											
Public Houses:											
Full	512					505					510
Beer and Cider	20					16					4
Wine or Cider	1					4					
Restaurant Licence											13
Residential Licence											1
Above Combined											17
Licensed Clubs											7
Total On Licences	**533**					**525**					**552**
Off Licences	**48**					**50**					**62**
Total On/Off Licences	**581**					**575**					**614**
Registered Clubs	**52**					**71**					**59**
Total Licences & Clubs	**633**					**646**					**673**

TABLE III 137
DRUNKENNESS OFFENCES, MOTORING OFFENCES AND LICENCES, 1953–63
PEMBROKESHIRE POLICE DISTRICT

	1953	1954	1955	1956	1957	1958	1959	1960	1961	1962	1963
Population '000	**92**					**94**					**95**
Proved Offences—											
Drunkenness											
Males											
Under 18	x	x	2		1	1	3	2	5	6	3
18 and under 21	5	10	14	14	13	18	15	15	21	41	17
21 and under 30	45	30	33	33	33	24	40	77	42	59	43
30 and under 60	66	57	61	60	44	49	84	94	62	64	57
60 and over	6	3	10	3	3	7	12	7	5	8	4
All ages	**119**	**98**	**118**	**110**	**94**	**99**	**154**	**195**	**135**	**178**	**124**
Females											
Under 18		(Included in									1
18 and under 21		the number						1			2
21 and under 30		of persons			1	1	1	1			2
30 and under 60		by ages		2	2		1	2	1	2	2
60 and over		given above)				1	1				
All ages	**3**	**2**	**2**	**2**	**3**	**2**	**3**	**4**	**2**	**2**	**7**
All Proved Offences	**122**	**100**	**120**	**112**	**97**	**101**	**157**	**199**	**137**	**180**	**131**
Motoring Offences											
Proceedings for:											
(a) Previously Convicted											
Unfit to drive											
Driving, undue alcohol											
Fail provide specimen											
(b) No Prev. Conviction											
Unfit to drive					20	20	20	37	31	27	23
Driving, undue alcohol											
Fail provide spec.											
In charge and:											
a nfit to drive					1	1	3	12	8	5	10
Undue alcohol											
Fail provide spec.											
Failure to provide breath specimen											
Total: All Proceedings	**23**	**15**	**33**	**29**	**21**	**21**	**23**	**49**	**39**	**32**	**33**
Licensed Premises											
Public Houses:											
Full	294					285					301
Beer and Cider											1
Wine or Cider											
Restaurant Licence											11
Residential Licence											15
Above Combined											24
Licensed Clubs											1
Total On Licences	**294**					**285**					**353**
Off Licences	**19**					**20**					**35**
Total On/Off Licences	**313**					**305**					**388**
Registered Clubs	**56**					**59**					**67**
Total Licences & Clubs	**369**					**364**					**455**

TABLE III 138

THE PRE-AMALGAMATION POLICE DISTRICTS MAKING UP EACH OF THE 47 1964–1973 POLICE DISTRICTS

1965–73 Title	Amalgamation of:
Bedfordshire and Luton	Bedfordshire, Luton
Cheshire	Cheshire, Birkenhead, Stockport, Wallasey
Cumbria	Cumberland, Westmorland, Carlisle
Derby County & Borough	Derby County, Derby Borough
Devon and Cornwall	Devon, Exeter, Cornwall, Plymouth
Durham	Durham, Gateshead, South Shields, Sunderland
Essex and Southend on Sea	Essex (beyond MPD), Southend
Gloucestershire	Gloucestershire
Bristol	Bristol
Gwent	Monmouthshire, Newport
Hampshire	Hampshire, Portsmouth, Southampton
Hertfordshire	Hertfordshire (beyond MPD)
Kent	Kent (beyond MPD)
Lancashire	Lancashire, Barrow, Blackburn, Blackpool, Bolton, Burnley, Oldham, Preston, Rochdale, St. Helens, Southport, Warrington, Wigan
Liverpool and Bootle	Liverpool, Bootle
Manchester and Salford	Manchester, Salford
Leicester and Rutland	Leicestershire and Rutland, Leicester Borough
Lincolnshire	Holland, Kesteven, Lindsey, Grimsby, Lincoln
City of London	City of London
Metropolitan Police District	Metropolitan Police District
Mid-Anglia	Cambridgeshire, Cambridge, Isle of Ely, Peterborough, Huntingdonshire
Norfolk	Norfolk, Great Yarmouth, Norwich
Northampton and County	Northamptonshire, Northampton
Northumberland	Northumberland, Newcastle, Tynemouth
Nottinghamshire combined	Nottinghamshire, Nottingham
Somerset and Bath	Somerset, Bath
Staffordshire County and Stoke on Trent	Staffordshire, Stoke on Trent, plus small part of West Mercia
Suffolk	Suffolk East, Ipswich, Suffolk West
Surrey	Surrey (beyond MPD)
Sussex	Sussex East, Brighton, Eastbourne, Hastings, Sussex West
Thames Valley	Buckinghamshire, Berkshire, Reading, Oxfordshire, Oxford
Warwickshire and Coventry	Warwickshire, Coventry
Birmingham	Birmingham
West Mercia	Herefordshire, Shropshire, Worcestershire, Worcester
West Midlands	Wolverhampton, Walsall, Dudley, small part of Staffordshire
West Yorkshire	West Riding, Barnsley, Dewsbury, Doncaster, Halifax, Huddersfield, Wakefield
Bradford	Bradford
Leeds	Leeds
Sheffield and Rotherham	Sheffield, Rotherham
Wiltshire	Wiltshire
York and North-East Yorkshire	Yorkshire East Riding, York, plus one-half of Yorkshire North Riding
Kingston upon Hull	Kingston upon Hull
Teeside	Middlesbrough, plus one half of Yorkshire North Riding
Dyfed Powis	Carmarthenshire, Cardigan, Midwales, Pembrokeshire
Gwynedd	Denbighshire, Flintshire, Anglesey, Carnarvonshire, Meriethshire (last three were entitled Gwynedd for some years)
South Wales	Glamorgan, Cardiff, Merthyr Tydvil, Swansea

TABLE III 139
DRUNKENNESS OFFENCES, MOTORING OFFENCES AND LICENCES, 1963–73
ENGLAND AND WALES

	1963	1964	1965	1966	1967	1968	1969	1970	1971	1972	1973
Population '000	**47000**					**48000**					**49000**
Proved Offences—											
Drunkenness											
Males											
Under 18	1478	1775	1810	1772	1919	2141	2436	2790	3032	3326	4396
18 and under 21	7446	7262	7902	7905	8791	9461	9859	10269	10430	10762	12987
21 and under 30	17937	16549	16254	15527	16324	17666	17906	18166	19178	19193	21657
30 and under 60	46423	42257	39035	36999	39250	40090	40275	41046	42938	45399	47356
60 and over	4944	4562	4090	4265	4883	4868	4996	4801	5428	5488	6588
All ages	**78228**	**72405**	**69091**	**66468**	**71167**	**74226**	**75472**	**77072**	**81006**	**84168**	**92974**
Females											
Under 18	88	77	97	108	129	163	139	196	245	279	329
18 and under 21	229	210	187	189	248	264	299	393	460	496	666
21 and under 30	630	609	533	503	642	657	685	817	984	1152	1207
30 and under 60	3146	2928	2535	2727	2752	3050	3215	3124	3218	3351	3486
60 and over	686	613	537	504	606	710	692	772	822	752	612
All ages	**4779**	**4437**	**3889**	**4031**	**4377**	**4844**	**5030**	**5302**	**5729**	**6030**	**6300**
All Proved Offences	**83007**	**76842**	**72980**	**70449**	**75544**	**79070**	**80502**	**82374**	**86735**	**90198**	**99274**
Motoring Offences											
Proceedings for:											
(a) Previously Convicted											
Unfit to drive		426	377	359	277	19	19	39	57	56	71
Driving, undue alcohol					24	259	328	502	866	1384	1947
Fail provide specimen					6	33	46	55	112	168	234
(b) No Prev. Conviction											
Unfit to drive	7348	7323	8053	8865	8632	1442	1635	1752	2229	2290	2902
Driving, undue alcohol					774	16461	22099	24127	35878	43616	49615
Fail provide spec.					139	1353	1704	1733	2405	2495	2984
In charge and:											
Unfit to drive	1928	1775	2070	2103	1913	274	275	274	276	288	461
Undue alcohol					41	751	689	612	756	873	871
Fail provide spec.					19	247	308	283	310	497	912
Failure to provide breath specimen					125	1907	2324	2457	3139	3925	5251
Total: All Proceedings	**9276**	**9524**	**10500**	**11327**	**11950**	**22746**	**29427**	**31794**	**46028**	**55590**	**65248**
Licensed Premises											
Public Houses:											
Full	65627					64827					63534
Beer and Cider	1748					660					281
Wine or Cider	75					54					63
Restaurant Licence	2130					5160					8664
Residential Licence	709					1365					2230
Above Combined	1180					1917					2598
Licensed Clubs	1938					2438					2702
Total On Licences	**73409**					**76421**					**80072**
Off Licences	**25258**					**26906**					**29710**
Total On/Off Licences	**98667**					**103327**					**109782**
Registered Clubs	**20663**					**22705**					**24593**
Total Licences & Clubs	**119330**					**126032**					**134375**

TABLE III 140
DRUNKENNESS OFFENCES, MOTORING OFFENCES AND LICENCES, 1963–73
BEDFORDSHIRE AND LUTON POLICE DISTRICT

	1963	1964	1965	1966	1967	1968	1969	1970	1971	1972	1973
Population '000	**404**					**439**					**481**
Proved Offences—											
Drunkenness											
Males											
Under 18	6	4	5	3	13	8	6	10	6	10	19
18 and under 21	35	31	45	41	42	50	51	36	45	54	58
21 and under 30	102	111	124	106	63	102	83	91	80	104	139
30 and under 60	275	293	247	271	222	179	166	206	225	234	291
60 and over	20	27	19	19	11	15	30	14	21	32	58
All ages	**438**	**466**	**440**	**440**	**351**	**354**	**336**	**357**	**377**	**434**	**565**
Females											
Under 18	1			2	2	3		4	1		4
18 and under 21	2			1		3			1	1	3
21 and under 30	13	5	7	1	7	3		2		1	4
30 and under 60	6	3	9	12	4	2	5	11	12	8	16
60 and over	2				2	1	2		1		
All ages	**24**	**8**	**16**	**16**	**15**	**12**	**7**	**17**	**15**	**10**	**27**
All Proved Offences	**462**	**474**	**456**	**456**	**366**	**366**	**343**	**374**	**392**	**444**	**592**
Motoring Offences											
Proceedings for:											
(a) Previously Convicted											
Unfit to drive		5	5	5	4		1		1	1	2
Driving, undue alcohol						10	8	5	14	15	29
Fail provide specimen									2	4	7
(b) No Prev. Conviction											
Unfit to drive	50	48	68	65	84	3	11	7	3	3	11
Driving, undue alcohol					14	172	259	241	402	540	641
Fail provide spec.					2	10	20	13	44	48	57
In charge and:											
Unfit to drive	22	17	18	19	13	4	2	3	2	3	7
Undue alcohol						10	58	47	13	16	8
Fail provide spec.						4	8	10	1	1	3
Failure to provide breath specimen					1	22	35	49	65	74	111
Total: All Proceedings	**72**	**70**	**91**	**89**	**118**	**235**	**402**	**375**	**547**	**705**	**876**
Licensed Premises											
Public Houses:											
Full	676					665					637
Beer and Cider	12					2					
Wine or Cider	2					1					1
Restaurant Licence	10					32					46
Residential Licence	1										2
Above Combined	1					3					10
Licensed Clubs	6					16					25
Total On Licences	**708**					**719**					**721**
Off Licences	**144**					**191**					**234**
Total On/Off Licences	**852**					**910**					**965**
Registered Clubs	**149**					**171**					**209**
Total Licences & Clubs	**1001**					**1081**					**1174**

TABLE III 141
DRUNKENNESS OFFENCES, MOTORING OFFENCES AND LICENCES, 1963–73
CHESHIRE POLICE DISTRICT

	1963	1964	1965	1966	1967	1968	1969	1970	1971	1972	1973
Population '000	**1267**					**1361**					**1441**
Proved Offences—Drunkenness											
Males											
Under 18	42	54	41	45	51	55	63	66	64	60	111
18 and under 21	138	162	178	173	183	170	176	160	237	203	270
21 and under 30	205	218	230	225	202	215	178	240	281	244	332
30 and under 60	280	291	329	379	359	314	265	280	345	333	431
60 and over	19	40	44	42	36	28	21	32	36	17	48
All ages	**684**	**765**	**822**	**864**	**831**	**782**	**703**	**778**	**963**	**857**	**1192**
Females											
Under 18			3	2	7	6	3	3	2	9	5
18 and under 21	6	2	6	5	5	4	2	6	8	9	14
21 and under 30	4	5	10	10	4	4	8	10	15	7	18
30 and under 60	19	26	23	19	24	11	13	18	29	21	37
60 and over	2		2	1	1	1		1	3	1	5
All ages	**31**	**33**	**44**	**37**	**41**	**26**	**26**	**38**	**57**	**47**	**79**
All Proved Offences	**715**	**798**	**866**	**901**	**872**	**808**	**729**	**816**	**1020**	**904**	**1271**
Motoring Offences											
Proceedings for:											
(a) Previously Convicted											
Unfit to drive		17	8	5	4						
Driving, undue alcohol						1	1	4	4	10	19
Fail provide specimen						1	1				4
(b) No Prev. Conviction											
Unfit to drive	111	129	138	167	191	13	11	13	8	6	10
Driving, undue alcohol					14	413	607	633	1069	1306	1592
Fail provide spec.					2	31	53	44	76	100	117
In charge and:											
Unfit to drive	29	36	43	47	34	4	6	3	4	1	2
Undue alcohol						6	20	16	10	23	33
Fail provide spec.						3		1	5	1	12
Failure to provide breath specimen					3	49	77	49	99	135	165
Total: All Proceedings	**140**	**182**	**189**	**219**	**248**	**521**	**776**	**763**	**1275**	**1582**	**1954**
Licensed Premises											
Public Houses:											
Full	1536					1538					1550
Beer and Cider	33					15					8
Wine or Cider	4					1					
Restaurant Licence	42					128					196
Residential Licence	4					5					15
Above Combined	19					29					39
Licensed Clubs	34					51					66
Total On Licences	**1672**					**1767**					**1874**
Off Licences	**601**					**657**					**784**
Total On/Off Licences	**2273**					**2424**					**2658**
Registered Clubs	**590**					**670**					**706**
Total Licences & Clubs	**2863**					**3094**					**3364**

TABLE III 142
DRUNKENNESS OFFENCES, MOTORING OFFENCES AND LICENCES, 1963–73
CUMBRIA POLICE DISTRICT

	1963	1964	1965	1966	1967	1968	1969	1970	1971	1972	1973
Population '000	**363**					**367**					**362**
Proved Offences—Drunkenness											
Males											
Under 18	17	33	16	17	15	26	34	24	40	49	55
18 and under 21	58	83	60	72	79	82	99	115	135	111	118
21 and under 30	113	75	78	69	80	100	140	111	115	85	133
30 and under 60	143	137	138	149	170	139	147	148	145	121	150
60 and over	16	22	12	20	15	13	23	23	38	34	30
All ages	**347**	**350**	**304**	**327**	**359**	**360**	**443**	**421**	**473**	**400**	**486**
Females											
Under 18	1			2	1	5	3	6	2	1	2
18 and under 21	1	5	1	1	2			2	3	3	8
21 and under 30	1	3			4		2	4	3		6
30 and under 60	10	6	11	10	10	10	6	8	10	13	7
60 and over	3	1	5	3	3	1	1	2	1		1
All ages	**16**	**15**	**17**	**16**	**20**	**16**	**12**	**22**	**19**	**17**	**24**
All Proved Offences	**363**	**365**	**321**	**343**	**379**	**376**	**455**	**443**	**492**	**417**	**510**
Motoring Offences											
Proceedings for:											
(a) Previously Convicted											
Unfit to drive		9	5	1	3						1
Driving, undue alcohol					1	6	2	6	6	14	11
Fail provide specimen						1	1	1	2	2	
(b) No Prev. Conviction											
Unfit to drive	86	47	59	52	66		3		4	3	
Driving, undue alcohol					5	229	337	354	516	580	501
Fail provide spec.					3	6	15	12	33	34	32
In charge and:											
Unfit to drive	18	14	21	12	31	1	3	1	1	4	4
Undue alcohol					1	3	5	5	3	2	3
Fail provide spec.					2	7	4	5	1	1	7
Failure to provide breath specimen					4	11	18	20	25	41	36
Total: All Proceedings	**104**	**70**	**85**	**65**	**116**	**264**	**388**	**404**	**591**	**681**	**595**
Licensed Premises											
Public Houses:											
Full	897					865					866
Beer and Cider	11					6					6
Wine or Cider											
Restaurant Licence	24					70					106
Residential Licence	6					8					10
Above Combined	33					55					102
Licensed Clubs	9					2					5
Total On Licences	**980**					**998**					**1095**
Off Licences	**104**					**124**					**206**
Total On/Off Licences	**1084**					**1122**					**1301**
Registered Clubs	**192**					**224**					**261**
Total Licences & Clubs	**1276**					**1346**					**1562**

TABLE III 143
DRUNKENNESS OFFENCES, MOTORING OFFENCES AND LICENCES, 1963–73
DERBY COUNTY AND BOROUGH POLICE DISTRICT

	1963	1964	1965	1966	1967	1968	1969	1970	1971	1972	1973
Population '000	**898**					**889**					**887**
Proved Offences—Drunkenness											
Males											
Under 18	12	20	22	13	8	9	12	10	17	13	19
18 and under 21	40	37	67	29	54	49	42	41	50	35	45
21 and under 30	94	95	125	73	88	72	48	49	67	61	87
30 and under 60	250	313	302	216	237	178	118	138	151	168	163
60 and over	33	48	32	56	72	24	15	14	19	10	34
All ages	**429**	**513**	**548**	**387**	**459**	**332**	**235**	**252**	**304**	**287**	**348**
Females											
Under 18	1			2	1			1	2		2
18 and under 21		6	1				1			1	
21 and under 30	1	3		3	1	1	1	1	2	2	6
30 and under 60	12	22	17	18	22	13	10	12	11	11	14
60 and over	2	1			3			1	1		2
All ages	**16**	**32**	**18**	**23**	**27**	**14**	**12**	**15**	**16**	**14**	**24**
All Proved Offences	**445**	**545**	**556**	**410**	**486**	**346**	**247**	**267**	**320**	**301**	**372**
Motoring Offences											
Proceedings for:											
(a) Previously Convicted											
Unfit to drive		14	6	2	4	1					
Driving, undue alcohol						4	6	2	19	14	7
Fail provide specimen							2	2	1	2	1
(b) No Prev. Conviction											
Unfit to drive	92	84	92	136	117	7	9	4	2	7	2
Driving, undue alcohol					14	167	143	213	271	371	522
Fail provide spec.					1	19	8	13	22	26	18
In charge and:											
Unfit to drive	30	24	28	32	25	3	3	2	1	3	
Undue alcohol					1	11	5	2	2	5	1
Fail provide spec.						3	1	1		1	19
Failure to provide breath specimen					2	25	30	28	36	59	91
Total: All Proceedings	**122**	**122**	**126**	**170**	**164**	**240**	**207**	**267**	**344**	**488**	**661**
Licensed Premises											
Public Houses:											
Full	1550					1514					1493
Beer and Cider	33					20					8
Wine or Cider	1					1					1
Restaurant Licence	18					45					67
Residential Licence	3					10					15
Above Combined	1					10					30
Licensed Clubs	21					28					27
Total On Licences	**1627**					**1628**					**1641**
Off Licences	**658**					**700**					**731**
Total On/Off Licences	**2285**					**2328**					**2372**
Registered Clubs	**416**					**432**					**453**
Total Licences & Clubs	**2701**					**2760**					**2825**

TABLE III 144
DRUNKENNESS OFFENCES, MOTORING OFFENCES AND LICENCES, 1963-73
DEVON AND CORNWALL

	1963	**1964**	**1965**	**1966**	**1967**	**1968**	**1969**	**1970**	**1971**	**1972**	**1973**
Population '000	**1226**					**1236**					**1314**
Proved Offences—Drunkenness											
Males											
Under 18	13	18	26	13	20	12	18	31	40	42	55
18 and under 21	44	71	78	70	104	89	115	112	181	251	258
21 and under 30	107	128	115	103	128	144	133	165	234	267	244
30 and under 60	398	376	397	343	356	320	315	344	485	495	522
60 and over	56	47	81	86	101	53	48	65	57	62	80
All ages	**618**	**640**	**697**	**615**	**709**	**618**	**629**	**717**	**997**	**1117**	**1259**
Females											
Under 18	1	6	3	2	2	5	4	2	3	6	6
18 and under 21	4	2	5	4		4	3	3	13	17	19
21 and under 30	2	5	9	4	5	9	5	5	10	21	29
30 and under 60	12	20	16	23	19	21	14	14	17	23	28
60 and over	1	1	1		2	3	1	2	2	3	9
All ages	**20**	**37**	**31**	**33**	**28**	**42**	**27**	**26**	**45**	**70**	**91**
All Proved Offences	**638**	**677**	**728**	**648**	**737**	**660**	**656**	**743**	**1042**	**1187**	**1350**
Motoring Offences											
Proceedings for:											
(a) Previously Convicted											
Unfit to drive		12	16	18	16			1			1
Driving, undue alcohol					1	9	10	15	33	45	94
Fail provide specimen							3	3	4	7	10
(b) No Prev. Conviction											
Unfit to drive	226	205	223	209	214	8	8	10	9	6	7
Driving, undue alcohol					17	317	497	552	929	1403	1484
Fail provide spec.					3	20	27	22	36	39	75
In charge and:											
Unfit to drive	45	50	48	59	47	5	4	3	4	6	4
Undue alcohol					4	22	20	20	42	36	38
Fail provide spec.						7	8	2	5	24	15
Failure to provide breath specimen						15	29	17	52	70	104
Total: All Proceedings	**271**	**267**	**287**	**286**	**302**	**403**	**606**	**645**	**1114**	**1636**	**1832**
Licensed Premises											
Public Houses:											
Full	2197					2370					2516
Beer and Cider	15					5					3
Wine or Cider	3					2					6
Restaurant Licence	94					422					742
Residential Licence	99					214					352
Above Combined	277					420					533
Licensed Clubs	139					180					184
Total On Licences	**2974**					**3613**					**4336**
Off Licences	**491**					**653**					**914**
Total On/Off Licences	**3465**					**4266**					**5250**
Registered Clubs	**549**					**614**					**687**
Total Licences & Clubs	**4014**					**4880**					**5937**

TABLE III 145
DRUNKENNESS OFFENCES, MOTORING OFFENCES AND LICENCES, 1963–73
DORSET AND BOURNEMOUTH POLICE DISTRICT

	1963	1964	1965	1966	1967	1968	1969	1970	1971	1972	1973
Population '000	**473**					**495**					**527**
Proved Offences—Drunkenness											
Males											
Under 18	9	5	5	8	8	7	4	10	16	11	12
18 and under 21	31	15	25	28	36	40	27	50	48	31	77
21 and under 30	61	51	52	46	51	73	66	66	88	76	92
30 and under 60	292	285	312	259	236	175	175	203	198	233	294
60 and over	33	42	54	49	71	25	25	32	37	39	54
All ages	**426**	**398**	**448**	**390**	**402**	**320**	**297**	**361**	**387**	**390**	**529**
Females											
Under 18		1	1		1	1	3	3	2	3	1
18 and under 21	1		3	2			4	1	2		3
21 and under 30	1		2			2	2	1	2	7	5
30 and under 60	7	11	10	10	7	10	8	12	10	20	20
60 and over	5	2	5		2	4		4	3	3	3
All ages	**14**	**14**	**21**	**12**	**10**	**17**	**17**	**21**	**19**	**33**	**32**
All Proved Offences	**440**	**412**	**469**	**402**	**412**	**337**	**314**	**382**	**406**	**423**	**561**
Motoring Offences											
Proceedings for:											
(a) Previously Convicted											
Unfit to drive		7	5	3	1	1		1	1		1
Driving, undue alcohol						2	2	5	1	7	11
Fail provide specimen							1			1	2
(b) No Prev. Conviction											
Unfit to drive	33	26	28	42	45	11	6	9	2	5	5
Driving, undue alcohol					7	114	113	157	240	273	384
Fail provide spec.						8	8	12	14	3	15
In charge and:											
Unfit to drive	27	22	7	18	26	2	3	2	8	2	2
Undue alcohol						3	13	10	10	8	5
Fail provide spec.						1	4	4	4	8	9
Failure to provide breath specimen						23	21	19	17	38	70
Total: All Proceedings	**60**	**55**	**40**	**63**	**79**	**165**	**171**	**219**	**298**	**345**	**504**
Licensed Premises											
Public Houses:											
Full	742					769					755
Beer and Cider	7					2					3
Wine or Cider											
Restaurant Licence	52					128					213
Residential Licence	41					77					146
Above Combined	76					105					125
Licensed Clubs	31					46					42
Total On Licences	**949**					**1127**					**1284**
Off Licences	**238**					**276**					**322**
Total On/Off Licences	**1187**					**1403**					**1606**
Registered Clubs	**209**					**236**					**261**
Total Licences & Clubs	**1396**					**1639**					**1867**

TABLE III 146
DRUNKENNESS OFFENCES, MOTORING OFFENCES AND LICENCES, 1963–73
DURHAM POLICE DISTRICT

	1963	1964	1965	1966	1967	1968	1969	1970	1971	1972	1973
Population '000	**1533**					**1434**					**1410**
Proved Offences—Drunkenness											
Males											
Under 18	76	97	87	105	102	92	64	114	104	139	163
18 and under 21	357	340	428	414	437	462	338	396	411	366	526
21 and under 30	534	496	508	566	560	559	369	470	498	437	596
30 and under 60	839	737	670	751	714	709	422	550	607	636	671
60 and over	70	62	64	74	77	96	302	87	79	80	81
All ages	**1876**	**1732**	**1757**	**1910**	**1890**	**1918**	**1495**	**1617**	**1699**	**1658**	**2037**
Females											
Under 18	4	4		4	1	4	3	5	4	6	8
18 and under 21	5	1	4	6	10	7	4	1	9	8	8
21 and under 30	10	6	8	8	13	7	6	5	11	14	4
30 and under 60	25	21	19	24	22	24	15	14	6	16	9
60 and over	3	1	2	3	2	4	1	3	3		2
All ages	**47**	**33**	**33**	**45**	**48**	**46**	**29**	**28**	**33**	**44**	**31**
All Proved Offences	**1923**	**1765**	**1790**	**1955**	**1938**	**1964**	**1524**	**1645**	**1732**	**1702**	**2068**
Motoring Offences											
Proceedings for:											
(a) Previously Convicted											
Unfit to drive		21	8	8	3	2		1			
Driving, undue alcohol						4			1	3	12
Fail provide specimen						1					
(b) No Prev. Conviction											
Unfit to drive	303	326	337	347	378	18	21	14	16	8	13
Driving, undue alcohol					35	652	765	827	1163	1356	1808
Fail provide spec.						21	7	4	2	1	
In charge and:											
Unfit to drive	56	58	59	69	56	9	6	5	2	2	8
Undue alcohol						26	7	2	2	1	1
Fail provide spec.					1	13	38	62	54	81	113
Failure to provide breath specimen					2	74	101	75	99	106	143
Total: All Proceedings	**359**	**405**	**404**	**424**	**475**	**820**	**945**	**990**	**1339**	**1558**	**2098**
Licensed Premises											
Public Houses:											
Full	1655					1489					1406
Beer and Cider	59					21					9
Wine or Cider											
Restaurant Licence	29					61					79
Residential Licence	1					6					7
Above Combined	5					8					16
Licensed Clubs	10					39					48
Total On Licences	**1759**					**1624**					**1565**
Off Licences	**907**					**944**					**1034**
Total On/Off Licences	**2666**					**2568**					**2599**
Registered Clubs	**737**					**751**					**809**
Total Licences & Clubs	**3403**					**3319**					**3408**

TABLE III 147
DRUNKENNESS OFFENCES, MOTORING OFFENCES AND LICENCES, 1963–73 ESSEX AND SOUTHEND-ON-SEA POLICE DISTRICT

	1963*	1964	1965	1966	1967	1968	1969	1970	1971	1972	1973
Population '000	**2084**					**1296**					**1398**
Proved Offences—Drunkenness											
Males											
Under 18	14	13	10	20	12	23	29	15	16	29	32
18 and under 21	49	58	72	73	45	66	54	56	58	49	63
21 and under 30	106	115	128	106	84	92	132	92	105	98	123
30 and under 60	209	206	216	170	165	214	179	199	253	230	241
60 and over	28	17	18	16	23	25	19	25	32	25	25
All ages	**406**	**409**	**444**	**385**	**329**	**420**	**413**	**387**	**464**	**431**	**484**
Females											
Under 18	1			1	1	1	2	1	6	3	2
18 and under 21		3		5	2		1	4	3	2	5
21 and under 30	4	3	2	5	4	3	2	2	3	6	2
30 and under 60	8	17	21	12	10	6	8	11	12	19	25
60 and over	3	4	5	1		2	1	4	4	1	3
All ages	**16**	**27**	**28**	**24**	**17**	**12**	**14**	**22**	**28**	**31**	**37**
All Proved Offences	**422**	**436**	**472**	**409**	**346**	**432**	**427**	**409**	**492**	**462**	**521**
Motoring Offences											
Proceedings for:											
(a) Previously Convicted											
Unfit to drive		7	4	3	4		2				1
Driving, undue alcohol						8	9	10	15	26	55
Fail provide specimen						1	1	1		2	7
(b) No Prev. Conviction											
Unfit to drive	128	133	134	127	108	7	21	17	35	51	55
Driving, undue alcohol					16	309	371	358	567	918	1198
Fail provide spec.					1	29	30	30	40	48	77
In charge and:											
Unfit to drive	25	52	31	25	36	2	3	2	6	10	18
Undue alcohol					2	17	11	5	8	16	22
Fail provide spec.					1	1			1	4	8
Failure to provide breath specimen					6	55	77	61	76	130	217
Total: All Proceedings	**153**	**192**	**169**	**155**	**174**	**429**	**525**	**484**	**748**	**1205**	**1658**
Licensed Premises											
Public Houses:											
Full	1708					1458					1510
Beer and Cider	16					6					1
Wine or Cider	5					2					2
Restaurant Licence	46					118					217
Residential Licence	14					28					37
Above Combined	26					29					44
Licensed Clubs	88					77					80
Total On Licences	**1913**					**1718**					**1891**
Off Licences	**647**					**466**					**592**
Total On/Off Licences	**2560**					**2184**					**2483**
Registered Clubs	**617**					**495**					**603**
Total Licences & Clubs	**3177**					**2679**					**3086**

*Licences and population data for 1963 include some of Metropolitan Police District.

TABLE III 148
DRUNKENNESS OFFENCES, MOTORING OFFENCES AND LICENCES, 1963-73
GLOUCESTERSHIRE POLICE DISTRICT

	1963	1964	1965	1966	1967	1968	1969	1970	1971	1972	1973
Population '000	**590**					**624**					**671**
Proved Offences—Drunkenness											
Males											
Under 18	8	10	4	7	3	8	8	6	13	8	14
18 and under 21	24	23	24	23	16	25	23	26	41	34	36
21 and under 30	34	69	44	61	61	34	48	37	39	46	42
30 and under 60	162	169	170	168	156	121	160	114	152	105	155
60 and over	30	28	17	14	20	18	26	22	28	24	30
All ages	**258**	**299**	**259**	**273**	**256**	**206**	**265**	**205**	**273**	**217**	**277**
Females											
Under 18	1		1			3	1		2		
18 and under 21			1		1		2	2	6		
21 and under 30	1				2		1		1	1	1
30 and under 60	8	3	3	3	5	4	5	2	2	5	5
60 and over	1		1	1			1	1	2		
All ages	**11**	**3**	**6**	**4**	**8**	**7**	**10**	**5**	**13**	**6**	**6**
All Proved Offences	**269**	**302**	**265**	**277**	**264**	**213**	**275**	**210**	**286**	**223**	**283**
Motoring Offences											
Proceedings for:											
(a) Previously Convicted											
Unfit to drive		4	4	4	6						
Driving, undue alcohol					1	5	10	6	18	16	39
Fail provide specimen							1		1	3	2
(b) No Prev. Conviction											
Unfit to drive	56	74	76	90	54		1	1	1	1	1
Driving, undue alcohol					13	149	176	202	283	340	522
Fail provide spec.					4	12	24	21	13	16	31
In charge and:											
Unfit to drive	25	31	30	35	22	1	3	1	4	2	8
Undue alcohol					2	12	22	19	26	31	31
Fail provide spec.						2	2		4	4	14
Failure to provide breath specimen					4	20	21	24	28	26	78
Total: All Proceedings	**81**	**109**	**110**	**129**	**106**	**201**	**260**	**274**	**378**	**439**	**726**
Licensed Premises											
Public Houses:											
Full	1132					1079					1013
Beer and Cider	21					2					
Wine or Cider	4					1					2
Restaurant Licence	25					60					114
Residential Licence	4					2					4
Above Combined	19					30					42
Licensed Clubs	37					29					32
Total On Licences	**1242**					**1203**					**1207**
Off Licences	**328**					**412**					**492**
Total On/Off Licences	**1570**					**1615**					**1699**
Registered Clubs	**233**					**262**					**328**
Total Licences & Clubs	**1803**					**1877**					**2027**

TABLE III 149
DRUNKENNESS OFFENCES, MOTORING OFFENCES AND LICENCES, 1963–73
BRISTOL POLICE DISTRICT

	1963	1964	1965	1966	1967	1968	1969	1970	1971	1972	1973
Population '000	**434**					**428**					**422**
Proved Offences—Drunkenness											
Males											
Under 18	4	5	2	6	2		3	2	1	4	3
18 and under 21	14	20	11	12	16	17	15	12	18	16	26
21 and under 30	19	54	41	29	20	32	39	29	27	39	39
30 and under 60	79	123	103	109	112	107	125	151	161	164	137
60 and over	6	13	9	9	8	13	12	16	9	11	22
All ages	**122**	**215**	**166**	**165**	**158**	**169**	**194**	**210**	**216**	**234**	**227**
Females											
Under 18			1		1		3		1		
18 and under 21			2	1		1	5	2	1	2	3
21 and under 30	1	2	2	1	1	2	8	3	1	5	9
30 and under 60	3	3	5	5	1	2	6	6	6	4	14
60 and over					1	2	3	2	2	2	
All ages	**4**	**5**	**10**	**7**	**4**	**7**	**25**	**13**	**11**	**13**	**26**
All Proved Offences	**126**	**220**	**176**	**172**	**162**	**176**	**219**	**223**	**227**	**247**	**253**
Motoring Offences											
Proceedings for:											
(a) Previously Convicted											
Unfit to drive							1			1	1
Driving, undue alcohol						2	3	8	10	25	30
Fail provide specimen						1		2	3	2	2
(b) No Prev. Conviction											
Unfit to drive	22	34	34	31	25	1		3	1	1	5
Driving, undue alcohol					6	81	128	171	223	289	403
Fail provide spec.						6	6	7	15	18	29
In charge and:											
Unfit to drive	19	13	6	11	3			2			2
Undue alcohol					2	42	14	2	2	4	4
Fail provide spec.					2	1	3	4	3	10	6
Failure to provide breath specimen					3	22	18	24	33	56	63
Total: All Proceedings	**41**	**47**	**40**	**42**	**41**	**156**	**173**	**223**	**290**	**406**	**545**
Licensed Premises											
Public Houses:											
Full	482					506					499
Beer and Cider	34					5					
Wine or Cider						1					
Restaurant Licence	9					54					90
Residential Licence	1					1					
Above Combined	2					6					11
Licensed Clubs	8					27					29
Total On Licences	**546**					**600**					**631**
Off Licences	**253**					**252**					**251**
Total On/Off Licences	**799**					**852**					**882**
Registered Clubs	**118**					**145**					**169**
Total Licences & Clubs	**917**					**997**					**1051**

TABLE III 150
DRUNKENNESS OFFENCES, MOTORING OFFENCES AND LICENCES, 1963–73
GWENT POLICE DISTRICT

	1963	1964	1965	1966	1967	1968	1969	1970	1971	1972	1973
Population '000	**451**					**463**					**462**
Proved Offences—Drunkenness											
Males											
Under 18	10	26	19	11	14	26	29	18	48	40	50
18 and under 21	41	56	66	57	47	61	75	123	102	148	155
21 and under 30	80	93	76	72	88	99	99	86	118	147	166
30 and under 60	159	157	114	171	178	138	113	92	121	136	174
60 and over	10	18	19	25	42	29	22	18	15	30	24
All ages	**300**	**350**	**294**	**336**	**369**	**353**	**338**	**337**	**404**	**501**	**569**
Females											
Under 18		3			1		1	2	3	2	4
18 and under 21	4	1					1	1	1	7	3
21 and under 30		2	1	2	3	1	1	2	3	12	7
30 and under 60	1	9	5	9	4	6	4	6		15	13
60 and over	1	2	4	2	11	2	1	1	1		1
All ages	**6**	**17**	**10**	**13**	**19**	**9**	**8**	**12**	**8**	**36**	**28**
All Proved Offences	**306**	**367**	**304**	**349**	**388**	**362**	**346**	**349**	**412**	**537**	**597**
Motoring Offences											
Proceedings for:											
(a) Previously Convicted											
Unfit to drive		1	1	3							
Driving, undue alcohol						3	4	1			
Fail provide specimen							1				
(b) No Prev. Conviction											
Unfit to drive	54	57	68	77	65	2	6		3	10	7
Driving, undue alcohol					4	175	290	267	414	398	452
Fail provide spec.					1	8	29	17	44	42	28
In charge and:											
Unfit to drive	12	12	13	14	5	1	2	7	4	3	2
Undue alcohol						3	6	1	1	1	
Fail provide spec.						1		2	3	2	6
Failure to provide breath specimen					1	22	32	26	34	34	30
Total: All Proceedings	**66**	**69**	**82**	**92**	**79**	**215**	**370**	**321**	**503**	**490**	**525**
Licensed Premises											
Public Houses:											
Full	717					667					623
Beer and Cider	14					6					21
Wine or Cider	2					1					1
Restaurant Licence	6					20					37
Residential Licence						1					1
Above Combined	5					9					8
Licensed Clubs	7					18					19
Total On Licences	**751**					**722**					**710**
Off Licences	**170**					**211**					**264**
Total On/Off Licences	**921**					**933**					**974**
Registered Clubs	**287**					**317**					**327**
Total Licences & Clubs	**1108**					**1250**					**1301**

TABLE III 151
DRUNKENNESS OFFENCES, MOTORING OFFENCES AND LICENCES, 1963–73
HAMPSHIRE POLICE DISTRICT

	1963	**1964**	**1965**	**1966**	**1967**	**1968**	**1969**	**1970**	**1971**	**1972**	**1973**
Population '000	**1349**					**1486**					**1571**
Proved Offences—											
Drunkenness											
Males											
Under 18	24	20	25	36	50	53	47	78	93	91	126
18 and under 21	130	145	153	137	261	276	277	291	289	297	380
21 and under 30	328	325	340	328	388	485	430	441	460	446	555
30 and under 60	753	701	736	753	727	752	759	704	870	869	1144
60 and over	88	75	84	95	78	106	119	88	97	130	181
All ages	**1323**	**1266**	**1338**	**1349**	**1504**	**1672**	**1632**	**1602**	**1800**	**1883**	**2386**
Females											
Under 18	2			1	4	2	2	10	5	6	3
18 and under 21	1	7	5	11	8	6	8	18	5	12	11
21 and under 30	13	37	12	16	10	12	14	21	19	14	25
30 and under 60	40	32	24	30	34	27	43	39	46	51	47
60 and over	15	23	10	13	12	7	2	17	5	3	9
All ages	**71**	**99**	**51**	**71**	**68**	**54**	**69**	**105**	**80**	**86**	**95**
All Proved Offences	**1394**	**1365**	**1389**	**1420**	**1572**	**1726**	**1701**	**1707**	**1889**	**1919**	**2481**
Motoring Offences											
Proceedings for:											
(a) Previously Convicted											
Unfit to drive		22	24	15	8	2	1	1	3	2	1
Driving, undue alcohol						7	17	18	22	35	35
Fail provide specimen						2	2	2	4	6	4
(b) No Prev. Conviction											
Unfit to drive	205	199	186	180	198	14	22	16	14	12	33
Driving, undue alcohol					12	424	492	602	988	1439	1833
Fail provide spec.					3	22	35	29	60	72	94
In charge and:											
Unfit to drive	56	49	61	78	56	7	8	7	6	6	7
Undue alcohol					3	73	55	31	28	41	31
Fail provide spec.						8	16	6	9	6	25
Failure to provide breath specimen					4	69	72	81	121	160	203
Total: All Proceedings	**261**	**270**	**271**	**273**	**284**	**628**	**720**	**793**	**1255**	**1779**	**2266**
Licensed Premises											
Public Houses:											
Full	2163					2155					2109
Beer and Cider	20					3					2
Wine or Cider						3					2
Restaurant Licence	67					171					288
Residential Licence	82					141					188
Above Combined	68					123					139
Licensed Clubs	110					127					126
Total On Licences	**2510**					**2723**					**2854**
Off Licences	**729**					**805**					**876**
Total On/Off Licences	**3239**					**3528**					**3730**
Registered Clubs	**588**					**674**					**756**
Total Licences & Clubs	**3827**					**4202**					**4486**

TABLE III 152
DRUNKENNESS OFFENCES, MOTORING OFFENCES AND LICENCES, 1963–73
HERTFORDSHIRE (Beyond M.P.D.) POLICE DISTRICT

	1963	1964	1965	1966	1967	1968	1969	1970	1971	1972	1973
Population '000	**874**					**892**					**940**
Proved Offences— Drunkenness											
Males											
Under 18	11	6	6	7	5	13	13	10	10	25	15
18 and under 21	21	32	40	33	36	38	46	29	30	48	54
21 and under 30	61	48	71	40	48	64	79	77	60	71	82
30 and under 60	85	90	95	70	83	113	100	134	146	113	161
60 and over	10	9	10	27	17	9	13	8	37	21	37
All ages	**188**	**185**	**222**	**177**	**189**	**237**	**251**	**258**	**283**	**278**	**349**
Females											
Under 18	1				1		1	3	1		1
18 and under 21			2		1		1	3		3	4
21 and under 30				3		1		4	2	3	3
30 and under 60	1	2	1		6	1	2	7	3	5	2
60 and over	2	4		1					1		1
All ages	**4**	**6**	**3**	**4**	**8**	**2**	**4**	**17**	**7**	**11**	**10**
All Proved Offences	**192**	**191**	**225**	**181**	**197**	**239**	**255**	**275**	**290**	**289**	**359**
Motoring Offences											
Proceedings for:											
(a) Previously Convicted											
Unfit to drive		3		1	2						
Driving, undue alcohol						1					16
Fail provide specimen											1
(b) No Prev. Conviction											
Unfit to drive	55	61	64	66	70	8	15	15	15	7	13
Driving, undue alcohol					6	139	264	293	413	583	612
Fail provide spec.						10	19	17	37	41	56
In charge and:											
Unfit to drive	13	13	11	10	11		3	2	2	2	6
Undue alcohol						4	1	3	3	10	7
Fail provide spec.						3	8	3	1		11
Failure to provide breath specimen					1	21	25	31	45	47	74
Total: All Proceedings	**68**	**77**	**75**	**77**	**90**	**186**	**335**	**364**	**516**	**692**	**796**
Licensed Premises											
Public Houses:											
Full	1043					1002					998
Beer and Cider	37					6					4
Wine or Cider						2					
Restaurant Licence	21					71					126
Residential Licence						5					6
Above Combined	9					14					18
Licensed Clubs	15					18					23
Total On Licences	**1125**					**1118**					**1175**
Off Licences	**285**					**295**					**351**
Total On/Off Licences	**1410**					**1413**					**1526**
Registered Clubs	**431**					**459**					**514**
Total Licences & Clubs	**1841**					**1872**					**2040**

TABLE III 153
DRUNKENNESS OFFENCES, MOTORING OFFENCES AND LICENCES, 1963–73
KENT POLICE DISTRICT

	1963*	1964	1965	1966	1967	1968	1969	1970	1971	1972	1973
Population '000	**1748**					**1371**					**1443**
Proved Offences—											
Drunkenness											
Males											
Under 18	18	9	14	11	17	13	11	16	27	30	36
18 and under 21	50	51	48	41	55	53	48	41	55	70	89
21 and under 30	98	86	81	79	75	75	79	89	87	106	117
30 and under 60	183	134	149	150	115	137	152	151	167	210	276
60 and over	10	24	24	34	54	28	21	26	29	19	37
All ages	**359**	**304**	**316**	**315**	**316**	**306**	**311**	**323**	**365**	**435**	**555**
Females											
Under 18		1			1	5	3	1	3	7	6
18 and under 21		2	1	1	3	3	2	10	2	4	11
21 and under 30	5	2	5	1	2	2	2		4	3	2
30 and under 60	5	11	6	11	12	11	9	11	19	12	16
60 and over	3	2	2	1	1	2	5	1	1	2	1
All ages	**13**	**18**	**14**	**14**	**19**	**23**	**21**	**23**	**30**	**26**	**36**
All Proved Offences	**372**	**322**	**330**	**329**	**335**	**329**	**332**	**346**	**395**	**461**	**591**
Motoring Offences											
Proceedings for:											
(a) Previously Convicted											
Unfit to drive		4		1	2					1	5
Driving, undue alcohol					1			4	9	21	33
Fail provide specimen										5	8
(b) No Prev. Conviction											
Unfit to drive	105	104	89	74	102	4	2	7	6	11	18
Driving, undue alcohol					5	211	330	391	657	805	952
Fail provide spec.					2	8	10	20	41	28	57
In charge and:											
Unfit to drive	27	22	41	39	19	3	3	1	5	5	2
Undue alcohol						21	17	20	26	47	38
Fail provide spec.					1	11	16	1	4	25	27
Failure to provide breath specimen					3	43	42	58	112	87	153
Total: All Proceedings	**132**	**130**	**130**	**114**	**135**	**301**	**420**	**502**	**860**	**1035**	**1297**
Licensed Premises											
Public Houses:											
Full	2700					2390					2304
Beer and Cider	33					13					8
Wine or Cider	2					3					2
Restaurant Licence	107					194					301
Residential Licence	111					139					168
Above Combined	56					78					87
Licensed Clubs	108					111					110
Total On Licences	**3117**					**2926**					**2980**
Off Licences	**755**					**654**					**723**
Total On/Off Licences	**3872**					**3580**					**3703**
Registered Clubs	**764**					**623**					**710**
Total Licences & Clubs	**4636**					**4203**					**4413**

*1963 includes some M.P.D. Licences.

TABLE III 154

DRUNKENNESS OFFENCES, MOTORING OFFENCES AND LICENCES, 1963–73
LANCASHIRE POLICE DISTRICT (excluding the Licensing Divisions of Manchester and Liverpool)

	1963	1964	1965	1966	1967	1968	1969	1970	1971	1972	1973
Population '000	**2187**					**2185**					**2234**
Proved Offences—Drunkenness											
Males											
Under 18	152	233	238	264	270	285	229	328	370	363	501
18 and under 21	674	703	867	791	892	1027	935	947	1043	988	1375
21 and under 30	1054	1134	1152	1140	1135	1329	1160	1239	1443	1258	1597
30 and under 60	1632	1630	1819	1839	1675	1820	1600	1425	1710	1693	2046
60 and over	168	176	190	248	241	244	196	125	105	143	204
All ages	**3680**	**3876**	**4266**	**4282**	**4213**	**4705**	**4120**	**4064**	**4671**	**4445**	**5723**
Females											
Under 18	14	4	16	13	25	22	13	21	18	24	36
18 and under 21	23	23	16	17	29	39	25	27	27	39	54
21 and under 30	20	39	26	27	41	48	49	60	61	77	77
30 and under 60	82	105	93	110	103	129	88	83	116	145	138
60 and over	28	15	11	14	18	10	3	9	6	7	11
All ages	**167**	**186**	**162**	**181**	**216**	**248**	**178**	**200**	**228**	**292**	**316**
All Proved Offences	**3847**	**4062**	**4428**	**4463**	**4429**	**4953**	**4298**	**4264**	**4899**	**4737**	**6039**
Motoring Offences											
Proceedings for:											
(a) Previously Convicted											
Unfit to drive		44	32	32	16		1	1	1	1	2
Driving, undue alcohol					4	30	19	43	84	144	206
Fail provide specimen						6	3	9	5	23	46
(b) No Prev. Conviction											
Unfit to drive	471	546	582	608	607	31	15	23	14	12	16
Driving, undue alcohol					84	1565	1792	2023	2969	3826	3737
Fail provide spec.					16	134	168	188	286	287	331
In charge and:											
Unfit to drive	122	122	126	141	115	11	21	9	4	5	8
Undue alcohol					2	96	95	26	53	57	85
Fail provide spec.					3	37	39	36	12	21	22
Failure to provide breath specimen					10	226	246	229	321	465	590
Total: All Proceedings	**593**	**712**	**740**	**781**	**857**	**2136**	**2399**	**2587**	**3759**	**4841**	**5043**
Licensed Premises*											
Public Houses:											
Full	3157					3148					3058
Beer and Cider	150					54					21
Wine or Cider	5					2					2
Restaurant Licence	76					163					277
Residential Licence	74					265					458
Above Combined	73					105					139
Licensed Clubs	65					94					107
Total On Licences	**3600**					**3831**					**4062**
Off Licences	**1578**					**1706**					**1751**
Total On/Off Licences	**5178**					**5537**					**5813**
Registered Clubs	**1132**					**1202**					**1239**
Total Licences & Clubs	**6310**					**6739**					**7052**

*Stockport C.B. included in Lancashire for licensing purposes.

TABLE III 155
DRUNKENNESS OFFENCES, MOTORING OFFENCES AND LICENCES, 1963–73
LIVERPOOL AND BOOTLE POLICE DISTRICT

	1963	1964	1965	1966	1967	1968	1969	1970	1971	1972	1973
Population '000	**1549**					**1581**					**1592**
Proved Offences—Drunkenness											
Males											
Under 18	184	227	182	124	158	207	472	381	214	250	246
18 and under 21	868	679	640	450	563	713	1449	1264	801	781	845
21 and under 30	1699	1112	901	610	710	858	1671	1663	1283	1253	1255
30 and under 60	3837	2494	1519	1190	1331	1506	2794	3068	2506	1758	2786
60 and over	491	309	159	126	210	227	284	283	313	308	359
All ages	**7079**	**4821**	**3401**	**2500**	**2972**	**3511**	**6670**	**6659**	**5117**	**5350**	**5491**
Females											
Under 18	12	5	5	7	5	9	11	12	20	16	20
18 and under 21	25	13	14	10	16	11	38	58	53	49	53
21 and under 30	52	33	18	22	25	49	36	57	68	80	70
30 and under 60	186	139	56	56	99	87	133	145	149	137	211
60 and over	45	21	6	7	11	26	15	26	16	19	26
All ages	**330**	**211**	**99**	**102**	**156**	**182**	**233**	**298**	**306**	**301**	**380**
All Proved Offences	**7409**	**5032**	**3500**	**2602**	**3120**	**3693**	**6903**	**6957**	**5423**	**5651**	**5871**
Motoring Offences											
Proceedings for:											
(a) Previously Convicted											
Unfit to drive		5	3	4	2						
Driving, undue alcohol						3	3	1	9		2
Fail provide specimen					2				1		
(b) No Prev. Conviction											
Unfit to drive	147	129	182	126	135	5		3	6	5	1
Driving, undue alcohol					1	243	276	334	589	626	669
Fail provide spec.					5	47	40	31	37		
In charge and:											
Unfit to drive	62	34	47	39	38		3		2	2	5
Undue alcohol						5	7	7	9	16	13
Fail provide spec.						1	6	29	37	88	112
Failure to provide breath specimen					4	34	34	52	58	111	118
Total: All Proceedings	**209**	**168**	**232**	**169**	**187**	**338**	**369**	**457**	**748**	**848**	**920**
Licensed Premises*											
Public Houses:											
Full	1777					1718					1552
Beer and Cider	56					12					4
Wine or Cider	1					1					1
Restaurant Licence	24					57					92
Residential Licence	2					2					3
Above Combined	5					12					17
Licensed Clubs	62					96					142
Total On Licences	**1927**					**1898**					**1811**
Off Licences	**416**					**445**					**554**
Total On/Off Licences	**2343**					**2343**					**2365**
Registered Clubs	**626**					**651**					**632**
Total Licences & Clubs	**2969**					**2994**					**2997**

*Includes the Liverpool Licensing Division of Lancashire.

TABLE III 156
DRUNKENNESS OFFENCES, MOTORING OFFENCES AND LICENCES, 1963–73
MANCHESTER AND SALFORD POLICE DISTRICT

	1963	1964	1965	1966	1967	1968	1969	1970	1971	1972	1973
Population '000	**1584**					**1555**					**1483**
Proved Offences—Drunkenness											
Males											
Under 18	114	123	82	73	87	90	99	116	130	142	171
18 and under 21	512	521	370	521	495	505	413	429	408	407	522
21 and under 30	1137	1207	768	939	868	844	789	756	694	753	971
30 and under 60	2266	2310	1675	1871	1921	1866	1418	1329	1243	1516	1811
60 and over	167	178	144	184	137	126	120	104	125	154	190
All ages	**4196**	**4339**	**3039**	**3588**	**3508**	**3431**	**2839**	**2734**	**2600**	**2972**	**3665**
Females											
Under 18	3	3	1	4	1	4	4	4	10	5	15
18 and under 21	26	23	9	6	26	16	12	23	36	19	45
21 and under 30	58	53	27	26	40	49	41	56	51	60	79
30 and under 60	178	200	107	172	151	151	130	120	140	144	160
60 and over	38	53	26	24	12	6	6	20	6	14	7
All ages	**303**	**332**	**170**	**232**	**230**	**226**	**193**	**223**	**243**	**242**	**306**
All Proved Offences	**4499**	**4671**	**3209**	**2820**	**3738**	**3657**	**3032**	**2957**	**2843**	**3214**	**3971**
Motoring Offences											
Proceedings for:											
(a) Previously Convicted											
Unfit to drive		31	37	43	27		4	3	2		7
Driving, undue alcohol					3	19	63	52	65	83	77
Fail provide specimen						3	5	2	2	6	4
(b) No Prev. Conviction											
Unfit to drive	481	543	602	693	557	43	51	56	47	69	38
Driving, undue alcohol					26	530	670	798	1098	1391	1894
Fail provide spec.					3	19	63	71	95	133	93
In charge and:											
Unfit to drive	128	141	142	154	140	12	10	6	10	5	3
Undue alcohol						21	25	25	18	8	16
Fail provide spec.						26	4	4	2	6	76
Failure to provide breath specimen					4	78	113	120	125	155	191
Total: All Proceedings	**609**	**715**	**781**	**890**	**760**	**751**	**1008**	**1137**	**1464**	**1856**	**2399**
Licensed Premises*											
Public Houses:											
Full	1934					1915					1831
Beer and Cider	224					97					30
Wine or Cider	1					1					
Restaurant Licence	36					88					135
Residential Licence	9					8					25
Above Combined	8					28					29
Licensed Clubs	85					91					82
Total On Licences	**2297**					**2228**					**2132**
Off Licences	**1504**					**1309**					**1094**
Total On/Off Licences	**3801**					**3337**					**3226**
Registered Clubs	**657**					**698**					**701**
Total Licences & Clubs	**4458**					**4035**					**3927**

*Includes the Manchester Licensing Division of Lancashire.

TABLE III 157

DRUNKENNESS OFFENCES, MOTORING OFFENCES AND LICENCES, 1963–73 LEICESTER AND RUTLAND POLICE DISTRICT

	1963	1964	1965	1966	1967	1968	1969	1970	1971	1972	1973
Population '000	**723**					**763**					**824**
Proved Offences— Drunkenness											
Males											
Under 18	3	17	6	11	2	3	2	5	9	7	13
18 and under 21	29	31	22	22	31	15	17	17	19	25	20
21 and under 30	58	66	71	76	51	50	45	25	34	35	66
30 and under 60	185	223	186	199	166	155	146	125	127	128	196
60 and over	22	27	28	16	21	35	15	5	29	18	24
All ages	**297**	**364**	**313**	**324**	**271**	**258**	**225**	**177**	**218**	**213**	**319**
Females											
Under 18	2	2	2	1		1		1	1		
18 and under 21	1	1			1		1			6	2
21 and under 30	4	4	1	1	1	3	3	2	1	3	1
30 and under 60	15	15	5	12	6	2	7	5	7	10	11
60 and over	9	4	6	2	1	1	1	1		1	2
All ages	**31**	**26**	**14**	**16**	**9**	**7**	**12**	**9**	**9**	**20**	**16**
All Proved Offences	**328**	**390**	**327**	**340**	**280**	**265**	**237**	**186**	**227**	**233**	**335**
Motoring Offences											
Proceedings for:											
(a) Previously Convicted											
Unfit to drive		6	7	2	3	2	2			1	
Driving, undue alcohol					1	6	5	5	7	15	30
Fail provide specimen						1		1		2	
(b) No Prev. Conviction											
Unfit to drive	59	56	73	64	73	11	7	3	13	3	2
Driving, undue alcohol					13	178	144	193	359	405	453
Fail provide spec.						7	7	6	21	24	25
In charge and:											
Unfit to drive	13	17	11	28	18	1	2	1	2		2
Undue alcohol						5	4	7	13	10	16
Fail provide spec.						4	6		1	3	2
Failure to provide breath specimen					1	7	10	13	21	28	24
Total: All Proceedings	**72**	**79**	**91**	**98**	**109**	**222**	**187**	**229**	**437**	**491**	**554**
Licensed Premises											
Public Houses:											
Full	1044					1049					1044
Beer and Cider	8					1					
Wine or Cider	2					1					
Restaurant Licence	27					66					96
Residential Licence	2					4					7
Above Combined	7					13					21
Licensed Clubs	10					17					23
Total On Licences	**1100**					**1151**					**1191**
Off Licences	**626**					**670**					**716**
Total On/Off Licences	**1726**					**1821**					**1907**
Registered Clubs	**314**					**343**					**354**
Total Licences & Clubs	**2040**					**2164**					**2261**

TABLE III 158
DRUNKENNESS OFFENCES, MOTORING OFFENCES AND LICENCES, 1963–73
LINCOLNSHIRE POLICE DISTRICT

	1963	1964	1965	1966	1967	1968	1969	1970	1971	1972	1973
Population '000	**764**					**795**					**820**
Proved Offences—Drunkenness											
Males											
Under 18	25	22	28	38	36	59	27	47	44	40	68
18 and under 21	70	81	58	88	98	149	121	111	127	115	134
21 and under 30	158	146	148	133	177	245	262	203	192	214	171
30 and under 60	343	343	294	283	280	401	360	354	417	428	394
60 and over	24	24	16	30	38	30	22	27	30	25	24
All ages	**620**	**616**	**544**	**572**	**629**	**884**	**792**	**742**	**810**	**822**	**791**
Females											
Under 18	5	2	1	2	2	2	4	7	2	5	8
18 and under 21	1	1	3	1	3	2	5	2	4	2	3
21 and under 30	6	3	3	1	7	8	4	5	9	7	8
30 and under 60	8	10	11	11	17	26	18	32	21	11	33
60 and over		1	1		1	3		2		2	
All ages	**20**	**17**	**19**	**15**	**30**	**41**	**31**	**48**	**36**	**27**	**52**
All Proved Offences	**640**	**633**	**563**	**587**	**659**	**925**	**823**	**790**	**846**	**849**	**843**
Motoring Offences											
Proceedings for:											
(a) Previously Convicted											
Unfit to drive		2	5	6	2			1		3	1
Driving, undue alcohol					2	17	14	21	22	28	45
Fail provide specimen						2	1	2	2	2	12
(b) No Prev. Conviction											
Unfit to drive	52	53	62	77	84	4	13	8	10	12	14
Driving, undue alcohol					16	275	279	361	557	626	834
Fail provide spec.					1	11	8	28	27	21	50
In charge and:											
Unfit to drive	23	20	25	21	16		4	6	3	3	4
Undue alcohol					1	19	11	23	18	43	20
Fail provide spec.						5	12	3	6	12	8
Failure to provide breath specimen					2	26	28	43	31	59	81
Total: All Proceedings	**75**	**75**	**92**	**104**	**124**	**359**	**370**	**496**	**676**	**809**	**1069**
Licensed Premises											
Public Houses:											
Full	1321					1285					1229
Beer and Cider	10					6					1
Wine or Cider						2					2
Restaurant Licence	44					95					127
Residential Licence	4					11					39
Above Combined	14					18					37
Licensed Clubs	11					17					31
Total On Licences	**1404**					**1434**					**1466**
Off Licences	**420**					**465**					**563**
Total On/Off Licences	**1824**					**1899**					**2029**
Registered Clubs	**374**					**411**					**448**
Total Licences & Clubs	**2198**					**2310**					**2477**

TABLE III 159
DRUNKENNESS OFFENCES, MOTORING OFFENCES AND LICENCES, 1963-73
CITY OF LONDON POLICE DISTRICT

	1963	1964	1965	1966	1967	1968	1969	1970	1971	1972	1973
Population '000	**5**					**4**					**5**
Proved Offences—Drunkenness											
Males											
Under 18	3		1	1		5	3	2	6	2	6
18 and under 21	7	8	4		6	8	10	9	11	14	19
21 and under 30	29	25	16	19	19	27	22	25	39	53	38
30 and under 60	157	160	144	196	144	161	145	145	193	212	199
60 and over	19	24	32	26	16	20	28	27	25	29	39
All ages	**215**	**217**	**197**	**242**	**185**	**221**	**208**	**208**	**274**	**310**	**301**
Females											
Under 18											2
18 and under 21					2				1		
21 and under 30	1		1	2					1	1	1
30 and under 60	14	11	16	11	4	7	8	6	11	5	9
60 and over	5	5	3	2	1	5	12	13			7
All ages	**20**	**16**	**20**	**15**	**7**	**12**	**20**	**19**	**13**	**6**	**19**
All Proved Offences	**235**	**233**	**217**	**257**	**192**	**233**	**228**	**227**	**287**	**316**	**320**
Motoring Offences											
Proceedings for:											
(a) Previously Convicted											
Unfit to drive		1	1	3							
Driving, undue alcohol							4	2	1	2	1
Fail provide specimen								1		1	
(b) No Prev. Conviction											
Unfit to drive	21	21	17	23	14	1		2	2	1	1
Driving, undue alcohol					1	37	48	50	47	59	51
Fail provide spec.					1	1	3	3	4	3	3
In charge and:											
Unfit to drive	9	6	7	7	7		1				2
Undue alcohol						4	1	3	3	3	2
Fail provide spec.							1	2	2	2	3
Failure to provide breath specimen					1	4	7	5	13	6	4
Total: All Proceedings	**30**	**28**	**25**	**33**	**24**	**47**	**65**	**70**	**72**	**73**	**67**
Licensed Premises											
Public Houses:											
Full	217					223					213
Beer and Cider	5					4					2
Wine or Cider											2
Restaurant Licence	14					33					40
Residential Licence											1
Above Combined											1
Licensed Clubs	19					25					34
Total On Licences	**255**					**285**					**292**
Off Licences	**93**					**79**					**43**
Total On/Off Licences	**348**					**364**					**335**
Registered Clubs	**84**					**78**					**82**
Total Licences & Clubs	**432**					**442**					**417**

TABLE III 160
DRUNKENNESS OFFENCES, MOTORING OFFENCES AND LICENCES, 1963–73
METROPOLITAN POLICE DISTRICT

	1963*	1964	1965	1966	1967	1968	1969	1970	1971	1972	1973
Population '000	**5416**					**7759**					**7275**
Proved Offences—Drunkenness											
Males											
Under 18	168	171	179	177	239	283	304	402	416	526	768
18 and under 21	1450	1283	1331	1434	1616	1857	1810	2091	2214	2230	2792
21 and under 30	6323	5728	5527	5187	5723	6030	6067	6221	6725	6954	7278
30 and under 60	22609	20824	19026	17152	19364	20628	20888	21018	22101	23156	22795
60 and over	2676	2458	2138	1977	2329	2469	2432	2652	2476	2670	2888
All ages	**33226**	**30468**	**28201**	**25297**	**29271**	**31267**	**31537**	**32384**	**33933**	**35536**	**36541**
Females											
Under 18	14	11	17	20	13	21	20	21	43	60	38
18 and under 21	48	46	33	45	48	66	86	98	124	146	178
21 and under 30	253	247	239	224	289	289	293	372	279	536	491
30 and under 60	1862	1761	1565	1614	1647	1973	2220	2078	2006	1984	1887
60 and over	380	356	340	340	426	545	552	582	657	572	370
All ages	**2557**	**2421**	**2194**	**2243**	**2423**	**2894**	**3171**	**3151**	**3309**	**3298**	**2964**
All Proved Offences	**35783**	**32889**	**30395**	**28170**	**31694**	**34161**	**34708**	**35535**	**37241**	**38834**	**39505**
Motoring Offences											
Proceedings for:											
(a) Previously Convicted											
Unfit to drive		55	66	71	32			23	44	28	26
Driving, undue alcohol					1	4	6	93	182	361	341
Fail provide specimen					1	1		2	15	9	
(b) No Prev. Conviction											
Unfit to drive	1952	1770	2053	2504	2340	1084	1128	1280	1763	1817	2424
Driving, undue alcohol					97	3394	5763	5920	8393	9283	8967
Fail provide spec.					52	430	527	507	651	604	583
In charge and:											
Unfit to drive	457	354	432	442	460	134	66	96	98	93	205
Undue alcohol						47	22	60	92	53	56
Fail provide spec.					3	9	12	13	41	17	161
Failure to provide breath specimen					31	295	339	292	279	199	239
Total: All Proceedings	**2409**	**2179**	**2551**	**3017**	**3017**	**5398**	**7863**	**8286**	**11558**	**12464**	**13002**
Licensed Premises											
Public Houses:											
Full	5166					6174					6110
Beer and Cider	111					45					28
Wine or Cider	10					9					19
Restaurant Licence	464					1273					2196
Residential Licence	16					45					73
Above Combined	50					96					144
Licensed Clubs	395					494					500
Total On Licences	**7212**					**8136**					**9070**
Off Licences	**2559**					**3404**					**3543**
Total On/Off Licences	**9771**					**11540**					**12613**
Registered Clubs	**1671**					**2546**					**2772**
Total Licences & Clubs	**11442**					**14086**					**15385**

*1963 Population and Licences exclude M.P.D. outside L.C.C. and Middlesex.

TABLE III 161
DRUNKENNESS OFFENCES, MOTORING OFFENCES AND LICENCES, 1963–73
MID-ANGLIA POLICE DISTRICT

	1963	1964	1965	1966	1967	1968	1969	1970	1971	1972	1973
Population '000	**451**					**494**					**533**
Proved Offences—Drunkenness											
Males											
Under 18	7	19	5	2	9	7	4	12	11	14	15
18 and under 21	32	21	24	24	23	19	22	21	24	19	39
21 and under 30	36	42	48	32	46	46	41	37	35	37	47
30 and under 60	103	102	96	85	114	103	127	129	154	143	181
60 and over	10	18	15	11	11	10	22	26	28	13	21
All ages	**188**	**202**	**188**	**154**	**203**	**185**	**216**	**225**	**252**	**226**	**303**
Females											
Under 18		2		1	2			1	3	1	2
18 and under 21	1		7	2	2			1	3		1
21 and under 30	1	1			4	2	1	1	3	5	4
30 and under 60		4	10	6	1	2	8	2	4	3	8
60 and over						1		1		2	2
All ages	**2**	**7**	**17**	**9**	**9**	**5**	**9**	**6**	**13**	**11**	**17**
All Proved Offences	**190**	**209**	**205**	**163**	**212**	**190**	**225**	**231**	**265**	**237**	**320**
Motoring Offences											
Proceedings for:											
(a) Previously Convicted											
Unfit to drive		3	6	5	1		1	1			
Driving, undue alcohol						5	4	7	8	12	28
Fail provide specimen							1	2	4	4	5
(b) No Prev. Conviction											
Unfit to drive	66	59	56	68	75	7	18	9	15	3	5
Driving, undue alcohol					7	138	182	166	284	298	385
Fail provide spec.					1	6	8	7	18	15	20
In charge and:											
Unfit to drive	24	18	15	12	12	2	5	5	5	3	1
Undue alcohol					1	7	7	8	18	10	11
Fail provide spec.						1	3			5	2
Failure to provide breath specimen						3	9	8	15	10	12
Total: All Proceedings	**90**	**80**	**77**	**85**	**97**	**169**	**238**	**213**	**367**	**360**	**469**
Licensed Premises											
Public Houses:											
Full	1055					993					880
Beer and Cider	28					12					2
Wine or Cider						1					2
Restaurant Licence	15					43					68
Residential Licence						2					3
Above Combined	1					5					12
Licensed Clubs	5					16					23
Total On Licences	**1104**					**1072**					**988**
Off Licences	**222**					**252**					**334**
Total On/Off Licences	**1326**					**1324**					**1322**
Registered Clubs	**220**					**247**					**285**
Total Licences & Clubs	**1546**					**1571**					**1607**

TABLE III 162
DRUNKENNESS OFFENCES, MOTORING OFFENCES AND LICENCES, 1963-73
NORFOLK POLICE DISTRICT

	1963	1964	1965	1966	1967	1968	1969	1970	1971	1972	1973
Population '000	**569**					**603**					**635**
Proved Offences—Drunkenness											
Males											
Under 18	7	4	4	6	11	1	8	13	5	11	14
18 and under 21	23	28	29	35	33	34	12	25	31	27	40
21 and under 30	20	40	39	43	48	58	48	44	30	47	78
30 and under 60	66	56	62	37	51	50	47	45	57	88	82
60 and over	10	4	6	16	3	4	5	7	8	10	11
All ages	**126**	**132**	**140**	**137**	**146**	**147**	**120**	**134**	**131**	**183**	**225**
Females											
Under 18	1	1				1	1	1		2	1
18 and under 21	4	2	2	1	1	1		1	2		1
21 and under 30	1	1		1	3	1	1		1	2	2
30 and under 60	1	1	3	1	1		1	4	2	7	8
60 and over				1							
All ages	**7**	**5**	**5**	**4**	**5**	**3**	**3**	**6**	**5**	**11**	**12**
All Proved Offences	**133**	**137**	**145**	**141**	**151**	**150**	**123**	**140**	**136**	**194**	**237**
Motoring Offences											
Proceedings for:											
(a) Previously Convicted											
Unfit to drive		1	6	1	2		1			1	2
Driving, undue alcohol							1		2	9	22
Fail provide specimen									1	2	3
(b) No Prev. Conviction											
Unfit to drive	25	27	38	48	52		11	16	14	15	6
Driving, undue alcohol					7	95	109	114	204	254	313
Fail provide spec.					2	17	13	9	18	22	18
In charge and:											
Unfit to drive	13	11	20	11	18	5	4	6	3	2	3
Undue alcohol					1	23	10	11	15	10	16
Fail provide spec.						3		1	2	5	6
Failure to provide breath specimen					4	11	15	14	27	29	45
Total: All Proceedings	**38**	**39**	**64**	**60**	**86**	**154**	**164**	**171**	**286**	**349**	**434**
Licensed Premises											
Public Houses:											
Full	1597					1435					1265
Beer and Cider	45					12					2
Wine or Cider	1										1
Restaurant Licence	31					71					122
Residential Licence	85					117					142
Above Combined	34					54					73
Licensed Clubs	25					23					37
Total On Licences	**1818**					**1712**					**1642**
Off Licences	**176**					**286**					**433**
Total On/Off Licences	**1994**					**1998**					**2075**
Registered Clubs	**182**					**213**					**238**
Total Licences & Clubs	**2176**					**2211**					**2313**

TABLE III 163
DRUNKENNESS OFFENCES, MOTORING OFFENCES AND LICENCES, 1963–73
NORTHAMPTON AND COUNTY POLICE DISTRICT

	1963	1964	1965	1966	1967	1968	1969	1970	1971	1972	1973
Population '000	**411**					**445**					**488**
Proved Offences—Drunkenness											
Males											
Under 18	2	9	9	10	9	20	9	14	16	6	20
18 and under 21	14	16	24	23	20	30	31	25	44	39	50
21 and under 30	29	55	49	63	45	54	43	61	73	76	97
30 and under 60	70	93	138	140	94	133	123	152	140	140	190
60 and over	4	16	11	18	5	7	12	9	12	15	14
All ages	**119**	**189**	**231**	**254**	**173**	**244**	**218**	**261**	**285**	**276**	**371**
Females											
Under 18				1				7	1	2	4
18 and under 21				2		1			2	3	5
21 and under 30	1		2		1		4	1	3	1	6
30 and under 60	3	2	4	7	2	8	11	14	10	14	17
60 and over			1	1	1					1	
All ages	**4**	**2**	**7**	**11**	**4**	**9**	**15**	**22**	**16**	**21**	**32**
All Proved Offences	**123**	**191**	**238**	**265**	**177**	**253**	**232**	**283**	**301**	**297**	**403**
Motoring Offences											
Proceedings for:											
(a) Previously Convicted											
Unfit to drive		2	5	1	4						
Driving, undue alcohol						1			5	2	1
Fail provide specimen										1	1
(b) No Prev. Conviction											
Unfit to drive	33	34	48	58	65	2	7	7	8	7	4
Driving, undue alcohol					5	133	143	143	235	238	324
Fail provide spec.					1	8	9	14	16	22	35
In charge and:											
Unfit to drive	17	9	15	13	17	4	8	6	1	5	6
Undue alcohol						7	6	4	3	14	10
Fail provide spec.						1	2	1			3
Failure to provide breath specimen					1	18	10	22	29	40	51
Total: All Proceedings	**50**	**45**	**68**	**72**	**93**	**174**	**185**	**197**	**297**	**329**	**435**
Licensed Premises											
Public Houses:											
Full	635					631					603
Beer and Cider	10					3					1
Wine or Cider	2										
Restaurant Licence	14					33					41
Residential Licence											3
Above Combined	4					11					12
Licensed Clubs	22					4					10
Total On Licences	**687**					**682**					**670**
Off Licences	**416**					**421**					**452**
Total On/Off Licences	**1103**					**1103**					**1122**
Registered Clubs	**195**					**233**					**285**
Total Licences & Clubs	**1298**					**1336**					**1407**

TABLE III 164
DRUNKENNESS OFFENCES, MOTORING OFFENCES AND LICENCES, 1963–73
NORTHUMBERLAND POLICE DISTRICT

	1963	1964	1965	1966	1967	1968	1969	1970	1971	1972	1973
Population '000	**826**					**822**					**789**
Proved Offences—Drunkenness											
Males											
Under 18	82	86	116	98	89	111	125	124	190	168	267
18 and under 21	378	390	447	452	440	529	424	454	513	559	708
21 and under 30	658	541	575	524	536	660	553	523	650	617	855
30 and under 60	1193	955	937	908	903	842	766	697	788	791	957
60 and over	79	69	63	80	91	82	75	62	84	76	110
All ages	**2390**	**2041**	**2138**	**2062**	**2059**	**2224**	**1943**	**1860**	**2225**	**2211**	**2897**
Females											
Under 18		4	6	4	3	8	3	15	17	21	31
18 and under 21	8	19	18	14	15	23	10	19	31	30	47
21 and under 30	39	29	34	20	28	25	24	23	42	43	50
30 and under 60	68	53	50	74	51	59	49	47	55	65	82
60 and over	12	12	10	6	11	6	7	7	5	2	3
All ages	**127**	**117**	**118**	**118**	**108**	**121**	**93**	**111**	**150**	**161**	**213**
All Proved Offences	**2517**	**2158**	**2256**	**2180**	**2167**	**2345**	**2036**	**1971**	**2375**	**2372**	**3110**
Motoring Offences											
Proceedings for:											
(a) Previously Convicted											
Unfit to drive		11	11	13	14						
Driving, undue alcohol					1	16	14	26	44	31	70
Fail provide specimen							3	4	5	6	11
(b) No Prev. Conviction											
Unfit to drive	153	153	170	178	173	3	4	3	8	1	
Driving, undue alcohol					17	436	475	502	681	655	893
Fail provide spec.					2	28	34	15	25	42	42
In charge and:											
Unfit to drive	26	36	32	27	21	3	1		4	1	3
Undue alcohol						5	9	9	13	10	1
Fail provide spec.						2	4	7	6	4	6
Failure to provide breath specimen					3	40	57	61	70	73	115
Total: All Proceedings	**179**	**200**	**213**	**218**	**231**	**533**	**601**	**627**	**856**	**823**	**1156**
Licensed Premises											
Public Houses:											
Full	924					873					870
Beer and Cider	11					6					4
Wine or Cider											
Restaurant Licence	22					45					62
Residential Licence	5					7					17
Above Combined	10					24					33
Licensed Clubs	21					42					41
Total On Licences	**993**					**997**					**1027**
Off Licences	**457**					**521**					**542**
Total On/Off Licences	**1450**					**1518**					**1569**
Registered Clubs	**449**					**477**					**509**
Total Licences & Clubs	**1899**					**1995**					**2078**

TABLE III 165
DRUNKENNESS OFFENCES, MOTORING OFFENCES AND LICENCES, 1963–73
NOTTINGHAMSHIRE COMBINED POLICE DISTRICT

	1963	1964	1965	1966	1967	1968	1969	1970	1971	1972	1973
Population '000	**926**					**964**					**985**
Proved Offences—Drunkenness											
Males											
Under 18	10	8	10	18	17	9	15	20	21	28	29
18 and under 21	32	46	57	57	64	64	70	53	50	23	48
21 and under 30	64	88	97	106	103	123	124	83	32	24	33
30 and under 60	164	175	230	215	275	266	237	107	345	290	566
60 and over	22	18	20	31	51	50	35	102	35	32	54
All ages	**292**	**335**	**414**	**427**	**510**	**512**	**481**	**365**	**501**	**397**	**730**
Females											
Under 18	3	1	1			2	1		1	2	2
18 and under 21	4		1	5	4	3	1	4			4
21 and under 30	2	4	1	2	7	5	7	3	2	3	1
30 and under 60	14	12	8	26	14	3	13	11	15	20	40
60 and over	5	2	1	3		2	1	6		3	3
All ages	**28**	**19**	**12**	**36**	**25**	**15**	**23**	**24**	**18**	**28**	**50**
All Proved Offences	**320**	**354**	**426**	**463**	**535**	**527**	**504**	**389**	**519**	**425**	**780**
Motoring Offences											
Proceedings for:											
(a) Previously Convicted											
Unfit to drive		8	6	4	6			1			
Driving, undue alcohol						5	4	7	4	3	
Fail provide specimen							1	1	2	1	
(b) No Prev. Conviction											
Unfit to drive	49	65	79	84	94	3	11			7	11
Driving, undue alcohol					9	239	295	328	404	527	737
Fail provide spec.					1	16	19	14	27	27	30
In charge and:											
Unfit to drive	9	15	21	16	21	1	7	3	3	2	10
Undue alcohol					1	18	9	12	38	12	17
Fail provide spec.						4	6	5	3	8	18
Failure to provide breath specimen						20	30	35	42	45	67
Total: All Proceedings	**58**	**88**	**106**	**104**	**132**	**306**	**382**	**406**	**523**	**632**	**890**
Licensed Premises											
Public Houses:											
Full	1120					1127					1120
Beer and Cider	15					8					1
Wine or Cider	1					1					
Restaurant Licence	24					44					91
Residential Licence	2					6					8
Above Combined	5					8					15
Licensed Clubs	30					35					50
Total On Licences	**1187**					**1229**					**1285**
Off Licences	**767**					**758**					**733**
Total On/Off Licences	**1954**					**1987**					**2018**
Registered Clubs	**332**					**365**					**386**
Total Licences & Clubs	**2286**					**2352**					**2404**

TABLE III 166
DRUNKENNESS OFFENCES, MOTORING OFFENCES AND LICENCES, 1963–73
SOMERSET AND BATH POLICE DISTRICT

	1963	1964	1965	1966	1967	1968	1969	1970	1971	1972	1973
Population '000	**616**					**658**					**702**
Proved Offences— Drunkenness											
Males											
Under 18	7	8	14	7	14	15	13	13	25	32	32
18 and under 21	29	31	33	34	29	56	56	64	92	86	100
21 and under 30	53	48	56	43	63	94	85	80	107	100	132
30 and under 60	147	141	121	118	118	144	142	145	200	222	237
60 and over	21	16	15	25	15	20	19	27	20	32	43
All ages	**257**	**244**	**239**	**227**	**239**	**329**	**315**	**329**	**444**	**472**	**544**
Females											
Under 18		1	2		1	5	4	2	4	8	3
18 and under 21	1	4	2		2	2	4	3	8	4	3
21 and under 30		1		1	1	1	3	1	2	8	3
30 and under 60	2	2	4	4	2	1	7	7	15	11	6
60 and over					2			3	5	1	1
All ages	**3**	**8**	**8**	**5**	**8**	**9**	**18**	**16**	**34**	**32**	**16**
All Proved Offences	**260**	**252**	**247**	**232**	**247**	**338**	**333**	**345**	**478**	**504**	**560**
Motoring Offences											
Proceedings for:											
(a) Previously Convicted											
Unfit to drive		1	4	2	6						2
Driving, undue alcohol						1	2	1	3	13	41
Fail provide specimen							1			3	5
(b) No Prev. Conviction											
Unfit to drive	55	36	63	47	47	4	2		2	5	3
Driving, undue alcohol					9	129	223	266	349	564	639
Fail provide spec.						10	11	12	30	29	23
In charge and:											
Unfit to drive	15	9	18	13	17			2	3	6	3
Undue alcohol					1	9	6	5	6	16	26
Fail provide spec.						2	1			8	3
Failure to provide breath specimen						10	10	11	16	15	16
Total: All Proceedings	**70**	**46**	**85**	**62**	**80**	**165**	**256**	**297**	**399**	**658**	**761**
Licensed Premises											
Public Houses:											
Full	1315					1332					1344
Beer and Cider	42					7					2
Wine or Cider											2
Restaurant Licence	39					108					190
Residential Licence	11					16					31
Above Combined	38					53					90
Licensed Clubs	17					24					22
Total On Licences	**1462**					**1540**					**1681**
Off Licences	**317**					**400**					**509**
Total On/Off Licences	**1779**					**1940**					**2190**
Registered Clubs	**278**					**340**					**377**
Total Licences & Clubs	**2057**					**2280**					**2567**

TABLE III 167
DRUNKENNESS OFFENCES, MOTORING OFFENCES AND LICENCES, 1963–73
STAFFORDSHIRE AND STOKE-ON-TRENT POLICE DISTRICT

	1963	1964	1965	1966*	1967	1968	1969	1970	1971	1972	1973
Population '000	**1300**					**1034**					**1073**
Proved Offences— Drunkenness											
Males											
Under 18	28	39	54	46	30	34	41	39	44	35	65
18 and under 21	115	200	221	170	156	131	155	149	150	141	148
21 and under 30	280	288	345	250	205	171	179	186	251	228	240
30 and under 60	455	470	531	343	319	272	275	233	268	298	314
60 and over	36	24	51	36	39	22	41	20	30	31	46
All ages	**914**	**1021**	**1202**	**845**	**749**	**630**	**691**	**627**	**743**	**733**	**813**
Females											
Under 18	1	1	3	3	5	4	3	5	3	1	4
18 and under 21	3	4	2	4	1	7	1	2	2		5
21 and under 30	6	2	5	1	4	2	5	4	4	5	6
30 and under 60	9	18	21	13	7	13	7	14	9	14	16
60 and over	2	4	4	3	1				1		2
All ages	**21**	**29**	**35**	**24**	**18**	**26**	**16**	**25**	**19**	**20**	**33**
All Proved Offences	**935**	**1050**	**1237**	**869**	**767**	**656**	**707**	**652**	**762**	**753**	**846**
Motoring Offences											
Proceedings for:											
(a) Previously Convicted											
Unfit to drive		5	9	6	10	1		2			
Driving, undue alcohol						8	11	3	25	20	55
Fail provide specimen						1		2	5	4	6
(b) No Prev. Conviction											
Unfit to drive	149	189	195	162	128	4	13	16	6	8	12
Driving, undue alcohol					15	261	447	534	678	757	917
Fail provide spec.					1	14	33	41	34	41	66
In charge and:											
Unfit to drive	40	33	48	35	45	4	9	11	6	5	18
Undue alcohol						9	20	4	11	8	9
Fail provide spec.					1	6	5	5	2		2
Failure to provide breath specimen					1	37	58	73	91	96	145
Total: All Proceedings	**189**	**227**	**252**	**203**	**201**	**345**	**596**	**691**	**858**	**939**	**1230**
Licensed Premises											
Public Houses:											
Full	2246					1557					1534
Beer and Cider	144					36					7
Wine or Cider	5					1					1
Restaurant Licence	26					59					84
Residential Licence	1					5					9
Above Combined	1					6					8
Licensed Clubs	19					16					23
Total On Licences	**2442**					**1680**					**1666**
Off Licences	**689**					**565**					**610**
Total On/Off Licences	**3131**					**2245**					**2276**
Registered Clubs	**665**					**522**					**571**
Total Licences & Clubs	**3796**					**2767**					**2847**

*Approximately 300,000 persons were transferred when parts of Staffordshire came under the West Midlands Police District.

TABLE III 168
DRUNKENNESS OFFENCES, MOTORING OFFENCES AND LICENCES, 1963-73
SUFFOLK POLICE DISTRICT

	1963	1964	1965	1966	1967	1968	1969	1970	1971	1972	1973
Population '000	**495**					**540**					**570**
Proved Offences—											
Drunkenness											
Males											
Under 18	11	8	13	11	10	13	10	29	36	19	31
18 and under 21	42	28	31	46	43	58	62	85	66	66	74
21 and under 30	46	55	48	66	68	123	117	111	118	113	153
30 and under 60	128	101	114	113	141	183	133	180	214	254	235
60 and over	9	6	8	11	32	21	18	21	29	22	31
All ages	**236**	**198**	**211**	**247**	**294**	**398**	**340**	**426**	**463**	**474**	**524**
Females											
Under 18	2			1	3		1	1	4	6	2
18 and under 21	2	1		1	2		1	1	3	2	5
21 and under 30	6	2	3	2		4	1	2		6	3
30 and under 60	2	6	4	4	6	9	6	7	5	9	7
60 and over	2	1	1	1	3	3	1	6	2	2	2
All ages	**14**	**10**	**8**	**9**	**14**	**16**	**10**	**17**	**14**	**25**	**19**
All Proved Offences	**250**	**208**	**219**	**256**	**308**	**414**	**350**	**443**	**477**	**499**	**543**
Motoring Offences											
Proceedings for:											
(a) Previously Convicted											
Unfit to drive		2	3	1	2	2		1		1	
Driving, undue alcohol						4	10	10	20	31	30
Fail provide specimen									1	6	
(b) No Prev. Conviction											
Unfit to drive	67	77	68	72	69	5	4	6	1	6	1
Driving, undue alcohol					4	235	241	319	455	545	577
Fail provide spec.					2	8	10	18	22	17	22
In charge and:											
Unfit to drive	20	16	21	28	23		2	9	6	4	7
Undue alcohol					3	12	13	9	10	13	7
Fail provide spec.						6	4	7	1	1	4
Failure to provide breath specimen						15	29	47	59	44	68
Total: All Proceedings	**87**	**95**	**92**	**101**	**103**	**287**	**313**	**426**	**575**	**668**	**716**
Licensed Premises											
Public Houses:											
Full	1111					1099					1046
Beer and Cider	39					6					1
Wine or Cider	1										
Restaurant Licence	19					43					75
Residential Licence	1					9					8
Above Combined	13					22					26
Licensed Clubs	13					13					10
Total On Licences	**1197**					**1192**					**1170**
Off Licences	**225**					**254**					**352**
Total On/Off Licences	**1422**					**1446**					**1522**
Registered Clubs	**221**					**254**					**292**
Total Licences & Clubs	**1643**					**1700**					**1814**

TABLE III 169
DRUNKENNESS OFFENCES, MOTORING OFFENCES AND LICENCES, 1963–73
SURREY (Beyond M.P.D.*) POLICE DISTRICT

	1963*	1964	1965	1966	1967	1968	1969	1970	1971	1972	1973
Population '000	**1756**					**991**					**1012**
Proved Offences—Drunkenness											
Males											
Under 18	4	2	9	5	5	5	14	7	13	6	17
18 and under 21	16	15	10	29	29	29	46	24	33	22	47
21 and under 30	36	33	37	19	34	34	54	41	43	49	57
30 and under 60	90	86	85	100	100	133	106	107	116	98	139
60 and over	8	6	11	25	36	28	11	5	16	18	17
All ages	**154**	**142**	**162**	**178**	**204**	**229**	**231**	**184**	**221**	**193**	**277**
Females											
Under 18		1					1		1	1	
18 and under 21	1			1		2					2
21 and under 30	1	1		1	1			1		2	1
30 and under 60	1	2	2	4	3	1	2	4	1	7	6
60 and over	1									2	1
All ages	**4**	**4**	**2**	**6**	**4**	**3**	**3**	**5**	**2**	**12**	**10**
All Proved Offences	**158**	**146**	**164**	**184**	**208**	**232**	**234**	**189**	**223**	**205**	**287**
Motoring Offences											
Proceedings for:											
(a) Previously Convicted											
Unfit to drive		3	7	8	9			1	2		1
Driving, undue alcohol						5	6	9	11	26	57
Fail provide specimen						1			1	5	8
(b) No Prev. Conviction											
Unfit to drive	101	86	100	120	108	7	9	6	8	3	17
Driving, undue alcohol					2	140	258	330	397	561	700
Fail provide spec.						11	21	32	18	29	52
In charge and:											
Unfit to drive	28	33	32	37	36	2	3	6	1	5	3
Undue alcohol						23	12	15	24	25	15
Fail provide spec.					1	3	13	8	4	4	7
Failure to provide breath specimen					1	28	26	46	38	67	89
Total: All Proceedings	**129**	**122**	**139**	**165**	**157**	**220**	**348**	**453**	**504**	**725**	**949**
Licensed Premises											
Public Houses:											
Full	1368					923					940
Beer and Cider	14					1					
Wine or Cider	1										1
Restaurant Licence	72					130					206
Residential Licence	3					3					9
Above Combined	18					23					22
Licensed Clubs	41					39					43
Total On Licences	**1517**					**1119**					**1221**
Off Licences	**734**					**422**					**487**
Total On/Off Licences	**2251**					**1541**					**1708**
Registered Clubs	**866**					**645**					**719**
Total Licences & Clubs	**3117**					**2186**					**2427**

*Population and licences in 1963 refer to the whole County of Surrey.

TABLE III 170
DRUNKENNESS OFFENCES, MOTORING OFFENCES AND LICENCES, 1963-73
SUSSEX POLICE DISTRICT

	1963	1964	1965	1966	1967	1968	1969	1970	1971	1972	1973
Population '000	**1108**					**1196**					**1270**
Proved Offences—Drunkenness											
Males											
Under 18	13	18	13	11	18	19	23	15	36	38	52
18 and under 21	61	61	67	72	63	73	84	84	75	110	163
21 and under 30	146	117	135	130	141	151	157	149	201	232	286
30 and under 60	407	396	368	331	358	428	395	456	542	632	685
60 and over	35	45	47	51	52	75	73	59	62	79	87
All ages	**662**	**637**	**630**	**595**	**632**	**746**	**732**	**763**	**916**	**1091**	**1273**
Females											
Under 18	2	1	1	3	4	10	5		7	6	5
18 and under 21	1	2	8	4	8	5	7	5	11	8	17
21 and under 30	7	2	6	7	3	3	5	12	14	18	35
30 and under 60	45	34	41	51	39	26	21	48	34	55	68
60 and over	17	12	12	11	19	10	13	8	7	13	16
All ages	**72**	**51**	**68**	**76**	**73**	**54**	**51**	**73**	**73**	**100**	**141**
All Proved Offences	**734**	**688**	**698**	**671**	**705**	**800**	**783**	**836**	**989**	**1191**	**1414**
Motoring Offences											
Proceedings for:											
(a) Previously Convicted											
Unfit to drive		15	12	11	12	1	3				1
Driving, undue alcohol						3	11	8	22	47	56
Fail provide specimen						1	4	3	2	10	12
(b) No Prev. Conviction											
Unfit to drive	126	132	162	163	151	12	16	16	11	9	6
Driving, undue alcohol					15	255	343	431	615	808	1012
Fail provide spec.						23	35	28	50	45	64
In charge and:											
Unfit to drive	47	38	44	45	48	5	6	7	6	9	6
Undue alcohol					2	19	13	20	18	28	26
Fail provide spec.						4	9	7	10	15	11
Failure to provide breath specimen					1	30	59	70	88	122	152
Total: All Proceedings	**173**	**185**	**218**	**219**	**229**	**353**	**499**	**590**	**822**	**1087**	**1346**

	1963	1968	1973
Licensed Premises			
Public Houses:			
Full	1734	1721	1707
Beer and Cider	27	12	7
Wine or Cider	8	5	6
Restaurant Licence	95	228	405
Residential Licence	30	41	54
Above Combined	65	97	101
Licensed Clubs	128	139	129
Total On Licences	**2087**	**2243**	**2409**
Off Licences	**668**	**706**	**771**
Total On/Off Licences	**2755**	**2949**	**3180**
Registered Clubs	**446**	**511**	**582**
Total Licences & Clubs	**3201**	**3460**	**3762**

TABLE III 171

DRUNKENNESS OFFENCES, MOTORING OFFENCES AND LICENCES, 1963-73
THAMES VALLEY POLICE DISTRICT

	1963	1964	1965	1966	1967	1968	1969	1970	1971	1972	1973
Population '000	**1379**					**1545**					**1670**
Proved Offences—Drunkenness											
Males											
Under 18	13	17	19	12	20	14	23	27	42	39	44
18 and under 21	60	39	61	54	91	72	66	87	101	119	169
21 and under 30	237	174	205	209	214	167	195	201	188	270	357
30 and under 60	497	435	495	415	543	433	539	557	619	822	1058
60 and over	39	30	35	51	48	56	60	55	73	63	98
All ages	**846**	**695**	**815**	**741**	**916**	**742**	**883**	**927**	**1023**	**1313**	**1726**
Females											
Under 18	2		4	1	3	2		3	3		3
18 and under 21	3		1	2	4	2	3	6	1	1	2
21 and under 30	3	1	3	4	2	4		4	4	4	6
30 and under 60	21	10	7	13	17	10	6	7	16	16	19
60 and over	1	1	2	2				2		2	2
All ages	**30**	**12**	**17**	**22**	**26**	**18**	**9**	**22**	**24**	**23**	**32**
All Proved Offences	**876**	**707**	**832**	**763**	**942**	**760**	**892**	**949**	**1047**	**1336**	**1758**
Motoring Offences											
Proceedings for:											
(a) Previously Convicted											
Unfit to drive		15	7	16	1	1			1	3	2
Driving, undue alcohol						2	1		4	10	59
Fail provide specimen									2		12
(b) No Prev. Conviction											
Unfit to drive	168	152	138	172	216	16	21	24	14	35	19
Driving, undue alcohol					21	379	591	689	983	1196	1387
Fail provide spec.					3	37	28	34	37	53	92
In charge and:											
Unfit to drive	47	47	53	50	66	8	9	8	7	6	16
Undue alcohol						11	14	7	12	16	31
Fail provide spec.						5	35	9	7	6	4
Failure to provide breath specimen					1	41	77	95	98	130	227
Total: All Proceedings	**215**	**214**	**198**	**238**	**308**	**500**	**776**	**866**	**1165**	**1455**	**1849**
Licensed Premises											
Public Houses:											
Full	2637					2589					2596
Beer and Cider	43					12					6
Wine or Cider	5					5					2
Restaurant Licence	52					128					244
Residential Licence	6					9					19
Above Combined	11					30					28
Licensed Clubs	24					38					77
Total On Licences	**2778**					**2811**					**2972**
Off Licences	**556**					**672**					**826**
Total On/Off Licences	**3334**					**3483**					**3798**
Registered Clubs	**700**					**802**					**913**
Total Licences & Clubs	**4034**					**4285**					**4711**

TABLE III 172
DRUNKENNESS OFFENCES, MOTORING OFFENCES AND LICENCES, 1963–73
WARWICKSHIRE AND COVENTRY POLICE DISTRICT

	1963	1964	1965	1966	1967	1968	1969	1970	1971	1972	1973
Population '000	**961**					**1026**					**1086**
Proved Offences—Drunkenness											
Males											
Under 18	18	30	32	26	31	33	43	28	62	31	59
18 and under 21	95	114	117	111	135	132	140	145	135	135	194
21 and under 30	199	207	220	258	204	236	211	189	185	174	290
30 and under 60	481	410	410	342	290	282	259	282	261	255	330
60 and over	28	28	29	33	48	32	30	24	40	49	55
All ages	**821**	**789**	**808**	**770**	**708**	**715**	**683**	**668**	**683**	**644**	**928**
Females											
Under 18			1	1	1	4	2	5	2	1	5
18 and under 21	2		2		1	1	3	3	1	8	12
21 and under 30	4	7	10	5	9	7	8	6	4	11	11
30 and under 60	23	27	19	21	23	26	16	12	20	20	25
60 and over	5	12	2	3	1	1		3	2	6	3
All ages	**34**	**43**	**34**	**30**	**35**	**39**	**29**	**29**	**29**	**46**	**56**
All Proved Offences	**855**	**832**	**842**	**800**	**743**	**754**	**712**	**697**	**712**	**690**	**984**
Motoring Offences											
Proceedings for:											
(a) Previously Convicted											
Unfit to drive		5	8	4	3						1
Driving, undue alcohol					1	2	8	19	20	35	48
Fail provide specimen						1	4		4	7	6
(b) No Prev. Conviction											
Unfit to drive	122	128	126	121	125	5	5	3	5	9	6
Driving, undue alcohol					22	302	379	384	618	838	1049
Fail provide spec.					4	28	33	41	36	42	61
In charge and:											
Unfit to drive	42	26	40	41	40	2	5	3	5	5	11
Undue alcohol						17	21	24	27	40	53
Fail provide spec.						4	5	8	6	12	36
Failure to provide breath specimen					3	31	36	43	38	65	86
Total: All Proceedings	**164**	**159**	**174**	**166**	**198**	**392**	**496**	**525**	**759**	**1053**	**1357**
Licensed Premises											
Public Houses:											
Full	1059					1055					1085
Beer and Cider	5					1					
Wine or Cider											
Restaurant Licence	34					79					118
Residential Licence	2					5					11
Above Combined	9					22					34
Licensed Clubs	28					36					35
Total On Licences	**1137**					**1198**					**1283**
Off Licences	**483**					**510**					**555**
Total On/Off Licences	**1620**					**1708**					**1838**
Registered Clubs	**562**					**604**					**644**
Total Licences & Clubs	**2182**					**2312**					**2482**

TABLE III 173
DRUNKENNESS OFFENCES, MOTORING OFFENCES AND LICENCES, 1963–73 BIRMINGHAM POLICE DISTRICT

	1963	1964	1965	1966	1967	1968	1969	1970	1971	1972	1973
Population '000	**1116**					**1075**					**1004**
Proved Offences—											
Drunkenness											
Males											
Under 18	42	43	69	66	56	91	139	140	151	159	234
18 and under 21	402	314	412	390	520	536	743	654	725	696	664
21 and under 30	1096	977	1208	1076	1152	1251	1502	1472	1499	1359	1205
30 and under 60	2049	1772	2266	2250	2028	1919	2213	2173	2357	2476	2208
60 and over	96	114	113	98	95	96	117	118	117	128	150
All ages	**3685**	**3220**	**4068**	**3880**	**3851**	**3893**	**4714**	**4557**	**4849**	**4818**	**4461**
Females											
Under 18	1		2	3	7	3	4	4	6	8	13
18 and under 21	5	5	7	4	9	8	18	20	25	26	22
21 and under 30	17	15	25	29	29	32	44	33	44	47	56
30 and under 60	109	63	65	62	111	105	99	82	114	120	134
60 and over	3	1	3	5	2	4	7	6	3	2	9
All ages	**135**	**84**	**102**	**103**	**158**	**152**	**172**	**145**	**192**	**203**	**234**
All Proved Offences	**3820**	**3304**	**4170**	**3983**	**4009**	**4045**	**4886**	**4702**	**5041**	**5021**	**4695**
Motoring Offences											
Proceedings for:											
(a) Previously Convicted											
Unfit to drive		14	15	14	17	4	1			1	
Driving, undue alcohol					1	11	17	20	23	40	38
Fail provide specimen						3	3	6	15	14	10
(b) No Prev. Conviction											
Unfit to drive	189	216	272	249	206	19	18	11	12	14	4
Driving, undue alcohol					10	286	395	335	472	512	711
Fail provide spec.					4	30	44	63	45	55	69
In charge and:											
Unfit to drive	48	76	129	82	59	13	18	10	4	5	3
Undue alcohol						7	17	14	12	12	24
Fail provide spec.						6	6	1	2	5	3
Failure to provide breath specimen					1	28	48	43	38	54	70
Total: All Proceedings	**237**	**306**	**416**	**345**	**298**	**407**	**568**	**503**	**623**	**712**	**932**
Licensed Premises											
Public Houses:											
Full	815					785					746
Beer and Cider	42					15					5
Wine or Cider											
Restaurant Licence	21					57					90
Residential Licence	1					3					8
Above Combined	3					8					12
Licensed Clubs	11					20					20
Total On Licences	**893**					**888**					**881**
Off Licences	**659**					**660**					**648**
Total On/Off Licences	**1552**					**1548**					**1529**
Registered Clubs	**398**					**412**					**438**
Total Licences & Clubs	**1950**					**1960**					**1967**

TABLE III 174
DRUNKENNESS OFFENCES, MOTORING OFFENCES AND LICENCES, 1963–73
WEST MERCIA POLICE DISTRICT

	1963	1964	1965	1966	1967	1968	1969	1970	1971	1972	1973
Population '000	**965**					**1149**					**1197**
Proved Offences—Drunkenness											
Males											
Under 18	21	17	21	19	14	23	24	26	31	50	52
18 and under 21	101	77	86	52	60	73	81	64	71	88	118
21 and under 30	159	124	92	92	93	98	98	101	108	134	158
30 and under 60	253	277	255	231	155	226	164	174	171	190	243
60 and over	38	26	27	29	46	46	37	34	30	38	38
All ages	**572**	**521**	**481**	**423**	**368**	**466**	**404**	**399**	**411**	**500**	**609**
Females											
Under 18		1	5		3	3	2	3	6	6	2
18 and under 21	1		1	3		1	3	4	4	3	6
21 and under 30	1	1	1	1		2	3	2	2	6	
30 and under 60	13	8	7	5	3	6	9	11	7	3	5
60 and over	3	3	3	1	2		1	1			
All ages	**18**	**13**	**17**	**10**	**8**	**12**	**18**	**21**	**19**	**18**	**13**
All Proved Offences	**590**	**534**	**498**	**433**	**376**	**478**	**422**	**420**	**430**	**518**	**622**
Motoring Offences											
Proceedings for:											
(a) Previously Convicted											
Unfit to drive		9	2	4	4						
Driving, undue alcohol							3	3	6	5	12
Fail provide specimen											1
(b) No Prev. Conviction											
Unfit to drive	148	164	154	147	155	8	19	8	7	6	12
Driving, undue alcohol					15	223	289	368	460	549	762
Fail provide spec.						8	33	27	25	16	57
In charge and:											
Unfit to drive	40	20	52	46	33	1	4	6	5	8	6
Undue alcohol					1	33	9	10	11	18	32
Fail provide spec.						15	1	2	9	15	12
Failure to provide breath specimen					1	32	49	43	75	57	103
Total: All Proceedings	**188**	**193**	**208**	**197**	**209**	**320**	**407**	**467**	**598**	**674**	**997**
Licensed Premises											
Public Houses:											
Full	2223					2343					2217
Beer and Cider	33					17					7
Wine or Cider	4					3					3
Restaurant Licence	37					91					141
Residential Licence	3					10					13
Above Combined	27					32					34
Licensed Clubs	24					45					51
Total On Licences	**2351**					**2541**					**2466**
Off Licences	**512**					**690**					**782**
Total On/Off Licences	**2863**					**3231**					**3248**
Registered Clubs	**544**					**661**					**705**
Total Licences & Clubs	**3407**					**3892**					**3953**

TABLE III 175
DRUNKENNESS OFFENCES, MOTORING OFFENCES AND LICENCES, 1963-73
WEST MIDLANDS POLICE DISTRICT

	1963	1964	1965	1966*	1967	1968	1969	1970	1971	1972	1973
Population '000	**451**					**801**					**802**
Proved Offences—Drunkenness											
Males											
Under 18	7	15	12	14	21	27	17	32	31	43	46
18 and under 21	25	34	57	86	133	91	97	106	113	104	130
21 and under 30	60	70	103	169	183	196	199	177	215	206	211
30 and under 60	144	148	153	274	379	312	291	321	348	385	375
60 and over	12	14	11	29	48	31	27	38	34	46	66
All ages	**248**	**271**	**336**	**572**	**764**	**657**	**631**	**674**	**741**	**784**	**828**
Females											
Under 18			1	2			5	3	4	4	
18 and under 21	2		2	1	2	1	7	4	4	8	5
21 and under 30	4	3	4	2	4	6	5	4	4	5	9
30 and under 60	6	6	5	6	11	9	7	9	14	13	21
60 and over	2	1	1	2	3	4	2	2	1	1	1
All ages	**14**	**11**	**13**	**13**	**20**	**20**	**26**	**22**	**27**	**31**	**36**
All Proved Offences	**262**	**282**	**349**	**585**	**784**	**677**	**657**	**696**	**768**	**815**	**864**
Motoring Offences											
Proceedings for:											
(a) Previously Convicted											
Unfit to drive		5	1	3	3					3	3
Driving, undue alcohol						5	11	11	32	27	44
Fail provide specimen							1	4	8	3	3
(b) No Prev. Conviction											
Unfit to drive	24	34	35	94	110	4	12	7	13	5	8
Driving, undue alcohol					12	296	458	540	1018	1089	1049
Fail provide spec.						17	33	24	39	34	83
In charge and:											
Unfit to drive	3	6	4	17	9	3	4	5	6	1	5
Undue alcohol					2	3	11	18	7	13	5
Fail provide spec.					2	1	3	2	3	8	7
Failure to provide breath specimen						30	46	56	92	96	129
Total: All Proceedings	**27**	**45**	**40**	**114**	**138**	**359**	**579**	**667**	**1218**	**1279**	**1336**
Licensed Premises											
Public Houses:											
Full	856					1302					1218
Beer and Cider	23					24					8
Wine or Cider											
Restaurant Licence	7					26					51
Residential Licence	1					3					3
Above Combined	2					2					4
Licensed Clubs	10					34					47
Total On Licences	**899**					**1391**					**1331**
Off Licences	**283**					**359**					**400**
Total On/Off Licences	**1182**					**1750**					**1731**
Registered Clubs	**218**					**370**					**382**
Total Licences & Clubs	**1404**					**2120**					**2113**

*Parts of Staffordshire attached in 1966.

TABLE III 176
DRUNKENNESS OFFENCES, MOTORING OFFENCES AND LICENCES, 1963–73
WEST YORKSHIRE POLICE DISTRICT

	1963	1964	1965	1966	1967	1968	1969	1970	1971	1972	1973
Population '000	**2201**					**2270**					**2309**
Proved Offences—Drunkenness											
Males											
Under 18	75	84	78	67	93	95	100	135	172	194	177
18 and under 21	293	322	341	331	367	365	343	364	423	423	448
21 and under 30	468	419	422	396	399	417	393	447	487	499	513
30 and under 60	718	708	654	551	570	505	496	495	515	501	573
60 and over	65	66	42	125	153	202	69	50	96	75	84
All ages	**1619**	**1599**	**1537**	**1470**	**1582**	**1584**	**1401**	**1491**	**1693**	**1692**	**1795**
Females											
Under 18	2	3	3	7	8	3	4	11	17	17	19
18 and under 21	6	9	9	6	5	8	6	8	7	15	19
21 and under 30	11	12	10	7	10	5	12	13	9	19	22
30 and under 60	51	37	34	15	22	15	28	27	30	27	53
60 and over	4	4	8	10	5	19	6	2	7	5	6
All ages	**74**	**65**	**64**	**45**	**50**	**50**	**56**	**61**	**70**	**83**	**119**
All Proved Offences	**1693**	**1664**	**1601**	**1515**	**1632**	**1634**	**1457**	**1552**	**1763**	**1775**	**1914**
Motoring Offences											
Proceedings for:											
(a) Previously Convicted											
Unfit to drive		9	3	4	2	1				2	1
Driving, undue alcohol						5			6	36	39
Fail provide specimen										2	5
(b) No Prev. Conviction											
Unfit to drive	291	276	287	332	329	26	72	77	76	48	41
Driving, undue alcohol					43	712	662	778	1357	1978	2154
Fail provide spec.					6	49	51	54	95	101	99
In charge and:											
Unfit to drive	52	39	62	84	62	5	8	10	22	23	13
Undue alcohol					2	19	12	15	23	21	13
Fail provide spec.						7	4	9	18	29	38
Failure to provide breath specimen					7	95	103	106	145	237	249
Total: All Proceedings	**343**	**324**	**352**	**420**	**451**	**919**	**912**	**1049**	**1742**	**2477**	**2652**
Licensed Premises											
Public Houses:											
Full	3042					3063					3043
Beer and Cider	82					23					5
Wine or Cider	4					3					2
Restaurant Licence	61					138					250
Residential Licence	3					10					18
Above Combined	19					32					49
Licensed Clubs	19					47					65
Total On Licences	**3230**					**3316**					**3432**
Off Licences	**1486**					**1593**					**1715**
Total On/Off Licences	**4716**					**4909**					**5147**
Registered Clubs	**1479**					**1471**					**1542**
Total Licences & Clubs	**6195**					**6380**					**6689**

TABLE III 177
DRUNKENNESS OFFENCES, MOTORING OFFENCES AND LICENCES, 1963–73
BRADFORD POLICE DISTRICT

	1963	**1964**	**1965**	**1966**	**1967**	**1968**	**1969**	**1970**	**1971**	**1972**	**1973**
Population '000	**297**					**294**					**292**
Proved Offences— Drunkenness											
Males											
Under 18	10	11	7	15	15	8	11	16	17	15	31
18 and under 21	66	34	45	34	49	47	30	54	70	59	90
21 and under 30	209	139	94	136	130	107	83	82	115	144	173
30 and under 60	846	601	385	388	391	391	311	272	410	540	502
60 and over	72	51	63	41	33	33	28	31	38	40	28
All ages	**1203**	**836**	**594**	**614**	**618**	**586**	**463**	**455**	**650**	**798**	**824**
Females											
Under 18	1	1	1		1	4		1	5	4	7
18 and under 21		2	1	1	1	1	3	2	4	1	5
21 and under 30	14	9	8	3	9	6	8	7	13	8	10
30 and under 60	55	36	30	36	46	47	38	26	75	76	70
60 and over	5	15	1	1	4	2	2	3	7	16	16
All ages	**75**	**63**	**41**	**41**	**61**	**60**	**51**	**39**	**104**	**105**	**108**
All Proved Offences	**1278**	**899**	**635**	**655**	**679**	**646**	**514**	**494**	**754**	**903**	**932**
Motoring Offences											
Proceedings for:											
(a) Previously Convicted											
Unfit to drive		3		1	2						2
Driving, undue alcohol					1	2		1	14	9	13
Fail provide specimen						1	3	1	2		5
(b) No Prev. Conviction											
Unfit to drive	50	37	38	31	40	2	2	2	1	1	1
Driving, undue alcohol					18	140	104	133	184	274	299
Fail provide spec.					2	16	6	7	10	10	26
In charge and:											
Unfit to drive	14	24	11	15	7		1	1		1	
Undue alcohol					1	13	7	5	6	4	6
Fail provide spec.						3			2	2	
Failure to provide breath specimen						13	11	18	28	45	53
Total: All Proceedings	**64**	**64**	**49**	**47**	**71**	**190**	**134**	**158**	**247**	**346**	**405**
Licensed Premises											
Public Houses:											
Full	348					358					343
Beer and Cider	25					17					4
Wine or Cider	1										
Restaurant Licence	11					18					33
Residential Licence	1										1
Above Combined	2					1					2
Licensed Clubs	5					10					6
Total On Licences	**393**					**404**					**389**
Off Licences	**388**					**384**					**362**
Total On/Off Licences	**781**					**788**					**751**
Registered Clubs	**158**					**158**					**156**
Total Licences & Clubs	**939**					**946**					**907**

TABLE III 178
DRUNKENNESS OFFENCES, MOTORING OFFENCES AND LICENCES, 1963-73 LEEDS POLICE DISTRICT

	1963	1964	1965	1966	1967	1968	1969	1970	1971	1972	1973
Population '000	**514**					**506**					**500**
Proved Offences—Drunkenness											
Males											
Under 18	26	32	40	39	46	43	62	79	70	78	83
18 and under 21	181	163	154	197	227	240	230	258	280	282	280
21 and under 30	466	444	365	420	611	641	633	600	619	488	520
30 and under 60	1068	1018	908	1214	1468	1207	1221	1460	1378	1254	1315
60 and over	156	161	127	117	175	157	194	192	153	141	153
All ages	**1897**	**1818**	**1594**	**1987**	**2527**	**2288**	**2340**	**2589**	**2500**	**2243**	**2351**
Females											
Under 18	2	4	5	2	4		3	7	4	5	7
18 and under 21	10	10	8	5	6	10	4	11	10	11	14
21 and under 30	25	23	16	18	27	25	37	35	34	27	25
30 and under 60	82	78	89	96	91	71	62	60	66	104	94
60 and over	19	17	13	15	15	9	14	11	25	23	24
All ages	**138**	**132**	**131**	**136**	**143**	**115**	**120**	**124**	**139**	**170**	**164**
All Proved Offences	**2035**	**1950**	**1725**	**2123**	**2670**	**2403**	**2460**	**2713**	**2639**	**2413**	**2515**
Motoring Offences											
Proceedings for:											
(a) Previously Convicted											
Unfit to drive		2			2						
Driving, undue alcohol					1	8	6			1	15
Fail provide specimen						1					4
(b) No Prev. Conviction											
Unfit to drive	124	121	106	131	129	4	4	2	3	1	5
Driving, undue alcohol					24	236	228	288	358	489	508
Fail provide spec.					4	47	44	49	40	57	54
In charge and:											
Unfit to drive	39	37	19	26	24		3	1		1	1
Undue alcohol						1	1			3	
Fail provide spec.										4	
Failure to provide breath specimen					8	60	25	36	51	90	69
Total: All Proceedings	**163**	**160**	**125**	**157**	**192**	**357**	**311**	**376**	**452**	**646**	**656**
Licensed Premises											
Public Houses:											
Full	385					395					396
Beer and Cider	34					12					4
Wine or Cider	1					1					1
Restaurant Licence	17					44					62
Residential Licence						1					5
Above Combined	2					5					7
Licensed Clubs	13					10					8
Total On Licences	**452**					**468**					**483**
Off Licences	**404**					**356**					**325**
Total On/Off Licences	**856**					**824**					**808**
Registered Clubs	**191**					**201**					**207**
Total Licences & Clubs	**1047**					**1025**					**1015**

TABLE III 179
DRUNKENNESS OFFENCES, MOTORING OFFENCES AND LICENCES, 1963-73
SHEFFIELD AND ROTHERHAM POLICE DISTRICT

	1963	1964	1965	1966	1967	1968	1969	1970	1971	1972	1973
Population '000	**582**					**618**					**597**
Proved Offences—											
Drunkenness											
Males											
Under 18	26	31	44	47	64	63	23	42	56	95	119
18 and under 21	173	194	192	197	245	191	145	198	185	301	381
21 and under 30	316	312	303	291	346	268	204	247	263	317	386
30 and under 60	744	662	542	535	602	455	375	445	429	448	532
60 and over	54	33	61	52	65	76	111	66	45	88	64
All ages	**1313**	**1252**	**1142**	**1122**	**1322**	**1053**	**858**	**998**	**978**	**1249**	**1482**
Females											
Under 18		2	2		3	7	1	3	3	5	7
18 and under 21	4	3	1	3	4	9	6	7	2	2	10
21 and under 30	6	4	5	6	6	7	7	6	13	15	11
30 and under 60	33	16	20	24	24	13	10	17	32	22	25
60 and over	4	2	2		4	3	4	2	2	4	3
All ages	**47**	**27**	**30**	**33**	**41**	**39**	**28**	**35**	**52**	**48**	**56**
All Proved Offences	**1360**	**1279**	**1172**	**1155**	**1363**	**1092**	**886**	**1035**	**1030**	**1297**	**1538**
Motoring Offences											
Proceedings for:											
(a) Previously Convicted											
Unfit to drive		3	1	2	9					1	
Driving, undue alcohol					1	11	6	6	19	40	52
Fail provide specimen									2	9	6
(b) No Prev. Conviction											
Unfit to drive	89	95	85	91	114		1	3	3	3	2
Driving, undue alcohol					31	287	310	268	458	552	674
Fail provide spec.						21	16	18	33	21	38
In charge and:											
Unfit to drive	22	18	17	19	23	1	2	3	3	2	
Undue alcohol					1	4	3	3	5	11	10
Fail provide spec.								3	2	1	2
Failure to provide breath specimen						20	21	20	29	45	54
Total: All Proceedings	**111**	**116**	**103**	**112**	**179**	**344**	**359**	**324**	**554**	**685**	**838**
Licensed Premises											
Public Houses:											
Full	589					640					650
Beer and Cider	118					80					45
Wine or Cider											
Restaurant Licence	13					31					40
Residential Licence						1					
Above Combined	3					3					4
Licensed Clubs	3					5					
Total On Licences	**726**					**760**					**741**
Off Licences	**504**					**452**					**373**
Total On/Off Licences	**1230**					**1212**					**1114**
Registered Clubs	**149**					**162**					**175**
Total Licences & Clubs	**1379**					**1374**					**1289**

TABLE III 180
DRUNKENNESS OFFENCES, MOTORING OFFENCES AND LICENCES, 1963–73
WILTSHIRE POLICE DISTRICT

	1963	1964	1965	1966	1967	1968	1969	1970	1971	1972	1973
Population '000	**447**					**490**					**501**
Proved Offences—Drunkenness											
Males											
Under 18	5	5	4	7	6	8	7	3	13	15	16
18 and under 21	19	20	23	33	22	9	15	35	43	41	52
21 and under 30	48	40	55	43	43	39	41	61	48	38	37
30 and under 60	87	68	75	83	83	63	92	92	49	56	51
60 and over	4	9	9	18	18	7	15	11	64	96	153
All ages	**163**	**142**	**166**	**184**	**172**	**126**	**170**	**202**	**217**	**246**	**309**
Females											
Under 18				2	2		1				3
18 and under 21	4		1		2	2	1	2	4	2	1
21 and under 30	3	3		3	1		3			1	2
30 and under 60	3	3	2		2	1	2	1	3	8	6
60 and over				1	4	1	5	3	1	2	4
All ages	**10**	**6**	**3**	**6**	**11**	**4**	**12**	**6**	**8**	**13**	**16**
All Proved Offences	**173**	**148**	**169**	**190**	**183**	**130**	**182**	**208**	**225**	**259**	**325**
Motoring Offences											
Proceedings for:											
(a) Previously Convicted											
Unfit to drive		2		2	2	1					
Driving, undue alcohol					1	4	4	2	4	9	14
Fail provide specimen					1				2		
(b) No Prev. Conviction											
Unfit to drive	12	24	38	29	35		3	1	2	1	3
Driving, undue alcohol					5	79	148	169	294	385	465
Fail provide spec.					1	5	10	12	16	23	14
In charge and:											
Unfit to drive	7	11	11	9	9	1	3	1	3	5	3
Undue alcohol						16	20	8	12	8	10
Fail provide spec.						5		3	3	2	7
Failure to provide breath specimen					1	10	15	19	40	38	36
Total: All Proceedings	**19**	**37**	**49**	**40**	**55**	**121**	**203**	**215**	**376**	**472**	**552**
Licensed Premises											
Public Houses:											
Full	820					811					802
Beer and Cider	5					1					1
Wine or Cider											
Restaurant Licence	19					43					67
Residential Licence	1					3					5
Above Combined	3					8					19
Licensed Clubs	3					4					5
Total On Licences	**851**					**870**					**899**
Off Licences	**194**					**246**					**295**
Total On/Off Licences	**1045**					**1116**					**1194**
Registered Clubs	**253**					**283**					**304**
Total Licences & Clubs	**1298**					**1399**					**1498**

TABLE III 181
DRUNKENNESS OFFENCES, MOTORING OFFENCES AND LICENCES, 1963–73
YORK AND NORTH EAST YORKSHIRE POLICE DISTRICT

	1963	1964	1965	1966	1967	1968	1969	1970	1971	1972	1973
Population '000	**749**					**683**					**717**
Proved Offences—Drunkenness											
Males											
Under 18	20	27	22	23	32	26	19	32	39	38	58
18 and under 21	79	78	88	97	93	88	78	96	74	114	122
21 and under 30	106	102	103	116	100	119	111	103	122	116	161
30 and under 60	109	118	137	150	145	133	131	137	160	172	207
60 and over	8	11	7	14	15	24	9	14	26	24	60
All ages	**322**	**336**	**357**	**400**	**385**	**390**	**348**	**382**	**421**	**464**	**608**
Females											
Under 18	1	3			1	1		3	1	3	5
18 and under 21	2	1		1	1	2	3	4	5	3	2
21 and under 30		4					1	4	1	6	5
30 and under 60	6	6	5	7	6	9	2	6	4	8	8
60 and over	1	1	1		1	1				2	3
All ages	**10**	**15**	**6**	**8**	**9**	**13**	**6**	**17**	**11**	**22**	**23**
All Proved Offences	**332**	**351**	**363**	**408**	**394**	**403**	**354**	**399**	**432**	**486**	**631**
Motoring Offences											
Proceedings for:											
(a) Previously Convicted											
Unfit to drive		4	4	6	3						
Driving, undue alcohol						2	2	1		1	1
Fail provide specimen						1					
(b) No Prev. Conviction											
Unfit to drive	102	97	91	137	129	6	7	7	6	6	11
Driving, undue alcohol					15	254	277	330	604	642	877
Fail provide spec.						10	19	20	30	28	25
In charge and:											
Unfit to drive	31	24	27	39	24	8	7	4	5	5	13
Undue alcohol					2	17	33	58	75	110	48
Fail provide spec.					1	5	4	7	11	24	34
Failure to provide breath specimen					2	34	23	34	40	68	90
Total: All Proceedings	**133**	**125**	**122**	**182**	**176**	**337**	**372**	**461**	**771**	**884**	**1099**
Licensed Premises											
Public Houses:											
Full	1462					1290					1312
Beer and Cider	5					2					1
Wine or Cider											
Restaurant Licence	32					78					115
Residential Licence	14					37					110
Above Combined	23					41					68
Licensed Clubs	25					38					31
Total On Licences	**1561**					**1486**					**1637**
Off Licences	**419**					**396**					**452**
Total On/Off Licences	**1980**					**1882**					**2089**
Registered Clubs	**310**					**272**					**283**
Total Licences & Clubs	**2290**					**2154**					**2372**

TABLE III 182
DRUNKENNESS OFFENCES, MOTORING OFFENCES AND LICENCES, 1963–73
KINGSTON-UPON-HULL POLICE DISTRICT

	1963	1964	1965	1966	1967	1968	1969	1970	1971	1972	1973
Population '000	**301**					**295**					**282**
Proved Offences—Drunkenness											
Males											
Under 18	30	35	39	42	38	32	32	38	46	50	58
18 and under 21	92	91	161	118	138	111	86	95	93	126	134
21 and under 30	135	117	127	141	117	127	100	137	150	155	183
30 and under 60	265	237	228	207	353	273	227	230	258	299	311
60 and over	18	20	26	18	43	25	21	22	29	29	36
All ages	**540**	**500**	**581**	**526**	**689**	**568**	**466**	**522**	**576**	**659**	**722**
Females											
Under 18	1	3	2	1	1	4	1		3	7	6
18 and under 21	5	4	4	2	4	4	1	3	5	8	16
21 and under 30	8	10	7	9	12	7	5	17	26	20	39
30 and under 60	18	14	6	13	4	6	6	6	16	16	20
60 and over	5	3	1	3	2	3	2	4	6	8	5
All ages	**37**	**34**	**20**	**28**	**23**	**24**	**25**	**30**	**56**	**59**	**86**
All Proved Offences	**577**	**534**	**601**	**554**	**712**	**592**	**481**	**552**	**632**	**718**	**808**
Motoring Offences											
Proceedings for:											
(a) Previously Convicted											
Unfit to drive			6	4	2		1		1		2
Driving, undue alcohol							2	5	18	12	12
Fail provide specimen							1		2	1	1
(b) No Prev. Conviction											
Unfit to drive	76	80	80	85	65	1	1	3	11	8	2
Driving, undue alcohol					10	125	151	199	313	350	341
Fail provide spec.					3	11	13	12	18	10	10
In charge and:											
Unfit to drive	24	12	20	12	13	1				4	2
Undue alcohol					1	2	1	7	4	14	10
Fail provide spec.						2	1	1		6	10
Failure to provide breath specimen					1	15	14	15	18	20	26
Total: All Proceedings	**100**	**92**	**106**	**101**	**95**	**157**	**185**	**242**	**385**	**425**	**416**
Licensed Premises											
Public Houses:											
Full	230					213					196
Beer and Cider	5					3					
Wine or Cider											
Restaurant Licence	11					16					24
Residential Licence											1
Above Combined	1					5					6
Licensed Clubs	58					55					58
Total On Licences	**305**					**295**					**285**
Off Licences	**224**					**170**					**132**
Total On/Off Licences	**529**					**462**					**417**
Registered Clubs	**65**					**65**					**82**
Total Licences & Clubs	**594**					**527**					**499**

TABLE III 183
DRUNKENNESS OFFENCES, MOTORING OFFENCES AND LICENCES, 1963–73
TEESSIDE POLICE DISTRICT

	1963	1964*	1965	1966	1967	1968	1969	1970	1971	1972	1973
Population '000	**158**					**393**					**390**
Proved Offences—Drunkenness											
Males											
Under 18	25	32	52	46	30	41	42	68	60	72	80
18 and under 21	138	169	232	267	147	190	189	221	184	265	254
21 and under 30	188	245	340	368	176	238	241	266	184	221	259
30 and under 60	385	437	465	443	272	319	360	490	264	413	421
60 and over	27	35	21	40	24	27	21	29	326	80	60
All ages	**763**	**918**	**1010**	**1164**	**649**	**815**	**853**	**1074**	**1018**	**1051**	**1074**
Females											
Under 18	1		1	2	5	3	1	9	4	4	13
18 and under 21	5	3	3	3	3	7	4	6	14	15	18
21 and under 30	6	5	8	13	10	5	13	12	9	16	18
30 and under 60	24	18	25	27	10	21	12	24	17	27	28
60 and over	5	3	2	9	2	3	3		13	4	3
All ages	**41**	**29**	**39**	**54**	**30**	**39**	**33**	**51**	**57**	**66**	**80**
All Proved Offences	**804**	**947**	**1049**	**1218**	**679**	**854**	**886**	**1125**	**1075**	**1117**	**1154**
Motoring Offences											
Proceedings for:											
(a) Previously Convicted											
Unfit to drive		3	5	3	2						2
Driving, undue alcohol						1	4	31	28	37	61
Fail provide specimen						1		3	5	2	10
(b) No Prev. Conviction											
Unfit to drive	80	73	101	117	110	1	1	3	4	4	1
Driving, undue alcohol					14	271	318	323	405	440	568
Fail provide spec.					1	12	20	13	14	20	27
In charge and:											
Unfit to drive	22	21	34	44	29			2	3	9	
Undue alcohol					1	7	5	3	5	14	13
Fail provide spec.					1			3	1	3	2
Failure to provide breath specimen					1	28	41	56	45	54	87
Total: All Proceedings	**102**	**97**	**140**	**164**	**159**	**321**	**389**	**437**	**510**	**583**	**771**
Licensed Premises											
Public Houses:											
Full	98					403					411
Beer and Cider	2					1					
Wine or Cider											
Restaurant Licence	3					22					33
Residential Licence						1					4
Above Combined						4					6
Licensed Clubs						16					6
Total On Licences	**103**					**447**					**460**
Off Licences	**84**					**263**					**339**
Total On/Off Licences	**187**					**710**					**799**
Registered Clubs	**60**					**192**					**187**
Total Licences & Clubs	**247**					**902**					**986**

*Parts of North Riding added to the area in 1964.

TABLE III 184
DRUNKENNESS OFFENCES, MOTORING OFFENCES AND LICENCES, 1963–73
DYFED-POWYS POLICE DISTRICT

	1963	1964	1965	1966	1967	1968	1969	1970	1971	1972	1973
Population '000	**469**					**472**					**468**
Proved Offences—Drunkenness											
Males											
Under 18	11	21	28	35	39	25	28	41	33	56	53
18 and under 21	67	79	91	118	117	83	96	122	106	126	143
21 and under 30	104	162	110	122	147	122	113	123	123	186	217
30 and under 60	155	170	156	160	157	146	95	145	160	211	219
60 and over	12	12	12	23	15	20	18	20	18	25	19
All ages	**349**	**444**	**397**	**458**	**475**	**396**	**350**	**451**	**440**	**604**	**651**
Females											
Under 18	1	4	2	2			5	2	6	1	4
18 and under 21	2		2	1	2	1	2	2	1	1	5
21 and under 30	4	2	2	2		1	1	2		1	3
30 and under 60	7	4	6	8	10	8	3	8	8	5	5
60 and over	1	3	3	1	3		4		1		3
All ages	**15**	**13**	**15**	**14**	**15**	**10**	**15**	**14**	**16**	**8**	**20**
All Proved Offences	**364**	**457**	**412**	**472**	**490**	**406**	**365**	**465**	**456**	**612**	**671**
Motoring Offences											
Proceedings for:											
(a) Previously Convicted											
Unfit to drive		12	9	11	7			1	1		1
Driving, undue alcohol					1	9	5	20	23	34	44
Fail provide specimen						2			5	7	5
(b) No Prev. Conviction											
Unfit to drive	81	74	56	68	81	2	1	7	2	2	5
Driving, undue alcohol					9	251	294	248	428	474	588
Fail provide spec.						9	6	14	32	26	43
In charge and:											
Unfit to drive	26	23	21	16	18		1		1	2	5
Undue alcohol						6	1	5	11	6	14
Fail provide spec.						1	1		1	2	
Failure to provide breath specimen						29	31	36	61	73	99
Total: All Proceedings	**107**	**109**	**86**	**93**	**116**	**309**	**340**	**331**	**569**	**626**	**804**
Licensed Premises											
Public Houses:											
Full	1472					1437					1421
Beer and Cider	6					3					3
Wine or Cider											
Restaurant Licence	41					86					140
Residential Licence	20					31					57
Above Combined	52					85					141
Licensed Clubs	16					28					45
Total On Licences	**1607**					**1670**					**1807**
Off Licences	**165**					**220**					**286**
Total On/Off Licences	**1772**					**1890**					**2093**
Registered Clubs	**215**					**298**					**322**
Total Licences & Clubs	**1987**					**2188**					**2415**

TABLE III 185

DRUNKENNESS OFFENCES, MOTORING OFFENCES AND LICENCES, 1963–73 GWYNEDD POLICE DISTRICT

	1963	1964	1965	1966	1967	1968	1969	1970	1971	1972	1973
Population '000	**499**					**526**					**558**
Proved Offences—											
Drunkenness											
Males											
Under 18	13	14	26	17	16	23	29	38	23	26	47
18 and under 21	54	72	62	67	99	103	97	118	98	86	88
21 and under 30	109	100	121	103	115	106	111	126	122	92	132
30 and under 60	141	163	127	129	110	101	116	102	112	116	157
60 and over	29	21	12	25	29	11	10	8	9	15	28
All ages	**346**	**370**	**348**	**341**	**369**	**344**	**363**	**392**	**364**	**335**	**542**
Females											
Under 18	2	2	3	8		3	1	1	4	5	6
18 and under 21				4	2		4	3	2	5	4
21 and under 30	5	2	1	3	1		2	3		1	8
30 and under 60	10	15	13	11	9	9	7	7	3	14	8
60 and over	4	2	1	1	1	1		1		1	1
All ages	**21**	**21**	**18**	**27**	**13**	**13**	**14**	**15**	**9**	**26**	**27**
All Proved Offences	**367**	**391**	**366**	**368**	**382**	**357**	**377**	**407**	**371**	**361**	**479**
Motoring Offences											
Proceedings for:											
(a) Previously Convicted											
Unfit to drive		9	4	3	4					1	1
Driving, undue alcohol						3	3	5	11	22	25
Fail provide specimen							1		2	3	3
(b) No Prev. Conviction											
Unfit to drive	80	81	98	105	95	7	6	3	5	6	3
Driving, undue alcohol					9	206	262	281	397	460	552
Fail provide spec.						10	5	5	19	17	5
In charge and:											
Unfit to drive	19	33	31	21	15	1	2	2	1	1	1
Undue alcohol						6	6	2	5	5	8
Fail provide spec.						7	12	6	13	12	36
Failure to provide breath specimen					1	27	37	43	48	55	78
Total: All Proceedings	**99**	**123**	**133**	**129**	**124**	**267**	**334**	**347**	**501**	**582**	**712**
Licensed Premises											
Public Houses:											
Full	988					1002					1036
Beer and Cider	24					11					3
Wine or Cider											
Restaurant Licence	44					81					147
Residential Licence	42					65					108
Above Combined	67					97					161
Licensed Clubs	41					45					44
Total On Licences	**1206**					**1301**					**1499**
Off Licences	**156**					**201**					**284**
Total On/Off Licences	**1362**					**1502**					**1783**
Registered Clubs	**221**					**249**					**273**
Total Licences & Clubs	**1583**					**1751**					**2050**

TABLE III 186
DRUNKENNESS OFFENCES, MOTORING OFFENCES AND LICENCES, 1963–73
SOUTH WALES POLICE DISTRICT

	1963	1964	1965	1966	1967	1968	1969	1970	1971	1972	1973
Population '000	**1242**					**1258**					**1264**
Proved Offences—Drunkenness											
Males											
Under 18	52	48	74	93	74	78	62	68	105	127	214
18 and under 21	207	196	230	309	336	355	320	312	328	432	441
21 and under 30	269	240	314	309	386	491	331	344	541	524	634
30 and under 60	522	458	457	488	520	638	487	542	610	625	733
60 and over	55	31	44	75	76	73	125	58	59	84	81
All ages	**1105**	**973**	**1119**	**1274**	**1392**	**1635**	**1325**	**1324**	**1643**	**1792**	**2103**
Females											
Under 18	2	1	1	1	2	2	9	2	5	7	11
18 and under 21	5	2	2	3	10	1	6	11	10	10	8
21 and under 30	5	13	9	6	11	14	7	9	6	12	23
30 and under 60	38	29	32	21	30	49	31	23	23	25	42
60 and over	37	17	35	9	10	12	13	9	3	4	4
All ages	**87**	**62**	**79**	**40**	**63**	**78**	**66**	**54**	**47**	**58**	**88**
All Proved Offences	**1192**	**1035**	**1198**	**1314**	**1455**	**1713**	**1391**	**1378**	**1690**	**1850**	**2191**
Motoring Offences											
Proceedings for:											
(a) Previously Convicted											
Unfit to drive		11	6	2	6					5	1
Driving, undue alcohol					1	5	7	6	2	8	17
Fail provide specimen					2		1	1		2	2
(b) No Prev. Conviction											
Unfit to drive	179	158	177	200	205	19	17	21	17	32	38
Driving, undue alcohol					20	579	773	721	1080	1362	1625
Fail provide spec.					1	43	43	52	70	105	138
In charge and:											
Unfit to drive	35	33	66	46	46	4	7	4	5	11	17
Undue alcohol					3	7	4	2	3	3	11
Fail provide spec.						7	2		8	1	
Failure to provide breath specimen						61	69	91	124	169	250
Total: All Proceedings	**214**	**202**	**249**	**248**	**284**	**725**	**923**	**899**	**1309**	**1698**	**2099**
Licensed Premises											
Public Houses:											
Full	1515					1463					1437
Beer and Cider	7					4					2
Wine or Cider											
Restaurant Licence	61					108					155
Residential Licence	2					9					24
Above Combined	13					27					39
Licensed Clubs	68					53					81
Total On Licences	**1666**					**1664**					**1738**
Off Licences	**444**					**496**					**672**
Total On/Off Licences	**2110**					**2160**					**2410**
Registered Clubs	**599**					**696**					**717**
Total Licences & Clubs	**2709**					**2856**					**3127**

TABLE III 187
LICENSED PREMISES (SCOTLAND), 1953–75

Year	Public Houses	Hotels	Restricted On-licences based on 1962 Licensing (Scotland Act) Restricted Hotels	Restricted On-licences based on 1962 Licensing (Scotland Act) Restaurants	Registered Clubs	Off-Licences	Totals
1953	4134	1800			990	2409	9333
1954	4156	1826			1021	2424	9427
1955	4162	1821			1056	2426	9465
1956	4176	1846			1132	2434	9588
1957	4201	1872			1169	2444	9686
1958	4181	1893			1219	2482	9775
1959	4177	1942			1245	2499	9863
1960	4186	1987			1297	2580	10050
1961	4206	2056			1326	2782	10370
1962	4218	2096	60	44	1379	2961	10758
1963	4212	2138	111	106	1421	3131	11119
1964	4222	2196	142	148	1497	3242	11447
1965	4213	2265	149	175	1554	3385	11741
1966	4222	2319	170	201	1607	3384	11903
1967	4230	2404	184	221	1686	3555	12280
1968	4198	2449	212	274	1793	3630	12556
1969	4111	2509	226	307	1890	3644	12687
1970	4190	2565	227	358	1938	3766	13044
1971	4176	2609	250	406	2073	3819	13333
1972	4064	2646	270	431	2148	3872	13431
1973	4086	2769	304	501	2214	4021	13895
1974	3923	2745	319	540	2306	4019	13852
1975	4002	2755	317	587	2404	4182	14247

TABLE III 188
"DRUNK AND INCAPABLE": PREVIOUS CONVICTIONS (SCOTLAND), 1953–75

Year	Not previously guilty of any offence	Previously guilty of some offence	Number of times previously guilty of some crime/offence: one	two	three	4–10	over 10 times
1953	2835	3118	469	257	316	859	1217
1954	2998	3134	457	318	338	786	1235
1955	3186	3364	541	342	360	851	1270
1956	3527	3581	593	417	360	940	1271
1957	3940	3858	670	387	488	992	1321
1958	3655	3666	596	378	500	916	1276
1959	3734	3909	610	390	530	1006	1373
1960	3933	3998	617	396	553	979	1453
1961	4368	4806	691	447	733	1209	1726
1962	4785	4882	770	481	694	1251	1686
1963	5171	5293	789	472	808	1424	1800
1964	4796	5653	764	557	775	1540	2017
1965	4855	5205	736	500	724	1366	1879
1966	4921	5315	762	568	558	1410	2017
1967	4878	5132	676	486	601	1427	1942
1968	4983	5452	673	535	683	1515	2046
1969	4905	5016	631	494	583	1410	1898
1970	5313	4921	585	452	496	1333	2055
1971	5267	5320	640	474	556	1473	2177
1972	5552	5812	701	502	474	1521	2614
1973	6241	6937	840	601	628	1716	3152
1974	6294	8028	970	658	768	2044	3588
1975	7043	7622	851	613	588	1893	3677

TABLE III 189
"DRUNK AND DISORDERLY": PREVIOUS CONVICTIONS (SCOTLAND), 1953–75

Year	Not previously guilty of any offence	Previously guilty of some offence	Number of times previously guilty of some crime/offence: one	two	three	4–10	over 10 times
1953	153	336	37	37	17	109	136
1954	152	340	38	27	23	91	161
1955	180	336	49	37	29	98	123
1956	180	377	64	36	23	104	150
1957	189	355	66	38	39	79	133
1958	166	343	57	30	20	103	133
1959	164	363	68	53	23	89	130
1960	151	281	47	21	21	74	118
1961	94	285	45	27	16	90	107
1962	49	125	13	11	10	43	48
1963	39	109	17	7	8	36	41
1964	32	120	18	8	10	44	40
1965	41	87	7	13	6	31	30
1966	69	158	16	17	12	51	62
1967	84	233	30	18	22	81	82
1968	101	225	33	25	26	70	71
1969	69	200	20	21	14	68	77
1970	56	150	20	16	16	45	53
1971	36	130	23	7	12	45	43
1972	45	101	11	10	7	21	52
1973	33	123	20	8	10	42	43
1974	58	134	12	14	9	41	58
1975	38	152	16	12	7	40	77

TABLE III 190
"OTHER DRUNKENNESS": PREVIOUS CONVICTIONS (SCOTLAND), 1953–75

Year	Not previously guilty of any offence	Previously guilty of some offence	Number of times previously guilty of some crime/offence: one	two	three	4–10	over 10 times
1953	65	59	16	4	5	16	18
1954	75	80	19	11	5	23	22
1955	81	89	20	14	8	25	22
1956	101	98	26	9	9	26	28
1957	87	95	13	12	12	32	26
1958	83	79	16	10	12	22	19
1959	72	78	20	9	8	25	16
1960	78	79	12	8	7	22	30
1961	96	64	16	9	8	17	14
1962	80	75	20	11	8	20	16
1963	104	83	21	7	6	24	25
1964	98	79	11	12	7	30	19
1965	106	86	13	5	11	31	26
1966	84	73	21	13	7	17	15
1967	101	62	13	13	8	13	15
1968	98	78	17	18	7	20	16
1969	72	65	11	6	5	30	13
1970	95	59	13	6	7	25	8
1971	79	66	18	5	8	20	15
1972	87	67	12	8	2	26	19
1973	105	77	19	13	6	24	15
1974	105	64	9	9	6	24	16
1975	73	71	12	10	5	25	19

TABLE III 191
"LIQUOR LAW OFFENCES": PREVIOUS CONVICTIONS (SCOTLAND), 1953–75

Year	Not previously guilty of any offence	Previously guilty of some offence	Number of times previously guilty of some crime/offence: one	two	three	4–10	over 10 times
1953	452	122	52	20	14	24	12
1954	421	130	58	19	17	25	11
1955	414	145	50	21	16	44	14
1956	578	201	97	35	9	43	17
1957	487	162	59	29	26	38	10
1958	382	151	64	30	13	28	16
1959	559	206	62	38	32	62	12
1960	462	203	78	55	22	39	9
1961	504	224	91	43	20	53	17
1962	450	198	70	43	31	41	13
1963	629	246	121	39	20	50	16
1964	781	307	131	54	37	70	15
1965	584	295	127	54	28	70	16
1966	677	273	122	50	33	59	9
1967	695	313	139	57	36	70	11
1968	915	351	155	81	44	60	11
1969	1013	363	163	63	39	76	22
1970	993	380	167	66	53	79	15
1971	1159	398	162	84	55	82	15
1972	1110	459	170	98	58	113	20
1973	1290	527	206	100	65	131	25
1974	1385	545	232	109	64	110	30
1975	1056	401	173	81	53	84	10

TABLE III 192
"UNFIT TO DRIVE": PREVIOUS CONVICTIONS (SCOTLAND), 1953–75

Year	Not previously guilty of any offence	Previously guilty of some offence	Number of times previously guilty of some crime/offence				
			one	two	three	4–10	over 10 times
1953	581	363	124	76	47	94	22
1954	606	406	137	100	40	96	33
1955	749	428	156	98	44	108	22
1956	902	586	238	106	65	145	32
1957	1023	580	211	106	69	151	43
1958	1054	724	296	138	79	159	52
1959	1251	872	333	162	97	222	58
1960	1334	1122	475	198	147	226	76
1961	1438	1428	603	284	174	290	77
1962	1633	1549	708	272	156	321	92
1963	1627	1909	675	372	229	510	123
1964	1650	2138	644	380	279	630	205
1965	1833	2380	703	479	306	687	205
1966	2158	2845	865	558	354	843	225
1967	2275	2932	886	615	419	764	248
1968	784	1148	318	215	171	320	124
1969	669	1029	318	179	118	305	109
1970	992	1300	378	262	154	385	121
1971	1108	1439	393	291	184	445	126
1972	950	1251	346	250	168	379	108
1973	844	1388	388	274	183	418	125
1974	910	1293	356	243	180	406	108
1975	893	1039	351	185	125	286	92

TABLE III 193
"DRIVING WITH EXCESS ALCOHOL": PREVIOUS CONVICTIONS (SCOTLAND), 1967–75

Year	Not previously guilty of any offence	Previously guilty of some offence	Number of times previously guilty of some crime/offence				
			one	two	three	4–10	over 10 times
1953							
1954							
1955							
1956							
1957							
1958							
1959							
1960							
1961							
1962							
1963							
1964							
1965							
1966							
1967	84	72	27	13	7	21	4
1968	1727	1938	611	364	255	548	160
1969	2600	2708	892	548	331	749	188
1970	3088	3034	995	594	395	824	226
1971	3628	3606	1253	688	427	964	274
1972	3769	4188	1351	846	519	1161	311
1973	4259	5074	1577	980	627	1474	516
1974	4466	5532	1618	1030	687	1707	490
1975	4564	5189	1594	978	639	1498	480

TABLE III 194
"DRUNK AND INCAPABLE": SEX AND AGE (SCOTLAND), 1953–75

Year	Under 14		14–16		17–20		21–29		30–49		50–59		60 & over		Totals	
	M	F	M	F	M	F	M	F	M	F	M	F	M	F	M	F
1953			15	2	160	15	800	94	2301	354	1057	179	775	201	5108	845
1954			18	1	196	13	797	84	2402	347	1090	208	765	211	5268	864
1955			14	1	244	13	970	83	2590	320	1131	185	801	198	5750	800
1956			25	2	243	16	1016	65	2812	374	1280	197	868	210	6244	864
1957			11	1	340	12	1219	71	3120	417	1312	187	888	220	6890	908
1958			31	3	368	16	1088	91	2887	416	1283	183	772	183	6429	892
1959			31	1	426	15	1161	83	2993	374	1356	153	857	194	6824	819
1960			35	4	441	16	1192	77	3604	358	1430	157	966	191	7128	803
1961			49	2	541	22	1460	75	3483	353	1643	190	1119	237	8295	879
1962			48	6	548	23	1398	71	3806	378	1788	192	1214	195	8802	865
1963			72	7	517	32	1625	72	4253	410	1833	216	1238	207	9520	944
1964			74	9	677	22	1578	92	4163	380	1876	225	1162	191	9530	919
1965			84	11	674	29	1539	81	3976	408	1764	190	1127	177	9164	896
1966	2		115	15	746	37	1559	86	4170	401	1719	175	1067	144	9378	858
1967			101	15	781	40	1518	99	4109	384	1614	176	1063	110	9186	824
1968	2	2	115	20	768	51	1516	111	4282	426	1716	187	1093	146	9492	943
1969	4		118	17	710	34	1386	99	4228	448	1580	178	996	123	9022	899
1970	1		165	31	779	65	1395	127	4276	432	1645	173	1023	122	9284	950

Year	8–15		16		17		18–20		21–29		30–49		50 & over		Totals	
	M	F	M	F	M	F	M	F	M	F	M	F	M	F	M	F
1971	40	16	145	36	159	25	655	59	1357	154	4300	512	2830	299	9486	1101
1972	2		186	50	196	37	674	73	1447	142	4474	544	3155	384	10134	1230
1973	3	3	216	39	234	34	814	83	1665	159	5144	645	3696	443	11772	1406
1974	1		217	36	259	20	882	106	1802	147	5658	676	4086	432	12905	1417
1975	7		213	43	233	38	933	96	1857	169	5673	847	4033	523	12949	1716

TABLE III 195
"DRUNK AND DISORDERLY": SEX AND AGE (SCOTLAND), 1953-75

Year	Under 14		14-16		17-20		21-29		30-49		50-59		60 & over		Totals	
	M	F	M	F	M	F	M	F	M	F	M	F	M	F	M	F
1953			2		28	3	136	23	168	46	48	12	17	6	399	90
1954					39	2	125	16	167	43	56	20	19	5	406	86
1955			3	1	41	7	159	22	165	34	46	16	14	8	428	88
1956					74	10	158	19	171	49	46	8	17	5	466	91
1957			2		81	6	153	15	147	49	50	12	27	2	460	84
1958			1		60	8	146	16	144	36	54	16	26	2	431	78
1959			3		72	6	146	21	185	33	35	9	17		458	69
1960			1		71	2	101	15	133	38	39	11	13	8	358	74
1961			1		61	1	96	10	131	23	21	14	16	5	326	53
1962			2		38		43	6	51	7	14	2	9	2	157	17
1963			1		36	2	49	1	34	5	14	1	5		139	9
1964					40	2	43		47	5	11		4		145	7
1965			3		25		48	2	36	3	9		2		123	5
1966			3		83	3	52	5	57	7	14		2	1	211	16
1967			8	1	87	1	90	4	92	8	21		5		303	14
1968			11		98	4	90	3	95	7	14	1	2	1	310	16
1969			5		57	4	76	6	87	11	14		8	1	247	22
1970			10	2	50	10	50		58	6	12	2	4		186	20

Year	8-15		16		17		18-20		21-29		30-49		50 & over		Totals	
	M	F	M	F	M	F	M	F	M	F	M	F	M	F	M	F
1971	1		9	3	9		44	3	21	1	45	9	21		150	16
1972			1	1	5	1	23		28	1	56	9	20	1	133	13
1973			6	2	9	1	26	4	32	3	49	10	14		136	20
1974			3	1	11		27	1	27	5	68	21	25	3	161	31
1975			1	1	3		23	3	34	6	70	15	28	6	159	31

TABLE III 196
"OTHER DRUNKENNESS": SEX AND AGE (SCOTLAND), 1953–75

Year	Under 14		14–16		17–20		21–29		30–49		50–59		60 & over		Totals	
	M	F	M	F	M	F	M	F	M	F	M	F	M	F	M	F
1953					5		13	3	71	5	20	2	5		114	10
1954					5	1	30	3	78	13	12	1	11	1	136	19
1955					3		36	4	80	16	27		4		150	20
1956			1		4		49	1	102	8	24	1	9		189	10
1957					4		38	3	85	16	23	2	9	2	159	23
1958			1		3		38	10	80	14	8	1	7		137	25
1959					4	1	29	4	70	15	21	1	4	1	128	22
1960					5		26	9	82	10	15	3	7		135	22
1961					5		28	5	86	14	13	4	4	1	136	24
1962					9		23	11	72	18	17		4	1	125	30
1963			1		7		31	16	91	18	16		7	1	153	34
1964					9		37	8	79	19	17	2	5	1	147	30
1965					12	2	46	5	80	27	10		9	1	157	35
1966			2		10	3	28	7	63	23	13	1	5	2	121	36
1967					12		38	9	60	25	17	2			127	36
1968			1		7	6	41	8	65	30	11	1	5	1	130	46
1969					9	1	31	13	54	20	4	2	3		101	36
1970					19	4	34	11	53	25	6	1		1	112	42
	8–15		**16**		**17**		**18–20**		**21–29**		**30–49**		**50 & over**		**Totals**	
	M	F	M	F	M	F	M	F	M	F	M	F	M	F	M	F
1971					2		7	1	31	9	53	29	9	4	102	43
1972				1	1		9	2	28	14	53	33	9	4	100	54
1973					2		15	2	40	20	57	32	9	5	123	59
1974			1		1	1	10	5	41	15	60	22	10	3	123	46
1975				1	1		6	3	36	16	40	24	12	5	95	49

TABLE III 197
"LIQUOR LAW OFFENCES": SEX AND AGE (SCOTLAND), 1953–75

Year	Under 14		14–16		17–20		21–29		30–49		50–59		60 & over		Totals	
	M	F	M	F	M	F	M	F	M	F	M	F	M	F	M	F
1953			15		63	1	128	9	232	13	69	3	36	5	543	31
1954			18		62	2	134	16	202	23	59	7	24	4	499	52
1955			27		70	2	148	6	207	8	69	7	14	1	535	24
1956			31		112	1	176	6	300	26	86	6	30	5	735	44
1957			34		108	2	166	5	225	14	62	4	25	4	620	29
1958			31		83	3	118	6	188	12	61	2	24	5	505	28
1959			44		128	4	146	6	298	21	82	10	23	3	721	44
1960			69	2	126	7	131	10	217	15	53	4	23	8	619	46
1961			67	3	168	12	130	11	230	19	48	14	20	6	663	65
1962			74	6	175	17	112	2	160	11	58	1	23	9	602	46
1963			175	29	242	19	128	5	171	22	50	12	18	4	784	91
1964			252	41	395	43	107	8	132	21	50	13	18	8	954	134
1965	1		159	23	291	44	102	10	159	18	48	7	15	2	775	104
1966			181	39	321	68	72	9	165	20	49	6	20		808	142
1967	1		218	57	325	70	117	4	134	19	39	5	13	6	847	161
1968			358	74	371	69	118	2	159	32	42	12	25	4	1073	193
1969		1	354	72	481	105	131	5	138	27	32	7	20	3	1156	220
1970	2	3	361	111	416	105	118	10	156	20	39	7	23	2	1115	258

Year	8–15		16		17		18–20		21–29		30–49		50 & over		Totals	
	M	F	M	F	M	F	M	F	M	F	M	F	M	F	M	F
1971	59	20	343	113	390	121	113	13	115	7	141	26	76	20	1237	320
1972	14	3	321	104	464	75	123	16	147	19	160	36	66	21	1295	274
1973	15	6	471	108	563	88	135	16	115	20	152	32	78	18	1529	288
1974	9		479	133	609	143	143	20	114	25	141	38	57	19	1552	378
1975	7	1	378	63	559	94	106	12	60	15	88	31	31	12	1229	228

TABLE III 198
"DRUNKEN DRIVING": SEX AND AGE (SCOTLAND), 1953–75

Year	under 17		17–20		21–29		30–49		50–59		60 & over		Totals	
	M	F	M	F	M	F	M	F	M	F	M	F	M	F
1953	1		10		178	1	601	6	116	6	31		937	7
1954			18		197	1	627	5	128		35	1	1005	7
1955			28		241		740	7	128	2	30	1	1167	10
1956	1		34		334	3	919	6	147	1	43		1478	10
1957			27		360		984	8	179	1	44		1594	9
1958	1		54		398	2	1062	5	208		48		1771	7
1959			62		512	3	1243	9	236	1	57		2110	13
1960	3		91	1	582	1	1399	14	307	1	57		2439	17
1961	1		133	1	664	1	1672	7	323	2	62		2855	11
1962	1		133		841	3	1781	13	314	7	89		3159	23
1963	2		154	2	882	4	1933	29	425	3	102		3498	38
1964	3		192		972	1	2103	24	400	4	89		3759	29
1965	5		239		1139	4	2254	14	447	6	103	2	4187	26
1966	6		303	2	1355	3	2667	23	520	6	117	1	4968	35
1967	4		340	3	1459	6	2806	36	585	8	115	1	5309	54
1968	14		491	2	1818	7	2630	36	454	8	133	4	5540	57
1969	15		661	3	2260	18	3288	38	580	5	165	3	6969	67
1970	13		704	11	2725	21	3994	34	702	12	195	2	8333	80

Year	under 17		17		18–20		21–29		30–49		50 & over		Totals	
	M	F	M	F	M	F	M	F	M	F	M	F	M	F
1971	17		67		825	5	3018	36	4605	81	1110	17	9642	139
1972	32		84		853	6	3361	49	4534	79	1138	21	10002	156
1973	22	1	112	2	1024	9	3779	56	5089	98	1353	21	11379	186
1974	30	1	124	1	1052	12	3809	43	5467	109	1430	23	12012	189
1975	31	3	153	3	1157	21	3544	79	5121	114	1419	30	11435	250

TABLE III 199
DRUNKENNESS OFFENCES AND MOTORING OFFENCES (SCOTLAND), 1953-74

Offence	**1953**	**1954**	**1955**	**1956**	**1957**	**1958**	**1959**	**1960**
Drunk and Incapable	10173	10618	11557	13086	13818	12616	12404	12847
Drunk and Disorderly	597	593	635	646	631	610	591	490
Other Drunkenness	188	220	240	292	237	239	257	330
Liquor Law Offences	617	608	609	846	701	589	839	726
Totals, Non-motoring	**11575**	**12039**	**13041**	**14870**	**15387**	**14054**	**14091**	**14393**
Drunk in Charge, Motor Vehicle	**1040**	**1080**	**1264**	**1609**	**1725**	**1898**	**2254**	**2613**
	1961	**1962**	**1963**	**1964**	**1965**	**1966**	**1967**	**1968**
Drunk and Incapable	14590	14832	14481	14039	13595	14018	13166	13153
Drunk and Disorderly	432	211	162	176	140	253	348	347
Other Drunkenness	193	191	227	195	216	172	188	193
Liquor Law Offences	815	730	989	1201	988	1076	1170	1385
Totals, Non-motoring	**16030**	**15964**	**15859**	**15611**	**14939**	**15519**	**14872**	**15078**
Drunk in Charge, Motor Vehicle	3064	3415	3759	4002	4470	5271	5481	2037
Driving, Excess Alcohol							159	3756
Totals, Motoring	**3064**	**3415**	**3759**	**4002**	**4470**	**5271**	**5640**	**5793**
	1969	**1970**	**1971**	**1972**	**1973**	**1974**		
Drunk and Incapable	12157	12475	12566	13473	15941	17370		
Drunk and Disorderly	293	219	182	154	170	196		
Other Drunkenness	155	170	151	170	205	186		
Liquor Law Offences	1537	1508	1731	1701	1975	2107		
Totals, Non-motoring	**14142**	**14372**	**14630**	**15498**	**18291**	**19849**		
Drunk in Charge, Motor Vehicle	1797	2382	2624	2267	2315	2298		
Driving, Excess Alcohol	5475	6246	7359	8090	9484	10163		
Totals, Motoring	**7272**	**8628**	**9983**	**10357**	**11799**	**12461**		

Population at risk, at five-year intervals, in thousands:
1953: 5123; 1958: 5169; 1963: 5204; 1968: 5195; 1973: 5210.

TABLE III 200
DRUNKENNESS OFFENCES AND MOTORING OFFENCES, 1953-74
CITY OF ABERDEEN

Offence	1953	1954	1955	1956	1957	1958	1959
Drunk and Incapable	305	329	325	319	367	343	391
Drunk and Disorderly	57	69	59	77	94	54	83
Other Drunkenness	5	6	10	9	18	11	11
Liquor Law Offences	53	58	27	32	35	52	39
Totals, Non-motoring	**420**	**462**	**421**	**437**	**514**	**460**	**524**
Drunk in Charge, Motor Vehicle	**33**	**43**	**36**	**40**	**36**	**42**	**69**

	1960	1961	1962	1963	1964	1965	1966	1967
Drunk and Incapable	306	337	319	312	339	253	280	254
Drunk and Disorderly	72	84	53	43	48	54	50	51
Other Drunkenness	4	5	8	3	3	2	1	
Liquor Law Offences	18	10	24	44	30	27	29	64
Totals, Non-motoring	**400**	**436**	**404**	**402**	**420**	**336**	**360**	**379**
Drunk in Charge, Motor Vehicle	82	117	116	120	175	129	145	153
Driving, Excess Alcohol								14
Totals, Motoring	**82**	**117**	**116**	**120**	**175**	**129**	**145**	**167**

	1968	1969	1970	1971	1972	1973	1974
Drunk and Incapable	238	247	273	272	322	346	359
Drunk and Disorderly	41	35	32	49	48	43	66
Other Drunkenness	1	2		1	2	5	4
Liquor Law Offences	134	159	192	205	87	170	146
Totals, Non-motoring	**414**	**443**	**497**	**529**	**459**	**564**	**575**
Drunk in Charge, Motor Vehicle	71	52	19	13	21	14	21
Driving, Excess Alcohol	116	145	243	308	347	367	546
Totals, Motoring	**187**	**197**	**262**	**321**	**368**	**381**	**567**

Population at risk, at five-year intervals, in thousands:
1953: 186; 1958: 186; 1963: 186; 1968: 181; 1973: 182.

TABLE III 201
DRUNKENNESS OFFENCES AND MOTORING OFFENCES, 1953-74
CITY OF DUNDEE

Offence	**1953**	**1954**	**1955**	**1956**	**1957**	**1958**	**1959**
Drunk and Incapable	749	826	829	1013	1268	1052	1062
Drunk and Disorderly	1	2	1				
Other Drunkenness		13	14	7	5	6	7
Liquor Law Offences	39	44	39	31	51	15	56
Totals, Non-motoring	**749**	**885**	**883**	**1051**	**1324**	**1073**	**1125**
Drunk in Charge, Motor Vehicle	**65**	**48**	**57**	**67**	**75**	**59**	**101**

	1960	**1961**	**1962**	**1963**	**1964**	**1965**	**1966**	**1967**
Drunk and Incapable	1034	1204	1104	1097	911	874	1042	906
Drunk and Disorderly						11	42	84
Other Drunkenness	10	3	7	12	4	12	7	6
Liquor Law Offences	37	40	37	71	34	50	32	75
Totals, Non-motoring	**1081**	**1247**	**1148**	**1180**	**949**	**947**	**1123**	**1071**
Drunk in Charge, Motor Vehicle	94	125	112	117	134	125	135	156
Driving, Excess Alcohol								7
Totals, Motoring	**94**	**125**	**112**	**117**	**134**	**125**	**135**	**163**

	1968	**1969**	**1970**	**1971**	**1972**	**1973**	**1974**
Drunk and Incapable	900	697	690	774	793	976	923
Drunk and Disorderly	69	93	71	38	56	87	91
Other Drunkenness	8	4	6	8	7	9	10
Liquor Law Offences	82	104	112	119	87	117	123
Totals, Non-motoring	**1059**	**898**	**879**	**939**	**943**	**1192**	**1147**
Drunk in Charge, Motor Vehicle	13	4	1	2	7	4	3
Driving, Excess Alcohol	237	199	237	278	316	418	421
Totals, Motoring	**250**	**203**	**238**	**280**	**323**	**422**	**424**

Population at risk, at five-year intervals, in thousands:
1953: 177; 1958: 180; 1963: 184; 1968: 182; 1973: 182.

TABLE III 202
DRUNKENNESS OFFENCES AND MOTORING OFFENCES, 1953–74
CITY OF EDINBURGH

Offence	**1953**	**1954**	**1955**	**1956**	**1957**	**1958**	**1959**
Drunk and Incapable	856	906	1057	1111	1035	1058	1076
Drunk and Disorderly	264	283	314	314	290	332	311
Other Drunkenness	5	9	7	12	9	9	11
Liquor Law Offences	31	75	51	31	35	42	106
Totals, Non-motoring	**1156**	**1273**	**1429**	**1478**	**1369**	**1441**	**1504**
Drunk in Charge, Motor Vehicle	**54**	**63**	**72**	**127**	**134**	**172**	**210**

	1960	**1961**	**1962**	**1963**	**1964**	**1965**	**1966**	**1967**
Drunk and Incapable	1071	1239	1283	1182	1169	1065	1006	869
Drunk and Disorderly	255	173	4					
Other Drunkenness	4	17	15	12	9	22	9	8
Liquor Law Offences	111	188	54	220	304	258	204	171
Totals, Non-motoring	**1441**	**1617**	**1356**	**1414**	**1482**	**1345**	**1219**	**1048**
Drunk in Charge, Motor Vehicle	262	309	327	446	430	414	565	637
Driving, Excess Alcohol								18
Totals, Motoring	**262**	**309**	**327**	**446**	**430**	**414**	**565**	**655**

	1968	**1969**	**1970**	**1971**	**1972**	**1973**	**1974**
Drunk and Incapable	985	842	956	1006	1190	1274	1427
Drunk and Disorderly							
Other Drunkenness	21	8	9	8	8	7	10
Liquor Law Offences	222	172	117	192	156	250	473
Totals, Non-motoring	**1228**	**1022**	**1072**	**1206**	**1354**	**1531**	**1910**
Drunk in Charge, Motor Vehicle	166	127	121	124	80	86	62
Driving, Excess Alcohol	339	507	518	505	635	669	701
Totals, Motoring	**505**	**634**	**639**	**629**	**715**	**755**	**763**

Population at risk, at five-year intervals, in thousands:
1953: 469; 1958: 467; 1963: 476; 1968: 465; 1973: 450.

TABLE III 203
DRUNKENNESS OFFENCES AND MOTORING OFFENCES, 1953–74
CITY OF GLASGOW

Offence	**1953**	**1954**	**1955**	**1956**	**1957**	**1958**	**1959**
Drunk and Incapable	3653	3717	4055	4813	4967	4593	4399
Drunk and Disorderly							
Other Drunkenness	38	33	39	39	41	81	108
Liquor Law Offences	67	44	68	71	80	85	189
Totals, Non-motoring	**3758**	**3794**	**4162**	**4923**	**5088**	**4759**	**4696**
Drunk in Charge, Motor Vehicle	**239**	**264**	**323**	**429**	**522**	**605**	**705**

	1960	**1961**	**1962**	**1963**	**1964**	**1965**	**1966**	**1967**
Drunk and Incapable	4690	5317	5477	5119	4855	4926	4581	4141
Drunk and Disorderly								
Other Drunkenness	189	58	66	82	68	68	68	88
Liquor Law Offences	134	128	109	143	172	109	136	118
Totals, Non-motoring	**5013**	**5503**	**5652**	**5344**	**5095**	**5103**	**4785**	**4347**
Drunk in Charge, Motor Vehicle	785	838	1107	1054	1114	1318	1455	1464
Driving, Excess Alcohol								25
Totals, Motoring	**785**	**838**	**1107**	**1054**	**1114**	**1318**	**1455**	**1489**

	1968	**1969**	**1970**	**1971**	**1972**	**1973**	**1974**
Drunk and Incapable	3966	4081	4179	3907	4178	4658	4366
Drunk and Disorderly	7		2	2	2	1	12
Other Drunkenness	64	52	49	59	71	73	70
Liquor Law Offences	225	388	343	424	396	434	306
Totals, Non-motoring	**4262**	**4521**	**4573**	**4392**	**4647**	**5166**	**4754**
Drunk in Charge, Motor Vehicle	870	773	1208	1379	1110	1177	1146
Driving, Excess Alcohol	539	761	899	967	963	1072	1121
Totals, Motoring	**1409**	**1434**	**2107**	**2346**	**2073**	**2249**	**2267**

Population at risk, at five-year intervals, in thousands:
1953: 1083; 1958: 1079; 1963: 1036; 1968: 928; 1973: 862.

TABLE III 204
DRUNKENNESS OFFENCES AND MOTORING OFFENCES, 1953–74
COUNTY OF ANGUS

Offence	**1953**	**1954**	**1955**	**1956**	**1957**	**1958**	**1959**
Drunk and Incapable	75	88	82	118	130	103	106
Drunk and Disorderly	1	2	5	9	1		3
Other Drunkenness	8	3	9	4	4	2	4
Liquor Law Offences	12	3	13	8	31	9	14
Totals, Non-motoring	**96**	**96**	**109**	**139**	**166**	**114**	**147**
Drunk in Charge, Motor Vehicle	**16**	**18**	**20**	**19**	**21**	**35**	**52**

	1960	**1961**	**1962**	**1963**	**1964**	**1965**	**1966**	**1967**
Drunk and Incapable	168	150	167	170	142	106	98	118
Drunk and Disorderly		1		1	1			
Other Drunkenness	7	1	8	4	4	3	2	6
Liquor Law Offences	25	24	61	36	42	19	22	25
Totals, Non-motoring	**200**	**176**	**236**	**211**	**189**	**128**	**122**	**149**
Drunk in Charge, Motor Vehicle	45	54	59	50	55	69	48	66
Driving, Excess Alcohol								5
Totals, Motoring	**45**	**54**	**59**	**50**	**55**	**69**	**48**	**71**

	1968	**1969**	**1970**	**1971**	**1972**	**1973**	**1974**
Drunk and Incapable	133	120	142	160	185	262	268
Drunk and Disorderly	1				2		1
Other Drunkenness	5	3	1		2	4	2
Liquor Law Offences	39	13	35	48	54	37	40
Totals, Non-motoring	**178**	**136**	**178**	**208**	**243**	**303**	**311**
Drunk in Charge, Motor Vehicle	6	4	1	1	5	2	9
Driving, Excess Alcohol	106	120	124	147	162	202	223
Totals, Motoring	**112**	**124**	**125**	**148**	**167**	**204**	**232**

Population at risk, at five-year intervals, in thousands:
1953: 98; 1958: 97; 1963: 96; 1968: 95; 1973: 98.

TABLE III 205
DRUNKENNESS OFFENCES AND MOTORING OFFENCES, 1953–74
COUNTY OF ARGYLL

Offence	1953	1954	1955	1956	1957	1958	1959
Drunk and Incapable	86	93	95	122	107	134	123
Drunk and Disorderly	18	9	15	6	1	6	5
Other Drunkenness	4	2	1	3	5		4
Liquor Law Offences	12	5	9	2		4	6
Totals, Non-motoring	**120**	**109**	**120**	**133**	**113**	**144**	**138**
Drunk in Charge, Motor Vehicle	**26**	**26**	**22**	**22**	**24**	**36**	**39**

	1960	1961	1962	1963	1964	1965	1966	1967
Drunk and Incapable	141	174	173	234	222	161	203	176
Drunk and Disorderly	11	16	10	4	1		8	6
Other Drunkenness	4	5	3	5	3	7	7	6
Liquor Law Offences	12	7	6	2	10	5	5	15
Totals, Non-motoring	**168**	**202**	**192**	**245**	**236**	**173**	**223**	**203**
Drunk in Charge, Motor Vehicle	41	68	62	105	104	100	114	95
Driving, Excess Alcohol								6
Totals, Motoring	**41**	**68**	**62**	**105**	**104**	**100**	**114**	**101**

	1968	1969	1970	1971	1972	1973	1974
Drunk and Incapable	212	150	191	197	164	243	292
Drunk and Disorderly	2	5	5	2	2	4	
Other Drunkenness	5	6	3	11	9	15	4
Liquor Law Offences	16	11	10	19	12	16	11
Totals, Non-motoring	**235**	**172**	**209**	**229**	**187**	**278**	**307**
Drunk in Charge, Motor Vehicle	42	24	22	28	25	27	27
Driving, Excess Alcohol	106	152	149	155	178	257	220
Totals, Motoring	**148**	**176**	**171**	**183**	**203**	**284**	**247**

Population at risk, at five-year intervals, in thousands:
1953: 60; 1958: 56; 1963: 60; 1968: 58; 1973: 58.

TABLE III 206
DRUNKENNESS OFFENCES AND MOTORING OFFENCES, 1953–74
COUNTY OF AYR

Offence	**1953**	**1954**	**1955**	**1956**	**1957**	**1958**	**1959**
Drunk and Incapable	476	551	614	687	676	647	623
Drunk and Disorderly	18	12	12	16	19	19	18
Other Drunkenness	11	23	26	15	26	14	24
Liquor Law Offences	37	52	65	49	73	53	84
Totals, Non-motoring	**542**	**638**	**717**	**767**	**794**	**733**	**749**
Drunk in Charge, Motor Vehicle	**65**	**71**	**70**	**110**	**95**	**92**	**116**

	1960	**1961**	**1962**	**1963**	**1964**	**1965**	**1966**	**1967**
Drunk and Incapable	637	658	736	689	753	654	738	705
Drunk and Disorderly	19	8	9	7	8	2	4	2
Other Drunkenness	16	22	13	21	13	11	5	11
Liquor Law Offences	59	44	59	52	108	67	87	88
Totals, Non-motoring	**731**	**732**	**817**	**769**	**882**	**734**	**834**	**806**
Drunk in Charge, Motor Vehicle	144	164	168	221	226	242	285	204
Driving, Excess Alcohol								1
Totals, Motoring	**144**	**164**	**168**	**221**	**226**	**242**	**285**	**205**

	1968	**1969**	**1970**	**1971**	**1972**	**1973**	**1974**
Drunk and Incapable	725	632	715	569	534	768	791
Drunk and Disorderly	1	1	3				1
Other Drunkenness	4	10	11	4	2	5	5
Liquor Law Offences	124	64	63	119	77	87	85
Totals, Non-motoring	**854**	**707**	**792**	**692**	**613**	**860**	**882**
Drunk in Charge, Motor Vehicle	164	232	330	356	340	396	486
Driving, Excess Alcohol	141	196	251	238	280	366	371
Totals, Motoring	**305**	**428**	**581**	**594**	**620**	**762**	**857**

Population at risk, at five-year intervals, in thousands:
1953: 326; 1958: 384; 1963: 346; 1968: 354; 1973: 364.

TABLE III 207
DRUNKENNESS OFFENCES AND MOTORING OFFENCES, 1953–74
COUNTY OF BERWICK, ROXBURGH AND SELKIRK

Offence	**1953**	**1954**	**1955**	**1956**	**1957**	**1958**	**1959**
Drunk and Incapable	96	102	128	93	65	90	96
Drunk and Disorderly	11	5	5	7	9	12	9
Other Drunkenness	7	6	7	7	3	3	3
Liquor Law Offences	24	17	22	25	10	20	16
Totals, Non-motoring	**138**	**130**	**162**	**132**	**87**	**125**	**124**
Drunk in Charge, Motor Vehicle	**21**	**11**	**21**	**18**	**20**	**28**	**31**

	1960	**1961**	**1962**	**1963**	**1964**	**1965**	**1966**	**1967**
Drunk and Incapable	87	89	89	78	88	90	145	137
Drunk and Disorderly	4	2	3		2	1	2	2
Other Drunkenness	4	2	2	3	7	3	9	
Liquor Law Offences	23	33	22	25	68	34	46	61
Totals, Non-motoring	**118**	**126**	**116**	**106**	**165**	**128**	**202**	**200**
Drunk in Charge, Motor Vehicle	35	39	27	41	51	56	63	84
Driving, Excess Alcohol								5
Totals, Motoring	**35**	**39**	**27**	**41**	**51**	**56**	**63**	**89**

	1968	**1969**	**1970**	**1971**	**1972**	**1973**	**1974**
Drunk and Incapable	144	106	108	82	76	128	158
Drunk and Disorderly	2						
Other Drunkenness	3		4	4	4	3	4
Liquor Law Offences	32	44	55	22	60	68	84
Totals, Non-motoring	**181**	**150**	**167**	**108**	**140**	**199**	**246**
Drunk in Charge, Motor Vehicle	15	6	10	12	12	5	4
Driving, Excess Alcohol	65	111	75	116	116	143	139
Totals, Motoring	**80**	**117**	**85**	**128**	**128**	**148**	**143**

Population at risk, at five-year intervals, in thousands:
1953: 91; 1958: 89; 1963: 85; 1968: 83; 1973: 83.

TABLE III 208
DRUNKENNESS OFFENCES AND MOTORING OFFENCES, 1953–74
COUNTY OF DUMBARTON

Offence	**1953**	**1954**	**1955**	**1956**	**1957**	**1958**	**1959**
Drunk and Incapable	249	275	294	394	344	381	355
Drunk and Disorderly	2	3	2	3	1		5
Other Drunkenness	6	9	10	7	3	6	6
Liquor Law Offences		4	4		2	6	4
Totals, Non-motoring	**257**	**291**	**310**	**359**	**350**	**393**	**370**
Drunk in Charge, Motor Vehicle	**21**	**24**	**34**	**48**	**37**	**45**	**37**

	1960	**1961**	**1962**	**1963**	**1964**	**1965**	**1966**	**1967**
Drunk and Incapable	401	488	534	622	508	611	643	657
Drunk and Disorderly					1			
Other Drunkenness	2	3	4	7	8	13	4	1
Liquor Law Offences			1	3		2	7	4
Totals, Non-motoring	**403**	**491**	**539**	**632**	**517**	**626**	**654**	**662**
Drunk in Charge, Motor Vehicle	76	80	96	93	90	134	158	205
Driving, Excess Alcohol								
Totals, Motoring	**76**	**80**	**96**	**93**	**90**	**134**	**158**	**205**

	1968	**1969**	**1970**	**1971**	**1972**	**1973**	**1974**
Drunk and Incapable	672	561	478	486	535	665	630
Drunk and Disorderly							
Other Drunkenness	6	3	1	5	1	5	1
Liquor Law Offences	9	15	18	6	14	15	6
Totals, Non-motoring	**687**	**579**	**497**	**497**	**550**	**685**	**637**
Drunk in Charge, Motor Vehicle	42	23	38	38	33	28	25
Driving, Excess Alcohol	118	451	376	473	412	448	423
Totals, Motoring	**160**	**474**	**414**	**511**	**445**	**476**	**448**

Population at risk, at five-year intervals, in thousands:
1953: 168; 1958: 177; 1963: 194; 1968: 228; 1973: 240.

TABLE III 209
DRUNKENNESS OFFENCES AND MOTORING OFFENCES, 1953–74
COUNTY OF DUMFRIES AND GALLOWAY

Offence	1953	1954	1955	1956	1957	1958	1959
Drunk and Incapable	74	79	101	117	90	91	120
Drunk and Disorderly	1		1			3	
Other Drunkenness	4	7	4	3	7	7	8
Liquor Law Offences	13	16	25	41	37	35	23
Totals, Non-motoring	**92**	**102**	**131**	**161**	**134**	**136**	**151**
Drunk in Charge, Motor Vehicle	**26**	**39**	**44**	**40**	**37**	**21**	**45**

Offence	1960	1961	1962	1963	1964	1965	1966	1967
Drunk and Incapable	102	106	97	75	92	86	80	51
Drunk and Disorderly							1	
Other Drunkenness	5	6	4	6	1	1	5	3
Liquor Law Offences	25	38	44	37	65	49	57	28
Totals, Non-motoring	**132**	**150**	**145**	**118**	**158**	**136**	**143**	**82**
Drunk in Charge, Motor Vehicle	47	51	43	67	73	83	81	78
Driving, Excess Alcohol								
Totals, Motoring	**47**	**51**	**43**	**67**	**73**	**83**	**81**	**78**

Offence	1968	1969	1970	1971	1972	1973	1974
Drunk and Incapable	62	45	49	64	57	91	94
Drunk and Disorderly							
Other Drunkenness		1	3	4		1	1
Liquor Law Offences	34	32	44	34	53	74	54
Totals, Non-motoring	**96**	**78**	**96**	**102**	**110**	**166**	**149**
Drunk in Charge, Motor Vehicle	39	39	49	39	34	23	34
Driving, Excess Alcohol	70	73	126	200	212	283	331
Totals, Motoring	**109**	**112**	**175**	**239**	**246**	**306**	**365**

Population at risk, at five-year intervals, in thousands:
1953: 148; 1958: 150; 1963: 146; 1968: 143; 1973: 143.

TABLE III 210

DRUNKENNESS OFFENCES AND MOTORING OFFENCES, 1953–74

COUNTY OF FIFE

Offence	**1953**	**1954**	**1955**	**1956**	**1957**	**1958**	**1959**
Drunk and Incapable	229	226	270	266	282	236	274
Drunk and Disorderly							1
Other Drunkenness	3	7	7	2	7	1	4
Liquor Law Offences	84	51	33	91	45	43	56
Totals, Non-motoring	**316**	**284**	**310**	**359**	**334**	**280**	**335**
Drunk in Charge, Motor Vehicle	**26**	**36**	**46**	**51**	**88**	**92**	**83**

	1960	**1961**	**1962**	**1963**	**1964**	**1965**	**1966**	**1967**
Drunk and Incapable	308	332	225	239	195	195	186	166
Drunk and Disorderly								
Other Drunkenness	12	2	4	10	2	3	1	
Liquor Law Offences	54	54	44	38	36	49	40	104
Totals, Non-motoring	**374**	**388**	**273**	**287**	**233**	**247**	**227**	**270**
Drunk in Charge, Motor Vehicle	92	96	101	114	134	186	215	210
Driving, Excess Alcohol								11
Totals, Motoring	**92**	**96**	**101**	**114**	**134**	**186**	**215**	**221**

	1968	**1969**	**1970**	**1971**	**1972**	**1973**	**1974**
Drunk and Incapable	174	148	130	128	157	210	259
Drunk and Disorderly							
Other Drunkenness	4	4	2	2	3	6	4
Liquor Law Offences	96	43	78	61	94	72	70
Totals, Non-motoring	**174**	**195**	**210**	**191**	**254**	**288**	**333**
Drunk in Charge, Motor Vehicle	23	15	8	6	6	8	12
Driving, Excess Alcohol	244	396	379	526	596	704	645
Totals, Motoring	**267**	**411**	**387**	**532**	**602**	**712**	**657**

Population at risk, at five-year intervals, in thousands:
1953: 313; 1958: 322; 1963: 323; 1968: 325; 1973: 332.

TABLE III 211
DRUNKENNESS OFFENCES AND MOTORING OFFENCES, 1953–74
COUNTY OF INVERNESS

Offence	**1953**	**1954**	**1955**	**1956**	**1957**	**1958**	**1959**
Drunk and Incapable	330	277	315	292	331	216	199
Drunk and Disorderly	2				2		
Other Drunkenness	9	7	7	5	4	2	1
Liquor Law Offences	23	10	9	2	5	8	10
Totals, Non-motoring	**364**	**294**	**331**	**299**	**342**	**226**	**210**
Drunk in Charge, Motor Vehicle	**76**	**54**	**52**	**78**	**57**	**87**	**89**

	1960	**1961**	**1962**	**1963**	**1964**	**1965**	**1966**	**1967**
Drunk and Incapable	265	370	298	327	356	387	397	431
Drunk and Disorderly								
Other Drunkenness	2	2	4	1	1	5	2	3
Liquor Law Offences	7	15	3		13	4	19	7
Totals, Non-motoring	**274**	**387**	**305**	**328**	**370**	**396**	**418**	**441**
Drunk in Charge, Motor Vehicle	117	134	112	139	120	145	186	176
Driving, Excess Alcohol								1
Totals, Motoring	**117**	**134**	**112**	**139**	**120**	**145**	**186**	**177**

	1968	**1969**	**1970**	**1971**	**1972**	**1973**	**1974**
Drunk and Incapable	393	339	344	324	530	577	745
Drunk and Disorderly							
Other Drunkenness	2	1	1		6	9	11
Liquor Law Offences	15	22	3	6	31	30	40
Totals, Non-motoring	**410**	**362**	**348**	**330**	**567**	**616**	**796**
Drunk in Charge, Motor Vehicle	84	111	131	177	146	131	105
Driving, Excess Alcohol	119	72	55	41	98	157	281
Totals, Motoring	**203**	**183**	**186**	**218**	**244**	**288**	**386**

Population at risk, at five-year intervals, in thousands:
1953: 85; 1958: 83; 1963: 82; 1968: 85; 1973: 89.

TABLE III 212
DRUNKENNESS OFFENCES AND MOTORING OFFENCES, 1953–74
COUNTY OF LANARK

Offence	1953	1954	1955	1956	1957	1958	1959
Drunk and Incapable	597	670	693	902	968	808	805
Drunk and Disorderly							
Other Drunkenness	12	13	16	22	12	12	8
Liquor Law Offences	65	56	53	220	74	54	57
Totals, Non-motoring	**674**	**739**	**762**	**1144**	**1054**	**874**	**870**
Drunk in Charge, Motor Vehicle	**68**	**82**	**92**	**107**	**114**	**132**	**175**

	1960	1961	1962	1963	1964	1965	1966	1967
Drunk and Incapable	869	1084	1098	1038	1224	1215	1179	1141
Drunk and Disorderly					1			2
Other Drunkenness	19	10	10	6	9	10	13	9
Liquor Law Offences	44	28	38	65	42	62	55	56
Totals, Non-motoring	**932**	**1122**	**1146**	**1109**	**1276**	**1287**	**1247**	**1208**
Drunk in Charge, Motor Vehicle	221	255	323	344	372	452	558	511
Driving, Excess Alcohol								16
Totals, Motoring	**221**	**255**	**323**	**344**	**372**	**452**	**558**	**527**

	1968	1969	1970	1971	1972	1973	1974
Drunk and Incapable	981	1077	1188	1118	1281	1416	1563
Drunk and Disorderly							
Other Drunkenness	10	19	34	15	23	17	15
Liquor Law Offences	66	52	73	59	99	98	90
Totals, Non-motoring	**1057**	**1148**	**1295**	**1192**	**1403**	**1531**	**1668**
Drunk in Charge, Motor Vehicle	161	115	156	152	139	135	145
Driving, Excess Alcohol	265	498	750	815	1019	1186	1043
Totals, Motoring	**426**	**613**	**906**	**967**	**1158**	**1321**	**1188**

Population at risk, at five-year intervals, in thousands:
1953: 532; 1958: 549; 1963: 582; 1968: 614; 1973: 632.

TABLE III 213
DRUNKENNESS OFFENCES AND MOTORING OFFENCES, 1953–74
COUNTY OF LOTHIANS AND PEEBLES

Offence	1953	1954	1955	1956	1957	1958	1959
Drunk and Incapable	100	154	151	218	276	218	187
Drunk and Disorderly	50	37	46	51	70	45	52
Other Drunkenness	3	9	5	19	12	7	13
Liquor Law Offences	26	32	53	73	76	37	42
Totals, Non-motoring	**179**	**232**	**255**	**361**	**434**	**307**	**294**
Drunk in Charge, Motor Vehicle	**38**	**31**	**44**	**63**	**60**	**58**	**49**

Offence	1960	1961	1962	1963	1964	1965	1966	1967
Drunk and Incapable	196	259	223	227	278	235	235	213
Drunk and Disorderly	37	29	36	28	31	21	36	34
Other Drunkenness	5	7	10	4	9	12	6	16
Liquor Law Offences	31	51	61	29	38	37	43	60
Totals, Non-motoring	**269**	**346**	**330**	**288**	**356**	**305**	**320**	**323**
Drunk in Charge, Motor Vehicle	79	83	99	144	129	148	134	111
Driving, Excess Alcohol								4
Totals, Motoring	**79**	**83**	**99**	**144**	**129**	**148**	**134**	**115**

Offence	1968	1969	1970	1971	1972	1973	1974
Drunk and Incapable	167	182	137	126	154	208	271
Drunk and Disorderly	36	31	14	6	25	8	9
Other Drunkenness	8	10	10	4	2	11	11
Liquor Law Offences	54	127	101	91	111	135	202
Totals, Non-motoring	**265**	**350**	**262**	**227**	**292**	**362**	**493**
Drunk in Charge, Motor Vehicle	28	21	18	22	29	18	9
Driving, Excess Alcohol	125	158	253	317	478	610	759
Totals, Motoring	**153**	**179**	**271**	**339**	**507**	**628**	**768**

Population at risk, at five-year intervals, in thousands:
1953: 261; 1958: 267; 1963: 280; 1968: 305; 1973: 328.

TABLE III 214
DRUNKENNESS OFFENCES AND MOTORING OFFENCES, 1953–74
NORTHERN CONSTABULARY

Offence	**1953**	**1954**	**1955**	**1956**	**1957**	**1958**	**1959**
Drunk and Incapable	59	56	86	116	133	63	53
Drunk and Disorderly	5	10	16	37	22	11	9
Other Drunkenness	6	6	4	7	5	7	1
Liquor Law Offences	8	12	3	1	1	5	
Totals, Non-motoring	**78**	**84**	**109**	**161**	**161**	**86**	**63**
Drunk in Charge, Motor Vehicle	**16**	**22**	**26**	**41**	**42**	**28**	**32**

	1960	**1961**	**1962**	**1963**	**1964**	**1965**	**1966**	**1967**
Drunk and Incapable	81	83	79	91	72	47	63	69
Drunk and Disorderly	5	5	4	4	2	1	1	
Other Drunkenness	2	5	3	4	1	4	2	1
Liquor Law Offences		5	3		4	2	5	13
Totals, Non-motoring	**88**	**98**	**89**	**99**	**79**	**54**	**71**	**83**
Drunk in Charge, Motor Vehicle	38	47	55	46	59	52	53	52
Driving, Excess Alcohol								1
Totals, Motoring	**38**	**47**	**55**	**46**	**59**	**52**	**53**	**53**

	1968	**1969**	**1970**	**1971**	**1972**	**1973**	**1974**
Drunk and Incapable	94	83	53	58	77	113	112
Drunk and Disorderly	1	2		3	1	4	
Other Drunkenness		1	2	1	3	6	2
Liquor Law Offences	9	9	9	5	7	24	25
Totals, Non-motoring	**104**	**95**	**64**	**67**	**88**	**147**	**139**
Drunk in Charge, Motor Vehicle	25	20	13	15	23	4	7
Driving, Excess Alcohol	41	47	62	73	103	138	179
Totals, Motoring	**66**	**67**	**75**	**88**	**126**	**142**	**186**

Population at risk, at five-year intervals, in thousands:
1953: 63; 1958: 63; 1963: 64; 1968: 63; 1973: 63.

TABLE III 215
DRUNKENNESS OFFENCES AND MOTORING OFFENCES, 1953–74
COUNTY OF PERTH AND KINROSS

Offence	1953	1954	1955	1956	1957	1958	1959
Drunk and Incapable	271	303	296	362	352	296	272
Drunk and Disorderly	42	53	41	50	44	38	26
Other Drunkenness	13	18	14	16	9	9	8
Liquor Law Offences	22	20	17	17	11	5	20
Totals, Non-motoring	**348**	**394**	**368**	**445**	**416**	**348**	**326**
Drunk in Charge, Motor Vehicle	**27**	**51**	**48**	**35**	**68**	**56**	**60**

	1960	1961	1962	1963	1964	1965	1966	1967
Drunk and Incapable	251	275	319	307	269	218	205	226
Drunk and Disorderly	22	23	27	3	4		1	4
Other Drunkenness	4	8	10	12	6	5	2	3
Liquor Law Offences	22	32	13	18	7	7	28	8
Totals, Non-motoring	**299**	**338**	**369**	**340**	**286**	**230**	**236**	**241**
Drunk in Charge, Motor Vehicle	67	75	77	91	75	92	94	110
Driving, Excess Alcohol								2
Totals, Motoring	**67**	**75**	**77**	**91**	**75**	**92**	**94**	**112**

	1968	1969	1970	1971	1972	1973	1974
Drunk and Incapable	254	208	213	218	258	308	378
Drunk and Disorderly	4	18	6	4	3	5	5
Other Drunkenness	11	10	10	8	2	3	3
Liquor Law Offences	9	17	15	37	37	62	33
Totals, Non-motoring	**278**	**253**	**244**	**257**	**300**	**378**	**419**
Drunk in Charge, Motor Vehicle	34	2	2	4	7	10	9
Driving, Excess Alcohol	179	236	236	304	338	333	391
Totals, Motoring	**213**	**238**	**238**	**308**	**345**	**343**	**400**

Population at risk, at five-year intervals, in thousands:
1953: 135; 1958: 134; 1963: 131; 1968: 131; 1973: 132.

TABLE III 216
DRUNKENNESS OFFENCES AND MOTORING OFFENCES, 1953-74
COUNTY OF RENFREW AND BUTE

Offence	1953	1954	1955	1956	1957	1958	1959	
Drunk and Incapable	1137	1185	1268	1206	1435	1388	1446	
Drunk and Disorderly	93	81	88	60	52	74	61	
Other Drunkenness	8	9	18	27	14	26	9	
Liquor Law Offences	32	20	9	17	13	4	21	
Totals, Non-motoring	**1270**	**1315**	**1383**	**1310**	**1514**	**1492**	**1537**	
Drunk in Charge, Motor Vehicle	**40**	**35**	**49**	**85**	**82**	**80**	**96**	
	1960	**1961**	**1962**	**1963**	**1964**	**1965**	**1966**	**1967**
Drunk and Incapable	1403	1580	1707	1784	1792	1695	2033	1945
Drunk and Disorderly	58	91	60	65	73	47	105	162
Other Drunkenness	13	13	10	18	29	17	10	15
Liquor Law Offences	10	13	26	26	41	49	20	23
Totals, Non-motoring	**1484**	**1697**	**1803**	**1893**	**1935**	**1808**	**2168**	**2145**
Drunk in Charge, Motor Vehicle	106	163	161	131	192	215	375	419
Driving, Excess Alcohol								27
Totals, Motoring	**106**	**163**	**161**	**131**	**192**	**215**	**375**	**446**
	1968	**1969**	**1970**	**1971**	**1972**	**1973**	**1974**	
Drunk and Incapable	1987	1769	1720	2208	2071	2614	3393	
Drunk and Disorderly	175	106	86	75	14	17	11	
Other Drunkenness	19	15	12	8	19	14	12	
Liquor Law Offences	31	64	60	76	137	120	163	
Totals, Non-motoring	**2212**	**1954**	**1878**	**2367**	**2241**	**1765**	**3579**	
Drunk in Charge, Motor Vehicle	84	74	91	132	103	141	95	
Driving, Excess Alcohol	366	546	593	664	582	700	665	
Totals, Motoring	**450**	**620**	**684**	**796**	**685**	**841**	**760**	

Population at risk, at five-year intervals, in thousands:
1953: 347; 1958: 351; 1963: 361; 1968: 372; 1973: 376.

TABLE III 217

DRUNKENNESS OFFENCES AND MOTORING OFFENCES, 1953–74
COUNTY OF ROSS AND SUTHERLAND

Offence	1953	1954	1955	1956	1957	1958	1959
Drunk and Incapable	58	63	77	78	87	86	83
Drunk and Disorderly		3		2			
Other Drunkenness	4	5	4	6	5	7	5
Liquor Law Offences		15	7	19	7	10	4
Totals, Non-motoring	**62**	**86**	**88**	**105**	**99**	**103**	**92**
Drunk in Charge, Motor Vehicle	**48**	**39**	**49**	**56**	**66**	**45**	**57**

Offence	1960	1961	1962	1963	1964	1965	1966	1967
Drunk and Incapable	99	81	79	77	91	102	111	131
Drunk and Disorderly	1				2	2	1	
Other Drunkenness	3	1	4	2		1	3	2
Liquor Law Offences	3	1	6	6	3	1	7	12
Totals, Non-motoring	**108**	**83**	**89**	**85**	**96**	**106**	**122**	**145**
Drunk in Charge, Motor Vehicle	58	61	57	56	78	80	96	102
Driving, Excess Alcohol								3
Totals, Motoring	**58**	**61**	**57**	**56**	**78**	**80**	**96**	**105**

Offence	1968	1969	1970	1971	1972	1973	1974
Drunk and Incapable	120	121	126	137	145	312	326
Drunk and Disorderly							
Other Drunkenness	1	3	4	2	2	1	1
Liquor Law Offences	7	10	15	14	6	5	3
Totals, Non-motoring	**128**	**134**	**145**	**151**	**153**	**318**	**330**
Drunk in Charge, Motor Vehicle	20	24	30	21	26	24	33
Driving, Excess Alcohol	102	119	151	236	269	395	357
Totals, Motoring	**122**	**143**	**181**	**257**	**295**	**419**	**390**

Population at risk, at five-year intervals, in thousands:
1953: 73; 1958: 73; 1963: 71; 1968: 70; 1973: 72.

TABLE III 218

DRUNKENNESS OFFENCES AND MOTORING OFFENCES, 1953–74 SCOTTISH NORTH-EAST COUNTIES

Offence	**1953**	**1954**	**1955**	**1956**	**1957**	**1958**	**1959**
Drunk and Incapable	388	324	365	352	416	310	332
Drunk and Disorderly	27	24	27	14	25	12	11
Other Drunkenness	30	25	23	24	25	8	16
Liquor Law Offences	37	47	43	58	64	61	67
Totals, Non-motoring	**482**	**420**	**458**	**448**	**530**	**391**	**426**
Drunk in Charge, Motor Vehicle	**91**	**75**	**95**	**113**	**99**	**112**	**110**

	1960	**1961**	**1962**	**1963**	**1964**	**1965**	**1966**	**1967**
Drunk and Incapable	332	351	357	383	299	306	291	345
Drunk and Disorderly	6		5	7	2	1	1	1
Other Drunkenness	6	10	1	11	10	2	4	3
Liquor Law Offences	59	71	91	140	141	125	171	174
Totals, Non-motoring	**403**	**432**	**454**	**541**	**542**	**434**	**467**	**523**
Drunk in Charge, Motor Vehicle	136	163	190	196	241	247	273	300
Driving, Excess Alcohol								9
Totals, Motoring	**136**	**163**	**190**	**196**	**241**	**247**	**273**	**309**

	1968	**1969**	**1970**	**1971**	**1972**	**1973**	**1974**
Drunk and Incapable	423	358	417	391	438	485	520
Drunk and Disorderly	8	2		3		1	
Other Drunkenness	7	2	3	4		5	9
Liquor Law Offences	140	155	138	156	127	134	111
Totals, Non-motoring	**578**	**517**	**558**	**554**	**565**	**625**	**640**
Drunk in Charge, Motor Vehicle	75	70	49	51	53	24	33
Driving, Excess Alcohol	249	293	432	644	619	707	899
Totals, Motoring	**324**	**363**	**481**	**695**	**672**	**731**	**932**

Population at risk, at five-year intervals, in thousands:
1953: 281; 1958: 273; 1963: 265; 1968: 266; 1973: 272.

TABLE III 219
DRUNKENNESS OFFENCES AND MOTORING OFFENCES, 1953–74
COUNTY OF STIRLING AND CLACKMANNAN

Offence	1953	1954	1955	1956	1957	1958	1959
Drunk and Incapable	385	394	456	552	489	503	382
Drunk and Disorderly	5		3		1	3	
Other Drunkenness	12	11	15	58	23	22	16
Liquor Law Offences	32	27	59	31	51	41	26
Totals, Non-motoring	**434**	**432**	**533**	**641**	**564**	**569**	**424**
Drunk in Charge, Motor Vehicle	**44**	**38**	**64**	**60**	**48**	**73**	**98**

	1960	1961	1962	1963	1964	1965	1966	1967
Drunk and Incapable	406	413	478	430	384	369	502	485
Drunk and Disorderly							1	
Other Drunkenness	19	13	5	4	8	15	12	7
Liquor Law Offences	52	33	28	34	43	32	63	64
Totals, Non-motoring	**477**	**459**	**511**	**468**	**435**	**416**	**578**	**556**
Drunk in Charge, Motor Vehicle	88	142	123	174	150	183	238	208
Driving, Excess Alcohol								4
Totals, Motoring	**88**	**142**	**123**	**174**	**150**	**183**	**238**	**212**

	1968	1969	1970	1971	1972	1973	1974
Drunk and Incapable	523	391	366	341	328	287	495
Drunk and Disorderly					1		
Other Drunkenness	14	1	5	5	4	6	7
Liquor Law Offences	41	36	27	38	56	27	42
Totals, Non-motoring	**578**	**428**	**398**	**384**	**389**	**320**	**544**
Drunk in Charge, Motor Vehicle	75	61	85	52	68	58	33
Driving, Excess Alcohol	229	395	337	352	367	329	448
Totals, Motoring	**304**	**456**	**422**	**404**	**435**	**387**	**481**

Population at risk, at five-year intervals, in thousands:
1953: 228; 1958: 233; 1963: 238; 1968: 248; 1973: 256.

SECTION IV

STATISTICAL TABLES, 1973–79

TABLE IV 1
DRUNKENNESS, MOTORING OFFENCES AND LICENCES (ENGLAND AND WALES), 1973–79

	1973	1974	1975	1976	1977	1978	1979*
Population '000							
Proved Offences—Drunkenness							
Males							
Under 18	4396	4624	4450	4653	4920	4769	5000
18 and under 21	12987	14293	14378	15785	16279	16231	18000
21 and under 30	21657	22998	23729	24183	24406	24146	27000
30 and under 60	47346	48580	48982	49781	49383	47809	51000
60 and over	6588	5779	5341	5654	5494	5426	6000
All ages	**92974**	**96294**	**96880**	**100056**	**100482**	**98381**	**107000**
Females							
Under 18	329	374	355	444	442	415	400
18 and under 21	666	839	854	1006	1036	962	950
21 and under 30	1207	1398	1762	1965	1923	2127	2000
30 and under 60	3486	3769	4126	4655	4369	4331	4100
60 and over	612	529	475	572	619	598	550
All ages	**6300**	**6909**	**7572**	**8642**	**8389**	**8433**	**8000**
All Proved Offences	**99274**	**103203**	**104452**	**108698**	**108871**	**106814**	**115000**
Motoring Offences Proceedings for:	Prosecutions			Findings of Guilt at Magistrates' Courts			
(a) Previously Convicted							
Unfit to drive	71	44	64	69	N/A	N/A	N/A
Driving, undue alcohol	1947	1793	1968	1919	N/A	N/A	N/A
Fail provide specimen	234	250	339	326	N/A	N/A	N/A
(b) No Prev. Conviction							
Unfit to drive	2902	2350	2714	2510	2524	2738	3000
Driving, undue alcohol	49615	46488	47903	40098	37431	42022	45000
Fail provide spec.	2984	2292	2647	2772	3082	3527	4000
In charge and:							
Unfit to drive	461	269	303	277	314	245	200
Undue alcohol	871	805	821	761	832	819	800
Fail provide spec.	912	796	901	980	848	503	500
Failure to provide breath specimen	5251	4180	4803	5570	5702	5996	6500
Total: All Proceedings	**65248**	**59267**	**62463**	**55282**	**50733**	**55850**	**60000**
Licensed Premises							
Public Houses:							
Full	63534				65148	65665	66000
Beer and Cider / Wine or Cider	344				395	392	350
Restaurant Licence	8664				10616	11257	12000
Residential Licence	2230				3156	3632	4000
Above Combined	2598				2916	3056	3250
Licensed Clubs	2702				2919	2980	3400
Total On Licences	**80072**				**85150**	**86982**	**89000**
Off Licences	**29710**				**33758**	**35009**	**36000**
Total On/Off Licences	**109782**				**118908**	**121991**	**125000**
Registered Clubs	**24593**				**25835**	**26229**	**27000**
Total Licences & Clubs	**134375**				**144743**	**148320**	**152000**

*Provisional

TABLE IV 2
DRUNKEN DRIVING, OTHER MOTORING OFFENCES AND LICENCES (SCOTLAND), 1973–79

	1973	1974	1975	1976	1977	1978	1979*
Population '000							
Proved Offences— Drunken Driving							
Males							
Under 18	134	154	194	126	144	N/A	N/A
18 and under 21	1024	1152	1157	946	829	N/A	N/A
21 and under 30	3779	3809	3544	3042	2623	N/A	N/A
30 and under 50	5089	5467	5121	4138	3722	N/A	N/A
50 and over	1353	1430	1419	1168	1142	N/A	N/A
All ages	**11379**	**12012**	**11435**	**9420**	**8460**	**N/A**	**N/A**
Females							
Under 18	2	2	6	2	1	N/A	N/A
18 and under 21	9	12	21	10	21	N/A	N/A
21 and under 30	56	43	79	59	55	N/A	N/A
30 and under 50	98	109	114	104	130	N/A	N/A
50 and over	21	23	30	26	24	N/A	N/A
All ages	**186**	**189**	**250**	**201**	**231**	**N/A**	**N/A**
All Proved Offences	**11565**	**12201**	**11685**	**9621**	**8691**	**N/A**	**N/A**
Motoring Offences							
Proceedings for:							
(a) Previously Convicted							
Unfit to drive							
Driving, undue alcohol							
Fail provide specimen							
(b) No Prev. Conviction							
Unfit to drive	2081	2251	1946	1555	1264	1265	1250
Driving, undue alcohol	9666	10553	10267	8546	7833	9548	10000
Fail provide spec.	966	1204	1235	1200	1212	1298	1350
In charge and:							
Unfit to drive	332	371	384	292	246	288	300
Undue alcohol	104	129	126	104	76	84	100
Fail provide spec.							
Failure to provide breath specimen							
Total: All Proceedings	**13149**	**14508**	**13967**	**11697**	**10631**	**12483**	**13000**
Licensed Premises							
Public Houses:							New
Full	4086				4192		Legislation
Beer and Cider							
Wine or Cider							
Hotels	2769				2865		”
Restricted Hotels	304				365		”
Restaurants	501				713		”
Licensed Clubs							
Total On Licences	**7660**				**8135**		”
Off Licences	**4021**				**4446**		”
Total On/Off Licences	**11681**				**12581**		”
Registered Clubs	**2214**				**2600**		”
Total Licences & Clubs	**13895**				**15181**		”

*Provisional

TABLE IV 3
DRUNKENNESS (SCOTLAND), 1973–79

	1973	1974	1975	1976	1977	1978	1979*
Population '000							
Proved Offences—Drunkenness							
Males							
Under 18	470	493	458	404	414	398	400
18 and under 21	855	919	962	909	766	783	800
21 and under 30	1737	1870	1927	1833	1459	1533	1500
30 and under 50	5250	5786	5783	5457	4819	4922	5000
50 and over	3719	4121	4073	3943	3364	3513	3300
All ages	**12031**	**13189**	**13203**	**12546**	**10822**	**11149**	**11000**
Females							
Under 18	79	58	83	50	42	60	50
18 and under 21	89	112	102	89	85	86	90
21 and under 30	182	167	191	222	226	217	230
30 and under 50	687	719	886	824	743	701	700
50 and over	448	438	534	425	428	430	430
All ages	**1485**	**1494**	**1796**	**1610**	**1524**	**1494**	**1500**
All Proved Offences	**13516**	**14683**	**14999**	**14156**	**12346**	**12643**	**12500**

*Provisional

APPENDIX I

ADVERTISING STANDARDS AUTHORITY'S LIQUOR ADVERTISING CODE OF PRACTICE

1. Normally, children should not be portrayed in advertisements for drink; however, in a scene where it would be natural for them to be present (e.g. a family situation), they may be included, provided that it is made clear that they are not drinking alcoholic beverages.
2. Advertisements should not be directed at young people nor in any way encourage them to start drinking. Anyone shown drinking should be obviously over eighteen.
3. Advertisements should not be based on a dare or impute any failing to those who do not accept the challenge of a particular drink.
4. Advertisements should not emphasize the stimulant, sedative or tranquillizing effects of any drink.
5. Advertisements should not give the general impression that a drink is being recommended mainly for its intoxicating effect, or that drinking is necessary for social success or acceptance.
6. The alcoholic strength of a drink should not be used as the principal subject of an advertisement.
   (This rule does not prevent the inclusion in advertisements of factual information as to strength).
7. The content of advertisements should never associate drink with driving.
8. Any claim that drink is, or might be, beneficial to health must comply with the provisions of Section V of the British Code of Advertising Practice.
9. Advertisements should neither claim nor suggest that any drink can contribute towards sexual success.

AMENDMENTS TO BRITISH CODE OF ADVERTISING PRACTICE

Amendments to the Appendix in the British Code of Advertising Practice which deals with the advertising of alcoholic drinks for all advertisements under the supervision of the Advertising Standards Authority were published in 1980. They will be progressively applied to all advertisements for alcohol in the United Kingdom.

Revised wording for Alcohol Appendix to British Code of Advertising Practice

1. Introduction

1.1 Moderate drinking is widely enjoyed and helps to make social occasions cheerful and pleasant.

1.2 Alcoholic Drinks Industry, with others, is aware that a small, but significant minority cause harm to themselves and others through misuse of alcohol. They share the concern about this social problem, the causes of which are complex and varied. There is no evidence connecting such misuse with the advertising of alcoholic drinks.

1.3 The industry is concerned that its advertisements should not exploit the immature, the young, the socially insecure, or those with physical, mental or social incapacity. The industry accepts that its advertising should be socially responsible and should not encourage excessive consumption.

1.4 The industry believes that it is proper for advertisements for alcoholic drinks:

(i) to indicate that they give pleasure to many, are of high quality and are widely enjoyed in all classes of society.

(ii) to seek to persuade people to change brands and/or types of drinks.

(iii) to provide information on products.

(iv) to employ such accepted techniques of advertising practice as are employed by other product groups and are not inconsistent with the detailed rules.

2. *Implementation and Interpretation*

2.1 The industry has therefore proposed the following rules for inclusion in the British Code of Advertising Practice. The CAP Committee has accepted this proposal and the Advertising Standards Authority has agreed to supervise the implementation of the rules.

2.2 The rules are to be interpreted in the light of the considerations set out in paragraphs 1.1 to 1.4 above. So far as the scope and general interpretation of the rules is concerned, the provisions of the BCAP apply, as they do to those aspects of drink advertisements not covered by the rules.

2.3 "Drink" for the purposes of this Appendix, is to be understood as referring to alcoholic beverages and their consumption.

Rules

Young people: Advertisements should not be directed at young people or in any way encourage them to start drinking. Anyone shown drinking must be and appear to be over 21. Children should not be depicted in advertisements except where it would be usual for them to appear (eg in family scenes or in background crowds) but they should never be shown drinking alcoholic beverages, nor should it be implied that they are.

Challenge: Advertisements should not be based on a dare, nor impute any failing to those who do not accept the challenge of a particular drink.

Health: Advertisements should not emphasise the stimulant, sedative or tranquillising effects of any drink, or imply that it can improve physical performance. However, references to the refreshing attributes of a drink are permissible.

Strength: Advertisements should not give the general impression of being inducements to prefer a drink because of its higher alcohol content or intoxicating effect. Factual information for the guidance of drinkers about such alcoholic strength may, however, be included.

Social success: Advertisements may emphasise the pleasure of companionship and social communication associated with the consumption of alcoholic drinks, but it should never be implied that drinking is necessary to social or business success or distinction, nor that those who do not drink are less likely to be acceptable or successful than those who do.

Advertisements should neither claim nor suggest that any drink can contribute towards sexual success, or make the drinker more attractive to the opposite sex.

Drinking and machinery: Advertisements should not associate drink with driving or dangerous machinery. Specific warnings of the dangers of drinking in these circumstances may, however, be used.

Excessive Drinking: Advertisements should not encourage or appear to condone over-indulgence. Repeated buying of large rounds should not be implied.

APPENDIX II

INDEPENDENT BROADCASTING AUTHORITY'S LIQUOR ADVERTISING CODE OF PRACTICE

1. Liquor advertising may not be addressed particularly to the young and no one associated with drinking in an advertisement should seem to be younger than about twenty-five. Children may not be seen or heard in an advertisement for alcoholic drink.
2. No liquor advertisement may feature any personality who commands the loyalty of the young.
3. Advertisements may not imply that drinking is essential to social success, or acceptance or that refusal is a sign of weakness.
4. Advertisements must not feature or foster immoderate drinking. This applies to the quantity of drink being consumed in the advertisement and to the act of drinking portrayed. References to buying of rounds of drink are not acceptable.
5. Advertisements must not claim that alcohol has therapeutic qualities nor offer it expressly as a stimulant, sedative or tranquillizer. While advertisements may refer to refreshment after physical performance, they must not give any impression that performance can be improved by drink.
6. Advertisements should not place undue emphasis on the alcoholic strength of drinks.
7. Nothing in an advertisement may link drinking with driving or with the use of potentially dangerous machinery.
8. No liquor advertisement may publicize a competition.
9. Advertisements must neither claim nor suggest that any drink can contribute towards sexual success.
10. Advertisements must not suggest that regular solitary drinking is acceptable.
11. Treatments featuring special daring or toughness must not be used in a way which is likely to associate the act of drinking with masculinity.

APPENDIX III

DRINK IN EUROPE

Now that Britain is a member of the European Community its pattern of drinking and its methods of control need to be seen in relation to those of other European countries. Membership of the Common Market has given a new dimension to almost every sector of British industry. Some specific industries may have their role in Europe clearly delineated, but this is not so for the liquor industry. The situation is complicated by the fact that there is not yet, and there may never be, a common policy on liquor licensing in the European Community. The E.E.C. is finding the ramifications of the production of the raw materials which are involved in the common agricultural policy, the manufacture of products which have deep-rooted traditional ties with various vineyards on the Continent, the marketing processes involving different levels of duty and surplus created by increased production, exceedingly complex. At the time of writing this chapter, the lack of uniform information from the different countries and the variations in licensing regulations impose serious limitations on any attempt to describe the situation in Western Europe as a whole. From Eastern Europe the amount of information is much more limited. All that can be attempted is a comparison between some European countries and Britain, insofar as information is available on such aspects as licensing and some of the social consequences of drinking.

Possibly the best-known feature is what has been commonly called "Europe's wine lake". There was much talk of this in 1974. However, three years later, in 1977, the main wine-producing countries in the E.E.C., France, Germany, Italy and Luxembourg, experienced the lowest grape harvest for ten years. Writing in *Wine and Spirit*[1] Jancis Robinson said this raised two questions – did this mean that the 1974 wine lake had been drained? Is the wine market in Europe now regulated by supply and demand? The table shows how the E.E.C. Commission in Brussels attempts to quantify the size of the European wine surplus in any given year.[2]

Wine production and consumption in the E.E.C. (m.hl.)

			1973/ 1974	1974/ 1975	1975/ 1976	1976/ 1977	1977/ 1978 (exp.)	1977/ 1978 (poss.)
1.	(a)	Amount produced for vinification	170.6	160.2	145.4	146.0	126.6	**150.00**
	(b)	Imports	7.2	5.3	5.0	5.2	5.1	**5.1**
		Total availability	177.8	165.5	149.4	151.2	131.17	**155.1**
2.	(a)	Use in EEC (not inc. assisted distillation)	143.0	148.9	146.8	142.6	135.0	**135.0**
	(b)	Exports	3.2	2.3	4.3	4.4	5.3	**5.3**
		Total usage	146.2	151.2	151.1	147.0	140.3	**140.3**
3.		Surplus	31.6	14.3	−1.7	4.2	−8.6	**14.8**
	(a)	of which distilled under article 7 of 816/70	5.9	20.3	2.2	4.7	5.1	
	(b)	EEC stocks exchange	+25.7	−6.0	−3.9	−0.5	−13.7	

This table shows just how much wine had been distilled since the bumper wine harvests of 1973 and E.E.C. estimates are that, particularly in France, consumption will continue to fall, although 1977's production of 126.6 m.hl. will fall short of requirements in the subsequent 1977/8 twelve months by 8.6 m.hl., so some of the 80 m.hl. in stock will have to be used up. The policy of massive distillation, 5.1 m.hl. in 1977/78 will be continued because there is such a backlog of poor-quality wine. Of the wine distilled, two-thirds is French and the rest Italian. 1977 happened to be a small vintage. The last column shows what might have happened if there had been a vintage of average size, as there probably will be in 1979.

The table shows that an apparent surplus of 31.6m. hectolitres in the year following the 1973 vintage fell to 4.2 m. hectolitres in 1977, with a projected shortfall of wine in 1978 because of the paucity of the 1977 vintage. This shortfall should be seen in the light of the fact that there were an estimated 80 m. hectolitres of wine in stock in the E.E.C. in 1978. This consisted chiefly of lower-grade wines from France. The intervention of the E.E.C. meant that most of the poor-quality wine, a total of 33.1 m. hectolitres, had gone to the distillers since 1973 to produce expensive wine-based alcohol. Jancis Robinson commented, "But there can be no doubt that the existence of a European wine lake which has now spilled over, by massive distillation, into an alcohol lake, has made the need for an alcohol regime all the more pressing."[3] She pointed out that the real problem facing the E.E.C. was the fact that in ten years the world's wine production had risen 24 per cent faster than consumption.

Because France is Britain's nearest European neighbour, the drinking habits and the regulations governing sale and consumption are often compared.[4] The sale of spirits at any time to young people under sixteen in France is forbidden; no alcohol of any kind may be sold on the premises to children under fourteen; and young people under sixteen are not allowed on on-licensed premises unless accompanied by a parent or an adult over eighteen who is responsible for them. There is, however, no national legislation relating to opening times which are controlled by the decree of the local mayor. Laws controlling the retail sale of liquor are enforced by the Ministry of the Interior and applied by the Gendarmerie or municipal police force depending on the size of the town. It is possible, under local legislation, to control the location of retail outlets as well as matters dealt with in England and Wales by planning authorities. In recent years laws relating to structural requirements, particularly fire safety, have been strengthened. Application to open a bar or café are made to the local mayor, or in Paris to the Prefect of Police.

In Belgium, control over retail outlets is exercised by the 596 communes whose detailed requirements vary greatly. In Brussels there are detailed regulations covering opening hours, police entry, safety precautions and other aspects. All local municipal authorities have power to close premises. Spirits for consumption off the premises can be bought only at shops other than those at which liquor is sold for consumption on the premises. The minimum amount which can be bought is two litres. Where beer is sold for on-consumption it is forbidden to have any quantity of spirits on the premises. There is no equivalent to a yearly renewal of licence, but premises are inspected by police. However, the possible introduction of a licensing system is under review. Hours of opening vary from commune to commune, but it is usually left to the owner to decide when to close. It is an offence to serve liquor on the premises to young people under sixteen. In practice beer is not usually reckoned to fall within that category. In neighbouring Holland, licences are issued by municipal authorities and enforced by the Ministry of Social Affairs. There are different kinds of licences for restaurants, bars, clubs, canteens and liquor shops. Shops such as grocery and dairy shops may sell beer and wine without a licence. Town councils have power to impose restrictions on types of liquor sold in various premises and to fix closing times. The maximum permitted hours are 8.30 a.m. – 6.00 p.m. for off-licences and 5.00 a.m. – 1.00 a.m. for on-sales. Night clubs may open from 10.00 p.m. to 4.00 a.m. There are various regulations imposing limits on the sale of liquor to and purchase of liquor by young persons.

Retail outlets in Italy are related to population: one in each commune for every 400 inhabitants and one for every 1,000 inhabitants in respect of beverages with an alcohol content of more than 4.5 per cent of volume. Minimum distances between outlets are also laid down by law, the exceptions being premises catering for residents. Outlets attached to railway stations and seaports and airports and motorways are excluded. Tourist centres may also be exempted from this regulation. Health and safety regulations apply to all premises. Licences are granted by the local chief of police. No licence is required if the liquor is sold in a closed container for consumption off the premises, provided it holds not less than one half litre for beverages of not more than 21 per cent volume and two-thirds of a litre in other instances. Hours of opening are fixed by the chief of police in consultation with the mayor. Premises may not be opened before 10 a.m. on weekdays (11 a.m. on holidays). Closing hours are also fixed. In hours when public outlets are closed, the sale of liquor in all other establishments is forbidden. Clubs come under the same regulations as other outlets. Alcohol may not be publicly consumed by people under sixteen, nor may it be publicly served to them.

There is no specific licence required for the sale of alcohol in Austria. The vendor must, however, have the licence required for his own particular trade. This means possessing a catering licence for public houses and similar establishments, and a retail trade licence for food stores. A licence for food stores costs Austrian Schilling 2,000 and for the catering industry between Austrian Schilling 3,000 and 5,000. Stamp duty in both cases amounts to Austrian Schilling 650. Self-service is allowed. The sale of alcohol in the retail trade depends upon normal business hours, usually 06.30 to 18.30 hours. On licensed premises the hours are fixed by the Provincial Governor and therefore vary from one province to another. There is no lower age limit for the sale of alcohol in commercially-bottled containers. However, innkeepers and similar persons may not serve alcohol for consumption on their premises to anyone under the age limit stipulated by law, which is usually eighteen. Food stores and butchers' shops are allowed to sell soft drinks and beer for consumption. There are no restrictions on spirits in bars during opening hours. Prices are not fixed by law. In 1979 the Austrian Commercial Delegate in Great Britain reported that currently there were about 36,000 licence-holders for inns and similar establishments in Austria.

What information is available about the social consequences of drinking in Europe does not support the popular belief that what is reckoned to be more relaxed drinking regulations than those in Britain result in less serious social consequences. In most countries of Europe there is an exceedingly high per capita consumption of various beverages. Wine is the most popular drink in France, the average Frenchman drinking 141.8 litres (31 gallons) of wine every year. France is the largest importer and consumer of port, and consumption continues to increase. In 1977 France imported 32,000 hectolitres more port than in the previous year, bringing the total to 192,000 hectolitres. This was two-and-a-half times more than the next most important importer, the United Kingdom. Consumption of beer in Belgium and Luxembourg is the same, that is an average of 132 litres a year. In Italy, in the last thirty years consumption of wine has risen by just under 100 per cent, and beer drinking by 600 per cent. Spirits drinking has risen by 700 per cent and Italy has become the third largest importer of Scotch whisky. For instance, during the first six months of 1974 Italy imported more than two million gallons of Scotch, the total value of which was £8,500,000. This was an increase of 32 per cent over the same period the previous year.

Consumption in West Germany is exceedingly high. West Germans are the biggest consumers of beer in Europe. The average per head of the population (including old people and babies) is 146 litres per year, with Bavarians averaging 200 litres per year. In 1974 West Germans spent five per cent of their national income on liquor, a total of DM31,000 million, which was three times more than fifteen years earlier.

In Austria annual campaigns are organized by the government to warn the public of the effects of excessive drinking, but they appear to have little effect. Austrians are said to drink about eleven litres of pure alcohol per head per year, chiefly in wine and beer.

The Nordic nations of Europe also have their problems. The Danes, who are proud of their relaxed attitude to the consumption of alcohol and the lack of restrictions are heavy drinkers. The average Dane is reported to drink almost twice as much as his Swedish and Norwegian neighbours put together. The Danes seem reluctant to use licensing controls as in Britain, nor do they seem willing to restrict or ban drink advertising as in Finland and Norway. In 1978 it was reported that in Sweden, when the government banned the sale of medium-strength beer in supermarkets in July 1977, Sweden's drinkers turned to stronger beer. The beer with a 3.6 per cent alcohol content was prohibited in a move to cut down heavy drinking by young people, but supermarkets were allowed to carry beer with a 2.8 per cent alcohol content. In 1978 a leading Swedish brewery claimed that the medium-strength ban had given an unexpected boost to sales of its strong beer (4.5 per cent alcohol content). Sales were up to 60 per cent over 1976 statistics, although strong beer could be purchased only through the state liquor monopoly.

With such high levels of consumption the social consequences are as evident in Western Europe as they are in Britain. There is, as one might expect, a serious drinking-driving problem. Statistical information is not available from every country, but there is sufficient to illustrate the seriousness of the problem. A study of all fatal traffic accidents in France between 1st January and 30th June 1977 showed that at least 38 per cent of fatal traffic accidents were caused by someone with a blood-alcohol level above the legal limit of 0.08 per cent. Professor Claude Got, head of the Department of Pathology at Hopital Raymond Poincare in Garches, said that in reality the proportion was probably 41 per cent to 45 per cent.[6] In 1978 France stepped up its anti-alcohol campaign by authorizing police to check on motorists' levels of alcohol, regardless of whether or not drivers were involved in road accidents. Drivers with more than 0.8 grammes of alcohol per litre of blood are now liable to lose their driving licences, face prison sentences and heavy fines. Motorists caught for the first time with between 0.8 and 1.2 grammes of alcohol are taken before a judge, who may order the suspension of their driving licence, sentence them to a prison term of between ten days and one month or fine them up to £60.

An indication of the problem in Belgium is given in statistics in 1972 when 10,372 blood tests were carried out on Belgian drivers, of which 95 per cent showed a blood-alcohol level of about 80 mg. per 100 ml. Drivers under the influence of drink were involved in 8,980 accidents in which 65 drivers, 49 passengers and 24 pedestrians were killed.

In 1977 it was reported that an insurance survey in Austria estimated that in non-traffic accidents in 1975 one-fifth of all Austrians injured were under the influence of alcohol at the material time. Of the 104,000 people injured either at work or during their leisure time, 20,000 had their judgement impaired by alcohol.

West Germany also has a serious drinking-driving problem. In 1972 drink caused 3,675 fatal accidents, which was more than one-fifth of all fatal road accidents. At least 4,000 lives were lost. The legal blood-alcohol level in West Germany is the same as in Britain, 80 mg. in 100 ml. In 1974–75 the West German government spent over one million pounds on a press, radio and TV advertising campaign aimed at sober driving.

The other social consequences of excessive drinking are equally dramatic. In France, in 1974, the Health Minister, Michael Poniatowski, declared that alcoholism was the national scourge of France. It cost the country 10,000 million francs (£1,000 million) a year. About 40 per cent of the beds in general hospitals were filled by alcoholics and the percentage was much higher in psychiatric hospitals. According to a government group set up to study the problem, 22,000 died each year from alcoholism. Statistics also showed that France had the highest number of liver cirrhosis cases in the world, with over 35,000 deaths a year from this condition and aneurism by alcoholism.

In West Germany the number of alcoholics is said to be 900,000 and in 1976 there were 750,000 other people classified as chronic drinkers. Surveys carried out at about the same time showed there were serious drinking habits among boys and girls over the age of fourteen. In Bavaria eight per cent of children between 12 and 14 were found to be drinking spirits "almost daily". Officials estimate that 100,000 young West Germans are becoming addicted to alcohol. Because the rising figures of alcohol abuse among teenagers could no longer be ignored, breweries in West Germany launched a campaign in 1979 to warn people of the dangers of excessive drinking. The German Brewery League (Deutscher Brauer Bund) composed of 1,500 breweries, spent DM700,000 on an advertising campaign to combat alcohol abuse. Posters were distributed to 64,000 taverns and restaurants explaining, in comic style, which alcoholic drinks could be sold to young people and at what age.

Following a warning from the Ministry of Health in Holland about rising alcohol consumption in 1976, the Dutch breweries announced voluntary restrictions on their advertising campaigns. The voluntary code declared that advertising should not encourage excessive drinking or the "misuse" of alcoholic drinks. It also declared that advertisements for low-alcohol-content drinks should not suggest they were any safer than stronger products. Young people should not be encouraged to drink, and there should be no featuring of young people or sports personalities in the advertisements.

The number of alcoholics in Austria is known to be at least 160,000 and it is reckoned there may be 100,000 more. A study by Professor Kornelius Kryspin-Exner claimed that spirits played a negligible role in Austrian alcoholism, the principal beverages consumed being wine and beer. An Austrian health report in 1971 showed that the country had the second biggest liver cirrhosis rate in Europe. In that year, 47.2 males out of 100,000 died of liver cirrhosis.

Italy, traditionally a wine-drinking country, is reputed to have a low rate of alcoholism.

There is evidence of a serious problem in Spain. In 1977 official estimates by the University of Madrid's professor of psychology, Dr Joaquin Santo-Domingo put the number of alcoholics at one-and-a-half million, with a further four to five million people being indirectly affected. In a bulletin issued by the government youth department, he said alcoholism was a serious problem in Spain and drinkers were becoming addicted younger. It is reckoned that drink problems cost Spain's economy at least 20,000 pesetas a year. An adviser to the Spanish government believed the rise in drink problems had been greatly influenced by Spain's tourist boom. The amount of alcohol consumed in Spain had not changed for 30 years, but traditional patterns had altered considerably. Tourism had helped to popularize spirits rather than wine or beer. Liquor advertising on television is prohibited in the early evening when children are most likely to be watching. Between 1968 and 1974 the number of 16–25 year-old patients at Madrid alcoholism treatment centre went up from 3 per cent of the total to 6 per cent. In 1968 young females accounted for 0.5 per cent of the patients and 2.5 per cent six years later.

Despite the reluctance of Communist governments to publish full statistics, it is possible from various pieces of information which have appeared in British journals and other publications to conclude that the problems associated with excessive drinking are at least as serious in Eastern Europe as they are in the West. The scale of the problem is probably summed up in a despairing comment in the Warsaw weekly *Czas* in 1978, "The way of drinking in Poland has not changed since the 15th century. We drink too much, too quickly and too often without food. There is no drinking without getting drunk".

Warsaw has indeed to wrestle with a far more serious problem than most other Eastern European capitals, Poland topping the world league in the consumption of spirits. In 1977, the per capita consumption of spirits was 3.83 gallons compared with Italy, in the twentieth position, with 1.30 gallons. The Polish Statistical Year Book for 1974 showed that half of all delinquencies and up to 70 per cent of serious crimes, were due to drink and alcohol was implicated in up to 85 per cent of the divorces. The statistics were likely to reflect more serious adverse trends because of the high increase in consumption. In 1975 it was reported that spirit drinking had increased by 25 per cent in two years. Heaviest drinkers were highly-paid skilled manual workers in the steel and mining industries.

Because statistics about drinking habits in Hungary were published for the first time in 1974, most of the known facts relate to very recent times. According to the newspaper *Kisalfold,* Hungary may rank among the leading alcohol-consuming countries in the world. In 1967, the paper said, per capita consumption was 7.5 litres compared with 5.9 litres in the United Kingdom. By 1970 the Hungarian figure was over 10 litres per capita though there was a slight decrease later, which the newspaper, *Magyar Hirlap,* suggested may have been illusory, and was caused by a drop in beer sales following a cool summer and price rises, whereas sales of other alcoholic drinks increased. Total consumption of wines went up by 14 per cent in 1970, by 8.6 per cent in 1971 and by 2.6 per cent in 1972. Consumption of spirits rose by 18 per cent in 1970, by 12 per cent in 1971 and by a further 7.8 per cent in 1972. For many years Hungary has had a total ban on drinking alcohol while driving. What is interesting is that the ownership of private cars has increased enormously in recent years. Prosperous Hungarians who have bought new cars are willing to forego drinking in order to enjoy owning a car. As recently as January 1978 strict new measures were brought in to control alcohol consumption. The sale of liquor before 9 a.m. on working days has been banned in all outlets except hotels and restaurants catering for international tourists. No alcohol may be sold in restaurants or refreshment-stands at railway stations, at bus terminals or at river embarkation points. A decree issued in 1977 by the Minister of Domestic Trade, limited the number of stores permitted to sell liquor. Vegetable, fruit, and meat shops are prohibited from selling it, and the range of beverages in other types of stores has been sharply curtailed. Those specializing in coffee, tea, sweets and high-quality foods are now limited to stocking only luxury drinks such as liqueurs, brandy, champagne and dessert wines. Self-service restaurants are allowed to serve only beer. No bars, wineshops or stores selling spirits may be located within a 200-metre radius of any factory or office employing one hundred or more people. Restaurants have been required to extend their range of non-alcoholic drinks, and those with a low-alcohol content. Water must be placed on every table. Mineral water must be available in smaller quantities than the one-litre bottles, and wine must be sold in carafes or by glass in addition to full bottles. Before the new regulations it was impossible to obtain anything less than a 0.7 litre bottle of wine in any Hungarian restaurant. The new measures followed a series of edicts issued in 1976 which prohibited advertising or publicity advocating alcohol consumption, and placed a total ban on the sale of any kind of liquor in the cafeterias, canteens, snackbars and refreshment-rooms of factories, business and government offices.

Bulgaria, another Eastern-bloc country, also has a serious alcohol problem. In 1974 it was reported that Bulgarians drank seven litres of wine and 26 litres of beer per head more in 1973 than in 1960. Dr Christo Popov of the Institute for the Prevention and Treatment of Drug Dependence in Sophia, who made the statement, claimed that in 1972 more than 70 per cent of all hooligans and 11 per cent of divorces were caused by alcohol abuse. At the end of 1973, of all the people registered in the psychiatric service, 12 per cent were alcohol abusers. Dr Popov said that he believed the root of the problem was the complacent view of the authorities that a law passed in 1947 to limit the number of taverns, so cutting down drunkenness, had made an alcohol education programme seem unnecessary, and it was also believed that Socialism would eliminate the problem. In its policy towards drinking-driving offences Bulgaria may have something to teach others where traffic accidents related to alcohol are much lower than in many other countries because of the continued determination of the authorities to stop drivers drinking. It is illegal for a driver to have even the smallest amount of alcohol in his blood.

Russia also has been reluctant to give much information about the drinking habits of her people. In 1974, however, the state-owned journals such as *Science and Life* published articles pointing out the immense damage done to individuals and the state by alcoholism. Despite recent restrictions, such as those relating to "hours" the Russians' fondness for vodka seems unabated. Attempts to wean vodka drinkers to beer have failed because of the inability of Russian breweries to cope with the demand. Official assurances that more breweries would be built have not been fulfilled. By 1990 the Soviet Food Ministry hopes to have built twenty new breweries, the first, with a 100-gallon capacity being planned to be ready in time for the 1980 Olympic Games. Reports coming out of Russia indicate that there is a serious problem of excessive drinking there especially among young people. Professor Roman Lirmyan of the U.S.S.R.'s Ministry of Internal Affairs Training Academy, said in an article in the Soviet teachers' gazette, "Alcohol has become 'fashionable' at schools. At some schools tenth-graders have even established the tradition of 'washing-down' every exam they pass. It is no secret that this trend peaks at graduation time when the militsia (police) really have their hands full". Also disturbing, he said, was their cynical bravado and the way they taunted their non-drinking peers. According to some studies 49.8 per cent of boys and 31.9 per cent of girls had tried alcoholic drinks before the age of ten, and 90 per cent of the Soviet Union's alcoholics made their first acquaintance with alcohol before they were fifteen. An official of a sobering-up centre in the Ural mountains told a Communist youth league daily paper that more and more juveniles were being sent for treatment. The paper reported that teenagers were being encouraged to drink by adults, even though in each of the fifteen republics there were laws under which adults could be severely punished for getting juveniles drunk. At Kermerovo, a coal-mining centre in Siberia, with a population of 400,000, during a six months' period in 1978 not a single adult was charged, but in the same period 46 teenagers were taken to sobering-up centres in a state of intoxication. Inevitably there are social consequences similar to those in other countries. In 1979 Soviet estimates reckoned that 10 per cent of industrial production is lost each year because of alcoholism. Up to 60 per cent of all fatal accidents and 50 per cent of murders were caused by drink, and the same cause lies behind more than half the divorces.

References

1. *Wine and Spirit* January 1978.
2. From *Wine and Spirit* January 1978.
3. Op cit.
4. Much of the information in the following paragraphs about licensing legislation and control in some countries of Western Europe is taken from *The Erroll Report* – Appendix G. p. 303 ff. More recent information has been obtained from Embassies in London or governments in Europe.
5. The information in the following section has come from a variety of sources. Some of the sources are identified in the text, but other details have come by various routes to the Christian Economic and Social Research Foundation and their authenticity verified.
6. For a detailed exposition of how Professor Got arrived at this conclusion see *Alliance News* July-August 1978 p. 16.

APPENDIX IV

MEASUREMENT OF ALCOHOLIC CONTENT

In 1979 new regulations[1] began to implement an E.E.C. directive which was due to come into force on 1st January 1980. The directive[2] was based on a recommendation[3] of the International Organization of Legal Metrology (OILM) of which the United Kingdom is a member and is designed to make things easier for Britain's international trade and cut down the likelihood of confusion and mistakes in converting measurements between overseas and British systems.

The British system used for spirits, liqueurs and fortified wines was the Sikes proof system which expressed the strength of such alcoholic beverages as so many degrees proof.

The new regulations provide definitions of alcoholic strengths by volume and by mass, the symbols or abbreviations to be used, and give statutory basis to the tables[4] to be used. The tables have been produced by computer from the formula given in the annex to the directive and are published by the E.E.C. Commission.

In outline the O.I.L.M. system will involve the measurement of the temperature of a mixture of ethanol (alcohol) and water and of its specific gravity with a glass alcohol hydrometer made to E.E.C. specification. The specific gravity value is corrected to 20°C by means of the tables and the alcoholic strength by volume is established.

The original British system was based on the work of Bartholomew Sikes (1730–1803) and used brass hydrometer instruments with a series of weights to provide a range of measurement and tables for computation purposes, and had been in used since 1816. Although it worked satisfactorily, it was a purely British system and differed from those in use in most other countries in the world.

References

1. The Alcohol Tables Regulations 1979 SI 132, available from H.M.S.O.
2. The E.E.C. directive No. 76/766/EEC relating to alcohol tables available from H.M.S.O. Agency Section, P.O. Box 569, London SE1.
3. International Recommendations No. 22 Alcoholometry – International Alcoholometric Tables, published on behalf of D.P.C.P. by the Technology Reports Centre, Department of Industry.
4. Practical Alcoholic Tables Volume 2 published by the E.E.C. Commission and available through H.M.S.O. Agency Section, P.O. Box 569, London, S.E.1.

APPENDIX V

THE ADVERTISING OF ALCOHOLIC BEVERAGES

There have been a number of estimates of the amount of money spent on the advertising and promotion of alcoholic drinks in Great Britain. None is attempted in this book. There are several reasons for the omission.

The first and obvious one is that the amount of money spent by the brewers, distillers and importers is no reliable measure of the effect that the promotion has on the habits of actual and potential consumers. As most advertisers know to their cost, there have been many expensive advertising campaigns which have produced no, or even deleterious, effects upon the sales of the goods featured. Conversely, some campaigns have brought about quite unexpected increases in consumption. It is not so much a matter of good or bad advertising as the general economic and social conditions holding at the time the advertisements appear and – importantly in markets where the consumer has a choice of goods or brands more or less equivalent in his eyes – what the competitors are doing.

Competitors do not necessarily take sales from the producers of similar goods. Together they can so expand the market that all benefit from a wider public demand. A classic example of this occurred between 1929 and 1939 in the case of malted-milk drinks. The market, a small one, had been dominated by Ovaltine, with Horlicks an important but more expensive substitute. Both firms advertised prudently, having due regard to the prevailing levels of their sales revenues. Cadbury entered the field with Bournvita, a product having a distinctive taste and spent heavily on advertising in order to persuade the chemists and grocers to take and hold stocks of the new product. Ovaltine and Horlicks reacted by sharply increasing their own advertising with the intention of preventing Bournvita succeeding at their expense. In the event, the impact of the much larger totality of advertising of malted-milk drinks was such that large numbers of consumers of cocoa switched to the malted-milk drinks in the evenings and "Night Starvation" moved into the national vocabulary. There had been an increase in the real value of the disposable income of the working and middle classes as the cost of imported food fell after 1929; they could afford to buy more milk; and cocoa was relatively more difficult to prepare.

On a much smaller scale, Rose's Lime Juice found a large new market when the advertising agents promoted the lime juice as a dilutant of gin, a sweetener of gin-laden breath, and a minimizer of the unwelcome after effects of over-indulgence. A proportionately small amount of money spent with considerable skill and imagination led to "Gin and Lime" displacing the "Gin and It" previously favoured by younger women – and which did none of the things that lime juice was held out as being able to do!

"Guinness is Good for You" will be remembered by many for the interest-compelling posters used to make sure that public houses stocked the Dublin stout. Guinness owned no licensed premises in Great Britain and had to persuade the public to ask for the product in the free houses as well as in the tied houses. The brewers of other stouts spent as much and more money than Guinness did but failed to displace Guinness as the market leader despite the advantage of having numerous tied houses which could be told to stock the brewer's brand.

It is not surprising that here as elsewhere it is not so much how loudly you shout as what you say and how you say it that matters. Alcoholic drinks are not the kind of products for which people will go far out of their way to secure a marginally better offering. All, or nearly all have a taste which needs, first, to be tolerated and then accepted. All, in the end, depend upon the same satisfaction-creating ingredient – the alcohol. But what can be done with the help of a little imagination is currently apparent in the campaign for Real Ale, in the posters in the London Underground advertising Smirnoff Vodka, and in the pages devoted to the discussion of wine and food in the magazines, in the more expensive daily papers and in the coloured Sunday supplements.

The first reason for not attempting an arithmetic summation and comparison of advertising expenditures as between types and brands of alcoholic drinks and over periods of time is clearly a sufficient one. But there are others.

A second reason for not doing so is that the published estimates of the expenditures by brands and types of alcoholic drinks are wrong.

The agencies specializing in the business of publishing such estimates are not given access to the records of the advertisers, the advertising agents or the advertisement departments of the various media. They do obtain the standard price lists for advertising space or time, as the case may be, for all the main media. The rest is monitoring which they do very thoroughly. Newspapers and magazines are monitored by the purchase of every edition of every issue of the publications known to carry even small amounts of display advertising. The staff comb through these looking for advertisements of each of the products and brands in respect of which the cutting agency offers an "expenditure analysis". The expenditures are arrived at by looking up the list price of the space occupied by the monitored advertisement so as to obtain the nominal cost of that advertisement. These costs are aggregated for all the papers and magazines taken and examined week by week and usually published to subscribers to the service at quarterly intervals. These carefully-calculated totals are wrong because the market for advertising space is a volatile and competitive one. Every advertising agency is seeking to buy space for its clients as cheaply as it can; the managers of the advertisement departments of the media are willing to give substantial discounts for pre-booked series of advertisements (such series discounts are quoted in most advertising space price lists and are known to the monitoring services, but the latter cannot know if a particular advertisement has been paid for at the series rate or not); and all such managers are confronted from time to time with under-sold issues or periods of commercial time. They will be eager to fill the empty spaces so as to keep up the pretence of being fully booked and will have to offer bargain prices to persuade the advertising agencies to upset their own schedules by bringing insertions forward or arranging repeats of previous advertisements. Indeed, the more astute advertisement managers make use of these unavoidable hiatuses to curry favour with the advertising agencies by anticipating the periods of shortage in the sense of offering each such agency in more or less turn the first option on expected "cancellations".

The method of calculation enforced upon the monitoring services is, therefore, bound to result in figures for the purchase of advertising space or time which are substantially higher than what will actually have been paid by the advertisers.

But they can also be substantially below the amount of money spent by the advertisers on the advertising campaign as a whole. This is because the advertiser has to pay for the production of the physical things which go to make the advertisement – artwork, blocks, typesetting, in the case of printed matter; artists, script-writers, studios and recording equipment and engineers in the case of radio or television commercials – and for the expertise which brings these things into being at the right time. The advertising agents obtain their remuneration in a number of ways, and these vary as between clients and over time with some clients. The traditional British method was for the agency to charge the client for the full list price of the space or commercial time, and to retain all discounts granted by the media. The American system was always different. Agents billed their clients with the net amounts paid to media, printers, etc., after deducting all discounts, and then made their own on-charge of an agreed percentage of the total outgoings by the client. Even by 1930, the American system was becoming more usual in Great Britian, and its prevalence is now greater. But not all clients, or even individual products within an advertiser's range, are charged in this way. For many years, the very small accounts (what is "small" depends on the size of the advertising agency) have had to find a servicing charge as a lump sum, and one which is higher on percentage terms than the normal commission on the general run of advertisers. The reverse is the case with some of the very large advertisers, especially if the campaigns have been running for some time. The lower administrative costs facing the agency in such instances are given effect through agreed lower commissions, on whatever basis, so long as no new advertising campaign is required. From time to time some of the larger clients attempt to set service fees independent of the amount to be spent, arguing that the direct relationship between the reward for the agency and the amounts spent by their clients tends to force the agencies to work towards higher advertising appropriations than they might in strict professional judgement deem to be sufficient. None of these alternatives is bruited abroad by either client or agency, and the monitors cannot know the position.

Advertising agency commissions, however, cannot distort the relativities substantially. The cost of producing the advertisement – printed or broadcast – must always do so. It is possible to fill a full-page advertisement space in a newspaper or magazine at practically no cost, simply by specifying a few words in large type and asking the newpaper or magazine to set the words within the space. It is equally possible to spend twice the cost of the space upon the production of the advertisement or announcement to go into it.

In the case of printed advertisements, the commissioning of special artwork or photographs and the preparation of the blocks necessary, given the types of paper used by the selected publications, to convey the required suggestion of luxury, romance or scientific precision desired by the advertiser and his agency, frequenty result in payments which are multiples of the cost of the space, especially in the smaller circulation and specialist publications. In all such cases the monitoring services will be underestimating the amounts being spent by the advertisers. Such kinds of advertisements are frequent in the wine and spirits campaigns when it is a case of persuading readers that products of no intrinsic difference possess such differences.

In pre-war days in commercial radio, when the advertiser who took the period of broadcast time also had the responsibility of filling it with the entertainment, and again today in television broadcasting when the client has only to provide content of the "advertisement slot", production costs were and are substantial and variable. The monitoring services cannot know the proportions between the cost of the "time" and the cost of the "commercial".

But in the case of broadcast advertising, a rule-of-thumb approach to the cost of "time" can be very misleading. The programme producer has to fill the network time for which he is responsible winter and summer, Mondays as well as Fridays, and the advertisement "slots" are programmed into the schedules more or less inflexibly. But advertisers have some very peculiar delusions. As a group they believe that there are always English summers, lasting from May until September, when all the evenings are so dry, so fine and so warm that no one watches television. They thought the same before the war when commercial radio was the cardinal medium despite the fact that Radio Luxembourg or Radio Normandie were making the evening air hideous, indoors or outdoors, throughout the summer. To make matters more difficult for the sellers of broadcast commercial "space", there is a complementary belief that none of *their* goods are ever featured in "Summer Sales".

In this context, the fixed number of hours of commercial television with the consequent immutability of the number of commercials poses considerable problems for the advertisement departments of the commercial networks. Some of the "holes" can be filled with "trailers" and self-advertisement, but there is a limit, and advertisers have to be found for most of them. Except when there are "world-series" sport broadcasts of one sort or another, the advertisers will only take space at substantial discounts, and these are kept as confidential as other commercial arrangements.

The estimation of advertising expenditure upon posters is even more difficult. It was generally held among media departments of advertising agencies before the war that the published estimates on posters and hoardings were little more than guesswork. There were so many contractors offering poster sites that it was not easy to obtain the nominal lists of charges of more than a proportion of them. It was well known that even the larger operators would vary their published prices according to the state of their forward bookings. Another complicating factor was the practice of leaving a relatively undamaged poster *in situ* until the following occupier of the space was due to appear. Under such circumstances, monitoring of the lengths of time particular brands were featured upon a sample of sites in order to obtain an idea of the number of weeks booked, and therefore the expenditure, was positively misleading. The situation became rather less confused as the various acts of parliament to do with planning and the control of the environment led to the gradual disappearance of most of the smaller sites and contractors, but there remains the problem of gaps between the end of one booking and the beginning of the next. Posters also experience the converse of the broadcasting problem of the seasonal illusion – in the autumn and the winter, fog and rain are such that no potential customer can be expected even to see a poster – unless both poster and viewer are under cover. The hoardings exposed to the inclement season still carry posters, however, and who knows if anyone is paying for these to stay on the boards?

The media departments of the larger advertising agencies are able to make useful allowances for the deficiencies in the published estimates because they will contain figures in respect of brands and clients for which the agency is placing the advertising, and the discrepancies will be apparent in each case. But investigators into the phenomenon without such points of reference and emendation can only be misled to an unknowable extent.

The third reason for the omission from this book of estimates of the expenditure on the advertising of alcoholic drinks is that the published figures are not only wrong; they are unreliably wrong.

Indicators which consistently under- or over-estimate the true data are often useful in showing the rates and directions of change. But the monitored advertising of alcoholic drinks takes in newspapers, coloured supplements, magazines, posters, commercial radio, commercial television and even cinema advertising as films and "commercial slides". As the previous discussion has indicated, each of these media has its own sources of mistaken conclusions so that, in any kind of aggregation, there will be no guarantee that the aggregations will be wrong to the same degree as in the preceding year. Given the continuance of technological change and progress in most of the media, the uncertainty that must accrue over lapses of time of five or ten years is such as to destroy all confidence in the purported trends emerging from comparisons.

The fourth and final reason for omitting a discussion of the estimated expenditures is that what is, or can be, monitored, is in important cases only a part and a small part of the promotional activity directed at actual and potential consumers of alcoholic drinks. We give some examples – the list is not exhaustive.

In nearly all cases, comparisons of periods prior to 1967 with periods after 1970 are hazardous. There was a substantial change in the ease of access to supplies of alcohol after the ending of Resale Price Maintenance and the mushroom growth of off-licence departments in grocers, co-operative stores and supermarkets. Before 1967, young persons and all ages of women had to go to public houses to get beer and to specialist off-licence shops if they preferred wines or spirits. This was actively disliked as a number of consumer surveys showed. The young would be likely to be questioned as to their ages and, in many pubs, their presence was a matter of resentment by the older *habitués.* Women ran the risk of arousing scandalous comment if observed by their neighbours and of unwelcome attentions in male-dominated bars and saloons. After 1970, both groups of potential consumers were free to go openly to the off-licence departments of the supermarkets, in particular, and to disguise the purchase of liquor by also buying cigarettes or sweets, which are almost invariably sold at the same counter.

But, not only do the supermarkets provide additional outlets for alcoholic drinks; they spend money on the promotion of the sales through these outlets in two ways. They cut the prices. They advertise the cut-prices. How much of the cost of such promotion is at the expense of the producer in reduced wholesale prices to the supermarkets, or in direct subsidy of the reatilers' advertising cannot be found out.

From 1970 to 1977, the liquor offered by the supermarkets was almost confined to wines and spirits and, as other chapters show, that period saw sustained growth in the consumption of these two forms of alcoholic drink while beers were more or less stagnant. From 1977 onwards, however, the emphasis has been changing. Canned beers and lagers, in sets of four tins, now constitute veritable medieval walls around the off-licence sections. Prices of beers and lagers have been reduced relatively – indeed, a pint of beer in cans had become 15 per cent cheaper than a pint of the same beer in a glass at a public house by the beginning of 1980. Subsidy of such beers by the brewers – inadvertent on the part of some, no doubt, but necessitated by the aggressive merchandising of competitive brewers – is obvious, but unknowable in any particular instance. It may be in addition to the more traditional advertising; it may be at the expense of the monitored media; there is no way for the outsider to find out.

Whisky and other spirits are not featured as paid advertisements on television. But when either the BBC or one of the ITV producers show outdoor sports, it is remarkable how often posters and placards displaying well-known brand names are in the eye of the camera when the action on the field is at its height. This is an early form of "sponsorship" in that the club or the arena owners are paid well for what in poster terms are "premium solus sites". But sponsorship now goes much further and deeper than this and the amounts of money involved are out of reach of estimate by any outside investigator. One of the more remarkable of the sponsorships by alcoholic drinks was that of *The Times* crossword by Cutty Sark Whisky. When *The Times* was itself forced to cease publication in November 1978, the sponsorship proved more lasting than the sponsored, for the competition continued to the finals early in 1979!

Wine has always indulged in a form of sponsorship which is difficult to assess in terms of money, either in cost or return. The wine and food societies at Oxford, Cambridge and a few other "select" universities have never lacked "wine and spirit tastings" in their annual programmes of events, and the longer-established wine merchants do the same for their clients at due seasons. Who pays for the occasions is not often clear, but it is a form of advertising that can be quite expensive. Recently, the practice of the same kind of "sampling" has spread to Co-operative stores and supermarkets.

Beer does not lend itself to such sampling, although some impresarios have ventured upon beer festivals. But it is, in fact, the public house that is the most expensive element in the promotion of all alcoholic drinks. The Monopolies Commission came to the conclusion that, allowing for maintenance at the minimum needed for the protection of the fabric, brewers owning tied houses were receiving only 3 per cent on the capital tied up in the pubs. With some 70,000 premises with an average market value of over £100,000 each, the promotional expenditure represented by the interest forgone by the brewers now exceeds a hundred millions every year. It will increase with inflation and vary wildly with fluctuations in the going rates of interest.

APPENDIX VI

BIBLIOGRAPHY

Adams, Junius and Leitch, Michael. *Alcohol:* Omnibus Press (1978).

Birdwood, George. *The Willing Victim:* Secker and Warbug (1969).

Bradley, Michael and Fenwick, David. *Public attitudes to Liquor Licensing Laws in Great Britain:* H.M.S.O. (1974).

Brimley Jones, R. (publisher). *Report of Committee under the chairmanship of the Bishop of Hereford* (1901).

Burton, Mary. *An Alcoholic in the Family:* Faber and Faber (1974).

Camberwell Council on Alocholism – *Where Erroll went wrong on liquor licensing* (1973).

Carter, Henry. *The Control of the Drink Trade:* Longmans and Co. (1919), (Second Edition).

Carter, Henry. *The English Temperance Movement – A study in objectives:* Epworth Press (1933).

Caruana, Cowley, Rutherford. *Teaching about Alcohol and Drinking:* TACADE (1978).

Caruana, S. (edited by). *Notes on Alcohol and Alcoholism:* Medical Council on Alcoholism (1972).

Chafetz, Morris E. *Liquor the Servant of Man:* Phoenix (1965).

Colvin, D. Leigh. *Prohibition in the United States:* George H. Doran and Co. New York (1926).

Cook, Timothy (Editor), Garth Dennis, Hensman Celia. *The Drunkenness Offence:* Pergamon (1969).

Cooper, Derek. *The Beverage Report:* Routledge and Kegan Paul (1970).

Davies, John and Stacey, Barrie. *Teenagers and Alcohol:* H.M.S.O. (1972).

Denney, Ronald C. *The Truth about Breath Tests:* Nelson (1970).

Denney, Ronald C. *Drinking and Driving:* Robert Hale (1979).

Dunn, Michael. *The Penguin Guide to Real Draught Beer:* Penguin Handbooks (1979).

Evans, Hilary and Mary. *The Man who drew the drunkard's daughter: The life and art of George Cruikshank 1792–1828:* Frederick Muller Ltd.

Foster, Terence. *Dr Foster's book of beer:* Adam and Charles Black (1979).

Fowler, J. W. *Edward Lee Hicks:* Christophers (1922).

French, R. Valpy. *Nineteen Centuries of Drink in England:* National Temperance Publication Depot.

Gwinner, Paul and Grant, Marcus. *What's your poison:* BBC Publications (1979).

Harrison, Brian. *Drink and the Victorians:* Faber and Faber (1971).

Hawker, Ann. *Adolescents and Alcohol:* B. Edsall and Co. Ltd. (1978).

Hawkins, K. H. and Pass, C. L. *The Brewing Industry:* Heinemann (1979).

Hayler, Mark H. C. *The Vision of a Century:* United Kingdom Alliance (1953).

Hutt, Christopher. *The death of the English pub:* Hutchinson (1973).

Keller, John E. *Ministry to Alcoholics:* Augsburg (1966).

Kessel, Neil and Walton, Henry. *Alcoholism:* Penguin (1965).

Leigh, John. *Young people and Leisure:* Routledge and Kegan Paul (1971).

Levy, Herman. *Drink – an Economic and Social Study:* Routledge and Kegan Paul (1951).

Longmate, Norman. *The Water Drinkers:* Hamish Hamilton (1968).

Luke, W. B. *Sir Wilfrid Lawson:* Simpkin, Marshall, Hamilton Kent and Co. Ltd. (1900).

Martin, J. N. *Paterson's Licensing Acts (Eighty-fifth edition):* Butterworth and Co., Shaw and Sons Ltd. (1977).

McKenzie, F. A. *"Pussyfoot" Johnson:* Hodder and Stoughton.

O'Connor, Joyce. *The Young Drinkers:* Tavistock Publications (1978).

Power, D. J. *Principles of Forensic Psychiatry:* B. Edsall & Co. Ltd (1979).

Protz, Roger. *Pulling a Fast one:* Pluto Press (1978).

Ritson, Bruce and Hassall, Christine. *The Management of Alcoholism:* E. and S. Livingstone (1970).

Robinson, David. *Talking out of Alcoholism:* Croom Helm (1979).

Rowntree, Joseph and Sherwell, Arthur. *British 'Gothenburg' experiments and Public House Trusts:* Hodder and Stoughton (1903).

Rowntree, Joseph and Sherwell, Arthur. *Public Control of the Liquor Traffic:* Grant Richards (1903).

Russell, G. W. E. (Editor). *Sir Wilfrid Lawson – A Memoir:* Smith, Elder and Co. Ltd. (1909).

Selley, Ernest. *The English public house as it is:* Longmans, Green and Co. Ltd. (1927).

Shadwell, Arthur. *Drink, Temperance and Legislation:* Longmans, Green and Co. Ltd. (1903).

Shadwell, Arthur. *Drink in 1914–1922 – A lesson in Control:* Longmans (1923).

Sinclair, Andrew. *Prohibition – The era of excess:* Faber and Faber (1926).

Swinson, R. P., and Eaves, Derek. *Alcoholism and Addiction:* Macdonald and Evans (1978).

Tapper, Ted. *Young people and Society:* Faber and Faber (1971).

Thomson, Robert. *Bill W. – Co-founder and Creator of Alcoholics Anonymous:* Hamish Hamilton (1976).

Townsend, Henry. *Robert Wilson Black:* Carey Kingsgate Press (1954).

Vaizey, John. *The Brewing Industry 1886–1951:* Pitman (1960).

Walker, John and Constable, Archibald. *The Commonwealth as Publican:* (1902).

Wilkins, R. H. *The hidden Alcoholic in General Practice:* Paul Elek (1975).

Williams, Lincoln. *Alcoholism – A manual for students and practitioners:* E & S Livingstone (1956).

Willett, T. C. *Criminal on the road:* Tavistock Publications (1964).

Wilson, G. B. *Alcohol and the Nation:* Nicholson and Watson (1940).

Winterton, Wilfrid. *Breath-taking history:* U.K. Alliance, London (1968).

REPORTS AND OFFICIAL PUBLICATIONS

Syllabus of lessons on "Temperance" for scholars attending public elementary schools: H.M.S.O. (1909).

Alcohol: its action on the human organism: H.M.S.O. (1918).

The hygiene of food and drink: H.M.S.O. (1922).

Evidence to and Report of the Royal Commission on Licensing (England and Wales) 1929–31: H.M.S.O. (1931).

Handbook of suggestions on health education: H.M.S.O. (1933).

Mass Observation – Report on Juvenile Drinking: Livesey-Clegg Youth Club. Sheffield (1943).

Health Education H.M.S.O. (1950).

Relation of alcohol to road accidents: British Medical Association, London (1960).

A survey of teenage drinking patterns and attitudes to drink: Institute for Social Research (1964).

The drinking driver: British Medical Association, London (1965).

A handbook of Health Education: H.M.S.O. (1968).

Beer: A report on the supply of beer: H.M.S.O. (1969).

Report of Departmental Committee on Liquor Licensing: H.M.S.O. (1972).

News Medium Forum: New Zealand Liquor Industry Council (1973).

Young drinkers: Report to the churches of Ireland (1974).

The Sale of Liquor in New Zealand: Report of New Zealand Royal Commission (1974).

Prevention and Health: Everybody's business: H.M.S.O. (1976).

Profile of Alcohol usage by Young persons in Coventry: Coventry and Warwickshire Council on Alcoholism (1976).

Indications of Alcohol usage and attitudes by young persons of school and college age in Somerset: Somerset Council on Alcoholism (1977).

Alcohol and Alcoholism: Report by the Royal College of Psychiatrists. Tavistock Publications (1979).

INDEX

Note: The subject headings throughout refer to England and Wales. Scotland, Northern Ireland and Ireland, Republic of, are treated separately as are other European countries and the U.S.A. The alphabetical order is letter by letter. The names of books and journals are italicised.